Barron's How to Prepare for the
Graduate Management Admission Test
GMAT
Fourth Edition

By

EUGENE D. JAFFE, M.B.A., Ph.D.
Associate Professor and
Director of the Management Training Center,
Bar-Ilan University, Israel
Formerly Professor of Marketing,
Graduate School of Business, St. John's University

and

STEPHEN HILBERT, Ph.D.
Associate Professor of Mathematics
Ithaca College

BARRON'S EDUCATIONAL SERIES, INC.
Woodbury, New York • London • Toronto

All inquiries should be addressed to:

Barron's Educational Series, Inc.
113 Crossways Park Drive
Woodbury, New York 11797

Library of Congress Catalog Card No. 81-3536

International Standard Book No. 0-8120-2350-1

Library of Congress Cataloging in Publication Data

Jaffe, Eugene D.
  Barron's how to prepare for the graduate management admission test (GMAT)

  1. Business education—Examinations, questions,
etc. I. Hilbert, Stephen. II. Title. III. Title: How to
prepare for the graduate management admission test
(GMAT)

| HF118.J33 1981 | 371.2′64 | 81-3536 |
| ISBN 0-8120-2350-1 | | AACR2 |

PRINTED IN THE UNITED STATES OF AMERICA

2345   051   987654

For Liora, Iris and Nurit
and for Susan

Table of Contents

Preface

Barron's How to Prepare for the Graduate Management Admission Test (GMAT) is designed to assist students planning to take the official Graduate Management Admission Test administered by the Educational Testing Service of Princeton, New Jersey. Since the results of the GMAT are used by many graduate schools of business as a means for measuring the qualifications of their applicants, it is important that the prospective student do as well as he possibly can on this exam. His admission to business school may well depend on it.

A study guide, although not able to guarantee a perfect score, can provide a good deal of assistance in test preparation by enabling the student to become familiar with the material he will encounter on the exam and supplying him with ample opportunity for practice and review. With this in mind, we have developed a study guide that goes further than the simple simulation of the official GMAT in its effort to offer a sound basis of test preparation. Besides containing six practice tests with questions (and answers) similar to those the student will encounter on the actual exam, it offers invaluable advice on how to prepare for the exam, ranging from a general discussion of the purpose and various formats of the GMAT to a step-by-step program of subject analysis and review designed to help the student discover his weak points and take measures to correct them.

Review sections for each subject area appearing on the exam have been especially developed to meet the specific needs of students who may feel a deficiency in any of these areas. Each review provides both an explanation of the material and exercises for practice work. The six practice exams included in the guide have self-scoring tables to help the student evaluate his results and check his progress. All answers to the test questions are fully explained to ensure complete understanding.

The authors would also like to extend their appreciation to Mrs. Susan Hilbert and Ms. Dawn Murcer for their excellent job in typing the manuscript, to Professor Shirley Hockett for several helpful discussions, and to Professor Justin Longenecker for his generous advice.

How to Use This Guide

The step-by-step study program appearing below outlines the recommended study plan you should follow when preparing for the GMAT. By making use of this procedure, you will be able to take full advantage of the material presented in this guide.

1. Familiarize yourself with the purpose and general format of the GMAT (Chapter I).

2. Study the analysis of each type of question on the exam (Chapter II).

3. Take the GMAT Diagnostic Test (Chapter III) and use the Self-scoring Table at the end of the test to evaluate your results.

4. Study the review sections (Chapter IV), spend-ing more time on areas where you scored poorly on the Diagnostic Test.

5. Take the five sample GMAT tests (Chapter V) and evaluate your results after completing each one.

6. Review again any areas you discover you are still weak in after you have evaluated your test results.

7. Use the list of Words Frequently Appearing on the GMAT (Chapter IV) to help increase your knowledge of word meanings and supplement your review.

8. Study the Experimental Question Types (Chapter VI) to be prepared in the event that one of these question forms appears on your exam.

Acknowledgments

The authors gratefully acknowledge the kindness of all organizations concerned with granting us permission to reprint passages, charts, and graphs. The copyright holders and publishers of quoted passages are listed on this and the following pages.

Sources and permissions for charts and graphs appear on the appropriate pages throughout the book through the courtesy of the following organizations: the New York Times Company; U.S. Department of Labor; Dow Jones & Company, Inc.; U.S. Department of Health, Education, and Welfare; United Nations Economics Bulletin for Europe; Social Security Bulletin, Statistical Abstract of the U.S., U.S. Department of Commerce, Bureau of Economic Analysis; Federal Reserve Bank of New York; European Economic Community; U.S. Department of Commerce, Bureau of the Census; New York State Department of Labor; Federal Power Commission; U.S. Treasury Department; U.S. Bureau of Labor Statistics; Institute of Life Insurance; and the Statistical Abstract of Latin America.

Page 7, Sample Passage: Reprinted with permission of the author, Virgil Thomson.

Page 17, Sample Passage: Maynard and Davis, *Sales Management*, © 1957, reprinted by permission of John Wiley & Sons, Inc., New York.

Page 29, Passage 1: Petra Karin Kelly, "Cancer A European Conquest?" *European Community*, April-May, 1976, pp. 23–24.

Page 31, Passage 2: Walter Sturdivant, "Loch Ness Monster," *European Community*, April-May, 1976, pp. 36–37.

Page 35, Passage 4: Reprinted from *The Bible on Broadway* by Arthur T. Buch © Arthur T. Buch 1968, Hamden, CT., Archon Books, with the permission of The Shoe String Press, Inc.

Portions of the "Reading Comprehension and Recall Review": Eugene J. Farley, *Barron's How to Prepare for the High School Equivalency Examination Reading Interpretation Test*, © 1970 Barron's Educational Series, Inc., Woodbury, N.Y.

Page 82, Example 2: "Skye, Lonely Scottish Isle," *Newark Sunday News*, June 9, 1968, C 16, Sec. 2.

Page 84, Example 4: David Gunter, "Kibbutz Life Growing Easier," *Newark News,* May 6, 1968, p. 5.

Page 89, Example 2: Reprinted with permission from "Understanding Foreign Policy," by Saul K. Padover, *Public Affairs Pamphlet #280.* Copyright, Public Affairs Committee, Inc.

Page 91, Exercise A: from *New Students and New Places* by the Carnegie Commission on Higher Education. Copyright 1971 The Carnegie Foundation for the Advancement of Teaching. Used with permission of McGraw-Hill Book Company.

Page 102, Exercise E: Marina Gazzo and Catherine Browne, "Venice Rising," *European Community,* November-December, 1975, pp. 15–16.

Portions of the "Verbal Aptitude Review": Samuel C. Brownstein and Mitchel Weiner, *Barron's How to Prepare for the Graduate Record Examination,* © 1981 Barron's Educational Series, Inc., Woodbury, N.Y.

"Writing Ability Review" and "Practical Judgment Review": Jerry Bobrow, *Barron's New Guide to the Law School Admission Test (LSAT),* Barron's Educational Series, Inc., Woodbury, N.Y. © 1979 by Jerry Bobrow.

Page 312, Passage 2: from *Our Dynamic World: A Survey in Modern Geography* by A. Joseph Wraight. © 1966 by the author. Reproduced by permission of the publisher Chilton Book Company, Radnor, Pennsylvania.

Page 359, Passage 1: *Improving Executive Development in the Federal Government,* copyright 1964 by the Committee for Economic Development.

Page 360, Passage 2: from *Legal Aspects of Marketing* by Marshall C. Howard. Copyright 1964 by McGraw-Hill Book Company. Used with permission of McGraw-Hill Book Company.

Page 392: reprinted with permission from Cruickshank and Davis, *Cases in Management* (Homewood, Ill.: Richard D. Irwin, Inc., 1954 c.).

Page 415, Passage 1: *The Hebrew Impact on Western Civilization,* edited by Dagobert Runes. The Philosophical Library.

Page 417, Passage 2: *Budgeting for National Objectives,* copyright 1966 by the Committee on Economic Development.

Page 419, Passage 3: from *The American Guide,* edited by Henry G. Alsberg, Copyright © 1949, by permission of Hastings House, Publishers.

Page 427: from *Basic Problems in Marketing Management* by Edwin G. Greif. © 1967 by Wadsworth Publishing Company, Inc., Belmont, California 94002. Reprinted by permission of the publisher.

ONE
AN INTRODUCTION TO THE GMAT

The most productive approach to undertaking the actual study and review necessary for any examination is, first to determine the answers to some basic questions: What? Where? When? and How? In this case, what is the purpose of the Graduate Management Admission Test (GMAT)? What does it measure? Where and when is the exam given? And most important, how can you prepare to demonstrate aptitude and ability to study business at the graduate level?

The following discussion centers on the purpose behind the Graduate Management Admission Test and presents a study program to follow in preparing for this exam, including a special section to acquaint you with the general format and procedure used on the GMAT.

The Purpose of the GMAT

The purpose of the GMAT is to measure your ability to think systematically and to employ the reading and analytical skills that you have acquired throughout your years of schooling. The types of questions that are used to test these abilities are discussed in the next chapter. It should be noted that the test does not aim to measure your knowledge of specific business or academic subjects. No specific business experience is necessary, nor will any specific academic subject area be covered. You are assumed to have knowledge of basic algebra, geometry, and arithmetic.

In effect, the GMAT provides business school admission officers with an objective measure of academic abilities to supplement subjective criteria used in the selection process, such as interviews, grades, and references. Suppose you are an average student in a college with high grading standards. Your overall grade average may be lower than that of a student from a college with lower grading standards. The GMAT allows you and the other student to be tested under similar conditions using the same grading standard. In this way, a more accurate picture of your all-around ability can be established.

Where to Apply

Information about the exact dates of the exam, fees, testing locations, and a test registration form can be found in the GMAT Bulletin of Information for Candidates published by ETS. You can obtain a copy by writing:

Graduate Management Admission Test
Educational Testing Service
Box 966-R
Princeton, New Jersey 08541

The GMAT is generally given in October, January, March, and July. Since the majority of business schools send out their acceptances in the spring, it is wise to take the exam as early as possible to ensure that the schools you are applying to receive your scores in time.

The Test Format

In recent years, the GMAT has contained questions of the following types: Reading Comprehension, Problem Solving, Practical Judgment, Data Sufficiency, Writing Ability (2 types: Usage and Sentence Correction), Verbal Ability, and Reading Recall. The following chart gives the two formats most commonly used on recent GMAT exams. Notice that not all types of questions appear on each exam, and that some types may be repeated. It is obviously impossible to predict the format of future exams, but in recent years most exams have contained Reading Comprehension, Problem Solving, Practical Judgment, Data Sufficiency, and Writing Ability sections.

Form A

SECTION	TYPE OF QUESTION	NUMBER OF QUESTIONS	TIME (MIN.)
I	Reading Comprehension	25	30
II	Problem Solving	30	40
III	Practical Judgment	20	20
	10 minute break		
IV	Data Sufficiency	30	30
V	Writing Ability	20	15
VI	Practical Judgment	20	20
VII	Verbal Ability	40	20
	or Writing Ability	25	20
	or Data Sufficiency	30	30
TOTAL		170-185	175-185

Form B

SECTION	TYPE OF QUESTION	NUMBER OF QUESTIONS	TIME (MIN.)
I	Reading Recall (Passages)	-	15
II	Reading Recall (Questions)	30	20
III	Problem Solving	55	75
	10 minute break		
IV	Practical Judgment	20	20
V	Data Sufficiency	15	15
VI	Verbal Ability	40	20
VII	Practical Judgment	20	20
VIII	Writing Ability	20	15
	or Data Sufficiency	15	15
TOTAL		195-200	200

Each section of the GMAT must be completed within a specified time limit. If you finish the section before the allotted time has elapsed, you must spend the remaining time working on that section *only*. You may *not* work on other sections of the test at all.

Specific directions telling you exactly how to answer the questions appear at the beginning of each section of the exam. Keep in mind that although the directions for answering the sample questions in this guide are designed to simulate as closely as possible those on the actual test, the format of the test you take may vary. Therefore, it is important that you read the directions on the actual test very carefully before attempting to answer the questions. You also should be certain of the exact time limit you are allowed.

GMAT Test-Taking Techniques

First, you must be prepared. Make sure you bring several sharpened number two pencils, a good eraser, and a watch (the test center may not have a visible clock).

Use your pencil and blacken your answer choices completely. Be sure erasures are done cleanly. If you skip a question, make sure you skip that answer space in your answer sheet.

Read the directions carefully. Make sure you answer the questions which are asked. Consider *all* choices. Remember you must pick the *best* choice, not just a good choice. For many questions, it is helpful to read the answers before trying to answer the question.

Budget your time. Calculate the time you may spend on each question, so that you will have time to look at each question. You want to answer as many questions correctly as you can, so try to work quickly but accurately. Check your watch a few times while you are working on each section to make sure you are working sufficiently fast. Be sure not to linger on a question you can't answer, or spend time worrying about questions you can't answer. You should not expect to answer every question correctly. If you have no idea what the answer to a question is, leave the space blank on your sheet and move on. Since one quarter of your wrong answers is subtracted from your total of correct answers to get your raw score, it is better to leave an answer blank if you can not eliminate any of the choices. However, if you can eliminate even one answer it is to your advantage to guess one of the remaining answers.

You will not be allowed to use rulers, slide rules, or calculators on the exam. If you usually use a calculator to do arithmetic, practice doing arithmetic without it.

The GMAT exam takes over three hours, and you will have only one ten-minute break. To ready yourself for this physical strain, do each practice exam entirely in one sitting. Try to be well rested and eat a good meal before the exam. Remember: a question answered correctly on the last section of the exam counts just as much as a question answered correctly on the first section. If you are tired by the end of the exam, you may not do as well as you could on the later sections.

Your Scores and What They Mean

You will receive three scores on the GMAT exam: a total score, a verbal score, and a quantitative score. The total score ranges from 200 to 800; the verbal and quantitative scores range from 0 to 60. You will also be given a percentile ranking for each of the three scores. The percentile ranking gives you the percentage of the test scores in the last three years lower than yours. Thus, a percentile ranking of 75 would mean that 75% of the test scores in the last three years were below your score.

All of the scores you receive are *scaled scores*. Since there are many different versions of the exam, the use of scaled scores allows test results based on different versions of the exam to be compared. The same *raw score* (total number of correct answers minus one fourth of the number of wrong answers) will be converted into a higher scaled score if you took a more difficult version of the exam. If you take several versions of the exam, your scaled scores should cluster about your "true" scaled score. Thus, your scaled score in some sense represents a range of possibilities. A score of 510 means that your "true" score is probably between 480 and 540.

In general, no particular score can be called good or bad, and no passing or failing grade has been established. Scores above 700 or below 250 are unusual. In recent years, about two thirds of all scores have fallen between 350 and 570, with the average between 460 and 470. In the verbal and quantitative scores, grades above 46 or below 10 are unusual. About two thirds of these scores fall between 17 and 35, with the average between 26 and 27.

Your score on the GMAT is only one of several factors examined by admissions officers. Your undergraduate record, for example, is at least as important as your GMAT score. Thus, a low score does not mean that no school will accept you, nor does a high GMAT score guarantee acceptance at the school of your choice. However, since your score is one important factor, you should try to do as well as you can on the exam. Using this book should help you to maximize your score.

How to Prepare for the GMAT

You should now be aware of the purpose of the GMAT and have a general idea of the format of the test. With this basic information, you are in a position to begin your study and review. The rest of this guide represents a study plan which will enable you to prepare for the GMAT. If used properly, it will help you diagnose your weak areas and take steps to remedy them.

Begin your preparation by becoming as familiar as possible with the various types of questions that appear on the exam. The analysis of typical GMAT questions in the next chapter is designed for this purpose. When you feel you understand this material completely, take the Diagnostic Test that follows and evaluate your results on the self-scoring table provided at the end of the test. (An explanation of how to use these tables appears below.) A low score in any area indicates that you should spend more time reviewing that particular material. Study the review section for that area until you feel you have mastered it and then take one of the sample GMATs at the back of the book. Continue this pattern of study until you are completely satisfied with your performance. For best results, try to simulate exam conditions as closely as possible when taking sample tests: no unscheduled breaks or interruptions, strict adherence to time limits, and no use of outside aids.

The Self-scoring Tables

The self-scoring tables for each sample test in this guide can be used as a means of evaluating your weaknesses in particular subject areas and should help you plan your study program most effectively.

After completing a sample test, first determine the number of *correct* answers you had for each section. Next, subtract *one-fourth* the number of *wrong* answers for each part from the number of correct answers. This is done to eliminate the benefits of wild guessing. Do *not* subtract for any answers left blank. For example, suppose that in Section I you answered 20 out of 30 questions correctly, with 6 incorrect responses and 4 blanks. Subtract ¼ of 6 (1½) from 20 to obtain a final score of 18½. Record this score in the appropriate score box in the Self-scoring Table as shown below.

Self-scoring Table

PART	SCORE	RATING
1	18½	GOOD
2		
3		
4		
5		
6		

Then compare this score with those contained in the Self-scoring Scale. Insert your rating, either POOR, FAIR, GOOD, or EXCELLENT, in the appropriate box in the Self-scoring Table.

Self-scoring Scale

RATING

PART	POOR	FAIR	GOOD	EXCELLENT
1-2	0-10	11-15	16-22	23-30
3	0-24	25-30	31-39	40-55
4	0-7	8-10	11-15	16-20
5	0-5	6-8	9-12	13-15
6	0-15	16-20	21-29	30-40
7	0-7	8-10	11-15	16-20
8	0-7	8-10	11-15	16-20

A rating of FAIR or POOR in any area indicates that you need to spend more time reviewing that material.

Scaled Scores

The rules below will give you a method for converting your raw score on a practice exam into a scaled score. This is not the same procedure that the GMAT uses, but it should give you some idea of what your scaled score would be on the exam. Note that your raw score on an exam is the number of correct answers minus one fourth of the incorrect answers, with no deduction for answers left blank.

Use the following rules to convert your raw score into a scaled score.

For tests with 195-200 questions:

RAW SCORE	SCALED SCORE
15 or less	250
16-65	250 plus 3 times (raw score minus 15)
66-165	400 plus 2 times (raw score minus 65)
166-185	600 plus 5 times (raw score minus 165)
185-194	700 plus 10 times (raw score minus 185)
195 or more	800

For tests with 170-185 questions:

RAW SCORE	SCALED SCORE
15 or less	250
16-55	250 plus 3 times (raw score minus 15)
56-145	400 plus 2 times (raw score minus 55)
146-160	600 plus 5 times (raw score minus 145)
161-169	700 plus 10 times (raw score minus 160)
170 or more	800

EXAMPLE:

Raw score on a test with 195 questions is 142.5
(A) Raw score is between 65 and 165
(B) Raw score minus 65 = 77.5
(C) Scaled Score is 400 + 2(77.5) = 400 + 155 = 555

If your scaled scores are low on the first practice exams you take, don't get discouraged. Your scaled score should improve on the later practice exams after you have used the various reviews to strengthen your weaknesses. The tests were made hard. That way you can discover your weaknesses and try to correct them. Easy practice tests are not good practice for a difficult exam. Remember that, on the GMAT itself, you shouldn't expect to be able to answer every single question. Don't worry about that. To maximize your score, you want to answer as many questions as you can correctly in the given amount of time.

After You Take the Exam

You will usually receive your scores about four weeks after the exam.

You may take the GMAT as many times as you wish. However, if you repeat the test, your scores from that test and the two most recent previous test results will be sent to all institutions you designate as score recipients. Many schools average your scores if you take the test more than once. So unless there is a reason to expect a substantial improvement in your score, it usually is *not* worthwhile to retake the exam.

Currently, you can receive a copy of your answer sheet, a booklet containing all questions that were counted in scoring your exam, an answer key, and the scale used to translate your raw scores into scaled scores. You should obtain this information if you are considering retaking the exam. You can see if there was any particular section which hurt your score and concentrate on those questions as you study.

You can also cancel your scores if you act *before* receiving them. If you wish to cancel your scores, you must indicate this on your answer sheet, notify the supervisor before you leave the test center, or notify ETS by mail within 7 days of the test administration. If you cancel your scores, the fact that you took the test will be reported to all the places you designated as score recipients. Thus, it is generally not advantageous to cancel your scores unless there is reason to believe that you have done substantially worse on the test than you would if you took the test again; for example, if you became ill while taking the exam. Once a score is cancelled from your record it can not be put back on your record or reported at a later date.

As a general rule, it is better to retake the exam after looking over your previous results (questions, answers, and so on) than it is to cancel your scores. You can do well on the exam without finishing every section of the exam. In addition, each version of the exam contains questions or sections which are experimental and are not counted towards your score, so your score may be better than you expect. Thus, you usually are better off waiting to see your score before deciding whether or not to retake the exam.

TWO
AN ANALYSIS OF TYPICAL GMAT QUESTIONS

A logical first step in preparing for the GMAT is to become as familiar as possible with the types of questions that usually appear on this exam. The following analysis of typical GMAT questions explains the purpose behind each type and the best method for answering it. Samples of the questions with a discussion of their answers are also presented. More detailed discussions and reviews for each type of question are presented elsewhere in this book.

Reading Comprehension

The Reading Comprehension section tests your ability to analyze written information, and includes passages from the humanities, the social sciences, and the physical and biological sciences. As you shall see, it differs from the Reading Recall section not only in the subject matter covered but also by the fact that you are allowed to refer to the passages while answering the questions.

The typical Reading Comprehension section consists of three or four passages with a total of 25 questions which must be completed in 30 minutes. You would normally be presented with *either* a Reading Recall or a Reading Comprehension section—almost never with both. In recent years, Reading Comprehension has been used more frequently.

The following passage will give you an idea of the format of the Reading Comprehension section. Read the passage through and then answer the questions, making sure to leave yourself enough time to complete them all.

Sample Passage

TIME—10 minutes

Political theories have, in fact, very little more to do with musical creation than electronic theories have. Both merely determine methods of distribution. The exploitation of these methods is subject to political regulation, is quite rigidly regulated in many countries. The revolutionary parties, both in Russia and elsewhere, have

(5) tried to turn composers on to supposedly revolutionary subject-matter. The net result for either art or revolution has not been very important. Neither has official fascist music accomplished much either for music or for Italy or Germany.

Political party-influence on music is just censorship anyway. Performances can be forbidden and composers disciplined for what they write, but the creative stimulus

(10) comes from elsewhere. Nothing really "inspires" an author but money or food or love.

That persons or parties subventioning musical uses should wish to retain veto power over the works used is not at all surprising. That our political masters (or our representatives) should exercise a certain negative authority, a censorship, over (15) the exploitation of works whose content they consider dangerous to public welfare is also in no way novel or surprising. But that such political executives should think to turn the musical profession into a college of political theorists or a bunch of hired propagandists is naïve of them. Our musical civilization is older than any political party. We can deal on terms of intellectual equality with acoustical engineers, with (20) architects, with poets, painters, and historians, even with the Roman clergy if necessary. We cannot be expected to take very seriously the inspirational dictates of persons or of groups who think they can pay us to get emotional about ideas. They can pay us to get emotional all right. Anybody can. Nothing is so emotion-producing as money. But emotions are factual; they are not generated by ideas. On the con- (25) trary, ideas are generated by emotions; and emotions, in turn, are visceral states produced directly by facts like money and food and sexual intercourse. To have any inspirational quality there must be present facts or immediate anticipations, not pie-in-the-sky.

Now pie-in-the-sky has its virtues as a political ideal, I presume. Certainly most (30) men want to work for an eventual common good. I simply want to make it quite clear that ideals about the common good (not to speak of mere political necessity) are not very stimulating subject-matter for music. They don't produce visceral movements the way facts do. It is notorious that musical descriptions of hell, which is something we can all imagine, are more varied and vigorous than the placid banal- (35) ities that even the best composers have used to describe heaven; and that all composers do better on really present matters than on either: matters like love and hatred and hunting and war and dancing around and around.

The moral of all this is that the vetoing of objective subject-matter is as far as political stimulation or censorship can go in advance. Style is personal and emo- (40) tional, not political at all. And form or design, which is impersonal, is not subject to any political differences of opinion.

1. The author is making a statement defending   Ⓐ Ⓑ Ⓒ Ⓓ Ⓔ

   I. intellectual freedom
  II. the apolitical stance of most musicians
 III. emotional honesty

  (A) I only
  (B) II only   (D) I and III only
  (C) I and II only   (E) I, II, and III

2. The tone of the author in the passage is   Ⓐ Ⓑ Ⓒ Ⓓ Ⓔ

  (A) exacting
  (B) pessimistic
  (C) critical
  (D) optimistic
  (E) fatalistic

3. The author's reaction to political influence on music is one of   Ⓐ Ⓑ Ⓒ Ⓓ Ⓔ

  (A) surprise
  (B) disbelief
  (C) resignation
  (D) deference
  (E) rancor

4. According to the author, political attempts to control the subject-matter of music   Ⓐ Ⓑ Ⓒ Ⓓ Ⓔ

    (A)   will be resisted by artists wherever they are made
    (B)   may succeed in censoring but not in inspiring musical works
    (C)   will succeed only if the eventual goal is the common good
    (D)   are less effective than the indirect use of social and economic pressure
    (E)   have profoundly influenced the course of modern musical history

5. The author refers to "musical descriptions of hell" (line 33) to make the point that   Ⓐ Ⓑ Ⓒ Ⓓ Ⓔ

    (A)   musical inspiration depends on the degree to which the composer's imagination is stimulated by his subject
    (B)   composers are better at evoking negative emotions and ideas than positive ones
    (C)   music is basically unsuited to a role in support of political tyranny
    (D)   religious doctrines have inspired numerous musical compositions
    (E)   political ideals are a basic motivating force for most contemporary composers

6. The author implies that political doctrines usually fail to generate artistic creativity   Ⓐ Ⓑ Ⓒ Ⓓ Ⓔ
because they are too

    (A)   naive
    (B)   abstract
    (C)   rigidly controlled
    (D)   concrete
    (E)   ambiguous

Answers to Sample Passages:

1. **(D)**   2. **(C)**   3. **(C)**   4. **(B)**   5. **(A)**   6. **(B)**

Analysis:

1. **(D)** The author is arguing that musicians will not conform to any control over their creativity. Thus, they want to be intellectually free and emotionally honest. It does not mean that they could not be active in politics (apolitical).

2. **(C)** The author is critical of attempts to censor the arts, especially music.

3. **(C)** The author does not find censorship surprising (line 13), nor does he take it seriously (line 21). He is resigned to attempts at censorship, although he does not believe it can inspire creativity.

4. **(B)** See paragraph 2.

5. **(A)** See lines 33-34.

6. **(B)** See paragraph 4, in which the author states that "ideals" do not inspire music as "facts" do; and also see lines 10-11 and 26-28.

Reading Recall

The purpose of these questions is to test your ability to understand and remember *main points* and *significant details* contained in material you have read and to determine how well you can draw inferences from this material. Generally, each Reading Recall section contains three passages of several paragraphs each. You are allowed 15 minutes to read all three passages. After this time has elapsed you are given another 20 minutes to answer questions based on these passages. You may not refer to the passages while answering the questions, but instead must rely on your memory to supply the desired information.

The best way to approach the Reading Recall question is to concentrate as much as possible on the *significant details* in the passages. A good method for fixing these ideas in your memory is to underline main points as you read. Try to budget your time so that you can cover all the material during the allotted 15 minutes. If you finish all three passages before time is called, you will be able to use the material you have underlined as a means of quick review.

The following passage will give you an idea of the format of the Reading Recall section. Like most Reading Recall passages, it deals with an *economic problem*. As you read, underline what you believe to be the main ideas presented. Limit your reading time to 5 minutes. Spend another 7 minutes answering the questions that follow, remembering not to refer back to the passage for assistance. When you have finished, compare your responses with the analysis of answers provided at the end.

Sample Passage

Part A: TIME—5 minutes

Some economists believe that the United States can be utilized as a "land bridge" for the shipment of containerized cargo between Europe and the Far East. Under the land-bridge concept, containerized freight traveling between Europe and the Far East would be shipped by ocean carrier to the United States East Coast, unloaded and placed on special railway flatcars, and shipped via railroad to a West Coast port. At this port, the containers would then be loaded on ships bound to a Far East port of entry. This procedure would be reversed for material traveling in the opposite direction. Thus, a land transportation system would be substituted for marine transportation during part of the movement of goods between Europe and the Far East.

If a land-bridge system of shipment were deemed feasible and competitive with alternative methods, it would open a completely new market for both United States steamship lines and railroads. At present, foreign lines carry all Far East–Europe freight. American carriers get none of this trade, and the all-water route excludes the railroads.

The system established by a land-bridge could also serve to handle goods now being shipped between the United States West Coast and Europe, or goods shipped between the Far East and the United States Gulf and East Coasts. Currently, there are 20 foreign lines carrying West Coast freight to Europe via the Panama Canal, but not one United States line. Thus, in addition to the land-bridge getting this new business for the railroads, it also gives the United States East Coast ships an opportunity to compete for this trade.

While this method of shipment will probably not add to the labor requirements at East and West Coast piers, it does have the potential of absorbing some of the jobs that the containerization of current cargo has eliminated or could eliminate. Thus, the possibility of creating new jobs for longshoremen is not an expected benefit of such a system, but it will most certainly create other labor requirements. The land-bridge concept has the potential of offering new job openings for United States railway workers and seamen. In addition, there would be expansion of labor requirements for people in the shipbuilding and container manufacturing business.

By making United States rail transportation an export service, the land-bridge system would have a favorable effect on our balance of payments. Such a system also has the potential of relieving the United States government of part of the burden it now bears in the form of subsidies to the shipping industry. The federal government subsidizes the construction and operation of scheduled vessels. Some 52 percent of the income from their operation comes from the government in that these ships are used for all our military and other government-related export shipments. The land-bridge requirement for scheduled sailings could effect a shift from the use of these subsidized lines for shipment of government goods to commercial cargo of the land bridge. This would then open some of the lucrative government business to the unscheduled, unsubsidized lines.

QUESTIONS TO

Sample Passage

Part B: TIME — 7 minutes

DIRECTIONS: Answer the following questions pertaining to information contained in the passage you have just read. You may not turn back to this passage for assistance.

1. According to the passage, if a land-bridge system were feasible, it would Ⓐ Ⓑ Ⓒ Ⓓ Ⓔ

    (A) create employment in the bridge-building industry
    (B) decrease the amount of air freight
    (C) create a new market for steamship lines and railroads
    (D) make American railroads more efficient
    (E) increase foreign trade

2. The author implies that which of the following would be provided employment by Ⓐ Ⓑ Ⓒ Ⓓ Ⓔ
    the development of a land-bridge?

      I. Longshoremen
     II. U.S. railway workers
   III. U.S. seamen

    (A) I only
    (B) III only
    (C) I and II only
    (D) II and III only
    (E) I, II, and III

3. According to the passage, the major alternative to a U.S. land-bridge is the Ⓐ Ⓑ Ⓒ Ⓓ Ⓔ

    (A) Panama Canal
    (B) Suez Canal
    (C) air-freight system
    (D) all land route
    (E) military transport system

Ⓐ Ⓑ Ⓒ Ⓓ Ⓔ   **4.** The passage states that a land-bridge would improve America's

        (A) foreign trade
        (B) balance of payments
        (C) rate of unemployment
        (D) international relations
        (E) gold reserves

Ⓐ Ⓑ Ⓒ Ⓓ Ⓔ   **5.** A land-bridge would *not*

        (A) aid U.S. steamship lines
        (B) handle goods shipped between Europe and the Far East
        (C) create new jobs for longshoremen
        (D) supply new business for U.S. railroads
        (E) create business for unscheduled shipping lines

Answers and Analysis

The sample passage with main points underlined appears below:

Some economists believe that the United States can be utilized as a "land bridge" for the shipment of containerized cargo between Europe and the Far East. Under the land-bridge concept, containerized freight traveling between Europe and the Far East would be shipped by ocean carrier to the United States East Coast, unloaded and placed on special railway flatcars, and shipped via railroad to a West Coast port. At this port, the containers would then be loaded on ships bound to a Far East port of entry. This procedure would be reversed for material traveling in the opposite direction. Thus, a land transportation system would be substituted for marine transportation during part of the movement of goods between Europe and the Far East.

If a land-bridge system of shipment were deemed feasible and competitive with alternative methods, it would open a completely new market for both United States steamship lines and railroads. At present, foreign lines carry all Far East-Europe freight. American carriers get none of this trade and the all-water route excludes the railroads.

The system established by a land-bridge could also serve to handle goods now being shipped between the United States West Coast and Europe, or goods shipped between the Far East and the United States Gulf and East Coasts. Currently, there are 20 foreign lines carrying West Coast freight to Europe via the Panama Canal, but not one United States line. Thus, in addition to the land-bridge getting this new business for the railroads, it also gives the United States East Coast ships an opportunity to compete for this trade.

While this method of shipment will probably not add to the labor requirements at East and West Coast piers, it does have the potential of absorbing some of the jobs that the containerization of current cargo has eliminated or could eliminate. Thus, the possibility of creating new jobs for longshoremen is not an expected benefit of such a system, but it will most certainly create other labor requirements. The land-bridge concept has the potential of offering new job openings for United States railway workers and seamen. In addition, there would be expansion of labor requirements for people in the shipbuilding and container manufacturing business.

By making United States rail transportation an export service, the land-bridge system would have a favorable effect on our balance of payments. Such a system also has the potential of relieving the United States government of part of the burden it now bears in the form of subsidies to the shipping industry. The federal government subsidizes the construction and operation of scheduled vessels. Some 52 percent of the income from their operation comes from the government in that these ships are used for all our military and other government-related export shipments. The land-bridge requirement for scheduled sailings could effect a shift from the use of these subsidized lines for shipment of government goods to commercial cargo of the land bridge. This would then open some of the lucrative government business to the unscheduled, unsubsidized lines.

ANSWERS TO PART B:

1. (C)   2. (D)   3. (A)   4. (B)   5. (C)

ANALYSIS:

1.   (C) See paragraph 2.

2.   (D) See paragraph 4.

3.   (A) Paragraph 3 discusses use of the Panama Canal as a route for freight lines.

4.   (B) See paragraph 5.

5.   (C) See paragraph 4. It specifically states that longshoremen wouldn't benefit.

Verbal Ability

This section of the GMAT is designed to test your ability to grasp the meanings of words and to determine the relationships that exist between words and ideas in a given situation. Verbal ability thus reflects your capacity for communication and understanding, and is a basic measure of your vocabulary range.

The Verbal Ability section of the exam usually consists of three types of questions: antonyms, analogies, and sentence completions. The following discussion will give you an idea of how to approach each of these types when you encounter them on the exam.

Antonyms

An antonym is a word that is opposite in meaning to another word. For example, an antonym for *good* would be *bad*. On the exam you are given a key word printed in capital letters accompanied by five lettered choices. You must select the lettered word that comes closest to being *opposite* in meaning to the capitalized word. Try the following sample question.

BUILD: (A) destroy (B) attack (C) furnish (D) demur (E) renovate   Ⓐ Ⓑ Ⓒ Ⓓ Ⓔ

ANSWER: (*A*) destroy

ANALYSIS: Build is a verb meaning to construct. (B) attack means to assault, (C) furnish means to equip, (D) demur means to hesitate, and (E) renovate means to refurbish. Clearly, (A) destroy, meaning to demolish, is the word that is opposite in meaning to the key word, build.

Analogies

In the context of the GMAT, an analogy can be defined as a similarity existing between two given sets of words. An example of this would be the analogy BOY : GIRL : : man : woman (read *boy is to girl as man is to woman*). The similarity between the two word-pairs should be apparent.

You are asked to select from five lettered word-pairs the combination which has a similar relationship to the key word-pair (or stem) which appears in capital letters. When making your selection, you should first establish the type of relationship existing between the key words. (In the example BOY : GIRL, this can be stated as "A is the male counterpart of B.") After the type of relationship has been determined, a corresponding word-pair can be logically located among the choices.

Try the sample question below.

RITUAL : WORSHIP :: (A) meal : recipe (B) paragon : person (C) pro-   Ⓐ Ⓑ Ⓒ Ⓓ Ⓔ
tocol : diplomacy (D) geography : geology (E) medicine : magic

ANSWER: (*C*) protocol : diplomacy

ANALYSIS: The rationale of the stem can be stated as A is the ceremony associated with B. Since protocol is the ceremony associated with diplomacy, the most similar word-pair is (C).

Sentence Completions

These questions require you to complete a sentence by selecting from five alternatives the word or set of words which, when inserted into blanks in the given sentence, best complete the meaning of that sentence. Look for key words in the sentence that will supply hints to the missing words. Make sure to choose only those words which are *logical* in the context of the sentence.

Try the sample questions below, choosing the set of words that best completes the meaning of the sentence.

SAMPLE 1:

A strike is employed as a last resort, to be used only when other _____ fail.   Ⓐ Ⓑ Ⓒ Ⓓ Ⓔ

(A) excuses
(B) companies
(C) movements

(D) measures
(E) admonitions

ANSWER: (*D*) measures

ANALYSIS: Strike is the key word here. In the context of the sentence, the answer will be a word describing a strike. Of the five alternatives, measures is the only logical choice.

SAMPLE 2:

Although the political controversies which occasioned it have long been _____,   Ⓐ Ⓑ Ⓒ Ⓓ Ⓔ
Milton's *Areopagitica* is still _____ today because of its vigorous, powerful style.

(A) settled . . . criticized
(B) discussed . . . controversial
(C) famous . . . obscure

(D) resolved . . . unpopular
(E) forgotten . . . admired

ANSWER: (*E*) forgotten . . . admired

ANALYSIS: The word "Although" suggests that the two clauses of the sentence will present ideas which conflict with one another. This eliminates choices (B) and (D), which would not establish any contrast. Choices (A) and (C) may be eliminated because a "vigorous, powerful style" would *not* lead to *Areopagitica*'s being either "criticized" or "obscure."

Writing Ability

The Writing Ability section tests your knowledge of basic English grammar. To succeed in this section, you need a command of sentence structure including tense and mood, subject and verb agreement, proper case, parallel structure, and other basics. No attempt is made to test for punctuation, spelling, or capitalization. Two question types have been used to test Writing Ability: Usage and Sentence Correction.

Writing Ability (Usage)

In this item type, each question consists of a sentence with four parts (words or phrases) underlined. These parts are labeled A, B, C, and D. There is also a fifth choice, No error, labeled E. You must choose the part of the sentence that is *incorrect* and blacken the corresponding letter on your answer sheet. If there are no incorrect parts, blacken letter E.

The following questions will give you an idea of the type of Writing Ability questions to expect. For each, choose the underlined word or phrase that is incorrect and blacken the appropriate letter in the answer grid.

After the fire whistle <u>blew to signal</u> lunch time, the foreman told <u>Joe and I</u> Ⓐ Ⓑ Ⓒ Ⓓ Ⓔ
                      A   B
<u>that we</u> would have to return early to finish <u>pouring the foundation</u>. <u>No error</u>
 C   D   E

ANSWER: **(B)**

ANALYSIS: *I* should be *me;* me is the objective case and, in this instance, the pronoun is the object of the verb *told*.

In order to identify a bird, <u>one must note</u> <u>it's peculiar markings</u> <u>and then find</u> a bird Ⓐ Ⓑ Ⓒ Ⓓ Ⓔ
      A   B   C   D
with similar markings in a guidebook. <u>No error</u>
                                         E

ANSWER: **(C)**

ANALYSIS: *it's* should be *its; it's* is a contraction of *it is*, not the possessive form that is needed here.

Writing Ability (Sentence Correction)

This item type has recently been introduced into the GMAT. The section consists of a series of sentences with some part of the sentence or the entire sentence underlined. The underlined part presents a problem in the appropriate use of language. Beneath each sentence, five different ways of writing the underlined part are presented. The first of these, (A), repeats the original; the other four choices are different.

Select the best version and blacken the appropriate space on your answer sheet.

Here is an example:

Since the advent of cable television, at the beginning of <u>this decade, the video industry took</u> a giant stride forward in this country.

(A) this decade, the video industry took
(B) this decade, the video industry had taken
(C) this decade, the video industry has taken
(D) this decade saw the video industry taking
(E) the decade that let the video industry take

ANSWER: **(C)**

ANALYSIS: The phrase, "Since the advent . . . . " demands a verb in the present perfect form; thus *"has taken"* and not *"took."* Choice (E) changes the meaning of the original sentence.

Practical Judgment

The objective of the Practical Judgment section is to test your ability to analyze business situations and draw conclusions about them. In this section, you are asked to read a passage discussing various aspects of a business situation leading to the need for a decision. After you complete the passage, you are given two sets of questions to answer.

The first set, consisting of Data Evaluation questions, contains a number of factors relating to the passage, each of which you must evaluate as being a *Major Objective,* a *Major Factor,* a *Minor Factor,* a *Major Assumption,* or an *Unimportant Issue* in the decision-making process. The second set, consisting of Data Application questions, contains general questions about the situation described in the passage. You are permitted to refer to the passage while answering the questions.

As in the Reading Recall passages, it is helpful to underline main points as you read. However, when reading the Practical Judgment passages, you should concentrate on defining decision-making factors that fit into the categories for evaluation in the Data Evaluation questions.

The sample passage below is considerably shorter than a typical Practical Judgment passage on the exam. Read the passage, underlining what you feel to be

1. Major Objectives
2. Major Factors
3. Minor Factors
4. Major Assumptions
5. Unimportant Issues

After you have finished, answer the questions that follow. Allow yourself 12 minutes to complete the entire exercise. You may consult the passage for assistance.

Sample Passage

TIME — 12 minutes

Early in 1953, the soft drink world began to watch an interesting experiment: the introduction of soft drinks in cans. Grocery outlets up to that time had enjoyed about one-half of all sales, but it was felt that if the new package was successful, local bottling plants might give way to great central plants, possibly operated by companies with established names in the grocery fields, with shipments being made in carload lots. Local bottlers faced a great decision. If the change were to prove permanent, they should perhaps hasten to add can-filling machines lest they lose their market. Coca-Cola, Canada Dry, White Rock, and many other bottlers experimented with the new plan. An eastern chain put out privately branded cans.

A basic limitation was the cost factor of about three cents per can, whereas bottle cost was but a fraction of a cent, since a bottle averaged about twenty-four round trips. It was known, however, that at that time about one third of all beer sales were made in cans and, furthermore, that other beverages had paved the way for consumer acceptance of a canned product. Beer prices were normally from three to four times those of soft drinks.

Many leaders in the industry felt that it might well be that consumer advertising emphasizing the convenience of using a nonreturnable package might offset both habit and the extra cost to the consumer. One of the principal bottling companies undertook a large-scale market research project to find useful guides to future action.

Sample Data Evaluation Questions

Directions: The questions that follow relate to the preceding passage. Evaluate, in terms of the passage, each of the items given. Then select your answer from one of the following classifications, and blacken the corresponding space on the answer sheet.

(A) A MAJOR OBJECTIVE in making the decision: one of the goals sought by the decision maker

(B) A MAJOR FACTOR in making the decision: an aspect of the problem, specifically mentioned in the passage, that fundamentally affects and/or determines the decision

(C) A MINOR FACTOR in making the decision: a less important element bearing on or affecting a Major Factor, rather than a Major Objective directly

(D) A MAJOR ASSUMPTION in making the decision: a projection or supposition arrived at by the decision maker before considering the factors and alternatives

(E) AN UNIMPORTANT ISSUE in making the decision: an item lacking significant impact on, or relationship to, the decision

1. Introduction of soft drinks in cans

2. Results of the market research project

3. Cost of soft drinks in cans

4. Inappropriateness of cans for more than a single use prior to scrapping

5. Size of the beer market as compared to that for soft drinks

6. Power of consumer advertising to eliminate resistance to canned soft drinks

Sample Data Application Question

DIRECTIONS: Answer the following question using information contained in the passage.

7. Which of the following reasons were given for the market research project launched by a bottling company?

   I. Desire to corner the soft-drink market
  II. Need to determine whether consumers would be willing to pay a higher price for canned soft drinks
 III. Desire to test consumer reaction to canned soft drinks

(A) I only
(B) III only
(C) I and II only
(D) II and III only
(E) I, II, and III

Answers and Analysis

The sample passage with suggested underlining appears below.

Early in 1953, the soft drink world began to watch an interesting experiment, the introduction of soft drinks in cans. Grocery outlets up to that time had enjoyed about one-half of all sales, but it was felt that if the new package was successful, local bottling plants might give way to great central plants, possibly operated by companies with established names in the grocery fields, with shipments being made in carload lots. Local bottlers faced a great decision. If the change were to prove permanent, they should perhaps hasten to add can-filling machines lest they lose their market. Coca Cola, Canada

Dry, White Rock, and many other bottlers experimented with the new plan. An eastern chain put out privately branded cans.

A basic limitation was a cost factor of about three cents per can, whereas bottle cost was but a fraction of a cent, since a bottle averaged about twenty-four round trips. It was, however, known that at that time about one-third of all beer sales were made in cases, and furthermore, that other beverages had paved the way for consumer acceptance of a canned product. Beer prices normally were from three or four times those of soft drinks.

Many leaders in the industry felt that it might well be that consumer advertising emphasizing the convenience of using a nonreturnable package might offset both habit and the extra cost to the consumer. One of the principal bottling companies undertook a rather large-scale market research project to find useful guides to future action.

Answers to Data Evaluation Questions:

1. (A) 2. (B) 3. (B) 4. (C) 5. (E) 6. (D)

Analysis:

1. (A) The introduction of soft drinks in cans is certainly the *Major Objective* here, since it is the ultimate goal toward which the executives were working.

2. (B) The market research project would gather information allowing management to make a decision; without such information, presumably, no decision could be reached. Therefore, the results of the project are a *Major Factor* influencing the decision.

3. (B) The cost of canned soft drinks is a *Major Factor* in making the decision because it is crucial to consumer acceptance. If the soft drinks are priced too high, consumers may not be willing to purchase them.

4. (C) Because cans may only be used once, their cost per use is higher than that of bottles. Since this factor has a peripheral effect on a major factor—namely, overall costs—it constitutes a *Minor Factor*.

5. (E) The size of the beer market is of minimal importance in the decision as to whether soft drinks in cans will prove a success. Therefore, the only possible answer to this question is (E), *Unimportant Issue*.

6. (D) The executives alluded to in the passage merely *suspect* that advertising will be capable of effecting the desired attitude change. No facts are given to support this belief. Thus, this item is a *Major Assumption*.

Answer to Data Application Question

7.   (D) II and III only.

ANALYSIS: The correct answer is (D) because the passage states that among the major uncertainties as to whether to offer canned soft drinks were their high cost and the purchasing habits of consumers, i.e., whether they would prefer canned soft drinks and be willing to pay a premium price for them. Alternative (A), I only, is factually incorrect, since no mention is made that the bottler in question desires to "corner the market."

Problem Solving

The Problem Solving section of the GMAT is designed to test your ability to work with numbers. There are a variety of questions in this section dealing with the basic principles of arithmetic, algebra, and geometry. These questions may take the form of word problems or require straight calculation. In addition, questions involving the interpretation of tables and graphs may be included.

The typical Problem Solving section consists of 30 questions that must be answered within a time limit of 40 minutes. Sometimes a longer section of 55 questions with a 75-minute time limit will appear. Although the majority of questions are not extremely difficult, it is sometimes impossible to answer all of them within the allotted time. For this reason, you should be aware of certain procedures that will help you make the most of the time you have.

Strategy for GMAT Problem Solving Questions

In order to maximize your score on this section, you must answer all the questions you can. *Don't waste time* on a question you can't figure out in a minute or two. You will score better if you answer 2 or 3 easy questions in the time it would take to answer one difficult one. Since the last questions may be easier for you than the first questions, try to *budget your time* so that you will have a chance to try each question.

Don't waste time on *unnecessary calculations*. If you can answer the question by *estimating* or doing a rough calculation, the time you save can be used to answer other questions. Keep this in mind especially when considering problems that involve tables and graphs. In many cases you can make estimates which will simplify your calculations and still be accurate enough to answer the question. Using estimates is a skill that can turn a good score into an excellent one.

For line and bar graphs, use your pencil as a ruler. It is more accurate than simply "eyeballing" columns which are not adjacent.

You should understand that random guessing will not help your score on these sections, since a percentage of your wrong answers is subtracted from your correct answers. If you can eliminate at least one of the answers for a particular question, it will probably help your score to guess an answer for that question.

Solve the sample questions below, allowing yourself 12 minutes to complete all of them. As you work, try to make use of the above strategy. Any figure that appears with a problem is drawn as accurately as possible to provide information that may help in answering the question. All numbers used are real numbers.

Sample Problem Solving Questions

TIME—12 minutes

1. Ⓐ Ⓑ Ⓒ Ⓓ Ⓔ   1.   A train travels from Albany to Syracuse, a distance of 120 miles, at the average rate of 50 miles per hour. The train then travels back to Albany from Syracuse. The total traveling

time of the train is 5 hours and 24 minutes. What was the average rate of speed of the train on the return trip to Albany?

(A) 60 mph

(B) 48 mph

(C) 40 mph

(D) 50 mph

(E) 35 mph

2. A parking lot charges a flat rate of X dollars for any amount of time up to two hours, and $\frac{1}{6}X$ for each hour or fraction of an hour after the first two hours. How much does it cost to park for 5 hours and 15 minutes?   2. Ⓐ Ⓑ ·Ⓒ Ⓓ Ⓔ

(A) $3X$

(B) $2X$

(C) $1\frac{2}{3}X$

(D) $1\frac{1}{2}X$

(E) $1\frac{1}{6}X$

Use the following table for questions 3–5.

Number of Students by major in State University		
	1950	1970
Division of Business	990	2,504
Division of Sciences	350	790
Division of Humanities	1,210	4,056
Division of Engineering	820	1,600
Division of Agriculture	630	1,050
TOTAL	4,000	10,000

3. From 1950 to 1970, the change in the percentage of university students enrolled in Engineering was   3. Ⓐ Ⓑ Ⓒ Ⓓ Ⓔ
   (A) roughly no change
   (B) an increase of more than 4%
   (C) an increase of more than 1% but less than 4%
   (D) a decrease of more than 4%
   (E) a decrease of more than 1% but less than 4%

4. The number of students enrolled in Business in 1970 divided by the number of Business students in 1950 is   4. Ⓐ Ⓑ Ⓒ Ⓓ Ⓔ
   (A) almost 3
   (B) about 2.5
   (C) roughly 2
   (D) about 1
   (E) about 40%

5. By 1970 how many of the divisions had an enrollment greater than 200% of the enrollment of that division in 1950?   5. Ⓐ Ⓑ Ⓒ Ⓓ Ⓔ

(A) 0

(B) 1

(C) 2

(D) 3

(E) 4

Use the graph below for questions 6 and 7.

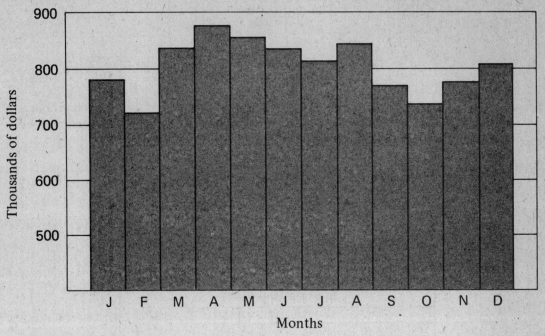

Months

The graph gives monthly sales of the XYZ corporation in thousands of dollars for each month in 1970.

Ⓐ Ⓑ Ⓒ Ⓓ Ⓔ **6.** In what month were sales the least?

(A) January   (D) December
(B) February   (E) March
(C) October

Ⓐ Ⓑ Ⓒ Ⓓ Ⓔ **7.** Which of the following statements are true?

  I. Of spring, summer, and fall, spring was the season which had the highest total sales.

  II. Sales in April were greater than the combined sales of January and February.

  III. The greatest change in sales occurred between August and September.

(A) I only   (D) II and III
(B) I and II   (E) I and III
(C) II only

Answers and Analysis

ANSWERS:

1. **(C)**   4. **(B)**   7. **(A)**
2. **(C)**   5. **(D)**
3. **(D)**   6. **(B)**

ANALYSIS:

1. **(C)** The train took $120/50 = 2\frac{2}{5}$ hours to travel from Albany to Syracuse. Since the total traveling time of the train was $5\frac{2}{5}$ hours, it must have taken the train 3 hours for the trip from Syracuse to Albany. Since the distance traveled is 120 miles, the average rate of speed on the return trip to Albany was $(1/3)(120)$ mph $= 40$ mph.

2. **(C)** It costs X for the first 2 hours. If you park 5 hours and 15 minutes there are 3 hours and 15 minutes left after the first 2 hours. Since this time is charged at the rate of $X/6$ for each hour or fraction thereof, it costs $4(X/6)$ for the last 3 hours and 15 minutes. Thus the total is $X + \frac{4}{6}X = 1\frac{2}{3}X$.

3. **(D)** Since $820/4,000 = .205$, the percentage of university students enrolled in Engineering in 1950 was 20.5%; since $1.600/10.000 = .16$, the percentage in 1970 was 16%. Thus the percentage of university students enrolled in Engineering was 4.5% less in 1970 than it was in 1950.

4. **(B)** In 1950 there were 990 Business students and in 1970 there were 2,504. Since $(2.5)(1,000) = 2,500$, the correct answer is thus (B) about 2.5. Note that this is an easy way to save yourself time. Instead of dividing 990 into 2,504 to find the exact answer, simply use numbers close to the original numbers to get an estimate. In many cases this gives enough information to answer the question and saves valuable time.

5. **(D)** If a division in 1970 has more than 200% of the number of students it had in 1950 that means that the number of students more than doubled between 1950 and 1970. Therefore simply double each entry in the 1950 column and if this is less than the corresponding entry in the 1970 column, that division has more than 200% of the number of students it had in 1950. Since $(2)(990) = 1980$ which is less than 2,504, the number of Business students more than doubled. Since $(2)(1,210) = 2,420$ which is less than 4,056, Humanities more than doubled, and because $(2)(350) = 700$ which is less than 790, Sciences more than doubled. Engineering did not double in size because $(2)(820) = 1640$ which is larger than 1,600. Also since $(2)(630) = 1,260$, which is larger than 1,050, the number of Agricultural students in 1970 was less than 200% of the number of Agricultural students in 1950. Therefore three of the divisions (Business, Humanities, and Sciences) more than doubled between 1950 and 1970.

6. **(B)** Use your pencil as a ruler to compare February to October; the other answers are obviously wrong.

7. **(A)** June and March were about the same; May was a little larger than August and April was much greater than July; so Spring sales were higher than Summer sales. It is easy to see Spring sales were higher than Fall sales. Therefore, statement I is true. (Use your pencil as a substitute for a ruler to compare columns which are not next to each other.) Since April sales were about $900,000 and sales in February and January were each larger than $700,000, the combined sales in January and February were larger than $1,400,000. Therefore, statement II is false. Between August and September the change was roughly $50,000 but between February and March the change was more than $100,000. Thus statement III is false.

Data Sufficiency

This section of the GMAT is designed to test your reasoning ability. Like the Problem Solving section, it requires a basic knowledge of the principles of arithmetic, algebra, and geometry.

Each Data Sufficiency question consists of a mathematical problem and two statements containing information relating to it. You must decide whether the problem can be solved by using information from: (A) the first statement alone, but not the second statement alone; (B) the second statement alone, but not the first statement alone; (C) both statements together, but neither alone; or (D) either of the statements alone. Choose (E) if the problem cannot be solved, even by using both statements together. Generally, you are allowed one minute to answer each question. Thus, if a section contains 15 questions, it will be 15 minutes in length. As in the Problem Solving section, time is of the utmost importance. Approaching Data Sufficiency problems properly will help you use this time wisely.

Always keep in mind the fact that you are never asked to supply an answer for the problem; you need only determine if there is sufficient data available to find the answer. Therefore, *don't waste time figuring out the exact answer*. Once you know whether or not it is possible to find the answer with the given information you are through. If you spend too much time doing unnecessary work on one question you may not be able to finish the entire section.

Because of the nature of these questions, it may be possible in certain instances to improve your score by making an educated guess. If, for example, you know that the first statement alone is sufficient but are not sure about the second one alone, you are already limited to just two choices—(A) the first statement alone but not the second statement alone is sufficient, or (D) either of the statements alone is sufficient. The same holds true if you are sure that the second statement alone is sufficient but are uncertain of the first statement. The answer must be either B or D. If you know that one of the statements is not sufficient by itself, then the answer must be either C or E. Since you get one raw score point for each correct answer and only lose ¼ of a point for an incorrect answer, you will probably raise your score by guessing.

Read the following directions carefully and then try the sample Data Sufficiency questions below. Allow yourself 6 minutes total time. All numbers used are real numbers. A figure given for a problem is intended to provide information consistent with that in the question, but not necessarily consistent with the additional information contained in the statements.

Sample Data Sufficiency Questions

TIME—6 minutes

DIRECTIONS: Each of the following problems has a question and two statements which are labeled (1) and (2). Use the data given in (1) and (2) together with other available information (such as the number of hours in a day, the definition of *clockwise*, mathematical facts, etc.) to decide whether the statements are *sufficient* to answer the question. Then choose

- (A) if you can get the answer from (1) alone but not from (2) alone;
- (B) if you can get the answer from (2) alone but not from (1) alone;
- (C) if you can get the answer from (1) and (2) together, although neither statement by itself suffices;
- (D) if statement (1) alone suffices *and* statement (2) alone suffices;
- (E) if you cannot get the answer from statements (1) and (2) together, but need even more data.

Ⓐ Ⓑ Ⓒ Ⓓ Ⓔ   1.   A rectangular field is 40 yards long. Find the area of the field.

    (1)   A fence around the entire boundary of the field is 140 yards long.
    (2)   The field is more than 20 yards wide.

2. Is X a number greater than zero?   2. Ⓐ Ⓑ Ⓒ Ⓓ Ⓔ

    (1) $X^2 - 1 = 0$

    (2) $X^3 + 8 = 0$

3. An industrial plant produces bottles. In 1961 the number of bottles produced by the   3. Ⓐ Ⓑ Ⓒ Ⓓ Ⓔ
plant was twice the number produced in 1960. How many bottles were produced
altogether in the years 1960, 1961 and 1962?

    (1) In 1962 the number of bottles produced was 3 times the number produced in
1960.

    (2) In 1963 the number of bottles produced was one half the total produced in the
years 1960, 1961, and 1962.

4. A man 6 feet tall is standing near a light on the top of a pole. What is the length of   4. Ⓐ Ⓑ Ⓒ Ⓓ Ⓔ
the shadow cast by the man?

    (1) The pole is 18 feet high.

    (2) The man is 12 feet from the pole.

5. Find the length of RS if z is $90°$ and $PS = 6$.   5. Ⓐ Ⓑ Ⓒ Ⓓ Ⓔ

    (1) $PR = 6$

    (2) $x = 45°$

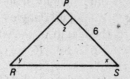

6. Working at a constant rate and by himself, it takes worker U 3 hours to fill up a ditch   6. Ⓐ Ⓑ Ⓒ Ⓓ Ⓔ
with sand. How long would it take for worker V to fill up the same ditch working by
himself?

    (1) Working together but at the same time U and V can fill in the ditch in 1 hour
$52\frac{1}{2}$ minutes.

    (2) In any length of time worker V fills in only 60% as much as worker U does in
the same time.

7. Did John go to the beach yesterday?   7. Ⓐ Ⓑ Ⓒ Ⓓ Ⓔ

    (1) If John goes to the beach, he will be sunburned the next day.

    (2) John is sunburned today.

Answers and Analysis

ANSWERS:

1.	(A)	4.	(C)
2.	(B)	5.	(D)
3.	(E)	6.	(D)
		7.	(E)

ANALYSIS:

1. **(A)** The area of a rectangle is the length multiplied by the width. Since you know the
length is 40 yards, you must find out the width in order to solve the problem. Since
statement (2) simply says the width is greater than 20 yards you can not find out the
exact width using (2). So (2) alone is not sufficient. Statement (1) says the length of
a fence around the entire boundary of the field is 140 yards. The length of this fence
is the perimeter of the rectangle, the sum of twice the length and twice the width.
If we replace the length by 40 in $P = 2L + 2W$ we have $140 = 2(40) + 2W$ and solving
for W yields $2W = 60$, or $W = 30$ yards. Hence the area is $(40)(30) = 1200$ square
yards. Thus (1) alone is sufficient but (2) alone is not.

2. **(B)** Statement (1) means $X^2 = 1$, but there are two possible solutions to this equation, $X = 1$, $X = -1$. Thus using (1) alone you can not deduce whether X is positive or negative. Statement (2) means $X^3 = -8$ but there is only one possible (real) solution to this, $X = -2$. Thus X is not greater than zero which answers the question. And (2) alone is sufficient.

3. **(E)** T, the total produced in the three years, is the sum of $P_0 + P_1 + P_2$, where P_0 is the number produced in 1960, P_1 the number produced in 1961, and P_2 the number produced in 1962. You are given that $P_1 = 2P_0$. Thus $T = P_0 + P_1 + P_2 = P_0 + 2P_0 + P_2 = 3P_0 + P_2$. So we must find out P_0 and P_2 to answer the question. Statement (1) says $P_2 = 3P_0$; thus by using (1) if we can find the value of P_0 we can find T. But (1) gives us no further information about P_0. Statement (2) says T equals the number produced in 1963, but it does not say what this number is. Since there are no relations given between production in 1963 and production in the individual years 1960, 1961, or 1962 you can not use (2) to find out what P_0 is. Thus (1) and (2) together are not sufficient.

4. **(C)** Sometimes it may help to draw a picture. By proportions or by similar triangles the height of the pole, h, is to 6 feet as the length of the shadow, s, + the distance to the pole, x, is to s. So $h/6 = (s + x)/s$. Thus $hs = 6s + 6x$ by cross-multiplication. Solving for s gives $hs - 6s = 6x$, or $s(h - 6) = 6x$, or, finally we have $s = 6x/(h - 6)$. Statement 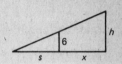 (1) says $h = 18$; thus $s = 6x/12 = x/2$, but using (1) alone we can not deduce the value x. Thus (1) alone is not sufficient. Statement (2) says x equals 12; thus, using (1) and (2) together we deduce $s = 6$, but using (2) alone all we can deduce is that $s = 72/(h - 6)$, which cannot be solved for s unless we know h. Thus using (1) and (2) together we can deduce the answer but (1) alone is not sufficient nor is (2) alone.

5. **(D)** Since z is a right angle, $(RS)^2 = (PS)^2 + (PR)^2$, so $(RS)^2 = (6)^2 + (PR)^2$, and RS will be the positive square root of $36 + (PR)^2$. Thus if you can find the length of PR the problem is solved. Statement (1) says $PR = 6$, thus $(RS)^2 = 36 + 36$, so $RS = 6\sqrt{2}$. Thus (1) alone is sufficient. Statement (2) says $x = 45°$ but since the sum of the angles in a triangle is $180°$ and z is $90°$ then $y = 45°$. So x and y are equal angles and that means the sides opposite x and opposite y must be equal or $PS = PR$. Thus $PR = 6$ and $RS = 6\sqrt{2}$ so (2) alone is also sufficient.

6. **(D)** (1) says U and V together can fill in the ditch in $1\frac{7}{8}$ hours. Since U can fill in the ditch in 3 hours, in 1 hour he can fill in one-third of the ditch. Hence, in $1\frac{7}{8}$ hours U would fill in $(1/3)(15/8) = \frac{5}{8}$ of the ditch. So V fills in $\frac{3}{8}$ of the ditch in $1\frac{7}{8}$ hours. Thus V would take $(8/3)(15/8) = 5$ hours to fill in the ditch working by himself. Therefore statement (1) alone is sufficient. According to statement (2) since U fills the ditch in 3 hours, V will fill $\frac{3}{5}$ of the ditch in 3 hours. Thus V will take 5 hours to fill in the ditch working by himself.

7. **(E)** Obviously, neither statement alone is sufficient. John *could* have gotten sunburned at the beach, but he might have gotten sunburned somewhere else. Therefore (1) and (2) together are not sufficient. This problem tests your grasp of an elementary rule of logic rather than your mathematical knowledge.

Answer Sheet — Diagnostic Test

Section I
Reading Comprehension

1. Ⓐ Ⓑ Ⓒ Ⓓ Ⓔ
2. Ⓐ Ⓑ Ⓒ Ⓓ Ⓔ
3. Ⓐ Ⓑ Ⓒ Ⓓ Ⓔ
4. Ⓐ Ⓑ Ⓒ Ⓓ Ⓔ
5. Ⓐ Ⓑ Ⓒ Ⓓ Ⓔ
6. Ⓐ Ⓑ Ⓒ Ⓓ Ⓔ
7. Ⓐ Ⓑ Ⓒ Ⓓ Ⓔ
8. Ⓐ Ⓑ Ⓒ Ⓓ Ⓔ
9. Ⓐ Ⓑ Ⓒ Ⓓ Ⓔ
10. Ⓐ Ⓑ Ⓒ Ⓓ Ⓔ
11. Ⓐ Ⓑ Ⓒ Ⓓ Ⓔ
12. Ⓐ Ⓑ Ⓒ Ⓓ Ⓔ
13. Ⓐ Ⓑ Ⓒ Ⓓ Ⓔ
14. Ⓐ Ⓑ Ⓒ Ⓓ Ⓔ
15. Ⓐ Ⓑ Ⓒ Ⓓ Ⓔ
16. Ⓐ Ⓑ Ⓒ Ⓓ Ⓔ
17. Ⓐ Ⓑ Ⓒ Ⓓ Ⓔ
18. Ⓐ Ⓑ Ⓒ Ⓓ Ⓔ
19. Ⓐ Ⓑ Ⓒ Ⓓ Ⓔ
20. Ⓐ Ⓑ Ⓒ Ⓓ Ⓔ
21. Ⓐ Ⓑ Ⓒ Ⓓ Ⓔ
22. Ⓐ Ⓑ Ⓒ Ⓓ Ⓔ
23. Ⓐ Ⓑ Ⓒ Ⓓ Ⓔ
24. Ⓐ Ⓑ Ⓒ Ⓓ Ⓔ
25. Ⓐ Ⓑ Ⓒ Ⓓ Ⓔ

Section II
Problem Solving

26. Ⓐ Ⓑ Ⓒ Ⓓ Ⓔ
27. Ⓐ Ⓑ Ⓒ Ⓓ Ⓔ
28. Ⓐ Ⓑ Ⓒ Ⓓ Ⓔ
29. Ⓐ Ⓑ Ⓒ Ⓓ Ⓔ
30. Ⓐ Ⓑ Ⓒ Ⓓ Ⓔ
31. Ⓐ Ⓑ Ⓒ Ⓓ Ⓔ
32. Ⓐ Ⓑ Ⓒ Ⓓ Ⓔ
33. Ⓐ Ⓑ Ⓒ Ⓓ Ⓔ
34. Ⓐ Ⓑ Ⓒ Ⓓ Ⓔ
35. Ⓐ Ⓑ Ⓒ Ⓓ Ⓔ

36. Ⓐ Ⓑ Ⓒ Ⓓ Ⓔ
37. Ⓐ Ⓑ Ⓒ Ⓓ Ⓔ
38. Ⓐ Ⓑ Ⓒ Ⓓ Ⓔ
39. Ⓐ Ⓑ Ⓒ Ⓓ Ⓔ
40. Ⓐ Ⓑ Ⓒ Ⓓ Ⓔ
41. Ⓐ Ⓑ Ⓒ Ⓓ Ⓔ
42. Ⓐ Ⓑ Ⓒ Ⓓ Ⓔ
43. Ⓐ Ⓑ Ⓒ Ⓓ Ⓔ
44. Ⓐ Ⓑ Ⓒ Ⓓ Ⓔ
45. Ⓐ Ⓑ Ⓒ Ⓓ Ⓔ
46. Ⓐ Ⓑ Ⓒ Ⓓ Ⓔ
47. Ⓐ Ⓑ Ⓒ Ⓓ Ⓔ
48. Ⓐ Ⓑ Ⓒ Ⓓ Ⓔ
49. Ⓐ Ⓑ Ⓒ Ⓓ Ⓔ
50. Ⓐ Ⓑ Ⓒ Ⓓ Ⓔ
51. Ⓐ Ⓑ Ⓒ Ⓓ Ⓔ
52. Ⓐ Ⓑ Ⓒ Ⓓ Ⓔ
53. Ⓐ Ⓑ Ⓒ Ⓓ Ⓔ
54. Ⓐ Ⓑ Ⓒ Ⓓ Ⓔ
55. Ⓐ Ⓑ Ⓒ Ⓓ Ⓔ

Section III
Practical Judgment

56. Ⓐ Ⓑ Ⓒ Ⓓ Ⓔ
57. Ⓐ Ⓑ Ⓒ Ⓓ Ⓔ
58. Ⓐ Ⓑ Ⓒ Ⓓ Ⓔ
59. Ⓐ Ⓑ Ⓒ Ⓓ Ⓔ
60. Ⓐ Ⓑ Ⓒ Ⓓ Ⓔ
61. Ⓐ Ⓑ Ⓒ Ⓓ Ⓔ
62. Ⓐ Ⓑ Ⓒ Ⓓ Ⓔ
63. Ⓐ Ⓑ Ⓒ Ⓓ Ⓔ
64. Ⓐ Ⓑ Ⓒ Ⓓ Ⓔ
65. Ⓐ Ⓑ Ⓒ Ⓓ Ⓔ
66. Ⓐ Ⓑ Ⓒ Ⓓ Ⓔ
67. Ⓐ Ⓑ Ⓒ Ⓓ Ⓔ
68. Ⓐ Ⓑ Ⓒ Ⓓ Ⓔ
69. Ⓐ Ⓑ Ⓒ Ⓓ Ⓔ
70. Ⓐ Ⓑ Ⓒ Ⓓ Ⓔ
71. Ⓐ Ⓑ Ⓒ Ⓓ Ⓔ
72. Ⓐ Ⓑ Ⓒ Ⓓ Ⓔ
73. Ⓐ Ⓑ Ⓒ Ⓓ Ⓔ
74. Ⓐ Ⓑ Ⓒ Ⓓ Ⓔ
75. Ⓐ Ⓑ Ⓒ Ⓓ Ⓔ

Section IV
Data Sufficiency

76. Ⓐ Ⓑ Ⓒ Ⓓ Ⓔ
77. Ⓐ Ⓑ Ⓒ Ⓓ Ⓔ
78. Ⓐ Ⓑ Ⓒ Ⓓ Ⓔ
79. Ⓐ Ⓑ Ⓒ Ⓓ Ⓔ
80. Ⓐ Ⓑ Ⓒ Ⓓ Ⓔ
81. Ⓐ Ⓑ Ⓒ Ⓓ Ⓔ
82. Ⓐ Ⓑ Ⓒ Ⓓ Ⓔ
83. Ⓐ Ⓑ Ⓒ Ⓓ Ⓔ
84. Ⓐ Ⓑ Ⓒ Ⓓ Ⓔ
85. Ⓐ Ⓑ Ⓒ Ⓓ Ⓔ
86. Ⓐ Ⓑ Ⓒ Ⓓ Ⓔ
87. Ⓐ Ⓑ Ⓒ Ⓓ Ⓔ
88. Ⓐ Ⓑ Ⓒ Ⓓ Ⓔ
89. Ⓐ Ⓑ Ⓒ Ⓓ Ⓔ
90. Ⓐ Ⓑ Ⓒ Ⓓ Ⓔ
91. Ⓐ Ⓑ Ⓒ Ⓓ Ⓔ
92. Ⓐ Ⓑ Ⓒ Ⓓ Ⓔ
93. Ⓐ Ⓑ Ⓒ Ⓓ Ⓔ
94. Ⓐ Ⓑ Ⓒ Ⓓ Ⓔ
95. Ⓐ Ⓑ Ⓒ Ⓓ Ⓔ
96. Ⓐ Ⓑ Ⓒ Ⓓ Ⓔ
97. Ⓐ Ⓑ Ⓒ Ⓓ Ⓔ
98. Ⓐ Ⓑ Ⓒ Ⓓ Ⓔ
99. Ⓐ Ⓑ Ⓒ Ⓓ Ⓔ
100. Ⓐ Ⓑ Ⓒ Ⓓ Ⓔ
101. Ⓐ Ⓑ Ⓒ Ⓓ Ⓔ
102. Ⓐ Ⓑ Ⓒ Ⓓ Ⓔ
103. Ⓐ Ⓑ Ⓒ Ⓓ Ⓔ
104. Ⓐ Ⓑ Ⓒ Ⓓ Ⓔ
105. Ⓐ Ⓑ Ⓒ Ⓓ Ⓔ

Section V
Writing Ability

106. Ⓐ Ⓑ Ⓒ Ⓓ Ⓔ
107. Ⓐ Ⓑ Ⓒ Ⓓ Ⓔ
108. Ⓐ Ⓑ Ⓒ Ⓓ Ⓔ
109. Ⓐ Ⓑ Ⓒ Ⓓ Ⓔ
110. Ⓐ Ⓑ Ⓒ Ⓓ Ⓔ

Section VI
Practical Judgment

126. Ⓐ Ⓑ Ⓒ Ⓓ Ⓔ
127. Ⓐ Ⓑ Ⓒ Ⓓ Ⓔ
128. Ⓐ Ⓑ Ⓒ Ⓓ Ⓔ
129. Ⓐ Ⓑ Ⓒ Ⓓ Ⓔ
130. Ⓐ Ⓑ Ⓒ Ⓓ Ⓔ
131. Ⓐ Ⓑ Ⓒ Ⓓ Ⓔ
132. Ⓐ Ⓑ Ⓒ Ⓓ Ⓔ
133. Ⓐ Ⓑ Ⓒ Ⓓ Ⓔ
134. Ⓐ Ⓑ Ⓒ Ⓓ Ⓔ
135. Ⓐ Ⓑ Ⓒ Ⓓ Ⓔ
136. Ⓐ Ⓑ Ⓒ Ⓓ Ⓔ
137. Ⓐ Ⓑ Ⓒ Ⓓ Ⓔ
138. Ⓐ Ⓑ Ⓒ Ⓓ Ⓔ
139. Ⓐ Ⓑ Ⓒ Ⓓ Ⓔ
140. Ⓐ Ⓑ Ⓒ Ⓓ Ⓔ
141. Ⓐ Ⓑ Ⓒ Ⓓ Ⓔ
142. Ⓐ Ⓑ Ⓒ Ⓓ Ⓔ
143. Ⓐ Ⓑ Ⓒ Ⓓ Ⓔ
144. Ⓐ Ⓑ Ⓒ Ⓓ Ⓔ
145. Ⓐ Ⓑ Ⓒ Ⓓ Ⓔ

Section IV Data Sufficiency (continued column)

111. Ⓐ Ⓑ Ⓒ Ⓓ Ⓔ
112. Ⓐ Ⓑ Ⓒ Ⓓ Ⓔ
113. Ⓐ Ⓑ Ⓒ Ⓓ Ⓔ
114. Ⓐ Ⓑ Ⓒ Ⓓ Ⓔ
115. Ⓐ Ⓑ Ⓒ Ⓓ Ⓔ
116. Ⓐ Ⓑ Ⓒ Ⓓ Ⓔ
117. Ⓐ Ⓑ Ⓒ Ⓓ Ⓔ
118. Ⓐ Ⓑ Ⓒ Ⓓ Ⓔ
119. Ⓐ Ⓑ Ⓒ Ⓓ Ⓔ
120. Ⓐ Ⓑ Ⓒ Ⓓ Ⓔ
121. Ⓐ Ⓑ Ⓒ Ⓓ Ⓔ
122. Ⓐ Ⓑ Ⓒ Ⓓ Ⓔ
123. Ⓐ Ⓑ Ⓒ Ⓓ Ⓔ
124. Ⓐ Ⓑ Ⓒ Ⓓ Ⓔ
125. Ⓐ Ⓑ Ⓒ Ⓓ Ⓔ

Section VII
Verbal Ability

146. Ⓐ Ⓑ Ⓒ Ⓓ Ⓔ
147. Ⓐ Ⓑ Ⓒ Ⓓ Ⓔ
148. Ⓐ Ⓑ Ⓒ Ⓓ Ⓔ
149. Ⓐ Ⓑ Ⓒ Ⓓ Ⓔ
150. Ⓐ Ⓑ Ⓒ Ⓓ Ⓔ
151. Ⓐ Ⓑ Ⓒ Ⓓ Ⓔ
152. Ⓐ Ⓑ Ⓒ Ⓓ Ⓔ
153. Ⓐ Ⓑ Ⓒ Ⓓ Ⓔ
154. Ⓐ Ⓑ Ⓒ Ⓓ Ⓔ
155. Ⓐ Ⓑ Ⓒ Ⓓ Ⓔ
156. Ⓐ Ⓑ Ⓒ Ⓓ Ⓔ
157. Ⓐ Ⓑ Ⓒ Ⓓ Ⓔ
158. Ⓐ Ⓑ Ⓒ Ⓓ Ⓔ
159. Ⓐ Ⓑ Ⓒ Ⓓ Ⓔ
160. Ⓐ Ⓑ Ⓒ Ⓓ Ⓔ
161. Ⓐ Ⓑ Ⓒ Ⓓ Ⓔ
162. Ⓐ Ⓑ Ⓒ Ⓓ Ⓔ
163. Ⓐ Ⓑ Ⓒ Ⓓ Ⓔ
164. Ⓐ Ⓑ Ⓒ Ⓓ Ⓔ
165. Ⓐ Ⓑ Ⓒ Ⓓ Ⓔ
166. Ⓐ Ⓑ Ⓒ Ⓓ Ⓔ
167. Ⓐ Ⓑ Ⓒ Ⓓ Ⓔ
168. Ⓐ Ⓑ Ⓒ Ⓓ Ⓔ
169. Ⓐ Ⓑ Ⓒ Ⓓ Ⓔ
170. Ⓐ Ⓑ Ⓒ Ⓓ Ⓔ
171. Ⓐ Ⓑ Ⓒ Ⓓ Ⓔ
172. Ⓐ Ⓑ Ⓒ Ⓓ Ⓔ
173. Ⓐ Ⓑ Ⓒ Ⓓ Ⓔ
174. Ⓐ Ⓑ Ⓒ Ⓓ Ⓔ
175. Ⓐ Ⓑ Ⓒ Ⓓ Ⓔ
176. Ⓐ Ⓑ Ⓒ Ⓓ Ⓔ
177. Ⓐ Ⓑ Ⓒ Ⓓ Ⓔ
178. Ⓐ Ⓑ Ⓒ Ⓓ Ⓔ
179. Ⓐ Ⓑ Ⓒ Ⓓ Ⓔ
180. Ⓐ Ⓑ Ⓒ Ⓓ Ⓔ
181. Ⓐ Ⓑ Ⓒ Ⓓ Ⓔ
182. Ⓐ Ⓑ Ⓒ Ⓓ Ⓔ
183. Ⓐ Ⓑ Ⓒ Ⓓ Ⓔ
184. Ⓐ Ⓑ Ⓒ Ⓓ Ⓔ
185. Ⓐ Ⓑ Ⓒ Ⓓ Ⓔ

THREE
GMAT DIAGNOSTIC TEST

Now that you have become familiar with the various types of questions appearing on the GMAT and have had a chance to sample each type, you probably have an idea of what to expect from an actual exam. The next step, then, is to take a sample test to see how you do.

The Diagnostic Test that follows has been designed to resemble the format of recent GMATs. When taking it, try to simulate actual test conditions as closely as possible. For example, time yourself as you work on each section so that you don't go over the allotted time limit for that section. After you have completed the test, check your answers and use the self-scoring chart to evaluate the results. Use these results to determine which review sections you should spend the most time studying before you attempt the 5 sample GMATs at the end of the book. To assist you in your review, all answers to mathematics questions are keyed so that you can easily refer to the section in the Mathematics Review that discusses the material tested by a particular question.

Diagnostic Test

Section I   Reading Comprehension

TIME: 30 minutes

DIRECTIONS: This part contains four reading passages. You are to read each one carefully. When answering the questions, you *will* be able to refer to the passages. The questions are based on what is *stated* or *implied* in each passage. You have thirty minutes to complete this section.

Passage 1:

In Aachen, Germany, and environs, many children have been found to have an unusually high lead content in their blood and hair. The amount of lead in the children tested has risen above the amount found in workers in heavy-metal industries. The general public is no longer surprised that the lead has been traced to Stol-
(5) berg near Aachen: Stolberg is surrounded by brass foundaries and slag heaps which supply building materials to construct schoolyards and sports halls.

This is but one example. In today's Europe, cancer-stricken children outnumber adults with the disease. And in the United States, cancer kills more children between the ages of one and four than any other disease.

(10)   When Dr. John W. Gofman, professor of medical physics at the University of California and a leading nuclear critic, speaks of "ecocide" in his adversary view of nuclear technology, he means the following: A large nuclear plant like that in Kalkar, the Netherlands, would produce about 200 pounds of plutonium each year. One pound, released into the atmosphere, could cause 9 billion cases of lung cancer.
(15)   This waste product must be stored for 500,000 years before it is of no further danger to man. In the anticipated reactor economy, it is estimated that there will be 10,000 tons of this material in western Europe, of which one tablespoonful of plutonium-239 represents the official maximum permissible body burden for 200,000 people. Rather than being biodegradable, plutonium destroys biological properties.

(20)   In 1972 the U.S. Occupational Safety and Health Administration ruled that the asbestos level in the work place should be lowered to 2 fibers per cubic centimeter of air, but the effective date of the ruling has been delayed until now. The International Federation of Chemical and General Workers' Unions report that the 2-fiber standard was based primarily on one study of 290 men at a British asbestos factory.
(25)   But when the workers at the British factory had been reexamined by another physician, 40–70 percent had x-ray evidence of lung abnormalities. According to present medical information at the factory in question, out of a total of 29 deaths thus far, seven were caused by lung cancer and three by mesothelima, a cancer of the lining of the chest-abdomen. An average European or American worker comes into con-
(30)   tact with six million fibers a day. And when this man returns home at night, samples of this fireproof product are on his clothes, in his hair, in his lunchpail. "We are now, in fact, finding cancer deaths within the family of the asbestos worker," states Dr. Irving Salikoff, of the Mount Sinai Medical School in New York

It is now also clear that vinyl chloride, a gas from which the most widely used
(35)   plastics are made, causes a fatal cancer of the blood-vessel cells of the liver. However, the history of the research on vinyl chloride is, in some ways, more disturbing than the "Watergate cover-up." "There has been evidence of potentially serious disease among polyvinyl chloride workers for 25 years that has been incompletely appreciated and inadequately approached by medical scientists and by regulatory
(40)   authorities," summed up by Dr. Salikoff in the *New Scientist*. At least 17 workers have been killed by vinyl chloride because research over the past 25 years was not followed up. And for over 10 years, workers have been exposed to concentrations of vinyl chloride 10 times the "safe limit" imposed by Dow Chemical Company. In the United Kingdom, a threshold limit value was set after the discovery of the causal
(45)   link with osteolysis, but the limit was still higher than that set by Dow Chemical. The Germans set a new maximum level in 1970, but also higher than that set by Dow. No other section of U.S. or European industry has followed Dow's lead.

1. Which of the following titles best describes the contents of the passage?

    (A) *The Problems of Nuclear Physics*
    (B) *Advanced Technology and Cancer*
    (C) *Occupational Diseases*
    (D) *Cancer in Germany*
    (E) *The Ecology of Cancer*

2. The author provides information that would answer which of the following questions?

    (A) What sort of legislation is needed to prevent cancer?
    (B) Should nuclear plants be built?
    (C) What are some causes of lung cancer?
    (D) What are the pros and cons of nuclear energy?
    (E) Which country has the lowest incidence of occupational disease?

3. According to the author, all the following are causes of lung cancer *except*

    (A) plutonium
    (B) asbestos
    (C) vinyl chloride
    (D) osteolysis
    (E) lead

4. The style of the passage is mainly

    (A) argumentative
    (B) emotional
    (C) factual
    (D) clinical
    (E) vitriolic

5. It can be inferred from the passage that the author believes that

    (A) industrialization must be halted to prevent further spread of cancer-producing agents
    (B) only voluntary, industry-wide application of anti-pollution devices can halt cancer
    (C) workers are partly to blame for the spread of disease because of poor work habits
    (D) more research is needed into the causes of cancer before further progress can be made
    (E) tougher legislation is needed to set lower limits of worker exposure to harmful chemicals and fibers

6. Some workers have been killed by harmful pollutants because

    (A) they failed to take the required precautions and safety measures
    (B) not enough research has been undertaken to find solutions to the pollution problem
    (C) available research was not followed up
    (D) production cannot be halted
    (E) factory owners have failed to provide safety equipment

Passage 2:

    The Great Glen is a 100-mile-long rift valley stretching across the Scottish Highlands from the Moray Firth in the northeast to the Firth of Lorne in the southwest, thus forming a natural link between the North Sea and the Atlantic Ocean. It is the result of a sideways slippage of the earth, a northeast-southwest trending fault of the
(5) Caledonian mountain system. During the Ice Age, Scotland was literally shoved

down into the earth, and when the ice melted, the sea rose for a time, then ceased. But the land kept on rising, some 50 feet above sea level, sealing off bodies of water from the oceans and leaving bizarre, white beaches about the edges of medieval forestry.

(10)   Loch Ness, the largest freshwater lake in the British Isles and the third largest in Europe, is the principal basin of the Great Glen. It receives a quantum runoff from neighboring glens—Glen Affric, Glen Cannich, Glen Moriston, Glen Farrar, Glen Urquhart—so that the water level may rise as much as 24 inches in an hour. Any
(15) possible underground passage from the loch to the North Sea has long ago been dammed by some two miles of river-brought silt, thus changing the original sea loch into a fresh-water lake. It has no curving outlines made by an indented shore or shallow bays; but, instead, its riparian walls slice straight down, giving the appearance of an enormous ditch widening to 1.5 miles and extending approximately 23
(20) miles from Inverness in the North to Fort Augustus at the southern end, where the Caledonian Canal continues on into the Atlantic. Its depth exceeds 700 feet over much of its length, with the deepest point so far discovered of 975 feet. The loch never freezes and acts like an inland Gulf Stream on its immediate environs, giving off in winter a vast amount of heat collected in the summer months. The coldest
(25) water remains at a fairly constant 42 degrees, warm enough to provide a home for literally millions of migrating eels, which, according to ichthyologists, have made their home here instead of going to the sea. Along the rocky shoreline a reddish brown algae adheres to the stones, and in the shallows around the mouths of tributary rivers and burns is an abundance of freshwater weeds and organic detritus—all
(30) a possible food source for eels, brown trout, salmon, and sticklebacks. Hence, the biomass of the loch is thought sufficient to support a population of large animals.

The loch inherits its name from the Greek water goddess Nesa, whose spirit was thought to cause the many "unnatural" occurrences in the area. If "Ness" is given a feminine diminutive ending, it becomes "Nessie"—the sobriquet for the Loch Ness Monster. The scientific name of *Nessiteras rhombopteryx* has been applied to Nessie
(35) by Sir Peter Scott, head of the world Wildlife Foundation and chancellor of Birmingham University. The word *Nessiteras* combines the name of the loch with the Greek word *teras*, genitive of *teratos*, which means a "marvel or wonder . . . arousing awe, amazement, and often fear." The word *rhombopteryx* is a combination of
(40) the Greek *rhombos*, meaning a diamond or rhomboid shape, and the Greek *pteryx*, meaning fin or wing. The name does not link the species to any animal or group of animals known to science but applies specifically to the creature first recorded by St. Columba in 565 A.D. From a zoological point of view, to base a name on photographs rather than the remains of an animal is quite unsatisfactory, however justi-
(45) fied by the urgency to protect an endangered species and therefore permitted by the International Code of Zoological Nomenclature.

In 1933 dynamite charges shook the loch-side, tumbling boulders, tree limbs, earth, and scree into the lake. For a year the blasting intermittently continued as steam shovels chuffed and gnawed their way through the forest, gradually surround-
(50) ing the once tranquil shoreline with the fresh macadam of a scenic highway. Such violent activity sent reverberations down through the waters beneath Fort Augustus, down into the deep holes off Urquhart Bay, and down into the shallows around Dores, Foyers, and Invermoriston. After the day's work a quietude descended, but only for an uncertain time. Then something that looked like a hump of sorts, per-
(55) haps only a wave or floating log (surely one that had been blasted that morning) or an upturned boat, would appear, drift, and disappear beneath a gibbous moon.

7. It can be assumed from the passage that the Loch Ness "monster" was thought to have been

   (A) a warm-water creature
   (B) observed in 565 A.D.
   (C) created during the ice age
   (D) fabricated during the Middle Ages
   (E) described in Greek mythology

8. The passage implies that which of the following has been offered as evidence of the existence of the Loch Ness "monster"?

   (A) Photographs of the creature
   (B) The lake's organic contents, which are suitable food for such creatures
   (C) The mild water temperature
   (D) Observations by zoologists
   (E) Discovery of the creature's remains

9. According to the passage, the surface area of Loch Ness is probably closest to

   (A) 1.5 square miles
   (B) 3.8 square miles
   (C) 25 square miles
   (D) 230 square miles
   (E) 345 square miles

10. The author is mainly concerned with

   (A) debunking the idea of a sea monster
   (B) describing Loch Ness and the "monster" it may contain
   (C) providing evidence for the existence of a sea monster
   (D) the scientific status of the Loch Ness "monster" myth
   (E) the geological characteristics of Scottish glens

11. When the author uses the word *ichthyologists* in line 26, he is referring to

   (A) a Scottish clan
   (B) zoologists who study fish
   (C) conservationists
   (D) wildlife experts
   (E) geologists

12. Which of the following can be inferred from the passage?

   (A) Loch Ness is a popular tourist resort.
   (B) Scotland's climate is very harsh.
   (C) Dynamite charges sealed off Loch Ness from the sea.
   (D) The inhabitants of Loch Ness are an endangered species protected by law.
   (E) None of the above.

Passage 3:

It is easy to accept Freud as an applied scientist, and, indeed he is widely regarded as the twentieth century's master clinician. However, in viewing Marx as an applied social scientist the stance needed is that of a Machiavellian operationalism. The ob-

(5) jective is neither to bury nor to praise him. The assumption is simply that he is better understood for being understood as an applied sociologist. This is in part the clear implication of Marx's *Theses on Feurbach*, which culminate in the resounding 11th thesis: "The philosophers have only interpreted the world in different ways; the point, however, is to change it." This would seem to be the tacit creed of applied scientists everywhere.

(10) Marx was no Faustian, concerned solely with understanding society, but a Promethean who sought to understand it well enough to influence and to change it. He was centrally concerned with the social problems of a lay group, the proletariat, and there can be little doubt that his work is motivated by an effort to reduce their suffering, as he saw it. His diagnosis was that their increasing misery and alienation (15) engendered endemic class struggle; his prognosis claimed that this would culminate in revolution; his therapeutic prescription was class consciousness and active struggle.

Here, as in assessing Durkheim or Freud, the issue is not whether this analysis is empirically correct or scientifically adequate. Furthermore, whether or not this formulation seems to eviscerate Marx's revolutionary core, as critics on the left may (20) charge, or whether the formulation provides Marx with a new veneer of academic respectability, as critics on the right may allege, is entirely irrelevant from the present standpoint. Insofar as Marx's or any other social scientist's work conforms to a generalized model of applied social science, insofar as it is professionally oriented to the values and social problems of laymen in his society, he may be treated as an (25) applied social scientist.

Despite Durkheim's intellectualistic proclivities and rationalistic pathos, he was too much the product of European turbulence to turn his back on the travail of his culture. "Why strive for knowledge of reality, if this knowledge cannot aid us in life," he asked. "Social science," he said, "can provide us with rules of action for the (30) future." Durkheim, like Marx, conceived of science as an agency of social action, and like him was professionally oriented to the values and problems of laymen in his society. Unless one sees that Durkheim was in some part an applied social scientist, it is impossible to understand why he concludes his monumental study of *Suicide* with a chapter on "Practical Consequences," and why, in the *Division of* (35) *Labor*, he proposes a specific remedy for anomie.

Durkheim is today widely regarded as a model of theoretic and methodologic sophistication, and is thus usually seen only in his capacity as a pure social scientist. Surely this is an incomplete view of the man who regarded the *practical* effectiveness of a science as its principal justification. To be more fully understood, Durk- (40) heim also needs to be seen as an applied sociologist. His interest in religious beliefs and organization, in crime and penology, in educational methods and organization, in suicide and anomie, are not casually chosen problem areas. Nor did he select them only because they provided occasions for the development of his theoretical orientation. These areas were in his time, as they are today, problems of indigenous (45) interest to applied sociologists in Western society, precisely because of their practical significance.

13. Which of the following best describes the author's conception of an applied social scientist?

    (A) A professional who listens to people's problems
    (B) A professional who seeks social action and change
    (C) A student of society
    (D) A proponent of class struggle
    (E) A philosopher who interprets the world in a unique way

14. According to the author, which of the folowing did Marx and Durkheim have in common?

   (A) A belief in the importance of class struggle
   (B) A desire to create a system of social organization
   (C) An interest in penology
   (D) Regard for the practical applications of science
   (E) A sense of the political organization of society

15. It may be inferred from the passage that the applied social scientist might be interested in all of the following subjects *except*

   (A) the theory of mechanics
   (B) how to make workers more efficient
   (C) rehabilitation of juvenile delinquents
   (D) reduction of social tensions
   (E) industrial safety

16. According to the passage, applied social science can be distinguished from pure social science by its

   (A) practical significance
   (B) universal application
   (C) cultural pluralism
   (D) objectivity
   (E) emphasis on the problems of the poor

17. Which of the following best summarizes the author's main point?

   (A) Marx and Durkheim were similar in their ideas.
   (B) Freud, Marx, and Durkheim were all social scientists.
   (C) Philosophers, among others, who are regarded as theoreticians can also be regarded as empiricists.
   (D) Marx and Durkheim were applied social scientists because they were concerned with the solution of social problems
   (E) Pure and applied sciences have fundamentally similar objectives.

18. All of the following are mentioned as topics of interest to Durkheim *except*

   (A) suicide
   (B) psychiatry
   (C) crime
   (D) education
   (E) religion

Passage 4:

Morally and culturally, American society, as reflected in our TV programs, our theatrical fare, our literature and art appears to have hit bottom.

Gen. David Sarnoff felt prompted to issue a statement in defense of the TV industry. He pointed out that there was much good in its programs that was being
(5) overlooked while its occasional derelictions were being overly stressed. It struck me that what he was saying about TV applied to other aspects of American culture as well, particularly to the theatrical productions.

Without necessarily resting on his conviction that the good outweighed the bad in American cultural activity, I saw further implications in Gen. Sarnoff's declaration.
(10) Audiences needed to be sensitized more and more to the positive qualities of the entertainment and cultural media. In addition, through such increased public sensitivity, producers would be encouraged to provide ever more of the fine, and less of the sordid.

Here is where questions arise. If the exemplary aspects of TV are not being rec-
(15) ognized, what is the reason for such a lack of appreciation? Similarly, and further, if the theatre, including in this term the legitimate stage, on and off Broadway as well as the moving pictures, has large measures of goodness, truth and beauty which are unappreciated, how are we to change this situation?

All in all, what should be done to encourage and condone the good, and to dis-
(20) courage and condemn the unsavory in the American cultural pattern?

These are serious and pressing questions—serious for the survival of the American Way of Life, and pressing for immediate and adequate answers. Indeed the simple truth is that the face that America shows the world affects seriously the future of democracy all over the globe.

(25) Since the theatre in its broadest sense is a large aspect of American culture—its expression as well as its creation—I saw the urgent importance of bringing the worthwhile elements in the American Theatre to the fore. Especially was this importance impressed on me when I realized how much Hollywood was involved in exporting American life to the world, and how much Broadway with all its theatres
(30) meant to the modern drama.

Then the thought of the Bible came to me in this connection. Was not the Bible the basis of Western civilization as far as morals are concerned? Why not use the Bible as guide and touchstone, as direction and goal in the matter of the cultural achievements of Western society? Thus was born "The Bible on Broadway."

(35) The birth of the idea accomplished, rearing it brought the usual difficulties of raising a child—albeit in this case a "brain" one. There was first the fact that the Bible, although the world's best seller, is not the world's best read book. Second was the current impression that "message-plays" must necessarily be dull and unpopular. What a combination! The Bible unknown, and Broadway (in the sense of
(40) theatre with an idea) unpopular!

Still, I was drawn to the project of a series of lectures on the Bible and the contemporary theatre. What if the Bible is not well known? Teach it! Plays with a message dull? All plays by reason of their being works of art have been created by their authors' selection and ordering of experience. As such, plays are proponents of
(45) ideas— and certainly they are not meant to be uninteresting.

Thus fortified, I turned to the subject of the Bible and the contemporary theatre and found it indeed appealing and full of interesting nuances.

That there are spiritual, even religious ideas, in the contemporary theatre should be no cause for wonderment. It is well known that the drama had its origin in re-
(50) ligion. The Greeks, the Romans, as well as the early Hebrews, all had forms of the drama which among the first two developed into our classical plays.

In the Middle Ages, it was the Church in the Western World that produced the morality and mystery plays. With such a long history it is not surprising to find an affinity between the Bible and the Theatre.

19. The author is primarily concerned with
    (A) the declining pattern of morality in America
    (B) promoting American theatre
    (C) the role of the Bible in the contemporary theatre
    (D) comparing the theatre with other art forms
    (E) preserving the "American Way of Life"

20. With which of the following statements regarding the theatre would the author most likely agree?
    (A) The theatre does not reflect American culture.
    (B) Critics of American cultural life are biased.
    (C) While the entertainment media can be criticized, they contain much wholesome material.
    (D) The advertising media are largely to blame for criticisms leveled at the theatre.
    (E) The Bible should be used as our primary source of entertainment ideas.

21. Which of the following statements best reflects the author's own ideas?

    (A) American art forms have degenerated to a new low.
    (B) The good outweighs the bad in American cultural activity.
    (C) American culture has positive content, but it is not appreciated by the public.
    (D) Only the Biblical content of American theatre has positive meaning.
    (E) American theatre is currently dull and unpopular.

22. The author implies that he will deal with which of the following questions?

    I.   What is the reason for the lack of appreciation of the theatre?
    II.   To what extent have Bible themes been used in or influenced American theatrical productions?
    III. What should be done to encourage the good in American culture?

    (A) I only
    (B) II only
    (C) I and II only
    (D) I and III only
    (E) I, II and III

23. It can be inferred from the passage that the author's background might be in any of the following occupations *except*

    (A) theatrical producer
    (B) thespian
    (C) humorist
    (D) writer
    (E) critic

24. The author implies that, if the public is made aware of the positive qualities of American entertainment, it will

   I.   demand more high quality entertainment
   II. demand less low quality entertainment
   III. attend the theatre more often

   (A) I only
   (B) II only
   (C) I and II only
   (D) I and III only
   (E) I, II, and III

25. When the author uses the expression "the Bible as guide and touchstone" in line 33, he probably means to refer to

   (A) the interrelationship of the Bible and the "American Way of Life"
   (B) an academic approach to researching the theatre and religion
   (C) the relationship of Biblical concepts to basic ideas and values contained in theatrical productions
   (D) the use of the Bible as a guide to everyday life
   (E) the Bible as a source of inspiration for all

   If there is still time remaining, you may review the questions in this section only.
   You may not turn to any other section of the test.

Section II   Problem Solving

DIRECTIONS: Solve each of the following problems; then indicate the correct answer on the answer sheet. [On the actual test you will be permitted to use any space available on the examination paper for scratch work.]

NOTE: A figure that appears with a problem is drawn as accurately as possible so as to provide information that may help in answering the question. Numbers in this test are real numbers.

TIME: 40 minutes

26. If the length of a rectangle is increased by 20% and the width is decreased by 20%, then the area

   (A) decreases by 20%
   (B) decreases by 4%
   (C) stays the same
   (D) increases by 10%
   (E) increases by 20%

27. If it is 250 miles from New York to Boston and 120 miles from New York to Hartford, what percentage of the distance from New York to Boston is the distance from New York to Hartford?

   (A) 12
   (B) 24
   (C) 36

   (D) 48
   (E) 52

28. The lead in a mechanical pencil is 5 inches long. After pieces $\frac{1}{8}$ of an inch long, $1\frac{3}{4}$ inches long, and $1\frac{1}{12}$ inches long are broken off, how long is the lead left in the pencil?

   (A) 2 in.
   (B) $2\frac{1}{24}$ in.
   (C) $2\frac{1}{12}$ in.

   (D) $2\frac{1}{4}$ in.
   (E) $2\frac{1}{2}$ in.

29. It costs $1.00 each to make the first thousand copies of a record and it costs x dollars to make each subsequent copy. How many dollars will it cost to make 4800 copies of a record?

   (A) 1,000
   (B) 4800
   (C) $4800x$

   (D) $1000x + 3800$
   (E) $1,000 + 3800x$

30. If a worker makes 4 boxes of labels in $1\frac{2}{3}$ hours, how many boxes of labels can he make in 50 minutes?

   (A) 2
   (B) $2\frac{1}{3}$
   (C) $2\frac{2}{3}$

   (D) $2\frac{5}{6}$
   (E) 3

31. If $x + y = 3$ and $y/x = 2$, then y is equal to

   (A) 0
   (B) $\frac{1}{2}$
   (C) 1

   (D) $\frac{3}{2}$
   (E) 2

32. A store buys paper towels for $9.00 a carton, each carton containing 20 rolls. The store sells a roll of paper towels for 50¢. About what percent of the cost is the selling price of a roll of paper towels?

(A) 11
(B) 89
(C) 100
(D) 111
(E) 119

33. A history book weighs 2.4 pounds. 12 copies of the history book and 8 copies of an English book together weigh 42.8 pounds. How much will one copy of the English book weigh?

(A) 1 pound
(B) 1.4 pounds
(C) 1.75 pounds
(D) 2.88 pounds
(E) 14 pounds

34. A car goes 15 miles on a gallon of gas when it is driven at 50 miles per hour. When the car is driven at 60 miles per hour it only goes 80% as far. How far will it travel on a gallon of gas at 60 miles per hour?

(A) 12 miles
(B) 13.5 miles
(C) 16.5 miles
(D) 18.75 miles
(E) 20 miles

35. If $x + y = z$ and x and y are positive, then which of the following statements can be inferred?

  I. $x < y$
  II. $x < z$
  III. $x < 2z$

(A) I only
(B) II only
(C) I and III only
(D) II and III only
(E) I, II, and III

36. If it costs x cents to produce a single sheet of paper for the first 800 sheets and if every subsequent sheet costs $x/15$ cents, how much will it cost to produce 5,000 sheets of paper?

(A) 800x¢
(B) 1,080x¢
(C) 1,400x¢
(D) 2,430x¢
(E) 3,500x¢

37. If in 1967, 1968, and 1969 a worker received 10% more in salary each year than he did the previous year, how much more did he receive in 1969 than in 1967?

(A) 10%
(B) 12%
(C) 19%
(D) 20%
(E) 21%

38. If factory A turns out a cars an hour and factory B turns out b cars every 2 hours, how many cars will both factories turn out in 8 hours?

(A) $a + b$
(B) $8a$
(C) $8b$.
(D) $8a + 4b$
(E) $8a + 8b$

39. If John makes a box every 5 minutes and Tim takes 7 minutes to make a box, what will be the ratio of the number of boxes produced by John to the number of boxes produced by Tim if they work 5 hours and 50 minutes?

(A) 5 to 6
(B) 5 to 7
(C) 6 to 5
(D) 7 to 5
(E) 2 to 1

40. If a store sells $3\frac{1}{4}$ crates of lettuce on Monday, $2\frac{1}{6}$ on Tuesday, $4\frac{1}{2}$ on Wednesday, and $1\frac{2}{3}$ on Thursday, how many crates has the store sold altogether?

(A) 10
(B) $11\frac{1}{2}$
(C) $11\frac{7}{12}$
(D) $11\frac{3}{4}$
(E) $12\frac{1}{3}$

41. If $x + y > 4$ and $x < 3$, then $y > 1$ is true

(A) always
(B) only if $x < 0$
(C) only if $x > 0$
(D) only if $x = 0$
(E) never

42. If 50 apprentices can finish a job in 4 hours and 30 journeymen can finish the same job in $4\frac{1}{2}$ hours, how much of the job should be completed by 10 apprentices and 15 journeymen in one hour?

(A) $\frac{1}{9}$
(B) $\frac{29}{180}$
(C) $\frac{26}{143}$
(D) $\frac{1}{5}$
(E) $\frac{39}{121}$

43. If 40% of all women are voters and 52% of the population are women, what percent of the population are women voters?

(A) 18.1
(B) 20.8
(C) 26.4
(D) 40
(E) 52

44. If a bus can travel 15 miles on a gallon of gas, how many gallons of gas will it use to travel 200 miles?

(A) 10
(B) $12\frac{1}{2}$
(C) $13\frac{1}{3}$

(D) 15
(E) $20\frac{1}{5}$

45. A tank contains 10 gallons of water. If a pump takes $15 - \frac{x}{10}$ minutes to pump one gallon of water out of the tank, how many minutes will it take for the pump to empty the tank?

(A) x
(B) $15 - 10x$
(C) $150 - 10x$

(D) $150 - x$
(E) $15 - 10x$

46. A company makes a profit of 6% on its first $1,000 of sales each day, and 5% on all sales in excess of $1,000 for that day. How many dollars in profit will the company make in a day when sales are $6,000?

(A) $250
(B) $300
(C) $310

(D) $320
(E) $360

47. If 15 men working independently and at the same rate can manufacture 27 baskets in an hour, how many baskets would 45 men working independently and at the same rate manufacture in 40 minutes?

(A) 27
(B) 35
(C) 40

(D) 54
(E) 81

48. A conveyer belt moves grain at the rate of 2 tons in 5 minutes and a second conveyer belt moves grain at the rate of 3 tons in 7 minutes. How many minutes will it take to move 20 tons of grain using both conveyer belts?

(A) 12
(B) $16\frac{4}{7}$
(C) $18\frac{3}{26}$

(D) 21
(E) $24\frac{4}{29}$

49. A field is rectangular and its width is $\frac{1}{3}$ as long as its length. What is the area of the field if the length of the field is 120 yards?

(A) 480 square yards
(B) 2,400 square yards
(C) 4,800 square yards

(D) 5,000 square yards
(E) 7,200 square yards

50. If the price of steak is currently $1.00 a pound, and the price triples every 6 months, how long will it be until the price of steak is $81.00 a pound?

(A) 1 year   (D) 13 years
(B) 2 years   (E) 13½ years
(C) 2½ years

51. If $\frac{x}{y} = \frac{2}{3}$, then $\frac{y^2}{x^2}$ is

(A) $\frac{4}{9}$ (D) $\frac{9}{4}$

(B) $\frac{2}{3}$ (E) $\frac{5}{2}$

(C) $\frac{3}{2}$

52. The entry following a_n in a sequence is determined by the rule $(a_n-1)^2$. If 1 is an entry in the sequence the next three entries are

(A) 0, −1, 2   (D) 2, 3, 4
(B) 0, −1, 1   (E) 0, 1, 0
(C) 0, 1, 2

53. An employer pays 3 workers X, Y, and Z a total of $610 a week. X is paid 125% of the amount Y is paid and 80% of the amount Z is paid. How much does X make a week?

(A) $150   (D) $195
(B) $175   (E) $200
(C) $180

54. What is the maximum number of points of intersection of two circles which have unequal radii?

(A) none   (D) 3
(B) 1   (E) infinite
(C) 2

55. If the area of a rectangle is equal to the area of a square, then the perimeter of the rectangle must be

(A) ½ the perimeter of the square
(B) equal to the perimeter of the square
(C) equal to twice the perimeter of the square
(D) equal to the square root of the perimeter of the square
(E) none of the above

If there is still time remaining, you may review the questions in this section only.
You may not turn to any other section of the test.

Section III   Practical Judgment

TIME: 20 minutes

DIRECTIONS: Read the following passage. After you have completed it, you will be asked to answer two sets of questions. The first of these, data evaluation, involves determining the importance of specific factors included in the passage. The second, data application, consists of general questions relating to the passage. When answering questions, you may consult the passage.

The B & S Manufacturing Co. for many years had held a dominant but stationary position in the industry which produces small gasoline engines for powering lawn mowers, chain saws, go-carts, compressors, pumps, and the like. Sales in 1970 were approximately $20,000,000. At a 1970 meeting, the board of directors approved a proposal by the corporate marketing manager to introduce a line of outboard motors. This proposal came as the result of a previous commitment by the board to develop a new product for a market related to those presently served.

The general plan involved the marketing of low horsepower motors for utility work and for fishing rather than the high horsepower units required for cruising, water skiing, and so on. A market study by a prominent outdoor magazine revealed that there were approximately 7.5 million active fishermen in 1970. About 15% of these actually owned outboard motors. Fishermen were located throughout the country, but there were major concentrations around inland waterways. Most of the fishermen who owned motors were located in these areas of concentration. A second market which seemed potentially good was the 2,500 fishing resort owners who rented boats and motors by the day or week. The marketing manager at B & S stressed that the company intended to get into the *user* market—not to supply motors for other outboard motor manufacturers, the situation which dominated the rest of the company's business. No consideration, therefore, was given to the possibility of developing O.E.M. customers.

B & S hoped it could establish a strong foothold in its target market by selling 50,000 units in 1971 and 1972. No fewer than 100,000 units should be sold each year thereafter. The general plan called for the development of a franchised distributor and retailer channel of distribution; an aggressive sales and advertising program; and a two-year marketing budget of $5,000,000. The average price of the motors was to be around $200.

The product strategy involved the development of three basic motors—a 2.2 hp unit, a 4.4 hp unit, and a 9.9 hp unit. These motors were all functionally designed to provide maximum convenience and service. Light in weight, relatively compact, and easy to install on almost any type or size of boat, the motors featured a built-in gasoline tank, a rewinding starter device, and a flexible (and adjustable) lower unit to permit operation in almost any depth of water. The motors were given the name of "Big Scout." Each had a very rugged appearance, designed to suggest durability, service, and reliability.

The product was tested under many kinds of conditions and received tremendous approval from fishermen who were asked to use it. However, the research and development expense and the actual costs of manufacturing ran considerably over the original estimates. The tentative introductory price was raised by about one-third.

The marketing manager did not foresee any great difficulty in obtaining distribution, in view of the great response to the initial product tests. He therefore assigned the task of designing the channel strategy to an assistant marketing manager. He told this assistant to prepare a detailed channel plan, studying the detailed marketing research reports if he needed additional information.

The distribution plan worked out by the assistant marketing manager involved the appointment of exclusive distributors and dealers in each of the major areas of concentration of fishermen. These dealers were to be marine and sporting goods retailers not presently handling a competitive line of fishing motors. As an incentive, the dealers would be offered a 40% discount, in contrast to the 33.3% usually expected by these kinds of retailers. A program of dealer training, especially in product service, was included in the channel strategy. It was anticipated that these same dealers would sell to the other market segment—the fishing resort owners.

Shortly after the assistant marketing manager submitted his report, one of the other people on the B & S marketing staff visited a regional trade show attended by marine and sporting goods dealers. He visited with more than a score of these dealers and left the show with the view that the distribution problem was going to be quite serious. He felt that there would be relatively few marine and sporting goods dealers who either could or would take on the new line. A very limited number of new boat dealers who could not get a Mercury, Johnson, or Evinrude franchise were likely to be interested, and some sporting goods shops which had not previously handled motors would probably be interested in at least discussing the possibility of taking on the "Big Scout" motors. But, in all, he judged that fewer than one-third of the major markets could be covered.

The marketing manager, leaning heavily on this report, decided that alternative channel directions would have to be pursued. The idea of exclusive distribution was abandoned. Instead, a wide range of retail outlets was proposed, including hardware stores, department stores, lawn and garden shops, and so on. The principle decision was that the sales estimate of 50,000 units for 1971 would have to be cut in half unless some other way of reaching users could be worked out. To offset this threatened cutback, the marketing manager proposed that Sears, Roebuck & Co. be approached. From informal conversations he had had with Sears personnel at an earlier date, he believed that Sears would be willing to take on the B & S motors, provided modest design modifications were incorporated and the Sears brand name were used.

In view of these overall changes in the plan, the original ideas on promotion had to be reconsidered. An advertising agency was appointed and assigned the task of developing a promotion strategy.

Data Evaluation Questions

DIRECTIONS: The questions that follow relate to the preceding passage. Evaluate, in terms of the passage, each of the items given. Then select your answer from one of the following classifications, and blacken the corresponding space on the answer sheet.

(A) A MAJOR OBJECTIVE in making the decision: one of the goals sought by the decision maker

(B) A MAJOR FACTOR in making the decision: an aspect of the problem, specifically mentioned in the passage, that fundamentally affects and/or determines the decision

(C) A MINOR FACTOR in making the decision: a less important element bearing on or affecting a Major Factor, rather than a Major Objective directly

(D) A MAJOR ASSUMPTION in making the decision: a projection or supposition arrived at by the decision maker before considering the factors and alternatives

(E) AN UNIMPORTANT ISSUE in making the decision: an item lacking significant impact on, or relationship to, the decision

56. 1970 company sales of $20,000,000

57. Likelihood that fishing resort owners would constitute a potential market

58. Marketing of a new product in order to increase market share

59. Penetration of the final user market

60. Suitability of "Big Scout" motors for any type of boat

61. Wide market coverage for the motors

62. Number of active fishermen in the U.S.

63. Percentage of fishermen currently owning outboard motors

64. Possibility of selling to O.E.M. customers

65. Desirability of the Sears brand name

66. Product service training for dealers

67. Possibility of maximizing sales through franchised distribution

68. Plausibility of achieving annual sales of 100,000 units

69. An aggressive sales and advertising program

Data Application Questions

DIRECTIONS: Answer each of the following questions using information contained in the passage.

70. The lack of dealer interest in "Big Scout" was attributed to

    I. insufficient trade discounts
    II. the poor B & S advertising campaign
    III. the availability of better-known motors

    (A) I only
    (B) III only
    (C) I and II only
    (D) I and III only
    (E) II and III only

71. The major potential markets for the "Big Scout" motors were

    I. water-ski enthusiasts
    II. fishermen
    III. fishing resorts

    (A) I only
    (B) II only
    (C) III only
    (D) II and III only
    (E) I, II, and III

72. It can be inferred from the passage that the B & S distribution plan was

    I. conceived before dealers were surveyed
    II. developed by a market research firm
    III. secondary to the advertising campaign

    (A) I only
    (B) II only
    (C) I and II only
    (D) I and III only
    (E) I, II, and III

73. B & S's business strategy was to

    I. sell "Big Scout" through the company's existing distribution channels
    II. rely mainly on an aggressive promotional campaign
    III. develop a product based on the company's present technological expertise

    (A) I only
    (B) III only
    (C) II and III only
    (D) I, II, and III
    (E) Neither I, II, nor III

74. The original sales forecast of "Big Scout" motors was revised because

    I. the price of "Big Scout" motors was too high
    II. the advertising campaign was ineffective
    III. a large enough number of distributors could not be found

    (A) II only
    (B) III only
    (C) I and III only
    (D) II and III only
    (E) I, II, and III

75. The impetus for the development of "Big Scout" motors came about because

    I. many dealers could not obtain a "big name" motor line
    II. the lawn mower market was saturated
    III. B & S management wanted to develop a new product for a related market

    (A) I only
    (B) III only
    (C) I and III only
    (D) II and III only
    (E) I, II, and III

If there is still time remaining, you may review the questions in this section only.
You may not turn to any other section of the test.

Section IV   Data Sufficiency

TIME: 30 minutes

DIRECTIONS: Each of the following problems has a question and two statements which are labeled (1) and (2). Use the data given in (1) and (2) together with other available information (such as the number of hours in a day, the definition of *clockwise*, mathematical facts, etc.) to decide whether the statements are *sufficient* to answer the question. Then fill in space

(A) if you can get the answer from (1) alone but not from (2) alone;

(B) if you can get the answer from (2) alone but not from (1) alone;

(C) if you can get the answer from (1) and (2) together, although neither statement by itself suffices;

(D) if statement (1) alone suffices *and* statement (2) alone suffices;

(E) if you cannot get the answer from statements (1) and (2) together, but need even more data.

All numbers used in this section are real numbers. A figure given for a problem is intended to provide information consistent with that in the question, but not necessarily with the additional information contained in the statements.

76.   A piece of wood 5 feet long is cut into three smaller pieces. How long is the longest of the three pieces?

(1) One piece is 2 feet, 7 inches long.
(2) One piece is 7 inches longer than another piece and the remaining piece is 5 inches long.

77. AC is a diameter of the circle. ACD is a straight line. What is the value of x?

(1) $AB = BC$
(2) $x = 2y$

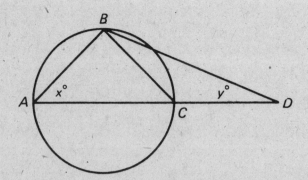

78.   What is the value of y?

(1) $x + 2y = 6$
(2) $y^2 - 2y + 1 = 0$

79. Two pipes, A and B, empty into a reservoir. Pipe A can fill the reservoir in 30 minutes by itself. How long will it take for pipe A and pipe B together to fill up the reservoir.

(1) By itself, pipe B can fill the reservoir in 20 minutes.
(2) Pipe B has a larger cross-sectional area than pipe A.

80. AB is perpendicular to CO. Is A or B closer to C?

(1) OA is less than OB.
(2) ACBD is not a parallelogram.

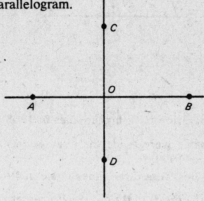

81. Is xy greater than 1? x and y are both positive.

(1) x is less than 1.
(2) y is greater than 1.

82. Does x = y?

(1) z = u
(2) ABCD is a parallelogram.

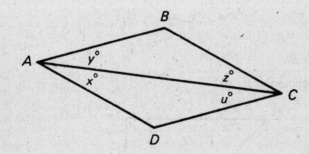

83. Train T leaves town A for town B and travels at a constant rate of speed. At the same time train S leaves town B for town A and also travels at a constant rate of speed. Town C is between A and B. Which train is traveling faster? Towns A, C, and B lie on a straight line.

(1) Train S arrives at town C before train T.
(2) C is closer to A than to B.

84. Does $x = y$?

    (1) BD is perpendicular to AC.
    (2) AB is equal to BC.

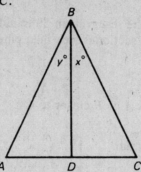

85. What is the value of $x + y$?

    (1) $x - y = 4$
    (2) $3x + 3y = 4$

86. Did the *XYZ* Corporation have higher sales in 1968 or in 1969?

    (1) In 1968 the sales were twice the average (arithmetic mean) of the sales in 1968, 1969, and 1970.
    (2) In 1970, the sales were three times those in 1969.

87. *AB* and *CD* are both chords of the circle with center *O*. Which is longer, *AB* or *CD*?

    (1) Arc *AEB* is smaller than arc *CFD*.
    (2) The area of the circular segment *CAEBD* is larger than the area of circular segment *ACFDB*.

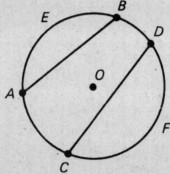

88. Is *ABCD* a square?

    (1) *BC* is perpendicular to *AD*.
    (2) *BE* = *EC*.

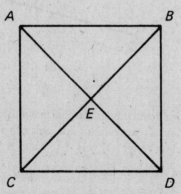

89. k is an integer. Is k divisible by 12?

(1) k is divisible by 4.
(2) k is divisible by 3.

90. How far is it from A to B?

(1) It is 15 miles from A to C.
(2) It is 25 miles from C to B.

91. Was Melissa Brown's novel published?

(1) If Melissa Brown's novel was published she would receive at least $1,000 in royalties during 1978.
(2) Melissa Brown's income for 1978 was over $1,000.

92. Is x an even integer? Assume n and p are integers.

(1) $x = (n+p)^2$
(2) $x = 2n+10p$

93. Did the price of lumber rise by more than 10% last year?

(1) Lumber exports increased by 20%.
(2) The amount of timber cut decreased by 10%.

94. Find the value of z if $x = 3$.

(1) $z = (x + 3)^4$
(2) $z = 2x + y$

95. What was the price of a dozen eggs during the 15th week of the year 1977?

(1) During the first week of 1977 the price of a dozen eggs was 75¢.
(2) The price of a dozen eggs rose 1¢ a week every week during the first four months of 1977.

96. Is DE parallel to BC? $DB = AD$.

(1) $AE = EC$
(2) $DB = EC$

97. There are two drains in the bottom of a water tank. If drain 1 is opened and drain 2 is closed a full tank will be empty in 15 minutes. How long will it take to empty a full tank if drain 1 and drain 2 are both opened?

(1) If drain 1 is closed and drain 2 is opened it takes 20 minutes to empty a full tank.
(2) In 3 minutes as much water flows through drain 1 as flows through drain 2 in 4 minutes.

98. Is $x > y$?

(1) $\dfrac{x}{y} = \dfrac{5}{4}$
(2) $x^2 > y^2$

99. Does every bird fly?

(1) Tigers do not fly.
(2) Ostriches do not fly.

100. Find $x + 2y$.

(1) $x - y = 12$
(2) $3x - 3y = 36$

101. Did the price of energy rise last year?

(1) If the price of energy rose last year then the price of food would rise this year.
(2) The price of food rose this year.

102. How much was a certain Rembrandt painting worth in Jan. 1971?

(1) In Jan. 1977 the painting was worth $2,000,000.
(2) Over the ten years 1968–1977 the painting increased in value by 10% each year.

103. A sequence of numbers $a_1, a_2, a_3, \ldots$ is given by the rule $a_n^2 = a_{n+1}$. Does 3 appear in the sequence?

(1) $a_1 = 2$
(2) $a_5 = 32$

104. Is AB greater than AC?

(1) $z > x$
(2) $AC > AD$

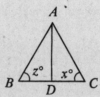

105. x and y are integers that are both less than 10. Is x greater than y?

(1) x is a multiple of 3.
(2) y is a multiple of 2.

If there is still time remaining, you may review the questions in this section only.
You may not turn to any other section of the test.

Section V Writing Ability

TIME: 30 minutes

DIRECTIONS: The following section contains a number of sentences with four underlined words or phrases. These sentences may have errors in grammar, tense, usage, diction (choice of words), idiom or structure. Choose the one underlined word or phrase that must be changed to make the sentence correct (for standard written English), and blacken the space provided to the right of the question. If you find no mistakes in a sentence, mark space E for No error; no sentence will contain more than one error. Note: Assume that all parts of the sentence that are not underlined are correct and cannot be changed.

106. The scheduled tasks of the director of this company are greater than the manager.
            A   B   C   D
      No error
      E

107. This young pianist is a person with great promise and who should be encouraged.
                          A   B   C   D
      No error
      E

108. An outstanding characteristic of each student was their ability to complete the exam
                                      A   B   C
      on time. No error
      D   E

109. If I would have arrived sooner, I would not have missed the fun. No error
            A   B   C   D   E

110. Our department was monitored by three supervisors, Sam, Bill and I. No error
      A   B   C D   E

111. The risks to the workers in contracting a work-related disease seems very great.
                  A   B   C   D
      No error
      E

112. The day progressed very quietly, fishing and eating at a picnic. No error
                    A   B   C   D   E

113. To join the club, a deposit must be made in advance. No error
      A B   C   D   E

114. It is not clear whether these are after-the-fact interpretations or something felt by the
                          A   B   C
      children at the time. No error
                  D   E

115. Only once before <u>have</u> <u>I</u> met a musician <u>who was so ready</u> to help a student.
                  A B   C   D
   <u>No error</u>
     E

116. My aunt, <u>whom we admire</u> almost too much, has <u>given</u> we <u>boys</u> ten dollars each
                A   B   C
   to spend <u>at the fair</u> tomorrow. <u>No error</u>
           D   E

117. When <u>I showed</u> my mother the suit <u>I had selected</u>, she objected to <u>me</u> buying it;
         A   B   C
   <u>she said it</u> was too expensive. <u>No error</u>
     D   E

118. <u>In her note</u> the teacher <u>asked the principal</u> to give some chalk from his supply
      A   B
   room to <u>whomever</u> of <u>us boys</u> would go down to pick it up. <u>No error</u>
           C   D   E

119. New York City <u>with</u> <u>it's many</u> tourist attractions is at once America's <u>most fabulous</u>
                  A   B   C
   metropolis, its dirtiest city, and its most exciting <u>place for a</u> brief vacation.
                                                               D
   <u>No error</u>
     E

120. Abraham <u>Lincolns Gettysburg</u> Address has been called a <u>model of brevity</u>, the
                    A   B
   greatest short speech that <u>anyone has ever</u> delivered, and a speech worth more than
               C   D
   a longer one <u>would have been. <u>No error</u>
                                 E

121. Please ask <u>whoever you</u> wish to serve as a fourth member of the <u>board I am</u> ap-
          A   B   C
   pointing to study the pollution situation <u>in your county</u>. <u>No error</u>
                                    D   E

122. <u>The United Nations</u> has performed many useful tasks <u>through its various</u> commis-
         A   B
   sions although there <u>are representatives</u> on these <u>commissions whom everyone</u> knows
                           C   D
   are Communists. <u>No error</u>
                  E

123. The Nobel Prize for Literature <u>has been awarded</u> to John Steinbeck, <u>who's novels</u>
                                  A   B

are now <u>considered among</u> the greatest which have been written in <u>the United States</u>
             C   D

in the twentieth century. <u>No error</u>
                            E

124. Even though we <u>know that</u> we are exercising our rights under the <u>United States</u>
                  A   B

<u>Constitution, Gail and myself</u> are arrested every <u>time we</u> picket police headquarters.
                   C   D

<u>No error</u>
 E

125. When the final story <u>has been written</u> for that final newspaper <u>sometime in the future</u>,
                    A   B

you can be sure <u>that it's substance</u> will be some violent <u>act that</u> has occurred.
                  C   D

<u>No error</u>
 E

If there is still time remaining, you may review the questions in this section only.
You may not turn to any other section of the test.

Section VI   Practical Judgment

TIME: 20 minutes

DIRECTIONS: Read the following passage. After you have completed it, you will be asked to answer two sets of questions. The first of these, data evaluation, involves determining the importance of specific factors included in the passage. The second, data application, consists of general questions relating to the passage. When answering questions, you may consult the passage.

Brooks and Company was a food manufacturer established in 1850. Until 1977, its major product lines had consisted of tomato specialties, such as catsup, pickles, and barbecue sauces. Its consumer products business accounted for 40% of sales; the balance consisted of institutional sales to restaurants, hospitals, and the armed forces. The company had advertised to the institutional market but never to final (household) consumers.

In 1977, the company introduced a new line of Italian specialty products aimed at the final consumer market. The line was composed of a number of prepared pasta dishes, such as spaghetti, lasagne, and ravioli. Each package contained all of the necessary ingredients (except meat) including seasoned tomato sauce, cheese, and noodles.

The idea for the line of Italian pasta products had been conceived by Joe Brooks, son of the company president. Joe's enthusiasm for the product idea was quickly picked up by other executives. The president had married an Italian woman after World War I and their only child, Joe, had been born in Naples. Because they lacked a Neapolitan background, William Johnson, production manager, and Carl Voght, treasurer, approved of the idea on less emotional grounds. Johnson saw in the Italian line certain production possibilities that fitted in well with the company's existing facilities. Mr. Voght had long argued for some type of expansion which would enable the company to solve a number of financial problems associated with its inability to attract outside capital.

Many planning meetings were held throughout the summer. These meetings were attended by both the Brookses, Johnson, and Voght. Charles Welch, an administrative assistant to the president, was instructed to sit in on the sessions after he returned from vacation on August 1. He acted as informal secretary for the group. The original thinking of the committee was that the product line should be introduced at the beginning of the fall food merchandising season, which started about October 1. This deadline, however, subsequently proved to be unrealistic. Production of the first items in the line did not get underway until September 30 and packaging difficulties prohibited introducing the product before mid-December.

In July the problems involved in the product introduction were not foremost in the planners' thoughts. Many hours were spent discussing the name of the product line. Finally, the name *Velsuvio* was adopted as a compromise, but without enthusiasm from Joe Brooks, who believed that a name such as *Valencia* better described the gourmet image that he thought the line should express. With the exception of the name, the younger Brooks directed most of the decisions related to the marketing program. From the beginning, he argued that there were already plenty of "middle class" spaghetti products on the grocers' shelves. What was needed, he believed, was a prestige—even a "gourmet"—line. The popularity of higher-priced Italian restaurants in many cities convinced young Brooks of the opportunity to market a prestige line of Italian food specialties.

Early in the planning it was decided not to limit distribution to those regional markets in which Brooks had previously established its reputation. National distribution would be undertaken from the beginning. It was planned that the *Velsuvio* line would be marketed in all major food chains except those handling only private or controlled brands. Sales to chain headquarters would be made by food brokers handling gourmet products rather than by brokers used to the handling of high-volume canned goods.

For the first time in its experience, Brooks planned to undertake an extensive consumer advertising program. A small Los Angeles advertising agency with slight experience in handling food products was appointed. However, by the time the agency had been selected and oriented to the marketing program, the time remaining before the scheduled introduction did not allow for the preparation of magazine advertisements or filmed television commercials. In order to break into the consumer market at the time of the scheduled product introduction on October 1, a consumer advertising program using newspapers, live television commercials, and radio was prepared. Except for the product introduction period, however, relatively little thought was given during the summer planning sessions to the total amount of money required to support the new product with consumer advertising.

A number of circumstances combined to prevent the introduction of the product in October as originally planned. No one had assumed personal responsibility for package design, and production was held up three weeks while the company waited for supplies of packaging materials. Brooks was forced to move very rapidly to obtain a package, and he was the first to admit that the result was neither very well designed functionally nor attractive from a promotional point of view. Time was short, however, and there was no choice but to use this package or abandon the project for the present season and possibly altogether, depending on competitive conditions.

A hastily put together advertising campaign was introduced in November. However, advertising costs had been greatly underestimated, so that the intensity of the campaign was much lower than Brooks had anticipated, even with the limited budget. As a result, most of the budget was allocated to newspapers and radio. Moreover, problems with the scripting of the TV commercials delayed broadcasting until the beginning of December. Newspaper advertisements and radio commercials did commence, however, as planned.

The new product was finally launched in mid-December. However, by February, two major competitors began marketing similar products. Shortly thereafter, a market research survey was sponsored by Brooks to determine whether the Velsuvio name made a favorable impression on housewives. The results of the survey were negative. Only twenty-two percent of the housewives interviewed could recall the Velsuvio name and of those, only twelve percent had tried the products. Consumer evaluation of the product line was far from encouraging. Of those who had tried the product for the first time, only four percent stated that they would buy it again.

Another indication that worried Brooks's management was that few major food chains showed interest in the line. By mid-year, Brooks's product sales were so poor that management established a special committee to determine without delay what immediate steps might be taken to reverse the poor sales record of Velsuvio.

Data Evaluation Questions

DIRECTIONS: The questions that follow relate to the preceding passage. Evaluate, in terms of the passage, each of the items given. Then select your answer from one of the following classifications, and blacken the corresponding space on the answer sheet.

(A) A MAJOR OBJECTIVE in making the decision: one of the goals sought by the decision maker

(B) A MAJOR FACTOR in making the decision: an aspect of the problem, specifically mentioned in the passage, that fundamentally affects and/or determines the decision

(C) A MINOR FACTOR in making the decision: a less important element bearing on or affecting a Major Factor, rather than a Major Objective directly

(D) A MAJOR ASSUMPTION in making the decision: a projection or supposition arrived at by the decision maker before considering the factors and alternatives

(E) AN UNIMPORTANT ISSUE in making the decision: an item lacking significant impact on, or relationship to, the decision

126. Possibility of using existing production facilities in manufacturing *Velsuvio* products

127. Likelihood of achieving wide consumer acceptance of the *Velsuvio* line

128. Company growth and expansion

129. Age of Brooks and Company

130. The popularity of high-priced Italian restaurants in the U.S.

131. Depth of Brooks's expertise in the sale of consumer products

132. Market survey results

133. Size of the advertising agency hired to promote the *Velsuvio* line

134. National distribution of the *Velsuvio* line

135. Brooks's inability to attract outside capital

136. Appointment of Welch as informal secretary

137. Difficulties with new package design

138. Need for a "gourmet" Italian food line

139. Market entry of competitors

Data Application Questions

DIRECTIONS: Answer each of the following questions using information contained in the passage.

140. Initial sales of the new product line were disappointing because of

    I. organizational problems
    II. lack of advertising objectives
    III. poor package design

    (A) I only
    (B) III only
    (C) I and II only
    (D) II and III only
    (E) I, II, and III

141. It can be inferred from the passage that Brooks and Company is

    I. consumer-oriented
    II. progressive
    III. organizationally deficient

    (A) I only
    (B) III only
    (C) I and II only
    (D) II and III only
    (E) I, II, and III

142. Brooks's advertising campaign was ill-conceived because of the

    I.   inexperienced advertising agency
   II. delay in the preparation of commercials
 III. company's decision not to use TV commercials

  (A) I only
  (B) III only
  (C) I and II only
  (D) II and III only
  (E) I, II, and III

143. According to the passage, it was planned to introduce the new product line

    I.   about October 1
   II. at the beginning of the fall food merchandising season
 III. in mid-December

  (A) I only
  (B) III only
  (C) I and II only
  (D) II and III only
  (E) I, II, and III

144. Analyzing the passage, it can be concluded that Brooks and Company's greatest weakness was in the area of

    I.   consumer marketing
   II. production
 III. public relations

  (A) I only
  (B) III only
  (C) I and II only
  (D) II and III only
  (E) I, II, and III

145. The marketing program for the new product line was mainly directed by

    I.   the marketing manager
   II. the planning committee
 III. the president's son

  (A) I only
  (B) III only
  (C) I and II only
  (D) II and III only
  (E) I, II, and III

If there is still time remaining, you may review the questions in this section only.
You may not turn to any other section of the test.

Section VII   Verbal Ability

TIME: 20 minutes

Antonyms

DIRECTIONS: For each question below, select the lettered word or phrase that comes closest to being *opposite* in meaning to the word appearing in capital letters. Be sure to consider all meanings carefully.

146. ABJURE: (A) injure (B) pledge (C) abdicate (D) realize (E) conjure

147. MITIGATE: (A) lose (B) transfer (C) intensify (D) abstain (E) extract

148. SPURIOUS: (A) soft (B) harmful (C) new (D) authentic (E) contradictory

149. TORRID: (A) wet (B) animated (C) cold (D) closed (E) even

150. CIRCUMSPECTION: (A) regret (B) humility (C) generosity (D) joy (E) recklessness

151. DESULTORY: (A) sad (B) methodical (C) rough (D) pleasant (E) contented

152. DISSONANCE: (A) heat (B) loudness (C) harmony (D) noise (E) identity

153. INCREDULOUS: (A) irreligious (B) creditable (C) indifferent (D) believing (E) confused

154. OBDURATE: (A) unsusceptible (B) tender (C) right (D) intelligent (E) meager

155. UNGAINLY: (A) graceful (B) exceptional (C) winning (D) sensible (E) average

156. DISCERN: (A) disobey (B) overlook (C) separate (D) include (E) disorganize

157. CONVIVIAL: (A) encouraging (B) unsociable (C) ignorant (D) tranquil (E) vicious

158. ALACRITY: (A) slowness (B) clarity (C) attractiveness (D) unfriendliness (E) culpability

159. PERFIDIOUS: (A) awkward (B) homely (C) faithful (D) comprehensible (E) ignorant

Analogies

DIRECTIONS: For each question below, determine the relationship between the pair of capitalized words and then select the lettered pair of words which have a similar relationship to the first pair.

160. COMPUTER : SLIDE RULE :: (A) car : driver (B) quadrant : teacher (C) reader : book (D) clock : sundial (E) solution : problem

161. BATTERY : FLASHLIGHT :: (A) sun : warmth (B) mercury : vapor (C) fertilizer : grass (D) tires : automobile (E) coal : furnace

162. MUFF : HANDS :: (A) helmet : head (B) polish : nails (C) glasses : eyes (D) anklet : legs (E) earring : ears

163. PHILATELIST : STAMPS :: (A) philanthropist : charity (B) entomologist : mosquitos (C) numismatist : coins (D) ornithologist : feathers (E) government : taxes

164. PLACID : TRANQUILIZER :: (A) jovial : liquor (B) somnolent : sedative (C) strong : pill (D) fearful : spectre (E) motionless : warning

165. MATURITY : INFANCY :: (A) culmination : inception (B) work : burden (C) applause : performance (D) seed : bulb (E) foundation : building

166. FLORICULTURE : FLOWERS :: (A) gold : ore (B) bushel : grain (C) horticulture : raisins (D) cultivation : vegetables (E) arboriculture : trees

167. SONNETEER : POET :: (A) sculptor : painter (B) layman : priest (C) director : actor (D) songwriter : composer (E) troubador : minstrel

168. MUSLIN : PLAIN :: (A) tile : square (B) brocade : ornate (C) montage : colored (D) wool : decorated (E) linen : fragile

169. DRAMA : EPILOGUE :: (A) music : coda (B) speech : applause (C) stanza : poetry (D) sunset : dark (E) beginning : end

170. PLANE : PILOT :: (A) election : politician (B) conduct : police (C) radar : repairman (D) arms : captain (E) store : manager

171. DECADE : CENTURY :: (A) decibel : unit (B) decimeter : meter (C) decimal : equation (D) delineate : boundary (E) deuce : ace

172. MODEL : REALITY :: (A) blueprint : house (B) design : prototype (C) formula : chemistry (D) hypothesis : theory (E) prognosis : diagnosis

Sentence Completions

DIRECTIONS: For each sentence below, select the lettered word or set of words which, when inserted in the sentence blanks, best completes the meaning of that sentence.

173. A free enterprise system depends upon the willingness of _____ to accept the risks involved in _____.

    (A) politicians ... elections (B) businesses ... competition (C) the people ... state control (D) workers ... unionization (E) government ... socialism

174. With some exceptions, _____ generally have criticized advertising as _____.

    (A) marketers ... innocuous (B) consumers ... helpful (C) economists ... wasteful (D) businessmen ... misleading (E) citizens ... ineffective

175. An attitude is a _____ to respond in an evaluative way toward a given object.

    (A) responsibility (B) desire (C) predisposition (D) need (E) failure

176. Far from being little-known, the relationship between advertising and subsequent _____ has been _____ studied.

    (A) prices ... rarely (B) research ... occasionally (C) sales ... closely (D) events ... secretly (E) commerce ... little

177. Election results showed that the voters had given the winner a _____ with a clear _____.

(A) parade . . . permit (B) majority . . . plurality (C) victory . . . mandate (D) plebiscite . . . referendum (E) majority . . . result

178. Statistical evidence can establish definite _____ between events, but usually cannot prove causal relationships.

(A) distinctions (B) intervals (C) similarities (D) correlations (E) divisions

179. In the interest of free speech, political advertising is not subject to the usual forms of _____ allowed by the Federal Communication Commission.

(A) broadcast (B) protection (C) censorship (D) sponsorship (E) discussion

180. In spite of heavy bombing, the bridge was still _____.

(A) extant (B) destroyed (C) needless (D) damaged (E) vital

181. The malingerer hoped to escape the _____.

(A) voyage (B) expense (C) work (D) crowd (E) criticism

182. Wars usually result from _____ among the parties involved and a failure to _____ them peacefully.

(A) hostilities . . . debate (B) doubts . . . dispel (C) treaties . . . amend (D) disagreements . . . resolve (E) frustrations . . . understand

183. The _____ action of the participants led the referee to _____ the fight.

(A) belligerent . . . cancel (B) enthusiastic . . . begin (C) unwarranted . . . stop (D) inert . . . postpone (E) wild . . . enter

184. Not far from the scene of the crime, the _____ was apprehended.

(A) victim (B) assailant (C) confessor (D) observer (E) detective

185. Logical progression in the flow of _____ is an essential part of good _____ writing.

(A) supposition . . . newspaper (B) words . . . order (C) information . . . report (D) facts . . . novel (E) fiction . . . chronicle

If there is still time remaining, you may review the questions in this section only.
You may not turn to any other section of the test.

Answers

Section I Reading Comprehension

1. (B)	8. (A)	15. (A)	21. (C)
2. (C)	9. (B)	16. (A)	22. (B)
3. (D)	10. (B)	17. (D)	23. (C)
4. (C)	11. (B)	18. (B)	24. (C)
5. (E)	12. (E)	19. (C)	25. (C)
6. (C)	13. (B)	20. (C)	
7. (B)	14. (D)		

Section II Problem Solving

(Numbers in parentheses indicate the section in the Mathematics Review where material concerning the question is discussed.)

26. (B) (I-4)	34. (A) (II-3)	42. (B) (II-3)	50. (B) (II-6)
27. (D) (I-4)	35. (D) (II-7)	43. (B) (II-4)	51. (D) (I-2, I-8)
28. (B) (I-2)	36. (B) (II-3)	44. (C) (I-2)	52. (E) (II-6, II-1)
29. (E) (II-3)	37. (E) (I-4)	45. (D) (II-3)	53. (E) (II-3)
30. (A) (II-5)	38. (D) (II-1)	46. (C) (I-4)	54. (C) (III-6)
31. (E) (II-2)	39. (D) (II-5)	47. (D) (II-5)	55. (E) (III-7)
32. (D) (I-4)	40. (C) (I-2)	48. (E) (II-3)	
33. (C) (II-3)	41. (A) (II-7)	49. (C) (III-7, II-3)	

Section III Practical Judgment

56. (E)	61. (B)	66. (C)	71. (D)
57. (D)	62. (B)	67. (D)	72. (A)
58. (A)	63. (B)	68. (D)	73. (B)
59. (A)	64. (E)	69. (B)	74. (B)
60. (C)	65. (B)	70. (B)	75. (B)

Section IV   Data Sufficiency

76.	(D)	84.	(C)	92.	(B)	100.	(E)
77.	(A)	85.	(B)	93.	(E)	101.	(E)
78.	(B)	86.	(A)	94.	(A)	102.	(C)
79.	(A)	87.	(D)	95.	(C)	103.	(D)
80.	(A)	88.	(E)	96.	(A)	104.	(A)
81.	(E)	89.	(C)	97.	(D)	105.	(E)
82.	(C)	90.	(E)	98.	(E)		
83.	(C)	91.	(E)	99.	(B)		

Section V   Writing Ability

106.	(D)	111.	(D)	116.	(B)	121.	(B)
107.	(C)	112.	(A)	117.	(C)	122.	(D)
108.	(B)	113.	(C)	118.	(C)	123.	(B)
109.	(A)	114.	(E)	119.	(B)	124.	(C)
110.	(D)	115.	(E)	120.	(A)	125.	(C)

Section VI   Practical Judgment

126.	(B)	131.	(D)	136.	(E)	141.	(B)
127.	(D)	132.	(B)	137.	(B)	142.	(C)
128.	(A)	133.	(E)	138.	(D)	143.	(C)
129.	(E)	134.	(A)	139.	(B)	144.	(A)
130.	(B)	135.	(B)	140.	(E)	145.	(B)

Section VII   Verbal Ability

146.	(B)	156.	(B)	166.	(E)	176.	(C)
147.	(C)	157.	(B)	167.	(D)	177.	(C)
148.	(D)	158.	(A)	168.	(B)	178.	(D)
149.	(C)	159.	(C)	169.	(A)	179.	(C)
150.	(E)	160.	(D)	170.	(E)	180.	(A)
151.	(B)	161.	(E)	171.	(B)	181.	(C)
152.	(C)	162.	(A)	172.	(A)	182.	(D)
153.	(D)	163.	(C)	173.	(B)	183.	(C)
154.	(B)	164.	(B)	174.	(C)	184.	(B)
155.	(A)	165.	(A)	175.	(C)	185.	(C)

Analysis

Section I   Reading Comprehension

1. **(B)** The passage deals with the harmful effects of certain production processes on workers and others.

2. **(C)** This answer is clear from lines 20-33 of the passage.

3. **(D)** Osteolysis is not mentioned as a cause. (A) can be found in lines 12-13; (B) in lines 20; (C) in line 34; and (E) in line 2.

4. **(C)** The author does not argue for remedial action in the passage, but merely presents the facts concerning cancer-producing occupational hazards.

5. **(E)** This is implied in lines 40ff. Existing legislated-maximum levels of vinyl chloride exposure are higher than that set by Dow Chemical, and apparently higher than a medically permissible safe limit.

6. **(C)** The passage relates that at least 17 workers were killed because of the failure by authorities to follow up on available research. See lines 40-41.

7. **(B)** The passage states that "a creature" was first observed by St. Columba in 565 A.D. See line 43.

8. **(A)** The statement beginning on line 43 indicates that the name of the monster is based on a specific shape and form (as discussed in lines 32ff) taken from a photograph of the animal.

9. **(C)** In line 19, the dimensions of the lake are given as approximately 23 miles long, with a maximum width of 1.5 miles. Therefore, answers (A) and (B) are almost certainly two small, while answers (D) and (E) are much too large.

10. **(B)** Most of the passage deals with the origins of Loch Ness and with the so-called "monster" within.

11. **(B)** Ichthyologists are zoologists who study fish.

12. **(E)** None can be inferred from the passage.

13. **(B)** Line 7 quotes Marx as saying that philosophers only want to interpret the world, when what should be done is to change it. Change, the author states on line 8, is the "creed of applied scientists everywhere."

14. **(D)** Durkheim also valued the application of science rather than theoretical constructs alone. See line 38.

15. **(A)** Items (B) through (E) deal with *applied* problems which are the main concern of the social scientist, according to the passage.

16. **(A)** See lines 38-40.

17. **(D)** This point is stressed in lines 5, 12, 17ff, 30, 32, 38, and 44ff.

18. **(B)** All but choice (B) are mentioned in the last paragraph.

19. **(C)** While the author is concerned with the moral and cultural aspects of American society (lines 1, 21-25), his major concern is to show how the Bible has been used as a guide for some theatrical productions. See especially lines 31-35, and 48ff.

20. **(C)** This central theme of the author's concern is contained in lines 3-12.

21. **(C)** Statements (A) and (B) were not originally voiced by the author, but rather by Gen. Sarnoff. See lines 1-2, 8-9. Statements (D) and (E) are taken out of context. See lines 32-40. Statement (C) reflects the author's own ideas. See lines 14-19.

22. **(B)** Question I is found in lines 14-18, question III in lines 19-20. However, the author does not present evidence that he intends to answer them. Only answers to question II are implied throughout. See lines 41-47.

23. **(C)** The author does not state his background or profession, but it might be any of the above except (C), since there are no traces of humor in this passage.

24. **(C)** Both these ideas are implied in lines 10-13.

25. **(C)** Examined in context, (C) is the most probable answer. See lines 32-34.

Section II   Problem Solving

26. **(B)** Let L be the original length and W the original width. The new length is 120% of L which is $(1.2)L$; the new width is 80% of W which is $(.8)W$. The area of a rectangle is length times width, so the original area is LW and the new area is $(1.2)(L)(.8)W$ or $(.96)LW$. Since the new area is 96% of the original area, the area has decreased by 4%.

27. **(D)** The distance from New York to Hartford divided by the distance from New York to Boston is $\frac{120}{250}$ or .48, and .48 = 48%.

28. **(B)** The amount broken off is $\frac{1}{8} + 1\frac{3}{4} + 1\frac{1}{12}$ inches. Since $\frac{1}{8} + 1\frac{3}{4} + 1\frac{1}{12} = \frac{3}{24} + \frac{42}{24} + \frac{26}{24} = \frac{71}{24}$ and the lead was 5 inches long to begin with, the amount left $= 5 - \frac{71}{24} = \frac{120}{24} - \frac{71}{24} = \frac{49}{24} = 2\frac{1}{24}$ inches.

29. **(E)** The first 1,000 copies cost $1 each; so altogether they will cost $1,000. The remaining 3,800 copies (4,800 − 1,000) cost x dollars each; so their cost is $3,800x. Therefore, the total cost of all 4,800 copies is $1,000 + $3,800x.

30. **(A)** Since $1\frac{2}{3}$ hours is 100 minutes, 50 minutes is $\frac{1}{2}$ of $1\frac{2}{3}$ hours. Therefore, he should make half as much in 50 minutes as he does in $1\frac{2}{3}$ hours. Since he made 4 boxes in $1\frac{2}{3}$ hours, he makes 2 boxes in 50 minutes.

31. **(E)** Since $\frac{y}{x} = 2$, $y = 2x$. Therefore, $x + y = x + 2x = 3x$ which equals 3. So $3x = 3$, which means $x = 1$. Thus, $y = 2$ because $y = 2x$.

32. **(D)** Since there are 20 rolls in a carton and a carton costs $9, each roll costs $\frac{1}{20}$ of $9 which is 45¢. The roll sells for 50¢, so the selling price divided by the cost is $\frac{50}{45} = \frac{10}{9}$ which is about 111%. (or divide the total income by the total cost: $\frac{20 \times .50}{9} = \frac{10}{9} = 111\%$.)

33. **(C)** 12 copies of the history book weigh (12)(2.4) or 28.8 pounds. Since the total weight of the books is 42.8 pounds, the weight of the English books is 42.8 − 28.8 or 14 pounds. Therefore, each English book weighs $\frac{14}{8}$ or 1.75 pounds.

34. **(A)** Let x be the number of miles the car travels on a gallon of gas when driven at 60 miles an hour. Then 80% of 15 is x; so $\frac{4}{5} \cdot 15 = x$ and $x = 12$.

35. **(D)**

STATEMENT I cannot be inferred since if $x = 2$ and $y = 1$, then x and y are positive but x is not less than y.

STATEMENT II is true since $x + y = z$ and y is positive so $x < z$.

STATEMENT III is true. z is positive since it is the sum of two positive numbers and so $z < 2z$. Since we know $x < z$ and $z < 2z$, then $x < 2z$.

Therefore, only STATEMENTS II and III can be inferred.

36. **(B)** The first 800 sheets cost $800x$ ¢. The remaining 4,200 sheets cost $\frac{x}{15}$ ¢ apiece which comes to $(4,200)\left(\frac{x}{15}\right)$¢ or $280x$ ¢. Therefore, the total cost of the 5,000 sheets of paper is $800x$ ¢ $+ 280x$ ¢, which is $1,080x$ ¢.

37. **(E)** Let S denote the worker's salary in 1967. In 1968 he received 110% of S which is $(1.1)S$, and in 1969 he received 110% of $(1.1)S$ which is $(1.1)(1.1)S$ or 1.21 S. Therefore, he received 21% more in 1969 than he did in 1967.

38. **(D)** Factory A turns out $8a$ cars in 8 hours. Since factory B turns out b cars in 2 hours, it turns out $4b$ cars in 8 hours. Therefore, the total is $8a + 4b$.

39. **(D)** In 35 minutes John makes 7 boxes and Tim makes 5. The required ratio, 7 to 5, is constant no matter how long they work.

40. **(C)** The total number of crates sold is $3\frac{1}{4} + 2\frac{1}{6} + 4\frac{1}{2} + 1\frac{2}{3}$ which is equal to $\frac{39}{12} + \frac{26}{12} + \frac{54}{12} + \frac{20}{12} = \frac{139}{12} = 11\frac{7}{12}$. A shorter method would be to add the integral parts of each of the numbers $3 + 2 + 4 + 1 = 10$. Next add the fractional parts $\frac{1}{4} + \frac{1}{6} + \frac{1}{2} + \frac{2}{3}$. Using 12 as a common denominator you get $\frac{(3+2+6+8)}{12}$ which is $\frac{19}{12} = 1\frac{7}{12}$. Therefore, the answer is $10 + 1\frac{7}{12} = 11\frac{7}{12}$.

41. **(A)** If $x + y$ exceeds 4 and x is less than 3, it is clear that y must exceed 1.

42. **(B)** Since 10 is $\frac{1}{5}$ of 50, the 10 apprentices should do $\frac{1}{5}$ as much work as 50 apprentices. 50 apprentices did the job in 4 hours, so in 1 hour 50 apprentices will do $\frac{1}{4}$ of the job.

Therefore, 10 apprentices should do $\frac{1}{5}$ of $\frac{1}{4} = \frac{1}{20}$ of the job in an hour.

Since 15 is $\frac{1}{2}$ of 30, 15 journeymen will do half as much work as 30 journeymen. The 30 journeymen finished the job in $4\frac{1}{4}$ hours, so in 1 hour they will do $\frac{2}{9}$ of the job. Therefore, 15 journeymen will do $\frac{1}{2}$ of $\frac{2}{9} = \frac{1}{9}$ of the job in an hour.

So both groups will do $\frac{1}{20} + \frac{1}{9} = \frac{9}{180} + \frac{20}{180} = \frac{29}{180}$ of the job in an hour.

43. **(B)** 40% of the 52% of the population who are women are voters. So $(.40)(.52) = .2080 = 20.8\%$ of the population are women voters.

44. **(C)** The amount of gas needed for a bus to travel 200 miles if the bus travels 15 miles on a gallon is $\frac{200}{15}$ or $13\frac{1}{3}$ gallons.

45. **(D)** The time required to pump 10 gallons of water out of the tank is $(10)\left(15 - \frac{x}{10}\right)$ which equals $150 - x$ minutes.

46. **(C)** The profit is 6% of $1,000 plus 5% of $6,000 − $1,000 which is $(.06)(\$1,000) + (.05)(\$5,000)$. Therefore, the profit equals $60 + $250 which is $310.

47. **(D)** Since the number of baskets manufactured in an hour is proportional to the number of workers, $\frac{15}{45} = \frac{27}{x}$, where x is the number of baskets manufactured by 45 men in an hour. Therefore, x is 81. Since 40 minutes is $\frac{2}{3}$ of an hour, 45 men will make $\frac{2}{3}$ of 81 or 54 baskets in 40 minutes.

48. **(E)** The first belt lifts $\frac{2}{5}$ of a ton per minute and the second belt lifts $\frac{3}{7}$ of a ton per minute, so both belts together will lift $\frac{2}{5} + \frac{3}{7} = \frac{29}{35}$ of a ton per minute. Therefore, using both belts it will take $\frac{20}{29/35} = \frac{35}{29} \times 20 = \frac{700}{29}$ or $24\frac{4}{29}$ minutes to lift 20 tons.

49. **(C)** Since the width is $^1/_3$ of the length and the length is 120 yards, the width of the field is 40 yards. The area of a rectangle is length times width, so the area of the field is 120 yards times 40 yards, which is 4,800 square yards.

50. **(B)** The price will be $3.00 a pound 6 months from now and $9.00 a pound a year from now. The price is a geometric progression of the form $\$3^j$ where j is the number of 6 month periods which have passed. Since $3^4 = 81$, after 4 six month periods, the price will be $81.00 a pound. Therefore, the answer is two years, since 24 months is 2 years.

51. **(D)** Since $\frac{x}{y} = \frac{2}{3}$, $\frac{y}{x}$, which is the reciprocal of $\frac{x}{y}$, must be equal to $\frac{3}{2}$. Also, $\frac{y^2}{x^2}$ is equal to $\left(\frac{y}{x}\right)^2$, so $\frac{y^2}{x^2}$ is equal to $\frac{9}{4}$.

52. **(E)** Starting with $a_n = 1$ the rule $(a_n - 1)^2 = (1 - 1)^2 = 0^2 = 0$ so the next entry is 0. Using 0 as a_n gives $(0 - 1)^2 = (-1)^2 = 1$ so the second entry is 1. Since using 1 as a_n gives 0 as the next entry, the entries after 1 should be 0,1,0.

53. **(E)** X is paid 125%, or $\frac{5}{4}$ of Y's salary, so Y makes $\frac{4}{5}$ of what X makes. X makes 80% or $\frac{4}{5}$ of Z's salary, so Z makes $\frac{5}{4}$ of what X makes. Thus, the total salary of X, Y, and Z is the total of X's salary, $\frac{4}{5}$ of X's salary and $\frac{5}{4}$ X's salary. Therefore, the total is $\frac{61}{20}$ of X's salary. Since the total of the salaries is $610, X makes $\frac{20}{61}$ of $610, or $200.

54. **(C)** Since the radii are unequal, the circles cannot be identical, thus (E) is incorrect. If two circles intersect in 3 points they must be identical, so (D) is also incorrect. Two different circles can intersect in 2 points without being identical, so (C) is the correct answer.

55. **(E)** Let L be the length and W be the width of the rectangle, and let S be the length of a side of the square. It is given that $LW = S^2$. A relation must be found between $2L + 2W$ and $4S$. It is possible to construct squares and rectangles so that (A), (B), (C), or (D) is false, so (E) is correct. For example, if the rectangle is a square, then the two figures are identical and (A), (C) and (D) are false. If the rectangle is not equal to a square, then the perimeter of the rectangle is larger than the perimeter of the square, so (B) is also false.

Section III   Practical Judgment

56. **(E)** The present sales level was not an important issue in the development of corporate strategy. What was important, however, was the fact that the company's *market share* was "stationary," which is an indicator of a lack of growth.

57. **(D)** Fishing resort owners were listed as a potential market in paragraph 2. However, the market research study did not mention any evidence that these resort owners were likely to purchase the proposed product.

58. **(A)** The commitment of the board of directors to the development of a new product to be sold to different (but related) markets was related to the stationary market position of the firm. Introduction of a new product to increase market share was a major objective of B & S.

59. **(A)** Sales to the 7.5 million fishermen—potential users of the product—was a major objective.

60. **(C)** The versatility of the motor was secondary to the consideration of whether fishermen had a *need* for a new low horsepower motor.

61. **(B)** In order to penetrate the diverse market ("located throughout the country"), B & S had to secure wide market coverage.

62. **(B)** The large potential market was a major consideration in the decision to develop the product.

63. **(B)** The fact that only 15% of active fishermen owned an outboard motor was a major consideration in the decision to develop the product.

64. **(E)** Selling to O.E.M. customers was not considered as a possibility by B & S.

65. **(B)** When it was realized that few independent dealers would take on the "Big Scout" line on a franchised basis, it was decided to abandon exclusive distribution (and the "Big Scout" name) and sell through the Sears Roebuck network.

66. **(C)** Provision of dealer training was an insignificant consideration in the decision to market the product.

67. **(D)** The assumption that many dealers would be willing to sell the product was not verified by the facts in the case.

68. **(D)** The sales forecast (in paragraph 3) was not supported by any cited evidence.

69. **(B)** An aggressive sales and advertising program was an important element in the general plan for marketing the new product (paragraph 3).

70. **(B)** It was clear that dealers—if given the option—would prefer a well-known brand name like Evinrude, rather than an unknown brand like Big Scout.

71. **(D)** Of the three, only water-ski enthusiasts were not considered.

72. **(A)** B & S's distribution plan was changed after it became clear that it would be difficult to attract dealers. This information came from the assistant marketing manager's talks with potential dealers at a trade show. It is obvious that if top management had had this information beforehand, they would not have planned for exclusive distribution.

73. **(B)** Although B & S held a dominant market position, its market share was not growing. Therefore, management strategy was to exploit the company's existing technological expertise to develop a new product for related—but different—markets. They did not plan to sell outboard motors through existing distribution channels, nor to rely *mainly* on an aggressive advertising campaign.

74. **(B)** Distributors were unwilling to take on the new line. See the last two paragraphs.

75. **(B)** Only relatively few dealers could not obtain a "big name" line. No evidence was presented in the case that the lawn mower market was saturated. In paragraph 1, it was stated that the board of directors was committed to the development of a new product.

Section IV   Data Sufficiency

76. **(D)**

    STATEMENT (1) alone is sufficient. 2 feet 7 inches is more than half of 5 feet, so the piece which is 2 feet 7 inches long must be longer than the other two pieces put together.

    STATEMENT (2) alone is sufficient. Since one piece is 5 inches long, the sum of the lengths of the remaining two pieces is 4 feet, 7 inches. Since one piece is 7 inches longer than the other, $L + (L + 7 \text{ in.}) = 4 \text{ ft. } 7 \text{ in.}$, where L is the length of the smaller of the two remaining pieces. Solving the equation yields $L + 7$ in. as the length of the longest piece.

77. **(A)** Since AC is a diameter, angle ABC is inscribed in a semicircle and is therefore a right angle.

    STATEMENT (1) alone is sufficient since it implies the two other angles in the triangle must be equal. Since the sum of the angles of a triangle is 180°, we can deduce that $x = 45$.

    STATEMENT (2) alone is not sufficient. There is no information about the angle ABD; so STATEMENT (2) cannot be used to find the angles of triangle ABD.

78. **(B)**

STATEMENT (2) alone is sufficient. $y^2 - 2y + 1$ equals $(y - 1)^2$, so the only solution to $(y - 1)^2 = 0$ is $y = 1$.

STATEMENT (1) alone is not sufficient. $x + 2y = 6$ implies $y = 3 - \dfrac{x}{2}$, but there is no data given about the value of x.

79. **(A)**

STATEMENT (1) alone is sufficient. Pipe A fills up $\dfrac{1}{30}$ of the reservoir per minute. STATEMENT (1) says pipe B fills up $\dfrac{1}{20}$ of the reservoir per minute, so A and B together fill up $\dfrac{1}{20} + \dfrac{1}{30}$ or $\dfrac{5}{60}$ or $\dfrac{1}{12}$ of the reservoir. Therefore, together pipe A and pipe B will take 12 minutes to fill the reservoir.

STATEMENT (2) alone is not sufficient. There is no information about how long it takes pipe B to fill the reservoir.

80. **(A)**

STATEMENT (1) alone is sufficient. Draw the lines AC and BC; then AOC and BOC are right triangles, since AB is perpendicular to CO. By the Pythagorean theorem, $(AC)^2 = (AO)^2 + (CO)^2$ and $(BC)^2 = (OB)^2 + (CO)^2$; so if AO is less than OB, then AC is less than BC.

STATEMENT (2) alone is not sufficient. There is no restriction on where the point D is.

81. **(E)**

STATEMENTS (1) and (2) together are not sufficient. If $x = \frac{1}{2}$ and $y = 3$, then xy is greater than 1, but if $x = \frac{1}{2}$ and $y = \frac{3}{2}$, then xy is less than 1.

82. **(C)**

STATEMENT (1) alone is not sufficient. By choosing B and D differently we can have either $x = y$ or $x \neq y$ and still have $z = u$.

STATEMENT (2) alone is not sufficient. It implies that $x = z$ and $y = u$, but gives no

information to compare x and y. STATEMENTS (1) and (2) together, however, yield $x = y$.

83. **(C)**

STATEMENT (1) alone is not sufficient. If town C were closer to B, even if S were going slower than T, S could arrive at C first. But if you also use STATEMENT (2), then train S must be traveling faster than train T, since it is further from B to C than it is from A to C.

So STATEMENTS (1) and (2) together are sufficient.

STATEMENT (2) alone is insufficient since it gives no information about the trains.

84. **(C)**

STATEMENT (2) alone is not sufficient, since D can be any point if we assume only STATEMENT (2).

STATEMENT (1) alone is not sufficient. Depending on the position of point C, x and y can be equal or unequal. For example, in both of the following triangles BD is perpendicular to AC.

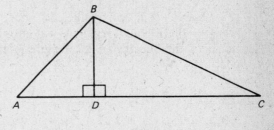

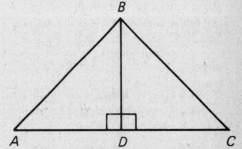

If STATEMENTS (1) and (2) are both true, then $x = y$. The triangles ABD and BDC are both right triangles with two pairs of corresponding sides equal; the triangles are therefore congruent and $x = y$.

85. **(B)**

   STATEMENT (2) alone is sufficient, since $3x + 3y$ is $3(x + y)$. (Therefore, if $3x + 3y = 4$, then $x + y = \frac{4}{3}$.)

   STATEMENT (1) alone is not sufficient, since you need another equation besides $x - y = 4$ to find the values of x and y.

86. **(A)**

   STATEMENT (1) alone is sufficient. We know that the total of sales for 1968, 1969, and 1970 is three times the average and that sales in 1968 were twice the average. Then the total of sales in 1969 and 1970 was equal to the average. Therefore, sales were less in 1969 than in 1968.

   STATEMENT (2) alone is insufficient, since it does not relate sales in 1969 to sales in 1968.

87. **(D)**

   Since the length of the arc of the circle is proportional to the length of the chord connecting the endpoints, STATEMENT (1) alone is sufficient.

   STATEMENT (2) alone is sufficient, since the areas of the circular segments are proportional to the squares of the lengths of the chord.

88. **(E)**

   STATEMENTS (1) and (2) together are not sufficient, since the points A and D can be moved and STATEMENTS (1) and (2) still be satisfied.

89. **(C)**

   STATEMENT (1) alone is not sufficient, since 24 and 16 are both divisible by 4 but only 24 is divisible by 12.

   STATEMENT (2) alone is not sufficient, since 24 and 15 are divisible by 3 but 15 is not divisible by 12.

   STATEMENT (1) implies that $k = 4m$ for some integer m. If you assume STATEMENT (2), then since k is divisible by 3, either 4 or m is divisible by 3. Since 4 is not divisible by 3, m must be. Therefore, $m = 3j$, where j

is some integer and $k = 4 \times 3j$ or $12j$. So k is divisible by 12. Therefore, STATEMENTS (1) and (2) together are sufficient.

90. **(E)**

   STATEMENTS (1) and (2) together are not sufficient, because there is no information about the location of C relative to the locations of A and B.

91. **(E)** Obviously a single statement is not sufficient. However, since Ms. Brown could have other sources of income, even both statements together are not sufficient. If you answered (C) you are making the additional assumption that Ms. Brown's only source of income was royalties from the novel.

92. **(B)** An even integer is an integer divisible by 2. Since $2n + 10p$ is 2 times $(n + 5p)$ using (2) lets you deduce that x is even. (1) by itself is not sufficient. If n were 2 and p were 3, $(n + p)^2$ would be 25 which is not even, but by choosing n to be 2 and p to be 4, $(n + p)^2$ is 36 which is even.

93. **(E)** Both statements give facts that *might* explain why the price of lumber rose. However, even using both statements you can't deduce what happened to the price of lumber.

94. **(A)** Since you know $x = 3$, statement (1) alone is sufficient. However, since no information is given about the value of y, statement (2) is insufficient.

95. **(C)** You need (1) to know what the price was at the beginning of 1977. Using (2) you could then compute the price during the fifteenth week. Either statement alone is insufficient. You should not actually compute the price since it would only waste time.

96. **(A)** (1) alone is sufficient since the line connecting the midpoints of 2 sides of a triangle is parallel to the third side. (2) alone is insufficient. In an isosceles triangle statement (2) would imply that ED is parallel to BC, but in a non-isosceles triangle, (2) would imply that ED and BC are not parallel.

97. **(D)** (1) alone is sufficient. For example, with both drains open, $\frac{1}{15} + \frac{1}{20}$ of the tank would be emptied each minute. You should not waste any time solving the problem. Remember, you only have to decide whether there is enough information to let you answer the question.

   (2) alone is also sufficient. You can deduce (1) from (2) and from the fact that drain 1 alone takes 15 minutes to empty the tank, and we just saw that (1) alone is sufficient.

98. **(E)** If you answered incorrectly you probably assumed that x and y were positive. If $x = 5$ and $y = 4$, then (1) and (2) are both true and $x > y$. However, if $x = -5$ and $y = -4$, (1) and (2) are both true but $x < y$.

99. **(B)** (2) alone is sufficient since ostriches are birds. (1) alone is not sufficient since tigers are not birds.

100. **(E)** Since the equation in (2) has exactly the same solutions as the equation in (1), $(3 (x - y) = 3x - 3y$ and $3 (12) = 36)$, you can't determine x and y even by using both (1) and (2). If $x = 12$ and $y = 0$, then (1) and (2) are true and $x + 2y = 12$, but if $x = 6$ and $y = -6$, (1) and (2) are again true but $x + 2y = -6$.

101. **(E)** (1) and (2) are not sufficient. The price of food could rise for other reasons besides the price of energy rising.

102. **(C)** (1) alone is obviously insufficient. To use (2) you need to know what the painting was worth at some time between 1968 and 1977. So (2) alone is insufficient, but by using (1) and (2) together you can figure out the worth of the painting in Jan. 1971.

103. **(D)** (1) alone is sufficient since the rule enables you to compute all successive values once you know a_1. Also the rule and (1) tell you that the numbers in the sequence will always increase. Thus since $a_2 = 4$, 3 will never appear. In the same way, by using (2) and the rule you can determine a_1, a_2, a_3, and a_4 and then a_6, etc.

104. **(A)** (1) alone is sufficient. If $z > x$ then the side opposite angle ABC is larger than the side opposite angle ACB. (2) alone is insufficient since D can be anywhere between B and C, so you can't decide whether AD is larger or smaller than AB.

105. **(E)** If $x = 9$ and $y = 8$, then (1) and (2) would be true and $x > y$. However, if $x = 6$ and $y = 8$, (1) and (2) would still be true although $x < y$.

Section V   Writing Ability

106. **(D)** *Tasks* and *manager* are being compared in this sentence rather than the *director* and the *manager*. A possible correct form is: The tasks of the director are greater than the *manager's*.

107. **(C)** In parallel writing, adjectives should be balanced with adjectives, phrases with phrases, etc. In this sentence, the *who* clause is incorrect. *And* is a conjunction connecting two ideas about the pianist. For parallel construction *she* (or *he*) is correct: The pianist is a person with great promise and *she* should be encouraged.

108. **(B)** The pronoun *their* does not agree in number with its antecedent (*each student*). The proper form is *his* (or *her*).

109. **(A)** Improper tense. The correct form is: *If I had*.

110. **(D)** The pronoun in this sentence should be in the objective case, since it is the object of the preposition *by*. The correct form is *me*.

111. **(D)** Verbs must agree in number with their subjects. The plural subject (risks) must have a plural verb (seem).

112. **(A)** This is an example of a dangling participle: fishing and eating should not refer to *day*, but to a subject such as *we*. For example: *We spent the day* very quietly, fishing and eating at a picnic.

113. **(C)** In this sentence it seems as if the deposit is joining the club, because of a dangling infinitive phrase. The phrase should modify a person, i.e., To join the club, *you must make a deposit* in advance.

114. **(E)** No error.

115. **(E)** No error.

116. **(B)** *We* should be *us*, because it is the indirect object of the verb *has given*.

117. **(C)** *me* should be *my*, because the possessive case is used with the gerund; the object of the preposition is *buying* and not *me*.

118. **(C)** *whomever* should be *whoever*, because it is the subject of *would go*.

119. **(B)** *it's* should be *its*, because the possessive case of *it* never has an apostrophe.

120. **(A)** *Lincolns* should be *Lincoln's*; this is a possessive, not a plural.

121. **(B)** *whoever* should be *whomever;* the objective case is needed, since the pronoun is the object of *wish*.

122. **(D)** *whom* should be *who;* it is the subject of the verb *are*.

123. **(B)** *who's* should be *whose*; who's is a contraction of *who is*.

124. **(C)** *myself* should be *I*; it is the subject of *are arrested; myself* is a reflexive pronoun.

125. **(C)** *it's* should be *its*; a possessive pronoun never has an apostrophe.

Section VI   Practical Judgment

126. **(B)** A major consideration of the production manager in endorsing the new product was that it "fit in well" with existing production facilities. See paragraph 3.

127. **(D)** The company's decision to market the new product line was based on the assumption that it would be purchased by consumers. However, nowhere in the passage was there mention of any consumer research to buttress this assumption.

128. **(A)** A *Major Objective* of the new product launching was to generate sales needed to expand the company and enable it to solve some of its financial problems. See paragraph 3.

129. **(E)** The age of the company was an unimportant issue in the passage.

130. **(B)** This fact convinced the president's son of the need for a gourmet line of Italian food products. See paragraph 5.

131. **(D)** The company's experience in the sale of consumer products was limited to the West Coast and the Southwest.

132. **(B)** The survey results indicated a lack of consumer enthusiasm for the product line, which prompted management to appoint the committee to determine the future of the new line.

133. **(E)** The size of the advertising company was not related to any decision alternative.

134. **(A)** National distribution was a *Major Objective* of the company early in the planning stage. See paragraph 6.

135. **(B)** Brooks's inability to attract outside capital was a *Major Factor* which influenced Voght's decision to press for expansion of the company.

136. **(E)** Welch's appointment was inconsequential to the decisions made by management.

137. **(B)** Packaging difficulties resulted in the postponement of the product introduction until mid-December. The failure to design the package in time was a *Major Factor* in management's decision to delay the product's market entry.

138. **(D)** Joe Brooks *believed* that there was an untapped market for a prestige line of Italian food specialties. According to the facts presented in the passage, he based his assumption on the popularity of higher-priced Italian restaurants in many cities. That the same people who patronized these restaurants would want to prepare such food themselves at home was not demonstrated by the facts.

139. **(B)** The fact that competitors had commenced selling similar products was a *Major Factor* influencing management's decision to establish the special committee with the task of determining the fate of the new product line.

140. **(E)** All these were mentioned as constraints on the sale of the line.

141. **(B)** The company had a poor organizational structure. This is evidenced by (1) poor planning and advertising, (2) lack of responsibility for package design, (3) poor production planning, and (4) absence of coordination of the marketing, production, and design functions.

142. **(C)** The selected advertising agency had little experience with food products, and the preparation of magazine advertisements and filmed TV commercials was delayed. See paragraph 7.

143. **(C)** It was decided to launch the new line at the beginning of the fall food merchandising season, which was about October 1. See paragraph 4.

144. **(A)** Before introducing the new line, 60% of the company's sales were to the institutional market; thus its experience in marketing to the final consumer was limited. Moreover, no evidence was given that even hinted at any consumer research to compensate for this deficiency.

145. **(B)** This is mentioned in paragraph 5: "With the exception of the name, the younger Brooks directed most of the decisions relating to the marketing program."

Section VII   Verbal Ability

146. **(B)** ABJURE: recant, revoke. *Antonym:* pledge

147. **(C)** MITIGATE: alleviate, abate. *Antonym:* intensify

148. **(D)** SPURIOUS: counterfeit, false. *Antonym:* authentic

149. **(C)** TORRID: hot, scorching. *Antonym:* cold

150. **(E)** CIRCUMSPECTION: watchfulness, caution. *Antonym:* recklessness

151. **(B)** DESULTORY: rambling, superficial. *Antonym:* methodical

152. **(C)** DISSONANCE: discord, lack of agreement. *Antonym:* harmony

153. **(D)** INCREDULOUS: skeptical, doubtful. *Antonym:* believing

154. **(B)** OBDURATE: callous, insensible. *Antonym:* tender

155. **(A)** UNGAINLY: clumsy, awkward. *Antonym:* graceful

156. **(B)** DISCERN: observe, perceive. *Antonym:* overlook

157. **(B)** CONVIVIAL: sociable, hospitable. *Antonym:* unsociable

158. **(A)** ALACRITY: willingness, quickness. *Antonym:* slowness

159. **(C)** PERFIDIOUS: faithless, insidious. *Antonym:* faithful

160. **(D)** A slide rule is a simple kind of computer. A sundial is a simple kind of clock.

161. **(E)** A battery powers a flashlight. Coal powers a furnace.

162. **(A)** A muff covers the hands. A helmet covers the head.

163. **(C)** Both are hobbyists. A philatelist collects stamps. A numismatist collects coins. Note that a government collects taxes (E), but not as a hobby!

164. **(B)** A tranquilizer makes one placid. A sedative makes one somnolent.

165. **(A)** Maturity is the opposite of infancy. Culmination is the opposite of inception.

166. **(E)** Floriculture is the raising of flowers. Arboriculture is the raising of trees.

167. **(D)** A sonneteer is a particular kind of poet. A songwriter is a particular kind of composer.

168. **(B)** Muslin is a plain cloth. Brocade is an ornate cloth.

169. **(A)** An epilogue is at the end of a dramatic work. A coda is the final passage of a musical work.

170. **(E)** A pilot has responsibility for running a plane. A manager is responsible for running a store.

171. **(B)** A decade is a tenth part of a century. A decimeter is a tenth part of a meter.

172. **(A)** A model is a representation of reality or a real situation; a blueprint is a model of a house.

173. **(B)** Competition necessarily goes along with free enterprise.

174. **(C)** The word criticized implies a negative word such as wasteful. Businessmen are not apt to be critical, as they continue to use advertising.

175. **(C)** A predisposition is an inclination.

176. **(C)** Economists and marketers are interested in determining the effect that advertising has on sales.

177. **(C)** A winner can gain a victory without a clear mandate. The other alternatives have little or no meaning in context.

178. **(D)** A correlation is a tendency for two events to occur together; it does not necessarily imply a causal relationship.

179. **(C)** Free speech and censorship are appropriately opposed concepts.

180. **(A)** Still standing; still existing.

181. **(C)** Malingerer means someone who shirks work.

182. **(D)** contains the best *meaning*.

183. **(C)** Alternatives (A), (B), and (E) have no meaning in context; a referee would not postpone a scheduled fight owing to the participants' ineptness, but he might stop the fight if the participants' behavior was unwarranted, i.e., unsportsmanlike.

184. **(B)** has the most *meaning*.

185. **(C)** Alternatives (A), (B), (D), and (E) are illogical.

Evaluating Your Score

Tabulate your score for each section of the Diagnostic Test according to the directions on pages 4-5 and record the results in the Self-scoring Table below. Then find your rating for each score on the Self-scoring Scale and record it in the appropriate blank.

Self-scoring Table

PART	SCORE	RATING
1		
2		
3		
4		
5		
6		
7		

Self-scoring Scale

RATING

PART	POOR	FAIR	GOOD	EXCELLENT
1	0-8	9-12	13-19	20-25
2	0-15	16-21	22-25	26-30
3	0-7	8-10	11-15	16-20
4	0-14	15-20	21-25	26-30
5	0-7	8-10	11-15	16-20
6	0-7	8-10	11-15	16-20
7	0-15	16-20	21-29	30-40

The following Review sections cover material for each type of question on the GMAT. Spend more time studying those sections for which you had a rating of FAIR or POOR on the Diagnostic Test.

To obtain an approximation of your actual GMAT score, see page 5.

FOUR
REVIEW AND PRACTICE FOR THE GMAT

Having taken the Diagnostic Test and evaluated your results, you now have an indication of what your strong and weak points are. Your next step is to begin a more intensive review of test material, concentrating particularly on those areas in which you rated FAIR or POOR, but also covering material you did well on so that you will be certain you fully understand all of the topics.

Study the following sections carefully and do all the practice exercises provided. The *Reading Comprehension Review* will assist you in preparing for both Reading Comprehension and Reading Recall as well as Practical Judgment questions. Problem Solving and Data Sufficiency are covered in the *Mathematics Review*, which is keyed to answers for sample tests for easy reference. The list of *Words Frequently Appearing on the GMAT* not only supplements the *Verbal Ability Review* but also presents words appearing throughout the GMAT.

READING COMPREHENSION AND RECALL REVIEW

A large proportion of the GMAT is designed to test your ability to comprehend material contained in reading passages. The Reading Recall sections of the exam are concerned with determining how well you remember the main points and significant details in material you have read and also your capacity for drawing inferences from this material. After you have read the material you are *not* allowed to turn back to the passages in order to answer the questions. Reading Comprehension sections, on the other hand, *do* allow you to turn back to the passages when answering the questions. However, many of the questions may be based on what is *implied* in the passages, rather than on what is explicitly stated. Your ability to draw inferences from the material is critical to successfully completing this section. Reading Comprehension now appears more frequently than Reading Recall on the GMAT.

The objective of the Practical Judgment sections is to test your ability to analyze business situations and draw conclusions about them. In each case, success depends on the extent of your reading comprehension skills. The following discussion is designed to help you formulate an approach to reading passages that will enable you to better understand the material you will be asked to read on the GMAT. Practice exercises at the end of this review will give you an opportunity to try out this approach.

Basic Reading Skills

A primary skill necessary for good reading comprehension and recall is the understanding of the meanings of individual words. Knowledge of a wide and diversified vocabulary enables you to detect subtle differences in sentence meaning that may hold the key to the meaning of an entire paragraph or passage. For this reason, it is important that you familiarize yourself with as many words as possible. The vocabulary list at the end of this chapter is a good place to begin.

A second reading skill to be developed is the ability to discover the central theme of a passage. By making yourself aware of what the entire passage is about, you are in a position to relate what you read to this central theme, logically picking out the main points and significant details as you go along. Although the manner in which the central theme is stated may vary from passage to passage, it can usually be found in the title (if one is presented), in the "topic sentence" of a paragraph in shorter passages, or, in longer passages, by reading several paragraphs.

A third essential skill is the capacity to organize mentally how the passage is put together and determine how each part is related to the whole. This is the skill you will have to use to the greatest degree on the GMAT, where you must pick out significant and insignificant factors, remember main details, and relate information you have read to the central theme.

In general, a mastery of these three basic skills will provide you with a solid basis for better reading comprehension wherein you will be able to read carefully to draw a conclusion from the material, decide the meanings of words and ideas presented and how they in turn affect the meaning of the passage, and recognize opinions and views that are expressed.

Applying Basic Reading Skills

The only way to become adept at the three basic reading skills outlined above is to practice using the techniques involved as much as possible. Studying the meanings of new words you encounter, not only in the vocabulary list in this guide but also in all your reading material, will soon help you establish a working knowledge of many words. In the same manner, making an effort to locate topic sentences, general themes, and specific details in material you read will enable you to improve your skills in these areas. The following drills will help. After you have read through them and answered the questions satisfactorily, you can try the longer practice exercises at the end.

Finding the Topic Sentence

The term "topic sentence" is used to describe the sentence that gives the key to an entire paragraph. Usually the topic sentence is found in the beginning of a paragraph. However, there is no absolute rule. A writer may build his paragraph to a conclusion, putting the key sentence at the end. Here is an example in which the topic sentence is located at the beginning:

EXAMPLE 1:

The world faces a serious problem of overpopulation. Right now many people starve from lack of adequate food. Efforts are being made to increase the rate of food production, but the number of people to be fed increases at a faster rate.

The idea is stated directly in the opening sentence. You know that the passage will be about "a serious problem of overpopulation." Like a heading or caption, the topic sentence sets the stage or gets your mind ready for what follows in that paragraph.

Before you try to locate the topic sentence in a paragraph you must remember that this technique depends upon reading and judgment. Read the whole passage first. Then try to decide which sentence comes closest to expressing the main point of the paragraph. Do not worry about the position of the topic sentence in the paragraph; look for the most important statement. Find the idea to which all the other sentences relate.

Try to identify the topic sentence in this passage:

EXAMPLE 2:

During the later years of the American Revolution, the Articles of Confederation government was formed. This government suffered severely from a lack of power. Each state distrusted the others and gave little authority to the central or federal government. The Articles of Confederation produced a government which could not raise money from taxes, prevent Indian raids, or force the British out of the United States.

What is the topic sentence? Certainly the paragraph is about the Articles of Confederation. However, is the key idea in the first sentence or in the second sentence? In this instance, the *second* sentence does a better job of giving you the key to this paragraph— the lack of centralized power that characterized the Articles of Confederation. The sentences that complete the paragraph relate more to the idea of "lack of power" than to the time when the government was formed. Don't assume that the topic sentence is always the first sentence of a paragraph. Try this:

EXAMPLE 3:

There is a strong relation between limited education and low income. Statistics show that unemployment rates are highest among those adults who attended school the fewest years. Most jobs in a modern industrial society require technical or advanced training. The best pay goes with jobs that demand thinking and decisions based on knowledge. A few people manage to overcome their limited education by personality or a "lucky break." However, studies of lifetime earnings show that the average high school graduate earns more than the average high school dropout, who in turn earns more than the average adult who has not finished eighth grade.

Here, the first sentence contains the main idea of the whole paragraph. One more example should be helpful:

EXAMPLE 4:

They had fewer men available as soldiers. Less than one third of the railroads and only a small proportion of the nation's industrial production was theirs. For most of the war their coastline was blockaded by Northern ships. It is a tribute to Southern leadership and the courage of the people that they were not defeated for four years.

In this case you will note that the passage builds up to its main point. The topic sentence is the last one. Practice picking out the topic sentences in other material you read until it becomes an easy task.

Finding the General Theme

A more advanced skill is the ability to read several paragraphs and relate them to one general theme or main idea. The procedure involves careful reading of the entire passage and deciding which idea is the central or main one. You can tell you have the right idea when it is most frequent or most important, or when every sentence relates to it. As you read the next passage, note the *underlined* parts.

EXAMPLE 1:

True democracy means direct <u>rule by the people.</u> A good example can be found in a modern town meeting in many small New England towns. All citizens aged twenty-one or over may vote. <u>They not only vote for officials, but they also get together to vote on local laws</u> (or ordinances). The small size of the town and the limited number of voters make this possible.

In the cities, voters cast ballots <u>for officials who get together to make the laws.</u> Because the voters do not make the laws directly, <u>this system is called indirect democracy or representative government.</u> There is no problem of distance to travel, but it is difficult to run a meeting with hundreds of thousands of citizens.

Representation of voters and a direct voice in making laws are more of a problem in state or national governments. <u>The numbers of citizens and the distances to travel make representative government the most practical way</u> to make laws.

Think about the passage in general and the underlined parts in particular. Several examples discuss voting for officials and making laws. In the first paragraph both of these are done by the voters. The second paragraph describes representative government in which voters elect officials who make laws. The last paragraph emphasizes the problem of size and numbers and says that representative government is more practical. In the following question, put all these ideas together.

The main theme of this passage is that

(A) the United States is not democratic
(B) citizens cannot vote for lawmakers
(C) representative government does not make laws
(D) every citizen makes laws directly
(E) increasing populations lead to less direct democracy

The answer is choice (E). Choices (B), (C), and (D) can be eliminated because they are not true of the passage. Choice (A) may have made you hesitate a little. The passage makes comments about *less direct* democracy, but it never says that representative government is *not democratic*.

The next 3 passages offer further practice in finding the main theme. Answer the question following each example and check the analysis to make sure you understand.

EXAMPLE 2:

Skye, 13 miles off the northwest coast of Scotland, is the largest and most famous of the Hebrides. Yet fame has neither marred its natural beauty nor brought affectation to its inhabitants. The scene and the people are almost as they were generations ago.

The first sight that impresses the visitor to Skye is its stark beauty. This is not beauty of the usual sort, for the island is not a lush green "paradise." It is, on the other hand, almost devoid of shrubbery. Mountains, moorlands, sky, and sea combine to create an overpowering landscape. Endless stretches of rocky hills dominate the horizon. Miles of treeless plains meet the eye. Yet this scene has a beauty all its own.

And then cutting into the stark landscape are the fantastic airborne peaks of the Cuillins, rising into the clear skies above. The Cuillins are the most beloved mountains in Scotland and are frequently climbed. Their rugged, naked grandeur, frost-sculptured ridges and acute peaks even attracted Sir Edmund Hilary.

The main idea of this passage is   Ⓐ Ⓑ Ⓒ Ⓓ Ⓔ

(A) the sky over Skye
(B) the lack of trees on Skye
(C) the natural beauty of Skye
(D) the lack of affectation on Skye
(E) the Cuillins in the skies of Skye

All of the answers have some truth to them. The problem is to find the *best* answer. Four of the choices are mentioned in the passage only by a small comment. But choice (C) is discussed throughout every part of the passage. The clue to the correct answer was how often the same theme was covered.

EXAMPLE 3:

Trade exists for many reasons. No doubt it started from a desire to have something different. Men also realized that different men could make different products. Trade encouraged specialization, which led to improvement in quality.

Trade started from person to person, but grew to involve different towns and different lands. Some found work in transporting the goods or selling them. Merchants grew rich as the demand for products increased. Craftsmen were able to sell more products at home and abroad. People in general had a greater variety of things to choose.

The knowledge of new products led to an interest in the lands which produced them. More daring persons went to see other lands. Others stayed at home, but asked many questions of the travellers. As people learned about the products and the conditions in other countries, they compared them with their own. This often led to a desire for better conditions or a hope for a better life. Trade was mainly an economic force, but it also had other effects.

The general theme of the passage is how   Ⓐ Ⓑ Ⓒ Ⓓ Ⓔ

(A) trade makes everyone rich
(B) trade divides the world
(C) products are made
(D) trade changes people's lives
(E) people find new jobs

This is not easy, as you may feel that all the choices are good. Most of them were mentioned in some part of the passage. However, you must select the *best* choice. If you had trouble, let us analyze the passage.

Paragraph one emphasizes a "desire for something different" and "improvement." The second paragraph refers to "found work," "merchants grew rich," "craftsmen sell more," and "greater variety of things to choose." The third paragraph covers "interest in the lands," "compared them with their own," "desire for better conditions" and "better life." All these are evidence of the same general theme of how trade brings changes in the lives of people. Choice (D) is the best answer.

Choice (A) is tempting because of the comment on merchants getting rich. However, this idea is not found all through the passage. Choice (B) may catch the careless thinker. Trade does not divide the world, even though the passage talks about dividing jobs. Choice (C) is weak. Some comment is made about making products, but not in all parts of the passage. Choice (E) is weak for the same reason as choice (C).

EXAMPLE 4:

The enormous problems of turning swamps and desert into fields and orchards, together with the ideal of share-and-share-alike, gave birth to the kibbutz.

In those days, the kibbutz member had to plow the fields with a rifle slung over his shoulder.

Today security is still a factor in the kibbutz. Shelters are furrowed into the ground along every walk among the shade trees, near the children's house, where all the young children of the kibbutz live, and near the communal dining room.

But the swamps have been conquered, and the desert is gradually becoming green. And while kibbutz members once faced deprivation and a monotonous diet, today they reap the harvest of hard work and success.

One such kibbutz is Dorot, at the gateway to the Negev desert and typical of the average size Israeli communal settlement.

Life on the kibbutz has become more complex through growth and prosperity. While once the land barely yielded enough for a living, Dorot, like many other kibbutzim, now exports some of its crops. It also has become industrialized, another trend among these settlements. Dorot has a factory which exports faucets to a dozen countries, including the United States.

Ⓐ Ⓑ Ⓒ Ⓓ Ⓔ The main theme of this article is

- (A)   the manufacture of faucets is a sign of growth and prosperity in the kibbutz
- (B)   with the solving of agricultural problems the kibbutz has become a more complex society
- (C)   since security is a problem for the kibbutz, it has become industrialized
- (D)   Dorot is the prosperous gateway to the Negev desert
- (E)   kibbutzim are good places to live, although they are located in swamps and deserts

Choice (A) receives brief mention at the end of the passage. It is an idea in the passage, but certainly not the general idea of the passage. Choice (D) is the same kind of answer as choice (A)—it is too specific a fact. Choice (E) is unrelated to the passage. We now have choices (B) and (C) as possible answers. Choice (C) seems reasonable until you analyze it. Did the need for security *cause* the industrialization? Or are there better examples of how life has become more complex now that agricultural problems have been solved? The evidence leans more to choice (B).

In summary, in order to find the general theme:

1. Read at your normal speed
2. Locate the topic sentence in each paragraph
3. Note ideas that are frequent or emphasized
4. Find the idea to which most of the passage is related

Finding Logical Relationships

In order to fully understand the meaning of a passage, you must first look for the general theme and then relate the ideas and opinions found in the passage to this general theme. In this way, you can determine not only what is important but also how the ideas interrelate to form the whole. From this understanding, you will be better able to answer questions that refer to the passage.

As you read the following passages, look for general theme and supporting facts, words or phrases that signal emphasis or shift in thought, and the relation of one idea to another.

EXAMPLE 1:

The candidate who wants to be elected pays close attention to statements and actions that will make the voters see him favorably. In ancient Rome candidates wore pure white togas (the Latin word *candidatus* means "clothed in white") to indicate that they were pure, clean, and above any "dirty work." However, it is interesting to note that such a toga was not worn after election.

In more modern history, candidates have allied themselves with political parties. Once a voter knows and favors the views of a certain political party, he may vote for anyone with that party's label. Nevertheless, divisions of opinion develop, so that today there is a wide range of candidate views in any major party.

1. The best conclusion to be drawn from the first paragraph is that after an election   Ⓐ Ⓑ Ⓒ Ⓓ Ⓔ

    (A) all candidates are dishonest
    (B) candidates are less concerned with symbols of integrity
    (C) candidates do not change their ideas
    (D) officials are always honest
    (E) policies always change

You noted the ideas about a candidate in Rome. You saw the word "however" signal a shift in ideas or thinking. Now the third step rests with your judgment. You cannot jump to a conclusion; you must see which conclusion is reasonable or fair. Choices (A), (D), and (E) should make you wary. They say "all" or "always" which means without exception. The last sentence is not that strong or positive. Choices (B) and (C) must be considered. There is nothing in the paragraph that supports the fact that candidates do not change their ideas. This forces you into choice (B) as the only statement logically related to what the paragraph said.

2. A fair statement is that most candidates from the same political party today are likely to

Ⓐ Ⓑ Ⓒ Ⓓ Ⓔ
    (A) have the same views
    (B) be different in every view
    (C) agree on almost all points
    (D) agree on some points and disagree on others
    (E) agree only by accident

Here again, the burden rests on your judgment after following ideas and word clues. The paragraph makes the point that there is a wide range of views. That eliminates choice (A). Choice (B) is not logical because the candidates would not likely be in the same party if they disagree on every view. The remaining choices are different degrees of agreement. Choice (E) is weak because candidates are too interested to arrive at agreement only by accident. The wide range mentioned seems to oppose choice (C) and favor choice (D) as a little more likely. You may say that choice (C) sounds pretty good. Again we stress that *you are picking the very best choice*, not just a good choice. This is what we mean by reflecting carefully on all possibilities and selecting the best available choice.

EXAMPLE 2:

In 1812 Napoleon had to withdraw his forces from Russia. The armies had invaded successfully and reached the city of Moscow. There was no question of French army disloyalty or unwillingness to fight. As winter came, the Russian army moved out of the way, leaving a wasted land and burned buildings. Other conquered European nations seized upon Napoleon's problems in Russia as their chance to rearm and to break loose from French control.

Ⓐ Ⓑ Ⓒ Ⓓ Ⓔ
    According to the passage, the main reason for Napoleon's withdrawal from Russia was the

    (A) disloyalty of the French troops
    (B) Russian winter
    (C) burned buildings
    (D) planned revolts in other countries
    (E) Russian army

In this passage, only choice (A) is totally incorrect. Choice (E) is very weak because the Russian army was not able to stop the invasion. The choices narrow to which is the best of (B), (C), and (D). It seems that all three answers are supported by the passage. There needs to be some thought and judgment by you. Which of these could be overcome easily and which could be the strongest reason for Napoleon leaving Russia? The burned buildings could be overcome by the troops making other shelters. The Russian winter was severe and the army did not want to face it. However, marching out of Russia in the winter was also a great problem. Napoleon probably would have stayed in Moscow except for a more serious problem—the loss of the control he had established over most of Europe. Thus, answer (D) is best.

EXAMPLE 3:

By 1915 events of World War I were already involving the United States and threatening its neutrality. The sinking of the British liner *Lusitania* in that year by a German submarine caused great resentment among Americans. Over a hundred United States citizens were killed in the incident. President Wilson had frequently deplored the use of submarines by Germany against the United States. Since the U.S. was neutral, it was not liable to acts of war by another nation.

However, Wilson resolved to represent the strong feeling in the country (notably in the Midwest) and in the Democratic Party that U.S. neutrality should be maintained. He felt that the United States should have "peace with honor," if possible.

There were also people, mostly in the East, that wanted to wage a preventive war against Germany. Such men as Theodore Roosevelt bitterly attacked Wilson as one who talked a great deal but did nothing.

By 1917 Germany again used unrestricted submarine warfare and Wilson broke off relations with Germany. In February British agents uncovered the Zimmerman Telegram. This was an attempt by the German ambassador to Mexico to involve that nation in a war against the United States. And in March several American merchant ships were sunk by German submarines. His patience at an end, Wilson at last took the position of a growing majority of Americans and asked Congress to declare war on Germany. Thus, United States entered World War I.

1. This passage tries to explain that   1. Ⓐ Ⓑ Ⓒ Ⓓ Ⓔ

    (A) Wilson wanted the U.S. to go to war against Germany
    (B) Wilson tried to avoid war with Germany
    (C) Germany wanted the U.S. to enter the war
    (D) Other nations were pressuring U.S. to enter the war
    (E) Mexico was our main enemy

2. We can conclude from the passage that most citizens of the United States in 1917 were   2. Ⓐ Ⓑ Ⓒ Ⓓ Ⓔ

    (A) totally opposed to war with Germany
    (B) in favor of war before Wilson was
    (C) willing to accept war after Wilson persuaded them
    (D) neutral
    (E) trying to avoid war

3. The last event in the series of happenings that led to a declaration of war against   3. Ⓐ Ⓑ Ⓒ Ⓓ Ⓔ
    Germany was

    (A) the Zimmerman Telegram
    (B) attacks on U.S. merchant ships
    (C) Wilson's war message to Congress
    (D) a change in public opinion
    (E) the sinking of the *Lusitania*

In question 1, the key is to note Wilson's actions discussed in paragraph two. Near the end of the passage there is a phrase about "his patience at an end." This describes a man who was trying to avoid a conflict, as in answer choice (B).

Question 2 rests on two ideas. There was a change in the feeling of the American people about war. The other idea is that Wilson responded after he felt that they had changed. The phrase "took the position of a growing majority of Americans" tells us that Wilson followed the change in opinion, as in answer choice (B).

In question 3, you need to check the sequence of events. The declaration of war followed the president's request.

Making Inferences

An inference is not stated. It is assumed by the reader from something said by the writer. An inference is the likely or probable conclusion rather than the direct, logical one. It usually involves an opinion or viewpoint that the writer wants the reader to follow or assume. In another kind of inference, the reader figures out the author's opinion even though it is not stated. The clues are generally found in which facts are presented and in the choice of words and phrases. Opinion is revealed by the one-sided nature of a passage in which no opposing facts are given. It is shown further by "loaded" words that reveal the author's feelings.

It is well worth noting that opinionated writing is often more interesting than straight factual accounts. Some writers are very colorful, forceful, or amusing in presenting their views. You should understand that there is nothing wrong with reading opinion. You should read varied opinions, but know that they are opinions. Then make up your own mind.

Not every writer will insert his opinion obviously. However, you can get clues from how often the same idea is said (frequency), whether arguments are balanced on both sides (fairness), and the choice of wording (emotional or loaded words). Look for the clues in this next passage.

EXAMPLE 1:

Slowly but surely the great passenger trains of the United States have been fading from the rails. Short-run commuter trains still rattle in and out of the cities. Between major cities you can still find a train, but the schedules are becoming less frequent. The Twentieth Century Limited, The Broadway Limited, and other luxury trains that sang along the rails at 60 to 80 miles an hour are no longer running. Passengers on other long runs complain of poor service, old equipment, and costs in time and money. The long distance traveller today accepts the noise of jets, the congestion at airports, and the traffic between airport and city. A more elegant and graceful way is becoming only a memory.

1. Ⓐ Ⓑ Ⓒ Ⓓ Ⓔ 1. With respect to the reduction of long run passenger trains, this writer expresses

   (A) regret   (D) elation
   (B) pleasure   (E) anger
   (C) grief

Before you choose the answer, you must deduce what the writer's feeling is. He does not actually state his feeling, but clues are available so that you may infer what it is. Choices (B) and (D) are impossible, because he gives no word that shows he is pleased by the change. Choice (C) is too strong, as is choice (E). Choice (A) is the most reasonable inference to make. He is sorry to see the change. He is expressing regret.

2. Ⓐ Ⓑ Ⓒ Ⓓ Ⓔ 2. The author seems to feel that air travel is

   (A) costly   (D) elegant
   (B) slow   (E) uncomfortable
   (C) streamlined

Here we must be careful because he says very little about air travel. However, his one sentence about it presents three negative or annoying points. The choice now becomes fairly clear. Answer (E) is correct.

EXAMPLE 2:

When the United States was founded at the end of the eighteenth century, it was a small and weak country, made up mostly of poor farmers. Foreign policy, reflecting this domestic condition, stressed "no entangling alliances." The State Department then had a staff of less than half a dozen persons, whose total salary was $6,600 (of which $3,500 went to the Secretary of State), and a diplomatic service budget (July, 1790) of $40,000. Militarily, too, the country was insignificant. The first United States army, soon after the American Revolution, was made up of one captain (John Doughty) and 80 men. Clearly, the United States did not consider itself a real power and was not taken seriously by the rest of the world.

It was not until immense changes took place *inside* the United States that the country began to play an important role in foreign affairs. By the beginning of the twentieth century, the United States had ceased to be a predominantly agricultural nation and had become an industrial one. Its population had grown to more than 30 times its original number. George Washington was president of 3,000,000 Americans: Theodore Roosevelt, of 100,000,000.

1. A country today cannot expect to play an important part in world affairs unless it   1. Ⓐ Ⓑ Ⓒ Ⓓ Ⓔ

   I. has wealth
  II. has a large population
 III. is strong internally

(A) I only
(B) III only
(C) I and II only
(D) II and III only
(E) I, II, and III

This is a slightly different style of question. You must look at each of the answer choices in I, II, and III. As you consider the passage and what it suggests, you note that each of the answer choices in I, II, and III make good sense. Therefore, answer choice (E) is the best answer because it includes all of the correct statements. Again, this is not designed to trick you. The purpose of such a question is to be sure that you have read all the choices.

2. The writer seems to think that a major factor in making the United States a world power   2. Ⓐ Ⓑ Ⓒ Ⓓ Ⓔ
was

(A) industrialization
(B) the passing of time
(C) a change in government policies
(D) the presidency of Theodore Roosevelt
(E) the avoidance of entangling alliances

The passage does not answer the question directly. You must infer what is meant by the author. However, there is a clue in the author's comment that changes inside a country make a big difference in its foreign policy. The big internal changes noted are the growth of America's population and industrial power. By correctly interpreting the passage, you will be led to choice (A) for this question.

In Example 3 you will find three short statements by three different writers. The questions will require that you make inferences about each writer and then make comparisons of one against the other two.

EXAMPLE 3:

Writer I

No nation should tolerate the slacker who will not defend his country in time of war. The so-called conscientious objector is a coward who accepts the benefits of his country but will not accept the responsibility. By shirking his fair share, he forces another person to assume an unfair burden.

Writer II

A democratic nation should have room for freedom of conscience. Religious training and belief may make a man conscientiously opposed to participation in war. The conscientious objector should be permitted to give labor service or some form of non-combat military duty. His beliefs should be respected.

Writer III

The rights of the conscientious objector should be decided by each individual. No government should dictate to any person or require him to endanger his life if the person, in conscience, objects. There need be no religious basis. It is enough for a free individual to think as he pleases and to reject laws or rules to which he conscientiously objects.

1. Ⓐ Ⓑ Ⓒ Ⓓ Ⓔ 1. A balanced opinion on this subject is presented by

    (A) Writer I
    (B) Writer II
    (C) Writer III
    (D) all of the writers
    (E) none of the writers

2. Ⓐ Ⓑ Ⓒ Ⓓ Ⓔ 2. We can conclude that the writer most likely to support a person who refuses any military service is

    (A) Writer I
    (B) Writer II
    (C) Writer III
    (D) all of the writers
    (E) none of the writers

3. Ⓐ Ⓑ Ⓒ Ⓓ Ⓔ 3. An authoritarian person is most likely to agree with

    (A) Writer I
    (B) Writer II
    (C) Writer III
    (D) all of the writers
    (E) none of the writers

Look for clues in the language or choice of words that are loaded with feeling such as "slacker," "so-called," and "shirking" by Writer I and "dictate," "endanger," and "as he pleases" by Writer III. Compare them with the language used by Writer II. The second help is to connect what these writers say with views you have heard or read. We are not asking you to accept any of these opinions. You are using your skill in reading what the writers think and adding it to your own knowledge. Then you make logical inferences. The correct answers are 1. (B), 2. (C), and 3. (A).

Now that you have spent time reviewing the three basic skills you should master for better reading comprehension ability, try the practice exercises that follow. Answers to these exercises appear after Exercise C. You should also try to spend time using this reading approach as you read other material not related to the GMAT.

Practice Exercises

The following five reading passages are similar to those found on the GMAT. The first three are Reading Recall sections; the latter two, Reading Comprehension. You should read each one and then answer the questions that follow according to the directions. Remember that in Reading Recall sections you cannot refer to the passage while answering the questions. Also, on the actual exam you are asked to read three or four Reading Recall passages before answering the questions. Passages are separated here for practice purposes.

Reading Recall

EXERCISE A

TOTAL TIME: 12 minutes

Part A: TIME — 5 minutes

DIRECTIONS: This part contains a reading passage. You will have 5 minutes to study the passage and 7 minutes to answer questions based on it. When answering the questions you will *not* be allowed to refer back to the passage.

The following passage was written in 1971.

For the most part, American institutions of higher education managed to expand their resources and facilities to absorb the rapidly increasing numbers of students seeking to enroll in the 1960s. Students who could not qualify for the most selective four-year institutions were admitted to less selective four-year institutions or to two-year colleges. Only toward the end of the decade were there signs of serious stresses and strains resulting from financial stringency in both public and private institutions.

The outlook for smooth absorption of the increased numbers of students who will be seeking higher education in the 1970s is at present very uncertain. Campus unrest, which is leading some state legislatures to "punish" public institutions of higher education by withholding funds and which is causing some alumni and other private donors to hold back on gifts to colleges and universities, may abate somewhat if we withdraw from the Indochina war, but most sophisticated observers do not expect unrest to disappear on campuses. Cutbacks in federal government support of higher education may prove to be temporary if a decline in military expenditures facilitates increased appropriations for education and other social services. But a more persistent problem is likely to be the fiscal stringency faced by state and local governments (with the latter representing a significant source of financing of two-year colleges).

Appropriations for higher education must compete at state and local levels with rapidly rising expenditures for welfare, elementary and secondary education, and other public services. State and local governments face serious difficulties in meeting these mounting costs because they tend to rely heavily on sales taxes and, in the case of local governments, property taxes—taxes yielding revenues that tend to rise less rapidly than personal income. In contrast, the tax revenues of the federal government, which rely in large part on personal and corporate income taxes, tend to rise more rapidly than personal income.

In fact, from the perspective of the fall of 1971, it appears likely that higher education will *not* be in a position to absorb the increased numbers of students seeking admission in the 1970s without greatly increased federal government support, along the lines recommended by the Carnegie Commission. In the absence of such increased federal government support, students and their parents in both public and private institutions will have to meet an increased proportion of the rising costs of education through greatly increased tuition and fees. That requirement will be to the detriment of enrollment of many students from low-income families and even of a good many students from middle-income families, and public institutions may continue to be forced to turn away qualified applicants on an increased scale.

Assuming, however, that adequate funds are forthcoming from public sources, that growth is not inhibited by changes in the demand for college graduates or by structural changes in higher education, and that the age distribution of students does not change very much, enrollment trends in the 1970s and the following two decades will be determined by (1) changes in the rate of growth of the college-age population and (2) a continuation of the long-run upward trend in enrollment rates, which in turn primarily reflects the influence of three interrelated and overlapping factors: (a) the upward trend in high school graduation rates, (b) the rise in real per-capita income, and (c) changes in the occupational structure which result in an increased demand for persons holding academic degrees.

How will enrollment be distributed among types of institutions in future years? If changes in the 1970s reflect the shifts that occurred from 1963 to 1970, the most rapid growth of enrollment to 1980 is likely to occur in the two-year institutions. Their enrollment will increase 70 percent and may be expected to increase these institutions' share of total enrollment from 28 to 31 percent. Most of this growth will occur in the public two-year colleges, which are likely to account for 96 percent of all enrollment in two-year institutions in 1980, as compared with 94 percent in 1970.

The comprehensive colleges are also estimated to experience rapid growth. Although their enrollment is likely to increase 58 percent in the 10-year period, their share of the total is projected to rise only from 31 to 32 percent. This estimate would be only slightly altered if, as seems likely, some of the public liberal arts colleges were to broaden their programs so that they would be entitled to classification as comprehensive colleges by 1980.

Interestingly, the projections suggest that the most slowly growing group of institutions will be the doctoral-granting institutions, although they will experience a substantial 37 percent increase in enrollment. But their share of the total is likely to fall from 30 to about 27 percent. Moreover, the more prestigious the institution, the less rapid the rate of enrollment growth is likely to be. This reflects the fact that the less prestigious doctoral-granting institutions tend to be younger, and thus in an earlier and more rapid stage of development.

If there is still time remaining, review the passage until all 5 minutes have elapsed.
Do not look at Part B until that time.

Part B: TIME — 7 minutes

DIRECTIONS: Answer the following questions pertaining to information in the passage you have just read. You may not turn back to that passage for assistance.

1. According to the passage, during the 1960s, American institutions of higher education   1. Ⓐ Ⓑ Ⓒ Ⓓ Ⓔ

    (A) failed to absorb all applicants
    (B) were financially strained
    (C) expanded their resources and facilities
    (D) worsened academically
    (E) increased in number

2. According to the author, the outlook for absorption of increased numbers of students   2. Ⓐ Ⓑ Ⓒ Ⓓ Ⓔ
during the 1970s is

    (A) favorable   (D) optimistic
    (B) varied   (E) plausible
    (C) uncertain

3. It is predicted in the passage that enrollment trends in the 1970s would be mainly   3. Ⓐ Ⓑ Ⓒ Ⓓ Ⓔ
influenced by

    (A) costs of education
    (B) changes in the rate of growth of educational institutions
    (C) changes in the educational system
    (D) changes in the rate of growth of college-age population
    (E) none of the above

4. Another factor mentioned by the author that would influence enrollment trends is   4. Ⓐ Ⓑ Ⓒ Ⓓ Ⓔ

    (A) changes in the demand for college graduates
    (B) attitudes of high school students
    (C) the general economic climate
    (D) growth of the service industry
    (E) the future of extra-curricular college activities

5. It can be inferred that the author believes that increased federal support   5. Ⓐ Ⓑ Ⓒ Ⓓ Ⓔ

    (A) should be welcomed only as a last resort
    (B) is essential to support increased enrollment
    (C) should be used only in public institutions
    (D) could lead to higher income taxes
    (E) would result in higher tuition costs

6. The author states that campus unrest has caused   6. Ⓐ Ⓑ Ⓒ Ⓓ Ⓔ

    (A) a decline in enrollment
    (B) disruption of classes
    (C) a decline in gift-giving to colleges
    (D) student support for the Indochina war
    (E) increased costs for police protection

7. Ⓐ Ⓑ Ⓒ Ⓓ Ⓔ   **7.** The author believes that campus unrest is

    (A) a passing phenomenon
    (B) of little effect on enrollment
    (C) unlikely to disappear quickly
    (D) of little consequence
    (E) the work of a minority

8. Ⓐ Ⓑ Ⓒ Ⓓ Ⓔ   **8.** It is the author's opinion that higher education will

    (A) not be able to absorb increased enrollments without more federal support
    (B) face a decrease in demand for a college degree
    (C) rely on higher personal and corporate income taxes
    (D) experience quite substantial enrollment increases
    (E) be affected by a changing labor market for Ph.D's

9. Ⓐ Ⓑ Ⓒ Ⓓ Ⓔ   **9.** According to the passage, enrollment in two-year institutions will

    (A) increase by 70 percent
    (B) increase by 20 percent
    (C) remain somewhat stable
    (D) decline slightly
    (E) decline rapidly

10. Ⓐ Ⓑ Ⓒ Ⓓ Ⓔ   **10.** The most slowly growing group of institutions will be

    (A) comprehensive colleges
    (B) four-year colleges
    (C) doctoral-granting institutions
    (D) two-year colleges
    (E) private colleges

EXERCISE B

TOTAL TIME: 12 minutes

Part A: TIME — 5 minutes

DIRECTIONS: This part contains a reading passage. You will have 5 minutes to study the passage and 7 minutes to answer questions based on it. When answering the questions you will *not* be allowed to refer back to the passage.

On August 15, 1971, the President announced a far-reaching New Economic Policy designed to check the rise in prices and wages, strengthen the nation's external economic position, and stimulate economic activity at home. To curb the rate of inflation, prices, wages, and rents were subjected to a 90-day freeze, which was followed by a comprehensive but more flexible system of controls. To improve the nation's balance of payments, the President suspended the convertibility of the dollar into gold and other reserve assets and imposed a temporary 10-percent surcharge on imports. And to strengthen the domestic economy, the President proposed, in addition to these measures, a fiscal package whose stimulus came from a set of tax cuts, which were passed by the Congress in December in somewhat altered form.

Results of the new program were visible in varying degrees by the end of the year. They were most apparent in the slowdown of price and wage increases during the freeze. On the international front the major industrial countries agreed to a realignment of currencies more favorable to the U.S. competitive position and to prompt discussions concerning trade barriers and long-term monetary reform. The strong upsurge in the purchases of automobiles from mid-August through November was partly a result of the proposed removal of the Federal excise tax, but much of it was apparently an attempt by consumers to buy automobiles before prices were increased in the post-freeze period. Perhaps the most significant effect of the combined package was the impact on public confidence. From mid-August to the end of the year, there was slow but steady improvement in confidence that the rate of inflation was subsiding and the pace of the economic recovery was gathering strength.

The decision to embark on the New Economic Policy (NEP) came from an increasing awareness in the Administration that the ambitious goals it had set in the beginning of the year were not being met. Progress in the fight against inflation was proceeding too slowly, and its future success was uncertain. At the same time, the recovery was also progressing, but not fast enough to cut the rate of unemployment. More crucial than either of these for the timing of the decisions was the serious weakening of the dollar in international markets. As the summer wore on, there were no signs of a resolution of the financial crisis that in May caused the Swiss franc and the Austrian schilling to be revalued and the German mark and the Netherlands guilder to be set free to float in value. In the second quarter, the U.S. balance of payments on the official reserve transactions basis had recorded a deficit of $23 billion at a seasonally adjusted annual rate, and in July and August pressure against the dollar reached enormous proportions. Funds totalling $3.7 billion moved into foreign official reserve accounts in the week ended August 15. The time had come to deal decisively with the international financial problem that had persisted for at least a dozen years despite the efforts of four successive Administrations.

If there is still time remaining, review the passage until all 5 minutes have elapsed.
Do not look at Part B until that time.

Part B: TIME—7 minutes

DIRECTIONS: Answer the following questions pertaining to information in the passage you have just read. You may not turn back to that passage for assistance.

1.   A provision of the President's New Economic Policy was   1. Ⓐ Ⓑ Ⓒ Ⓓ Ⓔ

    (A)   wage and price controls
    (B)   increased income taxes
    (C)   a surcharge on exports
    (D)   reduced tariffs
    (E)   devaluation of the dollar

2. Ⓐ Ⓑ Ⓒ Ⓓ Ⓔ **2.** Imports were subjected to a

    (A) 90-day freeze
    (B) system of price controls
    (C) quota system
    (D) 10-percent surcharge
    (E) most-favored nation basis

3. Ⓐ Ⓑ Ⓒ Ⓓ Ⓔ **3.** The decision to embark on the NEP came about because of

    (A) public pressure
    (B) devaluation of the dollar
    (C) an act of Congress
    (D) slowdown of inflation
    (E) failure to meet the Administration's economic goals

4. Ⓐ Ⓑ Ⓒ Ⓓ Ⓔ **4.** Which of the following currencies had been set free to float in value?

    (A) Dollar   (D) British pound
    (B) Swiss franc   (E) Italian lira
    (C) German mark

5. Ⓐ Ⓑ Ⓒ Ⓓ Ⓔ **5.** The international financial problem had persisted

    (A) for 12 years   (D) for 2 years
    (B) for 4 years   (E) since World War II
    (C) for 12 months

6. Ⓐ Ⓑ Ⓒ Ⓓ Ⓔ **6.** Increased automobile purchases in the United States were partly the result of

    (A) rising incomes
    (B) a surge in car imports
    (C) removal of the Federal excise tax
    (D) significant body restyling
    (E) unknown factors

7. Ⓐ Ⓑ Ⓒ Ⓓ Ⓔ **7.** The President suspended the convertibility of the dollar into gold to improve the country's

    (A) monetary system
    (B) balance of payments
    (C) dollar reserves
    (D) foreign exchange holdings
    (E) control over scarce resources

8. Ⓐ Ⓑ Ⓒ Ⓓ Ⓔ **8.** The passage states that, as a result of the president's NEP, the public's confidence

    (A) waned
    (B) showed little change
    (C) showed no change
    (D) showed slow but steady improvement
    (E) greatly increased

9. During the period under discussion in the passage, unemployment

9. Ⓐ Ⓑ Ⓒ Ⓓ Ⓔ

    (A) increased dramatically
    (B) increased slightly
    (C) stayed about the same
    (D) plummeted
    (E) first fell, then rose

10. As of the second quarter of 1971, the annual deficit of the U.S. balance of payments stood at

10. Ⓐ Ⓑ Ⓒ Ⓓ Ⓔ

    (A) $1.8 billion   (D) $74 billion
    (B) $3.7 billion   (E) $92 billion
    (C) $23 billion

EXERCISE C

TOTAL TIME: 12 minutes

Part A: TIME — 5 minutes

DIRECTIONS: This part contains a reading passage. You will have 5 minutes to study the passage and 7 minutes to answer questions based on it. When answering the questions you will *not* be allowed to refer back to the passage.

The following passage was written in 1971.

The sudden demise of the SST program supplied final evidence of a process that started in the mid-sixties: our generation stands, at present, at one of the sharp turning points of human culture characterized by fairly general rejection of an old value system.

We grew up in a world that regarded material progress through technological improvement as the main glory of our times. We learned to admire our productive machinery as a generator of greater self-fulfillment by freeing us from the toil of past generations. We interpreted the conquest of distance through rapid transportation as a way of creating freer and better understanding among the inhabitants of our planet. As our younger generation has taken stock of our hopes and actual accomplishments, however, it has found that a world built on technology is a hollow one. Our expectations were too utopian and, therefore, our actual achievements have lost the creditability of our ideals.

A new orientation is emerging. It does not build its hopes on the more efficient creation of goods and services as the ultimate answer to miseries. Instead, it regards technology as a source of our ills rather than the solution to them. The factories, once visited by streams of admiring townfolk, now stand in the public eye as the source of pollution. Supersonic planes are no longer the embodiment of the ultimate conquest of distance. The important element of their existence is now the nuisance of their noise. Automation is no longer valued as the source of leisure time; it draws criticism as the creator of structural unemployment.

Middle-aged men are ill advised to argue their ideological-social beliefs with the younger generation. As value systems replace each other, being "right" or "wrong" loses most of its meaning. Demography itself assures the ultimate domination by the younger generation; the young will outlive us.

There is, however, room for rational analysis in the economic impact of this change in cultures. The SST case has proven it; the preferences of the alienated are now a strong enough factor to determine the contractions and expansions of the public purse.

There can be little doubt that their attitudes as citizens, as consumers and even as investors will have a crucial impact upon the economic structure.

Mankind has experienced recurrent trouble in dealing with the intricacies of advanced civilizations. Saint Augustine's Christian purism was a rejection of Roman sophistication. Calvin's puritanistic views represented deep distrust of Renaissance worldliness. Jean Jacques Rousseau's eighteenth century turn to the natural life expressed the reservations of a sensitive man to complexities beyond his understanding. High moments of civilization have a general tendency to produce counter-cultures and alienated reactions: a yearning for a world with fewer complexities and closer to the intimate scale of man's own life.

Life at present abounds with similar symptoms. Leading schools report a growing interest among graduating collegians for careers in farming. Clothing styles among the young, a good indicator of cultural change, reflect a taste for the simple, non-commercial product. The traditionalist tweedy line is being replaced by items from the Army and Navy surplus store. Girls turn to home sewing and create their own styles inspired by folkloric elements. Over-urbanized vacation spots are losing out to wandering and camping. "Roughing it" is now in style. The rediscovery of nature mixes well with the embracing of conservationist causes. The latter, formerly a conservative movement among the landed gentry against the intrusion of new elements, is now a mass issue.

If there is still time remaining, review the passage until all 5 minutes have elapsed.
Do not look at Part B until that time.

Part B: TIME — 7 minutes

DIRECTIONS: Answer the following questions pertaining to information in the passage you have just read. You may not turn back to that passage for assistance.

1. Ⓐ Ⓑ Ⓒ Ⓓ Ⓔ 1. An appropriate title for the passage could be

   (A) Youth in Rebellion
   (B) Demographics of Youth
   (C) The Dethroning of Technology
   (D) Demise of the SST
   (E) Old and New Ideologies

2. Ⓐ Ⓑ Ⓒ Ⓓ Ⓔ 2. The demise of the SST is considered by the author to be indicative of

   (A) an upsurge of patriotism
   (B) a rejection of technology as a source of ills
   (C) a misunderstanding of progress
   (D) a costly failure
   (E) the rebellious nature of our youth

3. Ⓐ Ⓑ Ⓒ Ⓓ Ⓔ 3. Progress, according to the passage, used to mean

   (A) the spread of scientific knowledge
   (B) an increase in material goods
   (C) better transportation
   (D) greater self-fulfillment
   (E) more wealth

4. The author states that automation is viewed by young people as a(n) 4.Ⓐ Ⓑ Ⓒ Ⓓ Ⓔ

   (A) potential source of leisure time
   (B) labor saving trend
   (C) aid to economic growth
   (D) creator of structural unemployment
   (E) complement to technology

5. Some colleges report that graduates have taken a growing interest in 5.Ⓐ Ⓑ Ⓒ Ⓓ Ⓔ

   (A) politics   (D) farming
   (B) sewing   (E) auto mechanics
   (C) transportation·

6. To describe the desire by youth for a simpler life closer to nature, the author uses the 6.Ⓐ Ⓑ Ⓒ Ⓓ Ⓔ
   term
   (A) conservationism   (D) purism
   (B) counter-culture   (E) conservatism
   (C) renaissance

7. Which historical figure mentioned in the passage desired a return to the "natural life"? 7.Ⓐ Ⓑ Ⓒ Ⓓ Ⓔ

   (A) Rousseau   (D) Saint Augustine
   (B) Calvin   (E) Luther
   (C) Saint Simon

8. The author believes that the older generation should 8.Ⓐ Ⓑ Ⓒ Ⓓ Ⓔ

   (A) not argue their ideological beliefs with the young generation
   (B) take on the beliefs of the young generation
   (C) take a "business as usual" attitude
   (D) try to persuade young people to be more conservative
   (E) take no action at all

9. According to the passage, young people will have an impact on the economy 9.Ⓐ Ⓑ Ⓒ Ⓓ Ⓔ
   because of all of the following except

   (A) they will comprise a large number of the population
   (B) they will influence investment
   (C) their incomes will rise
   (D) they have more voting power
   (E) they will become more militant

10. In general, the passage points out that attitudes and values of the youth generation 10.Ⓐ Ⓑ Ⓒ Ⓓ Ⓔ
    are

    (A) basically the same as their parents
    (B) influenced by what they learn in college
    (C) basically different from that of their parents
    (D) volatile, in that they change every year or two
    (E) favorably disposed to conspicuous consumption

Reading Comprehension

EXERCISE   D

TIME: 9 minutes

DIRECTIONS: This part contains a reading passage. You are to read it carefully. When answering the questions, you *will* be able to refer to the passages. The questions are based on what is *stated* or *implied* in the passage. You have nine minutes to complete this part.

Above all, colonialism was hated for its explicit assumption that the civilizations of colonized peoples were inferior. Using slogans like *The White Man's Burden* and *La Mission Civilicatrice,* Europeans asserted their moral obligation to impose their way of life on those endowed with inferior cultures. This orientation was
(5)   particularly blatant among the French. In the colonies, business was conducted in French. Schools used that language and employed curricula designed for children in France. One scholar suggests that Muslim children probably learned no more about the Maghreb than they did about Australia. In the Metropole, intellectuals discoursed on the weakness of Arabo-Islamic culture. A noted historian accused Islam
(10)   of being hostile to science. An academician wrote that Arabic—the holy language of religion, art and the Muslim sciences—is "more of an encumbrance than an aid to the mind. It is absolutely devoid of precision." There was of course an element of truth in the criticisms. After all, Arab reformists had been engaging in self-criticism for decades. Also, at least some Frenchmen honestly believed they were help-
(15)   ing the colonized. A Resident General in Tunisia, for example, told an assemblage of of Muslims with sincerity, "We shall distribute to you all that we have of learning; we shall make you a party to everything that makes for the strength of our intelligence." But none of this could change or justify the cultural racism in colonial ideologies. To the French, North Africans were only partly civilized and could be saved
(20)   only by becoming Frenchmen. The reaction of the colonized was of course to defend his identity and to label colonial policy, in the words of Algerian writer Malek Hadad, "cultural asphyxia." Throughout North Africa, nationalists made the defense of Arabo-Islamic civilization a major objective, a value in whose name they demanded independence. Yet the crisis of identity, provoked by colonial experiences, has not
(25)   been readily assured and lingers into the post-colonial period. A French scholar describes the devasting impact of colonialism by likening it to "the role played for us (in Europe) by the doctrine of original sin." Frantz Fanon, especially in his *Studies in a Dying Colonialism,* well expresses the North African perspective.

Factors producing militant and romantic cultural nationalism are anchored in
(30)   time. Memories of colonialism are already beginning to fade and, when the Maghreb has had a few decades in which to grow, dislocations associated with social change can also be expected to be fewer. Whether this means that the cultural nationalism characteristic of the Maghreb today will disappear in the future cannot be known. But a preoccupation with identity and culture and an affirmation of Arabism and Islam
(35)   have characterized the Maghreb since independence and these still remain today important elements in North African life.

A second great preoccupation in independent North Africa is the promotion of a modernist social revolution. The countries of the Maghreb do not pursue development in the same way and there have been variations in policies within each coun-
(40)   try. But all three spend heavily on development. In Tunisia, for example, the government devotes 20-25% of its annual budget to education, and literacy has climbed from 15% in 1956 to about 50% today. A problem, however, is that such advances

are not always compatible with objectives flowing from North African nationalism. In Morocco, for instance, when the government decided to give children an "Arab" (45) education, it was forced to limit enrollments because, among other things, most Moroccans had been educated in French and the country consequently had few teachers qualified to teach in Arabic. Two years later, with literacy rates declining, this part of the Arabization program was postponed. The director of Arabization declared. "We are not fanatics; we want to enter the modern world."

1. Which of the following titles best describes the content of the passage? 1. Ⓐ Ⓑ Ⓒ Ⓓ Ⓔ

   (A) *Education in the Levant*
   (B) *Nationalism in North Africa*
   (C) *Civilization in the Middle East*
   (D) *Muslim Science*
   (E) *Culture and Language*

2. Which of the following is *not* used by the author in the presentation of his arguments? 2. Ⓐ Ⓑ Ⓒ Ⓓ Ⓔ

   (A) Colonialism demoralized the local inhabitants.
   (B) Colonialism produced an identity crisis.
   (C) Cultural nationalism will soon disappear.
   (D) Decolonization does not always run smoothly.
   (E) Colonialists assumed that local cultures were inferior.

3. The author's attitude toward colonialism is best described as one of 3. Ⓐ Ⓑ Ⓒ Ⓓ Ⓔ

   (A) sympathy
   (B) bewilderment
   (C) support
   (D) hostility
   (E) ambivalence

4. Which of the following does the author mention as evidence of cultural colonialism? 4. Ⓐ Ⓑ Ⓒ Ⓓ Ⓔ

   (A) Native children in North Africa learned little about local culture.
   (B) Science was not taught in the Arabic language.
   (C) Colonial policy was determined in France.
   (D) Colonialists spent little on development.
   (E) Native teachers were not employed in public schools.

5. The author provides information that would answer which of the following questions? 5. Ⓐ Ⓑ Ⓒ Ⓓ Ⓔ

   (A) What was the difference between French and German attitudes toward their colonies?
   (B) Why did Europeans impose their way of life on their colonies?
   (C) Why was colonialism bad?
   (D) Why was colonialism disliked?
   (E) When did colonialism end in North Africa?

EXERCISE   E

TIME: **9 minutes**

DIRECTIONS: This part contains a reading passage. You are to read it carefully. When answering the questions, you *will* be able to refer to the passages. The questions are based on what is *stated* or *implied* in the passage. You have nine minutes to complete this part.

Man and nature were the culprits as Venice sank hopelessly—or so it seemed—into the 177 canals on which the city is built. While nature's work took ages, man's work was much quicker and more brutal. But now man is using his ingenuity to save what he had almost destroyed. The sinking has been arrested and Venice
(5)   should start rising again, like an oceanic phoenix from the canals.

The saving of Venice is the problem of the Italian Government, of course, but Venice is also a concern for Europe. And it happened that in the second half of 1975 Italy was in the chair of the European Council of Ministers. But the EC as such has no program for the salvation of Venice. "The Community is not a cultural
(10)   community," explained one Commission official. "There are some areas where it just does not have competence, the preservation of historical landmarks being one of them." So the efforts to save Venice have taken on a worldwide, rather than a Community-wide dimension.

Industrialization of the Porto Marghera area brought economic benefits to Venice,
(15)   but it also raped the city as growing air and water pollution began to take their toll on the priceless works of art and architecture. The danger of the imminent disappearance of Venice's cultural heritage was first brought to public attention in November 1966 when tides rose over six feet to flood Venice's canals and squares. Since then, various national and international organizations have sought ways and
(20)   means to halt the destruction of the "queen of the Adriatic," though no one program has proved wholly satisfactory.

The US "Save Venice" group and the British "Venice in Peril" committee were formed to raise money for the restoration of priceless works of art and monuments. In 1967 the United Nations Educational, Scientific and Cultural Organization (UN-
(25)   ESCO) took on the task of helping to save Venice by setting up a joint international advisory committee with the Italian Government. Such distant lands as Pakistan, no stranger to aid programs itself, joined in the effort, giving UNESCO a gift of 10,000 postage stamps for "Venice in Peril." Even a group of famous cartoonists felt moved to draw attention to the fact that "Venice must be saved" and organized an exhibit
(30)   in 1973, with the Council of Europe in Strasbourg, France, and this year a ballet festival drew people and funds to Venice.

Though Venice, the city of bridge-linked islands, was built in the fifth century, the land on which it was built has been sinking "naturally" for a billion years. Movements of the earth's crust have caused the very slow and gradual descent of
(35)   the Po Valley. And nature's forces aren't easily countered. Each year, Venice has been sinking about one millimeter into the lagoon which holds this Adriatic jewel. To add to Venice's peril, the slow melting of the polar cap causes the level of the sea to rise another millimeter. If nothing is done to reverse nature's work, Venice is doomed to be another Atlantis, lost for ever beneath the murky sea.

(40)   Man's part in the sink-Venice movement has been for reasons mainly economic. For the last 400 years, the population of Venice has been drifting toward the mainland to escape the isolation and incovenience of living on a series of islets. Between 1951 and 1971, Venice lost 63,000 inhabitants. To curtail this migration, new, artificial land areas, on the Dutch model, were added to the old Venice. Venice's orig-
(45)   inal builders had not been far-sighted enough and set the ground level at only a few inches above what they expected to be the maximum tides. The combination of reclaimed land and Porto Marghera industrialization have "squeezed" the lagoon until its waters have no place to go but . . . up.

As Porto Marghera grows as an industrial port, and more and deeper channels
(50)   are added for larger ships, currents become faster and dikes make the ravaging tides

even more violent. The "acqua alta" has always been a problem for Venice, but with increased industrialization, flooding has become more frequent, sometimes occurring 50 times a year. Added to the violent "scirocco" that blows up to 60 miles an hour, Venice is rendered all the more vulnerable.

(55)   Yet Venice is not crumbling. Despite the visible decay caused by repeated floods and despite pollution that peels the stucco off the palazzi and eats away at their bottom-most steps, the structures are solid. The Rialto Bridge still stands safely on its ancient foundations supported by 6000 piles.

And something has been done to stop the damage done by water. Indeed, one (60) simple measure has proved to work miracles. The ban on pumping from the thousands of artesian wells in and around the city—an easy source of water, but also a folly that caused a further descent of 5 millimeters a year—has been so effective that Venice should rise an inch in the next twenty years.

1. According to the passage, between 1951 and 1971, Venice lost approximately how many residents annually?   1. Ⓐ Ⓑ Ⓒ Ⓓ Ⓔ

(A) 475
(B) 3,150
(C) 6,300
(D) 15,500
(E) 63,000

2. The author's point of view is that Venice   2. Ⓐ Ⓑ Ⓒ Ⓓ Ⓔ

(A) cannot be saved from destruction
(B) is in danger of imminent disappearance
(C) is doomed to become another "Atlantis"
(D) can be saved, but much work is necessary
(E) must become a member of the EC

3. Which of the following conditions has *not* contributed to Venice's peril?   3. Ⓐ Ⓑ Ⓒ Ⓓ Ⓔ

(A) Movement of the earth's crust
(B) Natural causes
(C) Melting of the polar cap
(D) Industrialization
(E) Shipping on the canals

4. According to the passage, which of the following figures indicates the approximate year when Venice first began sinking?   4. Ⓐ Ⓑ Ⓒ Ⓓ Ⓔ

(A) 400 B.C.
(B) A.D. 1400
(C) A.D. 1966
(D) A.D. 1970
(E) None of the above

5. The author feels that Venice is an example of   5. Ⓐ Ⓑ Ⓒ Ⓓ Ⓔ

(A) a doomed city like Atlantis
(B) uncontrolled conditions
(C) a combination of natural and human destruction
(D) international neglect
(E) benign concern by international agencies

Answers and Analysis

EXERCISE A

1. **(C)** See paragraph 1, line 1: ". . . American institutions of higher education managed to expand their resources and facilities. . . ."

2. **(C)** Paragraph 2, see line 1: "The outlook for smooth absorption of the increased numbers of students in the 1970s is at present very uncertain."

3. **(D)** See paragraph 5, item 1: "changes in the rate of growth of the college age population."

4. **(A)** See paragraph 5, item c: "changes in the occupational structure which result in an increased demand for persons holding academic degrees."

5. **(B)** See paragraph 5, line 1, and also paragraph 4, line 1: ". . . it appears likely that higher education will *not* be in a position to absorb the increased numbers of students seeking admission in the 1970s without greatly increased federal government support. . . ."

6. **(C)** See paragraph 2, line 2: "Campus unrest . . . is leading some state legislatures [to withhold] funds . . . and . . . is causing some alumni to hold back on gifts. . . ."

7. **(C)** See paragraph 2: ". . . most sophisticated observers do not expect unrest to disappear. . . ."

8. **(A)** See the explanation to question 5 above.

9. **(A)** This figure is given in paragraph 6.

10. **(C)** See paragraph 8, line 1: ". . . the most slowly growing group of institutions will be the doctoral-granting. . . ."

EXERCISE B

1. **(A)** This is implied in paragraph 1, line 1, and specifically mentioned in line 2.

2. **(D)** Also mentioned in paragraph 1: ". . . the President . . . imposed a temporary 10-percent surcharge on imports."

3. **(E)** See paragraph 3, line 1: "The decision to embark on the NEP came from. . . ." and following.

4. **(C)** See paragraph 3: ". . . the German mark and the Netherlands guilder to be set free to float in value."

5. **(A)** See the last line of the passage: ". . . the international financial problem that had persisted for at least a dozen years. . . ."

6. **(C)** Paragraph 2: "The strong upsurge in the purchases of automobiles . . . was partly a result of the proposed removal of the Federal excise tax. . . ."

7. **(B)** Paragraph 1: "To improve the Nation's balance of payments. the President suspended the convertibility of the dollar into gold. . . ."

8. **(D)** See paragraph 2: ". . . the most significant effect of the combined package [i.e. the NEP] was the impact on public confidence."

9. **(C)** Paragraph 3: ". . . the recovery was also progressing, but not fast enough to cut the rate of unemployment."

10. **(C)** Paragraph 3, sentence beginning "In the second quarter . . ."

EXERCISE C

1. **(C)** The passage deals with the supposed rejection of technology and material progress by youth.

2. **(B)** See for example. paragraph 3: ". . . it regards technology as a source of our ills. . . ."

3. **(B)** See paragraph 2: "We grew up in a world that regarded material progress through technological improvement. . . ."

4. **(D)** See paragraph 3: "Automation . . . draws criticism as the creator of structural unemployment."

5. **(D)** See paragraph 7. line 2.

6. **(B)** This is expressed in paragraph 6. last line.

7. **(A)** See paragraph 6.

8. **(A)** See paragraph 4: "Middle-aged men are ill-advised to argue . . . with the younger generation."

9. **(E)** These reasons are found in paragraphs 4 and 5.

10. **(C)** The youth have apparently rejected the value systems of their parents. as exemplified by the issues raised in the passage.

EXERCISE D

1. **(B)** Clearly, the main subject of the passage is nationalism. This is given in the statement on line 1, "Above all, colonialism was hatred . . ." and in lines 22ff and 29ff.

2. **(C)** Choice (E) is given in lines 1–2, (D) in lines 42–43, (B) in lines 24–25, and (A) is implied throughout; while the opposite of (C) is found in lines 34–36.

3. **(D)** See, for instance, the reference to "cultural racism" in line 18, as well as the general tone of paragraph 1.

4. **(A)** This is mentioned in lines 6-8. The fact that children were taught very little about their own culture and history was due to cultural colonialism.

5. **(D)** This theme begins on line 1 and continues throughout much of the passage.

EXERCISE E

1. **(B)** See lines 42-43.

2. **(D)** Venice can be saved, but much work is necessary. See lines 3–5.

3. Answer (A) appears in line 34, (B) in 33, (C) in 37, and (D) in lines 49–53. Choice **(E)** is not mentioned.

4. **(E)** In lines 32-33 it is stated that the land on which Venice is situated has been sinking for a billion years.

5. **(C)** The theme is given in the first line and repeated in lines 33, 37, 40, 46, 47, and 53.

PRACTICAL JUDGMENT REVIEW

The GMAT generally features two Practical Judgment sections. Each section usually contains one passage between 1000 and 1500 words in length. Each passage concerns a decision to be made by one or more of the characters. The passage will contain information regarding the characters, the available alternatives, and the facts and conditions under which the decision is to be made.

Two sets of questions follow each passage. The first (larger) set is composed of *Data Evaluation* questions. These questions require you to classify elements of the situation described in the passage as either (a) OBJECTIVES (of the decision maker[s]), (b) MAJOR FACTORS (bearing on the decision), (c) MINOR FACTORS (bearing on the decision), (d) MAJOR ASSUMPTIONS (by the decision makers), or (e) UNIMPORTANT ISSUES.

The second and briefer set comprises *Data Application* questions. These are multiple-choice questions. They may ask that you identify specific information from the passage, draw inferences from passage information, or make simple calculations based on facts and figures contained in the passage.

Answers to both *Data Evaluation* and *Data Application* questions should be based on the facts and conditions as presented in the passage, along with the assumptions, judgments, and perceptions of the passage characters.

A Discussion of Question Types

Data Evaluation Questions

On the actual exam the directions for the Data Evaluation questions will be very similar to the following:

DIRECTIONS: The questions that follow relate to the preceding passage. Evaluate, in terms of the passage, each of the items given. Then select your answer from one of the following classifications, and blacken the corresponding space on the answer sheet.

(A) A MAJOR OBJECTIVE in making the decision: one of the goals sought by the decision maker

(B) A MAJOR FACTOR in making the decision: an aspect of the problem, specifically mentioned in the passage, that fundamentally affects and/or determines the decision

(C) A MINOR FACTOR in making the decision: a less important element bearing on or affecting a Major Factor, rather than a Major Objective directly

(D) A MAJOR ASSUMPTION in making the decision: a projection or supposition arrived at by the decision maker before considering the factors and alternatives

(E) AN UNIMPORTANT ISSUE in making the decision: an item lacking significant impact on, or relationship to, the decision

In our practice tests, the basic format of the directions and the structure of the answer choices have not been altered. The balance of this section will discuss, at length, each of the five possible Data Evaluation answers.

Major Objectives

Practical Judgment passages normally contain several elements that can properly be labeled as Major Objectives of a decision maker. *Major Objectives are whatever a decision maker is trying to achieve by way of the decision being made;* that is, Major Objectives are those conditions which a decision maker wants to exist after having made a good decision. As an example, consider the following brief passage:

Reginald Crave wants to leave his present job because he wishes to work in a rural environment. Reggie has been employed as a charter company pilot for nearly eight years. Reggie's desire is to abandon the charter company and operate his own crop-dusting service. He must earn an income at least equal to his present one in order to meet his existing financial commitments. He is considering the purchase of one of four planes. The four aircraft represent both conventional and specialized (crop-dusting) design.

In any Practical Judgment passage one of the Major Objectives will be to make a major decision. In the example given, this objective could be stated as "selecting which plane to buy." Additional objectives may be by-products of the decision itself. Such by-product Major Objectives may refer to the personal wishes or happiness of a decision maker. Other Major Objectives are often presented as the measures of success—what is to be attained or avoided by the right decision. Additional Major Objectives in the preceding example may be stated as "working in a rural setting" and "operating his own crop-dusting company." Note the words "wishes" and "desire" in the passage. Such *key words* denote outcomes sought by the decision maker and are excellent clues in identifying Major Objectives.

When identifying Major Objectives, try to disregard the word "Major." In Practical Judgment passages Major Objectives often follow from one to another. (Do not try to weigh one apparent objective against another.) Be concerned only with whether or not an objective is one *held by a decision maker* and is *related to the decision at hand.*

Major Objectives in Practical Judgment passages are what a decision maker would like to achieve or have happen. In line with this, Data Evaluation questions which would be properly labeled as Major Objectives generally begin with *nouns formed from verbs*—that is, words connoting action. Examples are: "assuring," "establishment," "adoption," "completion," "avoidance," "providing," "acquiring," and so forth.

As a further aid in identifying questions to be labeled Major Objectives, ask yourself the following: Does the sentence fragment (Data Evaluation question) make sense when placed before the phrase "_____ is an outcome sought"? Returning to the case of Reginald Crave: *"Working in a rural setting* is an outcome sought" and *"Operating his own crop-dusting company* is an outcome sought" both make fine sense.

A final point. By the time you take the actual exam you should have memorized that Major Objectives are (A) (first column) on the answer sheet. This is not as trivial an exercise as it would first appear. The need to refer to the directions during the exam will cost you time and, quite possibly, points. Certainly, confusion in recording answers could prove disastrous.

Major Factors

Beyond a decision maker's objectives and assumptions (to be discussed later in this chapter), it is the Major Factors that play a decisive part in formulating the decision. Major Factors are the measures of relative strength and weakness associated with the various alternatives under consideration. Major Factors are the means by which the alternatives are compared and contrasted, weighed one against the other. *A Major Factor will be a large, general, comprehensive issue.* For example: a passage may mention a number of specific advantages associated with a particular new product being considerd for production. Let us say that the various advantages presented are lower price, easier cleaning, and greater durability. A Data Evaluation question reading "advantages of Product X" would best be described as a Major Factor in this case, because "advantages" is a large, general, comprehensive term. We might mention here that any one of the specific advantages listed, such as easier cleaning, would represent a Minor Factor.

Major Factors may also take the form of a consideration, explicit in the passage, that could likely determine the *success or failure* of the action under discussion in the passage. This form of Major Factor is most common in those passages dealing with "yes/no" or "go/no go" types of decision situations. To continue with the example in the paragraph on page 107: the passage could indicate that the firm has obtained an exclusive patent on the new product effectively screening out competitive encroachment for some time. A Data Evaluation question worded "patent rights held on Product X" would best be labeled a Major Factor in the decision process, because the holding of patent rights may determine the success or failure of the product.

Regardless of their form, the Major Factors will always be explicitly mentioned in the passage. Thus, if a Data Evaluation question were an item not explicitly mentioned in the subject passage, it could not be properly labeled a Major Factor.

Let us return to the story of Reginald Crave, begun on page 107. The passage continues with the introduction of Reggie's alternatives—that is, the various airplanes from which Reggie is trying to make a selection.

Reggie is considering four planes: a new crop-dusting craft, a new conventional craft (not modified for dusting or spraying), a used crop duster, and a used conventional plane. As Reggie evaluates the planes, he carefully computes the total cost of each. He considers in his calculation not only the purchase price but the expenditure necessary for any required repairs or modifications to each plane. Based upon the cost data he has assembled, Reggie realizes that he will need a sizeable business loan. In examining his financial position, Reggie is aware that, because the personal savings he is able to invest are small, he must make the best possible choice. His last dime is at stake. In addition to the cost, Reggie looks into the

versatility of each of the four planes. By talking with dealers, fellow pilots, and a large
crop-care company, Reggie gets good ideas of each plane's maneuverability, capacity, and
wet/dry delivery capability. Reggie recognizes that if he is to maintain his current level of
income he will need a craft that will allow him to work year-round, in a variety of settings, and
with a variety of chemicals. He is quite anxious to reach a decision. It has been at least eight
years since he has piloted a prop-driven aircraft. However, he feels confident that he can
handle that job when the time comes.

   Looking back at the passage just completed, you can identify two Major Factors: (1) total
cost of the planes under consideration and (2) the versatility of the planes considered. The
passage explains the importance of the two components. Both represent basic criteria
employed by Reggie in weighing the choices. A third Major Factor in the example passage
could be phrased as "level of Reggie's Personal Savings." Reggie's meager savings dictate the
extreme care with which he must make his decision. The level of his savings plays a major role
in determining the best (successful) choice.

   The first word in a Data Evaluation question is a valuable clue in determining if the
question does or does not represent a factor in the passage. A question's first word can often
distinguish factors from Major Objectives or Major Assumptions, because *both Major and
Minor Factors will usually be factual or tangible*. The first word of a Data Evaluation question
representing either Major or Minor Factors will usually be a *noun* such as "cost," "time,"
"sales," "age," "availability," "amount," "reliability," "date," or "location."

   Remember that Major Factors are (B) (second column) on the answer sheet. Memorize
this. It will save you time and reduce the probability of error in recording your answers.

Minor Factors

   Compared to Major Factors, those items properly designated as Minor Factors exert a
lesser and indirect influence on the overall decisions. Specifically, *Minor Factors are those
elements in the decision situation that relate to, or are associated with, Major Factors*. Often in
a passage a Major Factor, such as "total cost" in the Reginald Crave example, will be made up
of a number of component parts or pieces. In Reggie's case total cost was comprised of
purchase price and the cost of repairs and modifications; "purchase price of planes
considered" and "cost of repairs and modifications to planes considered" represent Minor
Factors. Continuing with Reggie's case, "versatility of the four planes" represents a Major
Factor. Within the passage one can identify a number of more specific or narrower
considerations associated with versatility. Data evaluation questions worded "Maneuverability of each plane considered," "capacity of the various planes considered," or "delivery
capabilities of the four planes" should all be labeled Minor Factors in our example.

   Minor Factors can also take the form of *considerations restricted in their impact to fewer
than all of the alternatives* being discussed. That is, a consideration associated or related to
only one or two of the decision choices. The restriction or limitation of a factor, thus making
it a Minor Factor, can come about in two ways. One, the impact of the factor can be restricted
to one or two alternatives by the passage presentation. Two, the factor can be restricted in its
application to one or two alternatives by the wording of the specific Data Evaluation
Question. Let us look at examples of each case. Suppose that the Reginald Crave passage
contained the following information: The two used aircrafts are required to pass a safety
inspection and be certified. Furthermore, this inspection necessitates a fee of $250 to be paid
by the buyer. Given this information in the passage, a Data Evaluation question
"Certification fee borne by buyer" would represent a Minor Factor. It is a factor in the
decision (relating to the Major Factor of the total cost). It is also restricted in association to
only two of Reggie's four alternatives (planes considered). The second way in which a Minor
Factor can be created is through the specific wording of the Data Evaluation question itself.
In this case a Major Factor is turned into a Minor one by the construction of the question. In

the Reginald Crave case, "Total cost of each aircraft considered" is a Major Factor. Note that no specific plane or pair of planes is identified in the question. The question applies to the entire set of choices. If the questions were phrased "Total cost of plane No. 3" the correct designation becomes Minor Factor. In this phrasing the issue of total cost has been restricted to only one of the planes (alternatives) under review. Along these same lines, a question phrased "Difference in total cost between planes No. 1 and No. 5" would also be properly labeled as a Minor Factor. The subject of this question is "Difference . . ." and this difference relates to only two of the five planes. Here again a Minor Factor question has been developed by restricting the issue of total cost to a lesser number of alternatives.

As with Major Factors, a Minor Factor will always be explicitly stated in the passage. Also, as with Major Factors, Data Evaluation questions which state Minor Factors will most likely begin with *tangible nouns* such as "durability," "variance," "quality," and so forth.

Remember, for Minor Factors mark (C) in the third column on the answer sheet.

Major Assumptions

Within every Practical Judgment passage the decision maker(s) will incorporate certain assumptions into the decision process. A decision maker will always make or accept certain suppositions or projections regarding factors, events, or conditions having a material impact on the decision. Major Assumptions contained in the passage will be stated very briefly. Supporting information will not be presented; Major Assumptions are those accepted by the decision maker without discussion or substantiation. Therefore, those passage elements representing Major Assumptions cannot be proved or disproved based upon the facts contained in the passage.

Assumptions, for Practical Judgment purposes, can take the form of (1) estimates, projections, or the continuation of trends, (2) the expectation or anticipation by a decision maker of an important future event, or (3) personal feelings, beliefs, or opinions held by a decision maker.

Returning to the Reginald Crave example: one Major Assumption might be stated as "ability to fly a crop duster." This Major Assumption represents both an expectation and a belief on Reggie's part. Look carefully at the last sentence of the Reginald Crave passage on page 107. It reads, "However, he feels confident that he can handle that job when the time comes." Note the words "feels" and "confident." These *key words signal feelings, beliefs, or opinions* on the part of the decision maker. Note also the final words of the sentence, "handle that job when the time comes." Reggie is proceeding with the decision under the assumption he will be able to fly the plane. He is acting in anticipation of a most important future consideration. *Major Assumptions* can often be identified in a passage by the presence of such words as "feels" and "believes." Another Major Assumption in Reggie's case, one more difficult to identify, may be phrased as "approval of a business loan." Reggie is proceeding with his decision with the expectation that he will be able to get the necessary business loan (an uncertain future occurrence). This form of Major Assumption is one *implied* within the passage by the decision maker's behavior, that is, the decision maker's (Reggie's) lack of hesitancy or tentativeness in proceeding with the decision. It is important to remember that, unlike Major and Minor Factors, *Major Assumptions may be implied* in a passage.

In considering Major Assumptions, the word "major" may, as it did with Major Objectives, prove confusing. You need not dwell on the relative importance of one assumption versus another. Your concern should be with whether or not an Assumption is one made by a decision maker and is one which limits, expands, weakens, or strengthens the Factors being considered.

As with Objectives and Factors, Data Evaluation questions properly labeled as Assumptions very often possess a clue in their wording. In general, *Major Assumption questions* will begin with *Abstract* works: words like "ability," "plausibility," "continuation," "validity," "prohibitiveness," and "likelihood."

Remember, use (D) (fourth column) of the answer sheet for Major Assumptions.

Unimportant Issues

Simply stated, Unimportant Issues are those items that are not Major Objectives, Major/Minor Factors, nor Major Assumptions related to the passage decision. *An Unimportant Issue is any issue that (1) does not appear to significantly influence the selection of the best alternatives, (2) does not represent a Major Objective, and (3) does not stand as a Major Assumption made by a decision maker.* In the case of Reginald Crave, examples of Unimportant Issues could be stated as "toxicity of pesticides to be used" and "number of years employed as a charter pilot."

Remember, Unimportant Issues are (E), the last column on the answer sheet.

Data Application Questions

The second set of questions following a passage are Data Application questions. *Data Application questions normally ask you to do one of three things: make simple computations, draw inferences from the passage, or identify specific elements in the passage.* It is not the intent of the Data Application section to test your mathematical or logical reasoning abilities. Rather, the section tests your ability to read carefully and critically. Data Application measures how well you can recall or relocate concrete facts and information in the passage.

Practical Judgment passages will often contain quantitative data—for example, facts and figures on cost, sales, profits, benefits, prices, and the like. Make a mental or marginal notation as to the location in the passage of such material. It will likely be the subject of Data Application questions. Data Application questions also take such forms as "Which of the following were seen as advantages of alternative C?" and "Which of the following was of concern to the management representatives?" As can be seen, questions such as these are similar to Data Evaluation questions. If a decision is not arrived at in the passage, you may be asked to make the decision in the Data Application section. Your choice will generally require both a computation and a review of the objectives and factors presented in the passage.

Test Tips

When answering Practical Judgment questions, do not reflect upon what *you* would do in the various passage situations. Your experiences and preferences have no place in answering Practical Judgment questions. You must confine your answers to the facts, assumptions, judgments, and perceptions disclosed in the passage. You are to answer the questions based only upon the passage.

Estimate Your Time

You will probably have 20 minutes to read a passage and answer 20 questions. Allowing about 30 seconds to answer each question, you should spend about 10 minutes pre-reading and reading each passage.

Pre-Read

Skim the questions and skim the passage. When skimming Data Evaluation questions, quickly underline an important word or phrase in each. For example:

1. *Operating* his own crop dusting company
2. *Advantages* of Product X
3. *Level* of Reggie's personal savings

4. *Cost* of repairs
5. *Difference in cost* between plane No. 4 and plane No. 5

Such underlining will help you to remember what to look for once you start reading the passage closely. Don't be concerned about which word or phrase to underline; just about anything you mark will guide your reading.

Read the Passage Actively

Mark important words and ideas. Skimming the questions will have helped you decide what to mark.

Answer All Questions

Be alert to the beginning words in Data Evaluation questions *(action word = Objective; tangible noun = Factor; abstract word = assumption)*. Answer easy questions first, but do return to the hard ones and mark your answers (or guesses) before going on to the next passage.

Summary
Data Evaluation Definitions

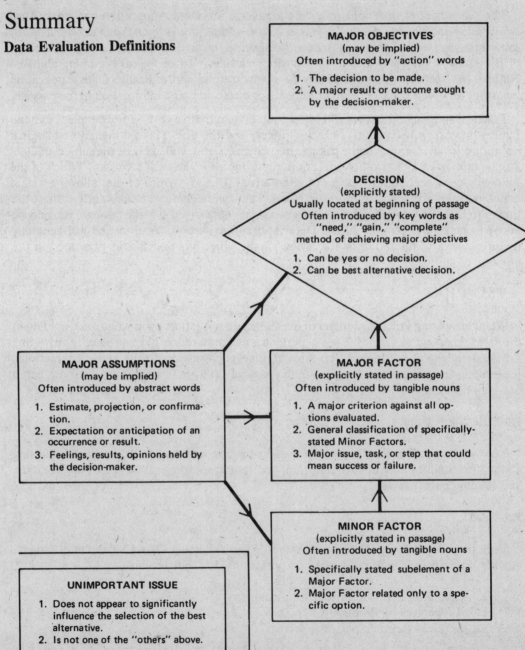

MAJOR OBJECTIVES
(may be implied)
Often introduced by "action" words

1. The decision to be made.
2. A major result or outcome sought by the decision-maker.

DECISION
(explicitly stated)
Usually located at beginning of passage
Often introduced by key words as
"need," "gain," "complete"
method of achieving major objectives

1. Can be yes or no decision.
2. Can be best alternative decision.

MAJOR ASSUMPTIONS
(may be implied)
Often introduced by abstract words

1. Estimate, projection, or confirmation.
2. Expectation or anticipation of an occurrence or result.
3. Feelings, results, opinions held by the decision-maker.

MAJOR FACTOR
(explicitly stated in passage)
Often introduced by tangible nouns

1. A major criterion against all options evaluated.
2. General classification of specifically-stated Minor Factors.
3. Major issue, task, or step that could mean success or failure.

MINOR FACTOR
(explicitly stated in passage)
Often introduced by tangible nouns

1. Specifically stated subelement of a Major Factor.
2. Major Factor related only to a specific option.

UNIMPORTANT ISSUE

1. Does not appear to significantly influence the selection of the best alternative.
2. Is not one of the "others" above.

Practice

This section is designed to give you some extra practice in Practical Judgment. The following pages contain a passage followed by Data Evaluation and data Application problems. On the actual GMAT, the usual time limit is 20 minutes for a passage followed by 20 questions.

DIRECTIONS: The passage below is followed by two sets of questions. The first question type, *data evaluation,* will require you to evaluate the importance of certain information in the passage. The second question type, *data application,* requires you to make judgments by comparing the five given alternatives for each question in terms of the pertinent criteria, in order to secure the desired objectives.
Read the passage carefully and answer the questions that follow.

Mrs. Miriam Privit had decided to purchase a second house, one she could manage as a rental. In addition to securing a needed augmentation to her monthly income, Miriam hoped she would soon be satisfying a long-standing desire to run her own business. In May, after months of looking, she located a desirable property: a "fixer-upper" for sale by sealed bid. Miriam was attracted to the property itself because she felt she would have little trouble finding renters for this two-bedroom home with a large yard. Miriam was also quite pleased with the property's location. It was within a relatively new and well-kept neighborhood, one very near Miriam's home. The property did have one serious shortcoming—its general condition. The house had apparently been abandoned. Vandalism, lack of upkeep, and an unchecked Mother Nature had taken their toll. Miriam was confident, however, that the house could be repaired and rented within two months. The time necessary to ready and rent out the house was quite important, because the cost of repairs and down payment would leave Miriam less than 5 percent of her available cash for contingencies. A major contingency was the number of house payments she herself would have to make. Deciding whether or not to bid on the house was difficult for Miriam. However, three days before the deadline for bids, she submitted what she felt to be a reasonable and attractive offer.

Data Evaluation Questions

DIRECTIONS: The questions that follow relate to the preceding passage. Evaluate, in terms of the passage, each of the items given. Then select your answer from one of the following classifications, and indicate your choice in the space provided.

(A)   A MAJOR OBJECTIVE in making the decision: one of the goals sought by the decision maker

(B)   A MAJOR FACTOR in making the decision: an aspect of the problem, specifically mentioned in the passage, that fundamentally affects and/or determines the decision

(C)   A MINOR FACTOR in making the decision: a less important element bearing on or affecting a Major Factor, rather than a Major Objective directly

(D)   A MAJOR ASSUMPTION in making the decision: a projection or supposition arrived at by the decision maker before considering the factors and alternatives

(E)   AN UNIMPORTANT ISSUE in making the decision: an item lacking significant impact on, or relationship to, the decision

1.   Likelihood of completing repairs within two months   1. Ⓐ Ⓑ Ⓒ Ⓓ Ⓔ

2.   Increasing monthly income   2. Ⓐ Ⓑ Ⓒ Ⓓ Ⓔ

3.   Proximity of property to Miriam's present home   3. Ⓐ Ⓑ Ⓒ Ⓓ Ⓔ

4.   Deadline for submitting bids   4. Ⓐ Ⓑ Ⓒ Ⓓ Ⓔ

5.   Condition of the property   5. Ⓐ Ⓑ Ⓒ Ⓓ Ⓔ

6. Ⓐ Ⓑ Ⓒ Ⓓ Ⓔ **6.** Ease of renting the house

7. Ⓐ Ⓑ Ⓒ Ⓓ Ⓔ **7.** Miriam's previous experience with home rentals

8. Ⓐ Ⓑ Ⓒ Ⓓ Ⓔ **8.** Location of the property

9. Ⓐ Ⓑ Ⓒ Ⓓ Ⓔ **9.** Damage done by vandals

10. Ⓐ Ⓑ Ⓒ Ⓓ Ⓔ **10.** Operating her own business

Data Application Questions

The following questions also relate to the preceding passage. Choose the most appropriate answer based on the information provided by the passage, and indicate your choice in the space provided.

11. Ⓐ Ⓑ Ⓒ Ⓓ Ⓔ **11.** Approximately what percentage of Miriam's cash would be devoted to the purchase and repair of the property?

(A) 5% (B) 96% (C) less than 95% (D) 95% (E) More then 95%

12. Ⓐ Ⓑ Ⓒ Ⓓ Ⓔ **12.** Which of the following is most likely viewed by Miriam as the property's greatest advantage?

(A) Its nearness to her present home
(B) Its affordability
(C) The size of the house and yard
(D) The nature of the surrounding neighborhood
(E) The speed with which it could be renovated

Answers and Analysis

Data Evaluation Questions

1. **(D)** Major Assumption. *Note the first word, "likelihood."* It is neither active, befitting an Objective, nor concrete, befitting a Factor. Major Assumption questions generally begin with abstract sorts of words, such as "likelihood." Looking at the passage, note the sentence, "Miriam was *confident* . . . house could be repaired . . . within two months." Miriam was proceeding with the decision based upon a personal belief (Assumption) regarding the likelihood of completing the necessary work within two months. The key word here is "confident." Note also that the passage does not provide any facts in support of Miriam's assumption. Finally, for a question to represent a Major Assumption, it must be a significant and relevant consideration in the decision process. For question 1, consider the passage sentence beginning, "The time necessary to ready . . . the house was quite important. . . ."

2. **(A)** Major Objective. *"Increasing monthly income* is an outcome sought." It makes sense. Look back to question 1. *"Likelihood . . . is an outcome sought"* does not make sense. "Likelihood" is not an Objective. "Likelihood" is an Assumption. *Note the first word of question 2, "Increasing."* It is an action word. Major Objective questions generally begin with words denoting action. Does question 2 represent an Objective of the decision maker relative to the decision? The passage tells us in its second sentence that the rental venture (subject of the decision) would provide a *needed* (key word) augmentation to Miriam's (decision maker) income.

3. **(C)** Minor Factor. *Note the first word, "proximity."* It is not as abstract as "likelihood" nor is it active like "increasing." "Proximity" is a more concrete word. Factors, both Major and Minor, generally begin with concrete, tangible words. Proximity of the

property to Miriam's home is *only one* of two Minor Factors (the other being the well-kept neighborhood) which comprise the Major Factor, "location of the property"; that is, "proximity" and "well-kept neighborhood" are the specific components of the larger and more general issue, "location." As the property's proximity to Miriam's home contributes significantly to her being pleased with the location, question 3 could hardly be labeled an Unimportant Issue.

4. **(E)** Unimportant Issue. The existence of a deadline is brought out in the passage. However, there is nothing in the passage to suggest that, for Miriam, the deadline played a significant role in the decision process.

5. **(B)** Major Factor. *Note the first word, "condition."* "Condition" is the type of concrete, tangible word with which Factor questions generally begin. Note, too, question 5 makes no sense when used to begin the sentence, "＿＿＿＿＿＿＿ is an outcome sought." The condition of the property is a physical reality to which Miriam is a witness. Therefore, question 5 is certainly not an Assumption. Finally, the relevance and importance of the property's condition in the decision process is established in the passage by the sentence "The property did have one serious shortcoming—its general condition."

6. **(D)** Major Assumption. *Note the first word, "Ease."* "Ease" is a bit more difficult to categorize. However, it should be seen as most befitting a Major Assumption. *"Ease of renting the house* is an outcome sought" is not a sound statement. The house in question is the particular property being considered in the passage. Ease of renting this particular property is not an *outcome* of either buying or not buying it. The tip-off on question 6 lies in the passage sentence ". . . she *felt* she would have little trouble finding renters. . . ." Question 6 then, deals with a feeling, opinion, or belief on the part of the decision maker. Is this Assumption important to the decision? Absolutely. It is this Assumption that renders the size of the house and yard one of the advantages of the property.

7. **(E)** Unimportant Issue. There is nothing in the passage which either explicitly or implicitly introduces this question into the decision process. The fact that the *reader* may feel that Miriam's experience is an important issue cannot be considered when answering Data Evaluation questions. You must confine yourself to what is available in the subject passage.

8. **(B)** Major Factor. *Note the first word, "location,"* a good Factor word. The answer cannot be (A), because "location" is not an outcome of either buying or not buying the subject property. The *location* of the property is by no means an Assumption; it is a fixed physical reality. Location is a Major Factor (general consideration) which is the sum of two more specific Minor Factors: proximity to Miriam's home (question 3) and the surrounding neighborhood. The importance of the property's location in the decision process is established in the passage by the sentence "Miriam was . . . pleased with . . . location." The property's location is one of the Major Factors weighing in favor of making the purchase.

9. **(C)** Minor Factor. *Note the first word, "damage."* Damage done by vandals is one of three Minor Factors (along with "lack of upkeep" and "unchecked Mother Nature") contributing to the Major Factor "condition of the property." Read the question 5 explanation as well.

10. **(A)** Major Objective. *Note the first word, "Operating."* *Operating her own business* is an outcome sought." Note the passage sentence ". . . Miriam (the decision maker) *hoped* she would . . . be *satisfying* . . . *desire* to run . . . own business."

Data Application Questions

11. **(E)** More than 95%. Refer to the passage sentence ". . . because the cost of repairs and down payment would *leave* Miriam *less than 5 percent* of her available cash. . . ." If

less than 5 percent would be *left,* then *more than 95 percent* would be *devoted* to the purchase and repair. Since it is not disclosed in the passage just how much less than 5 percent Miriam will have left, we cannot determine precisely how much more than 95 percent will have been spent. Therefore, answer (B), 96%, is less satisfactory than answer (E), more than 95%. The key word in the question is "devoted," that is, how much would be spent. The passage discusses how much would remain after the subject expenditures. Read questions carefully.

12. **(C)** The size of the house and yard. Answers (B) and (E) should be eliminated from consideration rather easily. (B) and (E) do not represent clear advantages to Miriam; answers (A), (C) and (D) do represent clear elements which the passage tells us Miriam finds *attractive* or *pleasing.* Answers (A) and (D) represent *Minor* Factor advantages; that is, (A) and (D) are each only a portion of the larger consideration, the property's location. "The location of the property" (a Major Factor) would be an excellent answer to question 12—if it were offered as a choice. Answer (C) is also a *Major* Factor. The size of the house and yard allow Miriam to feel that there would be little trouble in finding renters for the property. The size of the house and yard, then, serves as the basis for Miriam's being ". . . attracted to the property itself." The key words in the question are ". . . *most* likely . . ." and ". . . viewed *by Miriam.* . . ." *This type of question asks you to draw inferences from the passage and, therefore, requires a careful attention to passage wording and the distinguishing of "Major" from "Minor."*

VERBAL ABILITY REVIEW

The Verbal Ability section of the GMAT usually contains three parts—antonyms, analogies, and sentence completions—each designed to test your ability to grasp the meanings of words and to determine the relationships that exist between words and ideas in a given situation. Success with this section depends largely on your grasp of a wide range of vocabulary and your understanding of how to answer each type of question. A discussion of these questions with practice exercises for further review follows. You will also benefit by using the list of *Words Frequently Appearing on the GMAT* starting on page 291 to familiarize yourself with as many new words as possible.

Antonyms

You will recall that an antonym is a word that is *opposite* in meaning to another word as, for example, *fat* is an antonym for *thin.* On the exam you are given a key word printed in capital letters followed by five lettered choices. You must select the lettered word that comes closest to being *opposite* in meaning to the capitalized word.

There are two main points to remember in approaching questions of this type. First, when choosing the antonym for a key word, be sure that both words correspond in tense (present to present, past to past, etc.) or part of speech (noun to noun, adverb to adverb, etc.). Otherwise, your choice won't be a true opposite. Second, command of a large vocabulary is essential for success with antonym questions. You must know the meanings of all five choices and the key word in order to determine which choice is correct. Keeping these points in mind, try the following practice exercises. Answers are given after Exercise D.

Practice Exercises

Antonyms

EXERCISE A

DIRECTIONS: For each question below, select the lettered word or phrase that comes closest to being *opposite* in meaning to the word appearing in capital letters. Be sure to consider all meanings carefully.

1. ABOMINATE: (A) love (B) desire (C) seek (D) praise (E) attach   1. Ⓐ Ⓑ Ⓒ Ⓓ Ⓔ

2. RAVENOUS: (A) bored (B) nibbling (C) sated (D) thick (E) unsatisfied   2. Ⓐ Ⓑ Ⓒ Ⓓ Ⓔ

3. PITHY: (A) central (B) federal (C) homogeneous (D) verbose (E) gregarious   3. Ⓐ Ⓑ Ⓒ Ⓓ Ⓔ

4. ADAMANT: (A) yielding (B) primitive (C) elementary (D) primeval (E) emollient   4. Ⓐ Ⓑ Ⓒ Ⓓ Ⓔ

5.ⒶⒷⒸⒹⒺ **5.** EPHEMERAL: (A) evergreen (B) deciduous (C) biennial (D) everlasting (E) tactile

6.ⒶⒷⒸⒹⒺ **6.** SYNTHETIC: (A) cosmetic (B) raw (C) plastic (D) viscous (E) natural

7.ⒶⒷⒸⒹⒺ **7.** VIVACIOUS: (A) dry (B) dramatic (C) versatile (D) phlegmatic (E) vigilant

8.ⒶⒷⒸⒹⒺ **8.** AUDACITY: (A) quivering (B) cowardice (C) conciseness (D) patricide (E) reluctance

9.ⒶⒷⒸⒹⒺ **9.** IRASCIBLE: (A) pictorial (B) piscatorial (C) suave (D) sensitive (E) good-natured

10.ⒶⒷⒸⒹⒺ **10.** BUCOLIC: (A) citified (B) glossy (C) intoxicated (D) sick (E) healthy

11.ⒶⒷⒸⒹⒺ **11.** INFINITESIMAL: (A) everlasting (B) colossal (C) vague (D) universal (E) telescopic

12.ⒶⒷⒸⒹⒺ **12.** GELID: (A) lurid (B) torpid (C) torrid (D) piebald (E) vapid

13.ⒶⒷⒸⒹⒺ **13.** CIRCUITOUS: (A) diametric (B) direct (C) blunt (D) labyrinthine (E) radial

14.ⒶⒷⒸⒹⒺ **14.** PROVINCIAL: (A) urbane (B) governmental (C) famous (D) rural (E) native

15.ⒶⒷⒸⒹⒺ **15.** CLANDESTINE: (A) open (B) proud (C) salient (D) pugnacious (E) banal

16.ⒶⒷⒸⒹⒺ **16.** ABHOR: (A) protect (B) absolve (C) accuse (D) bedizen (E) adore

17.ⒶⒷⒸⒹⒺ **17.** FLAMBOYANT: (A) decorated (B) apparition (C) plain (D) dull (E) terse

18.ⒶⒷⒸⒹⒺ **18.** REDUNDANT: (A) frank (B) silent (C) concise (D) voluble (E) opulent

19.ⒶⒷⒸⒹⒺ **19.** IMPOVERISHED: (A) fertile (B) affluent (C) rococo (D) iniquitous (E) pendent

20.ⒶⒷⒸⒹⒺ **20.** OBSEQUIOUS: (A) severe (B) high (C) supercilious (D) improper (E) first

21. DISCRETE: (A) wise (B) foolish (C) unkempt (D) shameful (E) continuous 21.Ⓐ Ⓑ Ⓒ Ⓓ Ⓔ

22. FATUOUS: (A) scholarly (B) thin (C) witty (D) planned (E) stout 22.Ⓐ Ⓑ Ⓒ Ⓓ Ⓔ

23. AMENABLE: (A) rude (B) intractable (C) indifferent (D) stiff (E) correct 23.Ⓐ Ⓑ Ⓒ Ⓓ Ⓔ

24. FALLACIOUS: (A) clear (B) articulate (C) accurate (D) afraid (E) plucky 24.Ⓐ Ⓑ Ⓒ Ⓓ Ⓔ

25. ALTRUISM: (A) honesty (B) tolerance (C) bigotry (D) thievery (E) self-ishness 25.Ⓐ Ⓑ Ⓒ Ⓓ Ⓔ

EXERCISE B

DIRECTIONS: For each question below. select the lettered word or phrase that comes closest to being *opposite* in meaning to the word appearing in capital letters. Be sure to consider all meanings carefully.

1. INDIFFERENT: (A) curious (B) varied (C) uniform (D) alike (E) eager 1.Ⓐ Ⓑ Ⓒ Ⓓ Ⓔ

2. COHESIVE: (A) treacherous (B) detached (C) associated (D) affiliated (E) free 2.Ⓐ Ⓑ Ⓒ Ⓓ Ⓔ

3. INSIPID: (A) tasty (B) silly (C) angry (D) active (E) emaciated 3.Ⓐ Ⓑ Ⓒ Ⓓ Ⓔ

4. DISCORD: (A) noise (B) amity (C) irritation (D) scrap (E) use 4.Ⓐ Ⓑ Ⓒ Ⓓ Ⓔ

5. PRIOR: (A) anxious (B) irregular (C) subsequent (D) pious (E) impious 5.Ⓐ Ⓑ Ⓒ Ⓓ Ⓔ

6. CRABBED: (A) fished (B) saccharine (C) youthful (D) placid (E) soft 6.Ⓐ Ⓑ Ⓒ Ⓓ Ⓔ

7. CORROBORATION: (A) perjury (B) arrest (C) invalidation (D) alibi (E) alias 7.Ⓐ Ⓑ Ⓒ Ⓓ Ⓔ

8. DECORUM: (A) ribaldry (B) balladry (C) high collar (D) solo (E) freedom 8.Ⓐ Ⓑ Ⓒ Ⓓ Ⓔ

9.Ⓐ Ⓑ Ⓒ Ⓓ Ⓔ **9.** VOLATILE: (A) desiccated (B) awake (C) fireproof (D) inactive (E) boyish

10.Ⓐ Ⓑ Ⓒ Ⓓ Ⓔ **10.** INGENUOUS: (A) clever (B) stupid (C) profound (D) young (E) sophisticated

11.Ⓐ Ⓑ Ⓒ Ⓓ Ⓔ **11.** ALLEVIATE: (A) allow (B) aggravate (C) instigate (D) belittle (E) refuse

12.Ⓐ Ⓑ Ⓒ Ⓓ Ⓔ **12.** OBSOLETE: (A) recent (B) fancy (C) free (D) renovated (E) worthy

13.Ⓐ Ⓑ Ⓒ Ⓓ Ⓔ **13.** BLASÉ: (A) committed (B) awed (C) afraid (D) cultured (E) worldly

14.Ⓐ Ⓑ Ⓒ Ⓓ Ⓔ **14.** SANGUINE: (A) bloodless (B) gloomy (C) waxy (D) thin (E) red-faced

15.Ⓐ Ⓑ Ⓒ Ⓓ Ⓔ **15.** LANGUID: (A) pusillanimous (B) indifferent (C) sad (D) vigorous (E) motley

16.Ⓐ Ⓑ Ⓒ Ⓓ Ⓔ **16.** RESPITE: (A) agitation (B) repetition (C) exertion (D) friendship (E) anger

17.Ⓐ Ⓑ Ⓒ Ⓓ Ⓔ **17.** OBLOQUY: (A) recollection (B) fame (C) name (D) colloquy (E) inquiry

18.Ⓐ Ⓑ Ⓒ Ⓓ Ⓔ **18.** PLACATE: (A) nettle (B) label (C) toughen (D) reply (E) retaliate

19.Ⓐ Ⓑ Ⓒ Ⓓ Ⓔ **19.** COMPLACENT: (A) peevish (B) agreeable (C) nasty (D) unsatisfied (E) asking

20.Ⓐ Ⓑ Ⓒ Ⓓ Ⓔ **20.** ASSENT: (A) save (B) inquire (C) resent (D) introduce (E) disavow

21.Ⓐ Ⓑ Ⓒ Ⓓ Ⓔ **21.** HUSBANDRY: (A) munificence (B) expense (C) frugality (D) matrimony (E) widower

22.Ⓐ Ⓑ Ⓒ Ⓓ Ⓔ **22.** NOISOME: (A) quiet (B) salubrious (C) eager (D) memorable (E) deodorant

23.Ⓐ Ⓑ Ⓒ Ⓓ Ⓔ **23.** PERMANENT: (A) indifferent (B) tardy (C) mutable (D) improper (E) disheveled

24.Ⓐ Ⓑ Ⓒ Ⓓ Ⓔ **24.** COVETOUS: (A) unfinished (B) uncovered (C) undesirous (D) birdlike (E) plying

25.Ⓐ Ⓑ Ⓒ Ⓓ Ⓔ **25.** CORPOREAL: (A) fleeting (B) general (C) holy (D) spiritual (E) indistinct

EXERCISE C

DIRECTIONS: For each question below, select the lettered word or phrase that comes closest to being *opposite* in meaning to the word appearing in capital letters. Be sure to consider all meanings carefully.

1. ZEALOT: (A) heretic (B) hypocrite (C) person who is careless (D) person who is rich (E) person who is indifferent   1. Ⓐ Ⓑ Ⓒ Ⓓ Ⓔ

2. ABSTEMIOUS: (A) fastidious (B) punctilious (C) pusillanimous (D) dissipated (E) miserly   2. Ⓐ Ⓑ Ⓒ Ⓓ Ⓔ

3. SATIETY: (A) starvation (B) dissatisfaction (C) feigning (D) lowest class (E) grandeur   3. Ⓐ Ⓑ Ⓒ Ⓓ Ⓔ

4. DECIDUOUS: (A) undecided (B) hesitant (C) evergreen (D) floral (E) perennial   4. Ⓐ Ⓑ Ⓒ Ⓓ Ⓔ

5. INNOCUOUS: (A) large (B) toxic (C) spotless (D) impeccable (E) sober   5. Ⓐ Ⓑ Ⓒ Ⓓ Ⓔ

6. GERMANE: (A) moot (B) healthful (C) irrelevant (D) massive (E) puny   6. Ⓐ Ⓑ Ⓒ Ⓓ Ⓔ

7. EGREGIOUS: (A) notorious (B) obvious (C) abortive (D) maturing (E) birdlike   7. Ⓐ Ⓑ Ⓒ Ⓓ Ⓔ

8. FAVORITISM: (A) midnight (B) honesty (C) impartiality (D) temperance (E) integrity   8. Ⓐ Ⓑ Ⓒ Ⓓ Ⓔ

9. AUTONOMOUS: (A) magnanimous (B) ambiguous (C) exiguous (D) dependent (E) operated by hand   9. Ⓐ Ⓑ Ⓒ Ⓓ Ⓔ

10. EXCULPATE: (A) pardon (B) destroy (C) create (D) convict (E) admonish   10. Ⓐ Ⓑ Ⓒ Ⓓ Ⓔ

11. EARTHY: (A) pithy (B) salty (C) watery (D) refined (E) moldy   11. Ⓐ Ⓑ Ⓒ Ⓓ Ⓔ

12. CONTENTIOUS: (A) pacific (B) compromising (C) satisfied (D) dissatisfied (E) hungry   12. Ⓐ Ⓑ Ⓒ Ⓓ Ⓔ

13. GAINSAY: (A) pronounce (B) lose money (C) audit (D) applaud (E) affirm   13. Ⓐ Ⓑ Ⓒ Ⓓ Ⓔ

14.Ⓐ Ⓑ Ⓒ Ⓓ Ⓔ **14.** AMELIORATE: (A) harden (B) coarsen (C) aggravate (D) blacken (E) scrape

15.Ⓐ Ⓑ Ⓒ Ⓓ Ⓔ **15.** IGNOMINIOUS: (A) grandiose (B) erudite (C) scholarly (D) incognito (E) noble

16.Ⓐ Ⓑ Ⓒ Ⓓ Ⓔ **16.** EVANESCENT: (A) permanent (B) incandescent (C) motionless (D) putrid (E) perfunctory

17.Ⓐ Ⓑ Ⓒ Ⓓ Ⓔ **17.** CORPULENT: (A) sallow (B) fragile (C) emaciated (D) spiny (E) red-blooded

18.Ⓐ Ⓑ Ⓒ Ⓓ Ⓔ **18.** JOCUND: (A) round (B) flat (C) bleak (D) jugular (E) melancholy

19.Ⓐ Ⓑ Ⓒ Ⓓ Ⓔ **19.** HIBERNAL: (A) autumnal (B) estival (C) nocturnal (D) festive (E) wintry

20.Ⓐ Ⓑ Ⓒ Ⓓ Ⓔ **20.** EBULLIENT: (A) intoxicated (B) sluggish (C) wrathful (D) gregarious (E) bland

21.Ⓐ Ⓑ Ⓒ Ⓓ Ⓔ **21.** ASSUAGE: (A) meat (B) abate (C) individual (D) irritate (E) demonstrate

22.Ⓐ Ⓑ Ⓒ Ⓓ Ⓔ **22.** INDIGENOUS: (A) alien (B) digestible (C) roving (D) pleased (E) irate

23.Ⓐ Ⓑ Ⓒ Ⓓ Ⓔ **23.** DEARTH: (A) birth (B) frequency (C) abundance (D) brightness (E) morning

24.Ⓐ Ⓑ Ⓒ Ⓓ Ⓔ **24.** DELETERIOUS: (A) sane (B) intoxicated (C) sober (D) wholesome (E) adding

25.Ⓐ Ⓑ Ⓒ Ⓓ Ⓔ **25.** FELL: (A) downed (B) risen (C) propitious (D) cruel (E) genial

EXERCISE D

DIRECTIONS: For each question below, select the lettered word or phrase that comes closest to being *opposite* in meaning to the word appearing in capital letters. Be sure to consider all meanings carefully.

1.Ⓐ Ⓑ Ⓒ Ⓓ Ⓔ **1.** EXEMPLARY: (A) deplorable (B) imitative (C) devious (D) false (E) additive

2.Ⓐ Ⓑ Ⓒ Ⓓ Ⓔ **2.** CHOLERIC: (A) red (B) serene (C) severe (D) stern (E) meek

3. BAROQUE: (A) commoner (B) boat (C) rococo (D) simple (E) stupid   3. Ⓐ Ⓑ Ⓒ Ⓓ Ⓔ

4. DILETTANTE: (A) pedant (B) professional (C) tyro (D) cynic (E) advocate   4. Ⓐ Ⓑ Ⓒ Ⓓ Ⓔ

5. AMORPHOUS: (A) diaphanous (B) translucent (C) organized (D) opaque (E) sharp   5. Ⓐ Ⓑ Ⓒ Ⓓ Ⓔ

6. CAPRICIOUS: (A) justifiable (B) consistent (C) goatlike (D) honest (E) hypocritical   6. Ⓐ Ⓑ Ⓒ Ⓓ Ⓔ

7. SALUBRIOUS: (A) ill-tempered (B) plagued (C) rustic (D) fashioned (E) miasmic   7. Ⓐ Ⓑ Ⓒ Ⓓ Ⓔ

8. DISPARITY: (A) equality (B) aspersion (C) allusion (D) equanimity (E) suture   8. Ⓐ Ⓑ Ⓒ Ⓓ Ⓔ

9. APOTHEGM: (A) cliché (B) vague utterance (C) prolix statement (D) piety (E) letter   9. Ⓐ Ⓑ Ⓒ Ⓓ Ⓔ

10. CHARY: (A) lavish (B) malevolent (C) insinuating (D) sparing (E) irritable   10. Ⓐ Ⓑ Ⓒ Ⓓ Ⓔ

11. CANDOR: (A) hypocrisy (B) ingenuousness (C) sweetmeat (D) pleasure (E) velocity   11. Ⓐ Ⓑ Ⓒ Ⓓ Ⓔ

12. EQUIVOCATE: (A) lie (B) whisper (C) balance (D) state (E) be unequal   12. Ⓐ Ⓑ Ⓒ Ⓓ Ⓔ

13. ESTRANGED: (A) reconciled (B) similar (C) foreign (D) traded (E) embarrassed   13. Ⓐ Ⓑ Ⓒ Ⓓ Ⓔ

14. PRETENTIOUS: (A) real (B) excusing (C) modest (D) unpardonable (E) typical   14. Ⓐ Ⓑ Ⓒ Ⓓ Ⓔ

15. SUB ROSA: (A) shameless (B) oral (C) fashionable (D) open (E) simple   15. Ⓐ Ⓑ Ⓒ Ⓓ Ⓔ

16. SUBSERVIENT: (A) brutal (B) omnipresent (C) tyrannical (D) haughty (E) miserly   16. Ⓐ Ⓑ Ⓒ Ⓓ Ⓔ

17. UNTENABLE: (A) rented (B) verifiable (C) occupied (D) permanent (E) picayune   17. Ⓐ Ⓑ Ⓒ Ⓓ Ⓔ

18. Ⓐ Ⓑ Ⓒ Ⓓ Ⓔ **18.** HERBIVOROUS: (A) ravenous (B) omnivorous (C) carnivorous (D) voracious (E) veracious

19. Ⓐ Ⓑ Ⓒ Ⓓ Ⓔ **19.** OPULENCE: (A) glamor (B) sobriety (C) badinage (D) penury (E) petulance

20. Ⓐ Ⓑ Ⓒ Ⓓ Ⓔ **20.** PAEAN: (A) jeremiad (B) evaluation (C) lampoon (D) denunciation (E) elegy

21. Ⓐ Ⓑ Ⓒ Ⓓ Ⓔ **21.** VAUNTED: (A) nameless (B) belittled (C) crept (D) worried (E) wicked

22. Ⓐ Ⓑ Ⓒ Ⓓ Ⓔ **22.** CEDE: (A) request (B) harvest (C) annex (D) examine (E) mimic

23. Ⓐ Ⓑ Ⓒ Ⓓ Ⓔ **23.** OBFUSCATE: (A) clarify (B) magnify (C) intensify (D) belittle (E) describe

24. Ⓐ Ⓑ Ⓒ Ⓓ Ⓔ **24.** CONCAVE: (A) blunt (B) solid (C) convex (D) complex (E) broken

25. Ⓐ Ⓑ Ⓒ Ⓓ Ⓔ **25.** PRECIPITATE: (A) wary (B) level (C) audacious (D) masterly (E) conquered

Answer Key

Antonyms

EXERCISE A			EXERCISE B			EXERCISE C			EXERCISE D		
1. A	11. B	21. E	1. A	11. B	21. A	1. E	11. D	21. D	1. A	11. A	21. B
2. C	12. C	22. C	2. B	12. D	22. B	2. D	12. A	22. A	2. B	12. D	22. C
3. D	13. B	23. B	3. A	13. B	23. C	3. A	13. E	23. C	3. D	13. A	23. A
4. A	14. A	24. C	4. B	14. B	24. C	4. C	14. C	24. D	4. B	14. C	24. C
5. D	15. A	25. E	5. C	15. D	25. D	5. B	15. E	25. C	5. C	15. D	25. A
6. E	16. E		6. B	16. C		6. C	16. A		6. B	16. D	
7. D	17. C		7. C	17. B		7. B	17. C		7. E	17. B	
8. B	18. C		8. A	18. A		8. C	18. E		8. A	18. C	
9. E	19. B		9. D	19. D		9. D	19. B		9. C	19. D	
10. A	20. C		10. E	20. E		10. D	20. B		10. A	20. D	

Analogies

The purpose of this type of question is to test your ability to determine relationships between pairs of words. This may involve finding a relationship between a tangible situation and a more abstract one, or it may center around synonyms, antonyms, cause and effect, or other relationships.

On the GMAT you are given a pair of words printed in capital letters and five other lettered pairs. You must select the pair of words from among the five lettered choices that best matches the relationship of the first pair. For example:

TREE : FOREST :: (A) daisy : meadow (B) grass : lawn (C) wheat : farm (D) flower : garden (E) frog : pond

The first step in finding the answer to an analogy problem is to determine the relationship existing between the initial word-pair. In this instance, it is a part-to-whole relationship. Looking at the choices, you can see that B is the correct answer because a lawn would not exist without grass—TREE is to FOREST as *grass* is to *lawn*. The other choices are not satisfactory because daisies do not make up a meadow, wheat does not make up a farm, gardens don't necessarily have to have flowers (e.g., a vegetable garden), and ponds are not made up of frogs.

Consider the following example:

POSSESS : LOSE :: (A) hesitate : advance (B) cease : recur (C) undertake : perform (D) continue : desist (E) produce : supply

The initial words are opposite in meaning. Therefore, you can immediately eliminate choices C and E as they represent synonyms. Choice A is poor because hesitate and advance aren't clear opposites. Choice B is better, but the concept of repetition in recur is not found in lose. Choice D is the best answer—POSSESS is to LOSE as *continue* is to *desist*.

There are many possible relationships that can exist between words. The following list presents some of the more common ones you may encounter.

1. Worker and article created

> carpenter : house
> writer : book
> composer : symphony

2. Worker and tool used

> carpenter : saw
> writer : typewriter
> surgeon : scalpel

3. Tool and object worked on

> pencil : paper
> saw : wood

4. The act the tool does to the object it works on

> saw : cut
> knife : slice
> brake : stop

5. Time sequence

> early : late
> dawn : twilight
> inception : conclusion

6. Cause and effect

> germ : disease
> carelessness : accident
> explosion : debris

7. Degree of intensity

> tepid : hot
> joy : ecstasy
> fondness : love

8. Class — species

> furniture : chair
> insect : grasshopper
> mammal : whale
> dog : poodle

9. Type — characteristic

> cow : herbivorous
> tiger : carnivorous

10. Synonyms

> lie : prevaricate
> kind : benevolent

11. Antonyms

> never : always
> love : hate
> fancy : plain
> real : fictional

12. Person and thing he or she seeks

> alchemist : elixir
> prospector : bonanza

13. Person and thing he or she learns to avoid

      child : fire
      pilot : reef

14. Part to the whole

      soldier : regiment
      star : constellation

15. Sex

      duck : drake
      bull : cow

The following exercises will give you more practice in solving analogies. Answers to all exercises are located after Exercise D.

Practice Exercises

Analogies

EXERCISE A

DIRECTIONS: For each question below, determine the relationship between the pair of capitalized words and then select the lettered pair of words which have a similar relationship to the first pair.

1. QUIXOTIC : FEASIBLE :: (A) sudden : workable (B) theoretical : practical (C) fashionable : efficient (D) precise : practicable (E) sad : adept
    1. Ⓐ Ⓑ Ⓒ Ⓓ Ⓔ

2. DEBATE : FORENSIC :: (A) drama : histrionic (B) opera : spoken (C) concerto : harmonizing (D) argument : domestic (E) novel : original
    2. Ⓐ Ⓑ Ⓒ Ⓓ Ⓔ

3. ANTHOLOGY : POEMS :: (A) antipasto : hors d'oeuvres (B) volume : book (C) encyclopedia : words (D) thesaurus : synonyms (E) medley : arrangement
    3. Ⓐ Ⓑ Ⓒ Ⓓ Ⓔ

4. ANHYDROUS : SATURATED :: (A) dry : wet (B) sweet : wet (C) cloying : full (D) stolid : liquid (E) glorious : depleted
    4. Ⓐ Ⓑ Ⓒ Ⓓ Ⓔ

5. Ⓐ Ⓑ Ⓒ Ⓓ Ⓔ   5. WINE : GRAPES :: (A) champagne : bubbles   (B) cane : sugar   (C) vineyard : winery   (D) whiskey : hops   (E) vodka : potatoes

6. Ⓐ Ⓑ Ⓒ Ⓓ Ⓔ   6. NOTABLE : NOTORIOUS :: (A) philanthropic : benevolent   (B) philandering : pleasant   (C) heinous : atrocious   (D) nefarious : secret   (E) philanthropic : miserly

7. Ⓐ Ⓑ Ⓒ Ⓓ Ⓔ   7. ENTREPRENEUR : LABORER :: (A) profits : wages   (B) arbitrator : capitalist   (C) mediator : conflict   (D) employee : worker   (E) capitalism : communism

8. Ⓐ Ⓑ Ⓒ Ⓓ Ⓔ   8. MORPHINE : SEDATE :: (A) drug : addict   (B) liquor : intoxicate   (C) medicine : soothe   (D) oil : smear   (E) bandage : heal

9. Ⓐ Ⓑ Ⓒ Ⓓ Ⓔ   9. PLAY : SOLILOQUY :: (A) drama : tragedy   (B) trust : monopoly   (C) opera : aria   (D) novel : theme   (E) play : act

10. Ⓐ Ⓑ Ⓒ Ⓓ Ⓔ   10. CONTINENT : IMMORAL :: (A) wishful : evil   (B) dissolute : lascivious   (C) restrained : wanton   (D) dry : dismal   (E) conscientious : sinful

11. Ⓐ Ⓑ Ⓒ Ⓓ Ⓔ   11. MENDICANT : IMPECUNIOUS :: (A) critic : quizzical   (B) complainer : petulant   (C) hat : askew   (D) liar : poor   (E) philanthropist : prodigal

12. Ⓐ Ⓑ Ⓒ Ⓓ Ⓔ   12. APOSTATE : RELIGION :: (A) loyalist : faith   (B) traitor : country   (C) renegade : law   (D) vitality : church   (E) turncoat : colonies

13. Ⓐ Ⓑ Ⓒ Ⓓ Ⓔ   13. DERMATOLOGIST : SKIN :: (A) paleontologist : statues   (B) genealogist : genes   (C) cardiologist : heart   (D) astrologist : future   (E) psychologist : insanity

14. Ⓐ Ⓑ Ⓒ Ⓓ Ⓔ   14. SEE : EYES :: (A) grapple : iron   (B) grasp : hands   (C) lisp : speech   (D) limp : limbs   (E) sneeze : nostrils

15. Ⓐ Ⓑ Ⓒ Ⓓ Ⓔ   15. CYNOSURE : BRILLIANT :: (A) student : attentive   (B) map : legible   (C) rock : large   (D) word : common   (E) magnet : attractive

16. Ⓐ Ⓑ Ⓒ Ⓓ Ⓔ   16. NUMERATOR : DENOMINATOR :: (A) fraction : decimal   (B) divisor : quotient   (C) ratio : proportion   (D) dividend : divisor   (E) multiplication : division

17. Ⓐ Ⓑ Ⓒ Ⓓ Ⓔ   17. NOISOME : GARBAGE :: (A) liquid : perfume   (B) heavy : metal   (C) loud : music   (D) warm : snow   (E) fragrant : incense

18. SAD : DOLOROUS :: (A) rich : wealthy (B) smart : smug (C) weak :   18. Ⓐ Ⓑ Ⓒ Ⓓ Ⓔ
healthy (D) generous : free (E) grateful : frugal

19. SCHOOL : TUITION :: (A) game : loss (B) lawyer : client (C) hospital   19. Ⓐ Ⓑ Ⓒ Ⓓ Ⓔ
: insurance (D) church : tithe (E) library : fine

20. DISSERTATION : IDEAS :: (A) propaganda : facts (B) novel : theme   20. Ⓐ Ⓑ Ⓒ Ⓓ Ⓔ
(C) poem : emotions (D) play : acting (E) essay : novel

21. NAIVE : INGENUOUS :: (A) ordinary : ingenious (B) old : wise (C)   21. Ⓐ Ⓑ Ⓒ Ⓓ Ⓔ
simple : kind (D) eager : reserved (E) sophisticated : urbane

22. TERMAGANT : SHREW :: (A) anteater : mouse (B) virago : scold (C)   22. Ⓐ Ⓑ Ⓒ Ⓓ Ⓔ
supporter : nag (D) cuckold : lover (E) harpy : warlock

23. CLOUD : STORM :: (A) trembling : earthquake (B) portent : disaster   23. Ⓐ Ⓑ Ⓒ Ⓓ Ⓔ
(C) tornado : gale (D) thunder : lightning (E) rain : wind

24. CONDUIT : WATER :: (A) pump : oil (B) behavior : liquid (C) artery :   24. Ⓐ Ⓑ Ⓒ Ⓓ Ⓔ
blood (D) wire : sound (E) electricity : television

25. BREAD : OVEN :: (A) ceramics : kiln (B) silo : corn (C) pottery :   25. Ⓐ Ⓑ Ⓒ Ⓓ Ⓔ
wheel (D) iron : furnace (E) cake : stove

EXERCISE B

DIRECTIONS: For each question below, determine the relationship between the pair of
capitalized words and then select the lettered pair of words which have a similar relationship to
the first pair.

1. STARS : NAVIGATION :: (A) wheel : transportation (B) track : train   1. Ⓐ Ⓑ Ⓒ Ⓓ Ⓔ
(C) runway : flight (D) road map : motoring (E) trajectory : gun

2. ANTIMACASSAR : SOFA :: (A) rug : floor (B) table : chair (C) door   2. Ⓐ Ⓑ Ⓒ Ⓓ Ⓔ
: window (D) picture : frame (E) pillow : bed

3. PERIMETER : ADDITION :: (A) arithmetic : geometry (B) exponent :   3. Ⓐ Ⓑ Ⓒ Ⓓ Ⓔ
quadratic (C) line : logarithm (D) triangle : sphere (E) area :
multiplication

4. Ⓐ Ⓑ Ⓒ Ⓓ Ⓔ **4.** ACTUARY : INSURANCE :: (A) librarian : school (B) historian : dates (C) veterinarian : animal husbandry (D) agronomist : nutrition (E) vegetarian : meat

5. Ⓐ Ⓑ Ⓒ Ⓓ Ⓔ **5.** ISOLATIONIST : ALOOF :: (A) altruist : selfish (B) pessimist : hopeless (C) scholar : proud (D) bigot : tolerant (E) segregationist : gregarious

6. Ⓐ Ⓑ Ⓒ Ⓓ Ⓔ **6.** WATER : CONDUIT :: (A) electricity : magnet (B) elevator : shaft (C) rifle : shell (D) noise : cannon (E) soda : bottle

7. Ⓐ Ⓑ Ⓒ Ⓓ Ⓔ **7.** PLAINTIFF : DEFENDANT :: (A) court : law (B) injured : accused (C) judge : jury (D) attorney : lawyer (E) noble : serf

8. Ⓐ Ⓑ Ⓒ Ⓓ Ⓔ **8.** EXPLOSIVE : VOLCANO :: (A) cold : mountain (B) arid : desert (C) humid : valley (D) misty : morning (E) fertile : plain

9. Ⓐ Ⓑ Ⓒ Ⓓ Ⓔ **9.** BIZARRE : EXOTIC :: (A) tragic : convivial (B) commonplace : routine (C) wild : tame (D) ordinary : exceptional (E) lively : livid

10. Ⓐ Ⓑ Ⓒ Ⓓ Ⓔ **10.** DOCTOR : DISEASE :: (A) psychiatrist : maladjustment (B) teacher : pupil (C) scholar : knowledge (D) judge : crime (E) lawyer : law

11. Ⓐ Ⓑ Ⓒ Ⓓ Ⓔ **11.** SHOWER : DELUGE :: (A) irritation : rage (B) awe : rapture (C) passion : ardor (D) surprise : frustration (E) flow : surge

12. Ⓐ Ⓑ Ⓒ Ⓓ Ⓔ **12.** DRAMA : PLAYWRIGHT :: (A) act : actor (B) words : author (C) poetics : poet (D) review : critic (E) opera : musician

13. Ⓐ Ⓑ Ⓒ Ⓓ Ⓔ **13.** ALWAYS : NEVER :: (A) often : rarely (B) frequently : sometimes (C) constantly : frequently (D) intermittently : casually (E) occasionally : repeatedly

14. Ⓐ Ⓑ Ⓒ Ⓓ Ⓔ **14.** PRESIDENT : POPE :: (A) election : selection (B) ballot : smoke (C) proclamation : encyclical (D) cabinet : laiety (E) leader : religion

15. Ⓐ Ⓑ Ⓒ Ⓓ Ⓔ **15.** PERMANENT : EVANESCENT :: (A) durable : fleeting (B) lasting : glittering (C) eternal : everlasting (D) static : mobile (E) comparative : superlative

16. Ⓐ Ⓑ Ⓒ Ⓓ Ⓔ **16.** ORNITHOLOGIST : BIRDS :: (A) aquarium : fish (B) anthropologist : norms (C) archaeologist : artifacts (D) architect : buildings (E) botanist : leaves

17. VERBS : ACTION :: (A) nouns : amplification (B) pronouns : demonstration (C) adjectives : modification (D) adverbs : connection (E) prepositions : definition 17.Ⓐ Ⓑ Ⓒ Ⓓ Ⓔ

18. OAFISH : ASTUTE :: (A) selfish : crude (B) sharp : dull (C) wise : smart (D) pedantic : thorough (E) foolish : sagacious 18.Ⓐ Ⓑ Ⓒ Ⓓ Ⓔ

19. SUGGEST : DEMAND :: (A) deny : request (B) question : ask (C) hint : blunder (D) give : receive (E) take : grab 19.Ⓐ Ⓑ Ⓒ Ⓓ Ⓔ

20. VINDICABLE : REPREHENSIBLE :: (A) mild : serious (B) bitter : sad (C) petty : harsh (D) solid : porous (E) vivid : dull 20.Ⓐ Ⓑ Ⓒ Ⓓ Ⓔ

21. FILAMENT : BULB :: (A) flame : torch (B) wick : candle (C) log : hearth (D) glow : lamp (E) battery : flashlight 21.Ⓐ Ⓑ Ⓒ Ⓓ Ⓔ

22. RIPOSTE : PARRY :: (A) forbid : allow (B) upset : remove (C) lunge : block (D) attack : fail (E) bother : quieten 22.Ⓐ Ⓑ Ⓒ Ⓓ Ⓔ

23. TRIANGLE : QUADRILATERAL :: (A) plane : solid (B) pentagon : hexagon (C) rectangle : octagon (D) cone : cube (E) ellipse : circle 23.Ⓐ Ⓑ Ⓒ Ⓓ Ⓔ

24. FINE : IMPRISONMENT :: (A) sentence : judgment (B) bail : bond (C) jury : judge (D) magistrate : judge (E) misdemeanor : felony 24.Ⓐ Ⓑ Ⓒ Ⓓ Ⓔ

25. BREAD : WHEAT :: (A) oil : corn (B) wine : grape (C) butter : cow (D) fruit : tree (E) cake : icing 25.Ⓐ Ⓑ Ⓒ Ⓓ Ⓔ

EXERCISE C

DIRECTIONS: For each question below, determine the relationship between the pair of capitalized words and then select the lettered pair of words which have a similar relationship to the first pair.

1. LIQUEFY : PETRIFY :: (A) melt : freeze (B) soften : frighten (C) cash : invest (D) boil : condense (E) blend : separate 1.Ⓐ Ⓑ Ⓒ Ⓓ Ⓔ

2. BELT : TROUSERS :: (A) braces : garters (B) trunk : tree (C) pillar : society (D) cables : trolley (E) cables : bridge 2.Ⓐ Ⓑ Ⓒ Ⓓ Ⓔ

3. Ⓐ Ⓑ Ⓒ Ⓓ Ⓔ **3. GASOLINE : PETROL ::** (A) truck : car   (B) engine : trunk   (C) stove : furnace   (D) elevator : lift   (E) fuel : lubricant

4. Ⓐ Ⓑ Ⓒ Ⓓ Ⓔ **4. RHYTHM : RHYME ::** (A) poet : versifier   (B) accent : sound   (C) prose poetry   (D) versification : scansion   (E) verse : stanza

5. Ⓐ Ⓑ Ⓒ Ⓓ Ⓔ **5. SCHOLAR : ENTREPRENEUR ::** (A) books : superstition   (B) learning : study   (C) university : laboratory   (D) knowledge : profits   (E) knowledge : research

6. Ⓐ Ⓑ Ⓒ Ⓓ Ⓔ **6. NECTAR : AMBROSIA ::** (A) frankincense : myrrh   (B) vegetable : fruit   (C) taste : smell   (D) goddess : god   (E) drink : food

7. Ⓐ Ⓑ Ⓒ Ⓓ Ⓔ **7. MUSLIN : PLAIN ::** (A) robe : decorated   (B) rag : torn   (C) crown : rich   (D) brocade : figured   (E) ermine : variegated

8. Ⓐ Ⓑ Ⓒ Ⓓ Ⓔ **8. DERIVATION : LEXICOGRAPHER ::** (A) evolution : biologist   (B) origin : typographer   (C) politics : anarchist   (D) laws : court   (E) foundation : roofer

9. Ⓐ Ⓑ Ⓒ Ⓓ Ⓔ **9. EPAULET : SHOULDER ::** (A) medal : chest   (B) knapsack : head   (C) sash : window   (D) sword : scabbard   (E) decoration : uniform

10. Ⓐ Ⓑ Ⓒ Ⓓ Ⓔ **10. SHEEP : WOOL ::** (A) fodder : animal   (B) otter : fur   (C) flax : cotton   (D) animal : vegetable   (E) animal : commodity

11. Ⓐ Ⓑ Ⓒ Ⓓ Ⓔ **11. NAIL : PUNCTURE ::** (A) sword : scabbard   (B) scalpel : incision   (C) easel : picture   (D) needle : hem   (E) tire : rim

12. Ⓐ Ⓑ Ⓒ Ⓓ Ⓔ **12. FEAR : TERROR ::** (A) danger : anxiety   (B) joy : ecstasy   (C) apprehension : worry   (D) distress : discomfort   (E) relief : relaxation

13. Ⓐ Ⓑ Ⓒ Ⓓ Ⓔ **13. SPY : SECRET ::** (A) teacher : reality   (B) detective : law   (C) reporter : news   (D) sleuth : victim   (E) operative : agent

14. Ⓐ Ⓑ Ⓒ Ⓓ Ⓔ **14. FATUOUS : INANE ::** (A) clever : inchoate   (B) querulous : picayune   (C) fatal : mordant   (D) portentous : significant   (E) cloying : viscous

15. Ⓐ Ⓑ Ⓒ Ⓓ Ⓔ **15. LUNGS : BLOOD ::** (A) heart : circulation   (B) arteries : veins   (C) carburetor : car   (D) glands : secretions   (E) carburetor : gasoline

16. SCALES : JUSTICE :: (A) weights : measures (B) markets : courts (C) 16. Ⓐ Ⓑ Ⓒ Ⓓ Ⓔ
torch : liberty (D) laurel : peace (E) balance : right

17. DIAPHANOUS : CACOPHONOUS :: (A) twofold : multiple (B) sheer : 17. Ⓐ Ⓑ Ⓒ Ⓓ Ⓔ
transparent (C) sheer : opaque (D) harmonious : discordant (E) transparent
: noisy

18. BLEEDING : TOURNIQUET :: (A) drowning : resuscitation (B) sun- 18. Ⓐ Ⓑ Ⓒ Ⓓ Ⓔ
stroke : fatigue (C) traffic : roadblock (D) coughing : elixir (E) disease :
microbe

19. DETRITUS : GLACIERS :: (A) ice : icebergs (B) thaw : cold (C) silt 19. Ⓐ Ⓑ Ⓒ Ⓓ Ⓔ
: rivers (D) sediment : bottom (E) dregs : society

20. EXCULPATE : INCRIMINATE :: (A) exonerate : involve (B) free : 20. Ⓐ Ⓑ Ⓒ Ⓓ Ⓔ
fine (C) blame : criticize (D) blame : pardon (E) excuse : free

21. TRUMPET : BRASS :: (A) drums : hide (B) bugle : bronze (C) cello : 21. Ⓐ Ⓑ Ⓒ Ⓓ Ⓔ
string (D) orchestra : band (E) horn : metal

22. SANDPAPER : ABRASIVE :: (A) polish : detergent (B) pumice : 22. Ⓐ Ⓑ Ⓒ Ⓓ Ⓔ
emulsion (C) gasoline : refined (D) oil : lubricant (E) gratuity : irritant

23. TOBACCO : PIPE :: (A) incense : church (B) wood : stove (C) alcohol 23. Ⓐ Ⓑ Ⓒ Ⓓ Ⓔ
: bottle (D) coal : chute (E) smoke : chimney

24. HABITS : INSTINCTS :: (A) work : play (B) training : heredity (C) 24. Ⓐ Ⓑ Ⓒ Ⓓ Ⓔ
nerves : brain (D) learning : force (E) birds : animals

25. AMBULATORY : BEDRIDDEN :: (A) rapid : slow (B) healthy : sick 25. Ⓐ Ⓑ Ⓒ Ⓓ Ⓔ
(C) strong : restrained (D) venial : sinister (E) free : confined

EXERCISE D

DIRECTIONS: For each question below, determine the relationship between the pair of
capitalized words and then select the lettered pair of words which have a similar relationship
to the first pair.

1. PARIAH : FAVORITE :: (A) nephew : son (B) hypnotism : victim (C) 1. Ⓐ Ⓑ Ⓒ Ⓓ Ⓔ
sycophant : toady (D) outcast : chosen (E) chosen : accepted

2. Ⓐ Ⓑ Ⓒ Ⓓ Ⓔ   2.   GOLF : HOLES :: (A) badminton : feather (B) football : kick (C) baseball : innings (D) tennis : net (E) swimming : pool

3. Ⓐ Ⓑ Ⓒ Ⓓ Ⓔ   3.   INFANCY : SENILITY :: (A) conclusion : climax (B) helplessness : vigor (C) dawn : dusk (D) day : afternoon (E) incipience : crisis

4. Ⓐ Ⓑ Ⓒ Ⓓ Ⓔ   4.   TIRADE : ABUSIVE :: (A) monologue : lengthy (B) aphorism : boring (C) prologue : explanatory (D) encomium : laudatory (E) critique : insolent

5. Ⓐ Ⓑ Ⓒ Ⓓ Ⓔ   5.   GOOSE : GANDER :: (A) lion : lioness (B) shark : sharkskin (C) duck : drake (D) male : female (E) master : slave

6. Ⓐ Ⓑ Ⓒ Ⓓ Ⓔ   6.   GRAIN : DRUG :: (A) container : fruit (B) ounce : coal (C) bushel : fruit (D) point : diamond (E) mortar : bricks

7. Ⓐ Ⓑ Ⓒ Ⓓ Ⓔ   7.   PADDLE : CANOE :: (A) propellor : airplane (B) motor : auto (C) oar : steamship (D) wing : rocket (E) rudder : boat

8. Ⓐ Ⓑ Ⓒ Ⓓ Ⓔ   8.   THERMOMETER : TEMPERATURE :: (A) minute : time (B) gauge : pressure (C) calendar : year (D) stopwatch : speed (E) barometer : weather

9. Ⓐ Ⓑ Ⓒ Ⓓ Ⓔ   9.   SYNTHESIS : CONSTRUCTION :: (A) artifice : building (B) dissection : analysis (C) excuse : denial (D) induction : logic (E) elaboration : imagination

10. Ⓐ Ⓑ Ⓒ Ⓓ Ⓔ   10.   PLEBISCITE : UKASE :: (A) ballot : pen (B) lack : abundance (C) public : ruler (D) dictator : tyrant (E) democratic : political

11. Ⓐ Ⓑ Ⓒ Ⓓ Ⓔ   11.   IAMBIC : DACTYLIC :: (A) regular : bounding (B) poetic : musical (C) duple : triple (D) rhythmic : metrical (E) strict : loose

12. Ⓐ Ⓑ Ⓒ Ⓓ Ⓔ   12.   PARTY : AGREEMENT :: (A) owner : lease (B) partner : contract (C) henchman : plot (D) accessory : crime (E) signatory : treaty

13. Ⓐ Ⓑ Ⓒ Ⓓ Ⓔ   13.   INKBLOT : EYE CHART :: (A) blur : letter (B) blotter : spectacles (C) physician : specialist (D) psychiatrist : optometrist (E) oculist : ophthalmologist

14. TULIP : ZINNIA :: (A) autumn : fall (B) garden : meadow (C) bulb :   14. Ⓐ Ⓑ Ⓒ Ⓓ Ⓔ
seed (D) blossom : fruit (E) flower : grass

15. LIGAMENT : TEAR :: (A) fat : breakdown (B) muscle : train (C)   15. Ⓐ Ⓑ Ⓒ Ⓓ Ⓔ
bone : fracture (D) ankle : twist (E) heart : stroke

16. LEGISLATOR : LAW :: (A) judge : court (B) policeman : crime (C)   16. Ⓐ Ⓑ Ⓒ Ⓓ Ⓔ
attorney : suit (D) king : justice (E) magistrate : doctrine

17. DEBATER : LARYNGITIS :: (A) actor : applause (B) doctor :   17. Ⓐ Ⓑ Ⓒ Ⓓ Ⓔ
diagnosis (C) writer : paper (D) pedestrian : lameness

18. DAFFODILS : TREES :: (A) spring : summer (B) fish : frogs (C) lake :   18. Ⓐ Ⓑ Ⓒ Ⓓ Ⓔ
meadow (D) snakes : grass (E) garden : orchard

19. KNIGHT : SHIELD :: (A) fencer : saber (B) soldier : carbine (C)   19. Ⓐ Ⓑ Ⓒ Ⓓ Ⓔ
welder : goggles (D) mechanic : wrench (E) lord : escutcheon

20. FURLONG : MILE :: (A) second : time (B) degree : thermometer (C)   20. Ⓐ Ⓑ Ⓒ Ⓓ Ⓔ
foot : meter (D) ounce : weight (E) pint : gallon

21. CANINE : HOUND :: (A) equine : thoroughbred (B) feline : rat (C)   21. Ⓐ Ⓑ Ⓒ Ⓓ Ⓔ
ursine : cub (D) bovine : cattle (E) porcine : glutton

22. CONVICTION : INTELLECT :: (A) speech : propaganda (B) belief :   22. Ⓐ Ⓑ Ⓒ Ⓓ Ⓔ
religion (C) facts : statistics (D) court : home (E) response : emotion

23. BEREAVED : CONDOLENCES :: (A) guilty : accusation (B) faulty :   23. Ⓐ Ⓑ Ⓒ Ⓓ Ⓔ
eraser (C) robbed : insurance (D) victorious : wealth (E) destitute : charity

24. SAIL : MAST :: (A) wash : line (B) shade : lamp (C) tent : stake (D)   24. Ⓐ Ⓑ Ⓒ Ⓓ Ⓔ
flag : pole (E) sheet : scaffold

25. BRUSH : PAINT :: (A) hammer : nail (B) polish : floor (C) trowel :   25. Ⓐ Ⓑ Ⓒ Ⓓ Ⓔ
cement (D) match : fire (E) rake : lawn

Answer Key

Word-Pair Relationships

EXERCISE A			EXERCISE B			EXERCISE C			EXERCISE D		
1. B	11. B	21. E	1. D	11. A	21. B	1. A	11. B	21. C	1. D	11. C	21. A
2. A	12. B	22. B	2. A	12. D	22. C	2. E	12. B	22. D	2. C	12. E	22. E
3. D	13. C	23. B	3. E	13. A	23. B	3. D	13. C	23. B	3. C	13. D	23. E
4. A	14. B	24. C	4. C	14. C	24. E	4. B	14. D	24. B	4. D	14. C	24. D
5. E	15. E	25. A	5. B	15. A	25. B	5. D	15. E	25. E	5. C	15. C	25. C
6. E	16. D		6. B	16. C		6. E	16. C		6. D	16. C	
7. A	17. E		7. B	17. C		7. D	17. E		7. A	17. D	
8. B	18. A		8. B	18. E		8. A	18. C		8. B	18. E	
9. C	19. D		9. B	19. E		9. A	19. C		9. B	19. C	
10. C	20. C		10. A	20. A		10. B	20. A		10. C	20. E	

Sentence Completions

This type of question is designed to test your skills in vocabulary *usage* and your ability to recognize consistency among the elements in a sentence. You are given a sentence in which one or two words have been omitted. You must select from five lettered choices the word or words that when inserted in the sentence blanks best complete the meaning of the sentence.

In effect, these questions are a form of reading comprehension. If you are able to recognize the implications of a sentence, you will be able to choose the words that relate to these implications. At times, your knowledge of a particular fact may help you choose the correct answer, but, for the most part, you must depend upon your ability to understand and use language. For this reason you should make sure you understand the *usage* of all vocabulary words you learn.

When answering sentence completion questions, look for key words to assist you in determining the idea being expressed in each sentence. Consider the following examples.

(A) (B) (C) (D) (E) Because the enemy had a reputation for engaging in sneak attacks, we were forced to be —— on the alert.

(A) quietly
(B) frequently
(C) constantly

(D) periodically
(E) occasionally

The key words here are *sneak attacks* and *alert*. The missing word refers to the degree of alertness necessary for protection against sneak attacks. Since one must *always* be on the alert when faced with the possibility of sneak attacks, choice C, constantly, is the best answer. The other choices can be eliminated because they do not indicate constant alertness.

(A) (B) (C) (D) (E) —— has introduced the tremendous problem of the —— of the thousands of workers replaced by machines.

(A) Specialization . . . relocation
(B) Automation . . . retraining
(C) Unemployment . . . education

(D) Disease . . . recovery
(E) Machinery . . . hiring

In this sentence the key words are *problem* and *replaced by machines*. Choice B, automation . . . retraining and choice E, machinery . . . hiring, both pertain to machines. Choice B, however, is better because *automation* implies replacing people by machines, and *retraining* states the problem resulting from this replacement. The other choices don't fit into the context of the sentence.

The following exercises will help you become adept at sentence completions. Answers to the exercises appear after Exercise D.

Practice Exercises

Sentence Completions

EXERCISE A

DIRECTIONS: For each sentence below, select the lettered word or set of words which, when inserted in the sentence blanks, best completes the meaning of that sentence.

1. The literary artist, concerned solely with the creation of a book or story as close to perfection as his powers will permit, is generally a quiet individual, contemplative,   1. Ⓐ Ⓑ Ⓒ Ⓓ Ⓔ

    (A) jovial   (D) poetic
    (B) somnolent   (E) gregarious
    (C) retiring

2. He was so _____ at tying fishermen's flies that he was asked to demonstrate his technique at sports fairs and exhibitions.   2. Ⓐ Ⓑ Ⓒ Ⓓ Ⓔ

    (A) careful   (D) gauche
    (B) adroit   (E) deliberate
    (C) inept

3. No punishment is too severe for such an _____ crime; it is almost impossible to understand its enormity.   3. Ⓐ Ⓑ Ⓒ Ⓓ Ⓔ

    (A) purposeless   (D) arbitrary
    (B) unusual   (E) egregious
    (C) exemplary

4. He was so convinced that people were driven by _____ motives that he could not believe that anyone could be unselfish.   4. Ⓐ Ⓑ Ⓒ Ⓓ Ⓔ

    (A) selfless   (D) ulterior
    (B) emotional   (E) intrinsic
    (C) altruistic

5.Ⓐ Ⓑ Ⓒ Ⓓ Ⓔ **5.** When the infant displayed signs of illness, the anxious parents called in a _____ .

    (A) podiatrist   (D) pedagogue
    (B) pediatrician   (E) plagiarist
    (C) practitioner

6.Ⓐ Ⓑ Ⓒ Ⓓ Ⓔ **6.** I can recommend him for this position because I have always found him _____ and reliable.

    (A) voracious   (D) valorous
    (B) veracious   (E) mendacious
    (C) vindictive

7.Ⓐ Ⓑ Ⓒ Ⓓ Ⓔ **7.** No hero of ancient or modern times can surpass the Indian with his lofty contempt of death and the _____ with which he sustained the cruelest affliction.

    (A) assent   (D) concern
    (B) fortitude   (E) reverence
    (C) guile

8.Ⓐ Ⓑ Ⓒ Ⓓ Ⓔ **8.** Sitting so close to the _____ section of the orchestra, I found that the incessant beating of the drums gave me a headache.

    (A) string   (D) percussion
    (B) brass   (E) front
    (C) wind

9.Ⓐ Ⓑ Ⓒ Ⓓ Ⓔ **9.** I could not wish for a more _____ occasion on which to announce my plans for enlarging our establishment.

    (A) ominous   (D) serious
    (B) propitious   (E) portentous
    (C) poignant

10.Ⓐ Ⓑ Ⓒ Ⓓ Ⓔ **10.** We ask for _____ from others, yet we are never merciful ourselves.

    (A) clemency   (D) selectivity
    (B) culpability   (E) justice
    (C) sincerity

11.Ⓐ Ⓑ Ⓒ Ⓓ Ⓔ **11.** To prevent a repetition of this dreadful occurrence, we must discover the _____ element in the food that was served.

    (A) unknown   (D) unnecessary
    (B) toxic   (E) heinous
    (C) benign

12.Ⓐ Ⓑ Ⓒ Ⓓ Ⓔ **12.** The concept of _____ grouping of people with similar interests and abilities was very popular among educators.

    (A) segregated   (D) homogeneous
    (B) integrated   (E) congruent
    (C) heterogeneous

13. His theories were so ___ that few could see what he was trying to establish.　13. Ⓐ Ⓑ Ⓒ Ⓓ Ⓔ

    (A) logical   (D) theoretical
    (B) erudite   (E) nebulous
    (C) scholarly

14. When I first began to study words in families. I was unaware that *protagonist* was the opposite of *antagonist*, that ___ was the opposite of *zenith*.　14. Ⓐ Ⓑ Ⓒ Ⓓ Ⓔ

    (A) *apex*   (D) *nadir*
    (B) *rood*   (E) *hegira*
    (C) *solstice*

15. Your ___ attitude will alienate any supporters you may have won to your cause.　15. Ⓐ Ⓑ Ⓒ Ⓓ Ⓔ

    (A) fascinating   (D) truculent
    (B) humanitarian   (E) tortuous
    (C) logical

16. We do not mean to be disrespectful when we refuse to follow the advice of our ___ leader.　16. Ⓐ Ⓑ Ⓒ Ⓓ Ⓔ

    (A) venerable   (D) gracious
    (B) respectful   (E) dynamic
    (C) famous

17. I fail to understand why there is such a ___ atmosphere; we have lost a battle, not a war.　17. Ⓐ Ⓑ Ⓒ Ⓓ Ⓔ

    (A) funereal   (D) sanguine
    (B) blatant   (E) haughty
    (C) giddy

18. When he recited the passage by ___, he revealed that he was reproducing ___ without understanding their meaning.　18. Ⓐ Ⓑ Ⓒ Ⓓ Ⓔ

    (A) sounds – concepts   (D) rote – sounds
    (B) sounds – pronunciations   (E) ideas – messages
    (C) effects – causes

19. Something that is ___ is not ___.　19. Ⓐ Ⓑ Ⓒ Ⓓ Ⓔ

    (A) trite – boring   (D) elastic – resilient
    (B) violent – vivid   (E) hackneyed – original
    (C) common – a cliché

20. When he realized that he had been induced to sign the contract by ___, he threatened to institute legal proceedings to ___ the agreement.　20. Ⓐ Ⓑ Ⓒ Ⓓ Ⓔ

    (A) force – nullify   (D) flattery – liquidate
    (B) innuendo – negate   (E) hypnotism – validate
    (C) chicanery – cancel

21. Ⓐ Ⓑ Ⓒ Ⓓ Ⓔ   **21.** An individual who is _____ is incapable of _____.

        (A) fettered — flight   (D) militant — fear
        (B) modest — shame   (E) ambitious — failure
        (C) penurious — thought

22. Ⓐ Ⓑ Ⓒ Ⓓ Ⓔ   **22.** His _____ was so marked that I teasingly suggested that he had seen a _____.

        (A) clumsiness — vision   (D) separation — lawyer
        (B) pallor — spectre   (E) visage — ghost
        (C) demeanor — physician

23. Ⓐ Ⓑ Ⓒ Ⓓ Ⓔ   **23.** A _____ statement is an _____ comparison.

        (A) sarcastic — unfair   (D) metaphorical — implied
        (B) blatant — overt   (E) bellicose — ardent
        (C) sanguine — inherent

24. Ⓐ Ⓑ Ⓒ Ⓓ Ⓔ   **24.** The hostess attempted to _____ a romantic atmosphere that would help to bring the two young people together in _____.

        (A) simulate — conflict   (D) contrive — matrimony
        (B) expand — fealty   (E) present — collusion
        (C) eliminate – love

25. Ⓐ Ⓑ Ⓒ Ⓓ Ⓔ   **25.** Old legends of extinct religions come down to us as _____ and _____.

        (A) romance — chivalry   (D) predictions — prophecies
        (B) myths — fables   (E) miracles — epiphanies
        (C) dreams — visions

EXERCISE B

DIRECTIONS: For each sentence below, select the lettered word or set of words which, when inserted in the sentence blanks, best completes the meaning of that sentence.

1. Ⓐ Ⓑ Ⓒ Ⓓ Ⓔ   **1.** As I recall my plane trip around the world last July and August, I think my greatest difficulty was the adjustment to the different _____ served with the food in the various cities we visited.

        (A) ingredients   (D) grades
        (B) condiments   (E) varieties
        (C) qualities

2. Ⓐ Ⓑ Ⓒ Ⓓ Ⓔ   **2.** After several _____ attempts to send the missile into space, the spacecraft was finally launched successfully.

        (A) abortive   (D) careful
        (B) difficult   (E) excellent
        (C) experimental

3. He worked _____ at his task for weeks before he felt satisfied that the results would   3. Ⓐ Ⓑ Ⓒ Ⓓ Ⓔ
   justify his long effort.

   (A) occasionally   (D) assiduously
   (B) complacently   (E) intermittently
   (C) bravely

4. His book was marred by the many _____ remarks, which made us forget his main   4. Ⓐ Ⓑ Ⓒ Ⓓ Ⓔ
   theme.

   (A) interesting   (D) opinionated
   (B) humorous   (E) slanted
   (C) digressive

5. Overindulgence _____ character as well as physical stamina.   5. Ⓐ Ⓑ Ⓒ Ⓓ Ⓔ

   (A) strengthens   (D) maintains
   (B) stimulates   (E) provides
   (C) debilitates

6. He was not _____ and preferred to be alone most of the time.   6. Ⓐ Ⓑ Ⓒ Ⓓ Ⓔ

   (A) antisocial   (D) cordial
   (B) gracious   (E) handsome
   (C) gregarious

7. The reasoning in this editorial is so _____ that we cannot see how anyone can be   7. Ⓐ Ⓑ Ⓒ Ⓓ Ⓔ
   deceived by it.

   (A) coherent   (D) specious
   (B) controversial   (E) chauvinistic
   (C) cogent

8. Since you have failed three of the last four tests, you cannot afford to be _____ about   8. Ⓐ Ⓑ Ⓒ Ⓓ Ⓔ
   passing for the term.

   (A) courteous   (D) passive
   (B) pessimistic   (E) indolent
   (C) sanguine

9. You are afraid to attack him directly; you, therefore, are resorting to _____ .   9. Ⓐ Ⓑ Ⓒ Ⓓ Ⓔ

   (A) violence   (D) innuendo
   (B) effrontery   (E) condemnation
   (C) criticism

10. His _____ remarks are often embarrassing because of their frankness.   10. Ⓐ Ⓑ Ⓒ Ⓓ Ⓔ

   (A) sarcastic   (D) urbane
   (B) sadistic   (E) ingenuous
   (C) subtle

11. Ⓐ Ⓑ Ⓒ Ⓓ Ⓔ   **11.** The pioneers' greatest asset was not their material wealth but their _____.

    (A) fortitude   (D) companions
    (B) tribulations   (E) possessions
    (C) largesse

12. Ⓐ Ⓑ Ⓒ Ⓓ Ⓔ   **12.** Your _____ tactics may compel me to cancel the contract because the job must be finished on time.

    (A) dilatory   (D) infamous
    (B) offensive   (E) confiscatory
    (C) questionable

13. Ⓐ Ⓑ Ⓒ Ⓓ Ⓔ   **13.** Some students are _____ and want to take only the courses for which they see immediate value.

    (A) theoretical   (D) foolish
    (B) indolent   (E) opinionated
    (C) pragmatic

14. Ⓐ Ⓑ Ⓒ Ⓓ Ⓔ   **14.** Because I find that hot summer weather _____ me and leaves me very tired, I try to leave the city every August and go to Maine.

    (A) invigorates   (D) refreshes
    (B) bores   (E) disturbs
    (C) enervates

15. Ⓐ Ⓑ Ⓒ Ⓓ Ⓔ   **15.** Americans do not feel that _____ obedience and implicit submission to the will of another is necessary in order to maintain good government.

    (A) titular   (D) verbal
    (B) blind   (E) legal
    (C) partial

16. Ⓐ Ⓑ Ⓒ Ⓓ Ⓔ   **16.** Because his occupation required that he work at night and sleep during the day, he had an exceptionally _____ complexion.

    (A) ghastly   (D) plain
    (B) ruddy   (E) pallid
    (C) livid

17. Ⓐ Ⓑ Ⓒ Ⓓ Ⓔ   **17.** It is almost impossible at times to capture the _____ of words when we translate them into a foreign language.

    (A) grammar   (D) connotations
    (B) meanings   (E) sounds
    (C) denotations

18. As ____ head of the organization. he attended social functions and civic meetings   18. Ⓐ Ⓑ Ⓒ Ⓓ Ⓔ
but had no ____ in the formulation of company policy.

    (A) titular – voice   (D) real – competition
    (B) complete – vote   (E) actual – superior
    (C) nominal – equal

19. Unlike the Shakespearean plays. the "closet dramas" of the nineteenth century were   19. Ⓐ Ⓑ Ⓒ Ⓓ Ⓔ
meant to be ____ rather than ____

    (A) seen – acted   (D) sophisticated – urbane
    (B) read – acted   (E) produced – acted
    (C) quiet – loud

20. The collapse of the financial empire set up by the small group was more than a personal   20. Ⓐ Ⓑ Ⓒ Ⓓ Ⓔ
____; it affected millions of small ____.

    (A) threat – men   (D) disaster – homeowners
    (B) vision – speculators   (E) calamity – prospectors
    (C) misfortune – investors

21. Employers who retire people who are willing and able to continue working should   21. Ⓐ Ⓑ Ⓒ Ⓓ Ⓔ
realize that ____ age is not an effective ____ in determining whether an individual
is capable of working.

    (A) physical – barrier   (D) chronological – criterion
    (B) chronological – factor   (E) declining – standard
    (C) intellectual – criterion

22. Her true feelings ____ themselves in her sarcastic asides; only then was her ____   22. Ⓐ Ⓑ Ⓒ Ⓓ Ⓔ
revealed.

    (A) concealed – sweetness   (D) developed – anxiety
    (B) manifested – bitterness   (E) grieved – charm
    (C) hid – sarcasm

23. To ____ is to try to ____ an individual.   23. Ⓐ Ⓑ Ⓒ Ⓓ Ⓔ

    (A) gainsay – corrupt   (D) proselytize – convert
    (B) evacuate – dismiss   (E) inhibit – frighten
    (C) exhume – bury

24. When I listened to his cogent arguments, all my ____ were ____ and I was forced   24. Ⓐ Ⓑ Ⓒ Ⓓ Ⓔ
to agree with his point of view.

    (A) senses – stimulated   (D) questions – asked
    (B) doubts – confirmed   (E) doubts – dispelled
    (C) friends – present

25. Ⓐ Ⓑ Ⓒ Ⓓ Ⓔ **25.** She was _____ because her plans had gone _____.

    (A) pleased — awry   (D) importunate — splendidly
    (B) imminent — efficiently   (E) distraught — awry
    (C) foiled — well

EXERCISE C

DIRECTIONS: For each sentence below, select the lettered word or set of words which, when inserted in the sentence blanks, best completes the meaning of that sentence.

1. Ⓐ Ⓑ Ⓒ Ⓓ Ⓔ **1.** The ties that bind us together in common activity are so _____ that they can disappear at any moment.

    (A) numerous   (D) consistent
    (B) tenuous   (E) tenacious
    (C) restrictive

2. Ⓐ Ⓑ Ⓒ Ⓓ Ⓔ **2.** I did not anticipate reading such an _____ discussion of the international situation in the morning newspaper; normally, such a treatment could be found only in scholarly magazines.

    (A) erudite   (D) overt
    (B) arrogant   (E) interesting
    (C) ingenious

3. Ⓐ Ⓑ Ⓒ Ⓓ Ⓔ **3.** We need more men of culture and enlightenment; we have too many _____ among us.

    (A) statesmen   (D) artists
    (B) students   (E) philosophers
    (C) philistines

4. Ⓐ Ⓑ Ⓒ Ⓓ Ⓔ **4.** The Trojan War proved to the Greeks that cunning and _____ were often more effective than military might.

    (A) cruelty   (D) wisdom
    (B) artifice   (E) beauty
    (C) strength

5. Ⓐ Ⓑ Ⓒ Ⓓ Ⓔ **5.** His remarks were filled with _____, which sounded lofty but presented nothing new to the audience.

    (A) anecdotes   (D) digressions
    (B) platitudes   (E) symbols
    (C) examples

6. Ⓐ Ⓑ Ⓒ Ⓓ Ⓔ **6.** Achilles had his _____, Hitler had his Elite Corps.

    (A) myrmidons   (D) apostles
    (B) antagonists   (E) anchorites
    (C) brethren

7. In order to photograph ____ animals, elaborate flashlight equipment is necessary. 7. Ⓐ Ⓑ Ⓒ Ⓓ Ⓔ

(A) predatory   (D) live
(B) wild   (E) rare
(C) nocturnal

8. He was ____ by the charlatan who claimed he could cure all diseases with his miracle machine. 8. Ⓐ Ⓑ Ⓒ Ⓓ Ⓔ

(A) saved   (D) puzzled
(B) pleased   (E) inoculated
(C) deluded

9. The attorney protested that the testimony being offered was not ____ the case and asked that it be stricken from the record as irrelevant. 9. Ⓐ Ⓑ Ⓒ Ⓓ Ⓔ

(A) favorable to   (D) beneficial to
(B) accurate for   (E) germane to
(C) harmful to

10. Automation threatens mankind with an increased number of ____ hours. 10. Ⓐ Ⓑ Ⓒ Ⓓ Ⓔ

(A) meager   (D) complex
(B) useless   (E) leisure
(C) active

11. I was so bored with the verbose and redundant style of that writer that I welcomed the change to the ____ style of this author. 11. Ⓐ Ⓑ Ⓒ Ⓓ Ⓔ

(A) prolix   (D) logical
(B) consistent   (E) tacit
(C) terse

12. Such doltish behavior was not expected from so ____ an individual. 12. Ⓐ Ⓑ Ⓒ Ⓓ Ⓔ

(A) exasperating   (D) enigmatic
(B) astute   (E) democratic
(C) cowardly

13. Scandalized by the ____ nature of the plays being presented, the Puritans closed the theatres in 1642. 13. Ⓐ Ⓑ Ⓒ Ⓓ Ⓔ

(A) mediocre   (D) salacious
(B) fantastic   (E) witty
(C) moribund

14. John left his position with the company because he suspected that advancement was based on ____ rather than on ability. 14. Ⓐ Ⓑ Ⓒ Ⓓ Ⓔ

(A) merit   (D) salary
(B) seniority   (E) skill
(C) nepotism

15. Ⓐ Ⓑ Ⓒ Ⓓ Ⓔ

15. He became quite overbearing and domineering once he had become accustomed to the _____ shown to soldiers by the natives; he enjoyed his new sense of power.

(A) ability   (D) favor
(B) domesticity   (E) insolence
(C) deference

16. Ⓐ Ⓑ Ⓒ Ⓓ Ⓔ

16. Epicureans live for the _____ of their senses.

(A) mortification   (D) gravity
(B) removal   (E) repression
(C) gratification

17. Ⓐ Ⓑ Ⓒ Ⓓ Ⓔ

17. I grew more and more aware of Iago's _____ purpose as I watched him plant the seeds of suspicion in Othello's mind.

(A) noble   (D) unfathomable
(B) meritorious   (E) avowed
(C) fell

18. Ⓐ Ⓑ Ⓒ Ⓓ Ⓔ

18. Her reaction to his proposal was _____ ; she rejected it _____.

(A) inevitable – vehemently   (D) sympathetic – angrily
(B) subtle – violently   (E) garrulous – tersely
(C) clever – obtusely

19. Ⓐ Ⓑ Ⓒ Ⓓ Ⓔ

19. _____ is the mark of the _____.

(A) Timorousness – hero   (D) Trepidation – coward
(B) Thrift – impoverished   (E) Vanity – obsequious
(C) Avarice – philanthropist

20. Ⓐ Ⓑ Ⓒ Ⓓ Ⓔ

20. If you carry this _____ attitude to the conference, you will _____ any supporters you may have at this moment.

(A) belligerent – delight   (D) supercilious – attract
(B) truculent – alienate   (E) outspoken – alienate
(C) conciliatory – regain

21. Ⓐ Ⓑ Ⓒ Ⓓ Ⓔ

21. It hurt my pride to be forced to _____ a person who always insulted me; nevertheless, I tried to _____ him.

(A) rebuke – placate   (D) repudiate – evaluate
(B) respect – question   (E) intimidate – redeem
(C) propitiate – conciliate

22. Ⓐ Ⓑ Ⓒ Ⓓ Ⓔ

22. Because _____ is such an unsightly disease, its victims have frequently been _____.

(A) leprosy – shunned   (D) poverty – avoided
(B) cancer – numerous   (E) tuberculosis – unknown
(C) halitosis – admired

23. I am not attracted by the ____ life of the ____, always wandering through the   23. Ⓐ Ⓑ Ⓒ Ⓓ Ⓔ
countryside, begging for charity.

   (A) proud – almsgiver   (D) natural – philosopher
   (B) noble – philanthropic   (E) peripatetic – vagabond
   (C) urban – hobo

24. The sugar dissolved in the water ____; finally all that remained was an almost ____   24. Ⓐ Ⓑ Ⓒ Ⓓ Ⓔ
residue on the bottom of the glass.

   (A) quickly – lumpy   (D) subsequently – glassy
   (B) immediately – fragrant   (E) spectacularly – opaque
   (C) gradually – imperceptible

25. It is foolish to vent your spleen on an ____ object; still, you make ____ enemies that   25. Ⓐ Ⓑ Ⓒ Ⓓ Ⓔ
way.
   (A) inanimate – fewer   (D) invisible – lifelong
   (B) immobile – bitter   (E) appropriate – more
   (C) interesting – curious

EXERCISE D

DIRECTIONS: For each sentence below, select the lettered word or set of words which, when
inserted in the sentence blanks, best completes the meaning of that sentence.

1. Architects travel to Greece and Italy to ____ the Parthenon and the Pantheon.   1. Ⓐ Ⓑ Ⓒ Ⓓ Ⓔ

   (A) photograph   (D) teach about
   (B) rebuild   (E) study
   (C) demolish

2. The discoveries of science often are a mixed blessing; on the one hand, they give us
valuable pesticides that enable the farmer to grow more abundant crops, and on the   2. Ⓐ Ⓑ Ⓒ Ⓓ Ⓔ
other hand, they ____ the benefits by destroying the balance of nature.

   (A) underscore   (D) augment
   (B) misplace   (E) counteract
   (C) mollify

3. If we ____ these experienced people to positions of unimportance because of their   3. Ⓐ Ⓑ Ⓒ Ⓓ Ⓔ
political persuasions, we shall lose the services of valuably trained personnel.

   (A) define   (D) promote
   (B) elevate   (E) detract
   (C) relegate

4. Ⓐ Ⓑ Ⓒ Ⓓ Ⓔ   **4.** His ____ directions misled us; we did not know which of the two roads to take.

    (A) foolish   (D) ambiguous
    (B) painstaking   (E) arbitrary
    (C) extenuating

5. Ⓐ Ⓑ Ⓒ Ⓓ Ⓔ   **5.** I am afraid that you will have to alter your ____ views in the light of the tragic news that has just arrived.

    (A) roseate   (D) narrow
    (B) tragic   (E) dour
    (C) contrary

6. Ⓐ Ⓑ Ⓒ Ⓓ Ⓔ   **6.** You were frightened by a mere concept that you had ____ in your own mind.

    (A) rejected   (D) externalized
    (B) idealized   (E) created
    (C) sought

7. Ⓐ Ⓑ Ⓒ Ⓓ Ⓔ   **7.** Although there are still ____ outbursts of gunfire, we can report that the rebellion has been effectively suppressed.

    (A) bitter   (D) countless
    (B) heinous   (E) sporadic
    (C) meager

8. Ⓐ Ⓑ Ⓒ Ⓓ Ⓔ   **8.** He was guided by ____ rather than by ethical considerations.

    (A) expediency   (D) consequence
    (B) precepts   (E) religion
    (C) morality

9. Ⓐ Ⓑ Ⓒ Ⓓ Ⓔ   **9.** We now know that what constitutes practically all matter is empty space: relatively enormous ____ in which revolve with lightning velocity infinitesimal particles so small that they have never been seen or photographed.

    (A) seas   (D) skies
    (B) particles   (E) voids
    (C) constructs

10. Ⓐ Ⓑ Ⓒ Ⓓ Ⓔ   **10.** To be ____ is to be without ____ .

    (A) credulous – gullibility   (D) maudlin – intelligence
    (B) considerate – hostility   (E) gullible – skepticism
    (C) belligerent – pugnacity

11. Ⓐ Ⓑ Ⓒ Ⓓ Ⓔ   **11.** His listeners enjoyed his ____ wit but his victims often ____ at its satire.

    (A) lugubrious – suffered   (D) lugubrious – smiled
    (B) taut – smiled   (E) trenchant – winced
    (C) bitter – wondered

12. An occasional ____ remark spoiled the ____ that made the paper otherwise 12. Ⓐ Ⓑ Ⓒ Ⓓ Ⓔ
memorable.

(A) trite – clichés   (D) urbane – sophistication
(B) colloquial – verisimilitude   (E) jocund – gaiety
(C) hackneyed – originality

13. Unlike the carefully weighed and ____ compositions of Dante, Goethe's writings 13. Ⓐ Ⓑ Ⓒ Ⓓ Ⓔ
have always the sense of ____ and enthusiasm.

(A) inspired – vigor   (D) planned – immediacy
(B) spontaneous – immediacy   (E) developed – construction
(C) contrived – languor

14. In Homer's work, Achilles is the ____ of Greek warriors; Odysseus ____ the 14. Ⓐ Ⓑ Ⓒ Ⓓ Ⓔ
shrewd man.

(A) epitome – abhors   (D) prototype – eschews
(B) antithesis – exemplifies   (E) adversary – abhors
(C) paragon – exemplifies

15. ____ enables us to know the past and to use it in preparing for the future. 15. Ⓐ Ⓑ Ⓒ Ⓓ Ⓔ

(A) Beauty   (D) Antiquity
(B) Truth   (E) Prediction
(C) Language

16. Victims of glaucoma find that their ____ vision is impaired and that they can no 16. Ⓐ Ⓑ Ⓒ Ⓓ Ⓔ
longer see objects not directly in front of them.

(A) color   (D) ocular
(B) peripheral   (E) perspicacious
(C) nocturnal

17. The child's earliest words deal with concrete objects and actions; it is only much later 17. Ⓐ Ⓑ Ⓒ Ⓓ Ⓔ
that he is able to grapple with ____.

(A) decisions   (D) opponents
(B) abstractions   (E) mathematics
(C) maxims

18. It is regrettable that the playwright saved many of her most brilliant lines for the ____; 18. Ⓐ Ⓑ Ⓒ Ⓓ Ⓔ
by that time, most of the audience had left.

(A) ingenue   (D) prologue
(B) epilogue   (E) book
(C) intermission

19.Ⓐ Ⓑ Ⓒ Ⓓ Ⓔ **19.** It would be difficult for one so _____ to be led to believe that all men are equal and that we must disregard race, color, and creed.

    (A) emotional   (D) intolerant
    (B) broadminded   (E) democratic
    (C) tolerant

20.Ⓐ Ⓑ Ⓒ Ⓓ Ⓔ **20.** The _____ of our civilization from an agricultural society to today's complex industrial world was accompanied by upheaval and, all too often, war.

    (A) destruction   (D) metamorphosis
    (B) migration   (E) decline
    (C) contraction

21.Ⓐ Ⓑ Ⓒ Ⓓ Ⓔ **21.** To be _____ is to be _____ .

    (A) petulant – agreeable   (D) turgid – clear
    (B) turbid – swollen   (E) evergreen – deciduous
    (C) torpid – sluggish

22.Ⓐ Ⓑ Ⓒ Ⓓ Ⓔ **22.** Man is essentially a _____ animal and tends to _____ others.

    (A) selfish—deceive   (D) perverse – adopt
    (B) vicarious – work with   (E) gregarious – associate with
    (C) maudlin – belittle

23.Ⓐ Ⓑ Ⓒ Ⓓ Ⓔ **23.** Singers have a definite advantage over musicians who play an instrument; they can appeal to us through _____ as well as _____ .

    (A) personality – charm   (D) ideas – music
    (B) emotions—songs   (E) sight – personality
    (C) thoughts – ideas

24.Ⓐ Ⓑ Ⓒ Ⓓ Ⓔ **24.** Because the inspector gave the factory a _____ examination, he _____ many violations.

    (A) semiannual – uncovered   (D) pertinent – produced
    (B) significant – neglected   (E) routine – discovered
    (C) perfunctory – overlooked

25.Ⓐ Ⓑ Ⓒ Ⓓ Ⓔ **25.** The playwright was known not for his original ideas but for his _____ of ideas that had been propounded by others.

    (A) invention   (D) alteration
    (B) reiteration   (E) rejection
    (C) consideration

Answer Key

Sentence Completions

EXERCISE A			EXERCISE B			EXERCISE C			EXERCISE D		
1. C	11. B	21. A	1. B	11. A	21. D	1. B	11. C	21. C	1. E	11. E	21. C
2. B	12. D	22. B	2. A	12. A	22. B	2. A	12. B	22. A	2. E	12. C	22. E
3. E	13. E	23. D	3. D	13. C	23. D	3. C	13. D	23. E	3. C	13. D	23. D
4. D	14. D	24. D	4. C	14. C	24. E	4. B	14. C	24. C	4. D	14. C	24. C
5. B	15. D	25. B	5. C	15. B	25. E	5. B	15. C	25. A	5. A	15. C	25. B
6. B	16. A		6. C	16. E		6. A	16. C		6. E	16. B	
7. B	17. A		7. D	17. D		7. C	17. C		7. E	17. B	
8. D	18. D		8. C	18. A		8. C	18. A		8. A	18. B	
9. B	19. E		9. D	19. B		9. D	19. D		9. E	19. D	
10. A	20. C		10. E	20. C		10. B	20. B		10. E	20. D	

WRITING ABILITY REVIEW

Writing Ability questions test your understanding of the basic rules of English grammar, diction, and usage. Two types of Writing Ability questions have been used on the GMAT: Usage questions and Sentence Correction questions. Usage sections usually contain 25 questions to be answered in 15 minutes; Sentence Correction sections usually contain 25 questions to be answered in 20 minutes.

Sentence Correction

Each sentence in this section will be partially or totally underlined. You are asked to decide which of five multiple choices is the best phrasing of the underlined parts (Choice [A] is always the same as the original).

EXAMPLE
1. Old and withered, the child brought his great-grandmother a bouquet of roses.

    (A) Old and withered, the child brought his great-grandmother
    (B) The child brought his great-grandmother, old and withered
    (C) The old and withered child brought his great-grandmother
    (D) The child brought his old and withered great-grandmother
    (E) Old and withered, his great-grandmother brought the child

ANSWER AND ANALYSIS
The problem is where to place "old and withered" in order to clarify the meaning of the sentence. (D) is the best choice.

Usage

For each sentence in this section, four words or short phrases are underlined. Each underlined part is labeled (A), (B), (C), or (D). You are to decide if any underlined part is incorrect (e.g., contains an error in grammar, usage, diction, or idiom) and mark the appropriate letter on your answer sheet. If none of the choices is incorrect, mark E (No Error).

EXAMPLE

1. While I <u>swum</u> in the mountain lake, the <u>still trees</u> <u>around</u> me seemed <u>to be</u> watching.
         (A)   (B)   (C)   (D)

   <u>No error.</u>
      E

ANSWER AND ANALYSIS

"Swum" (A) is incorrect; the correct verb is "Swam."

Either question type may appear on the GMAT you take. It is even possible that both may be used. Therefore, you should be prepared to handle both types of questions.

Writing Ability—What is Measured

This section does not really test your ability to write; only a test in which you actually write essays can do that. Measured here is your skill at spotting the kinds of errors which are defined by the testmakers. You will not be required to make subjective judgments about style, tone, awkwardness, and so forth; the errors in the test problems will be fairly clear-cut.

Because this section is a limited test of language skills, it would be unwise for you to do unlimited study; a complete review of grammar and usage rules is probably not necessary. Efficient preparation for this section consists of reviewing the types of errors which are likely to appear on the test. This chapter provides such a review, classifying the errors which often show up on standardized tests such as the GMAT.

Certain grammar and usage testbooks emphasize the importance of knowing the *names* of sentence parts and suggest that you memorize the definitions of terms such as "nonrestrictive modifier," "conjunctive adverb," "pronomial reference," and so forth. But knowing such terms will be little help when you take the GMAT; you need only spot errors, not define them. In this book we will avoid using formal grammatical terms whenever possible. Following are brief definitions of some basic terms; you are probably familiar with most of them.

1. **Noun:** nouns name people, places, things, animals, concepts

                ↓   ↓   ↓   ↓   ↓

        boy   university car   dog   democracy

2. **Pronoun:** a substitute for a noun.

Noun	Pronoun
boy	he, his, him, who, whom
girl	she, her, who, whom
car	it, its, that, this, which, what
people	they, their, them, those

3. **Verbs:** name a present, past, or future action or state of being.

Present tense	I *am*	He *reads*	We *dance*
Past tense	I *was, have been*	He *read*	We *danced, have danced*
Future tense	I *will be*	He *will read*	We *will dance*

There are some other, slightly more complex verb forms which we will describe later with specific examples.

4. Subject—Object: The subject of a sentence is the *doer;* the object is the *receiver.* The subject usually comes before the verb, the object after the verb.

EXAMPLES

    a.   John   admires   Harry.
             ↓   ↓   ↓
       Subject Verb   Object

    b.   <u>John</u>, along with everyone of the players from all five teams in the division, Subject
       <u>admires Harry</u> for his great contribution to a successful season.
         Verb Object

A sentence with no object:

EXAMPLE

The <u>crate</u> of apples, oranges, and pears <u>arrived</u> safely.
    Subject   Verb

5. Adjective and Adverb:
    An adjective describes a *noun.*

EXAMPLES

    a. Be a *nice* boy.
    b. Jim was a *slow* runner.

An adverb describes an *action* and usually ends with *-ly.*

EXAMPLES

    a. He behaved very *nicely* at the party.
    b. Running *slowly,* Jim was the last to finish the race.

Review of Basic Rules of Diction and Grammar

Poor Diction

Diction refers to the choice of words used in writing. Errors in diction include words used improperly because they do not make sense in the sentence or because they are not acceptable in standard written Engish.

EXAMPLES

    a. Too busy to read *Gone with The Wind,* Harry relied on a *synthesis* of the novel.

ANSWER AND ANALYSIS

The meaning of "synthesis" (combination of parts to form a whole) does not make good sense in the sentence; the correct word is "synopsis" (summary).

    b. The explorers of the sixteenth century were willing to brave unknown regions, *irregardless* of the consequences.

ANSWER AND ANALYSIS

"Irregardless" is not acceptable in standard written English; "regardless" is.

The Most Common Diction Error: Confusion of Homonyms

A diction error often involves one word which might be confused with another because the two *sound alike*. Following is a list of many such pairs:

Homonyms and Words Easily Confused

1. **adapt/adept**
    adapt—change, adjust
    adept—highly skilled
2. **advice/advise**
    advice—counsel (n.)
    advise—to give advice to (v.)
3. **affect/effect**
    affect—influence (v.)
    effect—result (n.)
4. **afflicted/inflicted**
    afflicted—stricken, greatly distressed
    inflicted—caused (physical wounds); imposed (punishment)
5. **affront/confront**
    affront—to insult openly
    confront—to face boldly
6. **alteration/altercation**
    alteration—a change
    altercation—heated argument
7. **allude/elude**
    allude—to refer indirectly
    elude—to escape from; evade
8. **allusion/illusion/delusion**
    allusion—a casual reference
    illusion—unreal image
    delusion—a false belief
9. **apprise/appraise**
    apprise—to notify
    appraise—to estimate the value of
10. **beside/besides**
    beside—near
    besides—in addition
11. **capital/Capitol**
    capital—punishable by death; wealth
    Capitol—the U.S. house of legislature
12. **caret/carrot**
    caret—a mark (∧) used in sentence correction
    carrot—an orange vegetable
13. **censor/censure**
    censor—one who screens objectionable material
    censure—condemnation
14. **cite/sight/site**
    cite—to quote (v.)
    sight—vision (n.)
    site—location (n.)
15. **coherent/inherent**
    coherent—connected; intelligible
    inherent—a natural inseparable quality
16. **collaborate/corroborate**
    collaborate—to work together
    corroborate—to confirm; support

17. **command/commend**
command—to order
commend—to praise

18. **compile/comply**
compile—to collect, assemble
comply—to give in; consent

19. **complement/compliment**
complement—that which makes complete
compliment—something said in praise

20. **conscientious/conscious**
conscientious—governed by conscience; thorough
conscious—awake, aware

21. **continual/continuous**
continual—repeated often
continuous—uninterrupted

22. **contractual/contractural**
contractual—of a contract or written agreement
contractural—common misspelling of contractual

23. **credible/creditable/credulous**
credible—believable
creditable—deserving credit or praise
credulous—gullible

24. **depredation/deprecation**
depredation—a robbing
deprecation—an expression of disapproval

25. **detain/retain**
detain—to confine; slow down
retain—to keep in possession; to remember

26. **detracted/distracted**
detracted—taken away from
distracted—diverted; confused

27. **devise/revise**
devise—to create; invent
revise—to correct; improve

28. **devolve/develop**
devolve—to pass on to another (duties)
develop—evolve, grow

29. **discouraging/disparaging**
discouraging—dismaying
disparaging—belittling

30. **disinterested/uninterested**
disinterested—impartial; unbiased
uninterested—not interested; indifferent

31. **elegant/eloquent**
elegant—tastefully luxurious
eloquent—vivid; forceful (in speech or writing)

32. **elicit/illicit**
elicit—to extract
illicit—unlawful; improper

33. **elicit/solicit**
elicit—to extract
solicit—to appeal to; to lure

34. **emigrant/immigrant**
emigrant—one who leaves a country to settle in another
immigrant—one who comes into a new country

35. **eminent/imminent/immanent**
    eminent—lofty; prominent
    imminent—impending
    immanent—inherent; universal
36. **epaulet/epithet**
    epaulet—a shoulder ornament
    epithet—a word or phrase which characterizes a person or thing
37. **epic/epoch**
    epic—a long narrative poem dealing with heroic deeds (n.); heroic, grand (adj.)
    epoch—a period of time marked by noteworthy events or people
38. **flouting/flaunting**
    flouting—mocking; scorning
    flaunting—displaying; showing off
39. **foreword/forward**
    foreword—preface or introduction to a book
    forward—toward the front; onward
40. **formally/formerly**
    formally—ceremoniously
    formerly—in the past
41. **gorilla/guerilla**
    gorilla—an ape
    guerilla—member of a small band of irregular soldiers
42. **horde/hoard**
    horde—a crowd or swarm (n.)
    hoard—a stored up supply (n.); to accumulate and store away (v.)
43. **human/humane**
    human—having the qualities of mankind
    humane—kind; civilized
44. **immorality/immortality**
    immorality—being without morals; lewdness
    immortality—the ability to live forever
45. **imply/infer**
    imply—to hint; suggest
    infer—to conclude from a known fact by reasoning
46. **incandescent/clandestine**
    incandescent—glowing; very bright
    clandestine—secret or hidden
47. **incite/insight**
    incite—to urge to action; rouse (v.)
    insight—the quality of perceptiveness (n.)
48. **incorporate/incarcerate**
    incorporate—to combine, merge; to form into a corporation
    incarcerate—to imprison
49. **incredible/incredulous**
    incredible—unbelievable
    incredulous—doubting
50. **ingenious/ingenuous**
    ingenious—clever; resourceful
    ingenuous—frank; open
51. **irrelevant/irreverent**
    irrelevant—not to the point
    irreverent—showing disrespect
52. **lay/lie**
    lay—to place; put down
    lie—to recline; to make a false statement

53. **loath/loathe**
    loath—reluctant (adj.)
    loathe—to hate (v.)
54. **luxuriant/luxurious**
    luxuriant—growing in abundance; having rich ornamentation
    luxurious—fond of luxury; rich, comfortable
55. **perpetuate/perpetrate**
    perpetuate—to cause to continue
    perpetrate—to do (something evil); to commit
56. **persecute/prosecute**
    persecute—to afflict constantly in order to injure
    prosecute—to conduct legal proceedings against
57. **personal/personnel**
    personal—private; relating to a person
    personnel—employees
58. **perspective/prospective**
    perspective—appearance as determined by distance and position
    prospective—expected; likely
59. **precede/proceed**
    precede—to come before
    proceed—to go on, continue
60. **prescribe/proscribe**
    prescribe—to order, direct; advise (as medicine)
    proscribe—to outlaw; to banish; to forbid
61. **principal/principle**
    principal—the head of a school; the amount of a debt
    principle—a fundamental law
62. **profuse/profess**
    profuse—giving freely; excessive
    profess—to declare openly
63. **prophecy/prophesy**
    prophecy—prediction of the future (n.)
    prophesy—to predict (v.)
64. **raise/rise**
    raise—to lift
    rise—to stand up; to attain a higher level
65. **relay/relate**
    relay—a race between teams (n.); to convey (v.)
    relate—to narrate; to connect (v.)
66. **repel/repeal**
    repel—to drive back to reject
    repeal—to revoke; cancel
67. **respectful/respective**
    respectful—showing consideration, regard for
    respective—particular, individual
68. **rightly/rightfully/righteously**
    rightly—justly, with good reason
    rightfully—having a lawful claim
    righteously—acting in an upright or virtuous manner
69. **ruminating/fulminating**
    ruminating—meditating or reflecting (on)
    fulminating—exploding; shouting
70. **sensual/sensuous**
    sensual—of the body; carnal
    sensuous—appealing to the senses

71. **set/sit**
   set—to put in place
   sit—to rest as on a chair
72. **staple/stable**
   staple—chief commodity; regularly stocked item
   stable—firm; fixed
73. **stationary/stationery**
   stationary—not moving; still (adj.)
   stationery—writing materials (n.)
74. **supplement/supplant**
   supplement—something added; a section added to a book, newspaper
   supplant—to forcefully replace
75. **temerity/timidity**
   temerity—rash boldness
   timidity—shyness; hesitancy
76. **their/there/they're**
   their—of, belonging to
   there—in that place
   they're—they are
77. **troop/troupe**
   troop—a group of people or animals, soldiers
   troupe—a company of actors, singers
78. **trudgery/drudgery**
   trudgery—a common misspelling of drudgery (trudge means to march wearily)
   drudgery—hard menial work
79. **weather/whether**
   weather—atmospheric conditions
   whether—if; in case
80. **wholesome/fulsome**
   wholesome—healthful
   fulsome—disgusting because of excessiveness

   Don't sit down and memorize this list, unless you have a superb memory for such things. Rather, use it this way:
1. Several times a week, take a few minutes to read through the list. Don't try memorizing it, but do look at each pair of words carefully, and repeat them silently to yourself.
2. Several times a week, look up a few of the words on the list, and try making up your own "poor diction" sentences.
3. As you work through the practice tests in this book (an additional look in the GMAT Bulletin is recommended), add the diction errors you discover to the list.
In sum, what we are suggesting here is that you work actively with words, in short, regular sessions.

Another Diction Error: Confusion of Meanings

1. **amount/number**
   "Amount" refers to part of a whole and usually refers to bulk or weight.
   Example: He ate a large amount of food.

   "Number" applies to things which may be counted.
   Example: There were a number of reasons for the decision.

2. **between/among**
   "Between" is used to talk about *two* things.
   Example: "Let's keep this between you and me."

"Among" is used for more than two things.
Example: "The test was distributed among the students in the class."

3. **famous/notorious/infamous**
"Famous"—Well-known *good* people are famous.
Example: President Carter is famous.

"Notorious" or "Infamous"—Well-known *bad* people are notorious.
Example: Bluebeard was notorious.

4. **fewer/less**
"Less" refers to something not expressed in countable units.
Example: Less snow fell this summer.

"Fewer" refers to items which can be counted.
Example: Fewer voters than were expected showed up at the polls.

5. **than/then**
"Than" is used in a comparison.
Example: He is taller than I am.

"Then" means "at that time."
Example: He finished the exam and then began wondering about the results.

6. **leave/let**
"Leave" is unacceptable when used to mean "let."
Unacceptable: Leave us talk with each other in private.
Acceptable: Let us talk . . . in private.

7. **sure/certainly**
Unacceptable: "I sure am tired."
Acceptable: "I certainly am tired."

8. **learn/teach**
"Learn" is unacceptable when used to mean "teach."
Unacceptable: He learned us how to do well on the GMAT.
Acceptable: He taught us how to do well. . . .

9. **hanged/hung**
"Hanged" refers to people who are executed; "hung" refers to objects.
Example: They hanged people who hung treasonable signs on buildings.

More Diction Errors: Nonstandard Usage

So far we've covered words whose meanings may be inappropriate on the GMAT. The test directions additionally define poor diction as word choices which are unacceptable in standard written English: e.g., slang words, colloquialisms, or words associated with a particular regional or ethnic dialect (Western, Black English, Chicano English, etc.). There is nothing "bad" about ethnic or regional dialects, but they are not part of standard written

English, which is a kind of language in itself. Following is a list of terms generally associated with nonstandard usage:

1.	thisaway	21.	theirself
2.	being that	22.	clip joint
3.	hisself	23.	nowhere near
4.	drownded	24.	anywheres
5.	hadn't ought	25.	complected
6.	kind of a	26.	different than
7.	sort of a	27.	had of
8.	theirselves	28.	inferior than
9.	would of	29.	might of
10.	can't hardly	30.	nowheres
11.	but what	31.	wasn't scarcely
12.	these here	32.	seldom ever
13.	ain't	33.	take and
14.	anyways	34.	used to could
15.	being as how	35.	try and
16.	busted	36.	off of
17.	had ought to	37.	gig
18.	ought to of	38.	rap session
19.	suppose to	39.	shebang
20.	use to	40.	pigged out

Idiom

The Sentence Correction and Usage sections may also contain errors in idiom. Idiom refers to the way words are characteristically put together; they are usually particular phrases which "sound right" to us because we are native English speakers. Some common idioms are:

get the upper hand	rise to the occasion
to come in handy	strike a bargain
how do you do	look up an old friend
catch a cold	getting on in years

As you may have noticed, some idioms make little sense when they are taken apart. Defining "strike" does not help us understand "strike a bargain," and defining "come in " does not help us understand "to come in handy." The same holds true for "take" in "take a bath." Yet such phrases are characteristic and meaningful in our language, and correct just because they are widely accepted.

An expression may be unidiomatic if it does not conform to widely-accepted usage. It's easy enough to make up unidiomatic expressions by changing idiomatic ones.

Idiomatic	Unidiomatic
To come in handy	To come for handy
Catch a cold	Retrieve a cold
Look up an old friend	Look up the old friend

Watch out for slightly-changed familiar expressions on the GMAT. Also, watch out for *unidiomatic prepositions*. Correct, idiomatic prepositions should "sound right"; incorrect, unidiomatic ones will "sound wrong."

Idiomatic	Unidiomatic
abstain *from*	abstain *with*
addicted *to*	addicted *of*
adhere *to*	adhere *for*
capable *of*	capable *to*
characteristics *of*	characteristics *by*
desire *for*	desire *of*
disagree *with*	disagree *to*

expert *in*	expert *over*
independent *of*	independent *at*
obedient *to*	obedient *in*
plan *to, for*	plan *of*
profit *by*	profit *as*
regret *for*	regret *over*
try *to*	try *after*
vie *with*	vie *of*

Diction Errors: Summary

In many "poor diction" sentences, the misused word will be one which you don't often use; it will appear to be a *formal, intellectual term.*

EXAMPLE:

William Jennings Bryan, the *imminent* speaker, never won the election to the presidency.

ANSWER AND ANALYSIS

"Imminent" stands out; it is a less familiar word than any of the rest. The correct word is *eminent (famous).* The same is true of "temerity" in the following sentence:

EXAMPLE:

Displaying great *temerity (boldness),* the thief ran away when he spotted the police.

ANSWER AND ANALYSIS

The correct word is *timidity.*

Besides diction errors which sound too formal, beware of words or phrases that sound too informal.

EXAMPLE:

Many of the loneliest people in the hospital begin speaking to theirselves.

ANSWER AND ANALYSIS

"Theirselves" is a nonstandard word and stands out here as very different from the rest of the "normal" words in the sentence.

TO BECOME GOOD AT SPOTTING DICTION ERRORS

1. Several times a week, review the diction lists included in the book.
2. Add to the lists diction errors you spot in practice tests.
3. Using the diction lists we include, make up five or ten "poor diction" sentences on your own each week.
4. When taking a practice test, look for unfamiliar or unusual words (too *formal* or too *informal*). If a word or phrase stands out, it's probably a diction error.

Faulty Grammar

To recognize faulty grammar on the GMAT, become familiar with the following types of grammar errors:

1. Pronoun errors
2. Subject-verb agreement errors
3. Verb tense errors

4. Dangling elements errors
5. Faulty parallelism errors
6. Adjective-adverb confusion errors
7. Comparison errors

This list accounts for the majority of grammar errors in the Writing Ability sections of the GMAT.

Following is a general explanation of each type of grammar error listed. More specific explanations follow each practice test.

Pronoun Errors

Many of the grammar errors on the GMAT will involve *pronouns*. When you suspect a grammar error, *examine the pronouns in the sentence first*.

It is useful to remember the correct form of personal pronouns:

I	II
SUBJECT	*OBJECT*
(Doing the action)	(Receiving the action)
I	me
he	him
she	her
who	whom
they	them
we	us
whoever	whomever

Pronoun Rule No. 1. **Never join a pronoun from column I with a pronoun from Column II.**
The following sentences are incorrect:

    I   II
She and *him* went to the movies.

                      II   I
The drunk man stumbled against *him* and *I*.

Pronoun Rule No. 2. **Column I pronouns** *usually* **occur near the** *beginning* **of a sentence and** *before* **a verb.**
    Fred, Mary, and I arrived at the party early.
Another way to check the correctness of this pronoun is to try it by itself in the sentence:
    ~~Fred, Mary, and~~ I arrived at the party early.
It *sounds* right, and is!

Pronoun Rule No. 3. **Column II pronouns** *usually* **occur near the** *end* **of a sentence and** *follow* **the verb.**
    Many of the guests at the party liked Fred, Mary, and *me*.
If you consider "me" by *itself*, you'll "hear" whether it's correct or incorrect:
    Many of the guests at the party liked ~~Fred, Mary, and~~ me.
Each of the correctly parallel phrases begins with an adjective + noun.

EXCEPTION TO RULES 2 & 3

In some sentences, the verb can be replaced with an "equals sign":
    Those who passed the test were him and me.
    Those who passed the test = him and me.
"Equals sign" verbs include "am," "are," "is," "was," "were."
Whenever an "equals sign" verb precedes a pronoun, use column I pronouns:
    Those who passed the test were *he and I*.

Pronoun Rule No. 4. Make sure that all pronouns meant to refer to another word in the sentence do so clearly. Pronouns such as "that," "this," "which," or "it" often refer to some noun already expressed in the sentence.

He bowed before the audience, *which* applauded him heartily.

"Which" here clearly refers to "audience." But what about this sentence:

Lori remembers the Beatlemania of the 1960s but doubts that *they* warranted all that attention.

"They" seems to refer to "Beatles," a word which is never stated in the sentence. "They" is incorrect because it is a vague reference.

Pronoun Rule No. 5. To check for the correctness of "who" or "whom," try *substitution*. Consider the following sentence

My speech is directed toward *whoever* is interested.

"Whoever," an expanded form of "who," is the suspicious pronoun here. First, remove the "whoever" clause from the sentence (on the test itself, *underline* the clause):

whoever is interested

Because "whoever" is a column I pronoun, other column I pronouns may be substituted to test its correctness. When testing "whoever," try substituting "he/she" or "they."

he is interested

If *"he/she" or "they" sounds right when substituted for "whoever," "whoever" is correct.* How about this sentence:

We are not sure *whom* you have decided to bring along.

First, remove the "whom" clause from the rest of the sentence:

whom you have decided to bring along

When testing "whom" (a column II pronoun), *try substituting other column II pronouns, "him" or "them."*

him you have decided to bring along

This may sound all right, but so does—

he you have decided to bring along

Since "him" and "he" both sound right, we cannot yet tell whether "who" or "whom" is correct. In this case, when substitution alone doesn't yield a clear answer, *try moving the "who" or "whom" from the beginning of the phrase to the end:*

you have decided to bring *whom* along

Then substitute:

you have decided to bring *him* along

"Him" sounds right, so "whom" is right. "Them" would sound right too. "He" or "they" would not.

Here's the *who–whom* substitution process one more time:

Frank Henderson, treasurer of the local Elks Lodge, demanded an investigation of those members whom, he said, were withholding their dues.

First, remove the "whom" clause from the rest of the sentence:

whom, he said, were withholding their dues

Next, try substituting "him" or "them." In this case, since the subject is plural, "them" is the appropriate substitution:

them, he said, were withholding their dues

"Them" doesn't sound right, so try substituting "they":

they, he said, were withholding their dues

"They" sounds right, so "who," instead of "whom," is correct.

SUMMARY OF RULE 5

1. Separate the "who" or "whom" clause from the rest of the sentence.
2. Try substituting "he/she" or "they" for "who," "him/her" or "them" for "whom." If "he/she" or "they" sounds right, "who" is correct. If "him/her" or "them" sounds right, "whom" is correct.

3. If substitution doesn't yield a clear answer, try moving the "who" or "whom" to the end of the clause. In this sentence,
   a. *Who* do you want?
   Move the "whom,"
   b. Do you want *who?*
   and try substituting "he":
   c. Do you want *he?*
   "He" sounds awkward; try substituting "him":
   d. Do you want *him?*
   "Him sounds right, so "whom," not "who," is correct: *Whom* do you want?

ANOTHER WAY TO EXPLAIN THE WHO/WHOM DISTINCTIONS

"Who" takes the place of a *subject* in a sentence, and "whom" takes the place of an *object*. If such terms are familiar to you, (there are simple examples of these terms on page 161) and *if* you can easily distinguish between subject and object, skip the substitution game when you encounter "who" or "whom." However, if the terms "subject" and "object" are not clear to you, the substitution strategy we've outlined will work just fine.

Pronoun Rule No. 6.   Don't use "you" to refer to "a person" or "one."
   INCORRECT: If *a person* smokes cigarettes, *you* will die young.
   CORRECT: If *a person* smokes cigarettes, *he or she* will die young.

Pronoun Rule No. 7.   After a preposition (a word denoting *position* or *direction*), use only column II pronouns. Some prepositions are:

about	behind	onto
above	below	over
after	by	through
against	for	to
along	from	toward
among	in	under
at	into	upon
before	like	with

Here are some examples of prepositional phrases containing column II pronouns:

after me	upon whom	against me
for her and him	with whom	among us
like us	toward them	above him and me

Subject-Verb Agreement Errors

Other common problems on the test have to do with subject-verb agreement.

Subject-Verb Rule No. 1.   If a subject is singular, the verb must also be singular; if a subject is plural, the verb must also be plural.
   The <u>crate</u> full of hats and old shoes <u>is</u> very heavy.
        S   V
   NOT: The *crate* full of hats and old shoes *are* very heavy.
   It is correct to say, "The crate is" and incorrect to say, "The crate are." You might miss this error if you mistake "hats and old shoes" for the subject.

Subject-Verb Rule No. 2.   Only the word "and" may be used to form a compound (plural) subject:
   <u>Beethoven</u> and <u>Chopin</u> were great composers.
      Plural   Plural

All other combinations are singular:

Beethoven, as well as Chopin, *was* a great composer.

Beethoven, along with Chopin, *was* a great composer.

Beethoven, in addition to Chopin, *was* a great composer.

Either Beethoven or Chopin *was* a great composer.

Special Case of Subject-Verb Rule No. 2.   When two subjects are joined by "or" and one of the subjects is singular while the other is plural, the subject closer to the verb determines the verb:

Either <u>one apple</u> or <u>two oranges</u> <u>contain</u> 100 calories.
          singular   plural   plual

Either <u>two oranges</u> or <u>one apple</u> <u>contains</u> 100 calories.
        plural   singular singular

Subject-Verb Rule No. 3.   Collective nouns, money, and measurements *used as units* are singular:

Everybody *needs* milk.

Five dollars *is* a reasonable price.

Sixty inches *is* the average height in his family.

Verb Tense Errors

Watch out for sentences which contain HAVE, WOULD HAVE, COULD HAVE, or SHOULD HAVE combined with the following:

If he *would have* worked harder, he *could have* finished the job sooner.

"Would have" and "could have" indicate that both of the actions described (working hard and finishing the job) occurred at the same time. Of course, this is wrong. Working hard comes *before* finishing the job, and to show this, "would have" needs to be changed to "had":

If he *had* worked harder, he *could have* finished the job sooner.

Following is a verb tense error which is harder to spot, because it does not contain the "would have – should have – could have" clues:

Before she was twenty-one years old, she was married and divorced.

Two actions are described here, and one (marriage and divorce) occurs before the other (turning twenty-one). To indicate the earlier action, we once again use "had":

Before she was twenty-one years old, she had been married and divorced.

Irregular Verbs: "lay" and "lie." Some verbs are "irregular"; that is, their verb tenses are not formed in the usual way. "Lay" and "lie" are two of the irregular verbs which may appear on the GMAT:

lay—to put in place

PRESENT   I *lay* the newspaper on the table.

PAST   Yesterday, I *laid* the newspaper on the table.
              Often I *have laid* the newspaper on the table.
              I *have been laying* the newspaper on the table for years.

lie—to rest

PRESENT   I *lie* down.

PAST   Yesterday, I *lay* down.
              Often I *have lain* down.
              I *have been lying* down since this morning.

Dangling Element Errors

A dangling modifier is a phrase that does not clearly refer to some word in the sentence. Most sentences with dangling modifiers have a humorous effect:

Having many bumps and curves, she drove down the road.

"Having many bumps and curves" dangles. It seems to refer to "she," but logically it *must* refer to "road." To clarify the reference, the sentence should say—

She drove down the road, which had many bumps and curves.

A dangling modifier sentence often contains up to three obvious clues:
1. A comma around the middle of the sentence;
2. Nouns or pronouns preceding and following the comma;
3. An *-ing* word near the beginning of the sentence.

Any one of these three clues may signal a dangling element. When all three are present, a "dangler" is almost certainly present. Here is our example sentence with the clues marked:

Having many bumps and curves, she drove down the road.
   -ing word   comma   nouns or pronouns preceding and following

THE TEST: *Couple the noun following the comma with the "-ing" word* and ask yourself, "Is SHE *having* many bumps and curves?" If the answer is no, the sentence is in error.

Another example:

After running for more than a mile, my lungs began to ache.
   -ing word   comma   nouns

QUESTION: Are the *lungs running?*
No! So the sentence is incorrect.

Try labeling the dangling elements as you take the practice tests. Such work will help you to spot this error on the GMAT. Some sentences containing dangling elements are special cases which do not correspond to the clues we've mentioned. Such cases are fully explained following each practice test in which they occur.

Faulty Parallelisms

Watch out for sentences which contain a series of items separated by commas. For instance:

She found it unbearable to work all day, to lie awake all night, and eating only TV dinners.

Consider the series of three items:

to *work* all day
to *lie* awake all night
eating only TV dinners

To be grammatically correct, these three phrases must be parallel, as follows:

to *work* all day	*working* all day
to *lie* awake all night	*lying* awake all night
to *eat* only TV dinners	*eating* only TV dinners

Parallel phrases each begin with the same part of speech (in this case, "-ing" words).

Here is another example:

He admired the dog's shiny coat, strong teeth, and that his sense of smell was keen.

Incorrect	*Correct*
shiny coat	shiny coat
strong teeth	strong teeth
and that his sense	keen sense of smell

Each of the correctly parallel phrases begins with an adjective + noun.

Adjective-Adverb Confusions

Adjectives answer the question, "What kind?"
> *happy* man
> *ferocious* lion → **ADJECTIVES POINT**
> *clear* day   *toward things*

Adverbs answer the question, "How?"
> walking *happily* down the street
> roaring *ferociously* → **ADVERBS POINT**
> seeing things *clearly*   *toward actions*

(Adverbs often end with -*ly*.)

A REPRESENTATIVE ADJECTIVE/ADVERB LIST

Adjective	*Adverb*
considerable	considerably
careful	carefully
horrible	horribly
distant	distantly
deep	deeply
quick	quickly
hungry	hungrily
crazy	crazily
awful	awfully
good	well

Difficult sentences are those such as "I feel awful." "I feel awful" is correct; "I feel awfully" is incorrect, because "feel" refers to a *state of being* and requires an adjective to complete it. To test, replace "feel" with a state of being ("equals sign") verb such as *am, are, is, was, were*:

How *are* you?	I feel (*am*) *awful.* I = awful
How *is* the food?	The food tastes (*is*) *good.* food = good
How *are* the flowers?	The flowers smell (*are*) *sweet.* flowers = sweet

Comparison Errors

You might encounter two types of sentences which include comparison mistakes:
1. After reading both novels, he decided that neither was the greatest of the two.
2. His clothes were more expensive than the other men.

In sentence 1, two novels are being compared. When only two things are compard, -*er* words are used:
> the *smarter* of the two brothers
> the *cheaper* of the two cars

When *more than two* things are being compared, -*est* words are used:
> the *smartest* one in the family
> the *cheapest* car on the lot

NOTE: For adjectives of more than one syllable, *more* and *most* plus the adjective should be used rather than -*er* and -*est*, respectively.

Considering the rules above, sentence 1 should be corrected:
> After reading both novels, he decided that neither was the *greater* of the two.

Sentence 2 tips off a possible comparison error because it includes a "more . . . than" phrase. Other phrases which signal comparison are "better . . . than," "worse . . . than," "smarter . . . than," etc. Make sure the comparison is complete and balanced; sentence 2 is *not.* It seems to say that *clothes* are better than men. Here are some other errors of this sort:

3. Her fresh apple pie tasted better than the neighbors.
4. Thoreau's writings are more widely read than Swift.

Unless you're a cannibal, you don't compare the taste of apple pie to the taste of your neighbors, as does sentence 3. And it's equally illogical to compare writings to a person (Swift). Corrected, these sentences should read:

Her fresh apple pie tasted better than *that of* the neighbors.

Thoreau's writings are more widely read than *those of* Swift.

Other comparison errors look like this:

Bill is more reliable than any worker at the plant.

Bill is not more reliable than "any worker," because the phrase "any worker" includes him! Instead:

Bill is more reliable than any *other* worker at the plant.

The word "other" sets Bill apart from the workers to whom he is being compared.

Strategies For Sentence Correction Questions

In Sentence Correction questions, part or all of each sentence is underlined. Following each sentence are five choices for writing the underlined part. Answer (A) repeats the original and should be chosen only if the underlined portion is correct as it stands. Choices (B), (C), (D), and (E) are possible corrections of the original. You may not make a choice which changes the meaning of the sentence. A correct sentence is one which conforms to the rules of standard written English. You should look first for the sorts of grammar errors described on pages 161-168; such errors occur quite often in Sentence Correction. Errors of diction are less likely but may show up.

The best strategy for dealing with sentence correction is an *Elimination Strategy*. For instance, consider this sentence:

High oil prices infuriate Fred, who wonders if it is part of a plot by Middle Eastern oil magnates.

(A) who wonders if it is part of a plot by Middle Eastern oil magnates.
(B) who wonders if Middle East oil magnets are part of the plot.
(C) who wonders if they are part of a plot by Middle Eastern oil magnates.
(D) wondering if it is part of a plot by Middle Eastern oil magnates.
(E) who wonders if it is part of a plot by Middle Eastern oil magnets.

Look for faulty grammar first. When looking for faulty grammar, begin by examining pronouns. In this case, "it" is used incorrectly; "it" is singular and refers to "high oil prices," which is plural. Recognizing this, you can eliminate (A), (D), and (E) immediately, because none of them changes "it." (B) is incorrect because it unnecessarily changes "magnates" to "magnets." (C) is correct, changing the singular "it" to the plural "they."

In most cases, once you spot an error you will be able to eliminate several choices which repeat the same error. However, after eliminating obviously incorrect choices, you may need to choose between answers which are *all grammatically correct*. The following sentence illustrates this point:

Keeping to himself, the neighbors rarely knew where he was or what he was doing.

(A) Keeping to himself, the neighbors rarely knew where he was or what he was doing.
(B) Keeping to himself, he never told the neighbors where he was or what he was doing.
(C) The neighbors rarely knew where he was or what he was doing.

    (D)   Because he kept his whereabouts to himself, the neighbors rarely knew where he was or what he was doing.

    (E)   Because he kept to himself, the neighbors rarely knew where he was or what he was doing.

In this case there are no pronoun errors, but there is a dangling modifier ("keeping to himself"). Choices (B), (C), (D), and (E) all correct this error; however, only one of them is the *best* choice. (B) changes the meaning of the original; (C) unnecessarily deletes "keeping to himself" and thus changes the meaning of the original; (D) unnecessarily adds "his whereabouts." Only (E) *retains all of the information and most of the wording of the original*, and it is therefore the best choice.

Practice Run: Sentence Correction Strategies

1. <u>If Jack would have driven below the speed limit,</u> the policeman would not have pulled him over and issued a citation.

    (A)   If Jack would have driven below the speed limit,
    (B)   If only Jack would have driven below the speed limit,
    (C)   Being that Jack had driven below the speed limit,
    (D)   If Jack had driven below the speed limit,
    (E)   If Jack had driven far enough below the speed limit.

    CORRECTION PROCESS:
    1) Circle "would have" in the original. (See page 165.)
    2) Eliminate (A) and (B) because they retain "would have."
    3) Eliminate (C) because "being that" is poor diction.
    4) Eliminate (E) because it changes the meaning of the original.
    5) Choose (D)

2. Touring the English countryside, Andrea was <u>not surprised to see many of the homes she had admired</u> so often in movies.

    (A)   surprised to see many of the homes she had admired
    (B)   surprised at seeing many of the homes she had admired
    (C)   surprised to see many of the homes she'd admired
    (D)   surprising to admire many of the homes she had admired
    (E)   surprised to see many homes she'd admired

    CORRECTION PROCESS:
    1) The most obvious possibility is dangling modifier. Check the dangling modifier (see page 165). Ask yourself, "Is Andrea touring?" Yes. If the answer is yes, no dangling modifier exists.
    2) Reread the sentence, paying close attention to every underlined word.
    3) No error exists. Choose (A).

3. Having lived in New Jersey before moving to California, Bob treated all visitors from the <u>Garden State to great food, fine wine, and even invited them to sleep comfortably in his guest room.</u>

    (A)   Garden State to great food, fine wine, and even invited them to sleep comfortably in his guest room.
    (B)   Garden State to great food and fine wine, and even invited them to sleep comfortably in his guest room.
    (C)   Garden State to great food, fine wine, and comfortable sleep in his guest room.
    (D)   garden state to great food, fine wine, and comfortable sleep in his guest room.
    (E)   Garden State to great food, fine wine, and an invitation to comfortable sleep.

CORRECTION PROCESS:
1) Circle "great food, fine wine, and even invited . . . ." (faulty parallelism)
2) Eliminate (A); all other choices change the phrase in question and are therefore possible corrections.
3) Eliminate (D) for not capitalizing "Garden State."
4) Eliminate (E) for leaving out information from the original.
5) Eliminate (C) because it gives the impression that eating, drinking, and sleeping all take place in the guest room.
6) (B) is the best choice. Inserting "and" between "great food" and "fine wine" eliminated the need for parallel structure, and the remainder of the sentence *retains both the information and the wording of the original.*

SUMMARY OF SENTENCE CORRECTION STRATEGIES

1. Read the whole sentence carefully; make sure you see every word.
2. If you spot an error right away, circle it; identifying it in this way will help you to eliminate choices which include the same error.
3. Look for faulty grammar first (pronoun errors, subject-verb agreement errors, wrong verb tense, dangling modifiers, faulty parallelism, adjective-adverb confusion, comparison errors).
4. If no grammar error is apparent, there may be a diction or verbosity error.
5. The sentence may be *correct*; if so, choose (A).
6. If the sentence contains a mistake, immediately *eliminate* choice (A) and each other choice which contains the same mistake.
7. Eliminate all choices which change the meaning of the original.
8. You may be left with several choices which are *correct*. You must pick the *best* one.
9. The *best* one will be grammatically and structurally correct, and *will usually contain all of the information and most of the wording of the original.*

Strategies For Usage Questions

The Usage section is probably the easier of the Writing Ability tests on the GMAT. You don't have to make corrections, as in Sentence Correction. You need only recognize whether one of the underlined parts in each sentence contains an error in standard written English. A typical sentence looks like this:

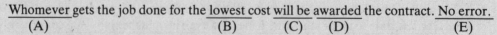

Whomever gets the job done for the lowest cost will be awarded the contract. No error.
(A)   (B)   (C)   (D)   (E)

You must decide whether the underlined portions (A), (B), (C), or (D) contain an error. If none of the underlined portions contains an error, you pick (E). In this case, (A) is incorrect. Applying the "Who—Whom" strategy outlined on page 163, we—
Separate the "Whom–Whom" clause: "Whomever gets the job."
Substitute "Him" or "Her": "Him gets the job."
"Him" doesn't sound right, so substitute "He": "He gets the job."
"He" sounds right, so "*who*ever," not "whomever," is correct.

IMPORTANT POINTS TO REMEMBER ABOUT THE USAGE SECTION

1. Only the underlined portions are to be considered for errors. If for some reason an error exists in a place which is not underlined, disregard the error entirely.
2. The following types of errors are common on this section of the test (each type has been explained earlier in this chapter):
   a. Pronoun errors
   b. Lack of agreement between subject and verb
   c. Incorrect verb tense
   d. Faulty parallelism
   e. Confusion of adjectives and adverbs
   f. Substandard usage
   g. Diction error

Practice in Writing Ability

This section is designed to give you some extra practice in Writing Ability. The following pages contain 31 problems with answers and explanations.

Sentence Correction

DIRECTIONS: This test consists of a number of sentences, in each of which some part or the whole is underlined. Each sentence is followed by five alternative versions of the underlined portion. Select the alternative you consider both most correct and most effective according to the requirements of standard written English. Answer A is the same as the original version; if you think the original version is best, select answer A.

In considering the answer choices, be attentive to matters of grammar, diction, and syntax, as well as clarity, precision, and fluency. Do not select an answer which alters the meaning of the original sentence.

1. The cause of the accident was <u>negligence rather than speeding in the court's judgment.</u>   1. Ⓐ Ⓑ Ⓒ Ⓓ Ⓔ

   (A) negligence rather than speeding in the court's judgment.
   (B) negligence instead of speeding in the court's judgment.
   (C) negligence rather than speeding, in the court's judgment.
   (D) negligence rather than speeding according to the court.
   (E) negligence rather then speeding, in the court's judgment.

2. Most of the other students <u>have had more experience giving oral reports than me,</u> and   2. Ⓐ Ⓑ Ⓒ Ⓓ Ⓔ
   laugh at my quavering voice, making matters worse.

   (A) have had more experience giving oral reports than me,
   (B) have had more experience with oral reports than me.
   (C) have had more experience giving oral reports than I,
   (D) have more experience giving oral reports than I,
   (E) had more experience giving oral reports than me,

3. When a person has worked overtime on a project, <u>one is reluctant to accept harsh</u>   3. Ⓐ Ⓑ Ⓒ Ⓓ Ⓔ
   <u>criticism of it.</u>

   (A) one is reluctant to accept harsh criticism of it.
   (B) one would be reluctant to accept harsh criticism of it.
   (C) they are reluctant to accept harsh criticism of it.
   (D) he or she is reluctant to accept harsh criticism of it.
   (E) he or she avoids criticism.

4. Ⓐ Ⓑ Ⓒ Ⓓ Ⓔ   4. Even before he started looking for the truth, <u>the philosopher sensed</u> the hopelessness of his search.

    (A) the philosopher sensed
    (B) the philosopher had sensed
    (C) the philosopher was sensing
    (D) the philosopher had a sense of
    (E) the philosopher will have sensed

5. Ⓐ Ⓑ Ⓒ Ⓓ Ⓔ   5. Our greatest problem <u>are guerrillas, who swarm out of the hills in great numbers as soon as evening falls.</u>

    (A) are guerrillas, who swarm out of the hills in great numbers as soon as evening falls.
    (B) are guerrillas, which swarm out of the hills in great numbers as soon as evening falls.
    (C) is guerrillas, who swarm out of the hills in great numbers as soon as evening falls.
    (D) is guerrillas, which swarm out of the hills in great numbers as soon as evening falls.
    (E) are guerrillas, who swarm out of the hills in great numbers at dark.

6. Ⓐ Ⓑ Ⓒ Ⓓ Ⓔ   6. Thirty-six hours, give or take a few minutes, <u>are the length of time for which</u> I should be paid.

    (A) are the length of time for which
    (B) is the length of time for which
    (C) is the length of time at which
    (D) is the approximate length of time for which
    (E) are the lengths of time for which

7. Ⓐ Ⓑ Ⓒ Ⓓ Ⓔ   7. A gymnasium is located on the first floor of the <u>Humanities building which</u> may be used by both students and faculty.

    (A) Humanities building which
    (B) humanities building which
    (C) Humanities building; which
    (D) Humanities building; it
    (E) Humanities building that

8. Ⓐ Ⓑ Ⓒ Ⓓ Ⓔ   8. <u>Friends who I had not contacted for months</u> surprised me by attending a party in my honor.

    (A) Friends who I had not contacted for months
    (B) Friends whom I had not contacted for months
    (C) Friends whom I have not contacted for months
    (D) Friends, who I had not contacted for months
    (E) Friends who I had not contacted in months

9. Ⓐ Ⓑ Ⓒ Ⓓ Ⓔ   9. When the candidate began to talk, he spoke <u>loudly and very defensive.</u>

    (A) loudly and very defensive.
    (B) loud and very defensive.
    (C) loudly and very defensively.
    (D) very loudly and very defensively.
    (E) loud and very defensively.

10. Ⓐ Ⓑ Ⓒ Ⓓ Ⓔ   10. <u>As I was leaving town, a storm began.</u>

    (A) As I was leaving town, a storm began.
    (B) Leaving town, a storm began.
    (C) As I was leaving town, a storm had begun.
    (D) As I was leaving town; a storm began.
    (E) Upon leaving town, a storm began.

11. After we <u>swam in the crystal mountain lake, my friends and I</u> decided to go canoeing.   11. Ⓐ Ⓑ Ⓒ Ⓓ Ⓔ

    (A) swam in the crystal mountain lake, my friends and I
    (B) had swum in the crystal lake, my friends and I
    (C) swam in the crystal mountain lake, my friends and me
    (D) swam in the clear mountain lake, my friends and me
    (E) had swam in the crystal mountain lake, my friends and I

12. The soprano performed <u>admirably well</u> during last night's presentation of *Rigoletto*.   12. Ⓐ Ⓑ Ⓒ Ⓓ Ⓔ

    (A) admirably well
    (B) admirable well
    (C) admirable and well
    (D) admirably and well
    (E) admiringly well

13. The family, <u>a happy bunch, were together once again at the reunion.</u>   13. Ⓐ Ⓑ Ⓒ Ⓓ Ⓔ

    (A) a happy bunch, were together once again at the reunion.
    (B) all a happy bunch, was together once again the reunion.
    (C) a happy bunch, was together once again at the reunion.
    (D) all a happy bunch, were together once again at the reunion.
    (E) a happy bunch was together once again at the reunion.

14. Even though he <u>had laid aside a great deal of money for whoever felt the sting</u> of   14. Ⓐ Ⓑ Ⓒ Ⓓ Ⓔ
poverty, the millionaire was accused of being stingy.

    (A) had laid aside a great deal of money for whoever felt the sting
    (B) had lain aside a great deal of money for whoever felt the sting
    (C) had laid aside a great deal of money for whomever felt the sting
    (D) had laid aside a great deal of money for whoever felt the bite
    (E) had lain aside a great deal of money for whomever felt the sting

15. The longer I think about love and marriage, <u>the more one question keeps entering my mind</u>.   15. Ⓐ Ⓑ Ⓒ Ⓓ Ⓔ

    (A) the more one question keeps entering my mind.
    (B) one more question keeps entering my mind.
    (C) the more one question keeps on entering my mind.
    (D) the longer one question kept entering my mind.
    (E) the more one question kept entering my mind.

Usage

DIRECTIONS: Each of the sentences in this section is either correct or contains one error in grammar, usage, diction (choice of words), idiom or punctuation. If there is an error it will be found in one of the underlined parts of the sentence, labeled (A), (B), (C), or (D). If you identify an error mark the appropriate letter on your answer sheet. If there is no error in the sentence mark (E)—no error.

Note: Assume that all parts of the sentence that are not underlined are correct and cannot be changed.

16. *Summer of My German Soldier* <u>it tells about</u> the <u>unlikely</u> friendship between a Jewish   16. Ⓐ Ⓑ Ⓒ Ⓓ Ⓔ
                               A   B

girl and a young German soldier <u>who</u> in other circumstances might have married and
                                            C

<u>"lived</u> happily ever after." <u>No error.</u>
  D   E

17. Ⓐ Ⓑ Ⓒ Ⓓ Ⓔ   17. Senator James, <u>a legislative leader</u> is a man <u>whom,</u> I think, <u>can</u> be trusted to consider
                                              A   B   C
the best interest of his constituency before <u>he votes.</u> <u>No error.</u>
                                          D   E

18. Ⓐ Ⓑ Ⓒ Ⓓ Ⓔ   18. The <u>principle</u> export of Hawaii <u>is</u> sugar, although tourism continues <u>to be</u> a growing
                   A   B   C
industry in its <u>own right.</u> <u>No error.</u>
                   D   E

19. Ⓐ Ⓑ Ⓒ Ⓓ Ⓔ   19. <u>Who's</u> book <u>was</u> <u>lying</u> on the table when the fire drill <u>occurred?</u> <u>No error.</u>
             A   B   C   D   E

20. Ⓐ Ⓑ Ⓒ Ⓓ Ⓔ   20. Although the class was a river <u>course,</u> the instructor <u>still considered</u> homework a must
                                    A   B
and an <u>indolent</u> attitude a <u>sort of an</u> unacceptable thing. <u>No error.</u>
                    C   D   E

21. Ⓐ Ⓑ Ⓒ Ⓓ Ⓔ   21. The hurricane, which <u>swept</u> across southern Arkansas, <u>destroyed</u> all the homes and
                              A   B
businesses <u>which</u> <u>laid</u> in the path of the violent winds and torrential downpour.
                C   D
<u>No error.</u>
   E

22. Ⓐ Ⓑ Ⓒ Ⓓ Ⓔ   22. The book was well written although most reviewers <u>disliked</u> the <u>conscious</u> verbosity,
                                                    A   B
<u>suggesting that</u> the author could have said the same thing in <u>less</u> words. <u>No error.</u>
             C   D   E

23. Ⓐ Ⓑ Ⓒ Ⓓ Ⓔ   23. <u>Because of</u> a very sophisticated advertising campaign, <u>lots of</u> people <u>bought many</u>
             A   B   C
<u>trinkets</u> they did not need. <u>No error.</u>
        D   E

24. Ⓐ Ⓑ Ⓒ Ⓓ Ⓔ   24. <u>Among</u> the questions that stumped the aspirants <u>were</u> the <u>ones</u> asking <u>him</u> to
             A   B   C   D
recognize three categories of sentence errors. <u>No error.</u>
                                        E

25. Ⓐ Ⓑ Ⓒ Ⓓ Ⓔ   25. The winter rain in the southland, <u>which</u> was late this year, is expected <u>to more than</u>
                                    A   B
<u>make up</u> for its tardiness <u>today.</u> <u>No error.</u>
        C   D   E

26. Ⓐ Ⓑ Ⓒ Ⓓ Ⓔ   26. Cyrano de Bergerac, <u>who</u> was unduly sensitive about the size of his nose, fought <u>duels</u>
                          A   B
with anyone <u>whom</u> <u>taunted</u> him about it. <u>No error.</u>
                C   D   E

27. Ⓐ Ⓑ Ⓒ Ⓓ Ⓔ   27. <u>Only after</u> the student served three hours' detention did <u>he</u> return to class to complete
             A   B
his assignments and <u>turn over</u> the homework to the principal, Mr. Stienman, and <u>I,</u> his
                            C   D
English teacher. <u>No error.</u>
                    E

28. This new labor contract, <u>together with</u> the fringe benefit package and inflation clause, 28. Ⓐ Ⓑ Ⓒ Ⓓ Ⓔ
    A
<u>have</u> only a limited chance <u>of being</u> approved by management during the next
    B   C
<u>collective bargaining sessions.</u> <u>No error.</u>
    D   E

29. The <u>president's day</u> was a <u>full one;</u> he was extremely busy throughout his tour <u>due to</u> 29. Ⓐ Ⓑ Ⓒ Ⓓ Ⓔ
        A   B   C
the poor planning of <u>his</u> press secretary. <u>No error.</u>
    D   E

30. After talking to the <u>accountant</u> Mr. Wright felt <u>he</u> should audit the report <u>in order to</u> 30. Ⓐ Ⓑ Ⓒ Ⓓ Ⓔ
                            A   B   C
have the job completed <u>prior to</u> the noon conference. <u>No error.</u>
                            D   E

31. <u>One of the</u> salesmen's cases <u>was</u> lost, because <u>he</u> had been careless <u>while checking out</u> 31. Ⓐ Ⓑ Ⓒ Ⓓ Ⓔ
    A   B   C   D
of the hotel. <u>No error.</u>
                  E

Answers and Analysis

Sentence Correction

1. **(C)** Where did the speeding take place? "In the court's judgment?" The sentence seems to say so, and should be completely rewritten as follows:
"In the court's judgment, the cause of the accident was negligence rather than speeding." Since none of the choices is a complete rewrite, the *best* choice is (C), which effectively separates "in the court's judgment" from "speeding."

2. **(C)** This sentence is understood to mean, "Most of the students have had more experience giving oral reports than I (have had)." Therefore, (C) is correct. (See page 162.)

3. **(D)** This sentence contains a pronoun error. The correct pronoun corresponding to "person" is "he" (or "she"). (E) is correct but changes the meaning of the original.

4. **(B)** Since the philosopher sensed the hopelessness *before* he started, "*had* sensed" is needed to indicate this earlier action.

5. **(C)** Since the subject ("problem") is singular, the verb must be singular ("is" instead of "are").

6. **(B)** Time expressed as a unit is always singular. In this case, "hours," the subject, is singular, so the verb must be singular ("is" instead of "are").

7. **(D)** It is unclear whether "which" refers to the gymnasium or the building. Ideally, the sentence should be rewritten as follows:
"A gymnasium which may be used by both students and faculty is located on the first floor of the Humanities building."
Since no choice offers a complete rewrite, the *best* choice is (D).

8. **(B)** "Who" is incorrect. Replacing "who" with "she" and "her" results in "I had not contacted she," which sounds wrong, and "I had not contacted her," which sounds right. If "her" sounds right, "whom" is right. (See page 163).

9. **(C)** "Describing *how* something is done, in this case how the candidate spoke, is the work of adverbs, "*-ly*" words like "defensively."

10. **(A)** This sentence is correct. (B) and (E) include a dangling modifier.

11. **(B)** "Had Swum" correctly indicates that this action took place before "decided."

12. **(A)** This sentence is correct. "Admirably" is an adverb describing how well she performed.

13. **(C)** Since the subject is the singular "family" and not the plural "people," the verb must be singular, "was" instead of "were."

14. **(A)** This sentence is correct. Replace "whoever" with "he" in "whoever felt the sting": "he felt the sting." If "he" sounds correct (as it does), "who" is correct.

15. **(A)** This sentence is correct. (B) changes the meaning of the original; (C) unnecessarily adds a word; (D) and (E) after the verb tense.

Usage

16. **(A)** "It" is repetitious.

17. **(B)** "Whom" is incorrect; "who" is correct.

18. **(A)** "Principle" (law or doctrine) is incorrect; "principal" (most important) would be correct.

19. **(A)** "Who's" means "who is" and is therefore incorrect. "Whose" is correct.

20. **(D)** "Sort of an" is nonstandard usage.

21. **(D)** "Laid" should be changed to "lay" (past tense of "lie").

22. **(D)** "Less" should be replaced by "fewer."

23. **(B)** "Lots of" is nonstandard usage.

24. **(D)** "Him" (singular) refers to "aspirants" (plural) and should be changed to "them."

25. **(E)** The sentence contains no error.

26. **(C)** "Whom" is incorrect; "who" is correct.

27. **(D)** "I" should be changed to "me."

28. **(B)** The subject, "contract," is singular, so the verb must be singular, "has" instead of "have."

29. **(C)** "Due to" is unacceptable usage; it should be changed to "because of."

30. **(B)** It is unclear whether "he" refers to the accountant or to Mr. Wright.

31. **(C)** "He" (singular) refers to "salesmen" (plural) and should be changed to "they."

MATHEMATICS REVIEW

The Mathematics and Data Sufficiency areas of the GMAT require a working knowledge of mathematical principles, including an understanding of the fundamentals of algebra, geometry, and arithmetic, and the ability to interpret graphs. The following review covers these areas thoroughly and if used properly, will prove helpful in preparing for the mathematical parts of the GMAT.

Read through the review carefully. You will notice that each topic is keyed for easy reference. Use the key number next to each answer given in the Sample Tests to refer to those sections in the review that cover material you may have missed and therefore will need to spend more time on.

I. Arithmetic

I-1. Whole Numbers

1-1

The numbers 0,1,2,3, . . . are called whole numbers or *integers*. So 75 is an integer but $4\frac{1}{3}$ is not an integer.

1-2

If the integer k divides m evenly, then we say *m is divisible by k* or *k is a factor of m*. For example, 12 is divisible by 4, but 12 is not divisible by 5. 1,2,3,4,6,12 are all factors of 12.

If k is a factor of m, then there is another integer n such that $m = k \times n$; in this case, m is called a *multiple of k*.

Since $12 = 4 \times 3$, 12 is a multiple of 4 and also 12 is a multiple of 3. 5,10,15, and 20 are all multiples of 5 but 15 and 5 are not multiples of 10.

Any integer is a multiple of each of its factors.

1-3

Any whole number is divisible by itself and by 1. If p is a whole number greater than 1, which has *only p* and 1 as factors, then p is called a *prime number*. 2,3,5,7,11,13,17,19 and 23 are all primes. 14 is not a prime since it is divisible by 2 and by 7.

A whole number which is divisible by 2 is called an *even* number; if a whole number is not even, then it is an *odd* number. 2,4,6,8,10 are even numbers, and 1,3,5,7 and 9 are odd numbers.

A collection of numbers is *consecutive* if each number is the successor of the number which precedes it. For example, 7,8,9 and 10 are consecutive, but 7,8,10,13 are not. 4,6,8,10 are consecutive even numbers. 7,11,13,17 are consecutive primes. 7,13,19,23 are not consecutive primes since 11 is a prime between 7 and 13.

1-4

> Any whole number can be written as a product of factors which are prime numbers.

To write a number as a *product of prime factors:*

(A) Divide the number by 2 if possible; continue to divide by 2 until the factor you get is not divisible by 2.

(B) Divide the result from (A) by 3 if possible; continue to divide by 3 until the factor you get is not divisible by 3.

(C) Divide the result from (B) by 5 if possible; continue to divide by 5 until the factor you get is not divisible by 5.

(D) Continue the procedure with 7, 11, and so on, until all the factors are primes.

EXAMPLE 1: Express 24 as a product of prime factors.

(A) $24 = 2 \times 12$, $12 = 2 \times 6$, $6 = 2 \times 3$ so $24 = 2 \times 2 \times 2 \times 3$. Since each factor (2 and 3) is prime, $24 = 2 \times 2 \times 2 \times 3$.

EXAMPLE 2: Express 252 as a product of primes.

(A) $252 = 2 \times 126$, $126 = 2 \times 63$ and 63 is not divisible by 2, so $252 = 2 \times 2 \times 63$.

(B) $63 = 3 \times 21$, $21 = 3 \times 7$ and 7 is not divisible by 3. Since 7 is a prime, then $252 = 2 \times 2 \times 3 \times 3 \times 7$ and all the factors are primes.

1-5

A number m is a *common multiple* of two other numbers k and j if it is a multiple of each of them. For example, 12 is a common multiple of 4 and 6, since $3 \times 4 = 12$ and $2 \times 6 = 12$. 15 is not a common multiple of 3 and 6, because 15 is not a multiple of 6.

A number k is a *common factor* of two other numbers m and n if k is a factor of m and k is a factor of n.

The *least common multiple* (L.C.M.) of two numbers is the smallest number which is a common multiple of both numbers. To find the least common multiple of two numbers k and j:

(A) Write k as a product of primes and j as a product of primes.

(B) If there are any common factors *delete* them in *one* of the products.

(C) Multiply the remaining factors; the result is the least common multiple.

EXAMPLE 1: Find the L.C.M. of 12 and 11.

(A) $12 = 2 \times 2 \times 3$, $11 = 11 \times 1$.
(B) There are no common factors.
(C) The L.C.M. is $12 \times 11 = 132$.

EXAMPLE 2: Find the L.C.M. of 27 and 63.

(A) $27 = 3 \times 3 \times 3$, $63 = 3 \times 3 \times 7$.
(B) $3 \times 3 = 9$ is a common factor so delete it once.
(C) The L.C.M. is $3 \times 3 \times 3 \times 7 = 189$.

You can find the L.C.M. of a collection of numbers in the same way except that if in step (B) the common factors are factors of more than two of the numbers, then delete the common factor in *all but one* of the products.

EXAMPLE 3: Find the L.C.M. of 27, 63 and 72.

(A) $27 = 3 \times 3 \times 3$, $63 = 3 \times 3 \times 7$, $72 = 2 \times 2 \times 2 \times 3 \times 3$.
(B) Delete 3×3 from two of the products.
(C) The L.C.M. is $3 \times 7 \times 2 \times 2 \times 2 \times 3 \times 3 = 21 \times 72 = 1,512$.

I-2. Fractions

2-1

A FRACTION is a number which represents a ratio or division of two whole numbers (integers). A fraction is written in the form $\frac{a}{b}$. The number on the top, a, is called the numerator; the number on the bottom, b, is called the denominator. The denominator tells how many equal parts there are (for example, parts of a pie); the numerator tells how many of these equal parts are taken. For example, $\frac{5}{8}$ is a fraction whose numerator is 5 and whose denominator is 8; it represents taking 5 of 8 equal parts, or dividing 8 into 5.

A fraction can not have 0 as a denominator since division by 0 is not defined. A fraction with 1 as the denominator is the same as the whole number which is its numerator. For example, $\frac{12}{1}$ is 12, $\frac{0}{1}$ is 0.

If the numerator and denominator of a fraction are identical, the fraction represents 1. For example, $\frac{3}{3} = \frac{9}{9} = \frac{13}{13} = 1$. Any whole number, k, is represented by a fraction with a numerator equal to k times the denominator. For example, $\frac{18}{6} = 3$, and $\frac{30}{5} = 6$.

2–2

Mixed Numbers. A mixed number consists of a whole number and a fraction. For example, $7\frac{1}{4}$ is a mixed number; it means $7 + \frac{1}{4}$ and $\frac{1}{4}$ is called the fractional part of the mixed number $7\frac{1}{4}$. Any mixed number can be changed into a fraction:

(A) Multiply the whole number by the denominator of the fractional part.

(B) Add the numerator of the fraction to the result of step A.

(C) Use the result of step B as the numerator and use the denominator of the fractional part of the mixed number as the denominator. This fraction is equal to the mixed number.

EXAMPLE 1:   Write $7\frac{1}{4}$ as a fraction.

(A) $4 \cdot 7 = 28$

(B) $28 + 1 = 29$

(C)   so $7\frac{1}{4} = \frac{29}{4}$.

A fraction whose numerator is larger than its denominator can be changed into a mixed number.

(A) Divide the denominator into the numerator; the result is the whole number of the mixed number.

(B) Put the remainder from step A over the denominator; this is the fractional part of the mixed number.

EXAMPLE 2:   Change $\frac{35}{8}$ into a mixed number.

(A) Divide 8 into 35; the result is 4 with a remainder of 3.

(B) $\frac{3}{8}$ is the fractional part of the mixed number.

(C) So $\frac{35}{8} = 4\frac{3}{8}$.

We can regard any whole number as a mixed number with 0 as the fractional part. For example, $\frac{18}{6} = 3$.

In calculations with mixed numbers, change the mixed numbers into fractions.

2–3

Multiplying Fractions. To multiply two fractions, multiply their numerators and divide this result by the product of their denominators.

In word problems, *of* usually indicates multiplication.

EXAMPLE: John saves $\frac{1}{3}$ of $240. How much does he save?

$$\frac{1}{3} \cdot \frac{240}{1} = \frac{240}{3} = \$80, \text{ the amount John saves.}$$

2–4

Dividing Fractions. One fraction is a *reciprocal* of another if their product is 1. So $\frac{1}{2}$ and 2 are reciprocals. To find the reciprocal of a fraction, simply interchange the numerator and denominator (turn the fraction upside down). This is called *inverting* the fractions. So when you invert $\frac{15}{17}$ you get $\frac{17}{15}$. When a fraction is inverted the inverted fraction and the original fraction are reciprocals. Thus $\frac{15}{17} \cdot \frac{17}{15} = \frac{255}{255} = \frac{1}{1} = 1$.

To divide one fraction (the dividend) by another fraction (the divisor), invert the divisor and multiply.

EXAMPLE 1: $\frac{5}{6} \div \frac{3}{4} = \frac{5}{6} \cdot \frac{4}{3} = \frac{20}{18}$

EXAMPLE 2: A worker makes a basket every $\frac{2}{3}$ hour. If the worker works for $7\frac{1}{2}$ hours, how many baskets will he make? We want to divide $\frac{2}{3}$ into $7\frac{1}{2}$, $7\frac{1}{2} = \frac{15}{2}$, so we want to divide $\frac{15}{2}$ by $\frac{2}{3}$. Thus

$$\frac{15}{2} \div \frac{2}{3} = \frac{15}{2} \cdot \frac{3}{2} = \frac{45}{4} = 11\frac{1}{4} \text{ baskets.}$$

2–5

Dividing and Multiplying by the Same Number. Since multiplication or division by 1 does not change the value of a number, you can multiply or divide any fraction by 1 and the fraction will remain the same. Remember that $\frac{a}{a} = 1$ for any non-zero number a. Therefore, if you multiply or divide any fraction by $\frac{a}{a}$, the result is the same as if you multiplied the numerator and denominator by a or divided the numerator and denominator by a.

If you multiply the numerator and denominator of a fraction by the same non-zero number the fraction remains the same.

If you divide the numerator and denominator of any fraction by the same non-zero number, the fraction remains the same.

Consider the fraction $\frac{3}{4}$. If we multiply 3 by 10 and 4 by 10, then $\frac{30}{40}$ must equal $\frac{3}{4}$.

When we multiply fractions, if any of the numerators and denominators have a common factor (see page 158 for factors) we can divide each of them by the common factor and the fraction remains the same. This process is called *cancelling* and can be a great time-saver.

EXAMPLE: Multiply $\frac{4}{9} \cdot \frac{75}{8}$. Since 4 is a common factor of 4 and 8, divide 4 and 8 by 4 getting $\frac{4}{9} \cdot \frac{75}{8} = \frac{1}{9} \cdot \frac{75}{2}$. Since 3 is a common factor of 9 and 75 divide 9 and 75 by 3 to get $\frac{1}{9} \cdot \frac{75}{2} = \frac{1}{3} \cdot \frac{25}{2}$. So $\frac{4}{9} \cdot \frac{75}{8} = \frac{1}{3} \cdot \frac{25}{2} = \frac{25}{6}$.

2-6
Equivalent Fractions. Two fractions are equivalent or equal if they represent the same ratio or number. In the last section, you saw that if you multiply or divide the numerator and denominator of a fraction by the same non-zero number the result is equivalent to the original fraction. For example, $\frac{7}{8} = \frac{70}{80}$ since $70 = 10 \times 7$ and $80 = 10 \times 8$.

> *In the test there will only be five choices, so your answer to a problem may not be the same as any of the given choices.* You may have to express a fraction as an equivalent fraction.

To find a fraction with a known denominator equal to a given fraction:

(A) divide the denominator of the given fraction into the known denominator;

(B) multiply the result of (A) by the numerator of the given fraction; this is the numerator of the required equivalent fraction.

EXAMPLE: Find a fraction with denominator 30 which is equal to $\frac{2}{5}$:

(A) 5 into 30 is 6;

(B) $6 \cdot 2 = 12$ so $\frac{12}{30} = \frac{2}{5}$.

2-7
Reducing a Fraction to Lowest Terms. A fraction has been reduced to lowest terms when the numerator and denominator have no common factors.

For example, $\frac{3}{4}$ is reduced to lowest terms, but $\frac{3}{6}$ is not because 3 is a common factor of 3 and 6.

> To reduce a fraction to lowest terms, cancel all the common factors of the numerator and denominator. (Cancelling common factors will not change the value of the fraction.)

For example, $\frac{100}{150} = \frac{10 \cdot 10}{10 \cdot 15} = \frac{10}{15} = \frac{5 \cdot 2}{5 \cdot 3} = \frac{2}{3}$. Since 2 and 3 have no common factors, $\frac{2}{3}$ is $\frac{100}{150}$ reduced to lowest terms. A fraction is equivalent to the fraction reduced to lowest terms.

If you write the numerator and denominator as products of primes, it is easy to cancel all the common factors.

$$\frac{63}{81} = \frac{3 \cdot 3 \cdot 7}{3 \cdot 3 \cdot 3 \cdot 3} = \frac{7}{9}$$

2–8

Adding Fractions. If the fractions have the same denominator, then the denominator is called a *common denominator*. Add the numerators, and use this sum as the new numerator with the common denominator as the denominator of the sum.

EXAMPLE 1: $\frac{5}{12} + \frac{3}{12} = \frac{5+3}{12} = \frac{8}{12} = \frac{2}{3}$

EXAMPLE 2: Jim uses 7 eggs to make breakfast and 8 eggs for supper. How many dozen eggs has he used? 7 eggs are $\frac{7}{12}$ of a dozen and 8 eggs are $\frac{8}{12}$ of a dozen. He used $\frac{7}{12} + \frac{8}{12} = \frac{7+8}{12} = \frac{15}{12} = \frac{5}{4} = 1\frac{1}{4}$ dozen eggs.

If the fractions don't have the same denominator, you must first find a common denominator. Multiply all the denominators together; the result is a common denominator.

EXAMPLE: To add $\frac{1}{2} + \frac{2}{3} + \frac{7}{4}$, $2 \cdot 3 \cdot 4 = 24$ is a common denominator.

There are many common denominators; the smallest one is called the *least common denominator*. For the previous example, 12 is the least common denominator.

Once you have found a common denominator, express each fraction as an equivalent fraction with the common denominator, and add as you did for the case when the fractions had the same denominator.

EXAMPLE: $\frac{1}{2} + \frac{2}{3} + \frac{7}{4} = ?$

(A) 24 is a common denominator.

(B) $\frac{1}{2} = \frac{12}{24}, \frac{2}{3} = \frac{16}{24}, \frac{7}{4} = \frac{42}{24}.$

(C) $\frac{1}{2} + \frac{2}{3} + \frac{7}{4} = \frac{12}{24} + \frac{16}{24} + \frac{42}{24} = \frac{12 + 16 + 42}{24} = \frac{70}{24} = \frac{35}{12}.$

2–9

Subtracting Fractions. When the fractions have the same denominator, subtract the numerators and place the result over the denominator.

EXAMPLE: $\frac{3}{5} - \frac{2}{5} = \frac{3 - 2}{5} = \frac{1}{5}$

When the fractions have different denominators

(A) Find a common denominator.
(B) Express the fractions as equivalent fractions with the same denominator.
(C) Subtract.

EXAMPLE: $\frac{3}{5} - \frac{2}{7} = ?$

(A) A common denominator is $5 \cdot 7 = 35$.

(B) $\frac{3}{5} = \frac{21}{35}, \frac{2}{7} = \frac{10}{35}.$

(C) $\frac{3}{5} - \frac{2}{7} = \frac{21}{35} - \frac{10}{35} = \frac{21 - 10}{35} = \frac{11}{35}.$

2–10

Complex Fractions. A fraction whose numerator and denominator are themselves fractions is called a *complex fraction*. For example $\frac{2/3}{4/5}$ is a complex fraction. A complex fraction can always be simplified by dividing the fraction.

EXAMPLE 1: $\frac{2}{3} \div \frac{4}{5} = \frac{\cancel{2}^{1}}{3} \cdot \frac{5}{\cancel{4}_{2}} = \frac{1}{3} \cdot \frac{5}{2} = \frac{5}{6}$

EXAMPLE 2: It takes $2\frac{1}{2}$ hours to get from Buffalo to Cleveland traveling at a constant rate of speed. What part of the distance is traveled in $\frac{3}{4}$ of an hour?

$\frac{3/4}{2\ 1/2} = \frac{3/4}{5/2} = \frac{3}{4} \cdot \frac{2}{5} = \frac{3}{2} \cdot \frac{1}{5} = \frac{3}{10}$ of the distance.

I-3. Decimals

3-1

A collection of digits (the digits are 0,1,2, . . . ,9) after a period (called the decimal point) is called a *decimal fraction*. For example, .503, .5602, .32, and .4 are all decimal fractions.

Every decimal fraction represents a fraction. To find the fraction a decimal fraction represents:

(A) Take the fraction whose denominator is 10 and whose numerator is the first digit to the right of the decimal point.

(B) Take the fraction whose denominator is 100 and whose numerator is the second digit to the right of the decimal point.

(C) Take the fraction whose denominator is 1,000 and whose numerator is the third digit to the right of the decimal point.

(D) Continue the procedure until you have used each digit to the right of the decimal place. The denominator in each step is 10 times the denominator in the previous step.

(E) The *sum* of the fractions you have obtained in (A), (B), (C), and (D) is the fraction that the decimal fraction represents.

EXAMPLE 1: Find the fraction .503 represents.

(A) $\dfrac{5}{10}$

(B) $\dfrac{0}{100}$

(C) $\dfrac{3}{1000}$

(D) All the digits have already been used.

(E) So $.503 = \dfrac{5}{10} + \dfrac{0}{100} + \dfrac{3}{1000} = \dfrac{500}{1000} + \dfrac{0}{1000} + \dfrac{3}{1000} = \dfrac{503}{1000}$.

EXAMPLE 2: What fraction does .78934 represent?

(A) $\dfrac{7}{10}$

(B) $\dfrac{8}{100}$

(C) $\dfrac{9}{1000}$

(D) $\dfrac{3}{10,000}, \dfrac{4}{100,000}$

(E) So $.78934 = \dfrac{7}{10} + \dfrac{8}{100} + \dfrac{9}{1000} + \dfrac{3}{10,000} + \dfrac{4}{100,000} = \dfrac{78,934}{100,000}$.

Notice that the denominator of the last fraction you obtain in step (D) is a common denominator for all the previous denominators. Since each denominator is 10 times the previous one, the denominator of the final fraction of part (D) will be the product of r copies of 10 multiplied together (called 10^r) where r is the number of digits which appear in the decimal fraction. Therefore, a decimal fraction represents a fraction whose denominator is 10^r where r is the number of digits in the decimal fraction and whose numerator is the number represented by the digits of the decimal fraction.

EXAMPLE 3: What fraction does .5702 represent?

There are 4 digits in .5702. Therefore, the denominator is $10 \times 10 \times 10 \times 10 = 10,000$, and the numerator is 5,702. Therefore, $.5702 = \dfrac{5,702}{10,000}$.

You can add any number of zeros to the right of a decimal fraction without changing its value.

EXAMPLE: $.3 = \dfrac{3}{10} = \dfrac{30}{100} = .30 = .30000 = \dfrac{30,000}{100,000} = .300000000 \ldots$

3-2

We call the first position to the right of the decimal point the tenths place, since the digit in that position tells you how many tenths you should take. (It is the numerator of a fraction whose denominator is 10.) In the same way, we call the second position to the right the hundredths place, the third position to the right the thousandths, and so on. This is similar to the way whole numbers are expressed, since 568 means $5 \times 100 + 6 \times 10 + 8 \times 1$. The various digits represent different numbers depending on their position: the first place to the left of the decimal point represents units, the second place to the left represents tens, and so on.

The following diagram may be helpful:

T	H	T	U		T	H	T
H	U	E	N		E	U	H
O	N	N	I	.	N	N	O
U	D	S	T		T	D	U
S	R		S		H	R	S
A	E				S	E	A
N	D					D	N
D	S					T	D
S						H	T
						S	H
							S

Thus, 5,342.061 means 5 thousands + 3 hundreds + 4 tens + 2 + 0 tenths + 6 hundredths + 1 thousandth.

3-3

A DECIMAL is a whole number plus a decimal fraction; the decimal point separates the whole number from the decimal fraction. For example, 4,307.206 is a decimal which represents 4,307 added to the decimal fraction .206. A decimal fraction is a decimal with zero as the whole number.

3–4

A fraction whose denominator is a multiple of 10 is equivalent to a decimal. The denominator tells you the last place that is filled to the right of the decimal point. Place the decimal point in the numerator so that the last place to the right of the decimal point corresponds to the denominator. If the numerator does not have enough digits, add the appropriate number of zeros *before* the numerator.

EXAMPLE 1: Find the decimal equivalent of $\frac{5,732}{100}$.

Since the denominator is 100, you need two places to the right of the decimal point so $\frac{5,732}{100} = 57.32$.

EXAMPLE 2: What is the decimal equivalent of $\frac{57}{10,000}$?

The denominator is 10,000, so you need 4 decimal places. Since 57 only has two places, we add two zeros in front of 57; thus, $\frac{57}{10,000} = .0057$.

Do not make the error of adding the zeros to the right instead of to the left of 57; .5700 means $\frac{5,700}{10,000}$ not $\frac{57}{10,000}$.

3–5

Adding Decimals.   Decimals are much easier to add than fractions. To add a collection of decimals:

(A) Write the decimals in a column with the decimal points vertically aligned.
(B) Add enough zeros to the right of the decimal point so that every number has an entry in each column to the right of the decimal point.
(C) Add the numbers in the same way as whole numbers.
(D) Place a decimal point in the sum so that it is directly beneath the decimal points in the decimals added.

EXAMPLE 1:   How much is $5 + 3.43 + 16.021 + 3.1$?

(A)   5
      3.43
   16.021
  + 3.1

(B)   5.000
    3.430
  16.021
 + 3.100

(C)   5.000
   3.430
 16.021
+ 3.100

(D)   27.551   The answer is **27.551**.

EXAMPLE 2: If John has $.50, $3.25, and $6.05, how much does he have altogether?

$$\begin{array}{r} \$\ .50 \\ 3.25 \\ +\ 6.05 \\ \hline \$9.80 \end{array}$$ So John has $9.80.

3–6

Subtracting Decimals. To subtract one decimal from another:

(A) Put the decimals in a column so that the decimal points are vertically aligned.

(B) Add zeros so that every decimal has an entry in each column to the right of the decimal point.

(C) Subtract the numbers as you would whole numbers.

(D) Place the decimal point in the result so that it is directly beneath the decimal points of the numbers you subtracted.

EXAMPLE 1: Solve $5.053 - 2.09$.

(A) $$\begin{array}{r} 5.053 \\ -\ 2.09 \\ \hline \end{array}$$ (B) $$\begin{array}{r} 5.053 \\ -\ 2.090 \\ \hline \end{array}$$

(C) $$\begin{array}{r} 5.053 \\ -\ 2.090 \\ \hline \end{array}$$
(D) $\quad 2.963$ The answer is **2.963.**

EXAMPLE 2: If Joe has $12 and he loses $8.40, how much money does he have left?

Since $12.00 - $8.40 = $3.60, he has $3.60 left.

3–7

Multiplying Decimals. Decimals are multiplied like whole numbers. *The decimal point of the product is placed so that the number of decimal places in the product is equal to the total of the number of decimal places in all of the numbers multiplied.*

EXAMPLE 1: What is $(5.02)(.6)$?

$(502)(6) = 3012$. There were 2 decimal places in 5.02 and 1 decimal place in .6, so the product must have $2 + 1 = 3$ decimal places. Therefore, $(5.02)(.6) = 3.012$.

EXAMPLE 2: If eggs cost $.06 each, how much should a dozen eggs cost?

Since $(12)(.06) = .72$, a dozen eggs should cost $.72.

> **Computing Tip.** To multiply a decimal by 10, just move the decimal point to the right one place; to multiply by 100, move the decimal point two places to the right and so on.

EXAMPLE: $9{,}983.456 \times 100 = 998{,}345.6$

3–8

Dividing Decimals. To divide one decimal (the dividend) by another decimal (the divisor):

(A) Move the decimal point in the divisor to the right until there is no decimal fraction in the divisor (this is the same as multiplying the divisor by a multiple of 10).

(B) Move the decimal point in the dividend the same number of places to the right as you moved the decimal point in step (A).

(C) Divide the result of (B) by the result of (A) as if they were whole numbers.

(D) The number of decimal places in the result (quotient) should be equal to the number of decimal places in the result of step (B).

EXAMPLE 1: Divide .05 into 25.155.

(A) Move the decimal point two places to the right in .05; the result is 5.

(B) Move the decimal point two places to the right in 25.155; the result is 2515.5.

(C) Divide 5 into 25155; the result is 5031.

(D) Since there was one decimal place in the result of (B); the answer is 503.1.

The work for this example might look like this:

$$.05\,\overline{)25.15\,5} \quad\to\quad 503.1$$

You can always check division by multiplying.

$(503.1)(.05) = 25.155$ so we were correct.

If you write division as a fraction, example 1 would be expressed as $\dfrac{25.155}{.05}$.

You can multiply both the numerator and denominator by 100 without changing the value of the fraction, so

$$\frac{25.155}{.05} = \frac{25.155 \times 100}{.05 \times 100} = \frac{2515.5}{5.}$$

So step (A) and (B) always change the division of a decimal by a decimal into the division of a decimal by a whole number.

To divide a decimal by a whole number, divide them as if they were whole numbers. Then place the decimal point in the quotient so that the quotient has as many decimal places as the dividend.

EXAMPLE 2: $\dfrac{55.033}{1.1} = \dfrac{550.33}{11.} = 50.03.$

EXAMPLE 3: If oranges cost 6¢ each, how many oranges can you buy for $2.52?

$$6¢ = \$.06,$$

so the number of oranges is

$$\dfrac{2.52}{.06} = \dfrac{252}{6} = 42.$$

Computing Tip. To divide a decimal by 10, move the decimal point *to the left* one place; to divide by 100, move the decimal point two places to the left, and so on.

EXAMPLE: Divide 5,637.6471 by 1,000.

The answer is 5.6376471, since to divide by 1,000 you move the decimal point 3 places to the left.

3–9

Converting a Fraction into a Decimal. To convert a fraction into a decimal, divide the denominator into the numerator. For example, $\dfrac{3}{4} = \dfrac{3.00}{4} = .75.$ Some fractions give an infinite decimal when you divide the denominator into the numerator, for example, $\dfrac{1}{3} = .333 \ldots$ where the three dots mean you keep on getting 3 with each step of division. $.333 \ldots$ is an *infinite decimal*.

If a fraction has an infinite decimal, use the fraction in any computation.

EXAMPLE 1: What is $\dfrac{2}{9}$ of $3,690.90?

Since the decimal for $\dfrac{2}{9}$ is $.2222 \ldots$ use the fraction $\dfrac{2}{9}$.
$\dfrac{2}{9} \times \$3,690.90 = 2 \times \$410.10 = \$820.20.$

You should know the following decimal equivalents of fractions:

$\frac{1}{100} = .01$	$\frac{1}{6} = .1666\ldots$
$\frac{1}{50} = .02$	$\frac{1}{5} = .2$
$\frac{1}{40} = .025$	$\frac{1}{4} = .25$
$\frac{1}{25} = .04$	$\frac{1}{3} = .333\ldots$
$\frac{1}{20} = .05$	$\frac{3}{8} = .375$
$\frac{1}{16} = .0625$	$\frac{2}{5} = .4$
$\frac{1}{15} = .0666\ldots$	$\frac{1}{2} = .5$
$\frac{1}{12} = .0833\ldots$	$\frac{5}{8} = .625$
$\frac{1}{10} = .1$	$\frac{2}{3} = .666\ldots$
$\frac{1}{9} = .111\ldots$	$\frac{3}{4} = .75$
$\frac{1}{8} = .125$	$\frac{7}{8} = .875$
	$\frac{3}{2} = 1.5$

Any decimal with . . . is an infinite decimal.

I-4. Percentage

4-1

PERCENTAGE is another method of expressing fractions or parts of an object. Percentages are expressed in terms of hundredths, so 100% means 100 hundredths or 1. 50% would be 50 hundredths or $\frac{1}{2}$.

A decimal is converted to a percentage by multiplying the decimal by 100. Since multiplying a decimal by 100 is accomplished by moving the decimal point two places to the right, *you convert a decimal into a percentage by moving the decimal point two places to the right.* For example, $.134 = 13.4\%$.

If you wish to convert a percentage into a decimal, you divide the percentage by 100. There is a shortcut for this also. To divide by 100 you move the decimal point two places to the left.

Therefore, *to convert a percentage into a decimal, move the decimal point two places to the left.* For example, $24\% = .24$.

A fraction is converted into a percentage by changing the fraction to a decimal and then changing the decimal to a percentage. A percentage is changed into a fraction by first converting the percentage into a decimal and then changing the decimal to a fraction. You should know the following fractional equivalents of percentages:

$$1\% = \frac{1}{100} \qquad 25\% = \frac{1}{4} \qquad 80\% = \frac{4}{5}$$

$$2\% = \frac{1}{50} \qquad 33\frac{1}{3}\% = \frac{1}{3} \qquad 83\frac{1}{3}\% = \frac{5}{6}$$

$$4\% = \frac{1}{25} \qquad 37\frac{1}{2}\% = \frac{3}{8} \qquad 87\frac{1}{2}\% = \frac{7}{8}$$

$$5\% = \frac{1}{20} \qquad 40\% = \frac{2}{5} \qquad 100\% = 1$$

$$8\frac{1}{3}\% = \frac{1}{12} \qquad 50\% = \frac{1}{2} \qquad 120\% = \frac{6}{5}$$

$$10\% = \frac{1}{10} \qquad 60\% = \frac{3}{5} \qquad 125\% = \frac{5}{4}$$

$$12\frac{1}{2}\% = \frac{1}{8} \qquad 62\frac{1}{2}\% = \frac{5}{8} \qquad 133\frac{1}{3}\% = \frac{4}{3}$$

$$16\frac{2}{3}\% = \frac{1}{6} \qquad 66\frac{2}{3}\% = \frac{2}{3} \qquad 150\% = \frac{3}{2}$$

$$20\% = \frac{1}{5} \qquad 75\% = \frac{3}{4}$$

Note, for example, that $133\frac{1}{3}\% = 1.33\frac{1}{3} = 1\frac{1}{3} = \frac{4}{3}$.

When you compute with percentages, it is usually easier to change the percentages to decimals or fractions.

EXAMPLE 1: A company has 6,435 bars of soap. If the company sells 20% of its bars of soap, how many bars of soap did it sell?

Change 20% into .2. Thus, the company sold $(.2)(6,435) = 1287.0 = 1,287$ bars of soap. An alternative method would be to convert 20% to $\frac{1}{5}$. Then, $\frac{1}{5} \times 6,435 = 1,287$.

EXAMPLE 2: In a class of 60 students, 18 students received a grade of B. What percentage of the class received a grade of B?

$\frac{18}{60}$ of the class received a grade of B. $\frac{18}{60} = \frac{3}{10} = .3$ and $.3 = 30\%$, so 30% of the class received a grade of B.

EXAMPLE 3: If the population of Dryden was 10,000 in 1960 and the population of Dryden increased by 15% between 1960 and 1970, what was the population of Dryden in 1970?

The population increased by 15% between 1960 and 1970, so the increase was (.15)(10,000) which is 1,500. The population in 1970 was 10,000 + 1,500 = 11,500.

A quicker method: the population increased 15%, so the population in 1970 is 115% of the population in 1960. Therefore, the population in 1970 is 115% of 10,000 which is (1.15)(10,000) = 11,500.

4–2

Interest and Discount. Two of the most common uses of percentages are in interest and discount problems.

The rate of interest is usually given as a percentage. The basic formula for interest problems is:

$$\boxed{\text{INTEREST} = \text{AMOUNT} \times \text{TIME} \times \text{RATE}}$$

You can assume the rate of interest is the annual rate of interest unless the problem states otherwise; so you should express the time in years.

EXAMPLE 1: How much interest will $10,000 earn in 9 months at an annual rate of 6%?

9 months is $\frac{3}{4}$ of a year and $6\% = \frac{3}{50}$, so using the formula, the interest is $10,000

$\times \frac{3}{4} \times \frac{3}{50} = \$50 \times 9 = \$450.$

EXAMPLE 2: What annual rate of interest was paid if $5,000 earned $300 in interest in 2 years?

Since the interest was earned in 2 years, $150 is the interest earned in one year. $\frac{150}{5,000} = .03 = 3\%$, so the annual rate of interest was 3%.

This type of interest is called *simple interest*.

There is another method of computing interest called *compound interest*. In computing compound interest, the interest is periodically added to the amount (or principal) which is earning interest.

EXAMPLE 3: What will $1,000 be worth after three years if it earns interest at the rate of 5% compounded annually?

Compounded annually means that the interest earned during one year is added to the amount (or principal) at the end of each year. The interest on $1,000 at

5% for one year is $(1,000)(.05) = 50. So you must compute the interest on $1,050(not $1,000) for the second year. The interest is $(1,050)(.05) = 52.50. Therefore, during the third year interest will be computed for $1,102.50. During the third year the interest is $(1,102.50)(.05) = $55.125 = 55.13. Therefore, after 3 years the original $1,000 will be worth $1,157.63.

If you calculated simple interest on $1,000 at 5% for three years, the answer would be $(1,000)(.05)(3) = 150. Therefore, using simple interest, $1,000 is worth $1,150 after 3 years. Notice that this is not the same as the money was worth using compound interest.

You can assume that interest means simple interest unless a problem states otherwise.

The basic formula for discount problems is:

$$\boxed{\text{DISCOUNT} = \text{COST} \times \text{RATE OF DISCOUNT}}$$

EXAMPLE 1: What is the discount if a car which cost $3,000 is discounted 7%?

The discount is $3,000 \times .07 = 210.00 since $7\% = .07$.

If we know the cost of an item and its discounted price, we can find the rate of discount by using the formula

$$\text{rate of discount} = \frac{\text{cost} - \text{price}}{\text{cost}}.$$

EXAMPLE 2. What was the rate of discount if a boat which cost $5,000 was sold for $4,800?

Using this formula, we find that the rate of discount equals

$$\frac{5,000 - 4,800}{5,000} = \frac{200}{5,000} = \frac{1}{25} = .04 = 4\%.$$

After an item has been discounted once, it may be discounted again. This procedure is called *successive* discounting.

EXAMPLE 3: A bicycle originally cost $100 and was discounted 10%. After three months it was sold after being discounted 15%. How much was the bicycle sold for?

After the 10% discount the bicycle was selling for $100(.90) = 90. An item which costs $90 and is discounted 15% will sell for $90(.85) = 76.50, so the bicycle was sold for $76.50.

Notice that if you added the two discounts of 10% and 15% and treated the successive discounts as a single discount of 25%, your answer would be that the bicycle sold for $75, which is incorrect. Successive discounts are *not* identical to a single discount of the sum of the discounts. The previous example shows that successive discounts of 10% and 15% are not identical to a single discount of 25%.

I-5. Rounding off Numbers

5-1

Many times an approximate answer can be found more quickly and may be more useful than the exact answer. For example, if a company had sales of $998,875.63 during a year, it is easier to remember that the sales were about $1 million.

Rounding off a number to a decimal place means finding the multiple of the representative of that decimal place which is closest to the original number. Thus, rounding off a number to the nearest hundred means finding the multiple of 100 which is closest to the original number. Rounding off to the nearest tenth means finding the multiple of $\frac{1}{10}$ which is closest to the original number. After a number has been rounded off to a particular decimal place, all the digits to the right of that particular decimal place will be zero.

EXAMPLE 1:   Round off 9,403,420.71 to the nearest hundred.

You must find the multiple of one hundred which is closest to 9,403,420.71.

The answer is 9,403,400.

To round off a number to the *r*th decimal place:

(A) Look at the digit in the place to the right of the *r*th place;
(B) *If the digit is 0,1,2,3, or 4, change all the digits in places to the right of the rth place to 0* to round off the number.
(C) *If the digit is 5,6,7,8, or 9, add 1 to the digit in the rth place and change all the digits in places to the right of the rth place to 0* to round off the number.

For example, the multiple of 100 which is closest to 5,342.1 is 5,300. Most problems dealing with money are rounded off if the answer contains a fractional part of a cent. This is common business practice.

EXAMPLE 2:   If 16 donuts cost $1.00, how much should three donuts cost?

Three donuts should cost $\frac{3}{16}$ of $1.00. Since $\frac{3}{16} \times 1. = .1875$, the cost would be $.1875. In practice, you would round it up to $.19 or 19¢.

Rounding off numbers can help you get quick, approximate answers. Since many questions require only rough answers, you can save time on the test by rounding off numbers.

EXAMPLE 3: If 5,301 of the 499,863 workers employed at the XYZ factory don't show up for work on Monday, about what percentage of the workers don't show up?

(A) 1   (B) 2   (C) 3   (D) 4   (E) 5

You can quickly see that the answer is (A) by rounding off both numbers to the nearest thousand before you divide, because $\frac{5,000}{500,000} = \frac{1}{100} = .01 = 1\%$. The exact answer is $\frac{5,301}{499,863} = .010604$, but it would take much longer to get an exact answer.

EXAMPLE 4: Round off 43.79 to the nearest tenth.

The place to the right of tenths is hundredths, so look in the hundredths place. Since 9 is bigger than 5, add 1 to the tenths place. Therefore, 43.79 is 43.8 rounded off to the nearest tenth.

If the digit in the rth place is 9 and you need to add 1 to the digit to round off the number to the rth decimal place, put a zero in the rth place and add 1 to the digit in the position to the left of the rth place. For example, 298 rounded off to the nearest 10 is 300; 99,752 to the nearest thousand is 100,000.

I–6.   Signed Numbers

6–1

A number preceded by either a plus or a minus sign is called a SIGNED NUMBER. For example, +5, −6, −4.2, and +¾ are all signed numbers. If no sign is given with a number, a plus sign is assumed; thus, 5 is interpreted as +5.

Signed numbers can often be used to distinguish different concepts. For example, a profit of $10 can be denoted by +$10 and a loss of $10 by −$10. A temperature of 20 degrees below zero can be denoted −20°.

6–2

Signed numbers are also called DIRECTED NUMBERS. You can think of numbers arranged on a line, called a number line, in the following manner:

Take a line which extends indefinitely in both directions, pick a point on the line and call it 0, pick another point on the line to the right of 0 and call it 1. The point to the right of 1 which is exactly as far from 1 as 1 is from 0 is called 2, the point to the right of 2 just as far from 2 as 1 is from 0 is called 3, and so on. The point halfway between 0 and 1 is called ½, the point halfway between ½ and 1 is called ¾. In this way, you can identify any whole number or any fraction with a point on the line.

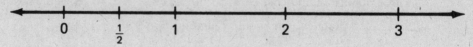

All the numbers which correspond to points to the right of 0 are called *positive numbers*. The sign of a positive number is +.

If you go to the left of zero the same distance as you did from 0 to 1, the point is called -1; in the same way as before, you can find $-2, -3, -\frac{1}{2}, -\frac{3}{2}$ and so on.

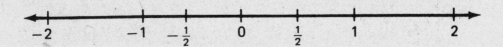

All the numbers which correspond to points to the left of zero are called *negative numbers*. Negative numbers are signed numbers whose sign is $-$. For example, $-3, -5.15, -.003$ are all negative numbers.

> *0 is neither positive nor negative; any nonzero number is positive or negative but not both.* So $-0 = 0$.

6-3
Absolute Value. The absolute value of a signed number is the distance of the number from 0. The absolute value of any nonzero number is *positive*. For example, the absolute value of 2 is 2; the absolute value of -2 is 2. The absolute value of a number a is denoted by $|a|$, so $|-2| = 2$. The absolute value of any number can be found by dropping its sign, $|-12| = 12, |4| = 4$. *Thus $|-a| = |a|$ for any number a.* The only number whose absolute value is zero is zero.

6-4
Adding Signed Numbers.
Case I. Adding numbers with the _same sign:_

  (A) The sign of the sum is the same as the sign of the numbers being added.
  (B) Add the absolute values.
  (C) Put the sign from step (A) in front of the number you obtained in step (B).

EXAMPLE 1: What is $-2 + (-3.1) + (-.02)$?

  (A) The sign of the sum will be $-$.
  (B) $|-2| = 2, |-3.1| = 3.1, |-.02| = .02$, and $2 + 3.1 + .02 = 5.12$.
  (C) The answer is -5.12.

Case II. Adding *two* numbers with *different signs:*

  (A) The sign of the sum is the sign of the number which is largest in absolute value.
  (B) Subtract the absolute value of the number with the smaller absolute value from the absolute value of the number with the larger absolute value.
  (C) The answer is the number you obtained in step (B) preceded by the sign from part (A).

EXAMPLE 2:   How much is $-5.1 + 3$?

   (A)   The absolute value of -5.1 is 5.1 and the absolute value of 3 is 3, so the sign of the sum will be $-$.
   (B)   5.1 is larger than 3, and $5.1 - 3 = 2.1$.
   (C)   The sum is -2.1.

Case III. Adding *more than two* numbers with *different signs:*

   (A)   Add all the positive numbers; the result is positive (this is Case I).
   (B)   Add all the negative numbers; the result is negative (this is Case I).
   (C)   Add the result of step (A) to the result of step (B), by using Case II.

EXAMPLE 3:   Find the value of $5 + 52 + (-3) + 7 + (-5.1)$.

   (A) $5 + 52 + 7 = 64$.
   (B) $-3 + (-5.1) = -8.1$.
   (C) $64 + (-8.1) = 55.9$, so the answer is 55.9.

EXAMPLE 4:   If a store made a profit of $23.50 on Monday, lost $2.05 on Tuesday, lost $5.03 on Wednesday, made a profit of $30.10 on Thursday, and made a profit of $41.25 on Friday, what was its total profit (or loss) for the week? Use $+$ for profit and $-$ for loss.

The total is $23.50 + (-2.05) + (-5.03) + 30.10 + 41.25$ which is $94.85 + (-7.08) = 87.77$. So the store made a profit of $87.77.

6-5

Subtracting Signed Numbers.   When subtracting signed numbers:

   (A)   Change the sign of the number you are subtracting (the subtrahend).
   (B)   <u>Add</u> the result of step (A) to the number being subtracted from (the minuend) using the rules of the preceding section.

EXAMPLE 1:   Subtract 4.1 from 6.5.

   (A)   4.1 becomes -4.1.
   (B) $6.5 + (-4.1) = 2.4$.

EXAMPLE 2:   What is $7.8 - (-10.1)$?

   (A) -10.1 becomes 10.1.
   (B) $7.8 + 10.1 = 17.9$.

So we subtract a negative number by adding a positive number with the same absolute value, and we subtract a positive number by adding a negative numbe of the same absolute value.

6–6

Multiplying Signed Numbers.

Case I. Multiplying two numbers:

(A) Multiply the absolute values of the numbers.

(B) If both numbers have the same sign, the result of step (A) is the answer, i.e. the product is positive. If the numbers have different signs, then the answer is the result of step (A) with a minus sign.

EXAMPLE 1: $(-5)(-12) = ?$

(A) $5 \times 12 = 60$

(B) Both signs are the same, so the answer is 60.

EXAMPLE 2: $(4)(-3) = ?$

(A) $4 \times 3 = 12$

(B) The signs are different, so the answer is -12. You can remember the sign of the product in the following way:

$$(-)(-) = +$$
$$(+)(+) = +$$
$$(-)(+) = -$$
$$(+)(-) = -$$

Case II. Multiplying more than two numbers:

(A) Multiply the first two factors using Case I.

(B) Multiply the result of (A) by the third factor.

(C) Multiply the result of (B) by the fourth factor.

(D) Continue until you have used each factor.

EXAMPLE 3: $(-5)(4)(2)(-\frac{1}{2})(\frac{3}{4}) = ?$

(A) $(-5)(4) = -20$

(B) $(-20)(2) = -40$

(C) $(-40)(-\frac{1}{2}) = 20$

(D) $(20)(\frac{3}{4}) = 15$, so the answer is 15.

> *The sign of the product is $+$ if there are no negative factors or an even number of negative factors. The sign of the product is $-$ if there are an odd number of negative factors.*

6–7

Dividing Signed Numbers.   Divide the absolute values of the numbers; the sign of the quotient is determined by the same rules as you used to determine the sign of a product. Thus,

$$+ \div + = +$$
$$- \div - = +$$
$$+ \div - = -$$
$$- \div + = -$$

EXAMPLE 1: Divide 53.2 by -4.

53.2 divided by 4 is 13.3. Since one of the numbers is positive and the other negative, the answer is -13.3.

EXAMPLE 2: $\dfrac{-5}{-2}=\dfrac{5}{2}$

I-7. Averages and Medians

7-1

Mean. The *average* or *arithmetic mean* of a collection of N numbers is the result of dividing the sum of all the numbers in the collection by N.

EXAMPLE 1: The scores of 9 students on a test were 72, 78, 81, 64, 85, 92, 95, 60, and 55. What was the average score of the students?

Since there are 9 students, the average is the total of all the scores divided by 9. So the average is $\dfrac{1}{9}$ of $(72+78+81+64+85+92+95+60+55)$, which is $\dfrac{1}{9}$ of 682 or $75\frac{7}{9}$.

EXAMPLE 2: The temperature at noon in Coldtown, U.S.A. was 5° on Monday, 10° on Tuesday, 2° below zero on Wednesday, 5° below zero on Thursday, 0° on Friday, 4° on Saturday, and 1° below zero on Sunday. What was the average temperature at noon for the week?

Use negative numbers for the temperatures below zero. The average temperature is the average of 5, 10, −2, −5, 0, 4 and −1, which is $\dfrac{5+10+(-2)+(-5)+0+4+(-1)}{7}=\dfrac{11}{7}=1\frac{4}{7}$. Therefore, the average temperature at noon for the week is $1\frac{4}{7}°$.

EXAMPLE 3: If the average annual income of 10 workers is $15,665 and two of the workers each made $20,000 for the year, what is the average annual income of the remaining 8 workers?

The total income of all 10 workers is 10 times the average income which is $156,650. The two workers made a total of $40,000, so the total income of the remaining 8 workers was $156,650 − $40,000 = $116,650. Therefore, the average annual income of the 8 remaining workers is $\dfrac{\$116,650}{8}=\$14,581.25$.

7-2

The Median. The number which is in the middle if the numbers in a collection of numbers are arranged in order is called the *median*. In example 1 above, the median score was 78, and in example 2, the median temperature for the week was 0. Notice that the medians were different from the averages. In example 3, we don't have enough data to find the median although we know the average.

In general, the median and the average of a collection of numbers are different.

If the number of objects in the collection is even, the median is the average of the two numbers in the middle of the array. For example, the median of 64, 66, 72, 75, 76, and 77 is the average of 72 and 75 which is 73.5.

I-8. Powers, Exponents, and Roots

8-1

If b is any number and n is a whole number greater than 0, b^n means the product of n factors each of which is equal to b. Thus,

$$b^n = b \times b \times b \times \cdots \times b \text{ where there are } n \text{ copies of } b.$$

If $n = 1$, there is only one copy of b so $b^1 = b$. Here are some examples,

$$2^5 = 2 \times 2 \times 2 \times 2 \times 2 = 32, (-4)^3 = (-4) \times (-4) \times (-4) = -64, \frac{3^2}{4} = \frac{3 \times 3}{4} = \frac{9}{4},$$
$$1^n = 1 \text{ for any } n, 0^n = 0 \text{ for any } n.$$

b^n is read as "b raised to the nth power." b^2 is read "b squared." b^2 is always greater than 0 (positive) if b is not zero, since the product of two negative numbers is positive. b^3 is read "b cubed," b^3 can be negative or positive.

You should know the following squares and cubes:

$1^2 = 1$	$8^2 = 64$
$2^2 = 4$	$9^2 = 81$
$3^2 = 9$	$10^2 = 100$
$4^2 = 16$	$11^2 = 121$
$5^2 = 25$	$12^2 = 144$
$6^2 = 36$	$13^2 = 169$
$7^2 = 49$	$14^2 = 196$
	$15^2 = 225$
$1^3 = 1$	$3^3 = 27$
$2^3 = 8$	$4^3 = 64$
	$5^3 = 125$

If you raise a fraction, $\frac{p}{q}$, to a power, then $\left(\frac{p}{q}\right)^n = \frac{p^n}{q^n}$. For example,

$$\left(\frac{5}{4}\right)^3 = \frac{5^3}{4^3} = \frac{125}{64}.$$

EXAMPLE 1: If the value of an investment triples each year, what percent of its value today will the investment be worth in 4 years?

The value increases by a factor of 3 each year. Since the time is 4 years, there will be four factors of 3. So the investment will be worth $3 \times 3 \times 3 \times 3 = 3^4$ as much as it is today. $3^4 = 81$, so the investment will be worth 8,100% of its value today in four years.

8–2

Exponents. In the expression b^n, b is called the base and n is called the *exponent*. In the expression 2^5, 2 is the base and 5 is the exponent. The exponent tells how many factors there are.

The *two basic formulas for problems involving exponents* are:

(A) $b^n \times b^m = b^{n+m}$

(B) $a^n \times b^n = (a \cdot b)^n$

(A) and (B) are called *laws of exponents*.

EXAMPLE 1: What is 6^3?

$$\text{Since } 6 = 3 \times 2, \; 6^3 = 3^3 \times 2^3 = 27 \times 8 = 216.$$
$$\text{or}$$
$$6^3 = 6 \times 6 \times 6 = 216.$$

EXAMPLE 2: Find the value of $2^3 \times 2^2$.

Using (A), $2^3 \times 2^2 = 2^{2+3} = 2^5$ which is 32. You can check this, since $2^3 = 8$ and $2^2 = 4$; $2^3 \times 2^2 = 8 \times 4 = 32$.

8–3

Negative Exponents. $b^0 = 1$ *for any nonzero number b.* By one of the laws of exponents (A) above, $b^n \times b^0$ should be $b^{n+0} = b^n$. If we still want (A) to be true, then b^0 must be 1. (NOTE: 0^0 is not defined.)

Using the law of exponents once more, you can define b^{-n} where n is a positive number. If (A) holds, $b^{-n} \times b^n = b^{-n+n} = b^0 = 1$, so $b^{-n} = \dfrac{1}{b^n}$. *Multiplying by b^{-n} is the same as dividing by b^n.*

EXAMPLE 1:

$$2^{-3} = \frac{1}{2^3} = \frac{1}{8}$$
$$2^0 = 1$$

EXAMPLE 2:

$$\left(\frac{1}{2}\right)^{-1} = \frac{1}{1/2} = 2$$

EXAMPLE 3: Find the value of $\dfrac{6^4}{3^3}$.

$$\frac{6^4}{3^3} = \frac{(3 \cdot 2)^4}{3^3} = \frac{3^4 \cdot 2^4}{3^3} = 3^4 \times 2^4 \times 3^{-3} = 3^4 \times 3^{-3} \times 2^4 = 3^1 \times 2^4 = 48.$$

8-4

Roots. If you raise a number d to the nth power and the result is b, then d is called the nth root of b, which is usually written $\sqrt[n]{b} = d$. Since $2^5 = 32$, then $\sqrt[5]{32} = 2$. The second root is called the square root and is written $\sqrt{}$; the third root is called the cube root. If you read the columns of the table on page 159 from right to left, you have a table of square roots and cube roots. For example, $\sqrt{225} = 15$; $\sqrt{81} = 9$; $\sqrt[3]{64} = 4$.

There are two possibilities for the square root of a positive number; the positive one is called the square root. Thus we say $\sqrt{9} = 3$ although $(-3) \times (-3) = 9$.

Since the square of any nonzero number is positive *the square root of a negative number is not defined as a real number.* Thus $\sqrt{-2}$ is not a real number. There are cube roots of negative numbers. $\sqrt[3]{-8} = -2$, because $(-2) \times (-2) \times (-2) = -8$.

You can also write roots as exponents; for example,

$$\sqrt[n]{b} = b^{1/n}; \text{ so } \sqrt{b} = b^{1/2}, \sqrt[3]{b} = b^{1/3}.$$

Since you can write roots as exponents, formula (B) above is especially useful.

$a^{1/n} \times b^{1/n} = (a \cdot b)^{1/n}$ or $\sqrt[n]{a \times b} = \sqrt[n]{a} \times \sqrt[n]{b}$. This formula is the basic formula for simplifying square roots, cube roots and so on. *On the test you must state your answer in a form which matches one of the choices given.*

EXAMPLE 1: $\sqrt{54} = ?$

Since $54 = 9 \times 6$, $\sqrt{54} = \sqrt{9 \times 6} = \sqrt{9} \times \sqrt{6}$. Since $\sqrt{9} = 3$, $\sqrt{54} = 3\sqrt{6}$.

You can not simplify by adding square roots unless you are taking square roots of the same number. For example,

$$\sqrt{3} + 2\sqrt{3} - 4\sqrt{3} = -\sqrt{3}, \text{ but } \sqrt{3} + \sqrt{2} \text{ is not equal to } \sqrt{5}.$$

EXAMPLE 2:   Simplify $6\sqrt{12} + 2\sqrt{75} - 3\sqrt{98}$.

Since $12 = 4 \times 3$, $\sqrt{12} = \sqrt{4 \times 3} = \sqrt{4} \times \sqrt{3} = 2\sqrt{3}$;
$75 = 25 \times 3$, so $\sqrt{75} = \sqrt{25} \times \sqrt{3} = 5\sqrt{3}$;
and $98 = 49 \times 2$, so $\sqrt{98} = \sqrt{49} \times \sqrt{2} = 7\sqrt{2}$.
Therefore, $6\sqrt{12} + 2\sqrt{75} - 3\sqrt{98} = 6 \times 2\sqrt{3} + 2 \times 5\sqrt{3} - 3 \times 7\sqrt{2} = 12\sqrt{3} + 10\sqrt{3} - 21\sqrt{2} = 22\sqrt{3} - 21\sqrt{2}$.

EXAMPLE 3:   Simplify $27^{1/3} \times 8^{1/3}$.

$27^{1/3} = \sqrt[3]{27} = 3$ and $8^{1/3} = 2$, so $27^{1/3} \times 8^{1/3} = 3 \times 2 = 6$. Notice that 6 is $\sqrt[3]{216}$ and $27^{1/3} \times 8^{1/3} = (27 \times 8)^{1/3} = 216^{1/3}$.

II. Algebra

II–1. Algebraic Expressions

1–1

Often it is necessary to deal with quantities which have a numerical value which is unknown. For example, we may know that Tom's salary is twice as much as Joe's salary. If we let the value of Tom's salary be called T and the value of Joe's salary be J, then T and J are numbers which are unknown. However, we do know that the value of T must be twice the value of J, or $T = 2J$.

T and $2J$ are examples of algebraic expressions. An algebraic expression may involve letters in addition to numbers and symbols; however, *in an algebraic expression a letter always stands for a number*. Therefore, you can multiply, divide, add, subtract and perform other mathematical operations on a letter. Thus, x^2 would mean x times x. Some examples of algebraic expressions are: $2x + y$, $y^3 + 9y$, $z^3 - 5ab$, $c + d + 4$, $5x + 2y(6x - 4y + z)$. When letters or numbers are written together without any sign or symbol between them, multiplication is assumed. Thus $6xy$ means 6 times x times y. $6xy$ is called a term; terms are separated by $+$ or $-$ signs. The expression $5z + 2 + 4x^2$ has three terms, $5z$, 2, and $4x^2$. Terms are often called monomials (mono = one). If an expression has more than one term, it is called a *polynomial*, (poly = many). The letters in an algebraic expression are called *variables* or *unknowns*. When a variable is multiplied by a number, the number is called the *coefficient* of the variable. So in the expression $5x^2 + 2yz$, the coefficient of x^2 is 5, and the coefficient of yz is 2.

1–2

Simplifying Algebraic Expressions. *Since there are only five choices of an answer given for the test questions, you must be able to recognize algebraic expressions which are equal.* It will also save time when you are working problems if you can change a complicated expression into a simpler one.

Case I. Simplifying expressions which don't contain parentheses:

- (A) Perform any multiplications or divisions before performing additions or subtractions. Thus, the expression $6x + y \div x$ means add $6x$ to the quotient of y divided by x. Another way of writing the expression would be $6x + \dfrac{y}{x}$. This is not the same as $\dfrac{6x + y}{x}$.
- (B) The order in which you multiply numbers and letters in a term does not matter. So $6xy$ is the same as $6yx$.
- (C) The order in which you add terms does not matter; for instance, $6x + 2y - x = 6x - x + 2y$.
- (D) If there are roots or powers in any terms, you may be able to simplify the term by using the laws of exponents. For example, $5xy \cdot 3x^2y = 15x^3y^2$.
- (E) Combine like terms. *Like terms* (or similar terms) are terms which have exactly the same letters raised to the same powers. So x, $-2x$, $\frac{1}{3}x$ are like terms. For example, $6x - 2x + x + y$ is equal to $5x + y$. In combining like terms, you simply add or subtract the coefficients of

the like terms, and the result is the coefficient of that term in the simplified expression. In our example above, the coefficients of x were $+6$, -2, and $+1$; since $6 - 2 + 1 = 5$ the coefficient of x in the simplified expression is 5.

(F) Algebraic expressions which involve divisions or factors can be simplified by using the techniques for handling fractions and the laws of exponents. Remember dividing by b^n is the same as multiplying by b^{-n}.

EXAMPLE 1: $3x^2 - 4\sqrt{x} + \sqrt{4x} + xy + 7x^2 = ?$

(D) $\sqrt{4x} = \sqrt{4}\sqrt{x} = 2\sqrt{x}$.

(E) $3x^2 + 7x^2 = 10x^2$, $-4\sqrt{x} + 2\sqrt{x} = -2\sqrt{x}$.

The original expression equals $3x^2 + 7x^2 - 4\sqrt{x} + 2\sqrt{x} + xy$. Therefore, the simplified expression is $10x^2 - 2\sqrt{x} + xy$.

EXAMPLE 2: Simplify $\dfrac{21x^4y^2}{3x^6y}$.

(F) $\dfrac{21}{3}x^4y^2x^{-6}y^{-1}$.

(B) $7x^4x^{-6}y^2y^{-1}$.

(D) $7x^{-2}y$, so the simplified term is $\dfrac{7y}{x^2}$.

EXAMPLE 3: Write $\dfrac{2x}{y} - \dfrac{4}{x}$ as a single fraction.

(F) A common denominator is xy so $\dfrac{2x}{y} = \dfrac{2x \cdot x}{y \cdot x} = \dfrac{2x^2}{xy}$, and $\dfrac{4}{x} = \dfrac{4y}{xy}$.

Therefore, $\dfrac{2x}{y} - \dfrac{4}{x} = \dfrac{2x^2}{xy} - \dfrac{4y}{xy} = \dfrac{2x^2 - 4y}{xy}$

Case II. Simplifying expressions which have parentheses:

The first rule is to perform the operations inside parentheses first. So $(6x + y) \div x$ means divide the sum of $6x$ and y by x. Notice that $(6x + y) \div x$ is different from $6x + y \div x$.

The main rule for getting rid of parentheses is the distributive law, which is expressed as $a(b + c) = ab + ac$. In other words, if any monomial is followed by an expression contained in a parenthesis, then *each* term of the expression is multiplied by the monomial. Once we have gotten rid of the parentheses, we proceed as we did in Case I.

EXAMPLE 4: $2x(6x - 4y + 2) = (2x)(6x) + (2x)(-4y) + (2x)(2) = 12x^2 - 8xy - 4x$.

If an expression has more than one set of parentheses, get rid of the *inner parentheses first* and then *work out* through the rest of the parentheses.

EXAMPLE 5: $2x - (x + 6(x - 3y) + 4y) = ?$

To remove the inner parentheses we multiply $6(x - 3y)$ getting $6x - 18y$. Now we have $2x - (x + 6x - 18y + 4y)$ which equals $2x - (7x - 14y)$. Distribute the minus sign (multiply by -1), getting $2x - 7x - (-14y) = -5x + 14y$. Sometimes brackets are used instead of parentheses.

EXAMPLE 6:   Simplify $-3x\left[\frac{1}{2}(3x - 2y) - 2(x(3 + y) + 4y)\right]$

$$= -3x\left[\frac{1}{2}(3x - 2y) - 2(3x + xy + 4y)\right]$$

$$= -3x\left[\frac{3}{2}x - y - 6x - 2xy - 8y\right]$$

$$= -3x\left[-\frac{9}{2}x - 2xy - 9y\right]$$

$$= \frac{27}{2}x^2 + 6x^2y + 27xy.$$

1-3

Adding and Subtracting Algebraic Expressions.   Since algebraic expressions are numbers, they can be added and subtracted.

> *The only algebraic terms which can be combined are like terms.*

EXAMPLE 1: $(3x + 4y - xy^2) + (3x + 2x(x - y)) = ?$

The expression $= (3x + 4y - xy^2) + (3x + 2x^2 - 2xy)$, removing the inner parentheses;
$= 6x + 4y + 2x^2 - xy^2 - 2xy$, combining like terms.

EXAMPLE 2: $(2a + 3a^2 - 4) - 2(4a^2 - 2(a + 4)) = ?$

It equals $(2a + 3a^2 - 4) - 2(4a^2 - 2a - 8)$, removing inner parentheses;
$= 2a + 3a^2 - 4 - 8a^2 + 4a + 16$, removing outer parentheses;
$= -5a^2 + 6a + 12$, combining like terms.

1-4

Multiplying Algebraic Expressions.   When you multiply two expressions, you multiply *each term of the first by each term of the second.*

EXAMPLE 1: $(b - 4)(b + a) = b(b + a) - 4(b + a) = ?$

$$= b^2 + ab - 4b - 4a.$$

EXAMPLE 2: $(2h - 4)(h + 2h^2 + h^3) = ?$

$$= 2h(h + 2h^2 + h^3) - 4(h + 2h^2 + h^3)$$
$$= 2h^2 + 4h^3 + 2h^4 - 4h - 8h^2 - 4h^3$$
$$= -4h - 6h^2 + 2h^4, \text{ which is the product.}$$

If you need to multiply more than two expressions, multiply the first two expressions, then multiply the result by the third expression, and so on until you have used each factor. Since algebraic expressions can be multiplied, they can be squared, cubed, or raised to other powers.

EXAMPLE 3: $(x - 2y)^3 = (x - 2y)(x - 2y)(x - 2y)$.

Since $(x - 2y)(x - 2y) = x^2 - 2yx - 2yx + 4y^2$
$$= x^2 - 4xy + 4y^2,$$

$$(x - y)^3 = (x^2 - 4xy + 4y^2)(x - 2y)$$
$$= x(x^2 - 4xy + 4y^2) - 2y(x^2 - 4xy + 4y^2)$$
$$= x^3 - 4x^2y + 4xy^2 - 2x^2y + 8xy^2 - 8y^3$$
$$= x^3 - 6x^2y + 12xy^2 - 8y^3.$$

The order in which you multiply algebraic expressions does not matter. Thus $(2a + b)(x^2 + 2x) = (x^2 + 2x)(2a + b)$.

1–5

Factoring Algebraic Expressions.   If an algebraic expression is the product of other algebraic expressions, then the expressions are called factors of the original expression. For instance, we claim that $(2h - 4)$ and $(h + 2h^2 + h^3)$ are factors of $-4h - 6h^2 + 2h^4$. We can always check to see if we have the correct factors by multiplying; so by example 2 above we see that our claim is correct. We need to be able to factor algebraic expressions in order to solve quadratic equations. It also can be helpful in dividing algebraic expressions.

First remove any monomial factor which appears in every term of the expression.

Some examples:

$$3x + 3y = 3(x + y): 3 \text{ is a monomial factor.}$$
$$15a^2b + 10ab = 5ab(3a + 2): 5ab \text{ is a monomial factor.}$$
$$\frac{1}{2}hy - 3h^3 + 4hy = h\left(\frac{1}{2}y - 3h^2 + 4y\right),$$

$$= h\left(\frac{9}{2}y - 3h^2\right): h \text{ is a monomial factor.}$$

You may also need to factor expressions which contain squares or higher powers into factors which only contain linear terms. (Linear terms are terms in which variables are raised only to the first power.) The first rule to remember is that since $(a + b)(a - b) = a^2 + ba - ba - b^2 = a^2 - b^2$, the difference of two squares can always be factored.

EXAMPLE 1:   Factor $(9m^2 - 16)$.

$9m^2 = (3m)^2$ and $16 = 4^2$, so the factors are $(3m - 4)(3m + 4)$.

Since $(3m - 4)(3m + 4) = 9m^2 - 16$, these factors are correct.

EXAMPLE 2:   Factor $x^4y^4 - 4x^2$.

$x^4y^4 = (x^2y^2)^2$ and $4x^2 = (2x)^2$, so the factors are $x^2y^2 + 2x$ and $x^2y^2 - 2x$.

You also may need to factor expressions which contain squared terms and linear terms, such as $x^2 + 4x + 3$. The factors will be of the form $(x + a)$ and $(x + b)$. Since $(x + a)(x + b) = x^2 + (a + b)x + ab$, you must look for a pair of numbers a and b such that $a \cdot b$ is the numerical term in the expression and $a + b$ is the coefficient of the linear term (the term with exponent 1).

EXAMPLE 3:   Factor $x^2 + 4x + 3$.

You want numbers whose product is 3 and whose sum is 4. Look at the possible factors of three and check whether they add up to 4. Since $3 = 3 \times 1$ and $3 + 1$ is 4, the factors are $(x + 3)$ and $(x + 1)$. Remember to check by multiplying.

EXAMPLE 4:   Factor $y^2 + y - 6$.

Since -6 is negative, the two numbers a and b must be of opposite sign. Possible pairs of factors for -6 are -6 and $+1$, 6 and -1, 3 and -2, and -3 and 2. Since $-2 + 3 = 1$, the factors are $(y + 3)$ and $(y - 2)$. So $(y + 3)(y - 2) = y^2 + y - 6$.

EXAMPLE 5:   Factor $a^3 + 4a^2 + 4a$.

Factor out a, so $a^3 + 4a^2 + 4a = a(a^2 + 4a + 4)$. Consider $a^2 + 4a + 4$; since $2 + 2 = 4$ and $2 \times 2 = 4$, the factors are $(a + 2)$ and $(a + 2)$. Therefore, $a^3 + 4a^2 + 4a = a(a + 2)^2$.

If the term with the highest exponent has a coefficient unequal to 1, divide the entire expression by that coefficient. For example, to factor $3a^3 + 12a^2 + 12a$, factor out a 3 from each term, and the result is $a^3 + 4a^2 + 4a$ which is $a(a + 2)^2$. Thus, $3a^3 + 12a^2 + 12a = 3a(a + 2)^2$.

There are some expressions which can not be factored, for example, $x^2 + 4x + 6$. In general, if you can't factor something by using the methods given above, don't waste a lot of time on the question. Sometimes you may be able to check the answers given to find out what the correct factors are.

1–6

Division of Algebraic Expressions.   The main things to remember in division are:

(1)   When you divide a sum, you can get the same result by dividing each term and adding quotients. For example, $\dfrac{9x + 4xy + y^2}{x} = \dfrac{9x}{x} + \dfrac{4xy}{x} + \dfrac{y^2}{x} = 9 + 4y + \dfrac{y^2}{x}$.

(2) You can cancel common factors, so the results on factoring will be helpful. For example, $\dfrac{x^2-2x}{x-2}=\dfrac{x(x-2)}{x-2}=x.$

You can also divide one algebraic expression by another using long division.

EXAMPLE 1: $(15x^2+2x-4)\div 3x-1.$

$$
\begin{array}{r}
5x+2 \\
3x-1\overline{)15x^2+2x-4} \\
\underline{15x^2-5x} \\
7x-4 \\
\underline{6x-2} \\
x-2
\end{array}
$$

So the answer is $5x+2$ with a remainder of $x-2$.
You can check by multiplying,

$(5x+2)(3x-1)=15x^2+6x-5x-2$

$\qquad = 15x^2+x-2$; now add the remainder $x-2$

and the result is $15x^2+x-2+x-2=15x^2+2x-4.$

Division problems where you need to use (1) and (2) are more likely than problems involving long division.

II–2. Equations

2–1

AN EQUATION is a statement that says two algebraic expressions are equal. $x+2=3,\ 4+2=6,\ 3x^2+2x-6=0,\ x^2+y^2=z^2,\ \dfrac{y}{x}=2+z,$ and $A=LW$ are all examples of equations. We will refer to the algebraic expressions on each side of the equals sign as the left side and the right side of the equation. Thus, in the equation $2x+4=6y+x$, $2x+4$ is the left side and $6y+x$ is the right side.

2–2

If we assign specific numbers to each variable or unknown in an algebraic expression, then the algebraic expression will be equal to a number. This is called *evaluating* the expression. For example, if you evaluate $2x+4y^2+3$ for $x=-1$ and $y=2$, the expression is equal to $2(-1)+4\cdot 2^2+3=-2+4\cdot 4+3=17.$

If we evaluate each side of an equation and the number obtained is the same for each side of the equation, then the specific values assigned to the unknowns are called a *solution of the equation*. Another way of saying this is that the choices for the unknowns satisfy the equation.

EXAMPLE 1:   Consider the equation $2x + 3 = 9$.

If $x = 3$, then the left side of the equation becomes $2 \cdot 3 + 3 = 6 + 3 = 9$, so both sides equal 9, and $x = 3$ is a solution of $2x + 3 = 9$. If $x = 4$, then the left side is $2 \cdot 4 + 3 = 11$. Since 11 is not equal to 9, $x = 4$ is *not* a solution of $2x + 3 = 9$.

EXAMPLE 2:   Consider the equation $x^2 + y^2 = 5x$.

If $x = 1$ and $y = 2$, then the left side is $1^2 + 2^2$ which equals $1 + 4 = 5$. The right side is $5 \cdot 1 = 5$, since both sides are equal to 5, $x = 1$ and $y = 2$ is a solution.

If $x = 5$ and $y = 0$, then the left side is $5^2 + 0^2 = 25$ and the right side is $5 \cdot 5 = 25$, so $x = 5$ and $y = 0$ is also a solution.

If $x = 1$ and $y = 1$, then the left side is $1^2 + 1^2 = 2$ and the right side is $5 \cdot 1 = 5$. Therefore, since $2 \neq 5$, $x = 1$ and $y = 1$ is not a solution.

There are some equations which *do not have any solutions which are real numbers*. Since the square of any real number is positive or zero, the equation $x^2 = -4$ does not have any solutions which are real numbers.

2-3

Equivalence.   One equation is *equivalent* to another equation, if they have exactly the same solutions. The basic idea in solving equations is to transform a given equation into an equivalent equation whose solutions are obvious.

The two main tools for solving equations are:

   (A)   If you add or subtract the same algebraic expression to or from *each side* of an equation, the resulting equation is equivalent to the original equation.

   (B)   If you multiply or divide both sides of an equation by the same *nonzero* algebraic expression, the resulting equation is equivalent to the original equation.

The most common type of equation is the linear equation with only one unknown. $6z = 4z - 3$, $3 + a = 2a - 4$, $3b + 2b = b - 4b$, are all examples of linear equations with only one unknown.

Using (A) and (B), you can solve a linear equation in one unknown in the following way:

   (1)   Group all the terms which involve the unknown on one side of the equation and all the terms which are purely numerical on the other side of the equation. This is called *isolating the unknown*.
   (2)   Combine the terms on each side.
   (3)   Divide each side by the coefficient of the unknown.

EXAMPLE 1: Solve $6x + 2 = 3$ for x.

(1) Using (A) subtract 2 from each side of the equation. Then $6x + 2 - 2 = 3 - 2$ or $6x = 3 - 2$.

(2) $6x = 1$.

(3) Divide each side by 6. Therefore, $x = \frac{1}{6}$.

You should always check your answer in the original equation.

$$\text{Since } 6\left(\frac{1}{6}\right) + 2 = 1 + 2 = 3, \ x = \frac{1}{6} \text{ is a solution.}$$

EXAMPLE 2: Solve $3x + 15 = 3 - 4x$ for x.

(1) Add $4x$ to each side and subtract 15 from each side; $3x + 15 - 15 + 4x = 3 - 15 - 4x + 4x$.

(2) $7x = -12$.

(3) Divide each side by 7, so $x = \frac{-12}{7}$ is the solution.

CHECK:

$$3\left(\frac{-12}{7}\right) + 15 = \frac{-36}{7} + 15 = \frac{69}{7} \text{ and } 3 - 4\left(\frac{-12}{7}\right) = 3 + \frac{48}{7} = \frac{69}{7}.$$

If you do the same thing to each side of an equation, the result is still an equation but it may not be equivalent to the original equation. Be especially careful if you square each side of an equation. For example, $x = -4$ is an equation; square both sides and you get $x^2 = 16$ which has both $x = 4$ and $x = -4$ as solutions. *Always check your answer in the original equation.*

If the equation you want to solve involves square roots, get rid of the square roots by squaring each side of the equation. Remember to check your answer since squaring each side does not always give an equivalent equation.

EXAMPLE 3: Solve $\sqrt{4x + 3} = 5$.

Square both sides: $(\sqrt{4x + 3})^2 = 4x + 3$ and $5^2 = 25$, so the new equation is $4x + 3 = 25$. Subtract 3 from each side to get $4x = 22$ and now divide each side by 4. The solution is $x = \frac{22}{4} = 5.5$. Since $4(5.5) + 3 = 25$ and $\sqrt{25} = 5$, $x = 5.5$ is a solution to the equation $\sqrt{4x + 3} = 5$.

If an equation involves fractions, multiply through by a common denominator and then solve. Check your answer to make sure you did not multiply or divide by zero.

EXAMPLE 4: Solve $\frac{3}{a} = 9$ for a.

Multiply each side by a: the result is $3 = 9a$. Divide each side by 9, and you obtain $\frac{3}{9} = a$ or $a = \frac{1}{3}$. Since $\frac{3}{1/3} = 3 \cdot 3 = 9$, $a = \frac{1}{3}$ is a solution.

You may be asked to solve two equations in two unknowns. Use one equation to solve for one unknown in terms of the other; now change the second equation into an equation in only one unknown which can be solved by the methods of the preceding section.

EXAMPLE 1: Solve for x and y: $\begin{cases} \dfrac{x}{y} = 3 \\ 2x + 4y = 20. \end{cases}$

The first equation gives $x = 3y$. Using $x = 3y$, the second equation is $2(3y) + 4y = 6y + 4y$ or $10y = 20$, so $y = \dfrac{20}{10} = 2$. Since $x = 3y$, $x = 6$.

CHECK:

$$\frac{6}{2} = 3, \text{ and } 2 \cdot 6 + 4 \cdot 2 = 20, \text{ so } x = 6 \text{ and } y = 2 \text{ is a solution.}$$

EXAMPLE 2: If $2x + y = 5$ and $x + y = 4$, find x and y.

Since $x + y = 4$, $y = 4 - x$, so $2x + y = 2x + 4 - x = x + 4 = 5$ and $x = 1$. If $x = 1$, then $y = 4 - 1 = 3$. So $x = 1$ and $y = 3$ is the solution.

CHECK:

$$2 \cdot 1 + 3 = 5 \text{ and } 1 + 3 = 4.$$

Sometimes we can solve two equations by adding them or by subtracting one from the other. If we subtract $x + y = 4$ from $2x + y = 5$ in example 2, we have $x = 1$. However, the previous method will work in cases when the addition method does not work.

2-5

Solving Quadratic Equations. If the terms of an equation contain squares of the unknown as well as linear terms, the equation is called *quadratic*. Some examples of quadratic equations are $x^2 + 4x = 3$, $2z^2 - 1 = 3z^2 - 2z$, and $a + 6 = a^2 + 6$.

To solve a quadratic equation:

(A) Group all the terms on one side of the equation so that the other side is *zero*.
(B) Combine the terms on the nonzero side.
(C) Factor the expression into linear expressions.
(D) Set the linear factors equal to zero and solve.

The method depends on the fact that if a product of expressions is zero then at least one of the expressions must be zero.

EXAMPLE 1:   Solve $x^2 + 4x = -3$.

  (A) $x^2 + 4x + 3 = 0$
  (C) $x^2 + 4x + 3 = (x + 3)(x + 1) = 0$
  (D) So $x + 3 = 0$ or $x + 1 = 0$. Therefore, the solutions are $x = -3$ and $x = -1$.

CHECK:

$$(-3)^2 + 4(-3) = 9 - 12 = -3$$
$$(-1)^2 + 4(-1) = 1 - 4 = -3, \text{ so } x = -3 \text{ and } x = -1$$
are solutions.

A quadratic equation will usually have 2 different solutions, but it is possible for a quadratic to have only one solution or even no real solution.

EXAMPLE 2:   If $2z^2 - 1 = 3z^2 - 2z$, what is z?

  (A) $0 = 3z^2 - 2z^2 - 2z + 1$
  (B) $z^2 - 2z + 1 = 0$
  (C) $z^2 - 2z + 1 = (z - 1)^2 = 0$
  (D) $z - 1 = 0$ or $z = 1$

CHECK:

$$2 \cdot 1^2 - 1 = 2 - 1 = 1 \text{ and } 3 \cdot 1^2 - 2 \cdot 1 = 3 - 2 = 1,$$
so $z = 1$ is a solution.

Equations which may not look like quadratics may be changed into quadratics.

EXAMPLE 3:   Find a if $a - 3 = \dfrac{10}{a}$.

Multiply each side of the equation by a to obtain $a^2 - 3a = 10$, which is quadratic.

  (A) $a^2 - 3a - 10 = 0$
  (C) $a^2 - 3a - 10 = (a - 5)(a + 2)$
  (D) So $a - 5 = 0$ or $a + 2 = 0$.

Therefore, $a = 5$ and $a = -2$ are the solutions.

CHECK:

$$5 - 3 = 2 = \frac{10}{5} \text{ so } a = 5 \text{ is a solution.}$$

$$-2 - 3 = -5 = \frac{10}{-2} \text{ so } a = -2 \text{ is a solution.}$$

You can also solve quadratic equations by using the *quadratic formula*. The quadratic formula states that the solutions of the quadratic equation

$ax^2 + bx + c = 0$ are $x = \dfrac{1}{2a} [-b + \sqrt{b^2 - 4ac}]$ and $x = \dfrac{1}{2a} [-b - \sqrt{b^2 - 4ac}]$.

This is usually written $x = \dfrac{1}{2a} [-b \pm \sqrt{b^2 - 4ac}]$. Use of the quadratic formula would replace steps (C) and (D).

EXAMPLE 4: Find x if $x^2 + 5x = 12 - x^2$.

(A) $x^2 + 5x + x^2 - 12 = 0$
(B) $2x^2 + 5x - 12 = 0$

So $a = 2, b = 5$ and $c = -12$. Therefore, using the quadratic formula, the solutions are $x = \frac{1}{4}[-5\pm \sqrt{25 - 4 \cdot 2 \cdot (-12)}] = \frac{1}{4}[-5\pm \sqrt{25 + 96}] = \frac{1}{4}[-5\pm \sqrt{121}]$. So we have $x = \frac{1}{4}[-5\pm 11]$. The solutions are $x = \frac{3}{2}$ and $x = -4$.

CHECK:

$$\left(\frac{3}{2}\right)^2 + 5\cdot\frac{3}{2} = \frac{9}{4} + \frac{15}{2} = \frac{39}{4} = 12 - \frac{9}{4} = 12 - \left(\frac{3}{2}\right)^2$$
$$(-4)^2 + 5(-4) = 16 - 20 = -4 = 12 - 16 = 12 - (-4)^2$$

NOTE: If $b^2 - 4ac$ is negative, then the quadratic equation $ax^2 + bx + c = 0$ has no real solutions because negative numbers do not have real square roots.

The quadratic formula will always give you the solutions to a quadratic equation. If you can factor the equation, factoring will usually give you the solution in less time. Remember, you want to answer as many questions as you can in the time given. So factor if you can. If you don't see the factor immediately, then use the formula.

II–3. Word Problems

3–1

The general method for solving word problems is to translate them into algebraic problems. The quantities you are seeking are the unknowns, which are usually represented by letters. The information you are given in the problem is then turned into equations. Words such as "is," "was," "are," and "were" mean equals, and words like "of" and "as much as" mean multiplication.

EXAMPLE 1: A coat was sold for $75. The coat was sold for 150% of the cost of the coat. How much did the coat cost?

You want to find the cost of the coat. Let $\$C$ be the cost of the coat. You know that the coat was sold for $75 and that $75 was 150% of the cost. So $\$75 = 150\%$ of $\$C$ or $75 = 1.5C$. Solving for C you get $C = \frac{75}{1.5} = 50$, so the coat cost $50.

CHECK:

$$(1.5)\,\$50 = \$75.$$

EXAMPLE 2: Tom's salary is 125% of Joe's salary; Mary's salary is 80% of Joe's salary. The total of all three salaries is $61,000. What is Mary's salary?

Let M = Mary's salary, J = Joe's salary and T = Tom's salary. The first sentence says T = 125% of J or $T = \frac{5}{4}J$, and M = 80% of J or $M = \frac{4}{5}J$. The second sentence says that $T + M + J = \$61{,}000$. Using the information from the first sentence, $T + M + J = \frac{5}{4}J + \frac{4}{5}J + J = \frac{25}{20}J + \frac{16}{20}J + J = \frac{61}{20}J$. So $\frac{61}{20}J = 61{,}000$; solving for J you have $J = \frac{20}{61} \times 61{,}000 = 20{,}000$. Therefore, $T = \frac{5}{4} \times \$20{,}000 = \$25{,}000$ and $M = \frac{4}{5} \times \$20{,}000 = \$16{,}000$.

CHECK:

$$\$25{,}000 + \$16{,}000 + \$20{,}000 = \$61{,}000.$$

So Mary's salary is $16,000.

EXAMPLE 3: Steve weighs 25 pounds more than Jim. The combined weight of Jim and Steve is 325 pounds. How much does Jim weigh?

Let S = Steve's weight in pounds and J = Jim's weight in pounds. The first sentence says $S = J + 25$, and the second sentence becomes $S + J = 325$. Since $S = J + 25$, $S + J = 325$ becomes $(J + 25) + J = 2J + 25 = 325$. So $2J = 300$ and $J = 150$. Therefore, Jim weighs 150 pounds.

CHECK:

If Jim weighs 150 pounds, then Steve weighs
175 pounds and $150 + 175 = 325$.

EXAMPLE 4: A carpenter is designing a closet. The floor will be in the shape of a rectangle whose length is 2 feet more than its width. How long should the closet be if the carpenter wants the area of the floor to be 15 square feet?

The area of a rectangle is length times width, usually written $A = LW$, where A is the area, L is the length, and W is the width. We know $A = 15$ and $L = 2 + W$. Therefore, $LW = (2 + W)W = W^2 + 2W$; this must equal 15. So we need to solve $W^2 + 2W = 15$ or $W^2 + 2W - 15 = 0$. Since $W^2 + 2W - 15$ factors into $(W + 5)(W - 3)$, the only possible solutions are $W = -5$ and $W = 3$. Since W represents a width, -5 cannot be the answer; therefore the width is 3 feet. The length is the width plus two feet, so the length is 5 feet. Since $5 \times 3 = 15$, the answer checks.

3–2

Distance Problems. A common type of word problem is a distance or velocity problem. The basic formula is

$$\boxed{\text{DISTANCE TRAVELED} = \text{RATE} \times \text{TIME.}}$$

The formula is abbreviated $d = rt$.

EXAMPLE 1: A train travels at an average speed of 50 miles per hour for $2\frac{1}{2}$ hours and then travels at a speed of 70 miles per hour for $1\frac{1}{2}$ hours. How far did the train travel in the entire 4 hours?

The train traveled for $2\frac{1}{2}$ hours at an average speed of 50 miles per hour, so it traveled $50 \times \frac{5}{2} = 125$ miles in the first $2\frac{1}{2}$ hours. Traveling at a speed of 70 miles per hour for $1\frac{1}{2}$ hours, the distance traveled will be equal to $r \times t$ where $r = 70$ m.p.h. and $t = 1\frac{1}{2}$, so the distance is $70 \times \frac{3}{2} = 105$ miles. Therefore, the total distance traveled is $125 + 105 = 230$ miles.

EXAMPLE 2: The distance from Cleveland to Buffalo is 200 miles. A train takes $3\frac{1}{2}$ hours to go from Buffalo to Cleveland and $4\frac{1}{2}$ hours to go back from Cleveland to Buffalo. What was the average speed of the train for the round trip from Buffalo to Cleveland and back?

The train took $3\frac{1}{2} + 4\frac{1}{2} = 8$ hours for the trip. The distance of a round trip is $2(200) = 400$ miles. Since $d = rt$ then 400 miles $= r \times 8$ hours. Solve for r and you have $r = \dfrac{400 \text{ miles}}{8 \text{ hours}} = 50$ miles per hour. Therefore the average speed is 50 miles per hour.

The speed in the formula is the average speed. If you know that there are different speeds for different lengths of time, then you must use the formula more than once, as we did in example 1.

3–3

Work Problems. In this type of problem you can always assume all workers in the same category work at the same rate. The main idea is: If it takes k

workers 1 hour to do a job then *each worker does* $\frac{1}{k}$ *of the job in an hour* or he works at the rate of $\frac{1}{k}$ of the job per hour. If it takes m workers h hours to finish a job then each worker does $\frac{1}{m}$ of the job in h hours so he does $\frac{1}{h}$ of $\frac{1}{m}$ in an hour. Therefore, each worker *works at the rate of* $\frac{1}{mh}$ *of the job per hour.*

EXAMPLE 1: If 5 men take an hour to dig a ditch, how long should it take 12 men to dig a ditch of the same type?

Since 5 workers took an hour, each worker does $\frac{1}{5}$ of the job in an hour. So 12 workers will work at the rate of $\frac{12}{5}$ of the job per hour. Thus if T is the time it takes for 12 workers to do the job, $\frac{12}{5} \times T = 1$ job and $T = \frac{5}{12} \times 1$, so

$$T = \frac{5}{12} \text{ hours or 25 minutes.}$$

EXAMPLE 2: Worker A takes 8 hours to do a job. Worker B takes 10 hours to do the same job. How long should it take worker A and worker B working together, but independently, to do the same job?

Worker A works at a rate of $\frac{1}{8}$ of the job per hour, since he takes 8 hours to finish the job. Worker B finished the job in 10 hours, so he works at a rate of $\frac{1}{10}$ of the job per hour. Therefore, if they work together they should complete $\frac{1}{8} + \frac{1}{10} = \frac{18}{80} = \frac{9}{40}$, so they work at a rate of $\frac{9}{40}$ of the job per hour together. So if T is the time it takes them to finish the job, $\frac{9}{40}$ of the job per hour $\times T$ hours must equal 1 job. Therefore,

$$\frac{9}{40} \times T = 1 \text{ and } T = \frac{40}{9} = 4\frac{4}{9} \text{ hours.}$$

EXAMPLE 3: There are two taps, tap 1 and tap 2, in a keg. If both taps are opened, the keg is drained in 20 minutes. If tap 1 is closed and tap 2 is open, the keg will be drained in 30 minutes. If tap 2 is closed and tap 1 is open, how long will it take to drain the keg?

Tap 1 and tap 2 together take 20 minutes to drain the keg, so together they drain the keg at a rate of $\frac{1}{20}$ of the keg per minute. Tap 2 takes 30 minutes to drain the keg by itself, so it drains the keg at the rate of $\frac{1}{30}$ of the keg per minute. Let r be the rate at which tap 1 will drain the keg by itself. Then $\left(r + \frac{1}{30}\right)$ of the keg per minute is the rate at which both taps together will drain the keg, so $r + \frac{1}{30} = \frac{1}{20}$. Therefore, $r = \frac{1}{20} - \frac{1}{30} = \frac{1}{60}$, and tap 1 drains the keg

at the rate of $\frac{1}{60}$ of the keg per minute, so it will take 60 minutes or 1 hour for tap 1 to drain the keg if tap 2 is closed.

II–4. Counting Problems

4–1

An example of the first type of counting problem is: 50 students signed up for both English and Math. 90 students signed up for either English or Math. If 25 students are taking English but not taking Math, how many students are taking Math but not taking English?

In these problems, "either . . . or . . ." means you can take both, so the people taking both are counted among the people taking either Math or English.

You must avoid counting the same people twice in these problems. The formula is:

   the number taking English or Math = the number taking English + the number taking Math − the number taking both.

You have to subtract the number taking both subjects since they are counted once with those taking English and counted again with those taking Math.

A person taking English is either taking Math or not taking Math, so there are $50 + 25 = 75$ people taking English, 50 taking English and Math and 25 taking English but not taking Math. Since 75 are taking English, $90 = 75 +$ number taking Math $- 50$; so there are $90 - 25 = 65$ people taking Math. 50 of the people taking Math are taking English so $65 - 50$ or 15 are taking Math but not English.

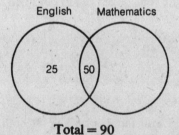

The figure shows what is given. Since 90 students signed up for English or Mathematics, 15 must be taking Mathematics but not English.

Total $= 90$

EXAMPLE 1: In a survey, 60% of those surveyed owned a car and 80% of those surveyed owned a T.V. If 55% owned both a car and a T.V., what percent of those surveyed owned a car or a T.V. or both?

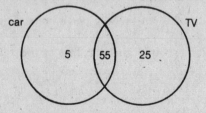

The basic formula is:

people who own a car or a T.V. = people who own a car
+ people who own a T.V. − people who own both a car and a T.V.

So the people who own a car or a T.V. = 60% + 80% − 55% = 85%. Therefore, 85% of the people surveyed own either a car or a T.V.

If we just add 60% and 80% the result is 140% which is impossible. This is because the 55% who own both are counted twice.

4–2

> If an event can happen in m different ways, and each of the m ways is followed by a second event which can occur in k different ways, then the first event can be followed by the second event in $m \cdot k$ different ways. This is called the *fundamental principle of counting*.

EXAMPLE 1: If there are 3 different roads from Syracuse to Binghamton and 4 different roads from Binghamton to Scranton, how many different routes are there from Syracuse to Scranton which go through Binghamton?

There are 3 different ways to go from Syracuse to Binghamton. Once you are in Binghamton, there are 4 different ways to get to Scranton. So using the fundamental principle of counting, there are $3 \times 4 = 12$ different ways to get from Syracuse to Scranton going through Binghamton.

EXAMPLE 2: A club has 20 members. They are electing a president and a vice president. How many different outcomes of the election are possible? (Assume the president and vice president must be different members of the club.)

There are 20 members, so there are 20 choices for president. Once a president is chosen, there are 19 members left who can be vice president. So there are $20 \cdot 19 = 380$ different possible outcomes of the election.

II–5. Ratio and Proportion

5–1

Ratio. A ratio is a comparison of two numbers by division. The ratio of a to b is written as $a{:}b = \frac{a}{b} = a \div b$. We can handle ratios as fractions, since a ratio is a fraction. In the ratio $a{:}b$, a and b are called the *terms* of the ratio. *Since* $a{:}b$ *is a fraction,* b *can never be zero.* The fraction $\frac{a}{b}$ is usually different from the fraction $\frac{b}{a}$ $\left(\text{for example } \frac{3}{2} \text{ is not the same as } \frac{2}{3}\right)$ so *the order of the terms in a ratio is important.*

EXAMPLE 1: If an orange costs 20¢ and an apple costs 12¢, what is the ratio of the cost of an orange to the cost of an apple?

The ratio is $\frac{20¢}{12¢} = \frac{5}{3}$ or 5:3. Notice that the ratio of the cost of an apple to the

cost of an orange is $\frac{12¢}{20¢} = \frac{3}{5}$ or 3:5. So the order of the terms is important.

A ratio is a number, so if you want to find the ratio of two quantities they must be expressed in the same units.

EXAMPLE 2: What is the ratio of 8 inches to 6 feet?

Change 6 feet into inches. Since there are 12 inches in a foot, 6 feet = 6 × 12 inches = 72 inches. So the ratio is $\frac{8 \text{ inches}}{72 \text{ inches}} = \frac{1}{9}$ or 1:9. If you regard ratios as fractions, the units must cancel out. In example 2, if you did not change units the ratio would be $\frac{8 \text{ inches}}{6 \text{ feet}} = \frac{4}{3}$ inches/feet, which is not a number.

If two numbers measure different quantities, their quotient is usually called a rate. For example, $\frac{50 \text{ miles}}{2 \text{ hours}}$ which equals 25 miles per hour is a rate of speed.

5–2

Proportion. A proportion is a statement that two ratios are equal. For example, $\frac{3}{12} = \frac{1}{4}$ is a proportion; it could also be expressed as 3:12 = 1:4 or 3:12 :: 1:4.

In the proportion $a:b = c:d$, the terms on the outside, (a and d), are called the *extremes*, and the terms on the inside, (b and c), are called the *means*. Since $a:b$ and $c:d$ are ratios, b and d are both different from zero, so $bd \neq 0$. Multiply each side of $\frac{a}{b} = \frac{c}{d}$ by bd; you get $(bd)\left(\frac{a}{b}\right) = ad$ and $(bd)\left(\frac{c}{d}\right) = bc$. Since $bd \neq 0$, the proportion $\frac{a}{b} = \frac{c}{d}$ is equivalent to the equation $ad = bc$. This is usually expressed in the following way.

In a proportion the product of the extremes is equal to the product of the means.

EXAMPLE 1: Find x if $\frac{4}{5} = \frac{10}{x}$.

In the proportion $\frac{4}{5} = \frac{10}{x}$, 4 and x are the extremes and 5 and 10 are the means, so $4x = 5 \cdot 10 = 50$.

Solve for x and we get $x = \frac{50}{4} = 12.5$.

Finding the products ad and bc is also called *cross-multiplying the proportion:*
$\frac{a}{b} \diagdown \frac{c}{d}$. So cross-multiplying a proportion gives two equal numbers. The proportion $\frac{a}{b} = \frac{c}{d}$ is read "a is to b as c is to d."

EXAMPLE 2: Two numbers are in the ratio 5:4 and their difference is 10. What is the larger number?

Let m and n be the two numbers. Then $\frac{m}{n} = \frac{5}{4}$ and $m - n = 10$. Cross-multiply the proportion and you get $5n = 4m$ or $n = \frac{4}{5}m$. So $m - n = m - \frac{4}{5}m = \frac{1}{5}m = 10$ and $m = 50$, which means $n = \frac{4}{5} \cdot 50 = 40$. Therefore, the larger number is 50.

CHECK:

$$\frac{50}{40} = \frac{5}{4} \text{ and } 50 - 40 = 10.$$

Two variables, a and b, are *directly proportional* if they satisfy a relationship of the form $a = kb$, where k is a number. The distance a car travels in two hours and its average speed for the two hours are directly proportional, since $d = 2s$ where d is the distance and s is the average speed expressed in miles per hour. Here $k = 2$. Sometimes the word *directly* is omitted, so a and b are proportional means $a = kb$.

EXAMPLE 3: If m is proportional to n and $m = 5$ when $n = 4$, what is the value of m when $n = 18$?

There are two different ways to work the problem.

I. Since m and n are directly proportional, $m = kn$; and $m = 5$ when $n = 4$, so $5 = k \cdot 4$ which means $k = \frac{5}{4}$. Therefore, $m = \frac{5}{4}n$. So when $n = 18$,

$m = \frac{5}{4} \cdot 18 = \frac{90}{4} = 22.5$.

II. Since m and n are directly proportional, $m = kn$. If n' is some value of n, then the value of m corresponding to n' we will call m', and $m' = kn'$. So $\frac{m}{n} = k$ and $\frac{m'}{n'} = k$; therefore, $\frac{m}{n} = \frac{m'}{n'}$ is a proportion. Since $m = 5$ when $n = 4$, $\frac{m}{n} = \frac{5}{4} = \frac{m'}{18}$. Cross-multiply and we have $4m' = 90$ or

$m' = \frac{90}{4} = 22.5$.

If two quantities are proportional, you can always set up a proportion in this manner.

EXAMPLE 4: If a machine makes 3 yards of cloth in 2 minutes, how many yards of cloth will the machine make in 50 minutes?

The amount of cloth is proportional to the time the machine operates. Let y be the number of yards of cloth the machine makes in 50 minutes; then $\frac{2\text{ minutes}}{50\text{ minutes}} = \frac{3\text{ yards}}{y\text{ yards}}$, so $\frac{2}{50} = \frac{3}{y}$. Cross multiply, and you have $2y = 150$, so $y = 75$. Therefore, the machine makes 75 yards of cloth in 50 minutes.

Since a ratio is a number, the units must cancel; so put the numbers which measure the same quantity in the same ratio.

> *Any two units of measurement of the same quantity are directly proportional.*

EXAMPLE 5: How many ounces are there in $4\frac{3}{4}$ pounds?

Let x be the number of ounces in $4\frac{3}{4}$ pounds. Since there are 16 ounces in a pound, $\frac{x\text{ ounces}}{16\text{ ounces}} = \frac{4\frac{3}{4}\text{ pounds}}{1\text{ pound}}$. Cross-multiply to get $x = 16 \cdot 4\frac{3}{4} = 16 \cdot \frac{19}{4} = 76$; so $4\frac{3}{4}$ pounds = 76 ounces.

You can always change units by using a proportion. You should know the following measurements:

LENGTH:	1 foot = 12 inches
	1 yard = 3 feet
AREA:	1 square foot = 144 square inches
	1 square yard = 9 square feet
TIME:	1 minute = 60 seconds
	1 hour = 60 minutes
	1 day = 24 hours
	1 week = 7 days
	1 year = 52 weeks
VOLUME:	1 quart = 2 pints
	1 gallon = 4 quarts
WEIGHT:	1 ounce = 16 drams
	1 pound = 16 ounces
	1 ton = 2000 pounds

EXAMPLE 6: On a map, it is $2\frac{1}{2}$ inches from Harrisburg to Gary. The actual distance from Harrisburg to Gary is 750 miles. What is the actual distance from town A to town B if they are 4 inches apart on the map?

Let d miles be the distance from A to B; then $\frac{2\frac{1}{2}\text{ inches}}{4\text{ inches}} = \frac{750\text{ miles}}{d\text{ miles}}$. Cross-multiply and we have $\left(2\frac{1}{2}\right)d = 4 \times 750 = 3{,}000$, so $d = \frac{2}{5} \times 3{,}000 = 1{,}200$.

Therefore, the distance from A to B is 1,200 miles. Problems like this one are often called scale problems.

Two variables, a and b, are *indirectly proportional* if they satisfy a relationship of the form $k = ab$, where k is a number. So the average speed of a car and the time it takes the car to travel 300 miles are indirectly proportional, since $st = 300$ where s is the speed and t is the time.

EXAMPLE 7: m is indirectly proportional to n and $m = 5$ when $n = 4$. What is the value of m when $n = 18$?

Since m and n are indirectly proportional, $m \cdot n = k$, and $k = 5 \cdot 4 = 20$ because $m = 5$ when n $= 4$. Therefore, $18m = k = 20$, so $m = \dfrac{20}{18} = \dfrac{10}{9}$ when $n = 18$.

Other examples of indirect proportion are work problems (see page 174).

If two quantities are directly proportional, then when one increases, the other increases. If two quantities are indirectly proportional when one quantity increases, the other decreases.

5–3

It is also possible to compare three or more numbers by a ratio. The numbers A, B, and C are in the ratio 2:4:3 means $A{:}B = 2{:}4$, $A{:}C = 2{:}3$, and $B{:}C = 4{:}3$. The order of the terms is important. $A{:}B{:}C$ is read A is to B is to C.

EXAMPLE 1: What is the ratio of Tom's salary to Martha's salary to Anne's salary if Tom makes \$15,000, Martha makes \$12,000 and Anne makes \$10,000?

The ratio is 15,000:12,000:10,000 which is the same as 15:12:10. You can cancel a factor which appears in *every* term.

EXAMPLE 2: The angles of a triangle are in the ratio 5:4:3; how many degrees are there is the largest angle?

The sum of the angles in a triangle is $180°$. If the angles are $a°$, $b°$, and $c°$, then $a + b + c = 180$, and $a{:}b{:}c{:} = 5{:}4{:}3$. You could find b in terms of a since $\dfrac{a}{b} = \dfrac{5}{4}$

and c in terms of a since $\dfrac{a}{c} = \dfrac{5}{3}$ and then solve the equation for a.

A quicker method for this type of problem is:

(1) Add all the numbers, so $5 + 4 + 3 = 12$.
(2) Use each number as the numerator of a fraction whose denominator is the result of step (1), getting $\dfrac{5}{12}, \dfrac{4}{12}, \dfrac{3}{12}$.
(3) Each quantity is the corresponding fraction (from step (2)), of the total.

Thus

$a = \dfrac{5}{12}$ of 180 or 75, $b = \dfrac{4}{12}$ of 180 or 60, and $c = \dfrac{3}{12}$ of 180 or 45.

So the largest angle is $75°$.

CHECK:

$$75{:}60{:}45 = 5{:}4{:}3 \text{ and } 75 + 60 + 45 = 180.$$

II–6. Sequence and Progressions

6–1

A SEQUENCE is an ordered collection of numbers. For example, 2,4,6,8,10, . . . is a sequence. 2,4,6,8,10 are called the *terms* of the sequence. We identify the terms by their position in the sequence; so 2 is the first term, 8 is the 4th term and so on. The dots mean the sequence continues; you should be able to figure out the succeeding terms. In the example, the sequence is the sequence of even integers, and the next term after 10 would be 12.

EXAMPLE 1:   What is the eighth term of the sequence 1,4,9,16,25, . . . ?

Since $1^2 = 1$, $2^2 = 4$, $3^2 = 9$, the sequence is the sequence of squares of integers, so the eighth term is $8^2 = 64$.

6–2

An *arithmetical progression* is a sequence of numbers with the property that the *difference* of any two consecutive numbers is always the same. The numbers 2,6,10,14,18,22, . . . constitute an arithmetic progression, since each term is 4 more than the term before it. 4 is called the common difference of the progression.

If d is the common difference and a is the first term of the progression, then the nth term will be $a + (n - 1)d$. So a progression with common difference 4 and initial term 5 will have $5 + 6(4) = 29$ as its 7th term. You can check your answer. The sequence would be 5,9,13,17,21,25,29, . . . so 29 is the seventh term.

A sequence of numbers is called a *geometric progression* if the *ratio* of consecutive terms is always the same. So 3,6,12,24,48, . . . is a geometric progression since $\frac{6}{3} = 2 = \frac{12}{6} = \frac{24}{12} = \frac{48}{24}$, ... *The nth term of a geometric series is* ar^{n-1} where a is the first term and r is the common ratio. If a geometric progression started with 2 and the common ratio was 3, then the fifth term should be $2 \cdot 3^4 = 2 \cdot 81 = 162$. The sequence would be 2,6,18,54,162, . . . so 162 is indeed the fifth term of the progression.

We can quickly add up the first *n* terms of a geometric progression which starts with *a* and has common ratio *r*. *The formula for the sum of the first n terms is* $\frac{ar^n - a}{r - 1}$ when $r \neq 1$. (If $r = 1$ all the terms are the same so the sum is *na*.)

EXAMPLE 1:   Find the sum of the first 7 terms of the sequence 5,10,20,40, ...

Since $\frac{10}{5} = \frac{20}{10} = \frac{40}{20} = 2$, the sequence is a geometric sequence with common ratio 2. The first term is 5, so $a = 5$ and the common ratio is 2. The sum of the first seven terms means $n = 7$, thus the sum is

$$\frac{5 \cdot 2^7 - 5}{2 - 1} = 5(2^7 - 1) = 5(128 - 1) = 5 \cdot 127 = 635.$$

CHECK:

The first seven terms are 5,10,20,40,80,160,320, and $5 + 10 + 20 + 40 + 80 + 160 + 320 = 635$.

II–7. Inequalities

7–1

A number is positive if it is greater than 0, so $1, \frac{1}{1000}$, and 53.4 are all positive numbers. Positive numbers are signed numbers whose sign is +. If you think of numbers as points on a number line (see section 6, page 155), positive numbers correspond to points to the right of 0.

A number is negative if it is less than 0. $-\frac{4}{5}, -50$, and $-.0001$ are all negative numbers. Negative numbers are signed numbers whose sign is −. Negative numbers correspond to points to the left of 0 on a number line.

0 is the only number which is neither positive nor negative.

$a > b$ means the number a is greater than the number b, that is $a = b + x$ where x is a positive number. If we look at a number line, $a > b$ means a is to the right of b. $a > b$ can also be read as b is less than a, which is also written $b < a$. For example, $-5 > -7.5$ because $-5 = -7.5 + 2.5$ and 2.5 is positive.

The notation $a \leq b$ means a is less than or equal to b, or b is greater than or equal to a. For example, $5 \geq 4$; also $4 \geq 4$. $a \neq b$ means a is not equal to b.

> If you need to know whether one fraction is greater than another fraction, put the fractions over a common denominator and compare the numerators.

EXAMPLE 1: Which is larger, $\frac{13}{16}$ or $\frac{31}{40}$?

A common denominator is 80.

$\frac{13}{16} = \frac{65}{80}$, and $\frac{31}{40} = \frac{62}{80}$;

since $65 > 62$,

$\frac{65}{80} > \frac{62}{80}$,

so $\frac{13}{16} > \frac{31}{40}$.

7–2

Inequalities have certain properties which are similar to equations. We can talk about the left side and the right side of an inequality, and we can use algebraic expressions for the sides of an inequality. For example, $6x < 5x + 4$. A value for an unknown *satisfies an inequality*, if when you evaluate each side of the inequality the numbers satisfy the inequality. So if $x = 2$, then $6x = 12$ and $5x + 4 = 14$ and since $12 < 14$, $x = 2$ satisfies $6x < 5x + 4$. Two inequalities are equivalent if the same collection of numbers satisfies both inequalities.

The following basic principles are used in work with inequalities:

(A) Adding the same expression to *each* side of an inequality gives an equivalent inequality (written $a < b \Leftrightarrow a + c < b + c$ where $\Leftrightarrow$ means equivalent).

(B) Subtracting the same expression from *each* side of an inequality gives an equivalent inequality ($a < b \Leftrightarrow a - c < b - c$).

(C) Multiplying or dividing *each* side of an inequality by the same *positive* expression gives an equivalent inequality ($a < b \Leftrightarrow ca < cb$ for $c > 0$).

(D) Multiplying or dividing each side of an inequality by the same *negative* expression *reverses* the inequality ($a < b \Leftrightarrow ca > cb$ for $c < 0$).

(E) If both sides of an inequality have the same sign, inverting both sides of the inequality *reverses* the inequality.

$$0 < a < b \Leftrightarrow 0 < \frac{1}{b} < \frac{1}{a}$$

$$a < b < 0 \Leftrightarrow \frac{1}{b} < \frac{1}{a} < 0$$

(F) If two inequalities are of the same type (both greater or both less), adding the respective sides gives the same type of inequality.

$$(a < b \text{ and } c < d, \text{ then } a + c < b + d)$$

Note that the inequalities are *not* equivalent.

(G) If $a < b$ and $b < c$ then $a < c$.

EXAMPLE 1: Find the values of x for which $5x - 4 < 7x + 2$.

Using **principle** (B) subtract $5x + 2$ from each side, so $(5x - 4 < 7x + 2) \Leftrightarrow -6 < 2x$. Now use **principle** (C) and divide each side by 2, so $-6 < 2x \Leftrightarrow -3 < x$.

So any x greater than -3 satisfies the inequality. It is a good idea to make a spot check. -1 is > -3; let $x = -1$ then $5x - 4 = -9$ and $7x + 2 = -5$. Since $-9 < -5$, the answer is correct for at least the particular value $x = -1$.

EXAMPLE 2: Find the values of a which satisfy $a^2 + 1 > 2a + 4$.

Subtract $2a$ from each side, so
$(a^2 + 1 > 2a + 4) \Leftrightarrow a^2 - 2a + 1 > 4$.
$a^2 - 2a + 1 = (a - 1)^2$ so
$a^2 - 2a + 1 > 4 \Leftrightarrow (a - 1)^2 > 2^2$.

We need to be careful when we take the square roots of inequalities. If $q^2 > 4$ and if $q > 0$, then $q > 2$; but if $q < 0$, then $q < -2$. We must look at two cases in example 2. First, if $(a - 1) \geq 0$ then

$(a - 1)^2 > 2^2 \Leftrightarrow a - 1 > 2$ or $a > 3$.
If $(a - 1) < 0$ then $(a - 1)^2 > 2^2 \Leftrightarrow a - 1 < -2 \Leftrightarrow a < -1$.
So the inequality is satisfied if $a > 3$ or if $a < -1$.

CHECK:

$$(-2)^2 + 1 = 5 > 2(-2) + 4 = 0, \text{ and } 5^2 + 1 = 26 > 14 = 2 \cdot 5 + 4.$$

Some inequalities are not satisfied by *any* real number. For example, since $x^2 \geq 0$ for all x, there is no real number x such that $x^2 < -9$.

You may be given an inequality and asked whether other inequalities follow from the original inequality. You should be able to answer such questions by using principles (A) through (G).

If there is any property of inequalities you can't remember, try out some specific numbers. If $x < y$, then what is the relation between $-x$ and $-y$? Since $4 < 5$ but $-5 < -4$, the relation is probably $-x > -y$, which is true by (D).

Probably the most common mistake is forgetting to reverse the inequalities if you multiply or divide by a negative number.

III. Geometry

III–1. Angles

1–1

If two straight lines meet at a point they form an *angle*. The point is called the *vertex* of the angle and the lines are called the *sides* or *rays* of the angle. The sign for angle is $\angle$ and an angle can be denoted in the following ways:

    (A) $\angle ABC$ where B is the vertex, A is a point on one side, and C a point on the other side.

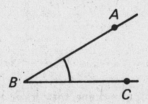

    (B) $\angle B$ where B is the vertex.

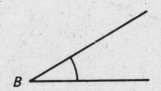

(C) $\angle 1$ or $\angle x$ where x or 1 is written inside the angle.

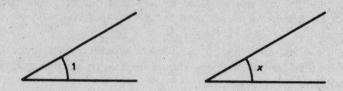

Angles are usually measured in degrees. We say that an angle equals x degrees, when its measure is x degrees. Degrees are denoted by °. An angle of 50 degrees is 50°. $60' = 1°$, $60'' = 1'$ where $'$ is read minutes and $''$ is read seconds.

1-2

Two angles are *adjacent* if they have the same vertex and a common side and one angle is not inside the other.

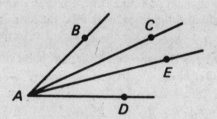

$\angle BAC$ and $\angle CAD$ are adjacent, but $\angle CAD$ and $\angle EAD$ are not adjacent.

If two lines intersect at a point, they form 4 angles. The angles opposite each other are called *vertical* angles. $\angle 1$ and $\angle 3$ are vertical angles. $\angle 2$ and $\angle 4$ are vertical angles.

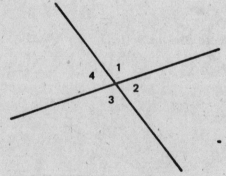

Vertical angles are equal,

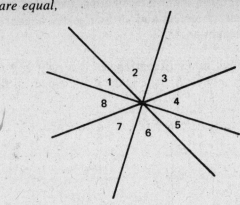

so $\angle 1 = \angle 5$, $\angle 2 = \angle 6$, $\angle 3 = \angle 7$, $\angle 4 = \angle 8$.

1–3

A straight angle is an angle whose sides lie on a straight line. *A straight angle equals 180°.*

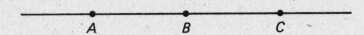

$\angle ABC$ is a straight angle.

If the sum of two adjacent angles is a straight angle, then the angles are *supplementary* and each angle is the supplement of the other.

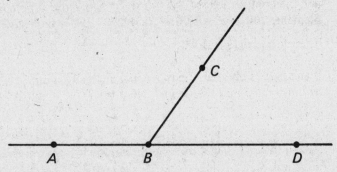

$\angle ABC$ and $\angle CBD$ are supplementary.

If an angle of $x°$ and an angle of $y°$ are supplements, then $x + y = 180$.

If two supplementary angles are equal, they are both *right angles*. A right angle is half of a straight angle. A right angle = 90°.

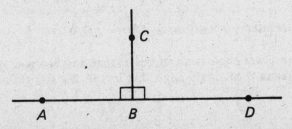

∠ABC = ∠CBD and they are both right angles. A right angle is denoted by ∟. When 2 lines intersect and all four of the angles are equal, then each of the angles is a right angle.

If the sum of two adjacent angles is a right angle, then the angles are *complementary* and each angle is the complement of the other.

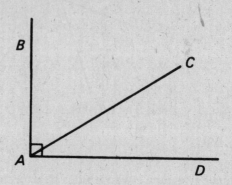

∠BAC and ∠CAD are complementary.

If an angle of x° and an angle of y° are complementary, then $x + y = 90$.

EXAMPLE 1:   If the supplement of angle x is three times as much as the complement of angle x, how many degrees is angle x?

Let d be the number of degrees in angle x; then the supplement of x is $(180 - d)°$, and the complement of x is $(90 - d)°$. Since the supplement is 3 times the complement, $180 - d = 3(90 - d) = 270 - 3d$ which gives $2d = 90$, so $d = 45$.

Therefore, angle x is 45°.

If an angle is divided into two equal angles by a straight line, then the angle has been *bisected* and the line is called the *bisector* of the angle.

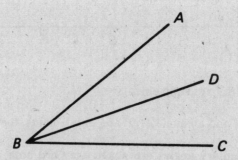

BD bisects ∠ABC; so ∠ABD = ∠DBC.

An *acute angle* is an angle less than a right angle. An *obtuse* angle is an angle greater than a right angle, but less than a straight angle.

∠1 is an acute angle, and ∠2 is an obtuse angle.

III–2. Lines

2–1

A line is understood to be a straight line. A line is assumed to extend indefinitely in both directions. *There is one and only one line between two distinct points.* There are two ways to denote a line:

(1) (A) by a single letter: l is a line;

l

(2) (B) by two points on the line: AB is a line.

A *B*

A *line segment* is the part of a line between two points called *endpoints*. A line segment is denoted by its endpoints.

A *B*

AB is a line segment. If a point P on a line segment is equidistant from the endpoints, then P is called the *midpoint* of the line segment.

A P B P is the midpoint of AB if the length of $AP=$

the length of PB.   Two line segments are equal if their lengths are equal; so $AP = PB$ means the line segment AP has the same length as the line segment PB.

When a line segment is extended indefinitely in one direction, it is called a *ray*. A ray has one endpoint.

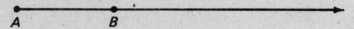

AB is a ray which has *A* as its endpoint.

2–2

P is a *point of intersection* of two lines if *P* is a point which is on both of the lines. *Two different lines can not have more than one point of intersection,* because there is only one line between two points.

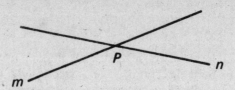

P is the point of intersection of *m* and *n*. We also say *m and n intersect at P*.

Two lines in the same plane are parallel if they do not intersect no matter how far they are extended.

m and *n* are parallel, but *k* and *l* are not parallel since if *k* and *l* are extended they will intersect. Parallel lines are denoted by the symbol ‖; so *m* ‖ *n* means *m* is parallel to *n*.

If two lines are parallel to a third line, then they are parallel to each other.

If a third line intersects two given lines, it is called a *transversal*. A transversal and the two given lines form eight angles. The four inside angles are called *interior* angles. The four outside angles are called *exterior* angles. If two angles are on opposite sides of the transversal they are called *alternate* angles.

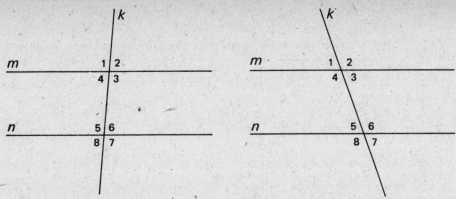

k is a transversal of the lines m and n. Angles 1, 2, 7, and 8 are the exterior angles, and angles 3, 4, 5, and 6 are the interior angles. ∠4 and ∠6 are an example of a pair of alternate angles. ∠1 and ∠5, ∠2 and ∠6, ∠3 and ∠7, and ∠4 and ∠8 are pairs of *corresponding* angles.

If two parallel lines are intersected by a transversal then:

  (1)   Alternate interior angles are equal.
  (2)   Corresponding angles are equal.
  (3)   Interior angles on the same side of the transversal are supplementary.

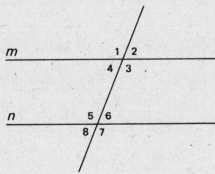

If we use the fact that vertical angles are equal, we can replace "interior" by "exterior" in (1) and (3).

m is parallel to n implies:

  (1)   ∠4 = ∠6 and ∠3 = ∠5
  (2)   ∠1 = ∠5, ∠2 = ∠6, ∠3 = ∠7 and ∠4 = ∠8
  (3)   ∠3 + ∠6 = 180° and ∠4 + ∠5 = 180°

The reverse is also true. Let m and n be two lines which have k as a transversal.

  (1)   If a pair of alternate interior angles are equal, then m and n are parallel.
  (2)   If a pair of corresponding angles are equal, then m and n are parallel.
  (3)   If a pair of interior angles on the same side of the transversal are supplementary, then m is parallel to n.

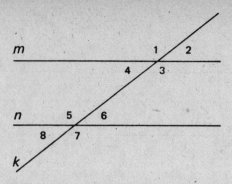

If $\angle 3 = \angle 5$, then $m \parallel n$. If $\angle 4 = \angle 6$ then $m \parallel n$. If $\angle 2 = \angle 6$ then $m \parallel n$. If $\angle 3 + \angle 6 = 180°$, then $m \parallel n$.

EXAMPLE 1: If m and n are two parallel lines and angle 1 is 60°, how many degrees is angle 2?

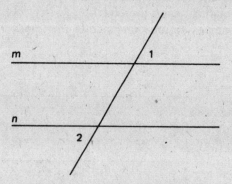

Let $\angle 3$ be the vertical angle equal to angle 2.

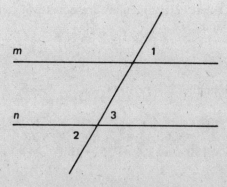

$\angle 3 = \angle 2$. Since m and n are parallel, corresponding angles are equal. Since $\angle 1$ and $\angle 3$ are corresponding angles, $\angle 1 = \angle 3$. Therefore, $\angle 1 = \angle 2$, and $\angle 2$ equals 60° since $\angle 1 = 60°$.

2-3

When two lines intersect and all four of the angles formed are equal, the lines are said to be *perpendicular*. If two lines are perpendicular, they are the sides of right angles whose vertex is the point of intersection.

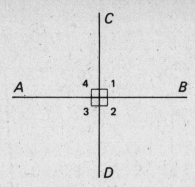

AB is perpendicular to CD, and angles 1, 2, 3, and 4 are all right angles. ⊥ is the symbol for perpendicular; so $AB \perp CD$.

If two lines in a plane are perpendicular to the same line, then the two lines are parallel.

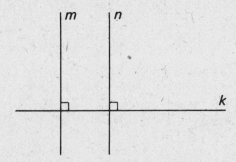

$m \perp k$ and $n \perp k$ implies that $m \parallel n$.

If *any one* of the angles formed when two lines intersect is a right angle, then the lines are perpendicular.

III–3. Polygons

A POLYGON is a closed figure in a plane which is composed of line segments which meet only at their endpoints. The line segments are called *sides* of the polygon, and a point where two sides meet is called a *vertex* (plural *vertices*) of the polygon.

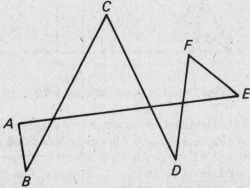

$ABCDEF$ is not a polygon since the line segments intersect at points which are not endpoints.

Some examples of polygons are:

A polygon is usually denoted by the vertices given in order.

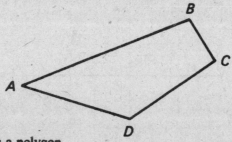

ABCD is a polygon.

A *diagonal* of a polygon is a line segment whose endpoints are nonadjacent vertices. The *altitude* from a vertex *P* to a side is the line segment with endpoint *P* which is perpendicular to the side.

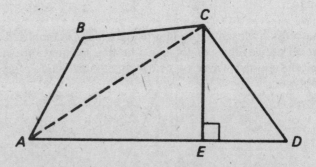

AC is a diagonal, and *CE* is the altitude from *C* to *AD*.

Polygons are classified by the number of angles or sides they have. A polygon with three angles is called a *triangle;* a four-sided polygon is a *quadrilateral;* a polygon with five angles is a *pentagon;* a polygon with six angles is a *hexagon;* an eight-sided polygon is an *octagon.* The number of angles is always equal to the number of sides in a polygon, so a six-sided polygon is a hexagon. The term *n*-gon refers to a polygon with *n* sides.

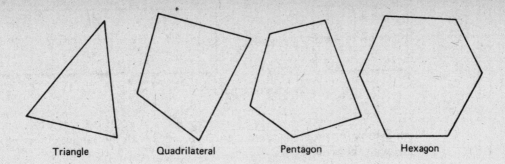

Triangle   Quadrilateral   Pentagon   Hexagon

If the sides of a polygon are all equal in length and if all the angles of a polygon are equal, the polygon is called a *regular* polygon.

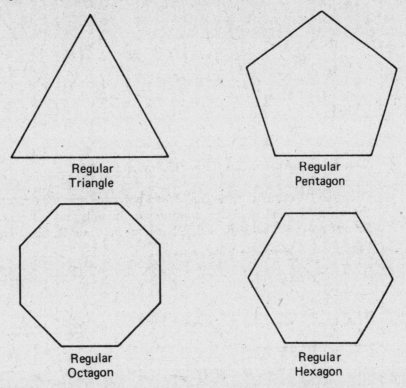

Regular
Triangle

Regular
Pentagon

Regular
Octagon

Regular
Hexagon

If the corresponding sides and the corresponding angles of two polygons are equal, the polygons are *congruent*. Congruent polygons have the same size and the same shape.

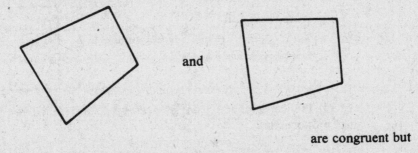

and

are congruent but

and

are not congruent.

In figures for problems on congruence, sides with the same number of strokes through them are equal.

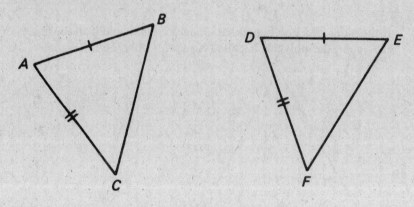

This figure indicates that $AB = DE$ and $AC = DF$.

If all the corresponding angles of two polygons are equal and the lengths of the corresponding sides are proportional, the polygons are said to be *similar*. Similar polygons have the same shape but need not be the same size.

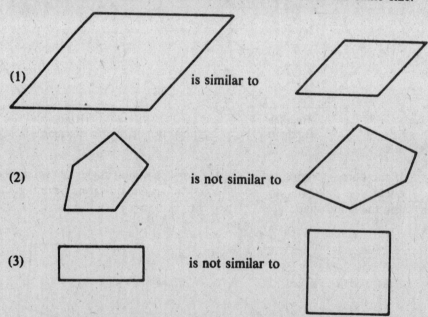

(1)   is similar to

(2)   is not similar to

(3)   is not similar to

In (3) the corresponding angles are equal, but the corresponding sides are not proportional.

The sum of all the angles of an *n*-gon is $(n - 2)180°$. So the sum of the angles in a hexagon is $(6 - 2)180° = 720°$.

III–4. Triangles

4–1

A TRIANGLE is a 3-sided polygon. If two sides of a triangle are equal, it is called *isosceles*. If all three sides are equal, it is an *equilateral* triangle. If all of the sides have different lengths, the triangle is *scalene*. When one of the angles in a triangle is a right angle, the triangle is a *right triangle*. If one of the angles is obtuse we have an *obtuse triangle*. If all the angles are acute, the triangle is an *acute triangle*.

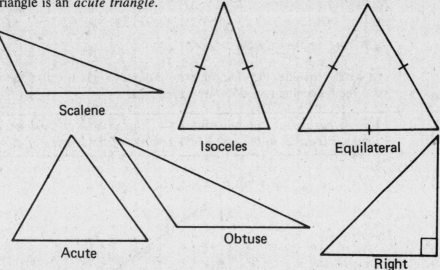

The symbol for a triangle is △; so △*ABC* means a triangle whose vertices are *A, B,* and *C*.

> *The sum of the angles in a triangle is 180°.*

The sum of the lengths of any two sides of a triangle must be longer than the remaining side.

If two angles in a triangle are equal, then the lengths of the sides opposite the equal angles are equal. If two sides of a triangle are equal, then the angles opposite the two equal sides are equal. In an equilateral triangle all the angles are equal and each angle = 60°. If each of the angles in a triangle is 60°, then the triangle is equilateral.

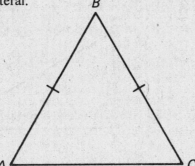

If *AB = BC*, then ∠*BAC* = ∠*BCA*.

If one angle in a triangle is larger than another angle, the side opposite the larger angle is longer than the side opposite the smaller angle. If one side is longer than another side, then the angle opposite the longer side is larger than the angle opposite the shorter side.

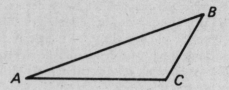

$AB > AC$ implies $\angle BCA > \angle ABC$.

In a right triangle, the side opposite the right angle is called the *hypotenuse*, and the remaining two sides are called *legs*.

> **The Pythagorean Theorem** states that *the square of the length of the hypotenuse is equal to the sum of the squares of the lengths of the legs.*

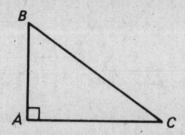

$$(BC)^2 = (AB)^2 + (AC)^2$$

If $AB = 4$ and $AC = 3$ then $(BC)^2 = 4^2 + 3^2 = 25$ so $BC = 5$. If $BC = 13$ and $AC = 5$, then $13^2 = 169 = (AB)^2 + 5^2$. So $(AB)^2 = 169 - 25 = 144$ and $AB = 12$.

If the lengths of the three sides of a triangle are a, b, and c and $a^2 = b^2 + c^2$, then the triangle is a right triangle where a is the length of the hypotenuse.

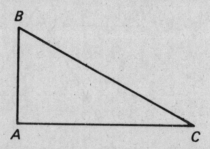

If $AB = 8$, $AC = 15$, and $BC = 17$, then since $17^2 = 8^2 + 15^2$, $\angle BAC$ is a right angle.

4–2

CONGRUENCE. Two triangles are congruent, if two pairs of corresponding sides and the corresponding *included* angles are equal. This is called *Side-Angle-Side* and is denoted by S.A.S.

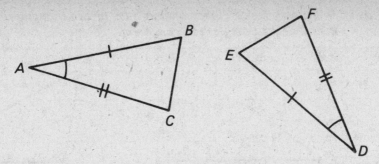

$AB = DE$, $AC = DF$ and $\angle BAC = \angle EDF$ imply that $\triangle ABC \cong \triangle DEF$. $\cong$ means congruent.

Two triangles are congruent if two pairs of corresponding angles and the corresponding *included* sides are equal. This is called *Angle-Side-Angle* or A.S.A.

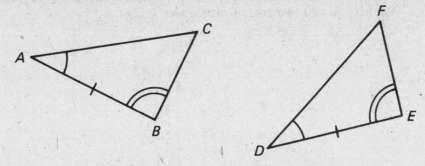

If $AB = DE$, $\angle BAC = \angle EDF$, and $\angle CBA = \angle FED$ then $\triangle ABC \cong \triangle DEF$.

If all three pairs of corresponding sides of two triangles are equal, then the triangles are congruent. This is called *Side-Side-Side* or S.S.S.

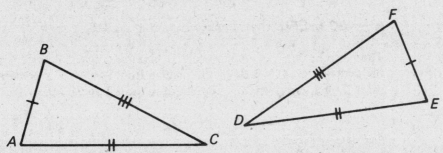

$AB = EF$, $AC = ED$, and $BC = FD$ imply that $\triangle ABC \cong \triangle EFD$.

Because of the Pythagorean Theorem, if any two corresponding sides of two right triangles are equal, the third sides are equal and the triangles are congruent.

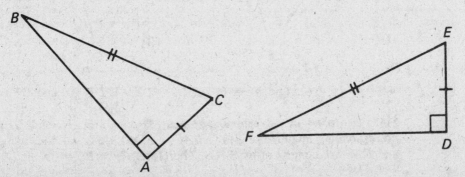

$AC = DE$ and $BC = EF$ imply $\triangle ABC \cong \triangle DFE$.

In general, if two corresponding sides of two triangles are equal, we cannot infer that the triangles are congruent.

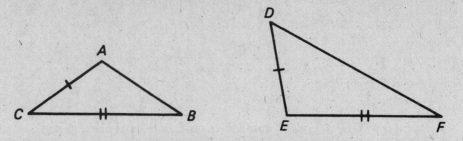

$AC = DE$ and $CB = EF$, but the triangles are not congruent.

If two sides of a triangle are equal, then the altitude to the third side divides the triangle into two congruent triangles.

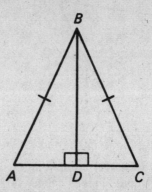

$AB = BC$ and $BD \perp AC$ implies $\triangle ADB \cong \triangle CDB$.

Therefore, $\angle ABD = \angle CBD$, so BD bisects $\angle ABC$. Since $AD = DC$, D is the midpoint of AC so BD is the median from B to AC. A *median* is the segment from a vertex to the midpoint of the side opposite the vertex.

EXAMPLE 1: $EF = ?$

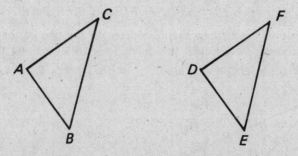

$AB = 4$, $AC = 4.5$ and $BC = 6$, $\angle BAC = \angle EDF$, $DE = 4$ and $DF = 4.5$

Since two pairs of corresponding sides (AB and DE, AC and DF) and the corresponding included angles ($\angle BAC$, $\angle EDF$) are equal, the triangles ABC and DEF are congruent by S.A.S. Therefore, $EF = BC = 6$.

4–3

Similarity. *Two triangles are similar if all three pairs of corresponding angles are equal.* Since the sum of the angles in a triangle is 180°, it follows that if two corresponding angles are equal, the third angles must be equal.

If you draw a line which passes through a triangle and is parallel to one of the sides of the triangle, the triangle formed is similar to the original triangle.

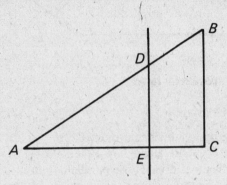

If $DE \parallel BC$ then $\triangle ADE \sim \triangle ABC$. The symbol $\sim$ means similar.

EXAMPLE 1:   A man 6 feet tall casts a shadow 4 feet long; at the same time a flagpole casts a shadow which is 50 feet long. How tall is the flagpole?

The man with his shadow and the flagpole with its shadow can be regarded as the pairs of corresponding sides of two similar triangles.

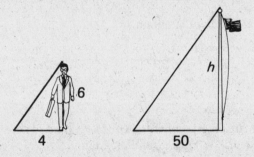

Let h be the height of the flagpole. Since corresponding sides of similar triangles are proportional, $\frac{4}{50} = \frac{6}{h}$. Cross-multiply getting $4h = 6 \cdot 50 = 300$; so $h = 75$. Therefore, the flagpole is 75 feet high.

III–5. Quadrilaterals

A QUADRILATERAL is a polygon with four sides. The sum of the angles in a quadrilateral is 360°. If the opposite sides of a quadrilateral are parallel, the figure is a *parallelogram*.

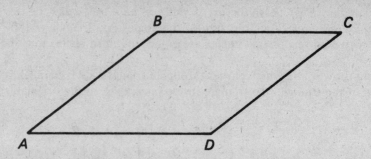

ABCD is a parallelogram.

In a parallelogram:

(1) The opposite sides are equal.
(2) The opposite angles are equal.
(3) A diagonal divides the parallelogram into two congruent triangles.
(4) The diagonals bisect each other. (A line *bisects* a line segment if it intersects the segment at the midpoint of the segment.)

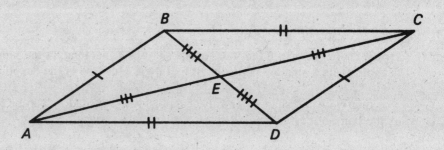

ABCD is a parallelogram.

(1) $AB = DC$, $BC = AD$.
(2) $\angle BCD = \angle BAD$, $\angle ABC = \angle ADC$.
(3) $\triangle ABC \cong \triangle ADC$, $\triangle ABD \cong \triangle CDB$.
(4) $AE = EC$ and $BE = ED$.

If *any* of the statements (1), (2), (3) and (4) are true for a quadrilateral, then the quadrilateral is a parallelogram.

If all of the sides of a parallelogram are equal, the figure is called a *rhombus*.

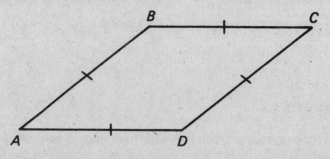

ABCD is a rhombus.

The diagonals of a rhombus are perpendicular.

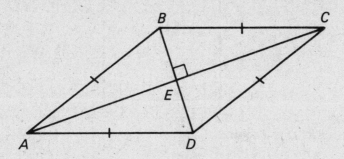

$BD \perp AC; \angle BEC = \angle CED = \angle AED = \angle AEB = 90°.$

If all the angles of a parallelogram are right angles, the figure is a *rectangle*.

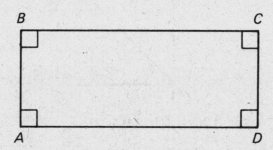

ABCD is a rectangle.

Since the sum of the angles in a quadrilateral is 360°, if *all* the angles of a quadrilateral are equal then the figure is a rectangle. The diagonals of a rectangle are equal. The length of a diagonal can be found by using the Pythagorean Theorem.

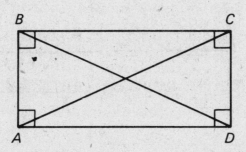

If *ABCD* is a rectangle, $AC = BD$ and $(AC)^2 = (AD)^2 + (DC)^2$.

If all the sides of a rectangle are equal, the figure is a *square*.

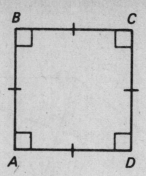

ABCD is a square.

If all the angles of a rhombus are equal, the figure is a square. The length of the diagonal of a square is $\sqrt{2}\,s$ where *s* is the length of a side.

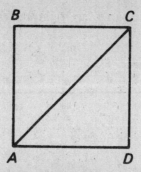

In square *ABCD*, $AC = (\sqrt{2})AD$.

A quadrilateral with two parallel sides and two sides which are not parallel is called a *trapezoid*. The parallel sides are called *bases*, and the non-parallel sides are called *legs*.

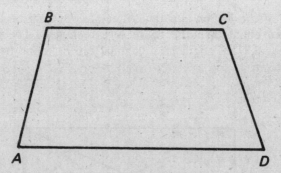

If *BC* ∥ *AD* then *ABCD* is a trapezoid; *BC* and *AD* are the bases.

III–6. Circles

A CIRCLE is a figure in a plane consisting of all the points which are the same distance from a fixed point called the *center* of the circle. A line segment from any point on the circle to the center of the circle is called a *radius* (plural: radii) of the circle. All radii of the same circle have the same length.

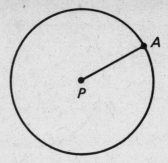

This circle has center *P* and radius *AP*.

A circle is **denoted** by a single letter, usually its center. Two circles with the same center are *concentric*.

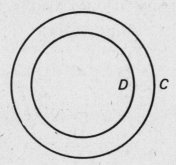

C and *D* are concentric circles.

A line segment whose endpoints are on a circle is called a *chord*. A chord which passes through the center of the circle is a *diameter*. *The length of a diameter is twice the length of a radius.* A diameter divides a circle into two congruent halves which are called *semicircles*.

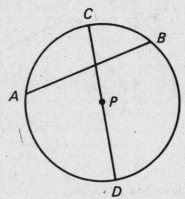

P is the center of the circle.
AB is a chord and *CD* is a diameter.

A diameter which is perpendicular to a chord bisects the chord.

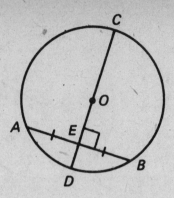

O is the center of this circle and $AB \perp CD$; then $AE = EB$.

If a line intersects a circle at one and only one point, the line is said to be a *tangent* to the circle. The point common to a circle and a tangent to the circle is called the *point of tangency*. The radius from the center to the point of tangency is perpendicular to the tangent.

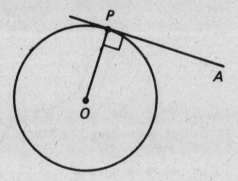

AP is tangent to the circle with center O. P is the point of tangency and $OP \perp PA$.

A polygon is *inscribed* in a circle if all of its vertices are points on the circle.

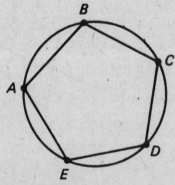

$ABCDE$ is an inscribed pentagon.

An angle whose vertex is a point on a circle and whose sides are chords of the circle is called an *inscribed angle*. An angle whose vertex is the center of a circle and whose sides are radii of the circle is called a *central angle*.

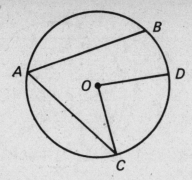

∠*BAC* is an inscribed angle.
∠*DOC* is a central angle.

An *arc* is a part of a circle.

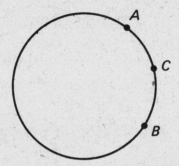

ACB is an arc. Arc *ACB* is written $\widehat{ACB}$.

If two letters are used to denote an arc, they represent the smaller of the two possible arcs. So $\widehat{AB} = \widehat{ACB}$.

An arc can be measured in degrees. The entire circle is 360°; thus an arc of 120° would be $\frac{1}{3}$ of a circle.

A central angle is equal in measure to the arc it intercepts.

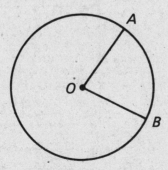

∠*AOB* = $\widehat{AB}$

An inscribed angle is equal in measure to $\frac{1}{2}$ the arc it intercepts.

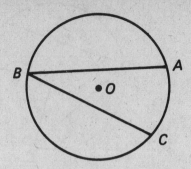

$\angle ABC = \frac{1}{2}\widehat{AC}$.

An angle inscribed in a semicircle is a *right angle*.

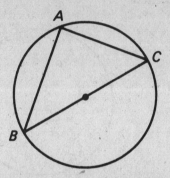

If BC is a diameter, then $\angle BAC$ is inscribed in a semicircle; so $\angle BAC = 90°$.

III–7.   Area and Perimeter

7–1

The area A of a square equals s^2, where s is the length of a side of the square. Thus, $A = s^2$.

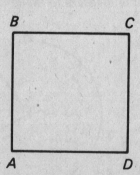

If $AD = 5$ inches, the area of square $ABCD$ is 25 square inches.

The area of a rectangle equals length times width; if L is the length of one side and W is the length of a perpendicular side, then the area $A = LW$.

If $AB = 5$ feet and $AD = 8$ feet, then the area of rectangle $ABCD$ is 40 square feet.

The area of a parallelogram is base × height; $A = bh$, where b is the length of a side and h is the length of an altitude to the base.

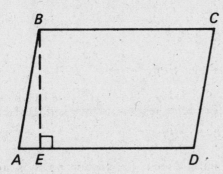

If $AD = 6$ yards and $BE = 4$ yards, then the area of the parallelogram $ABCD$ is $6 \cdot 4$ or 24 square yards.

The area of a trapezoid is the (average of the bases) × height. $A = [(b_1 + b_2)/2]h$ where b_1 and b_2 are the lengths of the parallel sides and h is the length of an altitude to one of the bases.

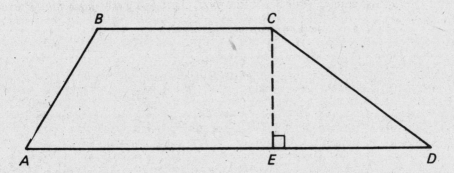

If $BC = 3$ miles, $AD = 7$ miles, and $CE = 2$ miles, then the area of trapezoid $ABCD$ is $[(3 + 7)/2] \cdot 2 = 10$ square miles.

The area of a triangle is $\frac{1}{2}$ (base × height); $A = \frac{1}{2}bh$, where b is the length of a side and h is the length of the altitude to that side.

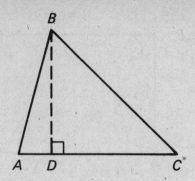

If $AC = 5$ miles and $BD = 4$ miles, then the area of the triangle is $\frac{1}{2} \times 5 \times 4 = 10$ square miles.

Since the legs of a right triangle are perpendicular to each other, the area of a right triangle is one-half the product of the lengths of the legs.

EXAMPLE 1:   If the lengths of the sides of a triangle are 5 feet, 12 feet, and 13 feet, what is the area of the triangle?

Since $5^2 + 12^2 = 25 + 144 = 169 = 13^2$, the triangle is a right triangle and the legs are the sides with lengths 5 feet and 12 feet. Therefore, the area is $\frac{1}{2} \times 5 \times 12 = 30$ square feet.

If we want to find the area of a polygon which is not of a type already mentioned, we break the polygon up into smaller figures such as triangles or rectangles, find the area of each piece, and add these to get the area of the given polygon.

The area of a circle is πr^2 where r is the length of a radius. Since $d = 2r$ where d is the length of a diameter, $A = \pi \left(\dfrac{d}{2}\right)^2 = \pi \dfrac{d^2}{4}$. π is a number which is approximately $\dfrac{22}{7}$ or 3.14; however, there is *no fraction which is exactly equal to π. π is called an irrational number.*

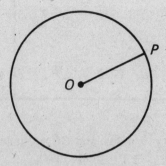

If $OP = 2$ inches, then the area of the circle with center O is $\pi 2^2$ or 4π square inches. The portion of the plane bounded by a circle and a central angle is called a *sector* of the circle.

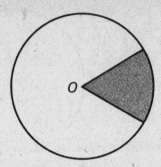

The shaded region is a sector of the circle with center O. The area of a sector with central angle $n°$ in a circle of radius r is $\frac{n}{360}\pi r^2$.

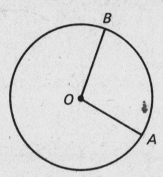

If $OB = 4$ inches and $\angle BOA = 100°$, then the area of the sector is $\frac{100}{360}\pi \cdot 4^2 =$ $\frac{5}{18} \cdot 16\pi = \frac{40}{9}\pi$ square inches.

7–2

The *perimeter* of a polygon is the sum of the lengths of the sides.

EXAMPLE 1: What is the perimeter of a regular pentagon whose sides are 6 inches long?

A pentagon has 5 sides. Since the pentagon is regular, all sides have the same length which is 6 inches. Therefore, the perimeter of the pentagon is 5×6 which equals 30 inches or 2.5 feet.

The *perimeter of a rectangle is* $2(L + W)$ where L is the length and W is the width.
The *perimeter of a square is* $4s$ where s is the length of a side of the square.

The *perimeter of a circle* is called the *circumference* of the circle. The *circumference of a circle is* πd *or* $2\pi r$, where d is the length of a diameter and r is the length of a radius.

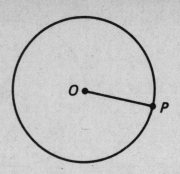

If O is the center of a circle and $OP = 5$ feet, then the circumference of the circle is $2 \times 5\pi$ or 10π feet.

The length of an arc of a circle is $(n/360)\,\pi d$ where the central angle of the arc is $n°$.

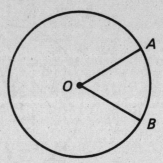

If O is the center of a circle where $OA = 5$ yards and $\angle AOB = 60°$, then the length of arc AB is $\dfrac{60}{360}\pi \times 10 = \dfrac{10}{6}\pi = \dfrac{5}{3}\pi$ yards.

EXAMPLE 2: How far will a wheel of radius 2 feet travel in 500 revolutions? (Assume the wheel does not slip.)

The diameter of the wheel is 4 feet; so the circumference is 4π feet. Therefore, the wheel will travel $500 \times 4\pi$ or $2,000\pi$ feet in 500 revolutions.

III–8. Volume and Surface Area

8–1

The volume of a rectangular prism or box is length times width times height.

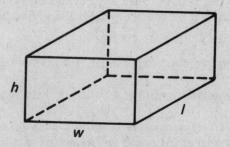

$$V = lwh$$

EXAMPLE 1: What is the volume of a box which is 5 feet long, 4 feet wide, and 6 feet high?

The volume is $5 \times 4 \times 6$ or 120 cubic feet.

If each of the faces of a rectangular prism is a congruent square, then the solid is a *cube*. The volume of a cube is the length of a side (or edge) cubed.

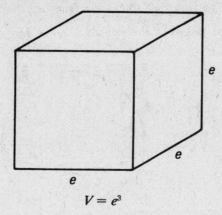

$$V = e^3$$

If the side of a cube is 4 feet long, then the volume of the cube is 4^3 or 64 cubic feet.

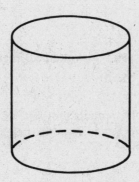

This solid is a circular cylinder. The top and the bottom are congruent circles. Most tin cans are circular cylinders. The volume of a circular cylinder is the product of the area of the circular base and the height.

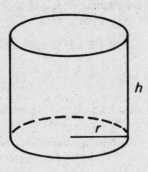

$$V = \pi r^2 h$$

EXAMPLE 2: A circular pipe has a diameter of 10 feet. A gallon of oil has a volume of 2 cubic feet. How many gallons of oil can fit into 50 feet of the pipe?

Think of the 50 feet of pipe as a circular cylinder on its side with a height of 50 feet and a radius of 5 feet. Its volume is $\pi \cdot 5^2 \cdot 50$ or $1,250\pi$ cubic feet. Since a gallon of oil has a volume of 2 cubic feet, 50 feet of pipe will hold $1,250\pi/2$ or 625π gallons of oil.

A *sphere* is the set of points in space equidistant from a fixed point called the center. The length of a segment from any point on the sphere to the center is called the radius of the sphere. *The volume of a sphere of radius r is $\frac{4}{3}\pi r^3$.*

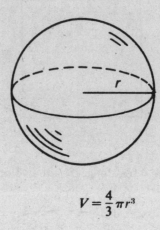

$$V = \frac{4}{3}\pi r^3$$

The volume of a sphere with radius 3 feet is $\frac{4}{3}\pi 3^3 = 36\pi$ cubic feet.

8–2

The surface area of a rectangle prism is $2LW + 2LH + 2WH$ where L is the length, W is the width, and H is the height.

EXAMPLE 1: If a roll of wallpaper covers 30 square feet, how many rolls are needed to cover the walls of a rectangular room 10 feet long by 8 feet wide by 9 feet high? There are no windows in the room.

We have to cover the surface area of the walls which equals $2(10 \times 9 + 8 \times 9)$ or $2(90 + 72)$ or 324 square feet. (Note that the product omits the area of the floor or the ceiling.) Since a roll covers 30 square feet, we need $\frac{324}{30} = 10\frac{4}{5}$ rolls.

The surface area of a cube is $6e^2$ where e is the length of an edge.

The area of the circular part of a cylinder is called the lateral area. The lateral area of a cylinder is $2\pi rh$, since if we unroll the circular part, we get a rectangle whose dimensions are the circumference of the circle and the height of the cylinder. The total surface area is the lateral surface area plus the areas of the circles on top and bottom, so the total surface area is $2\pi rh + \pi r^2$.

EXAMPLE 2: How much tin is needed to make a tin can in the shape of a circular cylinder whose radius is 3 inches and whose height is 5 inches?

The area of both the bottom and top is $\pi \cdot 3^2$ or 9π square inches. The lateral area is $2\pi \cdot 3 \cdot 5$ or 30π square inches. Therefore, we need $9\pi + 9\pi + 30\pi$ or 48π square inches of tin.

III–9. Coordinate Geometry

In coordinate geometry, every point in the plane is associated with an ordered pair of numbers called *coordinates*. Two perpendicular lines are drawn; the horizontal line is called the x-axis and the vertical line is called the y-axis. The point where the two axes intersect is called the *origin*. Both of the axes are number lines with the origin corresponding to zero (see I–6.) Positive numbers on the x-axis are to the right of the origin, negative numbers to the left. Positive numbers on the y-axis are above the origin, negative numbers below the origin. The coordinates of a point P are (x,y) if P is located by moving x units along the x-axis from the origin and then moving y units up or down. *The distance along the x-axis is always given first.*

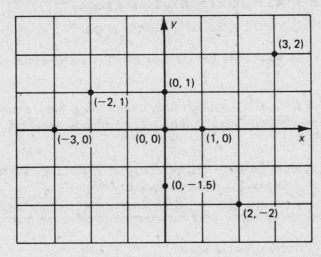

The numbers in parentheses are the coordinates of the point. Thus "$P = (3,2)$" means that the coordinates of P are $(3,2)$. *The distance between the point with coordinates (x,y) and the point with coordinates (a,b) is* $\sqrt{(x-a)^2 + (y-b)^2}$. You should be able to answer most questions by using the distance formula.

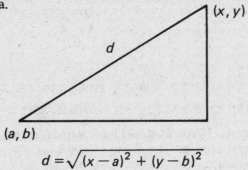

$$d = \sqrt{(x-a)^2 + (y-b)^2}$$

EXAMPLE 1: Is $ABCD$ a parallelogram? $A = (3,2)$, $B = (1,-2)$, $C = (-2,1)$, $D = (1,5)$.

The length of AB is $\sqrt{(3-1)^2+(2-(-2))^2} = \sqrt{2^2+4^2} = \sqrt{20}$. The length of CD is $\sqrt{(-2-1)^2+(1-5)^2} = \sqrt{(-3)^2+(-4)^2} = \sqrt{25}$. Therefore, $AB \neq CD$, so $ABCD$

cannot be a parallelogram, since in a parallelogram the lengths of opposite sides are equal.

Geometry problems occur frequently in the data sufficiency questions. *If you are not provided with a diagram, draw one for yourself.* Think of any conditions which will help you answer the question; perhaps you can see how to answer a different question which will lead to an answer to the original question. It may help to draw in some diagonals, altitudes, or other auxiliary lines in your diagram.

IV. Tables and Graphs

IV-1. Tables

General Hints. You *must* know how to interpret tables and graphs to score well on the Mathematics part of the test. In some recent tests, about half of the questions in the sections on mathematics have dealt with charts and graphs.

(A) Make sure to look at the *entire* table or graph.

(B) Figure out what *units* the table or graph is using. Make sure to express your answer in the correct units.

(C) Look at the possible answers before calculating. Since many questions only call for an approximate answer, it may be possible to round off (see I–5) saving time and effort.

(D) Don't confuse decimals and percentages. If the units are percentages, then an entry of .2 means .2% which is equal to .002.

(E) In inference questions, only the information given can be used.

(F) See if the answer makes sense.

EXAMPLE: (Refer to the table on page 259.)

1. Ⓐ Ⓑ Ⓒ Ⓓ Ⓔ 1. What percent of the babies born in the U.S. in 1947 died before the age of 1 year?

(A) 3.22
(B) 4.7
(C) 26.7

(D) 32.2
(E) 47

To find a percentage, use the information given in the rate columns. The rate is given *per thousand.* In 1947 the rate was 32.2 per thousand which is $\frac{32.2}{1000} = .0322$ or 3.22%. So the correct answer is (A). If you assumed incorrectly that the rate was per hundred, you would get the incorrect answer (D); if you looked in the wrong column you might get (B) or (E) as your answer.

2. Ⓐ Ⓑ Ⓒ Ⓓ Ⓔ 2. Which state had the most infant deaths in 1940?

(A) California
(B) New Mexico
(C) New York

(D) Pennsylvania
(E) Texas

INFANT DEATHS (UNDER 1 YEAR OF AGE) AND RATES PER 1,000 LIVE
BIRTHS, BY STATES: 1940 TO 1950

STATE	NUMBER OF INFANT DEATHS					RATE PER 1,000 LIVE BIRTHS				
	1940	1947	1948	1949	1950	1940	1947	1948	1949	1950
United States	110,984	119,173	113,169	111,531	103,825	47.0	32.2	32.0	31.3	29.2
Alabama	3,870	3,301	3,228	3,345	3,044	61.5	37.5	37.8	39.6	36.8
Arizona	983	973	1,083	1,034	953	85.5	50.8	56.4	51.0	45.8
Arkansas	1,810	1,445	1,363	1,539	1,209	47.0	29.5	28.4	33.7	26.5
California	4,403	7,233	6,885	6,574	6,115	39.2	29.4	28.6	26.8	25.0
Colorado	1,270	1,234	1,267	1,153	1,167	60.4	37.5	38.4	35.1	34.4
Connecticut	868	1,150	1,026	943	886	34.0	25.2	24.3	23.1	21.8
Delaware	217	239	214	224	235	47.7	31.0	29.5	30.4	30.7
District of Columbia	554	691	531	576	603	49.3	31.9	25.5	29.1	30.4
Florida	1,818	2,285	2,103	2,088	2,078	53.8	38.2	35.3	33.8	32.1
Georgia	3,744	3,251	3,169	3,101	3,064	57.8	34.2	34.2	33.3	33.5
Idaho	506	478	481	431	434	42.9	29.4	29.8	27.0	27.1
Illinois	4,398	5,672	5,123	5,195	4,868	35.3	28.9	27.7	27.4	25.6
Indiana	2,595	2,949	2,760	2,746	2,520	42.1	30.6	29.8	29.1	27.0
Iowa	1,636	1,817	1,610	1,591	1,555	36.5	28.5	26.6	25.7	24.8
Kansas	1,106	1,251	1,151	1,136	1,130	38.3	28.1	26.9	25.9	25.7
Kentucky	3,387	2,971	3,073	3,139	2,616	53.1	37.1	39.8	41.2	34.9
Louisiana	3,268	2,773	2,779	2,810	2,639	64.3	37.2	37.9	37.2	34.6
Maine	810	853	706	713	650	53.2	35.7	32.0	32.5	30.9
Maryland	1,590	1,794	1,537	1,636	1,465	49.1	31.6	28.8	30.5	27.0
Massachusetts	2,458	3,027	2,613	2,347	2,240	37.5	28.1	26.8	24.5	23.3
Michigan	4,032	5,080	4,639	4,545	4,230	40.7	31.5	30.0	28.9	26.3
Minnesota	1,758	2,165	1,959	1,893	1,889	33.2	28.6	26.9	25.6	25.1
Mississippi	2,869	2,448	2,474	2,631	2,385	54.4	36.8	37.9	39.6	36.7
Missouri	2,885	2,929	2,585	2,563	2,510	46.9	32.5	30.3	30.0	29.2
Montana	537	484	461	457	441	46.5	32.1	30.7	29.7	28.2
Nebraska	792	894	835	761	796	36.0	27.8	26.8	24.1	25.0
Nevada	109	134	147	118	139	51.7	33.2	39.8	32.1	37.9
New Hampshire	341	399	361	333	282	40.9	30.1	29.1	27.9	24.5
New Jersey	2,121	2,965	2,585	2,534	2,467	35.5	27.9	26.5	26.0	25.2
New Mexico	1,488	1,379	1,438	1,408	1,211	100.6	67.9	70.1	65.1	54.8
New York	7,297	9,123	8,258	7,878	7,429	37.2	28.2	27.3	26.1	24.7
North Carolina	4,631	3,938	3,858	4,113	3,674	57.6	34.9	35.3	38.1	34.5
North Dakota	593	523	487	517	453	45.1	30.6	29.4	30.7	26.6
Ohio	4,744	5,817	5,693	5,315	4,990	41.4	29.5	30.5	28.1	26.8
Oklahoma	2,238	1,733	1,731	1,531	1,514	49.9	32.3	34.4	30.8	30.2
Oregon	585	895	897	869	812	33.2	24.7	25.5	24.6	22.5
Pennsylvania	7,404	7,741	6,442	6,567	6,126	44.7	31.1	28.4	29.2	27.6
Rhode Island	410	522	444	395	450	37.9	28.2	26.3	24.0	27.8
South Carolina	3,042	2,352	2,331	2,283	2,220	68.2	39.5	40.4	39.0	38.6
South Dakota	466	511	525	448	473	38.7	30.9	32.0	26.0	26.6
Tennessee	2,954	3,144	3,098	3,331	2,961	53.5	36.3	37.7	40.2	36.4
Texas	8,675	8,161	9,131	8,628	7,630	68.3	41.1	46.2	42.7	37.4
Utah	539	545	568	535	503	40.4	25.1	27.4	25.3	23.7
Vermont	309	303	271	301	221	44.5	31.2	28.9	32.4	24.5
Virginia	3,335	3,142	3,163	3,162	2,836	58.5	36.6	38.5	38.1	34.6
Washington	992	1,643	1,537	1,530	1,522	35.2	28.1	27.5	27.1	27.3
West Virginia	2,269	2,091	2,108	2,082	1,822	53.7	38.0	40.2	39.6	36.1
Wisconsin	2,046	2,476	2,148	2,202	2,121	37.3	29.5	26.3	26.5	25.7
Wyoming	232	249	293	280	247	44.7	34.0	39.5	37.4	32.5

Source: Department of Health, Education, and Welfare, Public Health Service, National Office of Vital Statistics; annual report, *Vital Statistics of the United States.*

Source: Statistical Abstract of the U.S. 1957

Look in the numbers column under 1940. Only Texas had more than 8,000 in 1940, so the correct answer is (E). New Mexico had a *higher rate*, but the question asked for the *highest amount. Make sure you answer the question which is asked.*

3. Ⓐ Ⓑ Ⓒ Ⓓ Ⓔ   **3.** Which of the following statements can be inferred from the table?

    I.   In 1950 less than $\frac{1}{20}$ of the babies born in the U.S. died before the age of 1 year.
    II.   The number of infant deaths in the U.S. decreased from 1945 to 1950.
    III.   More than 5% of the infant deaths in the U.S. in 1950 occurred in California.
    IV.   The number of infant deaths in North America in 1950 was less than 150,000.

    (A)   I only
    (B)   II only
    (C)   I and III only
    (D)   I, III, IV only
    (E)   I, II, III, IV

Analysis:

Statement I can be inferred since $\frac{1}{20}$ of 1,000 = 50 which exceeds the rate per thousand of 29.2 in 1950.

Statement II can't be inferred since the table has no information about 1945. Infant deaths decreased between 1940 and 1950, but that doesn't mean they decreased between 1945 and 1950.

Statement III can be inferred from the table. The total number of infant deaths in 1950 was 103,825, and 6,115 occurred in California. A calculation of 6,115/103,825 could be made, but it is much quicker to find 5% of 103,825 which is 5,191. Since 6,115 is greater than 5,191, more than 5% of the infant deaths in the U.S. occurred in California.

Statement IV can't be inferred, because the table only gives information about the U.S. and there are other countries in North America.

So the correct answer is (C).

IV–2.   Circle Graphs

CIRCLE GRAPHS are used to show how various sectors share in the whole. Circle graphs are sometimes called pie charts. Circle graphs usually give the percentage that each sector receives.

EXAMPLE: (Refer to the graph on page 261.)

4. Ⓐ Ⓑ Ⓒ Ⓓ Ⓔ   **1.** The amount spent on materials in 1960 was 120% of the amount spent on

    (A)   research in 1960
    (B)   compensation in 1960
    (C)   advertising in 1970
    (D)   materials in 1970
    (E)   legal affairs in 1960

When using circle graphs to find ratios of various sectors, don't find the amounts each sector received and then the ratio of the amounts. Find the *ratio of the percentages,*

Expenditures of General Industries
By major categories

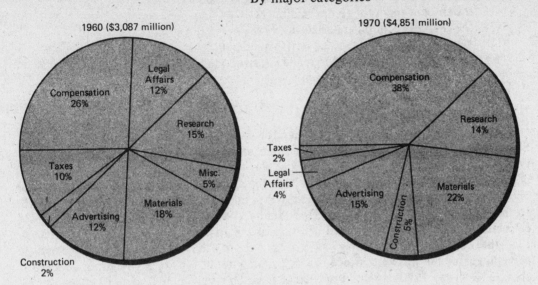

1960 ($3,087 million)

Compensation 26%
Legal Affairs 12%
Research 15%
Taxes 10%
Misc. 5%
Materials 18%
Advertising 12%
Construction 2%

1970 ($4,851 million)

Compensation 38%
Research 14%
Taxes 2%
Legal Affairs 4%
Advertising 15%
Construction 5%
Materials 22%

which is much quicker. In 1960, 18% of the expenditures were for materials. We want x where 120% of $x = 18\%$; so $x = 15\%$. Any category which received 15% of 1960 expenditures gives the correct answer, but only one of the five choices is correct. Here, the answer is (A) since research received 15% of the expenditure in 1960. Check the 1960 answers first since you need look only at the percentages, which can be done quickly. Notice that (C) is incorrect, since 15% of the expenditures for 1970 is different from 15% of the expenditures for 1960.

2. The fraction of the total expenditures for 1960 and 1970 spent on compensation was about

    2. Ⓐ Ⓑ Ⓒ Ⓓ Ⓔ

    (A) $\frac{1}{5}$ (D) $\frac{3}{7}$
    (B) $\frac{1}{4}$ (E) $\frac{1}{2}$
    (C) $\frac{1}{3}$

In 1960, 26% of $3,087 million was spent on compensation and in 1970 compensation received 38% of $4,851 million. The total expenditures for 1960 and 1970 are $(3,087 + 4,851)$ million. So the exact answer is $[(.26)(3,087) + (.38)(4,851)]/(3,087 + 4,851)$. Actually calculating the answer, you will waste a lot of time. Look at the answers and think for a second.

We are taking a weighted average of 26% and 38%. To find a weighted average, we multiply each value by a weight and divide by the total of all the weights. Here 26% is given a weight of 3,087 and 38% a weight of 4,851. The following general rule is often useful in average problems: The average or weighted average of a collection of values can *never* be:

(1) less than the smallest value in the collection, or
(2) greater than the largest value in the collection.

Therefore, the answer to the question must be greater than or equal to 26% and less than or equal to 38%.

Since $\frac{1}{5} = 20\%$ and $\frac{1}{4} = 25\%$, which are both less than 26%, neither (A) nor (B) can be the correct answer. Since $\frac{3}{7} = 42\frac{6}{7}\%$ and $\frac{1}{2} = 50\%$, which are both greater than 38%, neither (D) nor (E) can be correct. Therefore, by elimination (C) is the correct answer.

3. Ⓐ Ⓑ Ⓒ Ⓓ Ⓔ   **3.** The amount spent in 1960 for materials, advertising, and taxes was about the same as

   (A) $\frac{5}{4}$ of the amount spent for compensation in 1960
   (B) the amount spent for compensation in 1970
   (C) the amount spent on materials in 1970
   (D) $\frac{5}{3}$ of the amount spent on advertising in 1970
   (E) the amount spent on research and construction in 1970

First calculate the combined percentage for materials, advertising, and taxes in 1960. Since $18\% + 12\% + 10\% = 40\%$, these three categories accounted for 40% of the expenditures in 1960. You can check the one answer which involves 1960 now. Since $\frac{5}{4}$ of $26\% = 32.5\%$, (A) is incorrect. To check the answers which involve 1970, you must know the amount spent on the three categories above in 1960. 40% of 3,087 is 1234.8; so the amount spent on the three categories in 1960 was $1,234.8 million. You could calculate the amount spent in each of the possible answers, but there is a quicker way. Find the *approximate* percentage that 1,234.8 is of 4,851, and check this against the percentages of the answers. Since $\frac{12}{48} = \frac{1}{4}$, the amount for the 3 categories in 1960 is about 25% of the 1970 expenditures. Compensation received 38% of 1970 expenditures, so (B) is incorrect. Materials received 22% and research and construction together received 19%; since advertising received 15%, $\frac{5}{3}$ of the amount for advertising yields 25%. So (D) is probably correct. You can check by calculating 22% of 4,851 which is 1,067.22, while 25% of $4,851 = 1,212.75$. Therefore, (D) is correct.

In inference questions involving circle graphs, *do not compare different percentages.* Note in question 3 that the percentage of expenditures in 1960 for the three categories (40%) is *not equal* to 40% of the expenditures in 1970.

IV–3.   Line Graphs

LINE GRAPHS are used to show how a quantity changes continuously. Very often the quantity is measured as time changes. If the line goes up, the quantity is increasing; if the line goes down, the quantity is decreasing; if the line is horizontal, the quantity is not changing. To measure the height of a point on the graph, use your pencil or a piece of paper (for example, the admission card to the exam) as a straight edge.

EXAMPLE: (Refer to the graph on page 263.)

1. Ⓐ Ⓑ Ⓒ Ⓓ Ⓔ   **1.** The ratio of productivity in 1967 to productivity in 1940 was about

   (A) 1:4   (D) 4:1
   (B) 1:3   (E) 9:1
   (C) 3:1

In 1967 productivity had an index number of 400, and the index numbers are based on 1940 = 100. So the ratio is $400:100 = 4:1$. Therefore, the answer is (D). [If you used (incorrectly) output or employment (instead of productivity) you would get the wrong answer (E) or (C); if you confused the order of the ratio you would have incorrectly answered (A).]

TRENDS IN INDUSTRIAL INVESTMENT, LABOUR PRODUCTIVITY, EMPLOYMENT AND OUTPUT, 1940 TO 1967

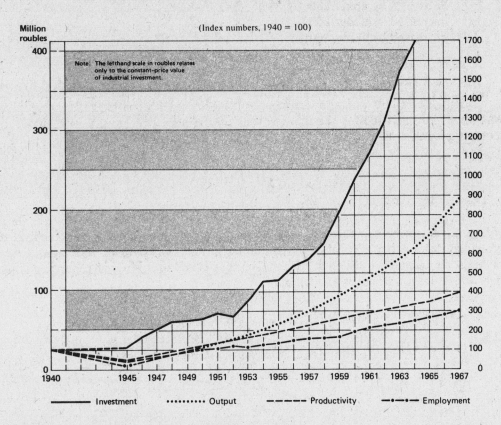

Source: United Nations Economics Bulletin for Europe

2. If 1 rouble = $3, then the constant-price value of industrial investment in 1959 was about   2. Ⓐ Ⓑ Ⓒ Ⓓ Ⓔ

   (A) $1.9 million
   (B) $200 million
   (C) $420,000,000
   (D) $570,000,000
   (E) $570,000 million

In 1959, the value was about 190 million roubles. (It was a little below 200 million.) The answers are all in dollars, so multiply 190 by 3 to get $570 million or $570,000,000 (D). If you are not careful about units, you may answer (B) or (E), which are incorrect.

3. Employment was at its minimum during the years shown in   3. Ⓐ Ⓑ Ⓒ Ⓓ Ⓔ

   (A) 1940   (D) 1953
   (B) 1943   (E) 1967
   (C) 1945

The minimum of a quantity displayed on a line graph is the lowest place on the line. Thus in 1945, (C), the minimum value of employment was reached.

4. Ⓐ Ⓑ Ⓒ Ⓓ Ⓔ   **4.** Between 1954 and 1965, output

    (A)   decreased by about 10%
    (B)   stayed about the same
    (C)   increased by about 200%
    (D)   increased by about 250%
    (E)   increased by about 500%

The line for output goes up between 1954 and 1965, so output increased between 1954 and 1965. Therefore, (A) and (B) are wrong. Output was about 200 in 1954 and about 700 in 1965, so the increase was 500. Since $\frac{500}{200} = 2.5 = 250\%$, the correct answer is (D).

IV–4. Bar Graphs

Quantities can be compared by the height or length of a bar in a bar graph. A bar graph can have either vertical or horizontal bars. You can compare different quantities or the same quantity at different times. Use your pencil or a piece of paper to compare bars which are not adjacent to each other.

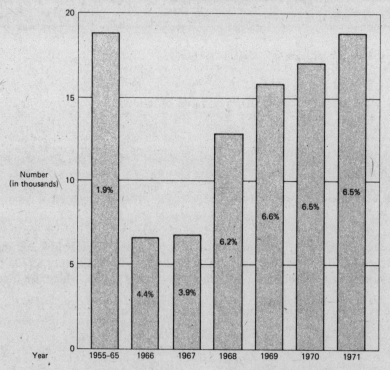

DISABILITY BENEFICIARIES REPORTED AS REHABILITATEI
Number, as percent of all rehabilitated clients
of State vocational rehabilitation agencies,
Years 1955–1971

Source: Social Security Bulletin

EXAMPLE: (Refer to the graph on page 264.)

1. Between 1967 and 1971, the largest number of disability beneficiaries were reported as rehabilitated in the year

   1. Ⓐ Ⓑ Ⓒ Ⓓ Ⓔ

   (A) 1967
   (B) 1968
   (C) 1969

   (D) 1970
   (E) 1971

   The answer is (E) since the highest bar is the bar for 1971. The percentage of disability beneficiaries out of all rehabilitated clients was higher in 1969, but the *number* was lower.

2. Between 1955 and 1965, about how many clients were rehabilitated by State vocational rehabilitation agencies?

   2. Ⓐ Ⓑ Ⓒ Ⓓ Ⓔ

   (A) 90,000
   (B) 400,000
   (C) 1,000,000

   (D) 1,900,000
   (E) 10,000,000

   1.9% of those rehabilitated were disability beneficiaries, and there were about 19,000 disability beneficiaries rehabilitated. So if T is the total number rehabilitated, then 1.9% of $T = 19,000$ or $.019T = 19,000$. Thus, $T = 19,000/.019 = 1,000,000$ and the answer is (C).

IV-5. Cumulative Graphs

You can compare several categories by a graph of the cumulative type. These are usually bar or line graphs where the height of the bar or line is divided up proportionately among different quantities.

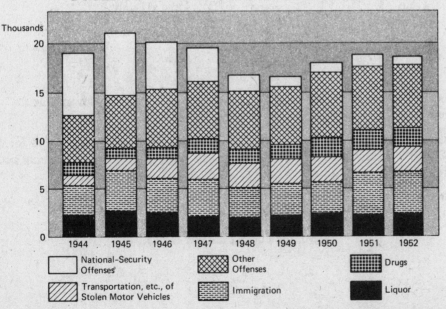

FEDERAL PRISONERS RECEIVED FROM THE COURTS,
BY MAJOR OFFENSE GROUPS: Years 1944–1952

Source: Statistical Abstract of the U.S. 1953

1, Ⓐ Ⓑ Ⓒ Ⓓ Ⓔ 1. In 1946, roughly what percent of the federal prisoners received from the courts were national-security offenders?

(A) 10   (D) 30
(B) 15   (E) 35
(C) 25

The total number of prisoners in 1946 was about 20,000, and national security offenders accounted for the part of the graph from just above 15,000 to just above 20,000. Therefore, there were about 20,000 − 15,000 = 5,000 prisoners convicted of national-security offenses. Since $5,000/20,000 = \frac{1}{4} = 25\%$, the correct answer is (C).

2. Ⓐ Ⓑ Ⓒ Ⓓ Ⓔ 2. Of the combined total for the four years 1947 through 1950, the largest number of offenders were in the category

(A) national-security offenses   (D) immigration
(B) other offenses   (E) liquor
(C) drugs

The correct answer is (B). Since other offenses had the most offenders in each year, that category must have the largest total number of offenders. [If you answered this question for the years 1944–1946, then (A) would be correct.]

3. Ⓐ Ⓑ Ⓒ Ⓓ Ⓔ 3. Which of the following statements can be inferred from the graph?

I. The number of federal prisoners received from the courts decreased each year from 1946 to 1948.

II. More than 40% of the prisoners between 1944 and 1952 came from the other offenses category.

III. 2% of the federal prisoners received in 1952 were convicted on heroin charges.

(A) I only   (D) I and III only
(B) III only   (E) I, II, and III
(C) I and II only

Statement I is true, since the height of the bar for each year was lower than the height of the bar for the previous year in 1946, 1947, and 1948.

Statement II is not true. For most of the years, other offenses accounted for about 25–30%, and it never was more than 40% in any year. Therefore, it could not account for more than 40% of the total.

Statement III can not be inferred. There is a category of drug offenders, but there is no information about specific drugs.

So, the correct answer is (A).

REVIEW OF FORMULAS

(Numbers next to the formulas refer to the section of the Math Review where the formula is discussed.)

Interest = Amount × Time × Rate	I–4
Discount = Cost × Rate of Discount	I–4
Price = Cost × (100% − Rate of Discount)	I–4
$x = \dfrac{1}{2a} \left[-b \pm \sqrt{b^2 - 4ac} \right]$ (quadratic formula)	II–2
Distance = Speed × Time	II–3
$a^2 + b^2 = c^2$ when a and b are the legs and c is the hypotenuse of a right triangle (Pythagorean Theorem)	III–4
Diameter of a circle = 2 × Radius	III–6
Area of a square = s^2	III–7
Area of a rectangle = LW	III–7
Area of a triangle = $\frac{1}{2} bh$	III–7
Area of a circle = πr^2	III–7
Area of a parallelogram = bh	III–7
Area of a trapezoid = $\frac{1}{2} (b_1 + b_2)h$	III–7
Circumference of a circle = πd	III–7
Perimeter of a square = $4s$	III–7
Perimeter of a rectangle = $2(L + W)$	III–7
Volume of a box = lwh	III–8
Volume of a cube = e^3	III–8
Volume of a cylinder = $\pi r^2 h$	III–8
Volume of a sphere = $\frac{4}{3} \pi r^3$	III–8
Surface area of a box = $2LW + 2LH + 2WH$	III–8
Surface area of a cube = $6e^2$	III–8
Surface area of a cylinder = $2\pi rh + 2\pi r^2$	III–8
Distance between points (x,y) and (a,b) is $\sqrt{(x - a)^2 + (y - b)^2}$	III–9

Hints for Answering Mathematics Questions

1. Make sure you answer the question you are asked to answer.

2. Look at the answers before you start to work out a problem; you can save a lot of time.

3. Don't waste time on superfluous computations.

4. *Estimate* whenever you can to save time.

5. Budget your time so you can try all the questions. (Bring a watch.)

6. You probably won't be able to answer all the questions; don't waste time worrying about it.

7. Do all the problems you know how to work *before* you start to think about those that you can't answer in a minute or two.

8. If you skip a question. make sure you skip that number on the answer sheet.

9. Don't make extra assumptions on inference questions.

10. Work efficiently; don't waste time worrying during the test.

11. Make sure you express your answer in the units asked for.

12. On data sufficiency questions, don't do any more work than is necessary. (Don't solve the problem; you only have to know that the problem can be solved.)

Further Practice Exercises

The four exercises that follow will give you an indication of your ability to handle these mathematics questions. The time for each exercise is 30 minutes. Scoring for each of the exercises may be interpreted as follows:

> 20–25—SUPERIOR
> 16–19—ABOVE AVERAGE
> 11–15—AVERAGE
> 7–10—BELOW AVERAGE
> 0– 6—UNSATISFACTORY

Your score should be determined by counting the number of correct answers minus ¼ the number of incorrect answers.

MATHEMATICS
EXERCISE A

1. In 1955, it cost $12 to purchase one hundred pounds of potatoes. In 1975, it cost $34 to purchase one hundred pounds of potatoes. The price of one hundred pounds of potatoes increased X dollars between 1955 and 1975 with X equal to:

    (A) 1.20   (B) 2.20   (C) 3.40   (D) 22   (E) 34

2. A house cost Ms. Jones C dollars in 1965. Three years later she sold the house for 25% more than she paid for it. She has to pay a tax of 50% of the gain. (The gain is the selling price minus the cost.) How much tax must Ms. Jones pay?

    (A) $\frac{1}{24}C$ (B) $\frac{C}{8}$ (C) $\frac{1}{4}C$ (D) $\frac{C}{2}$ (E) .6C

3. If the length of a rectangle is increased by 20%, and the width of the same rectangle is decreased by 20%, then the area of the rectangle

    (A) decreases by 20%   (B) decreases by 4%   (C) is unchanged   (D) increases by 20%   (E) increases by 40%

Use the following graph for questions 4-7.

Worldwide Military Expenditures

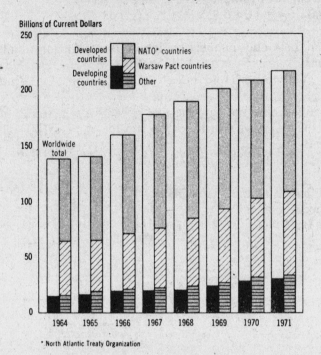

Billions of Current Dollars

Source: *Pocket Data Book U.S.A. 1973.*

4. Between 1964 and 1969, worldwide military expenditures

    (A) increased by about 50%   (B) roughly doubled   (C) increased by about 150%   (D) almost tripled   (E) increased by 10%

5. The average yearly military expenditure by the developing countries between 1964 and 1971 was approximately how many billions of current dollars?

    (A) 20   (B) 50   (C) 100   (D) 140   (E) 175

6. Which of the following statements can be inferred from the graph?
    I. The NATO countries have higher incomes than the Warsaw Pact countries.

    II. Worldwide military expenditures have increased each year between 1964 and 1971.

    III. In 1972 worldwide military expenditures were more than 230 billion current dollars.
    (A) I only   (B) II only   (C) I and II only   (D) II and III only   (E) I, II, and III

7. A speaker claims that the NATO countries customarily spend ⅓ of their combined incomes on military expenditures. According to the speaker, the combined incomes of the NATO countries (in billions of current dollars) in 1971 was about

    (A) 100   (B) 200   (C) 250   (D) 350   (E) 500

8. 8% of the people eligible to vote are between 18 and 21. In an election 85% of those eligible to vote who were between 18 and 21 actually voted. In that election, people between 18 and 21 who actually voted were what per cent of those people eligible to vote?
(A) 4.2   (B) 6.4   (C) 6.8   (D) 8   (E) 68

9. If n and p are both odd numbers, which of the following numbers *must* be an even number?
(A) $n + p$ (B) np (C) $np + 2$ (D) $n + p + 1$ (E) $2n + p$

10. It costs g cents a mile for gasoline and m cents a mile for all other costs to run a car. How many *dollars* will it cost to run the car for 100 miles?
(A) $\dfrac{g + m}{100}$ (B) $100g + 100m$ (C) $g + m$ (D) $g + .1m$ (E) g

11. What is the length of the line segment which connects A to B?
(A) $\sqrt{3}$ (B) 2   (C) $2\sqrt{2}$ (D) 4
(E) 8

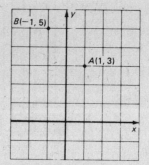

12. A cab driver's income consists of his salary and tips. His salary is $50 a week. During one week his tips were $\dfrac{5}{4}$ of his salary. What fraction of his income for the week came from tips?
(A) $\dfrac{4}{9}$ (B) $\dfrac{1}{2}$ (C) $\dfrac{5}{9}$ (D) $\dfrac{5}{8}$ (E) $\dfrac{5}{4}$

Use the table below for questions 13–17.

INCOME (IN DOLLARS)	TAX (IN DOLLARS)
0– 4,000	1% of income
4,000– 6,000	40 + 2 % of income over 4,000
6,000– 8,000	80 + 3% of income over 6,000
8,000–10,000	140 + 4% of income over 8,000
10,000–15,000	220 + 5% of income over 10,000
15,000–25,000	470 + 6% of income over 15,000
25,000–50,000	1,070 + 7% of income over 25,000

13. How much tax is due on an income of $7,500?
(A) $75   (B) $80   (C) $125   (D) $150   (E) $225

14. Your income for a year is $26,000. You receive a raise so that next year your income will be $29,000. How much *more* will you pay in taxes next year if the tax rate remains the same?
(A) $70   (B) $180   (C) $200   (D) $210   (E) $700

15. Joan paid $100 tax. If X was her income, which of the following statements is true?
(A) $0 < X < 4,000$ (B) $4,000 < X < 6,000$ (C) $6,000 < X < 8,000$
(D) $8,000 < X < 10,000$ (E) $10,000 < X < 15,000$

16. The town of Zenith has a population of 50,000. The average income of a person who lives in Zenith is $3,700 per year. What is the total amount paid in taxes by the people of Zenith? Assume each person pays tax on $3,700.
(A) $37   (B) $3700   (C) $50,000   (D) $185,000   (E) $1,850,000

17. A person who has an income of $10,000 pays what percent (to the nearest percent) of his or her income in taxes?
(A) 1   (B) 2   (C) 3   (D) 4   (E) 5

18. Given that x and y are real numbers, let $S(x,y) = x^2 - y^2$. Then $S(3, S(3,4)) =$
(A) -40 (B) -7 (C) 40 (D) 49 (E) 56

19. Eggs cost 90¢ a dozen. Peppers cost 20¢ each. An omelet consists of 3 eggs and ¼ of a pepper. How much will the ingredients for 8 omelets cost?
(A) $.90   (B) $1.30   (C) $1.80   (D) $2.20   (E) $2.70

20. It is 185 miles from Binghamton to New York City. If a bus takes 2 hours to travel the first 85 miles, how long must the bus take to travel the final 100 miles in order to average 50 miles an hour for the entire trip?
(A) 60 min.   (B) 75 min.   (C) 94 min.   (D) 102 min.   (E) 112 min.

21. What is the area of the figure below?
$ABDC$ is a rectangle and BDE is an isoceles right triangle.
(A) ab (B) ab^2 (C) $b\left(a + \dfrac{b}{2}\right)$
(D) cab (E) $\dfrac{1}{2}bc$

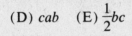

22. If $2x + y = 5$ then $4x + 2y$ is equal to
(A) 5   (B) 8   (C) 9   (D) 10   (E) none of these

23. In 1967, a new sedan cost $2,500; in 1975, the same type of sedan cost $4,800. The cost of that type of sedan has increased by what percent between 1967 and 1975?
(A) 48   (B) 52   (C) 92   (D) 152   (E) 192

24. What is the area of the square $ABCD$?
(A) 10   (B) 18   (C) 24   (D) 36
(E) 48

25. If $x + y = 6$ and $3x - y = 4$, then $x - y$ is equal to
(A) -1　(B) 0　(C) 2　(D) 4　(E) 6

MATHEMATICS
EXERCISE **B**

Use the graphs below for questions 1–5.

Women in the Labor Force

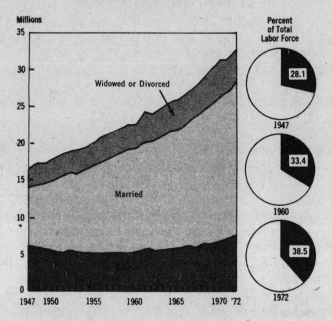

Source: *Pocket Data Book U.S.A. 1973. Bureau of the Census.*

1. The total labor force in 1960 was about y million with y equal to about
(A) 22　(B) 65　(C) 75　(D) 80　(E) 85

2. In 1947, the percentage of women in the labor force who were married was about
(A) 28　(B) 33　(C) 38　(D) 50　(E) 65

3. What was the first year when more than 20 million women were in the labor force?
(A) 1950　(B) 1953　(C) 1956　(D) 1958　(E) 1964

4. Between 1947 and 1972, the number of women in the labor force
(A) increased by about 50%　(B) increased by about 100%　(C) increased by about 150%　(D) increased by about 200%　(E) increased by about 250%

5. Which of the following statements about the labor force can be inferred from the graphs?
　I.　Between 1947 and 1957, there were no years when more than 5 million widowed or divorced women were in the labor force.
　II.　In every year between 1947 and 1972, the number of single women in the labor force has increased.
　III.　In 1965, women made up more than ⅓ of the total labor force.
(A) I only　(B) II only　(C) I and II only　(D) I and III only　(E) I, II, and III

6. If $\frac{x}{y} = \frac{2}{3}$ then $\frac{y^2}{x^2}$ is equal to

(A) $\frac{4}{9}$ (B) $\frac{2}{3}$ (C) $\frac{3}{2}$ (D) $\frac{9}{4}$ (E) $\frac{5}{2}$

7. In the figure, BD is perpendicular to AC. BA and BC have length a. What is the area of the triangle ABC?

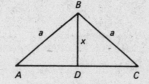

(A) $2x\sqrt{a^2 - x^2}$ (B) $x\sqrt{a^2 - x^2}$
(C) $a\sqrt{a^2 - x^2}$ (D) $2a\sqrt{x^2 - a^2}$
(E) $x\sqrt{x^2 - a^2}$

8. If two places are one inch apart on a map, then they are actually 160 miles apart. (The scale on the map is one inch equals 160 miles.) If Seton is 2⅞ inches from Monroe on the map, how many miles is it from Seton to Monroe?

(A) 3   (B) 27   (C) 300   (D) 360   (E) 460

9. In the accompanying diagram $ABCD$ is a rectangle. The area of isosceles right triangle $ABE = 7$, and $EC = 3(BE)$. The area of ABCD is

(A) 21   (B) 28
(C) 42   (D) 56
(E) 84

10. An automobile tire has two punctures. The first puncture by itself would make the tire flat in 9 minutes. The second puncture by itself would make the tire flat in 6 minutes. How long will it take for both punctures together to make the tire flat? (Assume the air leaks out at a constant rate.)

(A) $3\frac{3}{5}$ minutes   (B) 4 minutes   (C) $5\frac{1}{4}$ minutes   (D) $7\frac{1}{2}$ minutes

(E) 15 minutes

11. If n^3 is odd, which of the following statements are true?
    I. n is odd.
    II. n^2 is odd.
    III. n^2 is even.

(A) I only   (B) II only   (C) III only   (D) I and II only

(E) I and III only

Use the table below for questions 12–15.

Participation in National Elections

Persons in millions. Civilian noninstitutional population as of Nov. 1. Based on post-election surveys of persons reporting whether or not they voted; differs from table 103 data which are based on actual vote counts.

Characteristic	1964 Persons of voting age	1964 Percent voted	1968 Persons of voting age	1968 Percent voted	1972 Persons of voting age	1972 Percent voted
Total	111	69	117	68	136	63
Male	52	72	54	70	64	64
Female	58	67	62	66	72	62
White	99	71	105	69	121	64
Negro and other	11	57	12	56	15	51
Negro	10	58	11	58	13	52
Region:						
North and West	78	75	82	71	94	66
South	32	57	35	60	43	55
Age:						
18–24 years	10	51	12	50	25	50
25–44 years	45	69	46	67	49	63
45–64 years	38	76	40	75	42	71
65 years and over	17	66	18	66	20	63

Source: U.S. Bureau of the Census.

12. Which of the following groups had the highest percentage of voters in 1968?
    (A) 18–24 years (B) Female (C) South (D) 25–44 years (E) Male

13. In 1972, what percent (to the nearest percent) of persons of voting age were female?
    (A) 52 (B) 53 (C) 62 (D) 64 (E) 72

14. In 1968, how many males of voting age voted?
    (A) 37,440,000 (B) 37,800,000 (C) 42,160,000 (D) 62,000,000
    (E) 374,400,000

15. Let X be the number (in millions) of persons of voting age in the range 25–44 years who lived in the North and West in 1964. Which of the following includes all possible values and only possible values of X?
    (A) $0 \leqq X \leqq 45$ (B) $13 \leqq X \leqq 45$ (C) $13 \leqq X \leqq 78$ (D) $45 \leqq X \leqq 78$ (E) $75 \leqq X \leqq 78$

16. There are 50 students enrolled in Business 100. Of the enrolled students, 90% took the final exam. Two-thirds of the students who took the final exam passed the final exam. How many students passed the final exam?
    (A) 30 (B) 33 (C) 34 (D) 35 (E) 45

17. If a is less than b, which of the following numbers is greater than a and less than b?
    (A) $(a+b)/2$ (B) $(ab)/2$ (C) $b^2 - a^2$ (D) ab (E) $b - a$

18. In the figure, OR and PR are radii of circles. The length of OP is 4. If $OR = 2$, what is PR? PR is tangent to the circle with center O.

    (A) 2 (B) $\dfrac{5}{2}$ (C) 3 (D) $2\sqrt{3}$
    (E) $3\sqrt{2}$

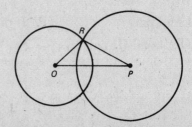

19. A bus uses one gallon of gasoline to travel 15 miles. After a tune-up, the bus travels 15% farther on one gallon. How many gallons of gasoline (to the nearest tenth) will it take for the bus to travel 150 miles after a tune-up?
(A) 8.5 (B) 8.7 (C) 8.9 (D) 9.0 (E) 10.0

20. If $x + 2y = 4$ and $x/y = 2$, then x is equal to
(A) 0 (B) $\frac{1}{2}$ (C) 1 (D) $\frac{3}{2}$ (E) 2

Use the following table for questions 21–23.

	SPEED OF A TRAIN OVER A 3 HOUR PERIOD							
TIMED PERIOD *(in minutes)*	0	30	45	60	90	120	150	180
SPEED AT TIME *(in m.p.h.)*	40	45	47.5	50	55	60	65	70

21. How fast was the train traveling 2½ hours after the beginning of the timed period?
(A) 50 m.p.h. (B) 55 m.p.h. (C) 60 m.p.h. (D) 65 m.p.h. (E) 70 m.p.h.

22. During the three hours shown on the table the speed of the train
(A) increased by 25% (B) increased by 50% (C) increased by 75%
(D) increased by 100% (E) increased by 125%

23. At time t measured in minutes after the beginning of the time period, which of the following gives the speed of the train in accordance with the table?
(A) $\frac{1}{6}t$ (B) $10t$ (C) $40 + t$ (D) $40 + \frac{1}{6}t$ (E) $40 + 10t$

24. It costs $1,000 to make the first thousand copies of a book and x dollars to make each subsequent copy. If it costs a total of $7,230 to make the first 8,000 copies of a book, what is x?
(A) .89 (B) .90375 (C) 1.00 (D) 89 (E) 90.375

25. If 16 workers can finish a job in three hours, how long should it take 5 workers to finish the same job?
(A) $3\frac{1}{2}$ hours (B) 4 hours (C) 5 hours (D) $7\frac{1}{16}$ hours (E) $9\frac{3}{5}$ hours

MATHEMATICS
EXERCISE C

1. A box contains 12 poles and 7 pieces of net. Each piece of net weighs .2 pounds; each pole weighs 1.1 pounds. The box and its contents together weigh 16.25 pounds. How much does the empty box weigh?
(A) 1.2 pounds (B) 1.65 pounds (C) 2.75 pounds (D) 6.15 pounds
(E) 16 pounds

2. If $a + b + c + d$ is a positive number, a minimum of x of the numbers a, b, c, and d must be positive where x is equal to
(A) 0 (B) 1 (C) 2 (D) 3 (E) 4

3. Consider the accompanying diagram. Which of the following statements is true?
(A) $KM < KL$ (B) $KM < LM$
(C) $KL + LM < KM$ (D) $KL < LM$ (E) $KL > LM$

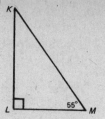

Use the graphs below for questions 4–6.

Population Characteristics

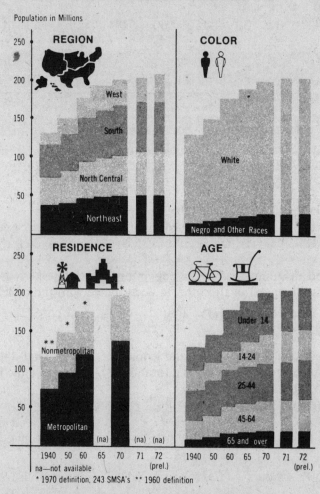

Source: *Pocket Data Book U.S.A. 1973. Bureau of the Census.*

4. In 1970, the ratio of the population living in metropolitan areas to the population living in nonmetropolitan areas was approximately
(A) 1 to 2   (B) 2 to 3   (C) 7 to 5   (D) 3 to 2   (E) 2 to 1

5. In 1950, the age group which had the fewest people was
(A) under 14   (B) 14–24   (C) 25–44   (D) 45–64   (E) 65 and over

6. How many of the regions shown had a population increase of less than 5% between 1940 and 1972?
(A) 0   (B) 1   (C) 2   (D) 3   (E) 4

7. Which of the following numbers is the largest?
   (A) $(2 + 2 + 2)^2$ (B) $[(2 + 2)^2]^2$ (C) $(2 \times 2 \times 2)^2$ (D) $2 + 2^2 + (2^2)^2$ (E) 4^3

8. In a survey of the town of Waso, it was found that 65% of the people surveyed watched the news on television, 40% read a newspaper, and 25% read a newspaper and watched the news on television. What percent of the people surveyed neither watched the news on television nor read a newspaper?
   (A) 0%   (B) 5%   (C) 10%   (D) 15%   (E) 20%

9. A worker is paid d dollars an hour for the first 8 hours she works in a day. For every hour after the first 8 hours, she is paid c dollars an hour. If she works 12 hours in one day, what is her average hourly wage for that day?
   (A) $(2d + c)/3$ (B) $8d + 4c$ (C) $(8d + 12c)/12$
   (D) $(4d + 8c)/12$ (E) $d + (\frac{1}{3})c$

10. A screwdriver and a hammer currently have the same price. If the price of a screwdriver rises by 5% and the price of a hammer goes up by 3%, how much more will it cost to buy 3 screwdrivers and 3 hammers?
    (A) 3%   (B) 4%   (C) 5%   (D) 8%   (E) 24%

11. If the radius of a circle is increased by 6%, then the area of the circle is increased by
    (A) .36%   (B) 3.6%   (C) 6%   (D) 12.36%   (E) 36%

12. Given that a and b are real numbers, let $f(a,b) = ab$ and let $g(a) = a^2 + 2$. Then $f[3, g(3)] =$
    (A) $3a^2 + 2$ (B) $3a^2 + 6$ (C) 27   (D) 29   (E) 33

13. A share of stock in Ace Enterprises cost D dollars on Jan. 1, 1975. One year later, a share increased to Q dollars. The fraction by which the cost of a share of stock has increased in the year is
    (A) $(Q - D)/D$ (B) $(D - Q)/Q$ (C) D/Q (D) Q/D (E) $(Q - D)/Q$

14. $ABCD$ is a square, $EFGH$ is a rectangle. $AB = 3$, $EF = 4$, $FG = 6$. The area of the region outside of $ABCD$ and inside $EFGH$ is
    (A) 6   (B) 9   (C) 12   (D) 15   (E) 24

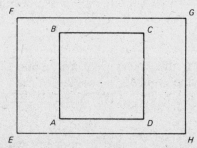

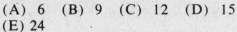

Use the graphs below for questions 15–17.

	% OF PROTEIN	% OF CARBOHYDRATES	% OF FAT	COST PER 100 GRAMS
FOOD A	10	20	30	$1.80
FOOD B	20	15	10	$3.00
FOOD C	20	10	40	$2.75

15. If you purchase x grams of Food A, y grams of Food B, and z grams of Food C, the cost will be
    (A) $(\frac{9}{5}x + 3y + \frac{11}{4}z)\cent$ (B) $\$(\frac{9}{5}x + 3y + \frac{11}{4}z)$ (C) $\$(1.8x + 3z + 2.75y)$
    (D) $(3x + 1.8y + 2.75z)\cent$ (E) $\$(x + y + z)$

16. Which of the following diets would supply the most grams of protein?

    (A) 500 grams of A   (B) 250 grams of B   (C) 350 grams of C   (D) 150 grams of A and 200 grams of B   (E) 200 grams of B and 200 grams of C

17. All of the following diets would supply at least 75 grams of fat. Which of the diets costs the least?

    (A) 200 grams of A, 150 grams of B   (B) 500 grams of B, 100 grams of A
    (C) 200 grams of C   (D) 150 grams of A, 100 grams of C
    (E) 300 grams of A

18. CD is parallel to EF. $AD = DF$, CD $= 4$, and $DF = 3$. What is EF?

    (A) 4   (B) 5   (C) 6   (D) 7
    (E) 8

19. Which of the following fractions is the largest?

    (A) $\frac{5}{6}$ (B) $\frac{11}{14}$ (C) $\frac{12}{15}$ (D) $\frac{17}{21}$ (E) $\frac{29}{35}$

20. How much simple interest will $2,000 earn in 18 months at an annual rate of 6%?

    (A) $120   (B) $180   (C) $216   (D) $1,800   (E) $2,160

21. If $x + y > 5$ and $x - y > 3$, then which of the following gives all possible values of x and only possible values of x?

    (A) $x > 3$ (B) $x > 4$ (C) $x > 5$ (D) $x < 5$ (E) $x < 3$

22. If the average (or arithmetic mean) of 6 numbers is 4.5, what is the sum of the numbers?

    (A) 4.5   (B) 24   (C) 27   (D) 30   (E) can not be determined

23. A silo is filled to capacity with W pounds of wheat. Rats eat r pounds a day. After 25 days, what percent of the silo's capacity have the rats eaten?

    (A) $25r/W$ (B) $25r/100W$ (C) $2,500(r/W)$ (D) r/W (E) $r/25W$

24. If $x^2 + 2x - 8 = 0$, then x is either -4 or

    (A) -2 (B) -1 (C) 0   (D) 2   (E) 8

25. The interest charged on a loan is p dollars per 1,000 for the first month and q dollars per $1,000 for each month after the first month. How much interest will be charged during the first three months on a loan of $10,000?

    (A) $30p$ (B) $30q$ (C) $p + 2q$ (D) $20p + 10p$ (E) $10p + 20q$

MATHEMATICS
EXERCISE **D**

Use the graph below for questions 1–2.

Annual Percentage Change in Social Welfare Expenditures

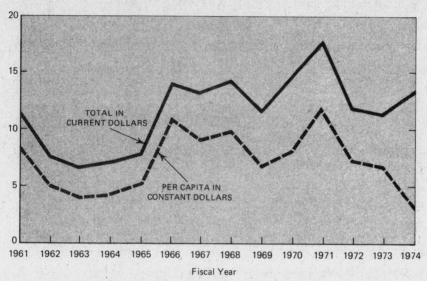

Fiscal Year

Source: Social Security Bulletin.

1. In which year between 1961 and 1974 were total social welfare expenditures in current dollars the highest?
   (A) 1961   (B) 1966   (C) 1970   (D) 1971   (E) 1974

2. If total social welfare expenditures were $10.8 billion in 1960, how many billion dollars were they in 1961?
   (A) .648   (B) 11.664   (C) 11.772   (D) 11.88   (E) 11.988

3. What is the area of the parallelogram *ABCD*?
   (A) 10   (B) 15   (C) 18
   (D) 20   (E) $4\sqrt{29}$

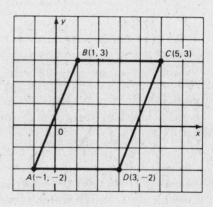

4. If k, m, and n are all integers which are divisible by 3, which of the following integers is divisible by 9?
   I. $k + m$
   II. km
   III. $k + m + n$
   (A) I only   (B) II only   (C) III only   (D) II and III only
   (E) I, II, and III

5. The Acme Company has 24 employees whose yearly salary is greater than $10,000. 15% of the employees of the Acme Company are paid yearly salaries which are greater than $10,000. How many employees does the Acme Company have?
   (A) 24 (B) 100 (C) 120 (D) 150 (E) 160

Use the table below for questions 6–9.

PAYROLL OF L.T.D. INC.		
RANK	NUMBER IN RANK	WAGES PAID TO EMPLOYEES IN RANK
Manager	5	$110,000
Supervisor	25	$350,000
Assembly worker	500	$600,000
Total	530	$1,060,000

6. The wages paid to managers make up what percent (to the nearest per cent) of the total payroll?
   (A) 5 (B) 9 (C) 10 (D) 11 (E) 42

7. The average wage for all employees is
   (A) $1,200 (B) $2,000 (C) $18,000 (D) $20,000 (E) $22,000

8. The ratio of the average salary of a manager to the average salary of an assembly worker is
   (A) 3 to 55 (B) 11 to 60 (C) 11 to 6 (D) 60 to 11 (E) 55 to 3

9. If 4 of the managers are paid wages of x dollars each, then the remaining manager is paid
   (A) $22,000   (B) $(110,000 − x)   (C) $(110,000 − x)/4
   (D) $(110,000 − 4x)   (E) $(22,000 − x)

10. A water tank has two drains. When only drain I is open, the tank will empty itself in 4 hours. When both drain I and II are open, the tank empties in $2\frac{1}{4}$ hours. How long does it take for the tank to empty if only drain II is open?
    (A) $1\frac{1}{2}$ hours (B) 2 hours (C) 4 hours (D) $5\frac{1}{2}$ hours (E) $6\frac{2}{3}$ hours

11. A drawer contains 6 red socks and 4 blue socks. What is the probability that if 2 socks are picked (without looking) from the drawer, both of the socks will be red?
    (A) $\frac{2}{15}$ (B) $\frac{4}{15}$ (C) $\frac{1}{3}$. (D) $\frac{2}{5}$ (E) $\frac{3}{5}$

12. A car originally was priced at $5,000. After one month, the price was discounted 10%. Two months later, the new price was discounted 20%, and the car was sold. How much did the buyer pay for the car?
    (A) $1,400 (B) $1,500 (C) $3,500 (D) $3,600 (E) $3,750

13. The area of the isosceles triangle *ABC* is 48. *AD = DC*, and *AE = EB*. Let *x* be the area of the rectangle *DEFG*. Then *x* equals
(A) 6 (B) 12 (C) 18 (D) 24
(E) 36

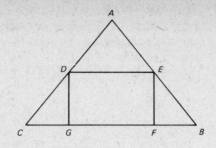

Use the graphs below for questions 14–17.

DISTRIBUTION OF U.S. LIFE INSURANCE COMPANIES BY REGION MID-1972

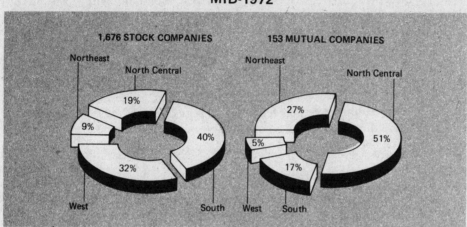

Source: Life Insurance Fact Book 1973, *Institute of Life Insurance.*

14. How many life insurance companies were there in the South in mid-1972?
(A) 26 (B) 670 (C) 696 (D) 732 (E) 1,043

15. Which region had the fewest life insurance companies in mid-1972?
(A) Northeast (B) North Central (C) South (D) West
(E) can't determine

16. The ratio of stock companies in the South to stock companies in the West in mid-1972 was
(A) 1 to 2 (B) 4 to 5 (C) 5 to 4 (D) 4 to 1 (E) 2 to 1

17. Which of the following statements about life insurance companies in mid-1972 can be inferred from the graph?
  I. There are more mutual companies in the North Central region than there are stock companies in the North Central Region.
  II. There are three times as many mutual companies as stock companies in the Northeast.
  III. There are fewer than 10 mutual companies in the West.
(A) I only (B) II only (C) III only (D) I and II only (E) I, II, and III

18. What is $\frac{\frac{4}{7}}{\frac{2}{3}}$ divided by $\frac{5}{12}$?
(A) $\frac{10}{63}$ (B) $\frac{5}{14}$ (C) $\frac{14}{15}$ (D) $\frac{72}{35}$ (E) $\frac{63}{10}$

19. In order for the line segment *AB* to be parallel to the line segment *CD*, the coordinates of *D* must be $(3,x)$ with *x* equal to
(A) 1   (B) 2   (C) 3   (D) 4   (E) 5

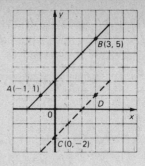

20. A farmer wishes to build a fence around a rectangular field. The field is 100 feet long and 60 feet wide. The fence will be of stone on one long side and of wire on the other three sides. Stone costs $5 a foot, and wire costs $2 a foot. How much will the fence cost?
(A) $320   (B) $620   (C) $760   (D) $800   (E) $940

21. Which of the following integers is the square of an integer for every integer *n*?
(A) $n^2 + 1$ (B) $n^2 + n$ (C) $n^2 + 2n$ (D) $n^2 + 2n + 1$ (E) $n^2 + 2n - 4$

22. A wheel with a diameter of 3 feet makes a revolution every 2 minutes. How many feet will the wheel travel in one hour?
(A) 3π (B) 6π (C) 60π (D) 90π (E) 180π

Use the information below for questions 23–25.

Territorial Expansion

		GROSS AREA
1	ORIGINAL 13 STATES 1790	888,685
2	LOUISIANA PURCHASE 1803	827,192
3	FLORIDA AND OTHER 1819	72,003
4	TEXAS 1845	390,144
5	OREGON TERRITORY 1846	285,580
6	MEXICAN CESSION 1848	529,017
7	GADSDEN PURCHASE 1853	29,640
8	ALASKA 1867	586,412
9	HAWAII 1898	6,450
	UNITED STATES TOTAL	3,615,123
	GUAM AND PUERTO RICO 1899	212 and 3,435
	AMERICAN SAMOA 1900	76
	VIRGIN ISLANDS 1917	133
	OTHER	9,083
	U.S. AND OUTLYING AREAS, TOTAL	3,628,062

GROSS AREA   Land and Water, square miles

Source: Pocket Data Book U.S.A. 1973. Bureau of the Census.

23. After the Louisiana Purchase the area of the United States had
(A) roughly tripled   (B) roughly doubled   (C) increased slightly   (D) stayed the same   (E) decreased slightly

24. Which of the following percentages is closest to the percent of the United States total that is Alaska?
(A) 10   (B) 15   (C) 20   (D) 25   (E) 30

25. The area of the United States in 1900 was about *x* times the area of the United States in 1800, where *x* is
(A) ¼   (B) 3   (C) 4   (D) 5   (E) 6

Answers

The letter following each question number is the correct answer. The numbers in parenthesis refer to the sections of this chapter which explain the necessary mathematics principles. A more detailed explanation of all answers follows:

Mathematics Exercise A

1.	D	(I-1)	14.	D	(I-4)
2.	B	(I-4)	15.	C	(I-4)
3.	B	(III-7, I-4)	16.	E	(I-7, I-4)
4.	A	(IV-4, IV-5, I-4)	17.	B	(I-4, I-5)
5.	A	(IV-4, I-7)	18.	A	(II-1)
6.	B	(IV-4)	19.	D	(I-2)
7.	D	(IV-4, I-2)	20.	D	(II-3)
8.	C	(I-4)	21.	C	(III-7, II-1, I-8)
9.	A	(I-1)	22.	D	(II-2)
10.	C	(II-1)	23.	C	(I-4)
11.	C	(III-9, I-8)	24.	D	(III-9, III-7)
12.	C	(I-2)	25.	A	(II-2)
13.	C	(I-4)			

Mathematics Exercise C

1.	B	(I-3)	14.	D	(III-7)
2.	B	(II-7, I-6)	15.	A	(II-1)
3.	E	(III-8)	16.	E	(I-4)
4.	E	(IV-5, II-5)	17.	E	(IV-1)
5.	E	(IV-5)	18.	E	(III-4)
6.	A	(IV-5)	19.	A	(I-1, I-2, III-7)
7.	B	(I-8)	20.	B	(I-4)
8.	E	(II-4)	21.	B	(II-7)
9.	A	(I-7, II-1)	22.	C	(I-7)
10.	B	(I-4)	23.	C	(I-4)
11.	D	(III-7)	24.	D	(II-1, II-2)
12.	E	(II-1)	25.	E	(II-1)
13.	A	(I-2)			

Mathematics Exercise B

1.	B	(IV-2, IV-3)	14.	B	(IV-1)
2.	D	(IV-3)	15.	B	(IV-1, II-7)
3.	C	(IV-3)	16.	A	(I-4, I-2)
4.	B	(IV-3)	17.	A	(II-7)
5.	A	(IV-3)	18.	D	(III-6, III-4)
6.	D	(I-8)	19.	B	(I-4)
7.	B	(III-4, III-7)	20.	E	(II-2)
8.	E	(II-5)	21.	D	(IV-1)
9.	D	(III-7)	22.	C	(IV-1)
10.	A	(II-3)	23.	D	(II-1)
11.	D	(I-1)	24.	A	(II-2)
12.	E	(IV-1)	25.	E	(II-3)
13.	B	(IV-1)			

Mathematics Exercise D

1.	E	(IV-3)	14.	C	(IV-2)
2.	E	(IV-3)	15.	A	(IV-2)
3.	D	(III-7, III-9)	16.	C	(IV-2)
4.	B	(I-1)	17.	C	(IV-2)
5.	E	(I-4)	18.	D	(I-2)
6.	C	(I-4)	19.	A	(III-9, III-2)
7.	B	(I-7)	20.	E	(III-7)
8.	E	(II-5)	21.	D	(I-1, I-8, II-1)
9.	D	(II-1)	22.	D	(III-7)
10.	E	(II-3)	23.	B	(IV-1)
11.	C	(II-4)	24.	B	(I-4)
12.	D	(I-4)	25.	C	(IV-1)
13.	D	(III-4, III-7)			

Explanation of Answers

Mathematics Exercise A

1. **D** The price increased by $34 - 12 = 22$ dollars.

2. **B** She sold the house for 125% of C or $\frac{5}{4}C$. Thus, the gain is $\frac{5}{4}C - C = \frac{C}{4}$

   She must pay a tax of 50% of $\frac{C}{4}$ or $\frac{1}{2}$ of $\frac{C}{4}$. Therefore, the tax is $\frac{C}{8}$. Notice that the three years has nothing to do with the problem. Sometimes a question contains unnecessary information.

3. **B** The area of a rectangle is length times width. Let L and W denote the original length and width. Then the new length is $1.2L$ and the new width is $.8W$. Therefore, the new area is $(1.2L)(.8W) = .96LW$ or 96% of the original area. So the area has decreased by 4%.

4. **A** In 1964 military expenditures were about 140 billion and by 1969 they had increased to about 200 billion. $\frac{60}{140} = \frac{3}{7}$ which is almost 50%. By using a straight edge, you may see that the bar for 1969 is about half again as long as the bar for 1964.

5. **A** Since the developing countries' military expenditures for every year were less than 30 billion, choice A is the only possible answer. Notice that by reading the possible answers first, you save time. You don't need the exact answer.

6. **B** I can not be inferred since the graph indicates *only* the dollars spent on military expenditures, not the percent of income and not total income. II is true since each bar is higher than the previous bar to the left. III can not be inferred since the graph gives no information about 1972. So only statement II can be be inferred from the graph.

7. **D** In 1971 the NATO countries spent over 100 billion and less than 150 billion on military expenditures. Since this was $\frac{1}{3}$ of their combined incomes the combined income is between 300 billion and 450 billion. Thus choice D must be the correct answer.

8. **C** Voters between 18 and 21 who voted are 85% of the 8% of eligible voters. Thus, $(.08)(.85) = .068$, so 6.8% of the eligible voters were voters between 18 and 21 who voted.

9. **A** Odd numbers are of the form $2x + 1$ where x is an integer. Thus if $n = 2x + 1$ and $p = 2k + 1$, then $n + p = 2x + 1 + 2k + 1 = 2x + 2k + 2$ which is even. Using $n = 3$ and $p = 5$, all the other choices give an odd number. In general, if a problem involves odd or even numbers, try using the fact that odd numbers are of the form $2x + 1$ and even numbers of the form $2y$ where x and y are integers.

10. **C** To run a car 100 miles will cost $100 (g + m)$ cents. Divide by 100 to convert to dollars. The result is $g + m$.

11. **C** Using the distance formula, the distance from A to B is $\sqrt{(1 - (-1))^2 + (3 - 5)^2} = \sqrt{4 + 4} = \sqrt{8} = \sqrt{4 \times 2} = \sqrt{4}\sqrt{2} = 2\sqrt{2}$. You have to be able to simplify $\sqrt{8}$ in order to obtain the correct answer.

12. **C** Tips for the week were $\frac{5}{4} \cdot 50$ so his total income was $50 + \frac{5}{4}(50) = \frac{9}{4}(50)$. Therefore, tips made up $\frac{5/4(50)}{9/4(50)} = \frac{5/4}{9/4} = \frac{5}{9}$ of his income. *Don't* waste time figuring out the total income and the tip income. You can use the time to answer other questions.

13. **C** 7,500 is in the 6,000–8,000 bracket so the tax will be 80 + 3% of the income over 6,000. Since 7,500 − 6,000 = 1,500, the income over 6,000 is 1,500. 3% of 1500 = (.03)(1500) = 45, so the tax is 80 + 45 = 125.

14. **D** The tax on 26,000 is 1,070 + 7% of (26,000 − 25,000). Thus, the tax is 1,070 + 70 = 1,140. The tax on 29,000 is 1.070 + 7% of (29,000 − 25,000). Thus, the tax on 29,000 is 1,070 + 280 = 1,350. Therefore, you will pay 1,350 − 1,140 = $210 more in taxes next year.
A faster method is to use the fact that the $3,000 raise is income over 25,000, so it will be taxed at 7%. Therefore, the tax on the extra $3,000 will be (.07)(3,000) = 210.

15. **C** If income is less than 6,000, then the tax is less than 80. If income is greater than 8,000, then the tax is greater than 140. Therefore, if the tax is 100, the income must be between 6,000 and 8,000. You *do not* have to calculate her exact income.

16. **E** Each person pays the tax on $3,700 which is 1% of 3700 or $37. Since there are 50,000 people in Zenith, the total taxes are (37)(50,000) = $1,850,000.

17. **B** The tax on 10,000 is 220, so taxes are $\frac{220}{10,000}$ = .022 = 2.2% of income. 2.2% is 2% after rounding to the nearest percent.

18. **A** $S(3,4) = 3^2 − 4^2 = 9 − 16 = −7$. Therefore, $S(3,S(3,4)) = S(3,−7) = 3^2 − (−7)^2 = 9 − 49 = −40$.

19. **D** 8 omelets will use 8 · 3 = 24 eggs and $8 · \frac{1}{4}$ = 2 peppers. Since 24 is two dozen, the cost will be (2)(90¢) + (2)(20¢) = 220¢ or $2.20.

20. **D** In order to average 50 m.p.h. for the trip, the bus must make the trip in $\frac{185}{50} = 3\frac{7}{10}$ hours which is 222 minutes. Since 2 hours or 120 minutes were needed for the first 85 miles, the final 100 miles must be completed in 222 − 120 which is 102 minutes.

21. **C** The area of a rectangle is length times width so the area of *ABDC* is *ab*. The area of a triangle is one half of the height times the base. Since *BDE* is an isosceles right triangle, the base and height both are equal to *b*. Thus, the area of *BDE* is $\frac{1}{2}b^2$ Therefore, the area of the figure is $ab + \frac{1}{2}b^2$ which is equl to $b(a + \frac{b}{2})$. You have to express your answer as one of the possible answers, so you need to be able to simplify.

22. **D** Since $4x + 2y$ is equal to $2(2x + y)$ and $2x + y = 5$, $4x + 2y$ is equal to 2(5) or 10.

23. **C** The cost has increased by $4800 minus $2500 or $2300 between 1967 and 1975. So the cost has increased by $\frac{2300}{2500}$ which is .92 or 92%. Answer (E) is incorrect. The price in 1975 is 192% of the price in 1967, but the *increase* is 92%.

24. **D** The distance from (−1, 2) to (5, 2) is 6. (You can use the distance formula or just count the blocks in this case.) The area of a square is the length of a side squared, so the area is 6^2 or 36.

25. **A** Since $x + y = 6$ and $3x − y = 4$, we may add the two equations to obtain $4x = 10$, or $x = 2.5$. Then, because $x + y = 6$, y must be 3.5. Therefore, $x − y = −1$.

Mathematics Exercise B

1. **B** In 1960 women made up 33.4% or about ⅓ of the labor force. Using the line graph, there were about 22 million women in the labor force in 1960.

So the labor force was about 3(22) or 66 million. The closest answer among the choices is 65 million.

2. **D** In 1947, there were about 16 million women in the labor force, and about 14 − 6 or 8 million of them were married. Therefore, the percentage of women in the labor force who were married is $\frac{8}{16}$ or 50%

3. **C** Look at the possible answers first. You can use your pencil and admission card as straight edges.

4. **B** In 1947, there were about 16 million women in the labor force. By 1972 there were about 32 million. Therefore, the number of women doubled which is an increase of 100%. (Not of 200%.)

5. **A** I is true since the width of the band for widowed or divorced women was never more than 5 million between 1947 and 1957. II is false since the number of single women in the labor force decreased from 1947 to 1948. III can not be inferred since there is no information about the total labor force or women as a percent of it in 1965. Thus, only I can be inferred.

6. **D** If $\frac{x}{y}$ is $\frac{2}{3}$, then $\frac{y}{x}$ is $\frac{3}{2}$. Since $\left(\frac{y}{x}\right)^2$ is equal to $\frac{y^2}{x^2}$, $\frac{y^2}{x^2}$ is $\left(\frac{3}{2}\right)^2$ or $\frac{9}{4}$.

7. **B** The area of a triangle is $\frac{1}{2}$ altitude times base. Since BD is perpendicular to AC, x is the altitude. Using the Pythagorean theorem, $x^2 + (AD)^2 = a^2$ and $x^2 + (DC)^2 = a^2$. Thus, $AD = DC$, and $AD = \sqrt{a^2 - x^2}$. So the base is $2\sqrt{a^2 - x^2}$. Therefore, the area is $\frac{1}{2}(x)(2\sqrt{a^2 - x^2})$ which is choice B.

8. **E** $1 : 160 :: 2\frac{7}{8} : x$. $x = 2\frac{7}{8}(160)$. $2\frac{7}{8}$ is $\frac{23}{8}$ so the distance from Seton to Monroe is $\frac{23}{8}(160) = 460$ miles

9. **D** Let $EF = FG = GC$. Therefore, $BE = EF = FG = GC$. Draw perpendiculars EH, FI, GJ. Draw diagonals HF, IG, JC. The 8 triangles are equal in area since they each have the same altitude (AB or DC) and equal bases (BE, EF, FG, GC, AH, HI, IJ, JD). Since the area of $ABE = 7$, the area of $ABCD = (8)(7)$ or 56.

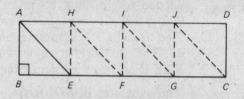

10. **A** In each minute the first puncture will leak $\frac{1}{9}$ of the air and the second puncture will leak $\frac{1}{6}$ of the air. Together $\frac{1}{9} + \frac{1}{6} = \frac{5}{18}$. So $\frac{5}{18}$ of the air will leak out in each minute. In $\frac{18}{5}$ or $3\frac{3}{5}$ minutes the tire will be flat.

11. **D** Since an even number times any number is even, and n times n^2 is odd, neither n or n^2 can be even. Therefore, n and n^2 must both be odd for n^3 to be odd. I and II are true, and III is false.

12. **E** Look in the fourth column.

13. **B** In 1972 there were 72 million females out of 136 million persons of voting age. $\frac{72}{136} = .529$ which is 53% to the nearest percent.

14. **B** In 1968, 70% of the 54 million males of voting age voted, and $(.7)(54,000,000) = 37,800,000$.

15. **B** Since 78 million persons of voting age lived in the North and West in 1964, and there were 65 million persons of voting age not in the 25–44 year range, there must be at least $78 − 65 = 13$ million people in the North and West in the 25–44 year range. X must be greater than or equal

to 13. Since there were 45 million people of voting age in the 25–44 year range, X must be less than or equal to 45.

16. **A** 90% of 50 is 45, so 45 students took the final. $\frac{2}{3}$ of 45 is 30. Therefore, 30 students passed the final.

17. **A** The average of two different numbers is always between the two. If $a = 2$ and $b = 3$, then $b^2 - a^2 = 5$, $ab = 6$, and $b - a = 1$ so C, D, and E must be false. If $a = \frac{1}{2}$ and $b = 1$, then $(ab)/2 = \frac{1}{4}$, so B is also false.

18. **D** Since the radius to the point of tangency is perpendicular to the tangent OR must be perpendicular to PR. Therefore, ORP is a right triangle, and $(PO)^2 = (OR)^2 + (PR)^2$. Then, $(PR)^2 = (PO)^2 - (OR)^2$. Thus, $(PR)^2 = 4^2 - 2^2$, and $PR = \sqrt{16 - 4} = \sqrt{12} = \sqrt{4}\sqrt{3} = 2\sqrt{3}$.

19. **B** After the tune-up, the bus will travel $(1.15)(15) = 17.25$ miles on a gallon of gas. Therefore, it will take $(150) \div (17.25) = 8.7$ (to the nearest tenth) gallons of gasoline to travel 150 miles.

20. **E** If $x/y = 2$, then $x = 2y$, so $x + 2y = 2y + 2y = 4y$. But $x + 2y = 4$, so $4y = 4$, or $y = 1$. Since $x = 2y$, x must be 2.

21. **D** 2½ hours is 150 minutes.

22. **C** The train's speed increased by $70 - 40$ which is 30 miles per hour. $30/40$ is 75%.

23. **D** When $t = 0$, the speed is 40, so A and B are incorrect. When $t = 180$, the speed is 70, so C and E are incorrect. Choice D gives all the values which appear in the table.

24. **A** The cost of producing the first 8,000 copies is $1,000 + 7,000x$. $1,000 + 7,000x = \$7,230$. Therefore, $7,000x = 6230$ and $x = .89$.

25. **E** Assume all workers work at the same rate unless given different information. Since 16 workers take 3 hours, each worker does $\frac{1}{48}$ of the job an hour. Thus, the 5 workers will finish $\frac{5}{48}$ of the job each hour. $\frac{5}{48}x = \frac{48}{48}$ It will take $\frac{48}{5} = 9\frac{3}{5}$ hours for them to finish the job.

Mathematics Exercise C

1. **B** The 12 poles weigh $(12)(1.1) = 13.2$ pounds and the 7 pieces of net weigh $7(.2) = 1.4$ pounds, so the contents of the box weigh $13.2 + 1.4 = 14.6$ pounds. Therefore, the box by itself must weigh $16.25 - 14.6 = 1.65$ pounds.

2. **B** If all the numbers were not positive, then the sum could not be positive so A is incorrect. If a, b, and c were all -1 and d were 5, then $a + b + c + d$ would be positive so C, D, and E are incorrect.

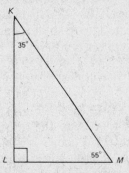

3. **E** Since the measure of angle M is 55°, the measure of angle K is 35°. Therefore, $KL > LM$ since the larger side is opposite the larger angle.

4. **E** The population in metropolitan areas in 1970 was about 140 million, and the population in nonmetropolitan areas was about $210 - 140$ or 70 million. Therefore, the ratio was about 140 to 70 or 2 to 1.

5. **E** Compare the segments of the second bar under "age."

6. **A** All regions increased by at least 10%. Compare the segments of the first bar with those of the last bar under "Region."

7. **B** Choice A gives 6^2 or 36. Choice B gives 4^4 or 256. Choice C is 8^2 or 64. Choice D is $2 + 4 + 16$ or 22. Choice E is 4^3 or 64.

8. **E** Since 25% read the newspaper and watched the news on television and 40% read the newspaper, $40\% - 25\%$ or 15% read the newspaper but did not watch the news on television. Thus $65\% + 15\%$ or 80% read the newspaper or watched the news on television, so $100\% - 80\%$ or 20% neither read the newspaper nor watched the news on television.

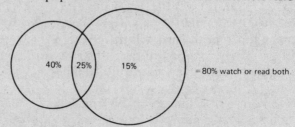

65% watch TV   40% read newspapers
$100\% - 80\% = 20\%$ neither watch nor read.

9. **A** For the first 8 hours, she is paid a total of $8d$. For the final 4 hours $(12 - 8)$, she is paid $4c$. Therefore, her total pay is $8d + 4c$. To find the average hourly pay, divide by 12. To find the correct answer among the choices, you have to reduce the fraction. Divide the numerator by four and the denominator by four.

10. **B** If the price of one screwdriver increases by 5%, then the price of three screwdrivers increases by 5% (not 15%). The percentage change is the same regardless of the number sold. Since a screwdriver and a hammer currently cost the same, the screwdrivers and the hammers each cost one half of the total price. So one half of the total is increased by 5%. The other half is increased by 3%. Therefore, the total price is increased by ½ $(5\%) +$ ½ $(3\%) = 4\%$.

11. **D** After the radius is increased by 6%, the radius will be 1.06 times the original radius. Since the area of a circle is πr^2, the new area will be $\pi(1.06r)^2 = \pi(1.1236r^2)$ or $1.1236\pi r^2$. Thus, the area has been increased by .1236 or by 12.36%.

12. **E** Since $g(a) = a^2 + 2$, $g(3)$ is $3^2 + 2$ or 11. So $f[3, g(3)]$ is $f(3,11) = 3 \times 11$ or 33.

13. **A** The difference in the price is $Q - D$. So the fraction by which it has increased is $Q - D/D$. Note that the denominator is the *original* price.

14. **D** Since $ABCD$ is a square, the area of $ABCD$ is 3^2 or 9. The area of the rectangle $EFGH$ is *length* times *width* or $4 \times 6 = 24$. Thus, the area outside the square and inside the rectangle is $24 - 9$ or 15.

15. **A** The cost of food A is $1.80 per hundred grams or 1.8¢ a gram, so x grams cost $(1.8x)$¢ or $(9/5)x$¢. Each gram of food B costs 3¢ so y grams of food B will cost $3y$¢. Each gram of food C costs 2.75¢ or 11/4¢; thus, z grams of food C will cost $(11/4)z$¢. Therefore, the total cost is $[(9/5)x + 3y + (11/4)z]$¢.

16. **E** Since food A is 10% protein, 500 grams of food A will supply 50 grams of protein. Food B is 20% protein so 250 grams of food B will supply 50 grams of protein. 350 grams of food C will supply 70 grams of protein. 150 grams of food A and 200 grams of food B will supply $15 + 40 = 55$ grams of protein. 200 grams of food B and 200 grams of food C will supply $40 + 40$ or 80 grams of protein. Choice E supplies the most protein.

17. **E** The diet of choice A will cost $2(\$1.80) + (3/2)(\$3) = \$3.60 + \$4.50 = \$8.10$. Choice B will cost $5(\$3) + \$1.80 = \$16.80$. Choice C costs $2(\$2.75) = \$5.50$. Choice D costs $(3/2)(\$1.80) + \$2.75 = \$2.70 + \$2.75 = \$5.45$. The diet of Choice E costs $3(\$1.80)$ or $\$5.40$ so Choice E costs the least.

18. **E** Since CD is parallel to EF, the triangles ACD and AEF are similar. Therefore, corresponding sides are proportional. So CD is to EF as AD is to AF. Since $AD = DF$, AD/AF is ½. Therefore, EF is twice CD or 8.

19. **A** You need to find a common denominator for the fractions. One method is to multiply all the denominators. A quicker method is to find the least common multiple of the denominators. Since $6 = 3 \times 2$, $14 = 2 \times 7$, $15 = 3 \times 5$, $21 = 3 \times 7$, and $35 = 5 \times 7$, the least common multiple is $2 \times 3 \times 5 \times 7 = 210$. 5/6 is 175/210, 11/14 is 165/210, 12/15 is 168/210, 17/21 is 170/210, and 29/35 is 174/210. 5/6 has the largest numerator.

20. **B** 18 months is 3/2 of a year. Interest = Amount × Time × Rate. $(\$2,000)(3/2)(.06) = \$180$.

21. **B** If $x + y > 5$ and $x - y > 3$, then, since both inequalities are of the same type, the corresponding sides can be added to obtain $2x > 8$ or $x > 4$.

22. **C** The average of 6 numbers is the sum of the numbers divided by 6. Thus, the sum of the numbers is the average multiplied by 6 or 4.5×6 which is 27.

23. **C** After 25 days the rats have eaten $25r$ pounds of wheat. So $(25r)/W$ is the fraction of the capacity eaten by the rats. To change this to percent, multiply by 100. $(25r)/W \times 100 = 2500 (r/W)$.

24. **D** Factor $x^2 + 2x - 8$ into $(x + 4)(x - 2)$. If x is either -4 or 2, $x^2 + 2x - 8 = 0$, and D is the correct answer.

25. **E** The interest on the $10,000 for the first month will be $10p$. For the next 2 months the interest will be $20q$. The total interest is $10p + 20q$.

Mathematics Exercise D

1. **E** Since the annual percentage change was positive in each year between 1961 and 1974, the total social welfare expenditures in current dollars increased in every year shown. Therefore, the expenditures were highest in the last year shown, 1974.

2. **E** In 1961, total social welfare expenditures increased by 11% from their value in 1960. Thus, in 1961, the total was 111% of $10.8 billion or $(1.11)(10.8) = \$11.988$ billion.

3. **D** The area of a parallelogram is altitude × base. AD has length 4 so the base is 4. The altitude is perpendicular to the base, so the altitude to point B would be 5. Therefore, the area is 5×4 or 20.

4. **B** I and III are false as can be seen by letting $k = 12$, $m = 3$, and $n = 6$. II is true since, if k and m are divisible by 3, then $k = 3i$ and $m = 3j$ when i and j are integers. Therefore, $km = (3i)(3j)$ or $9ij$ which means km is divisible by 9.

5. **E** 15% of the total number of employees is 24. 15% is equal to 15/100 or 3/20, so $(3/20)x = 24$ when x is the number of employees. Therefore $x = (24)(20/3) = 160$.

6. **C** The total payroll is $1,060,000, and the wages paid to managers = $110,000. Since $110,000/1,060,000 = 11/106 = .10$ (rounding to the nearest hundredth) or 10%.

7. **B** The average wage is $1,060,000 divided by 530 or $2,000.

8. **E** The average salary of a manager is $110,000/5 or $22,000. The average

salary of an assembly worker is $600,000 divided by 500 or $1,200. So the ratio is 220 to 12 or 55 to 3.

9. **D** All 5 managers together earn $110,000. Since each one of the four makes x dollars, the remaining manager is paid $(110,000 − 4x)$.

10. **E** Drain I alone empties ¼ of the tank in an hour since it takes 4 hours to empty the tank. If Drain II takes x hours to empty the tank by itself, then it will empty $1/x$ of the tank per hour. Both drains together will empty the tank in 5/2 hours so both drains together empty 2/5 of the tank in one hour. Therefore, $1/4 + 1/x = 2/5$. $1/x = 3/20$. $x = 20/3$ or 6 2/3.

11. **C** Since there are 10 socks in the drawer and 6 of them are red, there are 10×9 different ways to pick 2 socks from the drawer, and 6×5 different ways to pick 2 red socks. Therefore, the probability of picking 2 red socks is $(6 \times 5)/(10 \times 9) = 30/90$ or 1/3.

12. **D** After the 10% discount, the price of the car was 90% of $5,000 or $4,500. After the second discount of 20% the selling price was 80% of $4,500 or $3,600.

13. **D** Because the triangle is isosceles, the angles *DCG* and *EBF* are equal. Drop a perpendicular from *A* to *CB* which will intersect *DE* at *H*. Then the triangles *AHD*, *AHE*, *DGC*, and *EFB* are all congruent. So *DE* must equal *CG* + *FB* or half of *BC*. Also *DG* must be half of the altitude of *ABC*. Since 48 is ½ the altitude times *BC*, and the area of *DEFG* is ¼ of *BC* times the altitude, the area of *DEFG* is half of 48 or 24.

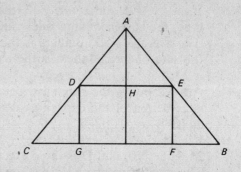

14. **C** The number of life insurance companies in the South is 40% of 1,676 + 17% of 153. $670 + 26 = 696$.

15. **A** Since most companies are stock companies, the Northeast is the most likely guess. The total in the Northeast is 9% (1,676) + 27% (153). Compare the result (191.8) with the nearest possibility which is the North Central. 19% of 1,676 is greater, even without adding mutual companies.

16. **C** The ratio is 40% to 32% or 5 to 4. Don't waste time figuring out the actual number of stock companies in the various regions.

17. **C** I is false since 51% of 153 is less than 19% of 1,676. II is false since 27% of 153 is less than 9% of 1,676. III is true since 5% of 153 is fewer than 10. Therefore, only III can be inferred from the graphs.

18. **D** 4/7 divided by 2/3 is $(4/7) \times (3/2)$ or 6/7. 6/7 divided by 5/12 is $6/7 \times 12/5$ or 72/35.

19. **A** If two lines are parallel, then the distance between the two lines along parallel lines must be equal. The easiest lines to use to calculate distances are lines parallel to the y axis. The distance along the y axis from *C* to *AB* is 4. *AB* intersects the y axis at the point (0,2). The distance from *D* to *AB* along the line parallel to the y axis must also be 4. *D* must have coordinates (3,1). $x = 1$.

20. **E** The fence will consist of 100 feet of stone and $100 + 60 + 60 = 220$ feet of wire. The cost will be $5(100) + $2(220) = $500 + $440 = $940.

21. **D** If $n = 1$ then Choice A is 2, Choice B is 2, Choice C is 3, Choice E is −1 so Choice D is the only possibility. Choice D is correct since $n^2 + 2n + 1 = (n + 1)^2$.

22. **D** The circumference of a circle is π times the diameter, so the circumference of the wheel is 3π feet. In one hour the wheel will make 30 revolutions, so it will travel $30(3\pi)$ or 90π feet in one hour.

23. **B** The Louisiana Purchase added about 830,000 square miles. The previous area was about 890,000 square miles, so the area almost doubled.

24. **B** Alaska is almost 600,000 square miles which is about 1/6 of 3,660,000 square miles. 1/6 is 16 2/3% so the correct answer is 15%. Save time by estimating; don't perform the calculations exactly.

25. **C** The area was about 3,600,000 square miles in 1900, and the area had been about 900,000 square miles in 1800. Since 4 times 900,000 is 3,600,000, x is about 4.

WORDS FREQUENTLY APPEARING ON THE GMAT

In your preparation for the GMAT, it is important that you become familiar with the meanings of as many words as possible. This is especially true for success on the Verbal Ability section of the test, but it is also necessary for better comprehension of Reading Comprehension, Reading Recall, and Practical Judgment passages, where a few key words may hold the meaning of an entire paragraph.

The vocabulary list presented here contains words that frequently appear on the GMAT and many terms that you may encounter in the course of the exam. Study it carefully to familiarize yourself with these words. Refer to it to check the meaning of any difficult words you may encounter in other parts of this Guide.

Abase—to humiliate, degrade
Abash—to bewilder, confound
Abate—to remove, lessen
Abdicate—to forsake, give up
Aberration—deviation
Abeyance—inactivity
Abhor—to detest, hate
Abject—degraded, miserable
Abjure—to recant, revoke
Abnegate—to deny, denounce
Abominate—to dislike
Abort—to be unsuccessful, fail to develop

Abrade—to scrape out
Abrogate—to abolish
Abscond—to bolt, decamp, flee
Absolve—to pardon
Abstemious—eating or drinking sparingly
Abstract—summary
Abstruse—profound, hidden, hard to understand
Accede—to consent
Accessory—accomplice
Acclivity—incline, rising slope
Accolade—honor, award
Accord—to grant, allow

Accost – to greet aggressively
Accretion – adhesion, concretion
Accrue – to accumulate
Acerbity – sharpness, bitterness
Acme – summit, peak
Acolyte – attendant, helper
Acrimonious – sharp, acrid
Actuate – to put into action
Adamant – immovable
Adduce – to give as proof
Adjudicate – to decide (a case)
Adjunct – auxiliary, appendage
Adjure – to state on oath
Admonish – to caution, warn
Adroit – skillful, clever
Adulation – flattery
Adulterate – to corrupt, contaminate
Advent – coming
Adventitious – accidental
Advocate – counsel, defender
Aegis – protection
Aesthetic – pertaining to beauty
Affability – politeness, courtesy
Affinity – relation, alliance
Affluence – wealth
Aggrandize – to increase in power
Agnostic – one who doubts the existence of God
Agrarian – relating to farming
Alacrity – willingness, agility
Albeit – although
Alchemy – chemistry of the middle ages
Alimentary – supplying food
Allay – to soothe, calm
Allegory – parable, fable
Allocate – to distribute
Allude – to insinuate, refer
Altercation – quarrel
Alternation – recurrence, succession
Altruism – unselfish devotion
Amalgamate – to combine, unite
Ambidextrous – using both hands equally well
Ameliorate – to amend, improve
Amenable – responsible, liable
Amenity – pleasantness
Amiable – pleasing, loving
Amorphous – shapeless
Anachronism – something misplaced in time
Analgesic – pain-reducing drug
Analogy – similarity, affinity
Anarchy – absence of government
Anathema – ban, curse
Anchorite – hermit
Ancillary – subordinate
Anecdote – tale, story

Animate – to inspire, encourage
Animosity – enmity, hatred
Annals – historical accounts
Anneal – to heat glass, metals, etc.
Annotator – commentator
Anomaly – abnormality, deviation
Antagonist – opponent
Antecede – to come before (in time or place)
Antedate – to assign a date earlier than the actual one
Anterior – front
Antimacassar – cover used to protect furniture
Antipathy – aversion, dislike
Antithesis – contrast, direct opposite
Aperture – opening
Apex – highest point
Aphorism – saying, adage
Apiary – place where bees are kept
Aplomb – self-confidence
Apochryphal – of questionable authenticity
Apogee – farthest orbit point from the earth
Apoplexy – sudden loss of consciousness
Apostasy – abandoning of faith
Apothecary – druggist
Apothegm – short, pithy statement
Appall – to terrify, shock
Appellation – name, title
Apposite – suitable, appropriate
Apprise – to inform
Approbation – approval, consent
Arbiter – arbitrator, judge
Archaic – no longer used
Archipelago – chain of islands
Archives – place where records are kept
Arduous – difficult
Argot – slang
Array – rank, order, finery
Arrears – in debt
Articulate – to speak or write clearly
Artifice – mastery, trickery
Asperity – acrimony, harshness
Aspersion – slander, false accusation
Assay – to analyze chemically
Asseverate – to state positively
Assiduity – care, diligence
Assimilate – to absorb
Assuage – to pacify, calm
Astral – starry
Astringent – contracting (tissues), severe
Astute – shrewd
Atheist – one who denies the existence of God
Atrophy – to waste away, deteriorate
Attenuate – to weaken
Attrition – a wearing away, weakening
Audacious – bold

Augment — to increase
Augur — to predict
August — majestic, noble
Auspice — protection
Auspicious — fortunate, favorable
Austere — rigid, severe
Authoritative — powerful, commanding
Autocratic — arrogant, dictatorial
Autonomy — self-government
Auxiliary — assistant, helping
Avarice — greed, cupidity
Aver — assert
Averse — unwilling
Aviary — place where birds are kept
Avidity — eagerness
Avoirdupois — weight
Avow — declare
Awry — crooked, bent
Axiomatic — principle accepted as self-evident

Badger — to harass, nag
Badinage — banter
Baleful — harmful, evil
Balm — something that soothes
Banal — meaningless, commonplace
Bandy — to exchange (words)
Bane — cause of harm
Barrister — court lawyer
Bedizen — to dress in a gaudy, vulgar manner
Beguile — to deceive
Belabor — to attack verbally, drag out
Bellicose — warlike
Beneficient — liberal, kind
Benign — gentle, mild
Berate — to scold
Bereft — bereaved, deprived of
Bestial — savage
Bestride — to mount
Bicameral — having two legislative chambers
Biennial — every two years
Bilious — bad-tempered
Biped — two-footed animal
Bivouac — encampment
Bland — mild
Blasé — indifferent
Blasphemy — profane abuse of anything sacred
Blatant — noisy, vociferous
Blazon — to adorn, proclaim
Bluster — to swagger, boast
Bogus — counterfeit
Boisterous — violent, furious
Bombast — pompous speech
Botch — to ruin
Bounty — generosity

Bourgeois — middle class
Bovine — ox or cow
Brandish — to wave menacingly
Bravado — pretense of bravery
Breech — lower part of the body
Brigand — robber, bandit
Broach — to start a discussion
Browbeat — to intimidate
Brusque — abrupt in manner
Bucolic — rustic
Buffoon — clown
Buoyancy — lightness, animation
Bureaucracy — government of specialized functions and
    hierarchy of officials
Burgeon — bud, sprout
Burnish — to polish
Butte — hill
Buttress — prop, protuberance

Cabal — intrigue, faction
Cache — hiding place
Cacophony — harsh sound
Cadence — measured movement
Cajole — to coax, flatter
Caldron — kettle
Calligraphy — penmanship
Callous — hard, obdurate
Callow — unfledged
Calumny — slander, defamation
Canard — hoax
Canker — ulcer
Cant — tilt, whining speech
Cantilever — supporting bracket
Canvass — to make a survey, solicit
Capacious — roomy, ample
Caper — frolic, mischievous act
Capitulate — to surrender
Caprice — whim, fancy
Captious — touchy, cross
Captivate — to charm, fascinate
Carnage — slaughter, massacre
Carniverous — flesh-eating
Carom — rebound
Carp — to complain constantly
Carrion — decaying flesh
Castigate — to punish
Casuistry — false reasoning
Cataclysm — violent change or upheaval
Catalyst — agent of change
Cathartic — purifying
Catholic — universal
Caustic — sarcastic, corrosive
Cavil — to quibble
Celerity — rapidity, velocity

Censorious – fault-finding
Censure – to criticize sharply
Centrifugal – moving away from center
Cephalic – of the head
Cerebration – thought process
Chafe – fret, irritate
Chaff – worthless material
Chagrin – embarrassment
Charlatan – faker
Charnel – place where corpses are deposited
Chary – discretely cautious
Chastise – to castigate, correct
Chattel – slave
Chauvinism – fanatical patriotism
Chicanery – deception
Chimerical – imaginary
Choleric – irascible, easily angered
Chronic – always present
Churlish – ill-bred
Circuitous – roundabout, tortuous
Circumlocution – evasion in speech
Circumspect – watchful, cautious
Circumvent – to avoid
Citadel – fortress
Civility – politeness, affability
Clairvoyant – able to perceive something not readily apparent
Clandestine – secret, hidden
Cloy – to overindulge with an initially pleasing thing
Coagulate – to thicken, clot
Coalesce – to unite, join forces
Coda – ending section distinct from the main body of a work
Coerce – to force
Cogent – forcible, convincing
Cogitate – to think seriously
Cognate – related
Cognizant – aware
Cohesion – a sticking together
Collate – to put together in proper order
Colligate – to group together
Collocate – to arrange in position
Colloquy – conversation, dialogue
Collusion – secret agreement to defraud
Colophon – inscription in a book
Colorable – plausible, ostensible
Comestible – edible
Commensurate – proportionate
Commodious – spacious
Commute – alter, exchange
Compatible – consistent
Compendious – brief, short
Compendium – abridgement, abstract
Compunction – uneasiness, remorse

Conclave – secret meeting
Concomitant – accompanying
Concupiscence – strong desire
Condign – appropriate
Condone – to overlook as unimportant
Conduce – to lead toward a desired end
Configuration – shape, arrangement
Confiscatory – seized by authority
Conflagration – destructive fire
Confute – to disprove, refute
Congeal – to change to a solid state
Congenital – existing from birth
Congruous – appropriate, in agreement
Coniferous – cone-bearing
Conjecture – guess, conclusion
Conjure – to summon solemnly
Connive – cooperate secretly
Connoisseur – expert, critic
Connote – suggest, imply
Conscript – to force into service, draft
Consecrate – to sanctify, dedicate
Consonance – harmony
Consort – associate, companion
Constellation – group of stars
Consternation – sudden confusion, panic
Constituency – voters in a district
Constrain – to restrict movement, limit
Constrict – to shrink
Consummate – to complete
Contemn – to despise, scorn
Contemptuous – scornful, insolent
Contentious – argumentative
Contiguous – adjacent, touching
Contingency – casualty, occurrence
Contravene – to contradict
Contrition – remorse, repentance
Contrivance – plan, scheme
Controvert – to debate, dispute
Contumely – rudeness
Contusion – bruise
Conundrum – riddle
Conversant – familiar with
Convivial – joyous, festal
Convoke – to assemble
Convulse – to shake violently, agitate
Copious – abundant
Corollary – inference, result
Corona – crown, luminous circle
Corporeal – pertaining to the body
Corpulent – fat, stout
Correlate – to be in mutual relation
Corrigible – amenable, tractable
Corroborate – to strengthen, confirm
Coterie – group

Countenance—facial expression, composure
Countermand—to cancel with a contrary order
Covenant—contract
Covert—clandestine, secret
Covet—to desire, aspire to
Cower—to cringe in fear
Cozen—to trick
Crag—steep projecting rock
Crass—grossly stupid
Credence—belief, faith
Credible—believable
Credulity—simplicity, gullibility
Crimp—to bend into shape, pinch together
Cruciate—cross-shaped
Crux—vital point
Cryptic—mysterious
Cudgel—club
Culmination—highest point, climax
Culpable—deserving blame
Cumbrous—unwieldy
Cupidity—avarice, greed
Curry—to seek favor by flattery
Cursory—hasty, superficial
Cynical—sarcastic, sneering
Cynosure—center of attraction

Dalliance—dawdling
Dank—chilly and wet
Dastard—coward
Dauntless—valiant, intrepid
Dearth—scarcity
Debacle—complete failure, fiasco
Debase—to degrade, lower
Debauch—to corrupt
Debility—weakness
Debonair—affable, jaunty
Decamp—to break camp, depart suddenly
Decant—to pour
Deciduous—shedding (leaves) annually
Declaim—speak, debate
Declaration—announcement
Declivity—descent, slope
Decorous—proper, in good taste
Decrepit—run-down, worn-out
Decry—censure
Deference—honor, respect
Definitive—explicit, conclusive
Defunct—no longer existing
Deign—to condescend
Deleterious—harmful
Delineate—to describe
Demean—to behave properly
Denigrate—to defame, belittle
Denizen—inhabitant

Denote—to stand for, mean
Denude—to strip, divest
Deposition—removal (from office), testimony
Depraved—sinful
Deprecate—to disapprove of
Depreciate—to lessen the value of
Depute—to appoint, entrust
Derogatory—disparaging
Descry—to discover, make known
Desecrate—to profane, abuse
Desiccate—to dry up
Desist—to cease, stop
Despicable—contemptible
Desultory—loose, rambling
Deterrent—constraint, preventative
Detritus—product of disintegration
Devious—rambling, errant, tricky
Diametric—opposite
Diaphanous—extremely delicate, insubstantial
Dichotomy—division into two parts
Dictum—positive statement
Didactic—instructive
Diffident—lacking confidence, reserved
Diffuse—to spread without restraint
Dilate—to stretch, widen
Dilatory—tardy, lagging
Dilettante—one who dabbles superficially
Diligent—industrious, assiduous
Diluvial—pertaining to floods
Discern—to observe, perceive
Discompose—to upset the order of
Disconcert—to confound, disturb
Disconsolate—sad, forlorn
Discord—disagreement
Discountenance—disapproval
Discursive—rambling
Disdain—to scorn
Disingenuous—without candor
Disparage—to belittle
Disparate—distinct in quality
Disputation—debate
Disseminate—to spread widely
Dissident—disagreeing
Dissimulate—to put on a false appearance
Dissipate—to scatter or use wastefully
Dissolute—morally loose
Dissonant—lacking harmony
Dissuade—to advise against
Distend—to stretch out
Distrait—absentminded, distracted
Distraught—mentally upset
Diverge—to branch off, deviate
Divers—various
Divest—to deprive, strip off

Doctrinate — impractical theorist
Dogmatic — arrogant stating of opinion
Doldrums — low spirits
Dole — something given sparingly
Doleful — dismal
Dolorous — mournful
Dolt — stupid person
Dotage — senility
Dour — stern, gloomy
Dowdy — shabby, styleless
Dregs — undesirable leftovers
Drivel — silly talk
Droll — funny, amusing
Dross — refuse, waste
Dubious — uncertain
Dubitable — open to doubt
Dupe — to deceive
Duplicity — deception
Duress — restraint, force

Ebony — hard durable wood, black
Ebullient — enthusiastic
Ecclesiastical — pertaining to the church
Echelon — formation of units or troops
Eclectic — made up of elements from a variety of sources
Ecology — study of the relationships in an environment
Ecumenical — general, worldwide
Edict — public announcement, decree
Edifice — large building
Edify — to enlighten
Educe — to bring forth
Effable — capable of being expressed
Efface — to wipe out, erase
Efficacious — effective
Effigy — image, crude likeness
Effluence — flowing out
Effrontery — impudence
Effulgent — illuminated
Effusive — highly emotional
Egocentric — self-centered
Egregious — flagrant
Egression — emergence
Electorate — voting body
Elicit — to cause a response
Elision — omission
Eloquent — pleasingly expressive
Elucidate — to make clear
Elusive — hard to grasp
Emaciate — to make thin
Emanate — to come out from
Embellish — to ornament
Embody — to make perceptible, personify
Embroil — involve in an argument
Emend — to correct or alter (as in a literary work)

Emissary — messenger
Emollient — soothing substance
Emolument — salary, compensation
Emulate — to rival or try to equal
Enclave — distinct unit surrounded by foreign territory
Encomium — glowing praise
Encroach — trespass
Encyclopedia — compendium of knowledge
Endemic — restricted to a given locality
Endogenous — originating from within
Enervate — to lessen the vitality of
Enfranchise — to give the right to vote
Engender — to bring into being
Engross — to take the entire attention of
Engulf — to swallow up
Enigmatic — hard to understand, puzzling
Enjoin — to impose by order, prohibit
Enmesh — to entangle
Enmity — hostility
Enormity — outrageous act
Ensconce — to conceal, settle snugly
Entity — something that exists independently
Entomology — study of insects
Entreat — to implore
Enunciate — to announce, pronounce clearly
Ephemeral — short-lived
Epic — long, narrative poem
Epicure — one who has discriminating tastes for foods and liquors
Epigram — terse, witty saying
Epilogue — closing section of a literary work
Epistle — letter
Epitaph — inscription
Epithet — word or phrase characterizing a person or thing
Epitome — ideal example, embodiment
Epoch — event or time that marks the start of a new period
Equable — uniform, even
Equanimity — composure
Equivocal — purposely ambiguous
Equivocate — to purposely deceive
Era — period of time marked by certain events
Ergo — therefore
Ersatz — artificial, substitute
Erudite — learned
Escapement — notched device regulating movement in a mechanism
Escarpment — steep slope between level areas
Eschew — to shun
Esculent — edible
Escutcheon — shield containing a coat of arms
Esoteric — limited to a chosen few
Esthetic — beautiful

Estival – pertaining to summer
Ethereal – airy
Etude – musical composition used for practice
Eulogy – speech in praise of a dead person
Euphemism – substitution of a less offensive word
Euphony – agreeable sounds
Euphoria – feeling of well-being
Evanescent – fading from sight
Evasion – avoidance
Evince – to show plainly
Evoke – to call forth, produce
Evolve – to develop gradually
Exacerbate – to aggravate
Exacting – making severe demands
Exclude – to bar
Excoriate – to strip the skin of
Exculpate – to free from blame
Execrable – detestable
Execrate – to curse
Exemplary – serving as a model
Exempt – to excuse from responsibility others are subject to
Exhort – to entreat, appeal urgently
Exhume – to dig up
Exigency – situation making extremely urgent demands
Exigent – urgent
Exiguous – scanty, meager
Exogenous – originating from outside
Exonerate – to clear from blame
Exorcise – to expel (an evil spirit)
Expatiate – to speak or write at length, wander
Expedite – to speed up
Expeditious – prompt
Expiate – to make amends
Expound – to state in detail
Expunge – to erase
Expurgate – to remove passages (from a book)
Exquisite – very beautiful, perfected
Extant – still existing
Extemporary – impromptu
Extemporize – to improvise
Extenuate – to lessen the seriousness of
Extirpate – to destroy completely
Extol – to laud
Extraneous – not pertinent to the whole
Extricate – to set free
Extrinsic – not essential
Extrude – to force out
Exude – to discharge
Exult – to rejoice

Fabricate – to manufacture, invent
Fabulous – fictitious
Facade – front or main face of a building

Facetious – lightly joking
Facile – easily done
Facilitate – to make easier
Facsimile – reproduction
Factious – producing dissention
Factitious – artificially produced
Factotum – general worker
Fallacious – tending to mislead
Fallible – capable of erring
Fallow – cultivated land not in use
Fastidious – hard to please, meticulous
Fatuous – foolish
Fawn – to court favor, grovel
Fealty – intense faithfulness
Feasible – possible
Feculent – impure
Fecund – fertile
Feign – to simulate, pretend
Felicitous – appropriate, pleasant
Fell – dangerous, cruel
Ferret – to search out
Fervid – ardent
Fervor – ardor, zeal
Festoon – decorative chain
Fetid – stinking
Fetish – an object believed to have magical powers
Fettle – condition, state of fitness
Fiasco – complete failure
Fickle – capricious
Figment – fabrication
Filament – fine thread
Filch – to pilfer
Finesse – skill
Fissure – cleft or crack
Flaccid – soft and limp
Flagitious – wicked
Flagrant – outrageous
Flail – implement for threshing grain
Flair – aptitude, attractive quality
Flamboyant – showy
Flaunt – to show off
Flex – to bend
Flinch – to draw back
Flippant – lacking proper respect
Florescence – flowering
Floriculture – care of ornamental plants
Flout – to mock or scoff
Fluctuate – to vary
Foible – minor weakness
Foment – to stir up
Foray – to plunder
Forensic – relating to court or public debate
Forerunner – predecessor, sign warning of something to follow

Forlorn — miserable
Formidable — dreadful, awesome
Fortitude — courage
Fortnight — two weeks
Fortuitous — by chance
Fractious — unruly
Fraught — laden
Fray — fight
Frenetic — wildly excited
Frugal — thrifty
Fruition — accomplishment
Fulminate — to explode, denounce
Fulsome — disgusting
Furtive — stealthy

Gainsay — to contradict
Gambol — to frolic
Gamut — entire range
Garble — to distort
Garish — showy, gaudy
Garrulous — talkative
Gastronomy — art of good eating
Gauntlet — glove (medieval), ordeal
Gelid — frozen
Genial — cordial
Genre — sort or type, category
Genus — class, group with similar characteristics
Germane — fitting
Germinate — to develop, sprout
Gestation — development, pregnancy
Gibber — to speak rapidly, chatter
Gibe — to scoff, deride
Gird — to encircle
Glib — superficial, unconvincing
Glut — to oversupply
Glutton — one who overindulges
Goad — to spur
Gourmet — expert on good food and drink
Gradient — slope
Grandeur — splendor
Gratuitous — free of charge
Gratuity — tip
Gregarious — sociable
Grimace — expression of pain
Grommet — metal ring
Grueling — very tiring
Guild — organization of persons with common interests
Guile — deceitful behavior
Guise — false pretense
Gyrate — to move in a circular fashion

Hackneyed — overused, trite
Haphazard — not planned, random
Harangue — long speech

Harass — to torment
Harbinger — forerunner
Haughty — extremely proud
Hauteur — disdainful pride
Havoc — great destruction
Hawser — strong rope
Heady — impetuous
Hearth — fireplace floor
Hegemony — dominance of authority
Heinous — hateful, evil
Heptagon — seven-sided polygon
Heresy — anti-religious thought
Hermetic — airtight
Heterodox — differing from the accepted standard
Heterogeneous — differing in structure, mixed
Hexapod — something with six legs
Hiatus — gap
Hibernal — pertaining to winter
Hierarchy — an ordering by rank or grade
Hinder — to thwart, impede
Histrionic — theatrical
Hoax — practical joke, trick
Holocaust — complete destruction
Homily — sermon
Homogeneous — uniform in structure
Homologous — corresponding in structure
Horology — science of measuring time
Horrendous — horrible
Hortative — exhorting, pleading
Horticulture — the art of growing flowers, plants, fruits
Huddle — to crowd together
Humus — fertilizer, organic part of soil
Hurtle — to speed
Husbandry — cultivation and care of plants and animals
Hybrid — of mixed origin
Hydrophobia — fear of water
Hyperbole — exaggeration
Hypothesis — assumption

Idiosyncrasy — peculiar mannerism
Idyllic — pleasing, simple, pastoral
Ignoble — mean, base
Ignominious — shameful, degrading
Illicit — unlawful
Illimitable — boundless
Illusory — deceptive
Imbibe — to absorb or drink
Imbroglio — confused situation
Imbue — to permeate
Immolate — to offer in sacrifice
Immutable — unchangeable
Impale — to pierce through
Impalpable — not understood, vague
Impasse — deadlock

Impassioned — ardent, fervent
Impeach — to accuse
Impeccable — flawless
Impecunious — having no money, poor
Imperceptible — slight, subtle
Imperious — domineering
Impertinent — rude
Impervious — not influenced
Impetuous — impulsive
Impious — lacking reverence
Implicit — implied, not apparent
Imply — to indicate by indirect statement
Importune — to urge persistently
Impromptu — without preparation
Impudence — insolence
Impugn — to challenge as false
Impunity — freedom from harm
Impute — to attribute (something bad) to another
Inadvertence — negligence, oversight
Inalienable — unable to be taken away
Inane — lacking sense
Inarticulate — unable to speak clearly
Incendiary — one who excites or agitates
Inception — beginning
Incessant — never ceasing
Inchoative — just begun, initial
Incipient — beginning to appear
Inclement — stormy
Inclusive — taking all factors into account
Incognito — disguised
Incongruous — unconforming, inconsistent
Inconsiderable — trivial, small
Inconspicuous — not readily apparent
Incorrigible — not able to be corrected, delinquent
Incredulous — skeptical
Increment — increase, addition
Inculpate — to incriminate
Incumbent — officeholder, obligatory
Indefatigable — tireless
Indigenous — native to
Indigent — poor
Indolent — lazy
Indurate — hardened
Ineffable — unspeakable, indescribable
Ineluctable — inevitable
Ineptitude — awkwardness, incompetence
Inert — without power to move or resist
Inexorable — unrelenting
Infamy — bad reputation
Inference — conclusion
Infernal — hellish, fiendish
Infinitesimal — immeasurably small
Infrastructure — basic framework of an organization
Infringe — to encroach upon

Ingenious — resourceful, inventive
Ingenuous — frank, naive
Ingratiate — to seek someone's favor
Inherent — belonging by nature
Inimical — hostile
Iniquitous — unjust
Injunction — court order, command
Innate — natural, existing from birth
Innocuous — harmless
Innuendo — hint, allusion
Inscrutable — enigmatic, mysterious
Insidious — treacherous
Insinuate — to suggest, hint at artfully
Insipid — dull, tasteless
Insolvent — bankrupt
Instigator — one who incites action
Insular — narrow-minded, limited
Insurgent — one who revolts against established authority
Intangible — incorporeal, vague
Intemperance — excessive indulgence
Interdict — to prohibit
Interment — burial
Interminable — endless
Internment — confinement (of enemies)
Interpolate — to change by inserting new material
Interstice — space, interval
Intractable — unruly, stubborn
Intransigent — refusing to compromise
Intrepid — fearless
Intrinsic — inherent
Introvert — to turn inward
Intuition — insight
Inundate — to overflow, overwhelm
Inure — habituate
Invective — denunciation
Inveigh — to complain bitterly
Inveigle — to trick, entice
Investiture — installation in office
Inveterate — firmly established
Invidious — offensive
Invincible — unconquerable
Inviolate — sacred
Irascible — easily angered
Ironical — contrary to what was expected, sarcastic
Isthmus — narrow strip of land
Iterate — to repeat over and over
Itinerant — traveling from place to place

Jaundice — yellow pigmentation of the skin
Jaunty — lively
Jettison — to throw overboard, discard as superfluous
Jocose — humorous
Jocund — cheerful
Jocular — playful, jolly

Jostle — to elbow, agitate
Judicious — showing sound judgment
Juggernaut — massive destructive force
Juridical — pertaining to law
Juxtapose — to put side by side

Kaleidoscopic — changing
Kindred — family relationship
Kinetic — active
Kismet — fate
Kith — friends
Knave — dishonest person
Kudos — credit for an achievement, praise

Labyrinth — maze
Lacerate — to mangle, tear
Laconic — concise
Lambaste — to scold, censure
Lampoon — satirical attack
Languid — weak, dull
Languish — to become weak
Languor — lack of vitality
Larcenous — thievish
Largess — generous giving
Lascivious — lustful
Lassitude — fatigue
Latent — hidden
Laudatory — expressing praise
Lethal — deadly
Lethargic — sluggish
Levity — lightness, frivolity
Lexicon — dictionary
Libation — ceremonial drinking
Licentious — morally unrestrained
Limpid — clear, transparent
Lineament — a distinctive feature
Lissome — nimble
Litany — prayer, chant
Lithe — flexible
Litigation — lawsuit
Livid — discolored by a bruise, enraged
Locution — style of speech
Loquacious — talkative
Lucid — shining, readily understood
Ludicrous — absurd
Lugubrious — affectedly mournful
Luminary — outstanding person
Lurid — sensational

Macabre — gruesome
Machination — evil plot
Macrocosm — entity representing on a larger scale, one of its smaller units
Madrigal — song, ballad

Magistrate — official who administers laws
Magnanimous — generous
Maladroit — awkward
Malefactor — evildoer
Malevolent — arising from an evil will
Malfeasance — wrongdoing
Malign — to slander
Malinger — to feign illness
Malleable — flexible, adaptable
Martinet — very strict disciplinarian
Masticate — to chew up
Maudlin — foolishly sentimental
Megalomania — illusions of grandeur
Meliorate — to make or become better
Mellifluous — flowing sweetly, smoothly
Ménage — household
Mendacious — untruthful
Mendicant — beggar
Menial — servile
Mercurial — changeable, fickle
Meretricious — falsely alluring, gaudy
Meritorious — deserving honor
Mesmerize — hypnotize
Metamorphosis — change of form
Metaphor — figure of speech using one idea in place of another to denote a likeness between the two
Mete — to allot
Meticulous — careful with details
Mettle — spirit, courage
Miasma — pervading corruptive atmosphere
Microcosm — a small unit that is the epitome of a larger entity
Mien — manner, appearance
Militate — to work (for or against)
Millenium — 1000 years
Minion — favored person
Miscreant — villain
Misgiving — doubt
Misnomer — name wrongly applied
Missive — letter
Mitigate — to ease
Mnemonic — memory aid
Modicum — small portion
Modulate — to regulate
Mollify — to appease
Moot — debatable
Mordant — sarcastic
Mores — customs
Moribund — dying
Morose — gloomy
Motley — composed of many elements
Multifarious — diverse
Mundane — worldly
Munificent — generous, lavish

Myopia – nearsightedness
Myriad – very large number

Nadir – lowest point
Nape – back of the neck
Narcissism – self-love
Narrative – story, account
Nascent – coming into being
Nebulous – vague
Nefarious – very wicked
Nemesis – formidable rival, one who inflicts just punishment
Neology – use of an established word in a new way
Neophyte – beginner, convert
Nepotism – favoritism shown relatives
Nettle – irritate
Nexus – link, connection
Niggardly – stingy
Nocturnal – pertaining to night
Noisome – offensive, harmful to health
Nomenclature – system of names
Nonpareil – unequaled
Nonplussed – perplexed
Nostalgia – sentimental yearning for the past
Notorious – widely known
Noxious – harmful
Numismatic – monetary
Nuptial – pertaining to marriage
Nurture – train, rear

Obdurate – stubborn
Obeisance – gesture of respect
Obesity – stoutness, fatness
Obfuscate – to obscure
Objurgate – to denounce
Oblation – solemn offering
Oblique – evasive
Obloquy – widespread censure
Obsequious – servile
Obsolescent – falling into disuse
Obstreperous – noisy, unruly
Obstruct – to stop, close
Obtrude – to push out
Obtuse – stupid, blunt
Obviate – to prevent
Occidental – Western
Odious – disgusting
Odoriferous – giving off a smell
Officious – meddlesome
Olfactory – pertaining to smell
Oligarchy – government by a small group often for corrupt purposes
Ominous – threatening
Omnipotent – having unlimited power

Omnivorous – eating all sorts of food
Onerous – burdensome
Onus – burden
Opaque – not translucent
Opprobrious – disgraceful, infamous
Opulent – wealthy
Opus – work, composition
Orbit – revolving path
Ordinance – statute
Ordnance – artillery
Ordure – excrement
Ornate – showy
Ornery – obstinate
Ornithology – study of birds
Oscillate – to fluctuate between two points
Ossify – to change to bone
Ostensible – apparent
Ostentatious – showy
Ostracize – to banish
Overt – done openly
Overweening – arrogant

Palatable – agreeable to the senses
Pall – to lose effectiveness
Palliate – to reduce the intensity of
Pallid – pale
Palpable – obvious, easily perceived
Paltry – petty
Panacea – remedy for all maladies
Pandemic – widely spread
Parable – short story showing a moral
Paradigm – model, example
Paradox – a statement that seems contradictory but may be true in fact
Paragon – model of excellence
Paramount – highest in rank
Paraphernalia – personal belongings
Pariah – outcast
Parity – equality in value
Parody – farcical imitation
Paroxysm – sudden outburst
Parsimony – stinginess, thrift
Parsonage – pastor's dwelling
Pastoral – of shepherds, rural
Patent – evident
Pathos – something which arouses pity
Patrimony – property inherited from ancestors
Paucity – scarcity
Peculate – to embezzle
Pecuniary – involving money
Pedant – one who emphasizes trivial points of learning
Pejorative – worsening
Penchant – strong liking
Pendant – hanging object

Penitence – sorrow for sins
Penology – study of prisons and prison reform
Pensile – hanging
Penurious – stingy
Perambulate – to walk
Perdition – damnation
Perennial – enduring
Perfidy – treachery
Perforce – of necessity
Perfunctory – routine, superficial
Perigee – point of an orbit nearest the earth
Peripatetic – itinerant
Periphery – outside boundary
Periphrasis – using long phrasing instead of shorter expressions
Permeable – passable, penetrable
Permutation – change, alteration
Pernicious – destructive, fatal
Peroration – end of a speech
Perpetrate – carry out, commit
Perpetuate – cause to continue
Perquisite – something in addition to regular pay, tip, bonus
Personage – important person
Perspective – sense of proportion
Perspicacity – keen judgment
Perspicuous – easily understood
Pert – bold, cocky
Pertinent – relevant
Perturb – to upset, agitate
Peruse – to read carefully
Pervade – to spread throughout
Perverse – deviating from what is considered normal
Petulance – impatience
Phalanx – massed group of individuals
Philander – to court with no intention of marriage
Philistine – one governed by material rather than intellectual values
Philology – study of linguistics
Phlegmatic – sluggish
Phobia – persistent irrational fear
Picayune – of little value, petty
Piebald – marked with splotches of color, heterogeneous
Pillory – to scorn publicly
Piquant – agreeably stimulating, pungent
Pique – to offend, provoke
Piscatorial – pertaining to fish
Pithy – terse
Pixilated – amusingly eccentric
Placate – to appease
Placid – calm
Plaintive – melancholy
Plait – to braid, pleat
Platitude – trite remark

Plaudit – expression of approval
Plausible – seemingly reasonable
Plebiscite – popular vote
Plenary – full, complete
Plethora – overabundance
Plicate – folded lengthwise
Plumb – straight down, vertically
Ply – to use or practice diligently
Poach – to trespass
Poignant – pungent, touching the emotions
Polemic – involving dispute
Politic – prudent, expedient
Polity – political organization
Ponderous – unwieldy, dull
Pontificate – to orate, make dogmatic statements
Portend – to warn, foreshadow
Portentous – ominous
Posit – to postulate
Posterity – future generations
Postulate – hypothesis, axiom
Potable – suitable for drinking
Potpourri – mixture
Poultice – soft heated dressing applied to wounds
Pragmatic – practical, relating to fact
Prate – to chatter
Precarious – uncertain, risky
Precipitous – steep
Precipitate – hasty
Preclude – to shut out, prevent
Precursor – forerunner
Predacious – predatory
Predatory – tending to exploit others for one's own gain
Predicate – to affirm
Predilection – preconceived liking
Predispose – to make susceptible
Preeminent – outstanding, high-ranking
Preen – to dress up or adorn (oneself)
Premeditation – preplanning
Premise – statement forming the basis of an argument
Preponderate – to surpass in weight or power
Preposterous – absurd, ridiculous
Prerequisite – something needed for performing a function
Prescience – foreboding
Prescribe – to establish as a means of action
Presumptuous – too bold or forward
Pretentious – showy, making unjustified claims
Prevaricate – to evade the truth
Pristine – uncorrupted by society
Probity – integrity, honesty
Proclaim – to declare proudly
Proclivity – inclination
Prodigal – spendthrift
Prodigious – wonderous, enormous
Profane – irreligious

Proffer — to present for approval
Profligate — recklessly wasteful
Progeny — offspring
Prognosticate — to predict
Proliferate — to increase in number
Prolific — producing abundantly
Prolix — prolonged unduly
Prominent — noticeable, well-known
Promontory — high peak that overlooks lower land or water
Promulgate — to announce openly
Propensity — natural tendency
Propinquity — nearness
Propitiate — to appease
Propitious — favorable
Proponent — one in favor of
Propound — to present for discussion
Prorate — to divide proportionately
Prosaic — commonplace, dull
Proscribe — to outlaw, prohibit
Proselytize — to convert from one belief to another
Protagonist — main character in novel
Prototype — standard example
Provincial — having a limited outlook
Prurient — lustful, lewd
Puerile — childish, silly
Pulchritude — beauty
Punctilious — very exact
Pundit — learned person
Pungent — sharp sensation of taste and smell
Pugnacious — belligerent
Purloin — to steal
Purport — to give an appearance of, intend
Pusillanimous — lacking courage and resolve
Putative — assumed to exist
Putrefy — to rot
Pythonic — monstrous

Quadrant — one-quarter of a plane
Quaint — unusual, old-fashioned
Qualm — misgiving
Quandary — perplexed state
Querulous — complaining
Query — inquiry
Quiescent — quiet, still
Quintessence — perfect form
Quivering — shaking, trembling slightly
Quixotic — having highly romantic or chivalrous ideals

Raillery — playful teasing
Raiment — clothing
Rambunctious — boisterous
Ramification — offshoot, consequence
Rampant — widespread, without restraint

Ramshackle — loosely made, dilapidated
Rancor — ill will
Rankle — to cause resentment
Rapacious — greedy
Rapine — plunder
Ratification — formal approval
Raucous — rough sounding, boisterous
Ravenous — extremely eager for gratification
Recalcitrant — disobedient
Recant — to renounce
Recidivist — confirmed criminal
Reciprocal — complementary, mutually responsive
Recluse — hermit
Recondite — beyond ordinary understanding, concealed
Reconnoiter — to survey
Recreant — cowardly
Recrimination — countercharge
Rectitude — integrity
Recumbent — lying down
Redact — to edit
Redolent — fragrant
Redoubt — temporary fortification
Redress — to remedy, compensate
Redundant — superfluous, wordy
Refectory — dining hall
Referendum — popular vote on a measure submitted by a legislative body
Refractory — obstinate, unresponsive
Refute — to prove wrong
Refurbish — to renovate
Regale — to entertain
Regent — one who rules
Regicide — killing of a king
Regimen — system of diet, ruling system
Regressive — going backward
Relegate — to exile, to assign to a lower position
Reliquary — container for sacred objects
Remission — pardon, forgiveness, abatement
Remonstrate — to protest
Remunerate — to pay for work done, compensate
Renascent — reborn
Renegade — deserter, outcast
Renege — to go back on a promise
Renunciation — repudiation
Repast — meal
Repine — to long for
Replete — well filled
Reprehend — to criticize
Repression — stopping by force
Reprisal — act of retaliation
Reproach — disgrace, cause of blame
Reprobate — depraved, unprincipled
Reproof — rebuke, criticism
Repudiate — to refuse, reject, disown

Repugnant – distasteful, disliked
Requisite – requirement
Requital – suitable repayment
Rescind – to repeal, take back
Resilient – able to spring back into shape
Resplendent – dazzling
Restitution – restoration, refund
Restive – impatient
Resurgent – rising again
Resuscitate – revive
Retaliate – to get even
Reticence – silence, reserve
Retort – to make a witty reply
Retribution – just reward
Retroactive – extending to previous conditions
Retrograde – to go backward
Reverberate – to throw back, echo
Revile – to abuse verbally
Ribald – offensive, vulgar
Rife – widespread, abounding
Rift – opening, breach
Rigor – strictness
Risibility – laughter
Robust – healthy, strong
Rote – mechanical repetition or action
Rotund – rounded
Ruckus – noisy confusion
Rudiment – first principle, beginning of something
Ruminant – meditative
Ruminate – to meditate, ponder

Saccharine – overly sweet, affectedly agreeable
Sacrilege – desecration
Sagacious – shrewdly discerning
Salacious – lustful
Salient – conspicuous
Saline – salty
Sallow – dull greenish-yellow
Salubrious – wholesome
Salutary – curative
Salutatory – welcoming address
Sanctimony – pretended piety
Sanguine – confident, optimistic
Sapient – wise
Sardonic – scornful
Sartorial – pertaining to tailoring
Satiate – to satisfy, glut
Saturate – to soak, fill completely
Saturnine – sullen, sluggish
Savor – to relish, enjoy
Scabbard – sword sheath
Scathing – searing, blasting
Schematic – diagrammatic
Schism – split, difference of opinion

Scintilla – particle, trace
Scion – descendent
Scoff – derision
Scourge – whip, devastation
Scruple – small quantity, principle
Scrutinize – to examine closely
Scurrilous – coarse, vulgar
Secular – worldly, not religious
Sedition – rebellion
Sedulous – diligent
Semblance – appearance
Senescent – growing old
Sententious – given to moralistic expression
Sequester – to isolate
Serrate – having sawlike notches
Shallop – small, open boat
Shamble – to walk clumsily
Shunt – to turn to one side
Sibling – brother or sister
Sidle – move sidewise
Simile – figure of speech comparing two unlike things
Similitude – likeness
Simony – buying or selling of church pardons
Sinecure – easy job
Sinuous – bending, winding
Slothful – lazy
Sluice – artificial water channel
Sojourn – to remain somewhere temporarily
Solace – to comfort, console
Solicitous – showing care or concern
Soluble – able to be dissolved
Somatic – physical, of the body
Somnolent – sleepy, drowsy
Sonorous – full of sound, resonant
Sophistry – misleading but clever reasoning
Soporific – causing sleep
Sordid – dirty, ignoble
Spasmodic – intermittent
Spawn – to deposit eggs, bring forth
Specious – deceptively appealing
Specter – ghost
Sporadic – occasional
Spurious – false, not genuine
Staid – sedate
Stigma – mark of disgrace
Stilted – pompous
Stint – restriction
Stoicism – impassiveness, indifference
Stolid – showing little emotion
Stratagem – trick, device
Strategy – careful plan
Stricture – adverse criticism
Strident – harsh-sounding
Stultify – to appear foolish, impair

Stupor — loss of sensibility
Suave — polite, urbane
Subjoin — to append
Subjugate — to force to submit
Sublimate — to direct actions into more socially acceptable forms
Subservient — inferior, submissive
Subterfuge — deception used to evade something difficult or unpleasant
Subversive — destructive
Succinct — clearly and briefly stated
Succor — to help
Succulent — juicy
Suffuse — to overspread
Sully — to soil, stain
Sumptuous — lavish
Supercilious — haughty, contemptuous
Supernal — exalted, celestial
Supersede — to replace
Supervene — to happen additionally or unexpectedly
Supine — indolent, prone
Supple — flexible
Supplicate — to ask for humbly
Suppress — to keep from public knowledge
Surfeit — overindulgence
Surreptitious — acting in a secret and stealthy way
Surrogate — deputy, substitute
Sustenance — nourishment
Sycophant — self-serving flatterer
Syllogism — conclusion based on two premises
Synchronous — occurring simultaneously
Synopsis — summary
Synthesis — combining of elements to make a whole
Synthetic — man-made

Tacit — silent
Taciturn — tending toward silence
Tactic — means of accomplishing a purpose
Tactile — perceived by the sense of touch
Tantamount — equal in value
Tautology — needless repetition of an idea
Tawdry — gaudy, cheap
Taxonomy — classification (of plants and animals)
Temerity — foolish boldness
Temperate — moderate
Temporize — compromise
Tenacious — persistent, tough
Tenet — doctrine
Tenuous — unsubstantial, flimsy
Termagant — nagging woman
Terminus — end point
Terse — brief, to the point
Tertiary — third in order
Thespian — actor

Thrall — slave
Timorous — timid
Tirade — long, vehement speech or denunciation
Tithe — tenth part of something paid as a tax to a church
Titular — having a title without performing the functions involved
Tome — large book
Torpid — inactive, sluggish
Torrid — very hot
Toxic — pertaining to poison
Tractable — easily managed
Traduce — to slander
Tranquility — calmness, serenity
Transfuse — to transmit, imbue
Transgression — violation
Transitory — temporary
Translucent — permitting the passage of light
Transpire — to become known, happen
Transverse — placed crosswise
Travail — hard work
Travesty — ridiculous representation
Treble — to increase threefold
Tremulous — trembling
Trenchant — sharp, clear-cut
Trepidation — fear
Tribulation — misery, distress
Truculent — cruel, belligerent
Truncated — shortened, curtailed
Truncheon — club
Tumid — swollen, inflated
Tumultuous — violently turbulent
Turbid — muddy
Turgid — swollen
Turpitude — vileness
Tutelage — guardianship
Twit — to taunt

Ubiquitous — present everywhere simultaneously
Ulterior — lying beyond what is openly expressed
Umbrage — offense
Unctuous — oily, suave
Undaunted — determined in spite of adverse conditions
Undulate — to move in waves
Unerring — without fault
Ungainly — awkward, clumsy
Unmitigated — not lessened, absolute
Unobtrusive — not aggressive
Untenable — unable to be occupied or defended
Untoward — unfavorable
Upbraid — to scold, reproach
Uproarious — boisterous
Urbane — refined
Usurp — to take by force
Uxorial — pertaining to a wife

Vacillate — to show indecision
Vacuous — empty, stupid
Vagary — eccentric idea or action
Valorous — courageous
Vanguard — front part of a movement
Vapid — tasteless, flat
Variegated — marked with different colors
Vaunt — display boastfully
Vegetate — to lead an inactive life
Vehement — impassioned
Venal — open to corruption
Vendetta — extended bitter feud
Venerate — to show deep respect
Venial — excusable
Veracious — honest
Verbosity — wordiness
Verdant — green in color
Verisimilitude — truth
Verity — truth
Vermillion — bright red pigment
Vernacular — native language of a region
Versatile — able to change easily
Versification — metrical structure
Vertex — highest point
Vestige — trace
Viable — capable of living or functioning
Vicarious — experienced through the activity of another person
Vicissitude — changeability
Vilify — to defame
Vindicate — to clear from blame
Vindictive — wanting revenge
Virago — domineering woman
Viridity — greenness, naiveness
Virility — masculinity

Virulent — deadly, hateful
Viscous — sticky, lacking easy movement
Vitiate — to debase
Vitreous — pertaining to glass
Vituperate — to berate
Vivacious — spirited, lively
Vivid — vigorous, clear
Vixen — female fox
Vociferous — noisy
Volatile — quickly evaporating, explosive
Volition — act of determining
Voluble — talkative
Voracious — greedy
Votary — zealous follower
Votive — expressing a wish or vow
Vouchsafe — to grant

Waft — odor or sound carried through the air
Wan — pale
Wanton — reckless, immoral
Weal — well-being
Welter — confusion, turmoil
Wheedle — to coax
Whet — to arouse, stimulate
Windfall — unexpected gain
Wizened — dried up, withered
Wraith — ghost, apparition
Wrangle — to quarrel
Wroth — angry
Wry — twisted

Zany — fool, clown
Zealot — fanatic
Zenith — highest point
Zephyr — mild breeze

Answer Sheet—Sample Test 1

Section I
Reading Comprehension
1. Ⓐ Ⓑ Ⓒ Ⓓ Ⓔ
2. Ⓐ Ⓑ Ⓒ Ⓓ Ⓔ
3. Ⓐ Ⓑ Ⓒ Ⓓ Ⓔ
4. Ⓐ Ⓑ Ⓒ Ⓓ Ⓔ
5. Ⓐ Ⓑ Ⓒ Ⓓ Ⓔ
6. Ⓐ Ⓑ Ⓒ Ⓓ Ⓔ
7. Ⓐ Ⓑ Ⓒ Ⓓ Ⓔ
8. Ⓐ Ⓑ Ⓒ Ⓓ Ⓔ
9. Ⓐ Ⓑ Ⓒ Ⓓ Ⓔ
10. Ⓐ Ⓑ Ⓒ Ⓓ Ⓔ
11. Ⓐ Ⓑ Ⓒ Ⓓ Ⓔ
12. Ⓐ Ⓑ Ⓒ Ⓓ Ⓔ
13. Ⓐ Ⓑ Ⓒ Ⓓ Ⓔ
14. Ⓐ Ⓑ Ⓒ Ⓓ Ⓔ
15. Ⓐ Ⓑ Ⓒ Ⓓ Ⓔ
16. Ⓐ Ⓑ Ⓒ Ⓓ Ⓔ
17. Ⓐ Ⓑ Ⓒ Ⓓ Ⓔ
18. Ⓐ Ⓑ Ⓒ Ⓓ Ⓔ
19. Ⓐ Ⓑ Ⓒ Ⓓ Ⓔ
20. Ⓐ Ⓑ Ⓒ Ⓓ Ⓔ
21. Ⓐ Ⓑ Ⓒ Ⓓ Ⓔ
22. Ⓐ Ⓑ Ⓒ Ⓓ Ⓔ
23. Ⓐ Ⓑ Ⓒ Ⓓ Ⓔ
24. Ⓐ Ⓑ Ⓒ Ⓓ Ⓔ
25. Ⓐ Ⓑ Ⓒ Ⓓ Ⓔ

Section II
Problem Solving
26. Ⓐ Ⓑ Ⓒ Ⓓ Ⓔ
27. Ⓐ Ⓑ Ⓒ Ⓓ Ⓔ
28. Ⓐ Ⓑ Ⓒ Ⓓ Ⓔ
29. Ⓐ Ⓑ Ⓒ Ⓓ Ⓔ
30. Ⓐ Ⓑ Ⓒ Ⓓ Ⓔ
31. Ⓐ Ⓑ Ⓒ Ⓓ Ⓔ
32. Ⓐ Ⓑ Ⓒ Ⓓ Ⓔ
33. Ⓐ Ⓑ Ⓒ Ⓓ Ⓔ
34. Ⓐ Ⓑ Ⓒ Ⓓ Ⓔ
35. Ⓐ Ⓑ Ⓒ Ⓓ Ⓔ

36. Ⓐ Ⓑ Ⓒ Ⓓ Ⓔ
37. Ⓐ Ⓑ Ⓒ Ⓓ Ⓔ
38. Ⓐ Ⓑ Ⓒ Ⓓ Ⓔ
39. Ⓐ Ⓑ Ⓒ Ⓓ Ⓔ
40. Ⓐ Ⓑ Ⓒ Ⓓ Ⓔ
41. Ⓐ Ⓑ Ⓒ Ⓓ Ⓔ
42. Ⓐ Ⓑ Ⓒ Ⓓ Ⓔ
43. Ⓐ Ⓑ Ⓒ Ⓓ Ⓔ
44. Ⓐ Ⓑ Ⓒ Ⓓ Ⓔ
45. Ⓐ Ⓑ Ⓒ Ⓓ Ⓔ
46. Ⓐ Ⓑ Ⓒ Ⓓ Ⓔ
47. Ⓐ Ⓑ Ⓒ Ⓓ Ⓔ
48. Ⓐ Ⓑ Ⓒ Ⓓ Ⓔ
49. Ⓐ Ⓑ Ⓒ Ⓓ Ⓔ
50. Ⓐ Ⓑ Ⓒ Ⓓ Ⓔ
51. Ⓐ Ⓑ Ⓒ Ⓓ Ⓔ
52. Ⓐ Ⓑ Ⓒ Ⓓ Ⓔ
53. Ⓐ Ⓑ Ⓒ Ⓓ Ⓔ
54. Ⓐ Ⓑ Ⓒ Ⓓ Ⓔ
55. Ⓐ Ⓑ Ⓒ Ⓓ Ⓔ

Section III
Practical Judgment
56. Ⓐ Ⓑ Ⓒ Ⓓ Ⓔ
57. Ⓐ Ⓑ Ⓒ Ⓓ Ⓔ
58. Ⓐ Ⓑ Ⓒ Ⓓ Ⓔ
59. Ⓐ Ⓑ Ⓒ Ⓓ Ⓔ
60. Ⓐ Ⓑ Ⓒ Ⓓ Ⓔ
61. Ⓐ Ⓑ Ⓒ Ⓓ Ⓔ
62. Ⓐ Ⓑ Ⓒ Ⓓ Ⓔ
63. Ⓐ Ⓑ Ⓒ Ⓓ Ⓔ
64. Ⓐ Ⓑ Ⓒ Ⓓ Ⓔ
65. Ⓐ Ⓑ Ⓒ Ⓓ Ⓔ
66. Ⓐ Ⓑ Ⓒ Ⓓ Ⓔ
67. Ⓐ Ⓑ Ⓒ Ⓓ Ⓔ
68. Ⓐ Ⓑ Ⓒ Ⓓ Ⓔ
69. Ⓐ Ⓑ Ⓒ Ⓓ Ⓔ
70. Ⓐ Ⓑ Ⓒ Ⓓ Ⓔ
71. Ⓐ Ⓑ Ⓒ Ⓓ Ⓔ
72. Ⓐ Ⓑ Ⓒ Ⓓ Ⓔ
73. Ⓐ Ⓑ Ⓒ Ⓓ Ⓔ
74. Ⓐ Ⓑ Ⓒ Ⓓ Ⓔ
75. Ⓐ Ⓑ Ⓒ Ⓓ Ⓔ

Section IV
Data Sufficiency
76. Ⓐ Ⓑ Ⓒ Ⓓ Ⓔ
77. Ⓐ Ⓑ Ⓒ Ⓓ Ⓔ
78. Ⓐ Ⓑ Ⓒ Ⓓ Ⓔ
79. Ⓐ Ⓑ Ⓒ Ⓓ Ⓔ
80. Ⓐ Ⓑ Ⓒ Ⓓ Ⓔ
81. Ⓐ Ⓑ Ⓒ Ⓓ Ⓔ
82. Ⓐ Ⓑ Ⓒ Ⓓ Ⓔ
83. Ⓐ Ⓑ Ⓒ Ⓓ Ⓔ
84. Ⓐ Ⓑ Ⓒ Ⓓ Ⓔ
85. Ⓐ Ⓑ Ⓒ Ⓓ Ⓔ
86. Ⓐ Ⓑ Ⓒ Ⓓ Ⓔ
87. Ⓐ Ⓑ Ⓒ Ⓓ Ⓔ
88. Ⓐ Ⓑ Ⓒ Ⓓ Ⓔ
89. Ⓐ Ⓑ Ⓒ Ⓓ Ⓔ
90. Ⓐ Ⓑ Ⓒ Ⓓ Ⓔ
91. Ⓐ Ⓑ Ⓒ Ⓓ Ⓔ
92. Ⓐ Ⓑ Ⓒ Ⓓ Ⓔ
93. Ⓐ Ⓑ Ⓒ Ⓓ Ⓔ
94. Ⓐ Ⓑ Ⓒ Ⓓ Ⓔ
95. Ⓐ Ⓑ Ⓒ Ⓓ Ⓔ
96. Ⓐ Ⓑ Ⓒ Ⓓ Ⓔ
97. Ⓐ Ⓑ Ⓒ Ⓓ Ⓔ
98. Ⓐ Ⓑ Ⓒ Ⓓ Ⓔ
99. Ⓐ Ⓑ Ⓒ Ⓓ Ⓔ
100. Ⓐ Ⓑ Ⓒ Ⓓ Ⓔ
101. Ⓐ Ⓑ Ⓒ Ⓓ Ⓔ
102. Ⓐ Ⓑ Ⓒ Ⓓ Ⓔ
103. Ⓐ Ⓑ Ⓒ Ⓓ Ⓔ
104. Ⓐ Ⓑ Ⓒ Ⓓ Ⓔ
105. Ⓐ Ⓑ Ⓒ Ⓓ Ⓔ

Section V
Writing Ability
106. Ⓐ Ⓑ Ⓒ Ⓓ Ⓔ
107. Ⓐ Ⓑ Ⓒ Ⓓ Ⓔ
108. Ⓐ Ⓑ Ⓒ Ⓓ Ⓔ
109. Ⓐ Ⓑ Ⓒ Ⓓ Ⓔ
110. Ⓐ Ⓑ Ⓒ Ⓓ Ⓔ

111. Ⓐ Ⓑ Ⓒ Ⓓ Ⓔ
112. Ⓐ Ⓑ Ⓒ Ⓓ Ⓔ
113. Ⓐ Ⓑ Ⓒ Ⓓ Ⓔ
114. Ⓐ Ⓑ Ⓒ Ⓓ Ⓔ
115. Ⓐ Ⓑ Ⓒ Ⓓ Ⓔ
116. Ⓐ Ⓑ Ⓒ Ⓓ Ⓔ
117. Ⓐ Ⓑ Ⓒ Ⓓ Ⓔ
118. Ⓐ Ⓑ Ⓒ Ⓓ Ⓔ
119. Ⓐ Ⓑ Ⓒ Ⓓ Ⓔ
120. Ⓐ Ⓑ Ⓒ Ⓓ Ⓔ
121. Ⓐ Ⓑ Ⓒ Ⓓ Ⓔ
122. Ⓐ Ⓑ Ⓒ Ⓓ Ⓔ
123. Ⓐ Ⓑ Ⓒ Ⓓ Ⓔ
124. Ⓐ Ⓑ Ⓒ Ⓓ Ⓔ
125. Ⓐ Ⓑ Ⓒ Ⓓ Ⓔ

Section VI
Practical Judgment
126. Ⓐ Ⓑ Ⓒ Ⓓ Ⓔ
127. Ⓐ Ⓑ Ⓒ Ⓓ Ⓔ
128. Ⓐ Ⓑ Ⓒ Ⓓ Ⓔ
129. Ⓐ Ⓑ Ⓒ Ⓓ Ⓔ
130. Ⓐ Ⓑ Ⓒ Ⓓ Ⓔ
131. Ⓐ Ⓑ Ⓒ Ⓓ Ⓔ
132. Ⓐ Ⓑ Ⓒ Ⓓ Ⓔ
133. Ⓐ Ⓑ Ⓒ Ⓓ Ⓔ
134. Ⓐ Ⓑ Ⓒ Ⓓ Ⓔ
135. Ⓐ Ⓑ Ⓒ Ⓓ Ⓔ
136. Ⓐ Ⓑ Ⓒ Ⓓ Ⓔ
137. Ⓐ Ⓑ Ⓒ Ⓓ Ⓔ
138. Ⓐ Ⓑ Ⓒ Ⓓ Ⓔ
139. Ⓐ Ⓑ Ⓒ Ⓓ Ⓔ
140. Ⓐ Ⓑ Ⓒ Ⓓ Ⓔ
141. Ⓐ Ⓑ Ⓒ Ⓓ Ⓔ
142. Ⓐ Ⓑ Ⓒ Ⓓ Ⓔ
143. Ⓐ Ⓑ Ⓒ Ⓓ Ⓔ
144. Ⓐ Ⓑ Ⓒ Ⓓ Ⓔ
145. Ⓐ Ⓑ Ⓒ Ⓓ Ⓔ

Section VII
Writing Ability
146. Ⓐ Ⓑ Ⓒ Ⓓ Ⓔ
147. Ⓐ Ⓑ Ⓒ Ⓓ Ⓔ
148. Ⓐ Ⓑ Ⓒ Ⓓ Ⓔ
149. Ⓐ Ⓑ Ⓒ Ⓓ Ⓔ
150. Ⓐ Ⓑ Ⓒ Ⓓ Ⓔ
151. Ⓐ Ⓑ Ⓒ Ⓓ Ⓔ
152. Ⓐ Ⓑ Ⓒ Ⓓ Ⓔ
153. Ⓐ Ⓑ Ⓒ Ⓓ Ⓔ
154. Ⓐ Ⓑ Ⓒ Ⓓ Ⓔ
155. Ⓐ Ⓑ Ⓒ Ⓓ Ⓔ
156. Ⓐ Ⓑ Ⓒ Ⓓ Ⓔ
157. Ⓐ Ⓑ Ⓒ Ⓓ Ⓔ
158. Ⓐ Ⓑ Ⓒ Ⓓ Ⓔ
159. Ⓐ Ⓑ Ⓒ Ⓓ Ⓔ
160. Ⓐ Ⓑ Ⓒ Ⓓ Ⓔ
161. Ⓐ Ⓑ Ⓒ Ⓓ Ⓔ
162. Ⓐ Ⓑ Ⓒ Ⓓ Ⓔ
163. Ⓐ Ⓑ Ⓒ Ⓓ Ⓔ
164. Ⓐ Ⓑ Ⓒ Ⓓ Ⓔ
165. Ⓐ Ⓑ Ⓒ Ⓓ Ⓔ
166. Ⓐ Ⓑ Ⓒ Ⓓ Ⓔ
167. Ⓐ Ⓑ Ⓒ Ⓓ Ⓔ
168. Ⓐ Ⓑ Ⓒ Ⓓ Ⓔ
169. Ⓐ Ⓑ Ⓒ Ⓓ Ⓔ
170. Ⓐ Ⓑ Ⓒ Ⓓ Ⓔ

FIVE SAMPLE GMATs WITH ANSWERS AND ANALYSIS

Sample Test 1

Section I   Reading Comprehension

TIME: 30 minutes

DIRECTIONS: This part contains three reading passages. You are to read each one carefully. When answering the questions, you *will* be allowed to refer back to the passages. The questions are based on what is *stated* or *implied* in each passage. You have thirty minutes to complete this section.

Passage 1:

This passage was written in 1972.

The United States economy made progress in reducing unemployment and moderating inflation. On the international side, this year was much calmer than last. Nevertheless, continuing imbalances in the pattern of world trade contributed to intermittent strains in the foreign exchange markets. These strains intensified to crisis proportions, precipitating a further devaluation of the dollar.

The domestic economy expanded in a remarkably vigorous and steady fashion. After a few lingering doubts about the strength of consumer demand in the opening weeks, the vitality of the expansion never came again into serious question. The resurgence in consumer confidence was reflected in the higher proportion of incomes spent for goods and services and the marked increase in consumer willingness to take on installment debt. A parallel strengthening in business psychology was manifested in a stepped-up rate of plant and equipment spending and a gradual pickup in outlays for inventory. Confidence in the economy was also reflected in the strength of the stock market and in the stability of the bond market, where rates showed little net change over the year as a whole despite the vigorous economic upturn. On several occasions during the year, the financial markets responded to shifting appraisals of the outlook for peace in Vietnam. For the year as a whole, consumer and business sentiment benefited from rising public expectations that a resolution of the conflict was in prospect and that East-West tensions were easing.

The underpinnings of the business expansion were to be found in part in the stimulative monetary and fiscal policies that had been pursued. Moreover, the restoration of sounder liquidity positions and tighter management control of production efficiency had also helped lay the groundwork for a strong expansion. In addition, the economic policy moves made by the President had served to renew optimism on the business outlook while boosting hopes that inflation would be brought under more effective control. Finally, of course, the economy was able to grow as vigorously as it did because sufficient leeway existed in terms of idle men and machines.

The United States balance of payments deficit declined sharply. Nevertheless, by any other test, the deficit remained very large, and there was actually a substantial deterioration in our trade account to a sizable deficit, almost two thirds of which was with Japan. It was to be expected that the immediate effect of devaluation would be a worsening in our trade accounts, with the benefits coming only later. While the overall trade performance proved disappointing, there are still good reasons for expecting the delayed impact of devaluation to produce in time a significant strengthening in our trade picture. Given the size of the Japanese component of our trade deficit, however, the outcome will depend importantly on the extent of the corrective measures undertaken by Japan. Also important will be our own efforts in the United States to fashion internal policies consistent with an improvement in our external balance.

The underlying task of public policy for the year ahead—and indeed for the longer run—remained a familiar one: to strike the right balance between encouraging healthy economic growth and avoiding inflationary pressures. With the economy showing sustained and vigorous growth, and with the currency crisis highlighting the need to improve our competitive posture internationally, the emphasis seemed to be shifting to the problem of inflation. The Phase Three program of wage and price restraint can contribute to dampening inflation. Unless productivity growth is unexpectedly large, however, the expansion of real output must eventually begin to slow down to the economy's larger run growth potential if generalized demand pressures on prices are to be avoided. Indeed, while the unemployment rates of a bit over five percent were still too high, it seems doubtful whether the much lower rates of four percent and below often cited as appropriate definitions of full employment do in fact represent feasible goals for the United States economy—unless there are improvements in the structure of labor and product markets and public policies influencing their operation. There is little doubt that overall unemployment rates can be brought down to four percent or less, for a time at least, by sufficient stimulation of aggregate demand. However, the resultant inflationary pressures have in the past proved exceedingly difficult to contain. After a point, moreover, it is questionable just how much, if any, additional reduction in unemployment can be permanently "bought" by accepting a stepped-up rate of inflation.

1. The passage was most likely published in a

   (A) popular magazine
   (B) general newspaper
   (C) science journal
   (D) financial journal
   (E) textbook

2. Confidence in the economy was expressed by all of the following except

   (A) a strong stock market
   (B) a stable bond market
   (C) increased installment debt
   (D) increased plant and equipment expenditures
   (E) rising interest rates

3. During the year in question, public confidence in the economy resulted in part from which of the following occurrences?

    I.   Possible peace in Vietnam
   II.   Reduction in East-West tensions
  III.   An entente with China

  (A) I only
  (B) III only
  (C) I and II only
  (D) II and III only
  (E) I, II, and III

4. According to the author, business expansion for the period under review was caused largely by

  (A) stimulative monetary and fiscal policies
  (B) rising interest rates
  (C) increased foreign trade
  (D) price and wage controls
  (E) implementation of the Phase Three program

5. Most of the trade deficit in the balance of payments was attributed to trade with which country?

  (A) United Kingdom   (D) France
  (B) Japan   (E) Saudi Arabia
  (C) Germany

6. Part of the public policy task, as outlined in the passage, is to

  (A) cut consumer spending
  (B) prevent balance of payments deficits
  (C) devalue the dollar
  (D) avoid inflationary pressures
  (E) increase the balance of trade

7. The Phase Three program contained

  (A) higher income taxes   (D) productivity measures
  (B) reduced government spending   (E) wage and price controls
  (C) devaluation of the dollar

8. The passage states that the unemployment rate at the time the article was written was

  (A) 6 percent   (D) a little over 4 percent
  (B) a little over 5 percent   (E) 4 percent
  (C) 5 percent

Passage 2:

These huge waves wreak terrific damage when they crash on the shores of distant lands or continents. Under a perfectly sunny sky and from an apparently calm sea, a wall of water may break twenty or thirty feet high over beaches and waterfronts, crushing houses and drowning unsuspecting residents and bathers in its path.

How are these waves formed? When a submarine earthquake occurs, it is likely to set up a tremendous amount of shock, disturbing the quiet waters of the deep ocean. This disturbance travels to the surface and forms a huge swell in the ocean many miles across. It rolls outward in all directions, and the water lowers in the center as another swell looms up. Thus, a series of concentric swells are formed similar to those made when a coin or small pebble is dropped into a basin of water. The big difference is in the size. Each of the concentric rings of basin water traveling out toward the edge is only about an inch across and less than a quarter of an inch high. The swells in the ocean are sometimes nearly a mile wide and rise to several multiples of ten feet in height.

Many of us have heard about these waves, often referred to by their Japanese name of "tsunami." For ages they have been dreaded in the Pacific, as no shore has been free from them. An underwater earthquake in the Aleutian Islands could start a swell that would break along the shores and cause severe damage in the southern part of Chile in South America. These waves travel hundreds of miles an hour, and one can understand how they would crash as violent breakers when caused to drag in the shallow waters of a coast.

Nothing was done about tsunamis until after World War II. In 1947 a particularly bad submarine earthquake took place south of the Aleutian Islands. A few hours later, people bathing in the sun along the quiet shores of Hawaii were dashed to death and shore-line property became a mass of shambles because a series of monstrous, breaking swells crashed along the shore and drove far inland. Hundreds of lives were lost in this catastrophe, and millions upon millions of dollars' worth of damage was done.

Hawaii (at that time a territory) and other Pacific areas then asked the U.S. Coast and Geodetic Survey to attempt to forecast these killer waves. With the blessing of the government, the Coast and Geodetic Survey initiated a program in 1948 known as the Seismic Seawave Warning System, using the earthquake-monitoring facilities of the agency, together with the world seismological data center, to locate submarine earthquakes as soon as they might occur. With this information they could then tell how severe a submarine earthquake was and could set up a tracking chart, with the center over the area of the earthquake, which would show by concentric time belts the rate of travel of the resulting wave. This system would indicate when and where, along the shores of the Pacific, the swells caused by the submarine earthquakes would strike.

9. One surprising aspect of the waves discussed in the passage is the fact that they

   (A) are formed in concentric patterns
   (B) often strike during clear weather
   (C) arise under conditions of cold temperature
   (D) are produced by deep swells
   (E) may be forecast scientifically

10. The waves discussed in the passage often strike

   (A) along the coasts of the Aleutian Islands
   (B) in regions outside the area monitored by the Coast and Geodetic Survey
   (C) at great distances from their place of origin
   (D) at the same time as the occurrence of earthquakes
   (E) in areas outside the Pacific region

11. It is believed that the waves are caused by

    (A) seismic changes   (D) underwater earthquakes
    (B) concentric time belts   (E) storms
    (C) atmospheric conditions

12. The normal maximum width of the waves is approximately

    (A) five feet   (D) five miles
    (B) ten feet   (E) thirty miles
    (C) one mile

13. The U.S. Coast and Geodetic Survey set up a program to

    I.   Prevent submarine earthquakes
    II. Locate submarine earthquakes
    III. Determine the severity of submarine earthquakes

    (A) I only
    (B) III only
    (C) I and II only
    (D) II and III only
    (E) I, II, and III

14. Nothing was done about the waves until

    (A) deaths occurred
    (B) the outbreak of World War II
    (C) a solution was found
    (D) millions of dollars worth of damage was incurred in Hawaii
    (E) large areas in Chile were devastated

15. The movement of the waves has been measured at a speed of

    (A) 30 miles an hour
    (B) 40 miles an hour
    (C) 50 miles an hour
    (D) 100 miles an hour
    (E) more than a hundred miles an hour

16. According to the passage, the waves occur most frequently in the area of

    (A) the Eastern U.S. seaboard   (D) Western Europe
    (B) the Pacific   (E) Asia
    (C) Argentina

17. Given present wave-tracking systems, scientists can forecast all of the following *except*

    (A) the severity of underwater earthquakes   (D) where a wave will strike
    (B) the wave's rate of travel   (E) the height of the wave
    (C) when a wave will strike

Passage 3:

It is indisputable that in order to fulfill its many functions, water should be clean and biologically valuable. The costs connected with the provision of biologically valuable water for food production with the maintenance of sufficiently clean water, therefore, are primarily production costs. Purely "environmental" costs seem to be in this respect only costs connected with the safeguarding of cultural, recreational and sports functions which the water courses and reservoirs fulfill both in nature and in human settlements.

The pollution problems of the atmosphere resemble those of the water only partly. So far, the supply of air has not been deficient as was the case with water, and the dimensions of the air-shed are so vast that a number of people still hold the opinion that air need not be economized. However, scientific forecasts have shown that the time may be already approaching when clear and biologically valuable air will become problem No. 1.

Air being ubiquitous, people are particularly sensitive about any reduction in the quality of the atmosphere, the increased contents of dust and gaseous exhalations, and particularly about the presence of odors. The demand for purity of atmosphere, therefore, emanates much more from the population itself than from the specific sectors of the national economy affected by a polluted or even biologically aggressive atmosphere.

The households' share in atmospheric pollution is far bigger than that of industry which, in turn, further complicates the economic problems of atmospheric purity. Some countries have already collected positive experience with the reconstruction of whole urban sectors on the basis of new heating appliances based on the combustion of solid fossil fuels; estimates of the economic consequences of such measures have also been put forward.

In contrast to water, where the maintenance of purity would seem primarily to be related to the costs of production and transport, a far higher proportion of the costs of maintaining the purity of the atmosphere derives from environmental considerations. Industrial sources of gaseous and dust emissions are well known and classified; their location can be accurately identified, which makes them controllable. With the exception, perhaps, of the elimination of sulphur dioxide, technical means and technological processes exist which can be used for the elimination of all excessive impurities of the air from the various emissions.

Atmospheric pollution caused by the private property of individuals (their dwellings, automobiles, etc.) is difficult to control. Some sources such as motor vehicles are very mobile, and they are thus capable of polluting vast territories. In this particular case, the cost of anti-pollution measures will have to be borne, to a considerable extent, by individuals, whether in the form of direct costs or indirectly in the form of taxes, dues, surcharges, etc.

The problem of noise is a typical example of an environmental problem which cannot be solved passively, i.e., merely by protective measures, but will require the adoption of active measures, i.e., direct interventions at the source. The costs of a complete protection against noise are so prohibitive as to make it unthinkable even in the economically most developed countries. At the same time it would not seem feasible, either economically or politically, to force the population to carry the costs of individual protection against noise, for example, by reinforcing the sound insulation of their homes. A solution of this problem probably cannot be found in the near future.

18. According to the passage, the population at large

   (A) is unconcerned about air pollution controls
   (B) is especially aware of problems concerning air quality and purity
   (C) regards water pollution as more serious than air pollution
   (D) has failed to recognize the economic consequences of pollution
   (E) is unwilling to make the sacrifices needed to ensure clean air

19. Scientific forecasts have shown that clear and biologically valuable air

    (A) is likely to remain abundant for some time
    (B) creates fewer economic difficulties than does water pollution
    (C) may soon be dangerously lacking
    (D) may be beyond the capacity of our technology to protect
    (E) has already become difficult to obtain

20. According to the passage, which of the following contributes *most* to atmospheric pollution?

    (A) industry   (D) mining
    (B) production   (E) waste disposal
    (C) households

21. The costs involved in the maintenance of pure water are determined primarily by

    I. production costs
    II. transport costs
    III. research costs

    (A) I only   (D) II and III only
    (B) III only   (E) I, II, and III
    (C) I and II only

22. According to the passage, atmospheric pollution caused by private property is

    (A) easy to control   (D) decreasing
    (B) impossible to control (E) negligible
    (C) difficult to control

23. According to the passage, the problem of noise can be solved through

    I. Active measures
    II. Passive measures
    III. Tax levies

    (A) I only   (D) II and III only
    (B) III only   (E) I, II, and III
    (C) I and II only

24. According to the passage, the costs of some anti-pollution measures will have to be borne by individuals because

    (A) individuals contribute to the creation of pollution
    (B) governments do not have adequate resources
    (C) industry is not willing to bear its share
    (D) individuals are more easily taxed than producers
    (E) individuals demand production, which causes pollution

25. Complete protection against noise

(A) may be forthcoming in the near future
(B) is impossible to achieve
(C) may have prohibitive costs
(D) is possible only in developed countries
(E) has been achieved in some countries

If there is still time remaining, you may review the questions in this section only.
You may not turn to any other section of the test.

Section II   Problem Solving

TIME: 40 minutes

DIRECTIONS: Solve each of the following problems; then indicate the correct answer on the answer sheet. [On the actual test you will be permitted to use any space available on the examination paper for scratch work.]

NOTE: A figure that appears with a problem is drawn as accurately as possible so as to provide information that may help in answering the question. Numbers in this test are real numbers.

26. A trip takes 6 hours to complete. After traveling $\frac{1}{4}$ of an hour, $1\frac{3}{8}$ hours, and $2\frac{1}{3}$ hours, how much time is necessary to complete the trip?

(A) $2\frac{1}{12}$ hours
(B) 2 hours, $2\frac{1}{2}$ minutes
(C) 2 hours, 5 minutes
(D) $2\frac{1}{8}$ hours
(E) 2 hours, $7\frac{1}{2}$ minutes

27. If a stock average was 500 points at the beginning of a week and 400 points at the end of the same week, by what percent has it decreased during the week?

(A) 20
(B) 22
(C) 25
(D) 27
(E) 30

28. A car wash can wash 8 cars in 18 minutes. At this rate, how many cars can the car wash wash in 3 hours?

(A) 13
(B) 40.5
(C) 80
(D) 125
(E) 405

29. If the ratio of the areas of 2 squares is 2:1, then the ratio of the perimeters of the squares is

   (A) 1:2
   (B) $1:\sqrt{2}$
   (C) $\sqrt{2}:1$

   (D) 2:1
   (E) 4:1

30. In Leesville, 70% of the cars have whitewall tires and 25% of the cars are air-conditioned. If 20% of the cars are air-conditioned and have whitewall tires, what percentage of the cars have neither air-conditioning nor whitewall tires?

   (A) 5
   (B) 10
   (C) 15

   (D) 20
   (E) 25

31. A company issued 100,000 shares of stock. In 1970, each share of stock was worth $122.50. In 1973, each share of the stock was worth $111.10. How much less were the 100,000 shares worth in 1973 than in 1970?

   (A) $114,000
   (B) $1,100,040
   (C) $1,140,000

   (D) $114,000,000
   (E) $1,140,000,000

32. A worker's daily salary varies each day. In one week he worked five days. His daily salaries were $51.90, $52.20, $49.80, $51.50, and $50.60. What was his average daily wage for the week?

   (A) $50.80
   (B) $51.20
   (C) $51.50

   (D) $51.60
   (E) $255.00

33. A borrower pays 8% interest per year on the first $600 he borrows and 7% per year on the part of the loan in excess of $600. How much interest will the borrower pay on a loan of $6,000 for 1 year?

   (A) $378
   (B) $420
   (C) $426

   (D) $436
   (E) $480

34. If $3x - 2y = 8$, then $4y - 6x$ is:

   (A) -16
   (B) -8
   (C) 8

   (D) 16
   (E) none of these

35. It costs 10¢ a mile to fly and 12¢ a mile to drive. If you travel 200 miles, flying x miles of the distance and driving the rest, then the cost of the trip in dollars is

   (A) 20
   (B) 24
   (C) $24 - 2x$

   (D) $24 - .02x$
   (E) $2400 - 2x$

36. If two identical rectangles R_1 and R_2 form a square when placed next to each other, and the length of R_1 is x times the width of R_1, then x is

(A) 1
(B) $\frac{3}{2}$
(C) $\frac{5}{4}$
(D) 2
(E) 3

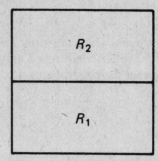

37. If the area of a square increases by 69%, then the side of the square increases by

(A) 13%
(B) 30%
(C) 39%
(D) 69%
(E) 130%

38. A used car dealer sells a car for $1,380 and makes a 20% profit. How much did the car cost the dealer?

(A) $1,100
(B) $1,120
(C) $1,150
(D) $1,180
(E) $1,560

39. If $x < z$ and $x < y$, which of the following statements are always true? Assume $x \geq 0$.

  I. $y < z$
 II. $x < yz$
III. $2x < y + z$

(A) only I
(B) only II
(C) only III
(D) II and III only
(E) I, II, and III

Use the following table for questions 40-42.

Distribution of Work Hours in a Factory

Numbers of Workers		Number of Hours Worked
20		45–50
15		40–44
25		35–39
16		30–34
4		0–29
80	TOTAL	3100

40. What percentage worked 40 or more hours?

(A) 18.75   (D) 40

(B) 25   (E) 43.75

(C) $33\frac{1}{3}$

41. The number of workers who worked from 40 to 44 hours is x times the number who worked up to 29 hours, where x is

(A) $^{15}/_{16}$ (D) 5

(B) $3\frac{3}{4}$ (E) $6\frac{1}{4}$

(C) 4

42. Which of the following statements can be inferred from the table?

   I. The average number of hours worked per worker is less than 40.

  II. At least 3 worked more than 48 hours.

 III. More than half of all the workers worked more than 40 hours.

(A) I only

(B) II only

(C) I and II only

(D) I and III only

(E) I, II, and III

43. A truck traveling at 70 miles per hour uses 30% more gasoline to travel a certain distance than it does when it travels at 50 miles per hour. If the truck can travel 19.5 miles on a gallon of gasoline at 50 miles per hour, how far can the truck travel on 10 gallons of gasoline at a speed of 70 miles per hour?

(A) 130   (D) 175

(B) 140   (E) 195

(C) 150

44. $\frac{2}{5} + \frac{1}{3} = \frac{x}{30}$, where x is

(A) 4   (D) 16

(B) 7   (E) 22

(C) 11

45. How many squares with sides $\frac{1}{2}$ inch long are needed to cover a rectangle which is 4 feet long and 6 feet wide?

(A) 24   (D) 13,824

(B) 96   (E) 14,266

(C) 3,456

Use the following graph for questions 46-48.

AVERAGE ANNUAL RECEIPTS AND OUTLAYS OF U.S. GOVERNMENT. 1967-1970

RECEIPTS

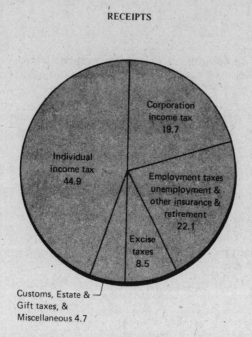

OUTLAYS

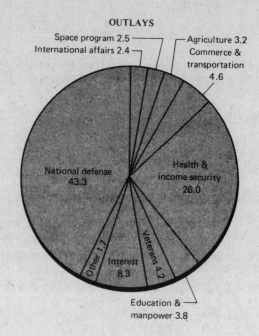

46. If the annual average receipts from the corporation income tax during the years 1967–1970 equal x, then the average annual receipts during this period were about

(A) $\dfrac{x}{4}$

(B) x^2

(C) $3x$

(D) $5x$

(E) x^5

47. The average annual combined outlay for veterans, education and manpower, and health and income security was roughly what fraction of the average annual outlays?

(A) $1/4$

(B) $1/3$

(C) $2/5$

(D) $1/2$

(E) $2/3$

48. If $5/8$ of the average annual outlays for agriculture was spent in the western U.S., what percentage of average annual outlays was spent on agriculture in the western U.S.?

(A) $5/8$

(B) 1

(C) $1\,1/4$

(D) 2

(E) 3.2

49. The next number in the geometric progression 5,10,20 . . . is

(A) 25
(B) 30
(C) 35

(D) 40
(E) 50

50. Eggs cost 8¢ each. If the price of eggs increases by ⅛, how much will a dozen eggs cost?

(A) 90¢
(B) $1.08
(C) $1.10

(D) $1.12
(E) $1.18

51. A trapezoid *ABCD* is formed by adding the isosceles right triangle *BCE* with base 5 inches to the rectangle *ABED* where *DE* is *t* inches. What is the area of the trapezoid in square inches?

(A) $5t + 12.5$
(B) $5t + 25$
(C) $2.5t + 12.5$

(D) $(t + 5)^2$
(E) $t^2 + 25$

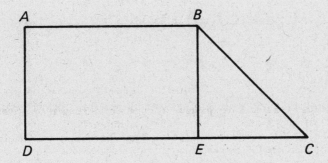

52. A manufacturer of jam wants to make a profit of $75 when he sells 300 jars of jam. It costs 65¢ each to make the first 100 jars of jam and 55¢ each to make each jar after the first 100. What price should he charge for the 300 jars of jam?

(A) $75
(B) $175
(C) $225

(D) $240
(E) $250

53. A farmer walks around the outside of a rectangular field at a constant speed. It takes him twice as long to walk the length of the field as it takes him to walk the width of the field. If he walked 300 yards when he walked around the field, what is the area of the field in square yards?

(A) 5,000
(B) 15,000
(C) 20,000

(D) 25,000
(E) 30,000

54. A company makes a profit of 7% selling goods which cost $2,000; it also makes a profit of 6% selling a machine which cost the company $5,000. How much total profit did the company make on both transactions?

(A) $300   (D) $440
(B) $400   (E) $490
(C) $420

55. If $\frac{x}{y} = \frac{3}{z}$, then $9y^2$ equals

(A) $\frac{x^2}{9}$ (D) $3x^2$
(B) x^3z (E) $\left(\frac{1}{9}\right)x^2z^2$
(C) x^2z^2

If there is still time remaining, you may review the questions in this section only. You may not turn to any other section of the test.

Section III   Practical Judgment

TIME: 20 minutes

DIRECTIONS: Read the following passage. After you have completed it, you will be asked to answer two sets of questions. The first of these, data evaluation, involves determining the importance of specific factors included in the passage. The second, data application, consists of general questions relating to the passage. When answering questions, you may consult the passage.

The success of the Abco Corporation in the investment-conscious country of Frieland was recently the subject of a government inquiry. Frieland is a developing country about the size of New York State with a population of ten million people. It has a small but growing industrial base, and several multinational business concerns have established manufacturing plants in various parts of the country.

Government policy in Frieland has traditionally favored foreign investment. Leaders of all political parties have been virtually unanimous in their belief that foreign investment in Frieland would contribute to speeding that country's economic development, a major priority of both the ruling coalition and opposition parties. Of special interest to the government were those industries that exported a significant share of their total output. Since Frieland had a relatively small population, there was a limit to the amount of goods that could be produced for the local market. Also, the government did not want to encourage foreign investors to compete with local industry, even though new industries might alleviate the already high unemployment rate.

A final reason for encouraging export-intensive industries was to earn badly needed foreign exchange. Frieland had a chronic deficit in its balance of trade; that is, its imports were regularly greater than its exports. This meant that it had to use scarce foreign exchange to pay for the growing deficit. Therefore, Frieland welcomed potential investors that would promise to export a significant share of their total output. So when executives of Abco Corporation proposed to establish a shoe manufacturing plant which would be export-intensive, it received ready approval from the government.

Government support for the enterprise was given not only because of the promise to export, but also because of the high unemployment rate in the country. However, approval was given despite the fact that there was at the time surplus shoe production in Frieland, most factories having large excess capacities and underworked labor forces. It was known that Abco had promised the government, among other things, to (1) employ hundreds of workers, (2) reduce the price of shoes by some 30 percent, and (3) export more than half its output.

In return for these promises, Abco received the following concessions from the government:

(1) Land was given the company on a lease basis for a period of 99 years, rent-free.
(2) A government-owned contracting firm built the factory at low subsidized prices.
(3) The company received loans at very low interest rates for an extended period of time. These loans could be renewed at company request at lower than the prevailing market interest rate.
(4) The government trained workers at the plant at no expense to the company.

Production commenced one year after the first equipment arrived at the new plant. It took another half year to properly train the new work force to operate the sophisticated equipment which was introduced. After the "running in" period, production continued smoothly for about a year until a labor dispute occurred. It appeared that management wanted to dismiss about 10 percent of the work force owing to what a company spokesman called "a temporary slack in demand" for Abco's products. The labor union representing the company's work force refused to accept any reduction in the work force and threatened a strike if workers were terminated. After some discussion, union representatives agreed that the company might be justified in laying off some workers, but nowhere near the 10 percent figure that management desired. At any rate, the union claimed that the company must first submit its request to a joint union-management grievance committee which was authorized under the current labor agreement to deal with such disputes. Management acquiesced to the union demand. After several days of bargaining, an agreement was worked out whereby Abco would be allowed to terminate most part-time workers, amounting to only one percent of the total work force. Although the agreement brought about a temporary solution to the current problem, labor-management relations at Abco continued to be strained, as management was convinced that more workers were redundant than the union cared to admit.

After another six months, it became apparent that what management had termed "a temporary slack in demand" was in reality a failure of the company to sell the quantity of shoes that had been forecast before production began. Actual sales never reached the target quantity, and, as a result, the company lost $1 million in each of its first two years of operation. The American representatives on the board of directors—who constituted a majority—voted to terminate the company's operations in Frieland. Shortly after the vote, bankruptcy hearings began.

Because Abco was located in an underdeveloped area of the country, the government was worried about the political ramifications if production ceased. The company employed 500 workers, and quite a few shopkeepers were dependent upon their patronage. When government representatives asked Abco management what could be done to keep the company operating, they received the following answer. Management was willing to continue production if the government granted the company an additional five-million-dollar loan on favorable terms. If the government could not grant such a loan, then another alternative was to purchase the company from Abco at a "reasonable" price.

The government was in a dilemma. On the one hand, it was concerned about the political consequences if Abco should continue the bankruptcy proceedings. On the other hand, if it granted the loan, it might be setting a precedent for any other company that was in financial difficulties. Moreover, there was a certain risk involved in lending the money to a company in bad shape. The government appointed a special committee to investigate the financial condition of Abco and decide the issue.

One month later, the committee submitted its report. The major finding was that Abco had not kept any of its original promises to the government. For one thing, Abco's shoe prices were no lower than those of any of its competitors. As for exports, not only had the company failed to reach its promised goal of 50 percent, but as of the bankruptcy hearings, its exports for a five-year period only amounted to 5 percent of total output. In light of these developments, the government felt that it had to make a quick decision in the Abco affair in such a way as to avoid criticism from the opposition.

Data Evaluation Questions

DIRECTIONS: The questions that follow relate to the preceding passage. Evaluate, in terms of the passage, each of the items given. Then select your answer from one of the following classifications, and blacken the corresponding space on the answer sheet.

(A)   A MAJOR OBJECTIVE in making the decision: one of the goals sought by the decision maker

(B)   A MAJOR FACTOR in making the decision: an aspect of the problem, specifically mentioned in the passage, that fundamentally affects and/or determines the decision

(C)   A MINOR FACTOR in making the decision: a less important element bearing on or affecting a Major Factor, rather than a Major Objective directly

(D)   A MAJOR ASSUMPTION in making the decision: a projection or supposition arrived at by the decision maker before considering the factors and alternatives

(E)   AN UNIMPORTANT ISSUE in making the decision: an item lacking significant impact on, or relationship to, the decision

56.   Ability of Abco to survive if the five-million-dollar loan were granted

57.   High unemployment in Frieland

58.   Dependence of shopkeepers on the existence of Abco

59.   Government investment incentives granted to Abco

60.   Status of Frieland as a developing country

61.   Continued operation of Abco

62.   Training of workers at no expense to Abco

63.   Strained worker-management relations at Abco

64.   Export potential of Abco

65.   Political philosophy of the opposition party

66.   Need for a quick decision by the government as to whether to grant the loan requested by Abco

67. Availability of government funds needed to support Abco

68. Prevention of layoffs of workers at Abco

69. Political consequence of an Abco bankruptcy

70. Frieland's small population

Data Application Questions

DIRECTIONS: Answer each of the following questions using information contained in the passage.

71. Abco's management looked with favor on the proposal that the company

    I. produce for the local market only
    II. be purchased by its workers
    III. be purchased by the government

    (A) I only
    (B) III only
    (C) I and II only
    (D) II and III only
    (E) I, II, and III

72. The government of Frieland approved the Abco operation despite the fact that

    I. Frieland shoe manufacturers had excess capacity
    II. world shoe prices had declined
    III. consumers were buying fewer shoes

    (A) I only
    (B) III only
    (C) I and II only
    (D) II and III only
    (E) I, II, and III

73. Of all the promises given to the government by Abco, which of the following were fulfilled?

    I. Exportation of 50 percent of its output.
    II. Lower shoe prices.
    III. Employment of hundreds of workers.

    (A) I only
    (B) III only
    (C) I and II only
    (D) II and III only
    (E) I, II, and III

74. It can be inferred from the passage that a major factor in the failure of the company was

    I. poor management
    II. inflation
    III. too much competition in the Frieland shoe industry

    (A) I only
    (B) III only
    (C) I and II only
    (D) II and III only
    (E) I, II, and III

75. The government's decision to help establish Abco may be described as

    I. overly optimistic
    II. short-sighted
    III. fortuitous

    (A) I only
    (B) III only
    (C) I and II only
    (D) II and III only
    (E) I, II, and III

*If there is still time remaining, you may review the questions in this section only.
You may not turn to any other section of the test.*

Section IV   Data Sufficiency

TIME: 30 minutes

DIRECTIONS: Each of the following problems has a question and two statements which are labeled (1) and (2). Use the data given in (1) and (2) together with other available information (such as the number of hours in a day, the definition of *clockwise*, mathematical facts, etc.) to decide whether the statements are *sufficient* to answer the question. Then fill in space

    (A) if you can get the answer from (1) alone but not from (2) alone;

    (B) if you can get the answer from (2) alone but not from (1) alone;

    (C) if you can get the answer from (1) and (2) together, although neither statement by itself suffices;

    (D) if statement (1) alone suffices *and* statement (2) alone suffices;

    (E) if you cannot get the answer from statements (1) and (2) together, but need even more data.

All numbers used in this section are real numbers. A figure given for a problem is intended to provide information consistent with that in the question, but not necessarily with the additional information contained in the statements.

76. Are two triangles congruent?

    (1) Both triangles are right triangles.
    (2) Both triangles have the same perimeter.

77. Is x greater than zero?

   (1) $x^4 - 16 = 0$
   (2) $x^3 - 8 = 0$

78. If both conveyer belt A and conveyer belt B are used, they can fill a hopper with coal in one hour. How long will it take for conveyer belt A to fill the hopper without conveyer belt B?

   (1) Conveyer belt A moves twice as much coal as conveyer belt B.
   (2) Conveyer belt B would take 3 hours to fill the hopper without belt A.

79. A fly crawls around the outside of a circle once. A second fly crawls around the outside of a square once. Which fly travels further?

   (1) The diagonal of the square is equal to the diameter of the circle.
   (2) The fly crawling around the circle took more time to complete his journey than the fly crawling around the square.

80. How much did it cost the XYZ Corporation to insure its factory from fire in 1972?

   (1) It cost $5,000 for fire insurance in 1971.
   (2) The total amount the corporation spent for fire insurance in 1970, 1971, and 1972 was $18,000.

81. Is y larger than 1?

   (1) y is larger than 0.
   (2) $y^2 - 4 = 0$.

82. A worker is hired for 6 days. He is paid $2 more for each day of work than he was paid for the preceding day of work. How much was he paid for the first day of work?

   (1) His total wages for the 6 days were $150.
   (2) He was paid 150% of his first day's pay for the sixth day.

83. A car originally sold for $3,000. After a month, the car was discounted $x\%$, and a month later the car's price was discounted $y\%$. Is the car's price after the discounts less than $2,600?

   (1) $y = 10$
   (2) $x = 15$

84. What is the value of *a*?

    (1) *a = f*
    (2) *a = b*

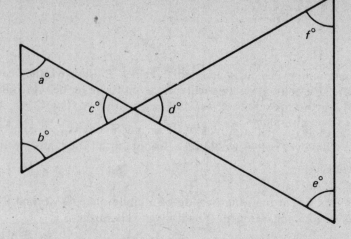

85. In triangle *ABC*, find *z* if *AB* = 5 and *y* = 40.

    (1) *BC* = 5
    (2) The bisector of angle *B* is perpendicular to *AC*.

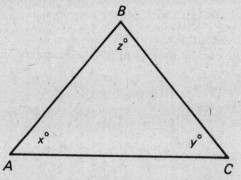

86. How much cardboard will it take to make an open cubical box with no top?

    (1) The area of the bottom of the box is 4 square feet.
    (2) The volume of the box is 8 cubic feet.

87. How many books are on a bookshelf?

    (1) The total weight of all the books on the bookshelf is 40 pounds.
    (2) The average weight of the books on the bookshelf is 2.5 pounds.

88. Is the figure *ABCD* a rectangle?

    (1) *x* = 90
    (2) *AB* = *CD*

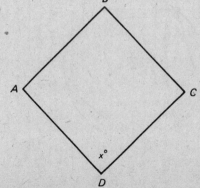

89. A sequence of numbers is given by the rule $a_n = (a_{n-1})^2$. What is a_5?

    (1) $a_1 = -1$
    (2) $a_3 = 1$

90. How much is John's weekly salary?

    (1) John's weekly salary is twice as much as Fred's weekly salary.
    (2) Fred's weekly salary is 40% of the total of Chuck's weekly salary and John's weekly salary.

91. Find $x + 2y$.

    (1) $x + y = 4$
    (2) $2x + 4y = 12$

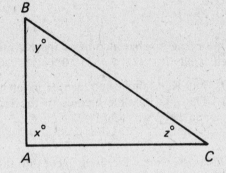

92. Is angle x a right angle?

    (1) $x = 2y$
    (2) $y = 1.5z$

93. Is x greater than y?

    (1) $x = 2k$
    (2) $k = 2y$

94. How much profit did Toyland make selling 65 dolls if each doll costs $8?

    (1) The amount the dolls sold for was $750.
    (2) The dolls cost $7 each last year.

95. 50% of the people in Teetown have blue eyes and blond hair. What percent of the people in Teetown have blue eyes but do not have blond hair?

    (1) 70% of the people in Teetown have blond hair.
    (2) 60% of the people in Teetown have blue eyes.

96. The pentagon $ABCDE$ is inscribed in the circle with center O. How many degrees is angle ABC?.

    (1) The pentagon $ABCDE$ is a regular pentagon.
    (2) The radius of the circle is 5 inches.

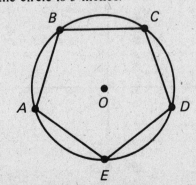

97. What is the area of the circle with center *O*? (*AB* and *DE* are straight lines)

    (1) *DE* = 5 inches
    (2) *AB* = 7 inches

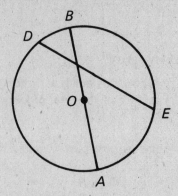

98. What is the taxable income of the Kell family in 1973? The taxable income of the Kell family in 1971 was $10,000.

    (1) The Kell family had taxable income of $12,000 in 1972.
    (2) The total taxable income of the Kell family for the three years 1971, 1972, and 1973 was $34,000.

99. A piece of string 6 feet long is cut into three smaller pieces. How long is the longest of the three pieces?

    (1) Two pieces are the same length.
    (2) One piece is 3 feet, 2 inches long.

100. If a group of 5 craftsmen take 3 hours to finish a job, how long will it take a group of 4 apprentices to do the same job?

    (1) An apprentice does $\frac{2}{3}$ as much work as a craftsman.
    (2) The 5 craftsmen and the 4 apprentices working together will take $1\frac{22}{23}$ hours to finish the job.

101. Is $\frac{1}{x}$ greater than $\frac{1}{y}$?

    (1) *x* is greater than 1.
    (2) *x* is less than *y*.

102. *AB* intersects *CD* at point *O*. Is *AB* perpendicular to *CD*? *AC* = *AD*.

    (1) Angle *CAD* is bisected by *AO*.
    (2) *BC* = *AD*

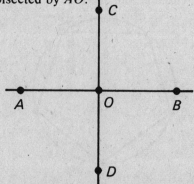

103. Plane *X* flies at *r* miles per hour from *A* to *B*. Plane *Y* flies at *S* miles per hour from *B* to *A*. Both planes take off at the same time. Which plane flies at a faster rate? Town *C* is between *A* and *B*.

(1) *C* is closer to *A* than it is to *B*.
(2) Plane *X* flies over *C* before plane *Y*.

104. What is the value of $x + y$?

(1) $2x + y = 4$
(2) $x + 2y = 5$

105. What is the area of the circular section *AOB*? *A* and *B* are points on the circle which has *O* as its center.

(1) Angle $AOB = 36°$
(2) $OB = OA$

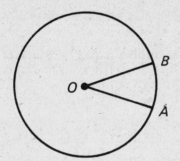

If there is still remaining, you may review the questions in this section only. You may not turn to any other section of the test.

Section V   Writing Ability

TIME: 15 minutes

DIRECTIONS: Each of the sentences in this section is either correct or contains one error in grammar, usage, diction (choice of words), idiom or punctuation. If there is an error it will be found in one of the underlined parts of the sentence, labeled (A), (B), (C), or (D). If you identify an error mark the appropriate letter on your answer sheet. If there is no error in the sentence mark (E)—no error.

Note: Assume that all parts of the sentence that are not underlined are correct and cannot be changed.

106.   Wear and tear on the human body during the course of everyday activities is a medical
       A   B   C
       problem well worth investigating. No error
                  D   E

107.   The team are waiting behind the main grandstand next to the playing field before the
              A   B   C
       second half begins. No error
                  D   E

108.   The First World War changed the world's major international financial relationships.
            A   B   C   D
       No error
       E

109.   A shot was fired in the dark, but a policeman seen where the bullet came from.
            A   B   C   D
       No error
       E

110.   He plays his violin every day in hopes that he would become concertmaster of the
          A   B   C
       orchestra. No error
          D   E

111.   The workers were enthused over the prospects for a wage increase. No error
                   A   B   C   D   E

112.   We were determined to arrive on time, irregardless of the inclement weather. No
          A   B   C   D
       error
       E

113.   After the battle was over, the soldiers will advance to the front lines. No error
              A   B   C   D   E

114. I read in the newspaper that in Nigeria they grow large tomatoes. No error
    A   B   C   D   E

115. To master the proper backstroke, your breathing must be carefully controlled.
    A   B   C   D
    No error
    E

116. The key to the persistence of the family farm is the difficulty of routinizing agricultural
    A   B   C   D
    operations. No error
              E

117. While one part of the TV program carried the football game, the other part shows
    A   B   C
    the training of the teams. No error
            D   E

118. The rainy season had already began by the time they arrived in Burma that year.
                    A   B   C   D
    No error
    E

119. How could you even dream of doing such a thing without me standing next to
       A   B   C   D
    you to make sure it was safe? No error
                                  E

120. Neither Arthur nor Mary has the slightest idea to whom this letter should be ad-
                        A   B
    dressed to because the original envelope has been lost. No error
       C   D   E

121. In this series of television programs, they want to show the corruption and graft that
          A   B   C
    lies beneath the surface even in the most progressive societies. No error
    D   E

122. Having been delayed by unfavorable weather, it was not possible for our plane to
              A   B   C
    arrive in time for the connecting flight. No error
    D   E

123. Despite what we had heard about Dr. Plunkett, we found him to be a considerable
                    A   B   C   D
    and kind man. No error
                  E

124. Whenever these three eminent scientists spoke to each other an argument was bound
                        A   B   C
    to ensue. No error
    D   E

125. The <u>less</u> chances you take, the greater your peace of mind <u>will be</u> but, <u>then again,</u>
       A   B   C

the high profits that you hope for may never <u>eventuate.</u> <u>No error</u>
                                               D   E

If there is still time remaining, you may review the questions in this section only.
You may not turn to any other section of the test.

Section VI   Practical Judgment

TIME: 20 minutes

DIRECTIONS: Read the following passage. After you have completed it, you will be asked to answer two sets of questions. The first of these, data evaluation, involves determining the importance of specific factors included in the passage. The second, data application, consists of general questions relating to the passage. When answering questions, you may consult the passage.

Mr. Ed Krim, a building contractor by profession, met with an old friend, Mr. Sam Sims, a marketing consultant. Mr. Krim was excited about a business opportunity and wanted to obtain Sims's evaluation of its prospects. Posturemat, a small company producing foam rubber mattresses, was in financial trouble, and its owners were anxious to sell it. The company had been established some twenty years, but its market share had steadily declined over the last five years. Since Mr. Krim had no previous experience in the mattress business, he requested that his friend find out what he could about the company.

Mr. Sims first analyzed the company's resources. Its best resource was its product and brand name. Foam rubber mattresses are made of imported latex and are extremely firm, unlike synthetic rubber mattresses made of polyurethane. However, synthetics are much cheaper than foam rubber mattresses. Latex mattresses are known for their orthopedic and anti-allergic qualities, among others. The Posturemat brand name had very nearly become a generic term for all types of rubber mattresses. Posturemat, however, was the only latex mattress produced locally.

Apart from a superior product, the company had few resources. Its equipment, while satisfactory, was old and had been fully depreciated. It operated in leased premises on a year-to-year basis, although the landlord was willing to conclude a long-term agreement on favorable terms. On the other hand, the company's labor force was experienced and dedicated and its production manager had more than ten years' experience in latex manufacturing.

Mr. Joe Caspi, president of the company, was past seventy years old and was anxious to retire. He had tried to retire previously, but had failed to train a successor. Apart from Fred Lefko, the sales manager, no one else shared responsibility for marketing or administration. Fred Lefko let Sam Sims know that if the company were sold, he had no intention of remaining. Lefko had eighteen years' experience in the mattress industry, including twelve years with Posturemat. If Lefko left the company, Krim might be hard pressed to find a suitable replacement. This was another issue that Sam Sims would have to study.

Posturemat's financial position was precarious. The company was heavily in debt and its line of credit fully extended. There was some question as to whether the company would be able to purchase enough latex to keep production going, but Mr. Caspi assured Sam Sims that the company had a bank letter of credit to purchase an additional three months' supply.

In spite of Mr Caspi's optimism, the fact was that his company had steadily lost market share. Once the dominant mattress manufacturer, with fifty percent of the local market, its market share had declined to less than ten percent. Mr. Caspi attributed this decline to inroads made by spring mattress manufacturers, who had only begun production five years ago. Spring mattresses now accounted for seventy percent of the total market, Caspi's company ten percent, with the remaining twenty percent shared by a number of small plants producing synthetic rubber mattresses. Spring mattresses had some attributes similar to those of foam rubber, such as orthopedic qualities. They were less costly to manufacture, but sold to the consumer at about the same price as Posturemat mattresses.

Because of Posturemat's financial difficulties, it ceased advertising in newspapers and on radio. Little if any advertising had been done in other media over the past five years. As a result, retailers were reluctant to handle the product line. By contrast, two of the larger spring mattress manufacturers had advertised heavily in the mass media. One of these manufacturer's products was sold exclusively by the largest furniture chain in the country. During his study of the mattress market, a number of retailers had expressed the opinion to Mr. Sims that a whole generation of young people were largely unaware of Posturemat products because of the lack of advertising. One retailer was quoted as saying: "It is true that older people remember Posturemat, but these mattresses last for almost twenty years. The big market is not the replacement market, but sales generated by family formation. Thousands of young couples get married every year, and every marriage means another mattress sale. But these young people only see advertisements for spring mattresses. It is obviously easier for my salesman to sell a mattress which his customers have seen in countless advertisements than one which is relatively unknown."

Sims was aware of the fact that if Posturemat was ever to regain some of its lost market share, it would have to launch a major advertising program to educate young adults about the important attributes found in its products. A major question that needed an immediate answer was: "To what extent are people aware of Posturemat mattresses and their attributes?" Other questions involved the attitudes of people toward foam rubber mattresses in general and how these attitudes compared to those toward spring mattresses. Mr. Sims ordered a market research survey to obtain answers to his questions. In brief, the study revealed that a large segment of the population over twenty-five years of age was aware of Posturemat mattresses and had favorable attitudes toward their attributes. About three-quarters of these people expressed a preference for foam rubber mattresses for their children (by contrast with other mattresses for their own use). Awareness among younger segments of the population of the attributes of foam rubber mattresses in general, and of Posturemat in particular, was very low. Few young people expressed an intention to buy foam rubber mattresses.

On the basis of the preliminary research results, Krim was optimistic that he could turn the company around. In support of his belief, he cited the recognition of the company among a significant portion of the population, and the fact that they would buy a Posturemat for their children. He believed that once retailers became aware that new management had taken over the company, they would be willing to stock the product. Krim was aware that the research findings were not always in agreement with his conclusions. However, the finding that young people were relatively unaware of Posturemat did not seem to worry him. He felt that a well-designed advertising program would convince many people to buy a foam rubber mattress, rather than any competing type. Moreover, the introduction of a new management team would instill confidence among Posturemat's bankers. Credit lines would be increased, thereby improving the company's financial position. However, before making a final decision as to whether to purchase Posturemat, Mr. Krim waited for Sam Sims's final report and recommendations.

Data Evaluation Questions

DIRECTIONS: The questions that follow relate to the preceding passage. Evaluate, in terms of the passage, each of the items given. Then select your answer from one of the following classifications, and blacken the corresponding space on the answer sheet.

- (A) A MAJOR OBJECTIVE in making the decision: one of the goals sought by the decision maker
- (B) A MAJOR FACTOR in making the decision: an aspect of the problem, specifically mentioned in the passage, that fundmentally affects and/or determines the decision
- (C) A MINOR FACTOR in making the decision: a less important element bearing on or affecting a Major Factor, rather than a Major Objective directly
- (D) A MAJOR ASSUMPTION in making the decision: a projection or supposition arrived at by the decision maker before considering the factors and alternatives
- (E) AN UNIMPORTANT ISSUE in making the decision: an item lacking significant impact on, or relationship to, the decision

126. Public awareness of the high quality of Posturemat mattresses

127. Joe Caspi's marketing ability

128. The anti-allergic qualities of Posturemat mattresses

129. Attitude of older consumers towards Posturemat mattresses

130. Willingness of retailers to stock Posturemat products in the future

131. Need to import latex rubber

132. Posturemat's present market share

133. Sam Sims's recommendations

134. Posturemat's present market share

135. Plausibility of changing consumer attitudes through advertising

136. Orthopedic qualities of Posturemat mattresses

137. Use of polyurethane in the production of synthetic mattresses

138. Lefko's intention to leave Posturemat

139. Age of Posturemat's manufacturing equipment

140. Likelihood that credit lines could be increased

141. Caspi's explanation for loss of market share

Data Application Questions

DIRECTIONS: Answer each of the following questions using information contained in the passage.

142. Sims found that Posturemat's best resource was its

    I.   manufacturing equipment
   II.   labor force
  III.   brand name

  (A) I only
  (B) III only
  (C) I and II only
  (D) II and III only
  (E) I, II, and III

143. As compared to synthetic mattresses, foam rubber mattresses are

    I.   more likely to cause an allergic reaction
   II.   relatively inexpensive
  III.   firmer to sleep on

  (A) I only
  (B) III only
  (C) I and II only
  (D) II and III only
  (E) I, II, and III

144. Krim postponed his retirement because

    I.   his sales manager threatened to leave
   II.   he could not pay the company's debts
  III.   he had not trained a successor

  (A) I only
  (B) III only
  (C) I and II only
  (D) II and III only
  (E) I, II, and III

145. Posturemat had completely ceased to advertise by means of

    I.   television
   II.   radio
  III.   newspapers

  (A) I only
  (B) III only
  (C) I and II only
  (D) II and III only
  (E) I, II, and III

If there is still time remaining, you may review the questions in this section only.
You may not turn to any other section of the test.

Section VII   Writing Ability

TIME: 20 minutes

DIRECTIONS: This test consists of a number of sentences, in each of which some part or the whole is underlined. Each sentence is followed by five alternative versions of the underlined portion. Select the alternative you consider both most correct and most effective according to the requirements of standard written English. Answer A is the same as the original version; if you think the original version is best, select answer A.

In considering the answer choices, be attentive to matters of grammar, diction, and syntax, as well as clarity, precision, and fluency. Do not select an answer which alters the meaning of the original sentence.

146. Give them several days more, they will have the report ready for you.

(A) Give them several days more, they will have the report ready for you.
(B) Give them several more days, they will have the report ready for you.
(C) Give them several days more; they will have the report ready for you.
(D) They will have the report ready for you, just give them several days more.
(E) They will have the report ready for you: just give them several days more.

147. Knowing the cost of the Space Shuttle program, its breakdown caused the director much irritation.

(A) Knowing the cost of the Space Shuttle program, its breakdown caused the director much irritation.
(B) Knowing the cost of the Space Shuttle program. Its breakdown caused the director much irritation.
(C) Knowing the cost of the Space Shuttle program, the director was greatly irritated by its breakdown.
(D) By knowing the cost of the Space Shuttle program, its breakdown greatly irritated the director.
(E) Knowledge of the cost of the Space Shuttle program: its breakdown greatly irritated the director.

148. In this particular job we have discovered that to be diligent is more important than being bright.

(A) to be diligent is more important than being bright
(B) for one to be diligent is more important than being bright
(C) diligence is more important than brightness
(D) being diligent is more important than to be bright
(E) by being diligent is more important than being bright

149. On their return, they not only witnessed the sinking ship but the amazing escape of the passengers as well.

(A) not only witnessed the sinking ship but the
(B) not only witnessed the sinking ship, but the
(C) did not only witness the sinking ship, but also the
(D) witnessed not only the sinking ship but the
(E) witnessed the sinking ship and also the

150. No one but <u>him could have told them that the thief was I</u>.

    (A) him could have told them that the thief was I
    (B) he could have told them that the thief was I
    (C) he could have told them that the thief was me
    (D) him could have told them that the thief was me
    (E) he could have told them the thief was me

151. <u>Either you transfer the data which was demanded</u> or file a report explaining the discrepancy in the over-all annual figures.

    (A) Either you transfer the data which was demanded
    (B) You either transfer the data, which was demanded,
    (C) You either transfer the data which were demanded
    (D) Either you transfer the data, which was demanded,
    (E) Either you transfer the data, which were demanded,

152. <u>On entering the stadium, cheers greeted them</u> as a sign of universal approval of their great achievement.

    (A) On entering the stadium, cheers greeted them
    (B) On entering the stadium, they were greeted by cheers
    (C) While entering the stadium, cheers greeted them
    (D) On entering the stadium cheers greeted them
    (E) On entering the stadium: cheers greeted them

153. The set of propositions <u>which was discussed by the panel have</u> been published in the society journal.

    (A) which was discussed by the panel have
    (B) which were discussed by the panel have
    (C) that was discussed by the panel has
    (D) which were discussed by the panel has
    (E) which was discussed, by the panel, has

154. <u>In a great amount of the requests, there have been very few</u> that the staff could deal with efficiently.

    (A) In a great amount of the requests, there have been very few
    (B) Out of the great amount of the requests, there have been very little
    (C) In a great amount of the requests, there has been very few
    (D) In a great number of the requests, there have been very few
    (E) Of the great number of requests, there have been very few

155. The results of the research have thus far proven to be <u>inconclusive, therefore, the report</u> can be postponed indefinitely without any fear of repercussions.

    (A) inconclusive, therefore, the report
    (B) inconclusive therefore the report
    (C) inconclusive; therefore, the report
    (D) inconclusive, therefore the report
    (E) inconclusive: therefore, the report

156. After a careful evaluation of the circumstances surrounding the incident, we decided that we <u>neither have the authority nor</u> the means to cope with the problem.

    (A) neither have the authority nor
    (B) neither have authority or
    (C) have neither the authority nor
    (D) have neither the authority or
    (E) have not either the authority nor

157. <u>Everyone of us have understood that without him helping us</u> we would not have succeeded in our program over the past six months.

    (A) Everyone of us have understood that without him helping us
    (B) Everyone of us has understood that without his helping us
    (C) Everyone of us have understood that without his help
    (D) Everyone of us has understood that without him helping us
    (E) Every single one of us have understood that without him helping us

158. On the African continent, the incidence of vitamin <u>deficiencies correlates positively with</u> the level of solar radiation.

    (A) deficiencies correlates positively with
    (B) deficiencies correlate positively with
    (C) deficiencies, correlate positively with,
    (D) deficiencies correlate positively to
    (E) deficiencies correlates positively to

159. The revolutionary cries of the underprivileged masses rise up <u>in the land, there is</u> an urgent need to act decisively.

    (A) in the land, there is
    (B) in the land. Because there is
    (C) in the land. There is
    (D) in the land: there is
    (E) in the land. And there is

160. <u>If they would have taken greater care</u> in the disposal of the nuclear waste, the disaster would not have occurred.

    (A) If they would have taken greater care
    (B) Unless they took greater care
    (C) Had they not taken greater care
    (D) If they had taken greater care
    (E) If they took greater care

161. <u>Neither the judge nor I am ready to announce who the winner is.</u>

    (A) Neither the judge nor I am ready to announce who the winner is.
    (B) Neither the judge nor I are ready to announce who the winner is.
    (C) Neither the judge nor I are ready to announce who is the winner.
    (D) Neither the judge nor I am ready to announce who is the winner.
    (E) Neither I or the judge are ready to announce who is the winner.

162. After adequate deliberation, the council <u>can see scarcely any valid reason for its</u> reviewing the request.

    (A) can see scarcely any valid reason for its
    (B) can not see scarcely any valid reason for its
    (C) can see any valid reason scarcely for its
    (D) can see scarcely any valid reason for it's
    (E) can scarcely see any valid reason for it's

163. There are two courses open <u>to us; we can demand</u> that the subject be brought up for discussion immediately, or we can wait until it appears on the agenda in about three months.

    (A) to us; we can demand
    (B) to us, we can demand
    (C) to us: we can demand
    (D) for us—we can demand
    (E) for us, we could demand

164. All of the possible combinations <u>having been considered, they</u> relaxed and waited for the results.

    (A) having been considered, they
    (B) having been considered. They
    (C) have been considered; they
    (D) have to be considered and they
    (E) having to be considered: they

165. We expect help <u>in providing adequate facilities and ample funds from everybody</u> in order to advance this vital program.

    (A) in providing adequate facilities and ample funds from everybody
    (B) in the provision of adequate facilities and ample funds from everybody
    (C) in providing adequate facilities and funds from everyone
    (D) with facilities and funds from everyone
    (E) from everyone in providing adequate facilities and ample funds

166. From the moment he took public office, his actions have <u>been loaded with significance and filled with worth</u>.

    (A) been loaded with significance and filled with worth
    (B) been significant and worthwhile
    (C) become loaded with significance and worth
    (D) to be loaded with significance and filled with worth
    (E) been actions of significance and worth

167. After several days' tour, we became convinced that <u>the climate of this deserted island was like Florida in winter</u>.

    (A) the climate of this deserted island was like Florida in winter
    (B) the climate of this deserted island was like that of Florida in winter
    (C) the climate of this desert Island was like Florida in winter
    (D) the climate of this deserted island in winter was like Florida
    (E) the climate of this desert island was as Florida in winter

168. The students have always had <u>a most sincere interest and admiration for</u> the important work of Professor Jakobsen.

    (A) a most sincere interest and admiration for
    (B) a most sincere interest in and admiration for
    (C) mostly a sincere interest and admiration for
    (D) a most sincere interest, and admiration for
    (E) a most sincere interest and an admiration for

169. I might have provided a happier <u>ending if I was the author of that novel</u>.

    (A) ending if I was the author of that novel
    (B) ending, if I were the author of that novel
    (C) ending. If I were the author of that novel
    (D) ending if I had been the author of that novel
    (E) ending, if I had to be the author of that novel

170. Last night, our guest lecturer spoke about the methods of controlling population growth, <u>the dangers involved in manipulating nature, and how to calculate</u> potential change in species' size.

    (A) the dangers involved in manipulating nature, and how to calculate
    (B) the dangers involved in manipulating nature and in calculating
    (C) how to manipulate nature, and how to calculate
    (D) the dangers involved in manipulating nature, and the method of calculating
    (E) how to manipulate nature and to calculate

If there is still time remaining, you may review the questions in this section only.
You may not turn to any other section of the test.

Answers

Section I   Reading Comprehension

1.	(D)	8.	(B)	15.	(E)	22.	(C)
2.	(E)	9.	(B)	16.	(B)	23.	(C)
3.	(C)	10.	(C)	17.	(E)	24.	(A)
4.	(A)	11.	(D)	18.	(B)	25.	(C)
5.	(B)	12.	(C)	19.	(C)		
6.	(D)	13.	(D)	20.	(C)		
7.	(E)	14.	(D)	21.	(C)		

Section II   Problem Solving

26.	(B) (I-2)	34.	(A) (II-2)	42.	(A) (IV-1)	50.	(B) (I-2)
27.	(A) (I-4)	35.	(D) (II-1)	43.	(C) (I-4, II-3)	51.	(A) (III-7)
28.	(C) (II-5)	36.	(D) (III-5)	44.	(E) (I-2)	52.	(E) (II-3)
29.	(C) (II-5, III-7)	37.	(B) (III-7, I-4)	45.	(D) (III-7)	53.	(A) (III-7)
30.	(E) (II-4)	38.	(C) (I-4)	46.	(D) (IV-2)	54.	(D) (I-4)
31.	(C) (I-3)	39.	(C) (II-7)	47.	(B) (IV-2)	55.	(C) (II-2)
32.	(B) (I-7)	40.	(E) (I-4)	48.	(D) (IV-2)		
33.	(C) (I-4)	41.	(B) (II-2)	49.	(D) (II-6)		

Section III   Practical Judgment

56.	(D)	61.	(A)	66.	(D)	71.	(B)
57.	(B)	62.	(E)	67.	(D)	72.	(A)
58.	(C)	63.	(B)	68.	(A)	73.	(B)
59.	(E)	64.	(B)	69.	(B)	74.	(B)
60.	(E)	65.	(E)	70.	(E)	75.	(C)

Section IV   Data Sufficiency

76. **(E)**	84. **(E)**	92. **(C)**	100. **(D)**
77. **(B)**	85. **(D)**	93. **(E)**	101. **(C)**
78. **(D)**	86. **(D)**	94. **(A)**	102. **(A)**
79. **(A)**	87. **(C)**	95. **(B)**	103. **(E)**
80. **(E)**	88. **(E)**	96. **(A)**	104. **(C)**
81. **(C)**	89. **(D)**	97. **(B)**	105. **(E)**
82. **(D)**	90. **(E)**	98. **(C)**	
83. **(B)**	91. **(B)**	99. **(B)**	

Section V   Writing Ability

106. **(E)**	111. **(B)**	116. **(E)**	121. **(B)**
107. **(A)**	112. **(C)**	117. **(C)**	122. **(C)**
108. **(E)**	113. **(C)**	118. **(A)**	123. **(D)**
109. **(C)**	114. **(C)**	119. **(D)**	124. **(B)**
110. **(A)**	115. **(B)**	120. **(C)**	125. **(A)**

Section VI   Practical Judgment

126. **(B)**	131. **(E)**	136. **(C)**	141. **(B)**
127. **(E)**	132. **(B)**	137. **(E)**	142. **(D)**
128. **(C)**	133. **(B)**	138. **(B)**	143. **(B)**
129. **(C)**	134. **(E)**	139. **(E)**	144. **(B)**
130. **(D)**	135. **(D)**	140. **(D)**	145. **(D)**

Section VII   Writing Ability

146. **(C)**	153. **(D)**	160. **(D)**	167. **(B)**
147. **(C)**	154. **(E)**	161. **(A)**	168. **(B)**
148. **(C)**	155. **(C)**	162. **(A)**	169. **(D)**
149. **(D)**	156. **(C)**	163. **(C)**	170. **(D)**
150. **(A)**	157. **(B)**	164. **(A)**	
151. **(C)**	158. **(A)**	165. **(E)**	
152. **(B)**	159. **(C)**	166. **(B)**	

Analysis

Section I   Reading Comprehension

1. **(D)** This is clearly a passage dealing with the economy and economic policy. Note that (E) is too vague; an *economic policy* textbook might have been a correct answer.

2. **(E)** All of the others are given in paragraph 2.

3. **(C)** See paragraph 2: "... consumer and business sentiment benefited from rising public expectations that a resolution of the conflict [Vietnam] was in prospect and that East-West tensions were easing."

4. **(A)** See paragraph 3, line 1: "The underpinnings of the business expansion were to be found in part in the stimulative monetary and fiscal policies that had been pursued."

5. **(B)** See paragraph 4: "... there was actually a substantial deterioration in our trade account to a sizable deficit, almost two thirds of which was with Japan."

6. **(D)** See paragraph 5, line 1: Only (D) was mentioned.

7. **(E)** See paragraph 5, sentence 2: "The Phase Three program of wage and price restraint can contribute to dampening inflation."

8. **(B)** See paragraph 5: "... the unemployment rates of a bit over 5 percent ..."

9. **(B)** See paragraph 1: "Under a perfectly sunny sky and from an apparently calm sea ..." None of the other answer choices is particularly suprising.

10. **(C)** See the first sentence of the passage: "... distant lands or continents."

11. **(D)** See paragraph 2, line 1: "How are these waves formed? When a submarine earthquake occurs. ..."

12. **(C)** See paragraph 2: "The swells in the ocean are sometimes nearly a mile wide. ..."

13. **(D)** See paragraph 5: "... the Coast and Geodetic Survey initiated a program ... to locate submarine earthquakes [and] tell how severe a submarine earthquake was. ..."

14. **(D)** See paragraph 4.

15. **(E)** See paragraph 3: "These waves travel hundreds of miles an hour. ..."

16. **(B)** See paragraph 3.

17. **(E)** All are mentioned in paragraph 5, except for the height of the wave.

18. **(B)** See paragraph 3, sentence 1: "... people are particularly sensitive about any reduction in the quality of the atmosphere."

19. **(C)** This is implied in paragraph 2.

20. **(C)** See paragraph 3: "The households' share in atmospheric pollution is far bigger than that of industry. ..." The key word in the question is "most."

21. **(C)** Both production *and* transportation costs are important. Although paragraph 1 states that the costs of maintaining clean water are

"primarily" production costs, paragraph 4 states that this problem is "related to the costs of production and transport . . ."

22. **(C)** See paragraph 5, line 1: "Atmospheric pollution caused by the private property of individuals . . . is difficult to control."

23. **(C)** See paragraph 6: both active and passive resources. No mention is made of levying taxes.

24. **(A)** See paragraph 5: "*In this particular case,* the cost of anti-pollution measures will have to be borne to a considerable extent by individuals." "In this particular case" refers to the situation also described in the paragraph where pollution is caused by the private property of individuals.

25. **(C)** See paragraph 6: While noise abatement is not impossible to achieve, the "costs of a complete protection against noise are so prohibitive. . . ."

Section II   Problem Solving

26. **(B)** The time needed to complete the trip is $\left(6 - \frac{1}{4} - 1\frac{3}{8} - 2\frac{1}{3}\right)$ hours. This equals $6 - (1 + 2) - \left(\frac{1}{4} + \frac{3}{8} + \frac{1}{3}\right) = 3 - \frac{6 + 9 + 8}{24} = 3 - \frac{23}{24} = 2\frac{1}{24} = 2$ hours $2\frac{1}{2}$ minutes.

27. **(A)** The average has decreased by $500 - 400$ or 100 points during the week, so the percentage of decrease is $100/500$ or 20%.

28. **(C)** Since there are 180 minutes in 3 hours, then $\frac{x}{8} = \frac{180}{18}$, where x is the number of cars washed in 3 hours. Therefore, $x = 8 \times 10 = 80$.

29. **(C)** If s and t denote the sides of the two squares, then $s^2 : t^2 = 2 : 1$, or $\frac{s^2}{t^2} = \frac{2}{1}$. Thus $\left(\frac{s}{t}\right)^2 = \frac{2}{1}$ and $\frac{s}{t} = \frac{\sqrt{2}}{1}$.

30. **(E)** The Venn diagram indicates the answer immediately. The region outside both circles denotes neither whitewall tires nor air-conditioning.

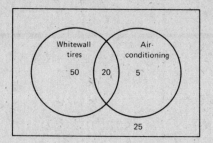

31. **(C)** Each share was worth $\$122.50 - \$111.10$ or $\$11.40$ less in 1973 than it was in 1970. Therefore, the 100,000 shares were worth $100,000 \times \$11.40$ or $\$1,140,000$ less in 1973 than in 1970.

32. **(B)** Add up the daily wages to get the total wages for the week. $\$51.90 + 52.20 + 49.80 + 51.50 + 50.60 = \$256.00$. Divide $\$256.00$ by 5 to get the average daily wage, $\$51.20$.

33. **(C)** The interest on the first $\$600$ is $(.08)(\$600)$ or $\$48.00$ for a year. There is $\$5,400$ of the loan in excess of $\$600$; so he must pay $(.07)(5,400)$ or $\$378.00$ interest for the year on the $\$5,400$. Therefore, the interest for one year will be $\$48 + \$378$ or $\$426$.

34. **(A)** $4y - 6x = -2(3x - 2y) = -2(8) = -16$.

35. **(D)** Since the total distance is 200 miles, of which you fly x miles, you drive $(200 - x)$ miles. Therefore, the cost is $10x + (200 - x)12$, which is $10x - 12x + 2400$ or $2400 - 2x$ cents. The answer in dollars is obtained by dividing by 100, which is $(24 - .02x)$ dollars.

36. **(D)** Since the sides of the square equal the length of the rectangles, which is twice the width, the length of R_1 is 2 times its width.

37. **(B)** If A_1 denotes the increased area and A the original area, then $A_1 = 1.69A$, since A_1 is A increased by 69%. Thus, $s_1^2 = A_1 = 1.69A = 1.69s^2$, where s_1 is the increased side and s the original side. Since the square root

of 1.69 is 1.3, we have $s_1 = 1.3s$ so s is increased by .3 or 30%.

38. **(C)** Since the dealer made a profit of 20%, he sold the car for 120% of what the car cost. Thus, if C is the cost of the car, 120% of $C = \$1,380$ or $(\%_5)C = \$1,380$. Therefore, $C = \%_6$ of $\$1,380$, which is $\$1,150$.

39. **(C)**

STATEMENT I is not always true. For example, 1 is less than 5 and 1 is less than 6, but 6 is not less than 5.

STATEMENT II is not always true, since $\%_8 <$ $\frac{1}{2}$ and $\%_8 < \frac{2}{3}$ but $\%_8$ is not less than $(\frac{1}{2})$ $(\frac{2}{3}) = \frac{1}{3}$.

Since STATEMENT III is always true, (C) is the correct answer.

40. **(E)** The total number of workers is 80, and 35 of them work 40 or more hours. Therefore, $\%_{80} = .4375 = 43.75\%$.

41. **(B)** 15 people worked 40 to 44 hours, and 4 worked up to 29 hours. So $4x = 15$, which means $x = \%_4 = 3\%_4$.

42. **(A)**

STATEMENT I can be inferred, since the average number of hours worked is $\frac{3100}{80} =$ $38\frac{3}{4}$ which is less than 40.

STATEMENT II can not be inferred, since there is no information about the number of workers who worked over 48 hours.

STATEMENT III is not true, since there are only 35 workers who worked 40 or more hours.

43. **(C)** The truck uses 30% more gasoline to travel the same distance at 70 mph than it does at 50 mph. Therefore, the truck requires 130% of a gallon of gasoline, which is 1.3 gallons, to travel 19.5 miles at 70 mph. So the truck will travel $(10/1.3)(19.5)$ or 150 miles on 10 gallons of gas at 70 mph.

44. **(E)** Convert $\frac{2}{5}$ and $\frac{2}{3}$ into fractions with denominators of 30. Since $\frac{2}{5} = \frac{12}{30}$ and $\frac{1}{3} = \frac{10}{30}$, $\frac{2}{5} + \frac{1}{3} = \frac{12}{30} + \frac{10}{30} = \frac{22}{30}$, and x is equal to 22.

45. **(D)** The area of the rectangle is $4 \times 6 = 24$ square feet. Since 1 square foot is 144 square inches, the area of the rectangle is 3,456 square inches. Each square has an area of $(\frac{1}{2})^2$ or $\frac{1}{4}$ square inches. Therefore, the number of squares needed $= 3,456 \div \frac{1}{4} =$ $3,456 \times 4 = 13,824$.

46. **(D)** The corporation income tax accounted for 19.7% of all average annual receipts for the years 1967–1970. Since 19.7% is about 20% or $\frac{1}{5}$, the average annual receipts were about 5 times the average annual receipts from the corporation income tax. Therefore, the answer is $5x$.

47. **(B)** Veterans received 4.2%, education and manpower 3.8%, and health and income security 26% of the average annual outlays; so together the three categories received $4.2\% + 3.8\% + 26\%$ or 34%. Since $\frac{1}{3}$ is $33\frac{1}{3}\%$, 34% is roughly $\frac{1}{3}$.

48. **(D)** Since $\frac{5}{8}$ of 3.2% $= 5 \times .4\% = 2.0\%$, the correct answer is (D).

49. **(D)** $\frac{10}{5} = 2 = \frac{20}{10}$, so the ratio of successive terms of the progression is 2. Therefore, the term which follows 20 is 2 times 20 or 40.

50. **(B)** Since $\frac{1}{8}$ of 8¢ is 1¢, each egg will cost 8¢ + 1¢ or 9¢ after the price has increased. The price of a dozen eggs will be $12 \times 9¢$ or $1.08.

51. **(A)** The area of trapezoid $ABCD$ equals the area of rectangle $ABED$, which is $t \times 5$ (since $BE = BC = 5$), plus the area of triangle BEC, which is $\frac{(5 \times 5)}{2}$. The answers is thus $5t + 12.5$.

52. **(E)** The selling price of the jars should equal cost + $75. The cost of making 300 jars = $(100)65¢ + (200)55¢ = \$65 + \$110 = \$175$. So the selling price should be $\$175 + \$75$ or $\$250$.

53. **(A)** Since it takes twice as long to walk the length as the width, $l = 2w$ where l is the length and w the width. The perimeter equals $2l + 2w = 3l = 300$ yards, so the length is 100 yards and the width is 50 yards. Therefore, the area is $50 \times 100 = 5,000$ square yards.

54. **(D)** The company's profit $= (2,000)(.07) + (5,000)(.06) = \$140 + \$300 = \$440.$

55. **(C)** Since $\dfrac{x}{y} = \dfrac{3}{z}$, $xz = 3y$ and $9y^2 = (3y)^2$; so $9y^2 = (xz)^2 = x^2z^2.$

Section III   Practical Judgment

56. **(D)** A *Major Assumption* of the government is that Abco will stay in business if the loan is granted.

57. **(B)** High unemployment in the country is a *Major Factor,* because it is a primary consideration in the decision as to whether to approve the additional loan.

58. **(C)** The dependence of shopkeepers on the existence of Abco is a *Minor Factor* in the government's weighing of the loan decision. Although not crucial in itself, the fact that shopkeepers may be harmed by an Abco bankruptcy helps to sway the government towards a decision to grant the loan.

59. **(E)** Investment incentives (concessions) were an important factor in Abco's decision to establish a plant in Frieland, but they do not figure in the government's decision as to whether to make the loan.

60. **(E)** The fact that Frieland is a developing country is not a consideration in the selection of an alternative course of action, nor is it a major assumption made by a decision maker.

61. **(A)** Finding a way to keep Abco operating is the *Major Objective* of the government, both for economic and political reasons.

62. **(E)** The initial training of workers at government expense has no bearing on the present decision.

63. **(B)** Poor worker-management relations is a *Major Factor* in the government's decision concerning the loan. It raises the problem of whether the company can become an economically viable institution.

64. **(B)** One of the government's economic policy goals is to increase exports. It is committed to supporting those companies that can contribute to this goal. Therefore, the export potential of Abco is a *Major Factor* in the decision, supporting the alternative of granting the company further financial support.

65. **(E)** There is nothing in the passage to suggest that the political *philosophy* of the opposition party is a consideration in the government's decision as to whether to make an additional loan. Of course, the political *consequence* (question 69) is important.

66. **(D)** The existence of a deadline ("a quick decision") is mentioned in the passage. The government *believes* that a quick decision is necessary to avoid criticism from the opposition. However, there are no facts cited to support this contention.

67. **(D)** The key word is "availability." No facts are mentioned to indicate that sufficient government funds are actually available to assist Abco.

68. **(A)** One *Major Objective* of the government is to prevent increased unemployment.

69. **(B)** The political consequence of Abco's pending bankruptcy is a *Major Factor* in the government's consideration of whether to grant the additional loan.

70. **(E)** The size of the population has no weight in the consideration of any decision alternative.

71. **(B)** See paragraph 8. One alternative for assuring the future of the company, was that it be purchased by the government at a "reasonable" price.

72. **(A)** Only the fact of excess capacity was mentioned.

73. **(B)** See paragraph 8. Abco did manage to employ some 500 workers.

74. **(B)** Whether the company suffered from poor management is unknown. However, since there was excess capacity in the industry, it can be concluded that there was too much competition.

75. **(C)** Based on the facts, the government was

overly optimistic in its assessment that Abco could succeed in such an industry, and certainly short-sighted not to have realized the consequences of some obvious indicators, e.g., the over-supply of shoes.

Section IV   Data Sufficiency

76. **(E)**

A triangle with sides of lengths 3, 4, and 5 is a right triangle since $3^2 + 4^2 = 5^2$, and its perimeter is 12. A triangle with sides of lengths 2, $4\frac{4}{5}$, and $5\frac{1}{5}$ also has a perimeter of 12. And since $2^2 + (4\frac{4}{5})^2 = (5\frac{1}{5})^2$, it too is a right triangle. Therefore, two triangles can satisfy STATEMENTS (1) and (2) yet not be congruent. On the other hand, any pair of congruent right triangles satisfy STATEMENTS (1) and (2). Thus, STATEMENTS (1) and (2) together are not sufficient to answer the question.

77. **(B)**

$x^3 - 8 = 0$ has only $x = 2$ as a real solution. And 2 is greater than 0, so STATEMENT (2) alone is sufficient.

Since $x = 2$ and $x = -2$ are both solutions of $x^4 - 16 = 0$, STATEMENT (1) alone is not sufficient.

78. **(D)**

STATEMENT (1) is sufficient since it implies that conveyer belt A loads $\frac{2}{3}$ of the hopper while conveyer belt B loads only $\frac{1}{3}$ with both working. Since conveyer belt A loads $\frac{2}{3}$ of the hopper in a hour, it will take $1 \div \frac{2}{3}$ or $1\frac{1}{2}$ hours to fill the hopper by itself.

STATEMENT (2) is also sufficient since it implies that conveyer belt B fills $\frac{1}{3}$ of the hopper in 1 hour. Thus, conveyer belt A loads $\frac{2}{3}$ in one hour, and that means conveyer belt A will take $1\frac{1}{2}$ hours by itself.

79. **(A)** The first fly will travel a distance equal to the circumference of the circle which is π times the diameter. The second fly will travel $4s$ where s is the length of a side. Since the diagonal of a square has length $\sqrt{2}S$, the second fly will travel $4/\sqrt{2}$ times the diagonal of the square. Therefore, (1) alone is sufficient, since $4/\sqrt{2} = 4\sqrt{2}/2 = 2\sqrt{2}$ which is less than π. (2) alone is not sufficient, since one fly might have crawled faster than the other.

80. **(E)** Using (1) and (2) together, it is only possible to determine the total amount paid for fire insurance in 1970 and 1972. Since no relation is given between the amounts paid in 1970 and 1972, there is not enough information to determine the cost in 1972.

81. **(C)** (2) alone is not sufficient since both $y = 2$ and $y = -2$ satisfy $y^2 - 4 = 0$. (1) alone is not sufficient, since $\frac{1}{2}$ is larger than 0 but less than 1 while 3 is larger than 0 and larger than 1. The only solution of $y^2 - 4 = 0$ which is larger than 0 is 2 which is larger than 1. Therefore, (1) and (2) are sufficient.

82. **(D)** Let $\$x$ be the amount he was paid the first day. Then he was paid $x + 2$, $x + 4$, $x + 6$, $x + 8$, and $x + 10$ dollars for the succeeding days. (1) alone is sufficient, since the total he was paid is $(6x + 30)$ dollars, and we can solve $6x + 30 = 150$ (to find that he was paid $20 for the first day). (2) alone is also sufficient. He was paid $\$(x + 10)$ on the sixth day, so (2) means that $(1.5)x = x + 10$ (which is the same as $x = 20$).

83. **(B)** Since 85% of $3,000 is $2,550, (2) alone is sufficient. (1) alone is not sufficient, since if x were 5% (1) would tell us the price of the car is less than $2,600. But if x were 1%, (1) would imply that the price of the car is greater than $2,600.

84. **(E)** Vertical angles are equal, so $c = d$. Since the sum of the angles in a triangle is 180°, $a + b + c = d + e + f$ which means $a + b = e + f$. If we use (1) and (2), we have $a + a = e + a$ so $e = a$. And we know the triangles are similar. However this does not give any information about the value of a, since any two similar triangles can be made to satisfy

conditions (1) and (2). Therefore, (1) and (2) together are not sufficient.

85. **(D)** (1) alone is sufficient since $BC = AB$ implies $x = y = 40$. Since the sum of the angles in a triangle is $180°$, z must equal 100. (2) alone is sufficient. Let D be the point where the bisector of angle B meets AC. Then according to (2), triangle BDC is a right triangle. Since angle y is $40°$, the remaining angle in triangle BDC is $50°$ and equals $\frac{1}{2}z$, so $z = 100$.

86. **(D)** Since there is a bottom and 4 sides, each a congruent square, the amount of cardboard needed will be $5e^2$ where e is the length of an edge of the box. So we need to find e. (1) alone is sufficient. Since the area of the bottom is e^2, (1) means $e^2 = 4$ with $e = 2$ feet. (2) alone is also sufficient. Since the volume of the box is e^3. (2) means $e^3 = 8$ and $e = 2$ feet.

87. **(C)** The average weight of the books is the total weight of all the books divided by the number of books on the shelf. Thus (1) and (2) together are sufficient. (Solve $2.5 = \frac{40}{x}$ for x, the number of books on the shelf.) (1) alone is not sufficient, nor is (2) alone sufficient.

88. **(E)** If $ABCD$ has the pairs of opposite sides equal and each angle is $90°$, then it is a rectangle. But there are many quadrilaterals which have two opposite sides equal with one angle a right angle. For example, the figure has $AB = DC$ and $x = 90$, but it is not a rectangle. Therefore, (1) and (2) together are insufficient.

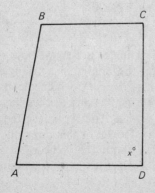

89. **(D)** (2) alone is sufficient, since if $a_3 = 1$ then $a_4 = (a_3)^2 = 1^2 = 1$; then $a_5 = (a_4)^2 = 1^2 = 1$. (1) alone is also sufficient. If $a_1 = -1$ then $a_2 = (a_1)^2 = 1$, and $a_3 = (a_2)^2 = 1$, but $a_3 = 1$ is given by (2) which we know is sufficient.

90. **(E)** Let J, F and C stand for the weekly salaries of John, Fred, and Chuck. (1) says $J = 2F$ and (2) says $F = .4(C + J)$. Since there is no information given about the values of C or F, we cannot deduce the value of J. Therefore, (1) and (2) together are insufficient.

91. **(B)**

STATEMENT (2) alone is sufficient. $2x + 4y = 2(x + 2y)$, so if $2x + 4y = 12$ then $2(x + 2y) = 12$ and $x + 2y = 6$.

STATEMENT (1) alone is insufficient. If you only use STATEMENT (1) then you can get $x + 2y = x + y + y = 4 + y$ but there is no information on the value of y.

92. **(C)**

Since the sum of the angles in a triangle is $180°$, $x + y + z = 180$. Using STATEMENT (1) alone we have $2y + y + z = 3y + z = 180$, which is insufficient to determine y or x.

Using STATEMENT (2) alone we have $x + 1.5z + z = x + 2.5z = 180$, which is not sufficient to determine x or z.

However, if we use both STATEMENTS (1) and (2) we obtain $3y + z = 4.5z + z = 5.5z = 180$, so $z = \frac{2}{11}$ of 180. Now $y = \frac{3}{2}$ of z, so $y = \frac{3}{11}$ of 180, and $x = \frac{6}{11}$ of 180. Therefore, x is not a right angle and STATEMENTS (1) and (2) are sufficient.

93. **(E)**

Since STATEMENT (1) only describes x and STATEMENT (2) only describes y both are needed to get an answer. Using STATEMENT (2), STATEMENT (1) becomes $x = 2k = 2 \cdot 2y = 4y$, so $x = 4y$. However, this is not sufficient, since if $y = -1$ then $x = -4$ and -4 is less than -1, but if $y = 1$ then $x = 4$ and x is greater than y.

94. **(A)**

If each doll costs $8, then 65 dolls will cost

$8 \times \$65 = \$520$. Using STATEMENT (1), the profit is selling price minus cost = $\$750 - \$520 = \$230$, so STATEMENT (1) alone is sufficient.

STATEMENT (2) alone is not sufficient since you need to know what price the dolls sell for to find the profit.

95. **(B)**

STATEMENT (2) alone is sufficient. 60% of the people have blue eyes and 50% of the people have blue eyes and blond hair, so $60\% - 50\% = 10\%$ of the people have blue eyes but do not have blond hair.

STATEMENT (1) alone is not sufficient. Using STATEMENT (1) alone we can only find out how many people have blond hair and do not have blue eyes, in addition to what is given.

96. **(A)**

The sum of the angles of the pentagon are 540°. (The sum of the angles of a polygon with n sides which is inscribed in a circle is $(n-2)180°$.) STATEMENT (1) alone is sufficient. If the polygon is regular, all angles are equal and so angle ABC is $\frac{1}{5}$ of 540° or 108°.

STATEMENT (2) alone is insufficient because the radius of the circle does not give any information about the angles of the pentagon.

97. **(B)**

The area of a circle is πr^2, where r is the radius of the circle. Since O is a point on the line AB, AB is a diameter of the circle. Therefore, since a radius is one half of a diameter, the radius of the circle is 3.5 inches. Thus, STATEMENT (2) alone is sufficient.

STATEMENT (1) alone is insufficient since there is no relation between DE and the radius.

98. **(C)**

Using STATEMENT (2) alone we have $\$10,000 + x + y = \$34,000$, where x is the taxable income for 1972 and y is the taxable income for 1973. So STATEMENT (2) alone is not sufficient.

STATEMENT (1) alone is not sufficient since no relation is given between taxable income in 1972 and 1973.

STATEMENTS (1) and (2) together give the equation $\$10,000 + \$12,000 + y = \$34,000$, which means $y = \$12,000$, where y is the taxable income for 1973.

99. **(B)**

STATEMENT (2) alone is sufficient. 3 feet, 2 inches is more than half of 6 feet so the piece of string 3 feet 2 inches long must be longer than the other 2 pieces put together.

STATEMENT (1) alone is insufficient. There is not enough information to find the length of *any* of the three pieces of string.

100. **(D)** Let r be the fraction of the job the 4 apprentices finish in 1 hour. Then $\frac{1}{r}$ is the amount of time in hours that it will take the 4 apprentices to finish the job. So it is sufficient to find r. The group of 5 craftsmen finishes $\frac{1}{3}$ of the job per hour, so each craftsman does $\frac{1}{15}$ of the job per hour.

STATEMENT (1) alone is sufficient. An apprentice will do $\frac{2}{3}$ of $\frac{1}{15} = \frac{2}{45}$ of the job per hour, so $r = \frac{8}{45}$.

STATEMENT (2) alone is sufficient. The craftsmen and the apprentices together will finish $\frac{1}{3} + r$ of the job per hour. Since it takes them $1\frac{22}{23}$ hours to finish the job, $(\frac{1}{3} + r)(\frac{45}{23}) = 1$ which can be solved for r.

101. **(C)**

STATEMENT (2) alone is not sufficient. -1 is less than 2 and $\frac{1}{-1}$ is less than $\frac{1}{2}$ but 1 is less than 2 and $\frac{1}{1}$ is greater than $\frac{1}{2}$.

STATEMENT (1) alone is insufficient since there is no information about y.

STATEMENTS (1) and (2) together imply that x and y are both greater than 1 and for two positive numbers x and y, if x is less than y then $\frac{1}{x}$ is greater than $\frac{1}{y}$.

102. **(A)**

STATEMENT (1) alone is sufficient. Since angle CAD is bisected by AO, the triangles AOD and AOC are congruent by side-angle-side ($AO = AO$). Therefore, angle

AOD = angle AOC. Since the sum of the angles is 180° (CD is a straight line) the two angles are right angles and AB is $\perp CD$.

STATEMENT (2) alone is insufficient. We can choose B so that $BC = AD$ whether or not $AB \perp CD$.

103. **(E)**

Since C is closer to A, if plane X is flying faster than plane Y it will certainly fly over C before plane Y. However, if plane X flys slower than plane Y, and C is very close to A, plane X would still fly over C before plane Y does. Thus, STATEMENTS (1) and (2) together are not sufficient.

104. **(C)**

STATEMENT (1) gives $x + y = 4 - x$ and since there is no further information about x, STATEMENT (1) alone is insufficient.

STATEMENT (2) alone is also insufficient because STATEMENT (2) only implies $x + y = 5 - y$. However, if you multiply STATEMENT (2) by -2 and add it to STATEMENT (1), the result is $-3y = -6$ or $y = 2$. So $x + y = 5 - 2 = 3$.

Therefore, STATEMENTS (1) and (2) together are sufficient and (C) is the answer.

105. **(E)**

Since the area of a circle is πr^2, the area of the circular section AOB is the fraction $^x/_{360}$ times πr^2, where angle $AOB = x°$. (There are 360° in the entire circle.) Using STATEMENT (1), we know $x = 36$ so $(^x/_{360})\pi r^2 = \frac{1}{10}\pi r^2$. However, STATEMENT (1) gives no information about the value of r, so STATEMENT (1) alone is insufficient.

STATEMENT (2) gives no information about the value of r, so STATEMENTS (1) and (2) together are insufficient.

Section V   Writing Ability

106. **(E)** Since both subjects are joined by the word *and*, they are considered as a single thing. Hence we use the single form *is* and not *and*.

107. **(A)** The word *team* is a collective noun and is considered singular when the group is regarded as a unit. Therefore, the singular form *is* should be used.

108. **(E)** No error.

109. **(C)** *Seen* is the wrong tense. *Saw* is the correct form.

110. **(A)** *Plays* is an illogical time form. The verb tense should be *played*.

111. **(B)** *Enthused* is a colloquial expression for *enthusiastic*, which is the preferred usage.

112. **(C)** An error in diction, or improper word usage. *Irregardless* is a substandard form of *regardless*.

113. **(C)** *After the battle* indicates the past, while the rest of the sentence is in the future tense. Part C should read *advanced*.

114. **(C)** The use of a personal pronoun (they) in an impersonal sense (as in the sentence) should be avoided. The sentence should read: "I read in the newspaper that in Nigeria the farmers grow large tomatoes."

115. **(B)** In this sentence, it seems as if *your breathing* is doing the swimming. The problem here is the dangling phrase, which must be given a word to modify. The sentence should read: "If you want to master the proper backstroke . . ."

116. **(E)** No error.

117. **(C)** This is a complex sentence with one main clause and one subordinate clause. The error is in tense. The main clause is in the past tense, while the subordinate clause is in the present. It should also be in the past tense, i.e., "the other part showed . . ."

118. **(A)** *Had . . . begun*; the past participle is required in the past perfect form and not *began*, which is the past simple form of the verb.

119. **(D)** The subject of the gerund *standing* should be in the possessive form; *my* and not *me*.

120. **(C)** The preposition *to* is redundant in this case as it appears earlier attached to the pronoun *whom.*

121. **(B)** The pronoun *they* has no antecedent.

122. **(C)** The subject of the modifying phrase *Having been delayed by unfavorable weather* is obviously *our plane,* which should follow directly after the phrase: "Having been delayed by unfavorable weather, our plane could not arrive . . ."

123. **(D)** The correct word is *considerate,* meaning *thoughtful of the needs of others* and not *considerable,* meaning *great in size or importance.*

124. **(B)** The expression *each other* is confined to relationships between two; in this case *one another* is required.

125. **(A)** The adjective *less* refers to quantity; *fewer,* which refers to countable units, e.g., *chances,* is required here.

Section VI   Practical Judgment

126. **(B)** A primary consideration in Mr. Krim's decision as to whether to buy the firm is the degree of public awareness of the company's products, since this will help determine the company's chances for future success.

127. **(E)** Caspi's marketing ability is not important to Krim's decision to buy the company, since Caspi will retire if the company is sold.

128. **(C)** While not crucial in itself, this feature of Posturemat mattresses is one of the strengths of the product and so of the company as a whole.

129. **(C)** This is a minor factor, since older consumers play only a small role in determining the present and future success of the company.

130. **(D)** Krim's assumption about retailers' attitudes is contrary to the facts given in the passage. Only if Posturemat launches an aggressive advertising campaign may retailers' attitudes change. But this is an assumption, not a fact.

131. **(E)** The importation of latex is not an issue in the decision as to whether to buy the company.

132. **(B)** Posturemat's declining market share is a *Major Factor* in the decision as to whether to buy the company. The issue is whether the decline can be halted and reversed.

133. **(B)** Although Krim had a preconceived notion of whether to buy the company, he nevertheless has asked Sims to prepare a marketing analysis upon which he will base his final decision.

134. **(E)** The ownership of the premises is not critical to the success of the firm or its viability as an enterprise.

135. **(D)** That attitudes toward foam rubber mattresses can be changed by advertising is an assumption of Mr. Krim not supported by any facts cited in the passage.

136. **(C)** The advantage or attribute of orthopedic qualities in particular is a *Minor Factor* in the decision as to whether to buy the company. The *overall* quality of Posturemat (including other attributes) would constitute a *Major Factor.*

137. **(E)** The fact that synthetic mattresses are made of polyurethane does not influence the selection of an alternative, and is neither related to a major objective nor an assumption of the decision maker.

138. **(B)** The passage states that Lefko handled the sales force of Posturemat. If he leaves, Krim will not have a single experienced manager to handle marketing and sales. Therefore, Krim must weigh the impact that Lefko's leaving would have on the management of the firm. It is, therefore, a *Major Factor.*

139. **(E)** The age of the machinery does not mean that the equipment was obsolete or useless (see paragraph 3). Therefore, the condition does not directly influence any of the decision alternatives.

140. **(E)** Krim *felt* that introduction of a new management team would instill confidence in the firm and allow for increased credit (see the last paragraph). However, no evidence is presented in the passage to support his feeling.

141. **(B)** Caspi attributed Posturemat's loss in market share to the competition of spring mattresses, which had "similar attributes" and were "cheaper to manufacture, but sold at about the same price as Posturemat." Whether Posturemat would in the future successfully compete against these conditions is a *Major Factor* in the decision to buy the company.

142. **(D)** The second resource (labor force) is mentioned in paragraph 3, and the third (brand name) in paragraph 2. Both are cited as positive factors. Its equipment was described as "satisfactory" but "old." (Paragraph 3).

143. **(B)** Synthetic mattresses are non-allergenic and less expensive for consumers to buy than foam rubber. However, foam rubber mattresses are firmer than synthetics (see paragraph 2).

144. **(B)** Krim did not retire because he had failed to train a successor. Lefko, the sales manager, threatened to leave only if the company was sold. There is no basis in fact for the second alternative given in the question (see paragraph 6).

145. **(D)** Posturemat had ceased to advertise in newspapers and radio. No specific mention is made of television (see paragraph 6).

Section VII   Writing Ability

146. **(C)** The two ideas cannot be joined by either a comma or a colon. The semicolon is the suitable way to connect independent clauses.

147. **(C)** *The director* is the proper subject of the dangling participle *knowing*.

148. **(C)** Parallelism: a similar form is required on either side of the comparison.

149. **(D)** They did witness two things, *not only the sinking ship* but the *escape* as well.

150. **(A)** *But* is always followed by the objective pronoun, and the copula *was* will take the subjective *I*.

151. **(C)** *Either . . . or* connect *transfer* and *file*. *Data* is plural and requires the verb *were*.

152. **(B)** *They* is the subject of the dangling participial phrase and must follow it directly.

153. **(D)** The *set has been* published, while the *propositions* (individually) *were* discussed.

154. **(E)** *Requests* as a countable noun requires *number,* whereas only a few *of* them could be dealt with.

155. **(C)** A semicolon is needed to join the two ideas, because *therefore* is an adverb and not a conjunction.

156. **(C)** *Neither . . . nor* apply to *authority* and *means* and must precede them directly.

157. **(B)** *Everyone* is singular and requires the singular *has*. The preposition *without* requires the gerund *helping* preceded by the possessive *his*.

158. **(A)** the *incidence* (singular) *correlates*. The preposition *with* is correct.

159. **(C)** Two separate ideas require punctuation separating them into two separate sentences.

160. **(D)** The correct form of the past conditional requires the past perfect in the conditional clause: *had taken*.

161. **(A)** In *neither . . . nor* constructions, the verb is matched to the noun or pronoun that immediately precedes it. The sentence is not a question, and thus does not become inverted.

162. **(A)** *Scarcely* applies to the *valid reason* and thus must precede it directly. *Scarcely,* having a negative connotation, does not require a negation of the verb.

163. **(C)** The correct punctuation is a colon.

164. **(A)** *They* is the subject of the participial phrase

having been considered and should be separated from it by a comma.

165. **(E)** *Everybody* is expected to help. The sense demands that *from everybody* be placed in the general position. *In the provision of* makes the sentence unnecessarily bulky.

166. **(B)** The original sentence is too wordy.

167. **(B)** The *climate* can only be compared to another climate.

168. **(B)** *Interest in* a subject and *admiration for* it: the prepositions must remain.

169. **(D)** This is a past conditional and requires the past perfect in the conditional clause. There is no punctuation before the *if*.

170. **(D)** Parallel structure demands a list of noun phrases: *the methods, the dangers,* and *the method*.

Evaluating Your Score

Tabulate your score for each section of Sample Test 1 according to the directions on pages 4–5 and record the results in the Self-scoring Table below. Then find your rating for each score on the Self-scoring Scale and record it in the appropriate blank.

Self-scoring Table

PART	SCORE	RATING
1		
2		
3		
4		
5		
6		
7		

Self-scoring Scale

PART	POOR	FAIR	GOOD	EXCELLENT
			RATING	
1	0-8	9-12	13-19	20-25
2	0-15	16-21	22-25	26-30
3	0-7	8-10	11-15	16-20
4	0-14	15-20	21-25	26-30
5	0-7	8-10	11-15	16-20
6	0-7	8-10	11-15	16-20
7	0-8	9-12	13-19	20-25

Study again the Review sections covering material in Sample Test 1 for which you had a rating of FAIR or POOR. Then go on to Sample Test 2.

To obtain an approximation of your actual GMAT score see page 5.

Sections I-II Reading Recall

1. Ⓐ Ⓑ Ⓒ Ⓓ Ⓔ
2. Ⓐ Ⓑ Ⓒ Ⓓ Ⓔ
3. Ⓐ Ⓑ Ⓒ Ⓓ Ⓔ
4. Ⓐ Ⓑ Ⓒ Ⓓ Ⓔ
5. Ⓐ Ⓑ Ⓒ Ⓓ Ⓔ
6. Ⓐ Ⓑ Ⓒ Ⓓ Ⓔ
7. Ⓐ Ⓑ Ⓒ Ⓓ Ⓔ
8. Ⓐ Ⓑ Ⓒ Ⓓ Ⓔ
9. Ⓐ Ⓑ Ⓒ Ⓓ Ⓔ
10. Ⓐ Ⓑ Ⓒ Ⓓ Ⓔ
11. Ⓐ Ⓑ Ⓒ Ⓓ Ⓔ
12. Ⓐ Ⓑ Ⓒ Ⓓ Ⓔ
13. Ⓐ Ⓑ Ⓒ Ⓓ Ⓔ
14. Ⓐ Ⓑ Ⓒ Ⓓ Ⓔ
15. Ⓐ Ⓑ Ⓒ Ⓓ Ⓔ
16. Ⓐ Ⓑ Ⓒ Ⓓ Ⓔ
17. Ⓐ Ⓑ Ⓒ Ⓓ Ⓔ
18. Ⓐ Ⓑ Ⓒ Ⓓ Ⓔ
19. Ⓐ Ⓑ Ⓒ Ⓓ Ⓔ
20. Ⓐ Ⓑ Ⓒ Ⓓ Ⓔ
21. Ⓐ Ⓑ Ⓒ Ⓓ Ⓔ
22. Ⓐ Ⓑ Ⓒ Ⓓ Ⓔ
23. Ⓐ Ⓑ Ⓒ Ⓓ Ⓔ
24. Ⓐ Ⓑ Ⓒ Ⓓ Ⓔ
25. Ⓐ Ⓑ Ⓒ Ⓓ Ⓔ
26. Ⓐ Ⓑ Ⓒ Ⓓ Ⓔ
27. Ⓐ Ⓑ Ⓒ Ⓓ Ⓔ
28. Ⓐ Ⓑ Ⓒ Ⓓ Ⓔ
29. Ⓐ Ⓑ Ⓒ Ⓓ Ⓔ
30. Ⓐ Ⓑ Ⓒ Ⓓ Ⓔ

Section III Problem Solving

31. Ⓐ Ⓑ Ⓒ Ⓓ Ⓔ
32. Ⓐ Ⓑ Ⓒ Ⓓ Ⓔ
33. Ⓐ Ⓑ Ⓒ Ⓓ Ⓔ
34. Ⓐ Ⓑ Ⓒ Ⓓ Ⓔ
35. Ⓐ Ⓑ Ⓒ Ⓓ Ⓔ
36. Ⓐ Ⓑ Ⓒ Ⓓ Ⓔ
37. Ⓐ Ⓑ Ⓒ Ⓓ Ⓔ
38. Ⓐ Ⓑ Ⓒ Ⓓ Ⓔ
39. Ⓐ Ⓑ Ⓒ Ⓓ Ⓔ
40. Ⓐ Ⓑ Ⓒ Ⓓ Ⓔ
41. Ⓐ Ⓑ Ⓒ Ⓓ Ⓔ
42. Ⓐ Ⓑ Ⓒ Ⓓ Ⓔ
43. Ⓐ Ⓑ Ⓒ Ⓓ Ⓔ
44. Ⓐ Ⓑ Ⓒ Ⓓ Ⓔ
45. Ⓐ Ⓑ Ⓒ Ⓓ Ⓔ
46. Ⓐ Ⓑ Ⓒ Ⓓ Ⓔ
47. Ⓐ Ⓑ Ⓒ Ⓓ Ⓔ
48. Ⓐ Ⓑ Ⓒ Ⓓ Ⓔ
49. Ⓐ Ⓑ Ⓒ Ⓓ Ⓔ
50. Ⓐ Ⓑ Ⓒ Ⓓ Ⓔ
51. Ⓐ Ⓑ Ⓒ Ⓓ Ⓔ
52. Ⓐ Ⓑ Ⓒ Ⓓ Ⓔ
53. Ⓐ Ⓑ Ⓒ Ⓓ Ⓔ
54. Ⓐ Ⓑ Ⓒ Ⓓ Ⓔ
55. Ⓐ Ⓑ Ⓒ Ⓓ Ⓔ
56. Ⓐ Ⓑ Ⓒ Ⓓ Ⓔ
57. Ⓐ Ⓑ Ⓒ Ⓓ Ⓔ
58. Ⓐ Ⓑ Ⓒ Ⓓ Ⓔ
59. Ⓐ Ⓑ Ⓒ Ⓓ Ⓔ
60. Ⓐ Ⓑ Ⓒ Ⓓ Ⓔ
61. Ⓐ Ⓑ Ⓒ Ⓓ Ⓔ
62. Ⓐ Ⓑ Ⓒ Ⓓ Ⓔ
63. Ⓐ Ⓑ Ⓒ Ⓓ Ⓔ
64. Ⓐ Ⓑ Ⓒ Ⓓ Ⓔ
65. Ⓐ Ⓑ Ⓒ Ⓓ Ⓔ
66. Ⓐ Ⓑ Ⓒ Ⓓ Ⓔ
67. Ⓐ Ⓑ Ⓒ Ⓓ Ⓔ
68. Ⓐ Ⓑ Ⓒ Ⓓ Ⓔ
69. Ⓐ Ⓑ Ⓒ Ⓓ Ⓔ
70. Ⓐ Ⓑ Ⓒ Ⓓ Ⓔ
71. Ⓐ Ⓑ Ⓒ Ⓓ Ⓔ
72. Ⓐ Ⓑ Ⓒ Ⓓ Ⓔ
73. Ⓐ Ⓑ Ⓒ Ⓓ Ⓔ
74. Ⓐ Ⓑ Ⓒ Ⓓ Ⓔ
75. Ⓐ Ⓑ Ⓒ Ⓓ Ⓔ
76. Ⓐ Ⓑ Ⓒ Ⓓ Ⓔ
77. Ⓐ Ⓑ Ⓒ Ⓓ Ⓔ
78. Ⓐ Ⓑ Ⓒ Ⓓ Ⓔ
79. Ⓐ Ⓑ Ⓒ Ⓓ Ⓔ
80. Ⓐ Ⓑ Ⓒ Ⓓ Ⓔ
81. Ⓐ Ⓑ Ⓒ Ⓓ Ⓔ
82. Ⓐ Ⓑ Ⓒ Ⓓ Ⓔ
83. Ⓐ Ⓑ Ⓒ Ⓓ Ⓔ
84. Ⓐ Ⓑ Ⓒ Ⓓ Ⓔ
85. Ⓐ Ⓑ Ⓒ Ⓓ Ⓔ

Section IV Practical Judgment

86. Ⓐ Ⓑ Ⓒ Ⓓ Ⓔ
87. Ⓐ Ⓑ Ⓒ Ⓓ Ⓔ
88. Ⓐ Ⓑ Ⓒ Ⓓ Ⓔ
89. Ⓐ Ⓑ Ⓒ Ⓓ Ⓔ
90. Ⓐ Ⓑ Ⓒ Ⓓ Ⓔ
91. Ⓐ Ⓑ Ⓒ Ⓓ Ⓔ
92. Ⓐ Ⓑ Ⓒ Ⓓ Ⓔ
93. Ⓐ Ⓑ Ⓒ Ⓓ Ⓔ
94. Ⓐ Ⓑ Ⓒ Ⓓ Ⓔ
95. Ⓐ Ⓑ Ⓒ Ⓓ Ⓔ
96. Ⓐ Ⓑ Ⓒ Ⓓ Ⓔ
97. Ⓐ Ⓑ Ⓒ Ⓓ Ⓔ
98. Ⓐ Ⓑ Ⓒ Ⓓ Ⓔ
99. Ⓐ Ⓑ Ⓒ Ⓓ Ⓔ
100. Ⓐ Ⓑ Ⓒ Ⓓ Ⓔ
101. Ⓐ Ⓑ Ⓒ Ⓓ Ⓔ
102. Ⓐ Ⓑ Ⓒ Ⓓ Ⓔ
103. Ⓐ Ⓑ Ⓒ Ⓓ Ⓔ
104. Ⓐ Ⓑ Ⓒ Ⓓ Ⓔ
105. Ⓐ Ⓑ Ⓒ Ⓓ Ⓔ

Section V Data Sufficiency

106. Ⓐ Ⓑ Ⓒ Ⓓ Ⓔ
107. Ⓐ Ⓑ Ⓒ Ⓓ Ⓔ
108. Ⓐ Ⓑ Ⓒ Ⓓ Ⓔ
109. Ⓐ Ⓑ Ⓒ Ⓓ Ⓔ
110. Ⓐ Ⓑ Ⓒ Ⓓ Ⓔ
111. Ⓐ Ⓑ Ⓒ Ⓓ Ⓔ
112. Ⓐ Ⓑ Ⓒ Ⓓ Ⓔ
113. Ⓐ Ⓑ Ⓒ Ⓓ Ⓔ
114. Ⓐ Ⓑ Ⓒ Ⓓ Ⓔ
115. Ⓐ Ⓑ Ⓒ Ⓓ Ⓔ
116. Ⓐ Ⓑ Ⓒ Ⓓ Ⓔ
117. Ⓐ Ⓑ Ⓒ Ⓓ Ⓔ
118. Ⓐ Ⓑ Ⓒ Ⓓ Ⓔ
119. Ⓐ Ⓑ Ⓒ Ⓓ Ⓔ
120. Ⓐ Ⓑ Ⓒ Ⓓ Ⓔ

Section VI Verbal Ability

121. Ⓐ Ⓑ Ⓒ Ⓓ Ⓔ
122. Ⓐ Ⓑ Ⓒ Ⓓ Ⓔ
123. Ⓐ Ⓑ Ⓒ Ⓓ Ⓔ
124. Ⓐ Ⓑ Ⓒ Ⓓ Ⓔ
125. Ⓐ Ⓑ Ⓒ Ⓓ Ⓔ
126. Ⓐ Ⓑ Ⓒ Ⓓ Ⓔ
127. Ⓐ Ⓑ Ⓒ Ⓓ Ⓔ
128. Ⓐ Ⓑ Ⓒ Ⓓ Ⓔ
129. Ⓐ Ⓑ Ⓒ Ⓓ Ⓔ
130. Ⓐ Ⓑ Ⓒ Ⓓ Ⓔ
131. Ⓐ Ⓑ Ⓒ Ⓓ Ⓔ
132. Ⓐ Ⓑ Ⓒ Ⓓ Ⓔ
133. Ⓐ Ⓑ Ⓒ Ⓓ Ⓔ
134. Ⓐ Ⓑ Ⓒ Ⓓ Ⓔ
135. Ⓐ Ⓑ Ⓒ Ⓓ Ⓔ
136. Ⓐ Ⓑ Ⓒ Ⓓ Ⓔ
137. Ⓐ Ⓑ Ⓒ Ⓓ Ⓔ
138. Ⓐ Ⓑ Ⓒ Ⓓ Ⓔ
139. Ⓐ Ⓑ Ⓒ Ⓓ Ⓔ
140. Ⓐ Ⓑ Ⓒ Ⓓ Ⓔ
141. Ⓐ Ⓑ Ⓒ Ⓓ Ⓔ
142. Ⓐ Ⓑ Ⓒ Ⓓ Ⓔ
143. Ⓐ Ⓑ Ⓒ Ⓓ Ⓔ
144. Ⓐ Ⓑ Ⓒ Ⓓ Ⓔ
145. Ⓐ Ⓑ Ⓒ Ⓓ Ⓔ
146. Ⓐ Ⓑ Ⓒ Ⓓ Ⓔ
147. Ⓐ Ⓑ Ⓒ Ⓓ Ⓔ
148. Ⓐ Ⓑ Ⓒ Ⓓ Ⓔ
149. Ⓐ Ⓑ Ⓒ Ⓓ Ⓔ
150. Ⓐ Ⓑ Ⓒ Ⓓ Ⓔ
151. Ⓐ Ⓑ Ⓒ Ⓓ Ⓔ
152. Ⓐ Ⓑ Ⓒ Ⓓ Ⓔ
153. Ⓐ Ⓑ Ⓒ Ⓓ Ⓔ
154. Ⓐ Ⓑ Ⓒ Ⓓ Ⓔ
155. Ⓐ Ⓑ Ⓒ Ⓓ Ⓔ
156. Ⓐ Ⓑ Ⓒ Ⓓ Ⓔ
157. Ⓐ Ⓑ Ⓒ Ⓓ Ⓔ
158. Ⓐ Ⓑ Ⓒ Ⓓ Ⓔ
159. Ⓐ Ⓑ Ⓒ Ⓓ Ⓔ
160. Ⓐ Ⓑ Ⓒ Ⓓ Ⓔ

Section VII Practical Judgment

161. Ⓐ Ⓑ Ⓒ Ⓓ Ⓔ
162. Ⓐ Ⓑ Ⓒ Ⓓ Ⓔ
163. Ⓐ Ⓑ Ⓒ Ⓓ Ⓔ
164. Ⓐ Ⓑ Ⓒ Ⓓ Ⓔ
165. Ⓐ Ⓑ Ⓒ Ⓓ Ⓔ
166. Ⓐ Ⓑ Ⓒ Ⓓ Ⓔ
167. Ⓐ Ⓑ Ⓒ Ⓓ Ⓔ
168. Ⓐ Ⓑ Ⓒ Ⓓ Ⓔ
169. Ⓐ Ⓑ Ⓒ Ⓓ Ⓔ
170. Ⓐ Ⓑ Ⓒ Ⓓ Ⓔ
171. Ⓐ Ⓑ Ⓒ Ⓓ Ⓔ
172. Ⓐ Ⓑ Ⓒ Ⓓ Ⓔ
173. Ⓐ Ⓑ Ⓒ Ⓓ Ⓔ
174. Ⓐ Ⓑ Ⓒ Ⓓ Ⓔ
175. Ⓐ Ⓑ Ⓒ Ⓓ Ⓔ
176. Ⓐ Ⓑ Ⓒ Ⓓ Ⓔ
177. Ⓐ Ⓑ Ⓒ Ⓓ Ⓔ
178. Ⓐ Ⓑ Ⓒ Ⓓ Ⓔ
179. Ⓐ Ⓑ Ⓒ Ⓓ Ⓔ
180. Ⓐ Ⓑ Ⓒ Ⓓ Ⓔ

Section VIII Writing Ability

181. Ⓐ Ⓑ Ⓒ Ⓓ Ⓔ
182. Ⓐ Ⓑ Ⓒ Ⓓ Ⓔ
183. Ⓐ Ⓑ Ⓒ Ⓓ Ⓔ
184. Ⓐ Ⓑ Ⓒ Ⓓ Ⓔ
185. Ⓐ Ⓑ Ⓒ Ⓓ Ⓔ
186. Ⓐ Ⓑ Ⓒ Ⓓ Ⓔ
187. Ⓐ Ⓑ Ⓒ Ⓓ Ⓔ
188. Ⓐ Ⓑ Ⓒ Ⓓ Ⓔ
189. Ⓐ Ⓑ Ⓒ Ⓓ Ⓔ
190. Ⓐ Ⓑ Ⓒ Ⓓ Ⓔ
191. Ⓐ Ⓑ Ⓒ Ⓓ Ⓔ
192. Ⓐ Ⓑ Ⓒ Ⓓ Ⓔ
193. Ⓐ Ⓑ Ⓒ Ⓓ Ⓔ
194. Ⓐ Ⓑ Ⓒ Ⓓ Ⓔ
195. Ⓐ Ⓑ Ⓒ Ⓓ Ⓔ
196. Ⓐ Ⓑ Ⓒ Ⓓ Ⓔ
197. Ⓐ Ⓑ Ⓒ Ⓓ Ⓔ
198. Ⓐ Ⓑ Ⓒ Ⓓ Ⓔ
199. Ⓐ Ⓑ Ⓒ Ⓓ Ⓔ
200. Ⓐ Ⓑ Ⓒ Ⓓ Ⓔ

Sample Test 2

Section I Reading Recall (Passages)

TIME: 15 minutes

DIRECTIONS: This part contains three reading passages. You are to read each one carefully. You will have fifteen minutes to study the three passages. In the next section, you will have twenty minutes to answer questions based on them. When answering the questions, you will *not* be allowed to refer back to the passages.

Passage 1:

The following passage was written in 1964.

The main burden of assuring that the resources of the federal government are well managed falls on relatively few of the five million men and women whom it employs. Under the department and agency heads there are 8,600 political, career, military, and foreign service executives—the top managers and professionals—who exert major influence on the manner in which the rest are directed and utilized. Below their level there are other thousands with assignments of some managerial significance, but we believe that the line of demarcation selected is the best available for our purposes in this attainment.

In addition to Presidential appointees in responsible posts, the 8,600 include the three highest grades under the Classification Act; the three highest grades in the postal field service; comparable grades in the foreign service; general officers in the military service; and similar classes in other special services and in agencies or positions excepted from the Classification Act.

There is no complete inventory of positions or people in federal service at this level. The lack may be explained by separate agency statutes and personnel systems, diffusion among so many special services, and absence of any central point (short of the President himself) with jurisdiction over all upper-level personnel of the government.

This Committee considers establishment and maintenance of a central inventory of these key people and positions to be an elementary necessity, a first step in improved management throughout the Executive Branch.

Top Presidential appointees, about 500 of them, bear the brunt of translating the philosophy and aims of the current administration into practical programs. This group includes the secretaries and assistant secretaries of cabinet departments, agency heads and their deputies, heads and members of boards and commissions with fixed terms, and chiefs and directors of major bureaus, divisions, and services. Appointments to many of these politically sensitive positions are made on recommendation by department or agency heads, but all are presumably responsible to Presidential leadership.

One qualification for office at this level is that there be no basic disagreement with Presidential political philosophy, at least so far as administrative judgments and actions are concerned. Apart from the bi-partisan boards and commissions, these men are normally identified with the political party of the President, or are sympathetic to it, although there are exceptions.

There are four distinguishable kinds of top Presidential appointees, including:

— Those whom the President selects at the outset to establish immediate and effective control over the government (e.g., Cabinet secretaries, agency heads, his own White House staff and Executive Office Personnel).

— Those selected by department and agency heads in order to establish control within their respective organizations (e.g.—assistant secretaries, deputies, assistants to, and major line posts in some bureaus and divisions).

— High-level appointees who—though often requiring clearance through political or interest group channels, or both—must have known scientific or technical competence (e.g.—the Surgeon General, the Commissioner of Education).

— Those named to residual positions traditionally filled on a partisan patronage basis.

These appointees are primarily regarded as policy makers and overseers of policy execution. In practice, however, they usually have substantial responsibilities in line management, often requiring a thorough knowledge of substantive agency programs.

Passage 2:

Under state fair trade acts, a producer or distributor of a good bearing his brand, trademark, or name can prescribe by contract either a minimum or stipulated resale price of that good, depending upon the particular state law. Prior to the passage of the fair trade laws, resale price maintenance agreements were considered illegal because such agreements by a producer with more than one distributor prevent price competition among those distributors. The effect is the same as if the distributors had combined and agreed to fix price.

In late 1963, forty states had fair trade laws; of these, twenty-three had "nonsigner" clauses. According to the nonsigner provision, all resellers are bound by the terms of the resale price maintenance contract signed by any *one* reseller. To be truly effective, a state fair trade law must contain a nonsigner provision; for unless the manufacturer has some control over the noncontracting price-cutter, there can be little effective control by the manufacturer over resale prices. In addition, in late 1963 special legislation in nine states made resale price maintenance with respect to alcoholic beverages either mandatory or subject to control by state liquor control agencies.

Not all branded goods are covered by the fair trade laws. Closeout sales are excepted. Exceptions are made in some of these laws on sales to colleges and libraries. Some make provisions to except damaged goods or those from which the brand or trade names have been removed or obliterated.

An obstacle to the success of fair trade is the fact that cut-price mail-order shipments of goods out of an area which has no fair trade law into a fair trade state cannot be prevented by an enforcement action under the fair trade law of the state into which the goods are shipped. For the buyer takes title to the goods in the location from which the goods are shipped. The mail-order business can thus be used to evade a state fair trade act. Likewise, an advertisement within a fair-trade state of cut prices of goods available in a non-fair-trade area has been judged not to be within the jurisdiction of the state fair trade law. Sales from within a fair-trade state to customers outside the state in a non-fair-trade area cannot, however, be made at cut prices.

Maintaining a fair-trade program is fraught with several legal problems. Responsibility for enforcement falls upon the producer or distributor, who must monitor and take legal action against the price-cutters. Legal enforcement must be continuous, vigorous, and effective; it cannot be selective. An assortment of marketing devices contrived by retailers to evade fair-trade prices, such as the granting of trading stamps in abnormally high volume or the placing of excessive value on the trade-in of durable consumer items, must be dealt with by court action. Further, utilization of fair trade prevents a manufacturer from itself selling in competition with those distributors, either wholesalers or retailers, who are governed by its fair-trade contracts, for the effect of such an arrangement is a horizontal agreement.

Passage 3:

When President Carter signed the synthetic fuels bill on June 30, 1980, he said that passage of the measure, designed to speed production of synthetic oil and gas from the vast U.S. coal and shale reserves, marked "a proud day for America." If all goes according to plan, the United States will be producing two million barrels of synthetic fuels daily by 1992, enough to substantially reduce U.S. dependence on imported oil. It is "the keystone of our national energy policy," he said, which "at last is being put in place."

The bill authorizes:
—Creation of a federally owned corporation, the U.S. Synthetic Fuels Corporation, to encourage production of oil and gas from coal and oil from shale.
—The hiring of up to 300 employees. The corporation's management would be by a seven-member board nominated by the President and confirmed by the U.S. Senate.
—Expenditure of $20 billion to be used by the corporation over the next five years for loans, loan guarantees, and other incentives to private industry to meet, by 1987, a production goal equivalent to 500,000 barrels of oil a day from synthetic sources. Another $68 billion is to be made available—subject to congressional appropriation—over the following seven years to meet the two-million-barrel-a-day goal.

The government's financial backing is intended to help private utilities and pipeline and energy companies borrow funds to build synthetic fuel plants. Hundreds of these firms have indicated their intention to seek the loans. There would be no direct cost to the government unless the projects failed to operate, or the finished product was so expensive that it required a subsidy to be marketed.

The new legislation also provides $5 billion to finance solar energy projects and for conservation measures, such as improved insulation for low-income households.

Speaking at the signing ceremony, President Carter said the measure would help the United States conserve considerably more energy than at present, thus further reducing its dependence on foreign oil. In this connection, he noted that U.S. oil imports have declined by 12.9 percent in the past year, gasoline consumption fell eight percent, and total oil consumption was off by more than nine percent.

Another benefit to be derived from synthetic fuels production is the increased employment it will provide for the nation's work force. A recent study by the Department of Energy found that designing and building a 60,000 barrel-a-day plant for turning coal directly into liquid fuel will take 22 million worker-hours of engineering time. To meet the President's goal of a million barrels of coal-based liquid fuel daily by 1990 would take 17 such plants. This would mean up to 85,000 persons employed at the construction sites by the middle of the 1980s.

Although there are already a few small experimental plants making synthetic gas and oil (including gasohol) in operation in the United States, the first large-scale production is to come from the huge oil-shale deposits underlying the high plains where the states of Colorado, Wyoming, and Utah meet. The Green River formation, a 16,500-square-mile area, contains an estimated 600 billion barrels of recoverable oil, almost as much as the total of proven worldwide oil reserves. A recent congressional study found that about 400 billion barrels of oil could be recovered from this source with existing technology at prices competitive with imported oil—though not without significant technological, economic, environmental and social problems yet to be resolved.

Indeed, the environmental aspects of synthetic fuel production may hamper its development despite the plans of government and industry. The possibility that a large-scale effort would cause massive air pollution and irreparable damage to the Western landscape, as well as deplete scarce water supplies essential for crops and livestock, has raised considerable apprehension, particularly among environmentalists. They contend that increased emphasis on solar energy, along with more energy conservation, would dispel the need for synthetic fuel development. Others believe, however, that the program is too vital to the economy and security of the nation to be postponed or sidetracked. A typical supporter of an all-out effort to produce synthetic fuels is a former governor or Colorado who now heads a business group advocating energy development. In his words, "We have got to face the fact that because our country needs these resources, they must be developed."

If there is still time remaining, review the passages until all 15 minutes have elapsed. You may not turn to any other section of the test.

Section II   Reading Recall (Questions)

TIME: 20 minutes

DIRECTIONS: Answer the following questions referring to information contained in the three passages from Section I. You may *not* turn back to those passages for assistance.

QUESTIONS TO

Passage 1:

1. According to the passage, about how many top managerial professionals work for the federal government?

    (A) five million
    (B) two million
    (C) twenty thousand
    (D) nine thousand
    (E) five hundred

2. No complete inventory exists of positions in the three highest levels of government service because

    (A) no one has bothered to count them
    (B) computers cannot handle all the data
    (C) separate agency personnel systems are used
    (D) the President has never requested such information
    (E) the Classification Act prohibits such a census

3. Top Presidential appointees have as their central responsibility the

    (A) prevention of politically motivated interference with the actions of their agencies
    (B) monitoring of government actions on behalf of the President's own political party
    (C) translation of the aims of the administration into practical programs
    (D) investigation of charges of corruption within the government
    (E) maintenance of adequate controls over the rate of government spending

4. One exception to the general rule that top Presidential appointees must be in agreement with the President's political philosophy may be found in

(A) most cabinet-level officers
(B) members of the White House staff
(C) bi-partisan boards and commissions
(D) those offices filled on a patronage basis
(E) offices requiring scientific or technical expertise

5. Applicants for Presidential appointments are usually identified with or are members of

(A) large corporations
(B) the foreign service
(C) government bureaus
(D) academic circles
(E) the President's political party

6. Appointees that are selected directly by the President include

(A) U.S. marshalls and attorneys
(B) military officers
(C) agency heads
(D) assistant secretaries
(E) congressional committee members

7. Appointees usually have to possess expertise in

(A) line management
(B) military affairs
(C) foreign affairs
(D) strategic planning
(E) constitutional law

8. According to the passage, Presidential appointees are regarded primarily as

(A) political spokesmen
(B) policy makers
(C) staff managers
(D) scientific or technical experts
(E) business executives

9. Appointees selected by department and agency heads include

(A) military men
(B) cabinet secretaries
(C) deputy secretaries
(D) diplomats
(E) residual position holders

10. This passage might have been extracted from a book about all of the following subjects except

(A) public administration
(B) political science
(C) management
(D) government
(E) marketing

QUESTIONS TO

Passage 2:

11. The essential purpose of fair trade legislation is to

    (A) allow manufacturers to stipulate the resale price of a good
    (B) allow manufacturers to bypass distributors in sales to retailers
    (C) provide that manufacturers engage in fair and equal trade with distributors
    (D) allow manufacturers to maintain a fair markup on their goods
    (E) exempt resale items from anti-trust legislation

12. A "nonsigner clause" stipulates that

    (A) all resellers who sign fair trade contracts are bound by them
    (B) all resellers are bound by the terms of the fair trade contract signed by one reseller
    (C) resellers are not bound by law to sign fair trade contracts
    (D) all branded goods are covered by the fair trade legislation
    (E) "nonsigners" are exempt from the provisions of fair trade legislation

13. It can be inferred from the passage that fair trade laws would probably be most welcomed by

    (A) discount stores
    (B) wholesale distributors
    (C) small-volume retailers
    (D) import-export houses
    (E) producers of raw materials

14. A direct obstacle to the success of fair trade laws is that

    (A) not all states have these laws
    (B) not all resellers are bound by the laws
    (C) cut-rate goods can be mailed from a non-fair-trade state
    (D) manufacturers may not avail themselves of all privileges given by the legislation
    (E) loss-leader selling is prohibited

15. Responsibility for enforcing fair trade laws falls on the

    (A) state
    (B) federal government
    (C) courts
    (D) manufacturer
    (E) retailer

16. Categories of goods exempted from fair trade laws include

    (A) pharmaceutical products
    (B) alcoholic beverages
    (C) imports
    (D) items in closeout sale
    (E) private label goods

17. At the time the passage was written, how many states had fair trade laws?

    (A) all states
    (B) about ten
    (C) about twenty
    (D) about thirty
    (E) about forty

18. Methods used by retailers to evade fair trade laws include

   (A) refusing to comply with the law
   (B) dealing with more than one supplier
   (C) giving extra trading stamps
   (D) giving extra discounts
   (E) refusal to deal with the manufacturer

19. It is stated in the passage that fair trade laws are enacted by

   (A) states
   (B) the federal government
   (C) local municipalities
   (D) both states and the federal government
   (E) both states and local municipalities

20. It can be inferred from the passage that fair trade laws

   (A) stimulate competition among retailers
   (B) stifle competition among retailers
   (C) make retailing less profitable
   (D) exempt many goods from legislation
   (E) are inexpensive to maintain and police

QUESTIONS TO

Passage 3:

21. According to the passage, the United States may be producing two million barrels of synthetic fuels daily by the year

   (A) 1985   (D) 1994
   (B) 1989   (E) 2000
   (C) 1992

22. The benefits derived from synthetic fuels production include

   I. energy conservation
   II. increased employment
   III. decreased pollution

   (A) I only
   (B) II only
   (C) I and II only
   (D) II and III only
   (E) I, II, and III

23. Which of the following synthetic fuel sources is (are) mentioned in the passage?

   I. Fossil fuels
   II. Coal
   III. Shale

   (A) I only
   (B) II only
   (C) I and II only
   (D) II and III only
   (E) I, II, and III

24. The synthetie fuels bill provides for funding a U.S. Synthetic Fuels Corporation, over a period of twelve years, in the amount of

(A) $20 billion   (D) $78 billion
(B) $30 billion   (E) $88 billion
(C) $68 billion

25. The legislation provides $5 billion to finance building of

   I. anti-pollution devices
  II. experimental plants
 III. solar energy projects

(A) II only
(B) III only
(C) I and II only
(D) II and III only
(E) I, II, and III

26. It is estimated that the U.S. Synthetic Fuels Corporation will hire up to

(A) 100 employees   (D) 800 employees
(B) 300 employees   (E) 1,200 employees
(C) 500 employees

27. According to the passage, those who favor solar energy over synthetic fuels development include

   I. environmentalists
  II. big business
 III. the U.S. Department of Energy

(A) I only
(B) III only
(C) I and III only
(D) II and III only
(E) I, II, and III

28. Oil shale deposits are concentrated in the states of

   I. Nevada
  II. Wyoming
 III. Utah

(A) I only
(B) III only
(C) I and III only
(D) II and III only
(E) I, II, and III

29. According to the passage, loans to synthetic fuel plants will cost the government nothing unless

(A) solar energy is perfected
(B) inflation reaches 15 percent or more
(C) the projects fail to operate
(D) oil consumption declines
(E) shale deposits are less than estimated

30. According to the passage, which of the following have declined?

    I. U.S. oil imports
   II. Gasoline consumption
 III. Heating fuel consumption

  (A) I only
  (B) II only
  (C) I and II only
  (D) II and III only
  (E) I, II, and III

If there is still time remaining, you may review the questions in this section only.
You may not look at Part A or turn to any other section of the test.

Section III   Problem Solving

TIME: 75 minutes

DIRECTIONS: Solve each of the following problems; then indicate the correct answer on the answer sheet. [On the actual test you will be permitted to use any space available on the examination paper for scratch work.]

NOTE: A figure that appears with a problem is drawn as accurately as possible so as to provide information that may help in answering the question. Numbers in this test are real numbers.

31. A borrower pays 6% interest on the first $500 he borrows and $5\frac{1}{2}$% on the part of the loan in excess of $500. How much interest will the borrower have to pay on a loan of $5,500?

  (A) $275   (D) $305
  (B) $280   (E) $330
  (C) $302.50

32. If $2x - y = 4$, then $6x - 3y$ is

  (A) 4   (D) 10
  (B) 6   (E) 12
  (C) 8

33. The next number in the arithmetical progression 5, 11, 17, . . . is

  (A) 18   (D) 28
  (B) 22   (E) 33
  (C) 23

Use the following graph for questions 34–36.

INSTALLED CAPACITY OF ELECTRIC UTILITY GENERATING PLANTS 1920-1952

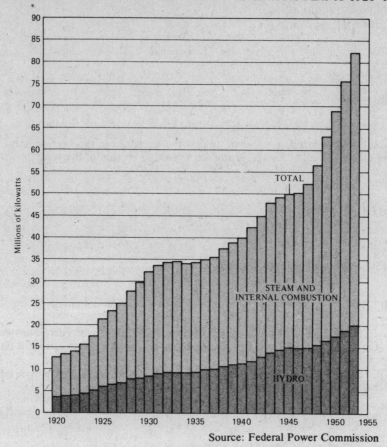

Source: Federal Power Commission

34. In what year did the installed capacity first reach 50 million kilowatts?

(A) 1939
(B) 1944
(C) 1945
(D) 1947
(E) 1950

35. In 1952, the installed capacity of steam and internal combustion plants was about x times the installed capacity of the hydro plants where x is

(A) ½
(B) 1
(C) 2
(D) 3
(E) 4

36. Which of the following statements about the installed capacity of electric utility generating plants between 1920 and 1952 can be inferred from the graph?

I.   In the period 1930–39, there was less of an increase in capacity than in either of the periods 1920–1929 or 1940–1949.
II. More than ⅕ of the capacity in 1925 was produced by hydro plants.
III. The increase in capacity in kilowatts between 1945 and 1952 was greater than the increase between 1925 and 1945.

(A) I only
(B) II only
(C) I and III only
(D) II and III only
(E) I, II, and III

37. A warehouse has 20 packers. Each packer can load ⅛ of a box in 9 minutes. How many boxes can be loaded in 1½ hours by all 20 packers?

(A) 1¼

(B) 10¼

(C) 12½

(D) 20

(E) 25

38. In Motor City 90% of the population owns a car, 15% owns a motorcycle, and everybody owns a car or motorcycle or both. What percent of the population owns a motorcycle but not a car?

(A) 5

(B) 8

(C) 9

(D) 10

(E) 15

Use the following table for questions 39–40.

TABLE 2.—Children under 18 years old, by age group, type of family, labor force status of mother, and race, March 1972

Type of family, labor force status of mother, and race	Number of children (thousands)		
	Under 18 years	Under 6 years	6 to 17 years
Total children	65,255	19,235	46,020
Mother in labor force	25,762	5,607	20,155
Husband-wife family	56,625	17,173	39,452
Mother in labor force	21,722	4,838	16,884
Mother not in labor force	34,903	12,335	22,568
Female family head	7,924	1,977	5,947
Mother in labor force	4,040	769	3,271
Mother not in labor force	3,884	1,208	2,676
Other male family head	706	85	621
White children, total	56,303	16,603	39,700
Mother in labor force	21,539	4,495	17,044
Husband-wife family	50,796	15,409	35,387
Mother in labor force	18,799	4,031	14,768
Mother not in labor force	31,997	11,378	20,619
Female family head	4,967	1,130	3,837
Mother in labor force	2,740	464	2,276
Mother not in labor force	2,227	666	1,561
Other male family head	540	64	476
Negro children, total	8,093	2,345	5,748
Mother in labor force	3,855	999	2,856
Husband-wife family	5,078	1,504	3,574
Mother in labor force	2,609	707	1,902
Mother not in labor force	2,469	797	1,672
Female family head	2,855	821	2,034
Mother in labor force	1,246	292	954
Mother not in labor force	1,609	529	1,080
Other male family head	160	20	140

Source: Social Security Bulletin

39. Approximately how many children between the ages of 6 to 17 did not have mothers in the labor force in 1972?

   (A) 20,000,000
   (B) 26,000,000
   (C) 28,000,000
   (D) 30,000,000
   (E) 46,000,000

40. Roughly x percent of the Negro children under 6 years of age had mothers in the labor force, where x is

   (A) 30
   (B) 35
   (C) 40
   (D) 50
   (E) 55

41. A chair originally cost $50.00. The chair was offered for sale at 108% of its cost. After a week the price was discounted 10% and the chair was sold. The chair was sold for

   (A) $45.00
   (B) $48.60
   (C) $49.00
   (D) $49.40
   (E) $54.00

42. A worker is paid x dollars for the first 8 hours he works each day. He is paid y dollars per hour for each hour he works in excess of 8 hours. During one week he works 8 hours on Monday, 11 hours on Tuesday, 9 hours on Wednesday, 10 hours on Thursday, and 9 hours on Friday. What is his average daily wage in dollars for the five day week?

   (A) $x + \dfrac{7}{5}y$
   (B) $2x + y$
   (C) $\dfrac{5x + 8y}{5}$
   (D) $x + 2y$
   (E) $5x + 7y$

43. What is the area of a rectangular field which is 25 yards wide and 50 yards long?

   (A) 625 square yards
   (B) 1,000 square yards
   (C) 1,250 square yards
   (D) 1600 square yards
   (E) 2,500 square yards

Use the chart below for questions 44–47.

CHANGE IN POPULATION OF THE UNITED STATES BETWEEN 1940 AND 1950

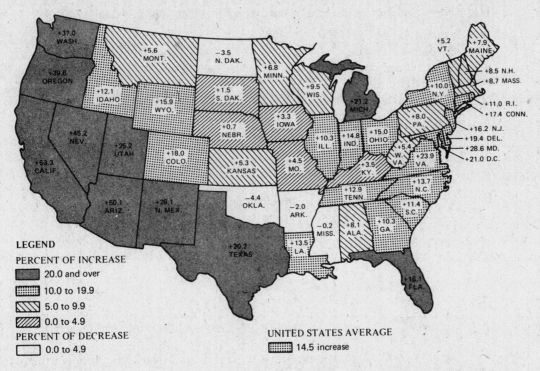

LEGEND

PERCENT OF INCREASE

20.0 and over

10.0 to 19.9

5.0 to 9.9

0.0 to 4.9

PERCENT OF DECREASE

0.0 to 4.9

UNITED STATES AVERAGE

14.5 increase

Source: Department of Commerce, Bureau of the Census

44. Which state had the largest percentage of increase in population between 1940 and 1950?

(A) Arizona
(B) Arkansas
(C) California

(D) Florida
(E) Maine

45. How many states had population decreases between 1940 and 1950?

(A) 1
(B) 2
(C) 3

(D) 4
(E) 5

46. If the population of the United States in 1940 was 100 million, then the population of the United States in 1950 was approximately

(A) 100 million
(B) 105 million
(C) 110 million

(D) 115 million
(E) 120 million

47. Which of the following statements about population changes between 1940 and 1950 can be inferred from the graph?

    I.   Less than 6 states had population increases of ⅓ or more.
   II. The number of people living in Oregon in 1950 was larger than the number of people living in Washington.
  III. The population of Nebraska was larger in 1950 than it was in 1940.

    (A) I only
    (B) III only
    (C) I and III only
    (D) II and III only
    (E) I, II and III

48. If 12 apples cost 63¢, how much should 4 apples cost?

    (A) 19¢   (D) 31¢
    (B) 21¢   (E) 32¢
    (C) 25¢

49. A car costs $2,500 when it is brand new. At the end of each year it is worth $\frac{4}{5}$ of what it was at the beginning of the year. What is the car worth when it is 3 years old?

    (A) $1,000   (D) $1,340
    (B) $1,200   (E) $1,430
    (C) $1,280

Use the following table for questions 50–52.

Type of vehicle	Cost of fuel for 500-mile trip
Automobile	$15
Motorcycle	$ 5
Bus	$20
Truck	$50
Airplane	$70

50. What is the cost of fuel for a 300-mile trip by automobile?

    (A) $5   (D) $15
    (B) $9   (E) $30
    (C) $12

51. If the wages of a bus driver for a 500-mile trip are $70, and the only costs for a bus are the fuel and the driver's wages, how much should a bus company charge to charter a bus and driver for a 500-mile trip in order to obtain 120% of the cost?

(A) $24
(B) $90
(C) $94

(D) $104
(E) $108

52. If 3 buses, 4 automobiles, 2 motorcycles, and one truck each make a 500-mile trip, what is the average fuel cost per vehicle?

(A) $5
(B) $15
(C) $18

(D) $20
(E) $24

53. If $x + 2y = 2x + y$, then $x - y$ is equal to

(A) 0
(B) 2
(C) 4

(D) 5
(E) none of the preceding

54. 15% of the families in state x have an income of $25,000 or more. $\frac{2}{3}$ of the families with income of $25,000 or more in state x own a boat. What fraction of the families own a boat and have an income of $25,000 or more in state x?

(A) $\frac{1}{15}$
(B) $\frac{1}{12}$
(C) $\frac{1}{10}$

(D) $\frac{4}{21}$
(E) $\frac{9}{40}$

55. If the angles of a triangle are in the ratio 1:2:2, then the triangle

(A) is isosceles
(B) is obtuse
(C) is a right triangle

(D) is equilateral
(E) has one angle greater than 80°

Use the following graphs for questions 56–60.

U.S. DEFENSE EXPENDITURES ABROAD
BY MAJOR CATEGORIES

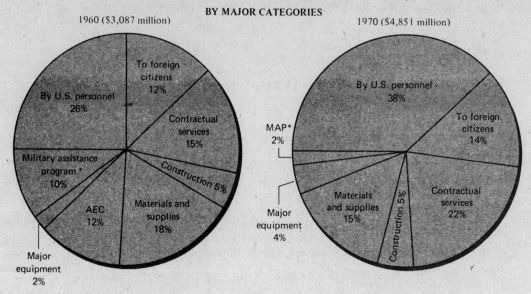

1960 ($3,087 million)   1970 ($4,851 million)

BY MAJOR COUNTRIES AND AREAS

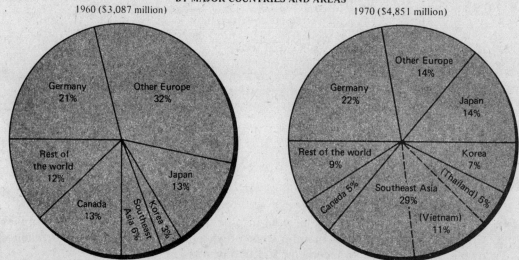

1960 ($3,087 million)   1970 ($4,851 million)

* Includes NATO Infrastructure

Source: U.S. Department of Commerce, Bureau of Economic Analysis

56. In 1970, $x was spent in Canada for defense where x is about

(A) 200 million
(B) 230 million
(C) 240 million
(D) 250 million
(E) 260 million

57. In 1960, what fraction of defense expenditures was used in all for the Military Assistance Program, AEC, and materials and supplies?

(A) $^3/_{10}$
(B) $^7/_{20}$
(C) $^{39}/_{100}$
(D) $^2/_5$
(E) $^{11}/_{25}$

58. Which of the following countries received the least amount of defense expenditures in 1970?

(A) Germany   (D) Korea
(B) Japan   (E) Thailand
(C) Vietnam

59. If $\frac{5}{7}$ of the defense expenditures in Europe other than Germany was spent in Spain, about how much was spent in Spain in 1970?

(A) $308 million   (D) $750 million
(B) $485 million   (E) $1,200 million
(C) $550 million

60. Which of the following statements about direct expenditures abroad for goods and services can be inferred from the graphs?

   I. In both 1960 and 1970, more than $\frac{1}{5}$ of the expenditures was spent in Germany.
   II. The total amount of expenditures increased by more than $\frac{1}{3}$ between 1960 and 1970.
   III. More than $\frac{2}{5}$ of the total expenditures for 1960 and 1970 together was spent by U.S. personnel.

(A) I only
(B) II only
(C) I and II only
(D) II and III only
(E) I, II, and III

61. If a car travels at a constant rate of 60 miles per hour, how long will it take to travel 255 miles?

(A) $3\frac{3}{4}$ hours   (D) $4\frac{1}{4}$ hours
(B) 4 hours   (E) $4\frac{1}{2}$ hours
(C) $4\frac{1}{8}$ hours

62. A car travels 15 miles on a gallon of gas but after a tune-up the car uses only $\frac{3}{4}$ as much gas as before. How many miles will the car travel on a gallon of gas after the tune-up?

(A) 15   (D) $18\frac{2}{3}$
(B) $16\frac{1}{2}$ (E) 20
(C) $17\frac{1}{2}$

63. Successive discounts of 20% and 15% are equal to a single discount of

(A) 30%   (D) 35%
(B) 32%   (E) 36%
(C) 34%

Use the following graphs for questions 64–67.

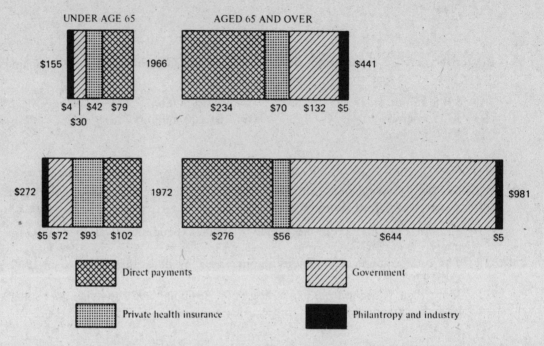

PER CAPITA PERSONAL HEALTH CARE EXPENDITURES

Source: Social Security Bulletin

64. If there were about 20 million people 65 and over in 1966, how much did the government spend on personal health care for people aged 65 and over in 1966?

(A) $26 million
(B) $264 million
(C) $2 billion

(D) $2.640 billion
(E) $3.6 billion

65. Between 1966 and 1972, the per capita amount spent by the government on personal health care for those under age 65 increased by *x*% where *x* is

(A) 100
(B) 120
(C) 140

(D) 220
(E) 240

66. In 1972, the fraction contributed by philanthropy and industry towards expenditures for personal health care for those aged 65 and over was about

(A) $\frac{1}{500}$
(B) $\frac{1}{196}$
(C) $\frac{1}{99}$

(D) $\frac{1}{88}$
(E) $\frac{2}{101}$

67. Which of the following statements about expenditures for personal health care between 1966 and 1972 can be inferred from the graphs?

    I.   The total amount spent for those aged 65 and over in 1972 was more than
3 times as much as the total amount spent on those under 65.

    II. Between 1966 and 1972, the amount spent per capita by those aged 65 and
over increased in each of the four categories (direct payments, government,
private health insurance, philanthropy).

    III. The government paid more than $\frac{1}{2}$ of the amount of expenditures for those
aged 65 and over in 1972.

    (A) I only
    (B) II only
    (C) III only
    (D) I and III only
    (E) II and III only

68. Oranges cost $1.00 for a crate containing 20 oranges. If oranges are sold for 6¢ each,
what percent of the selling price is the profit?

    (A) 5%   (D) 20%
    (B) 10%   (E) 25%
    (C) $16\frac{2}{3}$%

69. A hen lays $7\frac{1}{2}$ dozen eggs during the summer. There are 93 days in the summer
and it costs $10 to feed the hen for the summer. How much does it cost in food for
each egg produced?

    (A) 10¢   (D) $13\frac{1}{13}$¢
    (B) $11\frac{1}{9}$¢   (E) 15¢
    (C) $12\frac{3}{13}$¢

70. If the diameter of a circle has length d, the radius length r, and the area equals a,
then which of the following statements are true?

    I. $a = \pi d^2$
    II. $d = 2r$
    III. $\dfrac{a}{d} = \pi \dfrac{r}{2}$

    (A) only II
    (B) I and II only
    (C) I and III only
    (D) II and III only
    (E) I, II, and III

Use the following graph for questions 71–74.

SOCIAL WELFARE EXPENDITURES

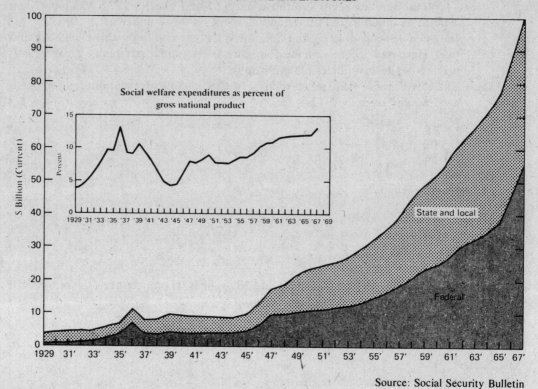

Source: Social Security Bulletin

71. During the period from 1929 to 1944 in what year were social welfare expenditures the highest?

(A) 1933   (D) 1939
(B) 1935   (E) 1944
(C) 1936

72. The Gross National Product in 1958 was about

(A) $100 billion   (D) $450 billion
(B) $200 billion   (E) $600 billion
(C) $300 billion

73. In 1957, the federal government spent about *x* times as much as state and local governments on social welfare, where *x* is

(A) ¼   (D) 2
(B) ½   (E) 3
(C) 1

74. Which of the following statements about social welfare expenditures can be inferred from the graph?

   I. The percentage of Gross National Product spent on social welfare decreased between 1939 and 1943.

  II. The state and local governments never spent more than $60 billion on social welfare in any of the years between 1929 and 1967.

 III. Between 1929 and 1933, the state and local government spent more on social welfare than did the federal government.

(A) I only
(B) II only
(C) I and III only
(D) II and III only
(E) I, II, and III

75. If hose A can fill up a tank in 20 minutes, and hose B can fill up the same tank in 15 minutes, how long will it take for the hoses together to fill up the tank?

(A) 5 minutes
(B) $7\frac{1}{2}$ minutes
(C) $8\frac{4}{7}$ minutes
(D) $9\frac{2}{7}$ minutes
(E) 12 minutes

76. If 5 men take 2 hours to dig a ditch, how long will it take 12 men to dig the ditch?

(A) 45 minutes
(B) 50 minutes
(C) 54 minutes
(D) 60 minutes
(E) 84 minutes

Use the following table for questions 77–79.

Car Production at Plant T for One Week

	Number of cars produced	Total daily wages
MONDAY	900	$30,000
TUESDAY	1200	$40,000
WEDNESDAY	1500	$52,000
THURSDAY	1400	$50,000
FRIDAY	1000	$32,000

77. What was the average number of cars produced per day for the week shown?

(A) 1,000
(B) 1,140
(C) 1,180
(D) 1,200
(E) 1,220

78. What was the average cost in wages per car produced for the week?

(A) $25
(B) $26
(C) $29
(D) $32
(E) $34

79. Which of the following statements about the production of cars and the wages paid for the week can be inferred from the table?

  I. $\frac{1}{4}$ of the cars were produced on Wednesday.
  II. More employees came to the plant on Friday than on Monday.
  III. $\frac{2}{5}$ of the days accounted for $\frac{1}{2}$ the wages paid for the week.

  (A) I only
  (B) II only
  (C) I and II only
  (D) I and III only
  (E) I, II, and III

80. How many rectangular plots 40 yards long by 30 yards wide can be obtained from a field which is a square with sides 1200 yards long?

  (A) 100   (D) 1200
  (B) 120   (E) 14000
  (C) 1000

81. A train travels from Cleveland to Toledo in 2 hours and 10 minutes. If the distance from Cleveland to Toledo is 150 miles, then the average speed of the train is about

  (A) 60 mph   (D) 72 mph
  (B) 66 mph   (E) 75 mph
  (C) 70 mph

82. If $x > 2$ and $y > -1$, then

  (A) $xy > -2$ (D) $-x > 2y$
  (B) $-x < 2y$ (E) $x < 2y$
  (C) $xy < -2$

83. What is the area of the rectangle $ABCD$, if the length of AC is 5 and the length of AD is 4?

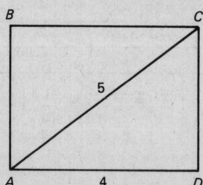

  (A) 3   (D) 15
  (B) 6   (E) 20
  (C) 12

84. If electricity costs k¢ an hour, heat $\$d$ an hour, and water w¢ an hour, how much will all three cost for 12 hours?

(A) $12(k + d + w)$¢

(B) $\$(12k + 12d + 12w)$

(C) $\$(k + 100d + w)$

(D) $\$\left(12k + \dfrac{12d}{100} + 12w\right)$

(E) $\$(.12k + 12d + .12w)$

85. If $x = y = 2z$ and $x \cdot y \cdot z = 256$, then x equals

(A)   2

(B) $2\sqrt[3]{2}$

(C)   4

(D) $4\sqrt[3]{2}$

(E)   8

If there is still time remaining, you may review the questions in this section only.
You may not turn to any other section of the test.

Section IV   Practical Judgment

TIME: 20 minutes

DIRECTIONS: Read the following passage. After you have completed it, you will be asked to answer two sets of questions. The first of these, data evaluation, involves determining the importance of specific factors included in the passage. The second, data application, consists of general questions relating to the passage. When answering questions, you may consult the passage.

Bill Kamil was director of Tibland's national lottery. The lottery had been established twenty years before to raise funds for health, education, and welfare projects. It was owned by the state and supervised by a board of directors selected from among leading businessmen, professional people such as lawyers and educators, and government officials. Throughout its history, lottery sales had increased faster than the annual growth of population and about 20 percent faster than the annual rate of inflation. However, during the last two years, sales—while increasing—had grown at a decreasing rate. Kamil was concerned that, should this trend continue, sales would soon level off, or even decrease. He therefore called a meeting of his staff, including Fred Fishman, Marketing Manager; Arnold Fox, Operations Manager; and Ron Davis, Statistician. Fishman was responsible for the lottery program, changes in prizes, new products, pricing policy, and advertising. Fox was responsible for the distribution of lottery tickets to dealers, collection of ticket sales, and the maintenance of sales booths. Davis's main duties involved preparing monthly statistical reports on lottery sales and data analysis.

Tibland's lottery consisted of three games. The most widely played of the three was a weekly game. All the participant had to do was purchase a ticket printed with a five-digit number. Every Monday a lottery was held wherein a computer selected the winning numbers at random. In a second game, the participant checked a series of numbers in boxes printed on a standard form. He or she might choose a birthdate, his or her children's ages, or any random series of numbers. Winning numbers were also selected at random by a computer. The third game was an instant lottery. Participants scraped off the foil on part of a card which revealed a series of numbers, symbols, or pictures, depending upon the game. Winning tickets were those that contained four of a kind (first prize), three of a kind (second prize), or two of a kind (third prize).

Top on the agenda of Kamil's staff meeting was a discussion of how sales of all lottery games could be increased. Kamil especially drew the staff's attention to a sales report prepared by Ron Davis.

Lottery Sales
(100,000 units of local currency)

Year	Weekly	Lottery Lotto	Instant	Total Sales
1961	38	—	—	38
1966	111	—	—	111
1971	136	31	—	167
1976	278	174	—	452
1977	356	233	—	589
1978	467	351	78	896
1979	616	494	142	1,252
1980	822	623	140	1,585

The report showed that total lottery sales in monetary units had increased every year. However, the rate of increase had declined since 1978. Ron Davis pointed out that Lotto sales had tapered off more than those of the weekly lottery. Instant lottery sales had actually declined slightly in 1980, and early sales returns for 1981 showed a similar downward trend. In all three games, the *number* of tickets sold had declined. If the trend continued, lottery sales growth in real terms (discounted for inflation) would be negative.

Kamil requested his staff to suggest alternative courses of action that would result in (1) an *annual* increase in the sales of all three games of not less than 30 percent, (2) a ten-percent increase in the number of tickets sold, and (3) the introduction of four new instant games every year. The following discussion ensued.

Fishman: Stagnating lottery sales are owing to bad publicity surrounding the introduction of the instant game in 1978. Initially, there were many buyers who even waited on long lines to purchase tickets. Media coverage of this frantic period was extensive, but negative. Rather than emphasize the positive aspects of the lottery, the news media pointed out that most of the purchasers seemed to be members of the lower social classes. We must do all we can to stimulate sales among upper income groups.

Fox: It wasn't the media that lowered sales, but simply that the initial enthusiasm wore off. Prizes are much smaller in the instant lottery compared to the weekly, even though the ticket prices of both are nearly the same. Participants feel that they are not getting their money's worth from the instant game.

Davis: There may be a third factor. Many people who were regular purchasers of weekly lottery tickets tried the instant game. Those who were disappointed with the instant game may have stopped purchasing other lottery games as well. This would explain the decrease in the number of tickets sold.

Fishman: An increase in sales of all lottery games can be made possible by, first, attracting new buyers, and, second, increasing the rate of purchase of existing buyers. According to a recent survey, the "non buyers" of most lottery games are mainly upper-income, professional people. We can best reach these people through a direct-mail compaign. One possibility is to sell them ticket subscriptions. Instead of buying one or a few tickets at a time of a single lottery, we should offer them a half year's subscription to the weekly lottery. Subscriptions can be paid for through the mail, at great convenience to the consumer.

Fox: Subscriptions might be the answer to the weekly lottery, but they will not work for the instant and Lotto games. Moreover, a six-month subscription would cost $52. Not enough people will pay such a sum in advance. Costs for printing special tickets and circulating them through the mail would be greater than the costs of our present distribution method.

Davis: We want to reach upper-income groups; they will be willing to pay for the convenience of subscribing to a series of lotteries in advance, without having to purchase tickets at a retail outlet. Present buyers who do not choose to subscribe may continue to purchase tickets at retail locations.

Fishman: Subscription sales work well in Germany and a few other European countries. I do not believe there is any difference between purchases in those countries and Tibland. People buy lottery tickets for two reasons: for the fun of playing, and to fulfill some sort of dream that only a large sum of money can make real. These motives are universal.

Fox: Subscriptions may induce non-buyers to purchase lottery tickets, but sales of the instant game and Lotto will not increase. We must increase advertising expenditures by at least fifty percent to stimulate sales. I have been in this business for twenty years. Based on my experience, advertising has always been the key to sales.

Davis: We have to operate within a budget. We do not have sufficient resources to undertake a subscription campaign, while at the same time increasing advertising expenditures by fifty percent. We may also be criticized by consumer councils for spending so much of our income on advertising, rather than allocating it to public projects.

Fishman: Let's consider trying to increase sales by making the games more attractive. For instance, we could immediately institute a plan to introduce new instant games every six weeks. The Lotto game could also be improved by adding a consolation prize. These changes would do more to stimulate sales than an increase in advertising. It is the product that counts, not the advertising.

Data Evaluation Questions

DIRECTIONS: The questions that follow relate to the preceding passage. Evaluate, in terms of the passage, each of the items given. Then select your answer from one of the following classifications, and blacken the corresponding space on the answer sheet.

(A) A MAJOR OBJECTIVE in making the decision: one of the goals sought by the decision maker

(B) A MAJOR FACTOR in making the decision: an aspect of the problem, specifically mentioned in the passage, that fundamentally affects and/or determines the decision

(C) A MINOR FACTOR in making the decision: a less important element bearing on or affecting a Major Factor, rather than a Major Objective directly

(D) A MAJOR ASSUMPTION in making the decision: a projection or supposition arrived at by the decision maker before considering the factors and alternatives

(E) AN UNIMPORTANT ISSUE in making the decision: an item lacking significant impact on, or relationship to, the decision

86. Fox's years of experience in the lottery business

87. Increasing the number of lottery games

88. Stagnating lottery sales

89. Cost of an advertising campaign

90. Increasing lottery sales by 30 percent

91. Number of tickets likely to be sold under each alternative

92. Predominance of members of the lower classes among purchasers of instant lottery tickets

93. Existence of lotteries in Tibland for the past twenty years

94. Printing costs for subscription tickets

95. Similarity of motives of purchasers of lottery tickets in Tibland and in Europe

96. Likelihood of stimulating sales through advertising

97. Attracting new buyers of lotteries

98. Amount of money available in the budget

99. Cost of proposed subscriptions to the weekly lottery game

100. Socio-economic status of members of the board of directors

Data Application Questions

DIRECTIONS: Answer each of the following questions using information contained in the passage.

101. Total lottery sales in monetary units had

  I. increased every year
  II. increased in real terms
  III. decreased in 1980

  (A) I only
  (B) III only
  (C) I and II only
  (D) II and III only
  (E) I, II, and III

102. Kamil's objectives for lottery games included

  I. a 30% annual increase in sales
  II. a 10% increase in tickets sold
  III. four new instant games per year

  (A) I only
  (B) III only
  (C) I and II only
  (D) II and III only
  (E) I, II, and III

103. According to Fishman, sales of lottery games could be increased by

  I. attracting new buyers
  II. lowering the price of tickets
  III. increasing advertising expenditures

  (A) I only
  (B) III only
  (C) I and II only

   (D) II and III only
   (E) I, II, and III

104. Fox was responsible for

   I. statistical reports
   II. distribution of lottery tickets
   III. maintenance of sales booths

   (A) I only
   (B) III only
   (C) I and II only
   (D) II and III only
   (E) I, II, and III

105. Davis was opposed to increasing advertising expenditures because of

   I. the lack of financial resources
   II. possible criticism by consumer groups
   III. the high cost of advertising media

   (A) I only
   (B) III only
   (C) I and II only
   (D) II and III only
   (E) I, II, and III

If there is still time remaining, you may review the questions in this section only.
You may not turn to any other section of the test.

Section V   Data Sufficiency

TIME: 15 minutes

DIRECTIONS: Each of the following problems has a question and two statements which are labeled (1) and (2). Use the data given in (1) and (2) together with other available information (such as the number of hours in a day, the definition of *clockwise,* mathematical facts, etc.) to decide whether the statements are *sufficient* to answer the question. Then fill in space

  (A) if you can get the answer from (1) alone but not from (2) alone;

  (B) if you can get the answer from (2) alone but not from (1) alone;

  (C) if you can get the answer from (1) and (2) together, although neither statement by itself suffices;

  (D) if statement (1) alone suffices *and* statement (2) alone suffices;

  (E) if you cannot get the answer from statements (1) and (2) together, but need even more data.

All numbers used in this section are real numbers. A figure given for a problem is intended to provide information consistent with that in the question, but not necessarily with the additional information contained in the statements.

106. Is x greater than y?

  (1) $3x = 2k$
  (2) $k = y^2$

107. Is *ABCD* a parallelogram?

(1) $AB = CD$
(2) *AB* is parallel to *CD*.

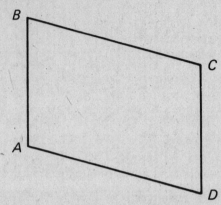

108. What was Mr. Smith's combined income for the years 1965–1970? In 1965 he made $10,000.

(1) His average yearly income for the years 1965–1970 was $12,000.
(2) In 1970, his income was $20,000.

109. How much profit did Walker's Emporium make selling dresses?

(1) Each dress cost $10.
(2) 600 dresses were sold.

110. *k* is a positive integer. Is *k* a prime number?

(1) No integer between 2 and $\sqrt{k}$ inclusive divides *k* evenly.

(2) No integer between 2 and $\frac{k}{2}$ inclusive divides *k* evenly, and *k* is greater than 5.

111. The towns *A, B,* and *C* lie on a straight line. *C* is between *A* and *B*. The distance from *A* to *B* is 100 miles. How far is it from *A* to *C*?

(1) The distance from *A* to *B* is 25% more than the distance from *C* to *B*.
(2) The distance from *A* to *C* is ¼ of the distance from *C* to *B*.

112. Is *AB* perpendicular to *CD*?

(1) $AC = BD$
(2) $x = y$

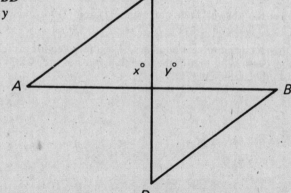

113. What is the value of $x - y$?

    (1) $x + 2y = 6$
    (2) $x = y$

114. The number of eligible voters is 100,000. How many eligible voters voted?

    (1)   63% of the eligible men voted.
    (2)   67% of the eligible women voted.

115. If $z = 50$, find the value of x.

    (1) $RS \neq ST$
    (2) $x + y = 60$

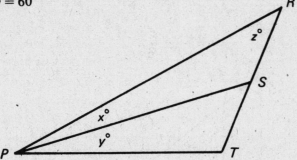

116. How much was the original cost of a car which sold for $2300?

    (1)   The car was sold for a discount of 10% from its original cost.
    (2)   The sales tax was $150.

117. The hexagon $ABCDEF$ is inscribed in the circle with center O. What is the length of AB?

    (1)   The radius of the circle is 4 inches.
    (2)   The hexagon is a regular hexagon.

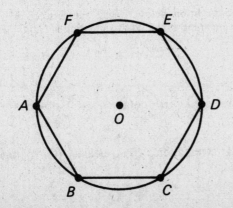

118. How many rolls of wallpaper are necessary to cover the walls of a room whose floor and ceiling are rectangles 12 feet wide and 15 feet long?

    (1) A roll of wallpaper covers 20 square feet.
    (2) There are no windows in the walls.

119. What is the average daily wage of a worker who works five days? He made $80 the first day.

    (1) The worker made a total of $400 for the first four days of work.
    (2) The worker made 20% more each day then he did on the previous day.

120. Is ABC a right triangle? $AB = 5$; $AC = 4$.

    (1) $BC = 3$
    (2) $AC = CD$

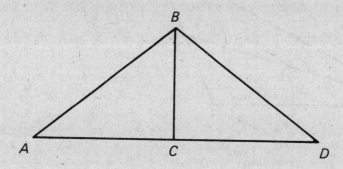

If there is still time remaining, you may review the questions in this section only. You may not turn to any other section of the test.

Section VI   Verbal Ability

TIME: 20 minutes

Antonyms

DIRECTIONS: For each question below, select the lettered word or phrase that comes closest to being *opposite* in meaning to the word appearing in capital letters. Be sure to consider all meanings carefully.

121. ABSTRUSE: (A) detested (B) detained (C) obvious (D) tight (E) rebuilt

122. COAGULATE: (A) strengthen (B) release (C) plunge (D) dissipate (E) prepare

123. PROCLIVITY: (A) proposition (B) propensity (C) aversion (D) activity (E) delay

124. TACIT: (A) late (B) open (C) brash (D) skilled (E) indiscreet

125. VORACIOUS: (A) bellicose (B) powerful (C) sated (D) inclined (E) stoic

126. SAGACIOUS: (A) fat (B) stupid (C) happy (D) unwelcome (E) irrational

127. RETICENT: (A) repellent (B) related (C) communicative (D) truthful (E) repetitious

128. FECUND: (A) barren (B) timid (C) sinister (D) determined (E) awful

129. FURTIVE: (A) active (B) expected (C) overt (D) abetting (E) fearful

130. INCLEMENT: (A) incipient (B) inevitable (C) new (D) mild (E) contrary

131. NOTORIOUS: (A) wicked (B) enigmatic (C) respected (D) open (E) political

132. DILATE: (A) darken (B) contract (C) remedy (D) include (E) concentrate

133. BOISTEROUS: (A) peaceful (B) undaunted (C) covert (D) auspicious (E) fatal

134. ECLECTIC: (A) agnostic (B) narrow (C) habitual (D) incisive (E) impulsive

Word-Pair Relationships

DIRECTIONS: For each question below, determine the relationship between the pair of capitalized words and then select the lettered pair of words which have a similar relationship to the first pair.

135. SAMPLE : UNIVERSE :: (A) plan : research (B) individual : population (C) mathematics : statistics (D) element : electron (E) tactic : strategy

136. CARBOHYDRATES : OBESITY :: (A) aversion : regression (B) sugar : cavities (C) pressure : extrusion (D) hostility : war (E) sickness : hospital

137. PROMISE : FULFILL :: (A) pawn : redeem (B) pledge : deny (C) law : enforce (D) confession : hedge (E) prisoner : release

138. ADDICTED : DEDICATED :: (A) slavish : kindly (B) fanatical : enthusiastic (C) acute : chronic (D) temporary : permanent (E) habitual : continuous

139. RECALL : REMEMBER :: (A) counterfeit : forge (B) behave : reenact (C) construct : terminate (D) predict : prove (E) believe : recant

140. ABUNDANCE : LUXURY :: (A) silence : stealth (B) humility : pretension (C) poverty : indigence (D) pilot : plane (E) wealth : miserliness

141. TOKEN : TURNSTILE :: (A) words : telegram (B) coin : telephone (C) gasoline : automobile (D) road : toll (E) profession : license

142. FUEL : PIPES :: (A) blood : veins (B) food : stomach (C) wood : trees (D) cars : expressway (E) power : generator

143. EXEMPTION : RULE :: (A) debarment : prevention (B) immunity : disease (C) forgiveness : crime (D) exile : nation (E) enclosure : gate

144. INDIGENOUS : FOREIGN :: (A) indifferent : interested (B) resident : nomadic (C) native : extraneous (D) partial : whole (E) local : universal

145. EFFICACIOUS : INEFFECTUAL :: (A) efficient : incompetent (B) effective : effortless (C) correct : faulty (D) legal : criminal (E) successful : attempted

146. EIGHT : OCTAVE :: (A) note : music (B) ten : meter (C) eight : quart (D) thousand : millenium (E) foot : yard

147. ARROW : TARGET :: (A) bat : glove (B) diver : water (C) tactic : objective (D) movement : destination (E) puck : stick

Sentence Completions

DIRECTIONS: For each sentence below, select the lettered word or set of words which, when inserted in the sentence blanks, best completes the meaning of that sentence.

148. We strongly favor fair ____ to victims of manufacturing defects, despite the financial costs it involves.

    (A) play (B) compensation (C) probity (D) apology (E) instruction

149. The ____ of a man might well be measured by his ____ of himself.

    (A) humility . . . opinion (B) weight . . . estimation (C) education . . . value (D) value . . . picture (E) ability . . . judgment

150. It was the practice for the President to offer a full ____ to political prisoners on the national holiday.

    (A) proclamation (B) defense (C) acquittal (D) pardon (E) expulsion

151. Police, prepared for a long ____, held a ____ on the street.

    (A) discussion . . . rally (B) seige . . . meeting (C) time . . . gathering (D) intercession . . . suspect (E) strike . . . trial

152. The meeting between the two was ____ with ____ significance.

    (A) begun . . . extraneous (B) complicated . . . no (C) fraught . . . historical (D) ended . . . reciprocal (E) described . . . little

153. It was not a(n) ____ beginning for the new railroad, as two trains ____.

    (A) early . . . were late (B) bad . . . were on time (C) auspicious . . . collided (D) inadequate . . . stalled (E) plausible . . . failed

154. Although the character of Sherlock Holmes has its ____ antecedents, the primary inspiration for its creation came from a(n) ____ person.

    (A) literary . . . actual (B) historical . . . real (C) dubious . . . original (D) fictional . . . unusual (E) reputed . . . famous

155. Medical frauds have always found a(n) ____ reception among the ignorant and ____.

    (A) hostile . . . naive (B) favorable . . . credulous (C) skeptical . . . educated (D) thoughtful . . . gullible (E) positive . . . wealthy

156. It was the first time the hostile parties had met since the _____ effort to _____ an accord last year.

(A) prohibitory . . . announce (B) reciprocal . . . purchase (C) abortive . . . reach (D) last . . convey (E) successful . . . establish

157. Like the United States, England was forced by economic events to embrace a program of _____ restraints, despite past pronouncements espousing less _____ in the economy.

(A) financial . . . change (B) voluntary . . . optimism (C) compulsory . . . intervention (D) fiscal . . . waste (E) temporary . . . freedom

158. Despite the existence of _____ difficulties with the hypothesis, experimenters have found it _____ as an instrument of prediction.

(A) theoretical . . . useful (B) numerous . . . invalid (C) practical . . . questionable (D) logical . . . costly (E) several . . . unreliable

159. Although he was once very loquacious, old age has made him less and less _____.

(A) lazy (B) independent (C) talkative (D) eloquent (E) tormented

160. The development of agriculture and that of industry act and react on each other; they are complementary, not _____.

(A) redundant (B) concentrated (C) associated (D) competitive (E) organized

If there is still time remaining, you may review the questions in this section only.
You may not turn to any other section of the test.

Section VII Practical Judgment

TIME: 20 minutes

DIRECTIONS: Read the following passage. After you have completed it, you will be asked to answer two sets of questions. The first of these, data evaluation, involves determining the importance of specific factors included in the passage. The second, data application, consists of general questions relating to the passage. When answering questions, you may consult the passage.

In 1967 Mr. Ed Carswell, a chemical engineer, began experimenting in his spare time with a new method for processing fresh orange juice. By 1970, he had perfected the process to such an extent that he was ready to begin production in a small way. His process enabled him to extract 18 percent more juice from oranges than was typically extracted by a pressure juicer of the type currently used in cafes. His process also removed some of the bitterness which got into the juice from the peelings when oranges were squeezed without peeling them.

Since many of the better quality restaurants preferred to serve fresh orange juice instead of canned or frozen juice, Mr. Carswell believed he could find a ready market for his product.

Another appeal of his product would be that he could maintain more consistent juice flavor than haphazard restaurant juicing usually produced.

Mr. Carswell patented the process and then started production. Since his capital was limited, he began production in a small building which previously had been a woodworking shop. With the help of his brother, Mr. Carswell marketed the juice through local restaurants. The juice was distributed in glass jugs, which proved to be rather expensive because of high breakage. The new product was favorably accepted by the public, however, and the business proved to be a success.

Mr. Carswell began to receive larger and more frequent orders from his customers and their business associates. In 1972, he quit his regular job in order to devote full time to his juice business. He soon reached his capacity because of his inability to personally cover a larger area with his pickup truck. Advertising was on a small scale because of limited funds. Faced with the problems of glass jug breakage and limited advertising and distribution, Mr. Carswell approached a regional food distributor for a solution. Mr. Carswell was offered a plan whereby the distributor would advertise and distribute the product on the basis of 25 percent of gross sales. The distributor would assist Mr. Carswell in securing a loan from the local bank to expand production.

Before he had an opportunity to contact the bank to borrow money, Mr. Carswell was introduced to Mr. Bernie Lubo, a plastics engineer, who produced plastic containers. Mr. Carswell mentioned his own problems in the expansion of his business. Mr. Lubo wanted to finance expanded juice production with the understanding that plastic containers would be used for marketing the orange juice. He would lend the money interest free, but he was to receive 40 percent of the net profits for the next ten years. Distribution and advertising were to be done through a local broker for 25 percent of gross sales. The principal on Mr. Lubo's invested money was to be repaid by Mr. Carswell on a basis of 10 percent of his share of the profits. Mr. Lubo was to retain an interest in the profits of the firm until the loan was repaid, or at least for ten years.

Mr. Carswell's current sales were 10,000 gallons of juice a month. If distribution could be expanded, sales could be doubled, given the potential demand. Of the possible total sales of 20,000 a month, about 75 percent would be sold to large restaurants and the remainder to small cafeterias and luncheonettes. As soon as the juice were bottled in plastic containers, sales could also be made to household consumers. Mr. Carswell was very optimistic that sales to the final consumer through retail shops would succeed. Some initial contacts were made with a local franchiser of drive-in dairy shops. The franchiser was sure that he could sell 4,000 gallons a month through his outlets.

Mr. Carswell also calculated his potential profits. His goal was to increase sales while at the same time earning a 10 percent rate of return on his prior capital investment in equipment and other assets. The present value of Mr. Carswell's investment was $250,000. Of this sum, machinery and equipment were valued at $100,000; real estate was worth $50,000 and his patent and know-how were valued at $100,000. On the basis of this evaluation, Mr. Carswell desired a return of $25,000 above salaries and other expenses after the first year of operation.

Both the regional distributor and Mr. Bernie Lubo believed that Mr. Carswell's sales could be increased to 15,000 gallons of juice per month by the end of the first year of expanded operations. However, the extent to which production could be expanded to meet demand depended on the availability of plastic containers (which would be supplied at factory cost under Mr. Lubo's proposal), and additional machinery. Increased market coverage would be obtained both under the regional food distributor and Lubo proposals. The critical deciding factor, as Mr. Carswell understood, was which plan would maximize his return on investment beyond the minimum figure of 10 percent.

Data Evaluation Questions

DIRECTIONS: The questions that follow relate to the preceding passage. Evaluate, in terms of the passage, each of the items given. Then select your answer from one of the following classifications, and blacken the corresponding space on the answer sheet.

    (A)   A MAJOR OBJECTIVE in making the decision: one of the goals sought by the decision maker

    (B)   A MAJOR FACTOR in making the decision: an aspect of the problem, specifically mentioned in the passage, that fundamentally affects and/or determines the decision

    (C)   A MINOR FACTOR in making the decision: a less important element bearing on or affecting a Major Factor, rather than a Major Objective directly

    (D)   A MAJOR ASSUMPTION in making the decision: a projection or supposition arrived at by the decision maker before considering the factors and alternatives

    (E)   AN UNIMPORTANT ISSUE in making the decision: an item lacking significant impact on, or relationship to, the decision

161. Cost of securing a loan

162. High breakage rate of glass jugs

163. Expansion of the business

164. Continued demand by the public for Carswell's orange juice

165. Availability of an interest-free loan

166. Possibility of doubling sales through expanded distribution

167. Current valuation of Carswell's real estate

168. Previous use of Mr. Carswell's building as a woodworking shop

169. Ten percent return on investment

170. Plausibility of monthly sales of 4,000 gallons in dairy shops

171. Small scale of current advertising

172. Availability of a loan from a local rather than a national bank

173. Sale of juice to cafeterias

174. Value of patent held by Mr. Carswell

175. Mr. Carswell's current level of sales

Data Application Questions

DIRECTIONS: Answer each of the following questions using information contained in the passage.

176. A major appeal of Carswell's process was its ability to

    I.   extract more juice

II.   remove the bitterness of juice
III. utilize orange peels

(A) I only
(B) III only
(C) I and II only
(D) II and III only
(E) I, II, and III

177. Which of the following reasons were given for the need to expand Mr. Carswell's business?

I.   High breakage rate of glass jugs
II.   Need for greater production capacity
III. Receipt of larger and more frequent orders

(A) I only
(B) III only
(C) I and II only
(D) II and III only
(E) I, II, and III

178. According to the expansion plan suggested by the food distributor, the distributor would

I.   advertise the product
II.   lend money to Mr. Carswell
III. receive 50 percent of gross sales

(A) I only
(B) III only
(C) I and II only
(D) II and III only
(E) I, II, and III

179. According to Mr. Lubo's plan, he would offer Mr. Carswell

I.   an interest-free loan
II.   a distribution channel
III. free use of plastic containers

(A) I only
(B) III only
(C) I and II only
(D) II and III only
(E) I, II, and III

180. Which of the following prevented immediate expansion of Mr. Carswell's business?

I.   He could not acquire a patent.
II.   His product was more expensive than frozen orange juice.
III. He lacked expansion capital.

(A) I only
(B) III only
(C) I and II only
(D) II and III only
(E) I, II, and III

If there is still time remaining, you may review the questions in this section only.
You may not turn to any other section of the test.

Section VIII   Writing Ability

TIME: 20 minutes

DIRECTIONS: Each of the sentences in this section is either correct or contains one error in grammar, usage, diction (choice of words), idiom or punctuation. If there is an error it will be found in one of the underlined parts of the sentence, labeled (A), (B), (C), or (D). If you identify an error mark the appropriate letter on your answer sheet. If there is no error in the sentence mark E—no error.

Note: Assume that all parts of the sentence that are not underlined are correct and cannot be changed.

181. Everyone in the family looks well in this family portrait except Uncle Robert and me.
                        A   B   C   D

     No error
     E

182. Neither Bob nor I am satisfied with the terms of the agreement we made. No error
              A   B   C   D   E

183. Although Eunice and I were seriously worried about the matter, the amount of hours
                           A   B   C   D

     we spent on it was ridiculously small. No error
                                          E

184. They met Simpson two or three months before they decided to open their
           A   B   C

     import-export business last summer. No error
        D   E

185. Realizing how much had been expected of me, my confidence grew until I was able to
                           A   B   C

     face my adversaries boldly. No error
                       D   E

186. Anybody who wishes to seek the nation's highest office must be prepared to devote
                   A   B   C

     two years or more to the quest. No error
             D   E

187. I read in the newspaper that the governor together with his wife and three daughters
       A   B

     are returning from New York by plane. No error
      C   D   E

188. The study concerned itself mainly with the affects of anxiety on decision making in
                     A   B   C

     high-risk situations. No error
        D   E

189. The queue of angry investors had by now grown until it ran the length of the block;
                         A   B   C

     Wentworth, acting as spokesman, rapped violently on the plate glass doors of the
                                    D

     bank. No error
          E

190. I am sure that <u>it would</u> be all right if no one <u>but him was allowed</u> to tender <u>their</u>
           A   B   C   D
resignation. <u>No error</u>
                E

191. Neither of my parents, <u>who were born</u> in Eastern Europe, <u>understand</u> the
                                    A   B
<u>full implications</u> of a democratic <u>electoral</u> system. <u>No error</u>
        C   D   E

192. If you <u>would have</u> come earlier, as I <u>had</u> advised, you <u>would</u> never have been
                     A   B   C
<u>misled</u> by that crude trick. <u>No error</u>
    D   E

193. Thomas <u>stated, moreover,</u> that Benson <u>had</u> not made an effort, <u>that</u> annoyed Benson
                       A   B   C
<u>even</u> more. <u>No error</u>
    D   E

194. <u>This</u> new model travels faster <u>then</u> last <u>year's</u> model, <u>which it supercedes.</u> <u>No error</u>
        A   B   C   D   E

195. Send it back to <u>whomever</u> you think <u>should receive it</u>; I <u>no longer</u> care <u>whose</u> it is.
                            A   B   C   D
<u>No error</u>
    E

196. When the fog descended <u>on us</u>, visibility became <u>so bad</u> that I <u>could not</u> hardly see
                                  A   B   C
the man who <u>was walking</u> one yard in front of me. <u>No error</u>
                 D   E

197. The set of texts required for this assignment is <u>to be found</u> in the library, so that
                                                              A
<u>everyone</u> of the students <u>is</u> able to refer to <u>it</u> at all times. <u>No error</u>
    B   C   D   E

198. The situation <u>would have been</u> <u>far different than</u> it is today <u>had</u> Carlo listened to the
                            A   B   C
good advice <u>given him</u> by his tutor. <u>No error</u>
                 D   E

199. The Vice President presides <u>not only</u> over the Senate <u>but</u> also <u>shoulders</u> any
                                        A   B   C
policy-making responsibilities <u>assigned him</u> by the President. <u>No error</u>
                                     D   E

200. We <u>strongly</u> recommend that Parker <u>is told</u> about his physical condition as soon
               A   B
as possible <u>in order</u> to <u>allow</u> him to make the necessary arrangements. <u>No error</u>
                 C   D   E

If there is still time remaining, you may review the questions in this section only.
You may not turn to any other section of the test.

Answers

Sections I and II   Reading Recall

1. **(D)**	9. **(C)**	17. **(E)**	25. **(B)**
2. **(C)**	10. **(E)**	18. **(C)**	26. **(B)**
3. **(C)**	11. **(A)**	19. **(A)**	27. **(A)**
4. **(C)**	12. **(B)**	20. **(B)**	28. **(D)**
5. **(E)**	13. **(C)**	21. **(C)**	29. **(C)**
6. **(C)**	14. **(C)**	22. **(C)**	30. **(C)**
7. **(A)**	15. **(D)**	23. **(D)**	
8. **(B)**	16. **(D)**	24. **(E)**	

Section III   Problem Solving

(Numbers in parentheses indicate the section in the Mathematics Review where material concerning the question is discussed.)

31. **(D)** (I–4)	50. **(B)** (II–7)	69. **(B)** (I–2)
32. **(E)** (II–2)	51. **(E)** (I–4)	70. **(D)** (III–6, III–7)
33. **(C)** (II–6)	52. **(C)** (I–7)	71. **(C)** (IV–3)
34. **(C)** (IV–4)	53. **(A)** (II–2)	72. **(D)** (IV–3)
35. **(D)** (IV–4)	54. **(C)** (I–2)	73. **(C)** (IV–3)
36. **(E)** (IV–4)	55. **(A)** (III–4)	74. **(E)** (IV–3)
37. **(E)** (II–5)	56. **(C)** (IV–2)	75. **(C)** (II–3)
38. **(D)** (II–4)	57. **(D)** (IV–2)	76. **(B)** (II–3)
39. **(B)** (IV–1)	58. **(E)** (IV–2)	77. **(D)** (IV–1, I–7)
40. **(C)** (IV–1)	59. **(B)** (IV–2)	78. **(E)** (IV–1, I–7)
41. **(B)** (I–4)	60. **(C)** (IV–2)	79. **(D)** (IV–1)
42. **(A)** (II–3)	61. **(D)** (II–3)	80. **(D)** (III–7)
43. **(C)** (III–7)	62. **(E)** (I–2)	81. **(C)** (II–3)
44. **(C)** (IV–1)	63. **(B)** (I–4)	82. **(B)** (II–7)
45. **(D)** (IV–1)	64. **(D)** (IV–5)	83. **(C)** (III–4, III–7)
46. **(D)** (IV–1, I–4)	65. **(C)** (IV–5)	84. **(E)** (II–3)
47. **(C)** (IV–1)	66. **(B)** (IV–5)	85. **(E)** (II–2)
48. **(B)** (II–5)	67. **(C)** (IV–5)	
49. **(C)** (II–6)	68. **(C)** (I–4)	

Section IV   Practical Judgment

86. **(E)**	91. **(B)**	96. **(D)**	101. **(A)**
87. **(A)**	92. **(D)**	97. **(A)**	102. **(E)**
88. **(B)**	93. **(E)**	98. **(B)**	103. **(A)**
89. **(C)**	94. **(C)**	99. **(C)**	104. **(D)**
90. **(A)**	95. **(D)**	100. **(E)**	105. **(C)**

Section V   Data Sufficiency

106.	(E)	110.	(D)	114.	(E)	118.	(E)
107.	(C)	111.	(D)	115.	(E)	119.	(B)
108.	(A)	112.	(B)	116.	(A)	120.	(A)
109.	(E)	113.	(B)	117.	(C)		

Section VI   Verbal Ability

121.	(C)	131.	(C)	141.	(B)	151.	(B)
122.	(D)	132.	(B)	142.	(A)	152.	(C)
123.	(C)	133.	(A)	143.	(B)	153.	(C)
124.	(B)	134.	(B)	144.	(C)	154.	(A)
125.	(C)	135.	(B)	145.	(A)	155.	(B)
126.	(B)	136.	(B)	146.	(D)	156.	(C)
127.	(C)	137.	(C)	147.	(B)	157.	(C)
128.	(A)	138.	(B)	148.	(B)	158.	(A)
129.	(C)	139.	(A)	149.	(A)	159.	(C)
130.	(D)	140.	(C)	150.	(D)	160.	(D)

Section VII   Practical Judgment

161.	(B)	166.	(D)	171.	(B)	176.	(C)
162.	(B)	167.	(C)	172.	(E)	177.	(D)
163.	(A)	168.	(E)	173.	(C)	178.	(A)
164.	(D)	169.	(A)	174.	(E)	179.	(A)
165.	(B)	170.	(D)	175.	(C)	180.	(B)

Section VIII   Writing Ability

181.	(B)	186.	(E)	191.	(B)	196.	(C)
182.	(E)	187.	(C)	192.	(A)	197.	(E)
183.	(D)	188.	(B)	193.	(C)	198.	(B)
184.	(A)	189.	(E)	194.	(B)	199.	(A)
185.	(C)	190.	(D)	195.	(E)	200.	(B)

Analysis

Sections I and II   Reading Recall

1. **(D)** Note that the question asks "about how many" which requires an approximate figure. Of all the alternative answers, (D) comes closest to the 8,600 employees given in paragraph 1.

2. **(C)** See paragraph 3, lines 1 and 2.

3. **(C)** See paragraph 5, line 1: "Top Presidential appointees, . . . bear the brunt of translating the philosophy and aims of the current administration into practical programs."

4. **(C)** See paragraph 6, sentence 2.

5. **(E)** See paragraph 6, last line.

6. **(C)** See paragraph 7: "Those whom the President selects. . . ." and following.

7. **(A)** See paragraph 8: ". . . they usually have substantial responsibilities in basic management."

8. **(B)** Paragraph 8, line 1: "These appointees are primarily regarded as policy makers. . . ."

9. **(C)** See paragraph 7: "Those selected by department and agency heads . . ." and following.

10. **(E)** Alternatives (A) through (D) are definitely acceptable, leaving (E) as the only possible answer.

11. **(A)** See paragraph 1.

12. **(B)** See paragraph 2: ". . . all resellers are bound by the terms of the . . . contract. . . ."

13. **(C)** This is implied throughout the passage.

14. **(C)** See paragraph 4, line 1.

15. **(D)** Paragraph 5: "Responsibility for enforcement falls upon the producer or distributor. . . ."

16. **(D)** See paragraph 3: "Closeout sales are excepted."

17. **(E)** This is found in paragraph 2, line 1.

18. **(C)** See paragraph 5: ". . . granting of trading stamps in abnormally high volume. . . ."

19. **(A)** See paragraph 2, line 1.

20. **(B)** These laws stifle competition because retailers cannot compete on a price basis.

21. **(C)** See paragraph 1.

22. **(C)** Energy savings are mentioned in paragraph 7, employment benefits in paragraph 8. Pollution, on the contrary, would increase: see paragraph 10.

23. **(D)** Only coal and shale are mentioned.

24. **(E)** $20 billion is to be appropriated over the first five years and another $68 billion over the following seven years, i.e. $88 billion over a period of twelve years.

25. **(B)** See paragraph 6.

26. **(B)** See paragraph 3.

27. **(A)** See paragraph 10.

28. **(D)** See paragraph 9.

29. **(C)** Two circumstances under which the government might incur some expense were given: (1) if the projects failed to operate, or (2) if the finished product was so expensive that it required a subsidy. See paragraph 5.

30. **(C)** U.S. oil imports and gasoline consumption have declined. See paragraph 7.

Section III   Problem Solving

31. **(D)** Since he pays 6% on the first $500, this equals (.06)(500) or $30 interest on the first $500. He is borrowing $5,500 which is $5,000 in excess of the first $500. Thus, he also pays $5\frac{1}{2}$% of $5,000, which is (.055)(5,000) or $275.00. Therefore, the total interest is $305.

32. **(E)** $6x - 3y$ is $3(2x - y)$. Since $2x - y = 4$, $6x - 3y = 3 \cdot 4$ or 12.

33. **(C)** The progression is arithmetic and $11 - 5 = 6 = 17 - 11$, so every term is 6 more than the previous term. Therefore, the next term after 17 is $17 + 6$ or 23.

34. **(C)** The bar first touched 50 in 1945.

35. **(D)** In 1952, hydro plants had about 21 million kilowatts, while the total capacity was about 84 million kilowatts. Therefore, the capacity of the steam and internal combustion plants in 1952 was about $(84 - 21)$ or 63 million kilowatts. Since $\frac{63}{21} = 3$, x is 3.

36. **(E)**

    STATEMENT I is true since the graph is almost horizontal between 1930 and 1939, whereas it rises between 1920 and 1929 and between 1940 and 1949.

    Since the total capacity in 1952 was less than 25 million kilowatts and the capacity of the hydro plants in 1925 was more than 5 million kilowatts, STATEMENT II can be inferred.

    STATEMENT III is also true. Between 1925 and 1945, the capacity went from about 22 million to about 50 million kilowatts, which is an increase of about 28 million kilowatts. However, the capacity in 1952 was about 84 million kilowatts, so the increase between 1945 and 1952 was about 34 million kilowatts.

    Therefore, STATEMENTS I, II, and III can all be inferred from the graph.

37. **(E)** Since each packer loads $\frac{1}{8}$ of a box in 9 minutes, the 20 packers will load $\frac{20}{8}$ or $2\frac{1}{2}$ boxes in 9 minutes. There are 90 minutes in $1\frac{1}{2}$ hours; so the 20 packers will load $10 \times 2\frac{1}{2}$ or 25 boxes in $1\frac{1}{2}$ hours.

38. **(D)** The entire population can be divided into three nonoverlapping parts: owns both a car and a motorcycle, owns a car but not a motorcycle, and owns a motorcycle but not a car. If we denote these categories by A, B, and C respectively, we know that $A + B + C = 100\%$. Also, since $A + B$ consists of all the people who own a car, we have $A + B = 90\%$. Therefore, C must be 10%. But C is the category of people who own a motorcycle but do not own a car.

39. **(B)** The total number of children between 6 and 17 in 1972 was about 46,000,000 and of these 20,155,000 had mothers in the labor force. Therefore, about 46,000,000 minus 20,000,000, or 26,000,000, did not have mothers in the labor force.

40. **(C)** There were 2,345,000 Negro children under 6, of whom 999,000 had mothers in the labor force. $\frac{999,000}{2,345,000}$ is about $\frac{1,000,000}{2,350,000}$ or $\frac{100}{235}$, which is roughly $\frac{5}{12} \cdot \frac{5}{12} = 5 \times 8\frac{1}{3}\% = 41\frac{2}{3}\%$.

41. **(B)** Since 108% of $50 = (1.08)(50) = $54, the chair was offered for sale at $54.00. It was sold for 90% of $54 since there was a 10% discount. Therefore, the chair was sold for $(.9)($54)$ or $48.60.

42. **(A)** Here's a table of the hours worked:

	Mon.	Tues.	Wed.	Thurs.	Fri.	Wages for week
	8	8	8	8	8	$5x$
excess over 8 hrs	0	3	1	2	1	$(0 + 3 + 1 + 2 + 1)y = 7y$.

    The average daily wage equals

    $\frac{(5x + 7y)}{5}$, or $x + \frac{7}{5}y$.

43. **(C)** The area of a rectangle is length times width; so the area of the field is 50×25 square yards or 1,250 square yards.

44. **(C)** California's population increased by 53.3%.

45. **(D)** Arkansas, Mississippi, North Dakota, and Oklahoma had decreases in population.

46. **(D)** The population of the United States increased by 14.5% between 1940 and 1950. So if the population was 100 million in 1940, it would have been 114.5 million in 1950. Therefore, the correct answer is 115 million.

47. **(C)**

STATEMENT I is true. $\frac{1}{3}$ is $33\frac{1}{3}\%$ and only California, Arizona, Florida, Nevada, Oregon, and Washington had population increases of more than $33\frac{1}{3}\%$.

STATEMENT II cannot be inferred since the graph tells us only that the *percentage* increase in Oregon's population was larger than the *percentage* increase in Washington's population. There is no information about the number of people living in each state.

STATEMENT III is true because Nebraska's population increased by .7%.

Therefore, only STATEMENTS I and III can be inferred from the graph.

48. **(B)** Since 4 is $\frac{1}{3}$ of 12, 4 apples cost $\frac{1}{3}$ of 63¢, which is 21¢.

49. **(C)** Let x_n be what the car is worth after n years. Then we know $x_0 = \$2,500$ and $x_{n+1} = \frac{4}{5} x_n$. So $x_1 = \frac{4}{5} \times 2,500$, which is $2,000$, x_2 is $\frac{4}{5} \times 2,000$, which is $1,600$, and finally x_3 is $\frac{4}{5} \times 1,600$, which is $1,280$. Therefore, the car is worth $1,280 at the end of three years.

OR

$x_3 = \frac{4}{5} x_2 = \frac{4}{5} (\frac{4}{5} x_1) = (\frac{4}{5})(\frac{4}{5})(\frac{4}{5} x_0) = \frac{64}{125} x_0$. $(\frac{64}{125})2500 = 1280$.

50. **(B)** Since 300 miles is $\frac{3}{5}$ of 500 miles, it should cost $\frac{3}{5}$ of $15 to travel 300 miles by automobile. Therefore, the cost is $9.

51. **(E)** Since the only costs are $20 for fuel and $70 for the drivers wages, the total cost is $90. Therefore, the company should charge 120% of $90, which is (1.2)($90) or $108.00.

52. **(C)** The total fuel cost will be $3 \cdot 20 + 4 \cdot 15 + 2 \cdot 5 + 1 \cdot 50$, which is $180. Since there are 10 vehicles, the average fuel cost is 180/10 or $18 per vehicle.

53. **(A)** Since $x + 2y = 2x + y$, we can subtract $x + 2y$ from each side of the equation and the result is $0 = x - y$.

54. **(C)** $\frac{2}{3}$ of the 15% of the families with income over $25,000 own boats. Since $\frac{2}{3}$ of 15% = 10%, $\frac{1}{10}$ of the families own boats and have an income of $25,000 or more.

55. **(A)** The angles are in the ratio of 1:2:2, so 2 angles are equal to each other, and both are twice as large as the third angle of the triangle. Since a triangle with two equal angles must have the sides opposite equal, the triangle is isosceles. (Using the fact that the sum of the angles of a triangle is 180°, you can see that the angles of the triangle are 72°, 72° and 36°, so only (A) is true.)

56. **(C)** In 1970, total expenditures were $4,851 million, of which 5% was spent in Canada; so x is 5% of $4,851 million, or $242.55 million. Therefore, the correct answer is about 240 million.

57. **(D)** In 1960, the military assistance program used 10%, the AEC 12%, and materials and supplies 18%. So all together the three programs received $(10 + 12 + 18)\%$ or 40% of defense expenditures; $40\% = \frac{2}{5}$.

58. **(E)** Thailand received 5% of defense expenditures in 1970.

59. **(B)** Since 14% was spent in "other Europe" in 1970, $\frac{5}{7}$ of 14% or 10% was spent in Spain in 1970. Thus, 10% of $4,851 million, or about $485 million, was spent in Spain in 1970.

60. **(C)**

STATEMENT I can be inferred since $\frac{1}{5} = 20\%$ and in both years more than 20% was spent in Germany.

The expenditures for 1970 were $4,851 million and for 1960 $3,087 million; so the expenditures increased by $(4,851 - 3,087)$ million or $1,764 million. Since $1,764 million is more than $\frac{1}{3}$ of $3,087 million, STATEMENT II can be inferred from the graph.

STATEMENT III is false. $\frac{2}{5} = 40\%$; U.S. personnel spent 26% in 1960 and 38% in 1970, so it is impossible for U.S. personnel to have spent 40% of the total for 1960 and 1970.

Therefore, only STATEMENTS I and II can be inferred from the graphs.

61. **(D)** The car travels at 60 mph; so the time to travel 255 miles is $\frac{255}{60}$ hours. Since $\frac{255}{60} = 4\frac{15}{60} = 4\frac{1}{4}$, it takes $4\frac{1}{4}$ hours.

62. **(E)** After the tune-up, the car will travel 15 miles on $\frac{3}{4}$ of a gallon of gas. So it will travel $\frac{15}{3/4}$ or $\frac{4}{3} \times 15$ or 20 miles on one gallon of gas.

63. **(B)** The price after a discount of 20% is 80% of P, the original price. After another 15% discount, the price is 85% of 80% of P or $(.85)(.80)$ P, which equals $.68P$. Therefore, after the successive discounts, the price is 68% of what it was originally, which is the same as a single discount of 32%.

64. **(D)** Since the government spent $132 per capita on personal health care for people aged 65 and over in 1966, the total expenditure by the government was $(20)(132) million, which is $2,640 million, or $2.640 billion.

65. **(C)** In 1966, the government spent $30 per capita on people under 65; by 1972 the per capita amount for those under 65 was $72. Therefore, the increase was $42. Since $\frac{42}{30} = 1.4 = 140\%$, the correct answer is (C).

66. **(B)** In 1972, philanthropy and industry contributed $5 out of the $981 per capita spent on personal health care for those aged 65 and over. Therefore, the fraction is $\frac{5}{981}$, which is about $\frac{5}{980} = \frac{1}{196}$.

67. **(C)**

STATEMENT I cannot be inferred since the graph gives only per capita amounts. The total amount will also depend on the number of people in each group.

STATEMENT II is false since private health insurance decreased from $70 to $56 per capita.

STATEMENT III is true since $644 is more than $\frac{1}{2}$ of $981.

Therefore, only STATEMENT III can be inferred from the graphs.

68. **(C)** Since there are 20 oranges in a crate, a crate of oranges is sold for $20 \times 6¢$ or $1.20. A crate of oranges costs $1.00; so the profit on a crate is $1.20 - $1.00 or $.20. Therefore, the rate of profit $= \frac{.20}{1.20} = \frac{1}{6} = 16\frac{2}{3}\%$.

69. **(B)** $7\frac{1}{2}$ dozen is $\frac{15}{2} \times 12 = 90$, so during the summer the hen lays 90 eggs. The food for the summer costs $10, so the cost in food per egg is $\frac{\$10}{90} = \frac{\$1}{9} = 11\frac{1}{9}¢$.

70. **(D)**

STATEMENT I is not true since the diameter is not equal to the radius and the area of the circle is πr^2.

STATEMENT II is true since the length of a diameter is twice the length of a radius.

STATEMENT III is true since $a = \pi r^2 = \pi r(d/2) = \pi(r/2)d$. Therefore, $a/d = \pi(r/2)$.

Therefore, only STATEMENTS II and III are true.

71. **(C)** The graph was highest in 1935.

72. **(D)** In 1958 about 10% of the Gross National Product was spent on social welfare and about $45 billion on social welfare. Therefore, the Gross National Product was about $450 billion.

73. **(C)** The federal government spent about $20 billion in 1957, and the total was about $40 billion. Therefore, the state and local governments spent about $20 billion. So the federal government and state and local governments spent about the same amount.

74. **(E)**

STATEMENT I is true since the graph giving the percentage of Gross National Product falls from 1939 to 1943.

STATEMENT II is true since the state and local expenditures have never reached $50 billion ($\frac{1}{2}$ of the height of the whole scale).

STATEMENT III is true because the state and local portion is greater than the federal government portion between 1929 and 1933.

Therefore, STATEMENTS I, II and III can all be inferred from the graph.

75. **(C)** Since hose A takes 20 minutes to fill the tank, it fills up $\frac{1}{20}$ of the tank each minute. Since hose B fills up the tank in 15 minutes, it fills up $\frac{1}{15}$ of the tank each minute. Therefore, hose A and hose B together will fill up $\frac{1}{20}+\frac{1}{15}$ or $\frac{3+4}{60}$ or $\frac{7}{60}$ of the tank each minute. Thus, it will take $\frac{60}{7}$ or $8\frac{4}{7}$ minutes to fill the tank.

76. **(B)** If T is the amount of time it takes for 12 men to dig the ditch, then $T = \frac{5}{12}$ of $2 = \frac{5}{6}$ of an hour. Therefore, the 12 men will take 50 minutes.

77. **(D)** The total number of cars produced was $900 + 1200 + 1500 + 1400 + 1000$ or $6,000$. So the average per day is $\frac{6,000}{5}$ or 1,200 cars per day.

78. **(E)** There were 6,000 cars produced and the total wages paid for the week was ($30,000 + $40,000 + $52,000 + $50,000 + $32,000) or $204,000. Therefore, the average cost in wages per car $= \frac{\$204,000}{6,000} = \$34$.

79. **(D)**

STATEMENT I is true since the total number of cars produced was 6,000 and $\frac{1}{4}$ of 6,000 is 1,500.

STATEMENT II cannot be inferred since there is no data about the number of employees. If some employees are paid more than others, there may be fewer employees present who receive higher wages.

STATEMENT III is true since $102,000 was paid on Wednesday and Thursday and $102,000 is $\frac{1}{2}$ of the weekly total of $204,000.

Therefore, only STATEMENTS I and III can be inferred from the graph.

80. **(D)** The area of the field is $(1200)^2$ or $1,440,000$ square yards. The area of each plot is 40×30 or 1200 square yards. Therefore, the number of plots $= \frac{1,440,000}{1,200} = 1,200$.

81. **(C)** The train travels 150 miles in 2 hours and 10 minutes which is $2\frac{1}{6}$ hours. Therefore, the average speed is $\frac{150}{2\frac{1}{6}} = 150 \times \frac{6}{13} = \frac{900}{13} = 69\frac{3}{13}$ or about 70 miles per hour.

82. **(B)** Since $x > 2$, then $-x < -2$; but $y > -1$ implies $2y > -2$. Therefore, $-x < -2 < 2y$ so $-x < 2y$. None of the other statements is always true. (A) is false if x is 5 and $y = -\frac{1}{2}$; (C) is false if $x = 3$ and $y = -\frac{1}{2}$; (D) is false if $x = 3$ and $y = 3$, and (E) is false if $x = 3$ and $y = -\frac{1}{2}$.

83. **(C)** Since $ABCD$ is a rectangle, all angles are right angles. The area of a rectangle is length times width; and the length of AD is 4. Using the Pythagorean theorem we have $4^2 + (\text{width})^2 = 5^2$, so the $(\text{width})^2$ is $25 - 16 = 9$. Therefore, the width is 3, and the area is $4 \times 3 = 12$.

84. **(E)** The electricity costs $12k¢$ for 12 hours, the heat costs $\$12d$ for 12 hours, and the water costs $12w¢$ for 12 hours. So the total is $12k¢ + \$12d + 12w¢$ or $\$.12k + \$12d + \$.12w$ which is $\$(.12k + 12d + .12w)$.

85. **(E)** Since $x = 2z$ and $y = 2z$, $x \cdot y \cdot z = (2z)(2z)(z) = 4z^3$; but $x \cdot y \cdot z = 256$ so $4z^3 = 256$. Therefore, $z^3 = 64$ and z is 4; so $x = 8$.

Section IV   Practical Judgment

86. **(E)** Fox's twenty years experience have no significant impact on the decision as to how to increase lottery sales.

87. **(A)** Increasing the number of instant lottery games was a *Major Objective* of Kamil, aimed at boosting lottery sales. *Increasing* the number of games, therefore, was an outcome sought.

88. **(B)** Note the word "stagnating." Stagnation is certainly not an outcome sought; rather, it is a condition which must be changed. The levelling off of lottery sales is a *Major Factor* in the decision process, since it forces the lottery directors to search for means of reversing this trend.

89. **(C)** The cost of the advertising campaign, while a factor in the decision, was limited to only one of the alternatives considered in the decision as to how to increase lottery sales.

90. **(A)** Increasing sales of lottery games by at least 30 percent was a major outcome desired by Kamil.

91. **(B)** The number of tickets to be sold was a *Major Factor* associated with all decision alternatives. In paragraph 4, the situation is described. In other parts of the passage, decision alternatives such as subscriptions, increasing the number of instant games (to sell more tickets), and the introduction of consolation prizes for the Lotto, all deal with increasing the *number* of tickets sold.

92. **(D)** Fishman raised the issue that members of the lower classes were the main purchasers of instant game tickets. Although this contention appeared in the press, management had no definite evidence that non-buyers were from the upper income groups. It is possible that there were lottery ticket buyers from upper-income groups and middle-income groups as well.

93. **(E)** The long history of lottery sales in Tibland has no bearing on any of the decision alternatives.

94. **(C)** The printing costs of special tickets is a *Minor Factor*. It is only one element in the *overall* cost of the decision alternative to issue subscriptions. The other element is circulation cost. The entire cost of introducing subscriptions would be a *Major Factor*.

95. **(D)** Fishman *believed* that the purchasing behavior of lottery buyers in Europe and Tibland was similar. No facts were presented to support his contention.

96. **(D)** That advertising stimulates sales must be taken as an *assumption* in this case. The argument for more advertising is put forward by Fox, based on his "experience." He did not present any facts to show, for example, that when advertising expenditures increased, sales increased, or some similar, clearly demonstrable relationship.

97. **(A)** Attracting new buyers is one of the outcomes desired by the decision makers. See paragraph 7.

98. **(B)** According to the passage, the limited budget within which the lottery must operate would make certain expensive schemes impossible. This restriction is a *Major Factor* in selecting a decision alternative.

99. **(C)** Cost of the subscriptions is a major determinant of whether consumers will purchase them and therefore a factor in management's decision as to whether to offer the product. It is a *Minor Factor* since it relates only to one alternative.

100. **(E)** The type of people serving on the board of directors is not an element in the decision making process.

101. **(A)** Davis's report—given in paragraph 3—shows total sales in monetary units increasing every year. Alternative II does not refer to any time period, while alternative III is not true. The key word is *total* sales. Note that sales of instant games actually *decreased* in 1980.

102. **(E)** All three are objectives given in paragraph 4.

103. **(A)** Only I was suggested by Fishman (see paragraph 8). No one suggested lowering ticket prices. Fox, not Fishman, suggested increasing advertising expenditures.

104. **(D)** Fox was responsible for distribution of lottery tickets, the maintenance of sales booths, and the collection of ticket sales. Davis was the statistician. See paragraph 1.

105. **(C)** Alternatives I and II are mentioned by Davis in the next to last paragraph. No mention was made of alternative III.

Section V   Data Sufficiency

106. **(E)**

Since STATEMENT (1) describes only x and STATEMENT (2) describes only y, both are needed to get an answer. Using STATEMENT (2), STATEMENT (1) becomes $3x = 2k = 2y^2$, so $x = \dfrac{2y^2}{3}$. However, this is not sufficient, since if $y = -1$ then $x = \frac{2}{3}$ and x is greater than y, but if $y = 1$ then again $x = \frac{2}{3}$ but now x is less than y.

Therefore, STATEMENTS (1) and (2) together are not sufficient.

107. **(C)**

$ABCD$ is a parallelogram if AB is parallel to CD and BC is parallel to AD. STATEMENT (2) tells you that AB is parallel to CD, but this is not sufficient since a trapezoid has only one pair of opposite sides parallel. Thus, STATEMENT (2) alone is not sufficient.

STATEMENT (1) alone is not sufficient since a trapezoid can have the two nonparallel sides equal.

However, using STATEMENTS (1) and (2) together we can deduce that BC is parallel to AD, since the distance from BC to AD is equal along two different parallel lines.

108. **(A)**

STATEMENT (1) alone is sufficient. The average is the combined income for 1965–1970 divided by 6 (the number of years). Therefore, the combined income is 6 times the average yearly income.

STATEMENT (2) alone is not sufficient since there is no information about his income for the years 1966–1969.

109. **(E)**

To find the profit, we must know the selling price of the dress as well as its cost. STATEMENTS (1) and (2) together are not sufficient, since there is no information about the selling price of the dresses.

110. **(D)**

k is a prime if none of the integers 2, 3, 4, . . . up to $k - 1$ divide k evenly. STATEMENT (1)

alone is sufficient since if k is not a prime then $k = (m)(n)$ where m and n must be integers less than k. But this means either m or n must be less than or equal to $\sqrt{k}$, since if m and n are both larger than $\sqrt{k}$, $(m)(n)$ is larger than $(\sqrt{k})(\sqrt{k})$ or k. So STATEMENT (1) implies k is a prime.

STATEMENT (2) alone is also sufficient, since if $k = (m)(n)$ and m and n are both larger than $\dfrac{k}{2}$, then $(m)(n)$ is greater than $\dfrac{k^2}{4}$; but $\dfrac{k^2}{4}$ is greater than k when k is larger than 5.

Therefore, if no integer between 2 and $\dfrac{k}{2}$ inclusive divides k evenly, then k is a prime.

111. **(D)**

Since we are given the fact that 100 miles is the distance from A to B, it is sufficient to find the distance from C to B. This is because 100 minus the distance from C to B is the distance from A to C. STATEMENT (1) says that 125% of the distance from C to B is 100 miles. Thus, we can find the distance from C to B, which is sufficient. Since the distance from A to C plus the distance from C to B is the distance from A to B, we can use STATEMENT (2) to set up the equation 5 times the distance from A to C equals 100 miles.

Therefore, STATEMENTS (1) and (2) are each sufficient.

112. **(B)**

STATEMENT (1) alone is not sufficient. If the segment AC is moved further away from the segment BD, then the angles x and y will change. So STATEMENT (1) does not ensure that CD and AB are perpendicular.

STATEMENT (2) alone is sufficient. Since AB is a straight line, $x + y$ equals 180. Thus, if $x = y$, x and y both equal 90 and AB is perpendicular to CD. So the correct answer is (B).

113. **(B)**

STATEMENT (2) alone is sufficient, since $x = y$ implies $x - y = 0$.

STATEMENT (1) alone is not sufficient. An

infinite number of pairs satisfy STATEMENT (1), for example, $x = 2$, $y = 2$, for which $x - y = 0$, or $x = 4$, $y = 1$, for which $x - y = 3$.

114. **(E)**

Since there is no information on how many of the eligible voters are men or how many are women, STATEMENTS (1) and (2) together are not sufficient.

115. **(E)**

We need to find the measure of angle PSR or of angle PST. Using STATEMENT (2), we can find angle PTR, but STATEMENT (1) does not give any information about either of the angles needed.

116. **(A)**

STATEMENT (1) is sufficient since it means 90% of the original cost is $2300. Thus, we can solve the equation for the original cost.

STATEMENT (2) alone is insufficient, since it gives no information about the cost.

117. **(C)**

Draw the radii from O to each of the vertices. These lines divide the hexagon into six triangles. STATEMENT (2) says that all the triangles are congruent since each of their pairs of corresponding sides is equal. Since there are 360° in a circle, the central angle of each triangle is 60°. And, since all radii are equal, each angle of the triangle equals 60°. Therefore, the triangles are equilateral, and AB is equal to the radius of the circle. Thus, if we assume STATEMENT (1), we know the length of AB. Without STATEMENT (1), we can't find the length of AB.

Also, STATEMENT (1) alone is not sufficient, since AB need not equal the radius unless the hexagon is regular.

118. **(E)**

We need to know the area of the walls. To find the area of the walls, we need the distance from the floor to the ceiling. Since neither STATEMENT (1) nor (2) gives any information about the height of the room, together they are not sufficient.

119. **(B)**

STATEMENT (2) alone is sufficient, since we know $80 was the amount the worker made the first day. We can use STATEMENT (2) to find his pay for each day thereafter and then find the average daily wage.

STATEMENT (1) alone is not sufficient, since there is no way to find out how much the worker made on the fifth day.

120. **(A)**

STATEMENT (1) alone is sufficient. Since $3^2 + 4^2 = 5^2$, ABC is a right triangle by the Pythagorean theorem.

STATEMENT (2) alone is not sufficient since you can choose a point D so that $AC = CD$ for *any* triangle ABC.

Section VI   Verbal Ability

121. **(C)** ABSTRUSE: arcane, enigmatic. *Antonym:* obvious

122. **(D)** COAGULATE: congeal, thicken. *Antonym:* dissipate

123. **(C)** PROCLIVITY: tendency, propensity. *Antonym:* aversion

124. **(B)** TACIT: implied, silent. *Antonym:* open

125. **(C)** VORACIOUS: greedy, ravenous. *Antonym:* sated

126. **(B)** SAGACIOUS: discerning, wise. *Antonym:* stupid

127. **(C)** RETICENT: reserved, secretive. *Antonym:* communicative

128. **(A)** FECUND: fertile, productive. *Antonym:* barren

129. **(C)** FURTIVE: sly, stealthy. *Antonym:* overt

130. **(D)** INCLEMENT: severe, harsh. *Antonym:* mild

131. **(C)** NOTORIOUS: infamous, ignoble. *Antonym:* respected

132. **(B)** DILATE: expand, stretch. *Antonym:* contract

133. **(A)** BOISTEROUS: violent, loud. *Antonym:* peaceful

134. **(B)** ECLECTIC: selecting what appears best from various sources. *Antonym:* narrow

135. **(B)** A sample (as in a survey) is part of the universe. An individual is part of a population.

136. **(B)** Carbohydrates may cause obesity. Sugar may cause cavities.

137. **(C)** One fulfills a promise, just as one enforces a law.

138. **(B)** One who is addicted gives himself up habitually, e.g. for food, for a drug, for a cause, etc.; dedicated is a milder form of the same idea. A similar relationship exists between fanaticism and enthusiasm.

139. **(A)** Recall and remember are synonyms, as are counterfeit and forge.

140. **(C)** Again, the relationship is one of synonyms. Abundance : luxury :: poverty : indigence.

141. **(B)** A token is inserted into a turnstile (in a subway, for instance), while a coin is inserted into a pay telephone.

142. **(A)** Fuel flows through pipes as blood flows through veins.

143. **(B)** To be exempt from a rule is to be free from the obligation to follow it; to be immune to a disease is to be free from the possibility of contracting it.

144. **(C)** Indigenous is an antonym of foreign, as native is an antonym of extraneous. While other alternatives may also be considered antonyms, e.g. local : universal, only (C) has the same meaning as indigenous : foreign.

145. **(A)** Efficacious is the opposite of ineffectual, as efficient is an antonym of incompetent.

146. **(D)** An octave consists of eight notes; a millenium consists of a thousand years.

147. **(B)** The goal of the arrow is the target, just as the goal of the diver is the water.

148. **(B)** Alternative (B) has the most meaning in a context which refers to "financial costs."

149. **(A)** Alternatives (C) and (E) can be ruled out, because one does not judge ability by subjective factors. Alternatives (D) and (B) do not make sense in the context.

150. **(D)** Alternatives (A) and (C) are incorrect because their meaning is not clear, and prisoners are not "acquitted" once they have been sentenced to a prison term. Alternative (E), clemency (leniency), is also unclear; i.e., what form does clemency take? Amnesty (B) is usually only granted to political prisoners, but in any case, it also means pardon, which is alternative (D).

151. **(B)** The police would hardly hold a rally or trial on the street for purposes of a strike or a discussion, but they would likely meet to discuss a seige.

152. **(C)** All the first word fill-ins are acceptable, but (C) has the most meaning when both words are used.

153. **(C)** Alternative (D) might be acceptable, but (C) has more meaning.

154. **(A)** Only choice (A) establishes the expected *contrast* implied by the word "Although."

155. **(B)** has the most logical meaning.

156. **(C)** An effort is not prohibitory (A). Alternative (B) hardly makes sense; and one does not convey an accord (D). If the effort had been successful (E), the parties would not now be hostile.

157. **(C)** Choices (B) and (E) are unclear; and (D) has little meaning.

158. **(A)** Only (A) carries out the logical connection implied by the word despite.

159. **(C)** Loquacious means talkative.

160. **(D)** If they are complementary, they are *not* competitive.

Section VII   Practical Judgment

161. **(B)** The cost of securing a loan is a *Major Factor* in making the decision.

162. **(B)** *Major Factor.* The breakage of glass jugs was a consideration in the decision to expand sales.

163. **(A)** Business expansion is clearly the *Major Objective* of Mr. Carswell.

164. **(D)** Continued public acceptance of the product is a *Major Assumption* which has led Mr. Carswell to want to expand his business.

165. **(B)** The availability of the loan was a *Major Factor* in the decision as to whether to accept Mr. Lubo's offer.

166. **(D)** The possibility of doubling his sales was a *Major Assumption* of Mr. Carswell, not an objective.

167. **(C)** Mr. Carswell's total investment was valued at $250,000, of which $50,000 was real estate. Real estate, then, was only one element in the total investment evaluation.

168. **(E)** The *previous* use of the building was of no importance to the present operation or to the decision to expand.

169. **(A)** Receiving a 10 percent rate of return is a *Major Objective* of Mr. Carswell.

170. **(D)** The franchiser was *sure* that 4,000 gallons of juice could be sold monthly through drive-in dairy shops. This figure is an estimate not substantiated by any facts cited in the passage.

171. **(B)** *Major Factor.* Mr. Carswell could advertise only on a small scale owing to lack of funds. In order to expand his business, Mr. Carswell would have to increase his advertising.

172. **(E)** The specific *source* of a business loan was an *Unimportant Issue* to Mr. Carswell.

173. **(C)** *Minor Factor.* Only 25 percent of total expected sales would be made through cafeterias.

174. **(E)** Mr. Carswell's patent—while important to protect his process—was only one part of the overall value of his business.

175. **(C)** Mr. Carswell's current sales served only as a baseline as far as expansion was concerned. Of far more importance to his decision to expand were potential sales and the expected rate of return on his investment.

176. **(C)** See paragraph 1: Among the major appeals of Mr. Carswell's process were its ability to extract 18 percent more juice than conventional means, and the removal of bitterness from the peelings.

177. **(D)** See paragraph 4: Mr. Sim needed to expand his business because he had reached production capacity and could not fill the growing demand for his product.

178. **(A)** See paragraph 4: Among the alternatives listed in this question, only the first, the promise to advertise the product, was given by the distributor.

179. **(A)** See paragraph 5: Among the alternatives listed in the question, only the first, an interest free loan, was offered by Mr. Lubo.

180. **(B)** See paragraph 3: Mr. Sim had a patent; whether his product was more expensive than the use of frozen orange juice was not an issue. Of most importance, he lacked expansion capital.

Section VIII   Writing Ability

181. **(B)** The linking verb *looks* requires the adjective *good* and not the adverb *well.*

182. **(E)** No error.

183. **(D)** The *number* of hours should be used instead of *amount,* since the countable unit *hours* is mentioned.

184. **(A)** The past perfect *had met* is required, since the action preceded past action.

185. **(C)** The participle *realizing* dangles, as *my confidence* cannot do the realizing. Phrase (C) should read *I became more confident.*

186. **(E)** No error.

187. **(C)** The verb *are* should be *is*, as the subject, *the governor,* is singular; *together with his wife,* etc., is parenthetical.

188. **(B)** The required noun is *effects*, i.e., *the results of* and not *affects* which is a verb only.

189. **(E)** No error.

190. **(D)** The singular pronoun *one* requires the singular *his* and not the plural *their*.

191. **(B)** The verb must be the third person singular *understands* to agree with the singular *Neither* (one).

192. **(A)** The past conditional requires the past perfect *had come* in the conditional clause.

193. **(C)** The pronoun *that* must refer to a specific word; in this case it has no clear antecedent.

194. **(B)** The required conjunction is *than* and not the adverb *then*.

195. **(E)** No error.

196. **(C)** The adverb *hardly* already carries a negative connotation and therefore does not take the negative *not*.

197. **(E)** No error.

198. **(B)** The standard idiom is *different from*. The sentence should read: "The situation would have been far *different from what* it is today . . . "

199. **(A)** The phrase *not only* should precede *presides*.

200. **(B)** The subjunctive requires the use of the base form of the verb; *be told* and not the present form *is told*.

Evaluating Your Score

Tabulate your score for each section of Sample Test 2 according to the directions on pages 4–5 and record the results in the Self-scoring Table below. Then find your rating for each score on the Self-scoring Scale and record it in the appropriate blank.

Self-scoring Table

PART	SCORE	RATING
1-2		
3		
4		
5		
6		
7		
8		

Self-scoring Scale

PART	RATING			
	POOR	FAIR	GOOD	EXCELLENT
1-2	0-10	11-15	16-22	23-30
3	0-24	25-30	31-39	40-55
4	0-7	8-10	11-15	16-20
5	0-5	6-8	9-12	13-15
6	0-15	16-20	21-29	30-40
7	0-7	8-10	11-15	16-20
8	0-7	8-10	11-15	16-20

Study again the Review sections covering material in Sample Test 2 for which you had a rating of FAIR or POOR. Then go on to Sample Test 3.

To obtain an approximation of your actual GMAT score, see page 5.

Section I
Reading Comprehension

1. Ⓐ Ⓑ Ⓒ Ⓓ Ⓔ
2. Ⓐ Ⓑ Ⓒ Ⓓ Ⓔ
3. Ⓐ Ⓑ Ⓒ Ⓓ Ⓔ
4. Ⓐ Ⓑ Ⓒ Ⓓ Ⓔ
5. Ⓐ Ⓑ Ⓒ Ⓓ Ⓔ
6. Ⓐ Ⓑ Ⓒ Ⓓ Ⓔ
7. Ⓐ Ⓑ Ⓒ Ⓓ Ⓔ
8. Ⓐ Ⓑ Ⓒ Ⓓ Ⓔ
9. Ⓐ Ⓑ Ⓒ Ⓓ Ⓔ
10. Ⓐ Ⓑ Ⓒ Ⓓ Ⓔ
11. Ⓐ Ⓑ Ⓒ Ⓓ Ⓔ
12. Ⓐ Ⓑ Ⓒ Ⓓ Ⓔ
13. Ⓐ Ⓑ Ⓒ Ⓓ Ⓔ
14. Ⓐ Ⓑ Ⓒ Ⓓ Ⓔ
15. Ⓐ Ⓑ Ⓒ Ⓓ Ⓔ
16. Ⓐ Ⓑ Ⓒ Ⓓ Ⓔ
17. Ⓐ Ⓑ Ⓒ Ⓓ Ⓔ
18. Ⓐ Ⓑ Ⓒ Ⓓ Ⓔ
19. Ⓐ Ⓑ Ⓒ Ⓓ Ⓔ
20. Ⓐ Ⓑ Ⓒ Ⓓ Ⓔ
21. Ⓐ Ⓑ Ⓒ Ⓓ Ⓔ
22. Ⓐ Ⓑ Ⓒ Ⓓ Ⓔ
23. Ⓐ Ⓑ Ⓒ Ⓓ Ⓔ
24. Ⓐ Ⓑ Ⓒ Ⓓ Ⓔ
25. Ⓐ Ⓑ Ⓒ Ⓓ Ⓔ

Section II
Problem Solving

26. Ⓐ Ⓑ Ⓒ Ⓓ Ⓔ
27. Ⓐ Ⓑ Ⓒ Ⓓ Ⓔ
28. Ⓐ Ⓑ Ⓒ Ⓓ Ⓔ
29. Ⓐ Ⓑ Ⓒ Ⓓ Ⓔ
30. Ⓐ Ⓑ Ⓒ Ⓓ Ⓔ
31. Ⓐ Ⓑ Ⓒ Ⓓ Ⓔ
32. Ⓐ Ⓑ Ⓒ Ⓓ Ⓔ
33. Ⓐ Ⓑ Ⓒ Ⓓ Ⓔ
34. Ⓐ Ⓑ Ⓒ Ⓓ Ⓔ
35. Ⓐ Ⓑ Ⓒ Ⓓ Ⓔ

36. Ⓐ Ⓑ Ⓒ Ⓓ Ⓔ
37. Ⓐ Ⓑ Ⓒ Ⓓ Ⓔ
38. Ⓐ Ⓑ Ⓒ Ⓓ Ⓔ
39. Ⓐ Ⓑ Ⓒ Ⓓ Ⓔ
40. Ⓐ Ⓑ Ⓒ Ⓓ Ⓔ
41. Ⓐ Ⓑ Ⓒ Ⓓ Ⓔ
42. Ⓐ Ⓑ Ⓒ Ⓓ Ⓔ
43. Ⓐ Ⓑ Ⓒ Ⓓ Ⓔ
44. Ⓐ Ⓑ Ⓒ Ⓓ Ⓔ
45. Ⓐ Ⓑ Ⓒ Ⓓ Ⓔ
46. Ⓐ Ⓑ Ⓒ Ⓓ Ⓔ
47. Ⓐ Ⓑ Ⓒ Ⓓ Ⓔ
48. Ⓐ Ⓑ Ⓒ Ⓓ Ⓔ
49. Ⓐ Ⓑ Ⓒ Ⓓ Ⓔ
50. Ⓐ Ⓑ Ⓒ Ⓓ Ⓔ
51. Ⓐ Ⓑ Ⓒ Ⓓ Ⓔ
52. Ⓐ Ⓑ Ⓒ Ⓓ Ⓔ
53. Ⓐ Ⓑ Ⓒ Ⓓ Ⓔ
54. Ⓐ Ⓑ Ⓒ Ⓓ Ⓔ
55. Ⓐ Ⓑ Ⓒ Ⓓ Ⓔ

Section III
Practical Judgment

56. Ⓐ Ⓑ Ⓒ Ⓓ Ⓔ
57. Ⓐ Ⓑ Ⓒ Ⓓ Ⓔ
58. Ⓐ Ⓑ Ⓒ Ⓓ Ⓔ
59. Ⓐ Ⓑ Ⓒ Ⓓ Ⓔ
60. Ⓐ Ⓑ Ⓒ Ⓓ Ⓔ
61. Ⓐ Ⓑ Ⓒ Ⓓ Ⓔ
62. Ⓐ Ⓑ Ⓒ Ⓓ Ⓔ
63. Ⓐ Ⓑ Ⓒ Ⓓ Ⓔ
64. Ⓐ Ⓑ Ⓒ Ⓓ Ⓔ
65. Ⓐ Ⓑ Ⓒ Ⓓ Ⓔ
66. Ⓐ Ⓑ Ⓒ Ⓓ Ⓔ
67. Ⓐ Ⓑ Ⓒ Ⓓ Ⓔ
68. Ⓐ Ⓑ Ⓒ Ⓓ Ⓔ
69. Ⓐ Ⓑ Ⓒ Ⓓ Ⓔ
70. Ⓐ Ⓑ Ⓒ Ⓓ Ⓔ
71. Ⓐ Ⓑ Ⓒ Ⓓ Ⓔ
72. Ⓐ Ⓑ Ⓒ Ⓓ Ⓔ
73. Ⓐ Ⓑ Ⓒ Ⓓ Ⓔ
74. Ⓐ Ⓑ Ⓒ Ⓓ Ⓔ
75. Ⓐ Ⓑ Ⓒ Ⓓ Ⓔ

Section IV
Data Sufficiency

76. Ⓐ Ⓑ Ⓒ Ⓓ Ⓔ
77. Ⓐ Ⓑ Ⓒ Ⓓ Ⓔ
78. Ⓐ Ⓑ Ⓒ Ⓓ Ⓔ
79. Ⓐ Ⓑ Ⓒ Ⓓ Ⓔ
80. Ⓐ Ⓑ Ⓒ Ⓓ Ⓔ
81. Ⓐ Ⓑ Ⓒ Ⓓ Ⓔ
82. Ⓐ Ⓑ Ⓒ Ⓓ Ⓔ
83. Ⓐ Ⓑ Ⓒ Ⓓ Ⓔ
84. Ⓐ Ⓑ Ⓒ Ⓓ Ⓔ
85. Ⓐ Ⓑ Ⓒ Ⓓ Ⓔ
86. Ⓐ Ⓑ Ⓒ Ⓓ Ⓔ
87. Ⓐ Ⓑ Ⓒ Ⓓ Ⓔ
88. Ⓐ Ⓑ Ⓒ Ⓓ Ⓔ
89. Ⓐ Ⓑ Ⓒ Ⓓ Ⓔ
90. Ⓐ Ⓑ Ⓒ Ⓓ Ⓔ
91. Ⓐ Ⓑ Ⓒ Ⓓ Ⓔ
92. Ⓐ Ⓑ Ⓒ Ⓓ Ⓔ
93. Ⓐ Ⓑ Ⓒ Ⓓ Ⓔ
94. Ⓐ Ⓑ Ⓒ Ⓓ Ⓔ
95. Ⓐ Ⓑ Ⓒ Ⓓ Ⓔ
96. Ⓐ Ⓑ Ⓒ Ⓓ Ⓔ
97. Ⓐ Ⓑ Ⓒ Ⓓ Ⓔ
98. Ⓐ Ⓑ Ⓒ Ⓓ Ⓔ
99. Ⓐ Ⓑ Ⓒ Ⓓ Ⓔ
100. Ⓐ Ⓑ Ⓒ Ⓓ Ⓔ
101. Ⓐ Ⓑ Ⓒ Ⓓ Ⓔ
102. Ⓐ Ⓑ Ⓒ Ⓓ Ⓔ
103. Ⓐ Ⓑ Ⓒ Ⓓ Ⓔ
104. Ⓐ Ⓑ Ⓒ Ⓓ Ⓔ
105. Ⓐ Ⓑ Ⓒ Ⓓ Ⓔ

Section V
Writing Ability

106. Ⓐ Ⓑ Ⓒ Ⓓ Ⓔ
107. Ⓐ Ⓑ Ⓒ Ⓓ Ⓔ
108. Ⓐ Ⓑ Ⓒ Ⓓ Ⓔ
109. Ⓐ Ⓑ Ⓒ Ⓓ Ⓔ
110. Ⓐ Ⓑ Ⓒ Ⓓ Ⓔ

Section VI
Practical Judgment

126. Ⓐ Ⓑ Ⓒ Ⓓ Ⓔ
127. Ⓐ Ⓑ Ⓒ Ⓓ Ⓔ
128. Ⓐ Ⓑ Ⓒ Ⓓ Ⓔ
129. Ⓐ Ⓑ Ⓒ Ⓓ Ⓔ
130. Ⓐ Ⓑ Ⓒ Ⓓ Ⓔ
131. Ⓐ Ⓑ Ⓒ Ⓓ Ⓔ
132. Ⓐ Ⓑ Ⓒ Ⓓ Ⓔ
133. Ⓐ Ⓑ Ⓒ Ⓓ Ⓔ
134. Ⓐ Ⓑ Ⓒ Ⓓ Ⓔ
135. Ⓐ Ⓑ Ⓒ Ⓓ Ⓔ
136. Ⓐ Ⓑ Ⓒ Ⓓ Ⓔ
137. Ⓐ Ⓑ Ⓒ Ⓓ Ⓔ
138. Ⓐ Ⓑ Ⓒ Ⓓ Ⓔ
139. Ⓐ Ⓑ Ⓒ Ⓓ Ⓔ
140. Ⓐ Ⓑ Ⓒ Ⓓ Ⓔ
141. Ⓐ Ⓑ Ⓒ Ⓓ Ⓔ
142. Ⓐ Ⓑ Ⓒ Ⓓ Ⓔ
143. Ⓐ Ⓑ Ⓒ Ⓓ Ⓔ
144. Ⓐ Ⓑ Ⓒ Ⓓ Ⓔ
145. Ⓐ Ⓑ Ⓒ Ⓓ Ⓔ

Section VII
Data Sufficiency

111. Ⓐ Ⓑ Ⓒ Ⓓ Ⓔ
112. Ⓐ Ⓑ Ⓒ Ⓓ Ⓔ
113. Ⓐ Ⓑ Ⓒ Ⓓ Ⓔ
114. Ⓐ Ⓑ Ⓒ Ⓓ Ⓔ
115. Ⓐ Ⓑ Ⓒ Ⓓ Ⓔ
116. Ⓐ Ⓑ Ⓒ Ⓓ Ⓔ
117. Ⓐ Ⓑ Ⓒ Ⓓ Ⓔ
118. Ⓐ Ⓑ Ⓒ Ⓓ Ⓔ
119. Ⓐ Ⓑ Ⓒ Ⓓ Ⓔ
120. Ⓐ Ⓑ Ⓒ Ⓓ Ⓔ
121. Ⓐ Ⓑ Ⓒ Ⓓ Ⓔ
122. Ⓐ Ⓑ Ⓒ Ⓓ Ⓔ
123. Ⓐ Ⓑ Ⓒ Ⓓ Ⓔ
124. Ⓐ Ⓑ Ⓒ Ⓓ Ⓔ
125. Ⓐ Ⓑ Ⓒ Ⓓ Ⓔ

146. Ⓐ Ⓑ Ⓒ Ⓓ Ⓔ
147. Ⓐ Ⓑ Ⓒ Ⓓ Ⓔ
148. Ⓐ Ⓑ Ⓒ Ⓓ Ⓔ
149. Ⓐ Ⓑ Ⓒ Ⓓ Ⓔ
150. Ⓐ Ⓑ Ⓒ Ⓓ Ⓔ
151. Ⓐ Ⓑ Ⓒ Ⓓ Ⓔ
152. Ⓐ Ⓑ Ⓒ Ⓓ Ⓔ
153. Ⓐ Ⓑ Ⓒ Ⓓ Ⓔ
154. Ⓐ Ⓑ Ⓒ Ⓓ Ⓔ
155. Ⓐ Ⓑ Ⓒ Ⓓ Ⓔ
156. Ⓐ Ⓑ Ⓒ Ⓓ Ⓔ
157. Ⓐ Ⓑ Ⓒ Ⓓ Ⓔ
158. Ⓐ Ⓑ Ⓒ Ⓓ Ⓔ
159. Ⓐ Ⓑ Ⓒ Ⓓ Ⓔ
160. Ⓐ Ⓑ Ⓒ Ⓓ Ⓔ
161. Ⓐ Ⓑ Ⓒ Ⓓ Ⓔ
162. Ⓐ Ⓑ Ⓒ Ⓓ Ⓔ
163. Ⓐ Ⓑ Ⓒ Ⓓ Ⓔ
164. Ⓐ Ⓑ Ⓒ Ⓓ Ⓔ
165. Ⓐ Ⓑ Ⓒ Ⓓ Ⓔ
166. Ⓐ Ⓑ Ⓒ Ⓓ Ⓔ
167. Ⓐ Ⓑ Ⓒ Ⓓ Ⓔ
168. Ⓐ Ⓑ Ⓒ Ⓓ Ⓔ
169. Ⓐ Ⓑ Ⓒ Ⓓ Ⓔ
170. Ⓐ Ⓑ Ⓒ Ⓓ Ⓔ
171. Ⓐ Ⓑ Ⓒ Ⓓ Ⓔ
172. Ⓐ Ⓑ Ⓒ Ⓓ Ⓔ
173. Ⓐ Ⓑ Ⓒ Ⓓ Ⓔ
174. Ⓐ Ⓑ Ⓒ Ⓓ Ⓔ
175. Ⓐ Ⓑ Ⓒ Ⓓ Ⓔ

Sample Test 3

Section I   Reading Comprehension

TIME: 30 minutes

DIRECTIONS: This part contains three reading passages. You are to read each one carefully. When answering the questions, you *will* be allowed to refer back to the passages. The questions are based on what is *stated* or *implied* in each passage. You have thirty minutes to complete this section.

Passage 1:

With Friedrich Engels, Karl Marx in 1848 published the *Communist Manifesto,* calling upon the masses to rise and throw off their economic chains. His maturer theories of society were later elaborated in his large and abstruse work *Das Capital.* Starting as a non-violent revolutionist, he ended life as a major social theorist more or less sympathetic with violent revolution, if such became necessary in order to change the social system which he believed to be frankly predatory upon the masses.

On the theoretical side, Marx set up the doctrine of surplus value as the chief element in capitalistic exploitation. According to this theory, the ruling classes no longer employed military force primarily as a means to plundering the people. Instead, they used their control over employment and working conditions under the bourgeois capitalistic system for this purpose, paying only a bare subsistence wage to the worker while they appropriated all surplus values in the productive process. He further taught that the strategic disadvantage of the worker in industry prevented him from obtaining a fairer share of the earnings by bargaining methods and drove him to revolutionary procedures as a means to establishing his economic and social rights. This revolution might be peacefully consummated by parliamentary procedures if the people prepared themselves for political action by mastering the materialistic interpretation of history and by organizing politically for the final event. It was his belief that the aggressions of the capitalist class would eventually destroy the middle class and take over all their sources of income by a process of capitalistic absorption of industry—a process which has failed to occur in most countries.

With minor exceptions, Marx's social philosophy is now generally accepted by left-wing labor movements in many countries, but rejected by centrist labor groups, especially those in the United States. In Russia and other Eastern European countries, however, Socialist leaders adopted the methods of violent revolution because of the opposition of the ruling classes. Yet, many now hold that the present Communist regime in Russia and her satellite countries is no longer a proletarian movement based on Marxist social and political theory, but a camouflaged imperialistic effort to dominate the world in the interest of a new ruling class.

It is important, however, that those who wish to approach Marx as a teacher should not be "buffaloed" by his philosophic approach. They are very likely to in these days, because those most interested in propogating the ideas of Marx, the Russian Bolsheviks, have swallowed down his Hegelian philosophy along with his science of revolutionary engineering, and they look upon us irreverent peoples who presume to meditate social and even revolutionary problems without making our obeisance to the mysteries of Dialectic Materialism, as a species of unredeemed and well-nigh unredeemable barbarians. They are right in scorning our ignorance of the scientific ideas of Karl Marx and our indifference to them. They are wrong in scorning our distaste for having practical programs presented in the form of systems of philosophy. In that we simply represent a more progressive intellectual culture than that in which Marx received his education—a culture farther emerged from the dominance of religious attitudes.

1. According to the passage, the chief element in Marx's analysis of capitalist exploitation was the doctrine of

   (A) just wages   (D) predatory production
   (B) the price system   (E) subsistence work
   (C) surplus value

2. *Das Capital* differs from the *Communist Manifesto* in that it

   (A) was written with the help of Friedrich Engels
   (B) retreated from Marx's earlier revolutionary stance
   (C) expressed a more fully developed form of Marxist theory
   (D) denounced the predatory nature of the capitalist system
   (E) expressed sympathy for the plight of the middle class

3. According to the passage, Marx ended his life

   I. a believer in non-violent revolution
   II. accepting violent revolution
   III. a major social theorist

   (A) I only
   (B) III only
   (C) I and III only
   (D) II and III only
   (E) Neither I, II, nor III

4. The author suggests that the present Communist regime in Russia may best be categorized as a(n)

   (A) proletarian movement   (D) revolutionary government
   (B) socialist government   (E) social democracy
   (C) imperialistic state

5. Marx's social philosophy is now generally accepted by

   (A) centrist labor groups
   (B) most labor unions
   (C) left-wing labor unions
   (D) only those in Communist countries
   (E) only those in Russia

6. It can be concluded that the author of the passage is

   (A) sympathetic to Marx's ideas
   (B) unsympathetic to Marx's ideas
   (C) uncritical of Marx's interpretation of history
   (D) a believer in Hegelian philosophy
   (E) a Leninist-Marxist

7. Which of the following classes did Marx believe should control the economy?

   (A) The working class   (D) The lower class
   (B) The upper class   (E) The capitalist class
   (C) The middle class

8. According to Marx, a social and economic revolution could take place through

   I. parliamentary procedures
   II. political action
   III. violent revolution

   (A) I only
   (B) III only
   (C) I or II only
   (D) II or III only
   (E) I, II, or III

Passage 2:

The basic character of our governmental and political institutions conditions the federal budgetary system. The working relationships between branches, and between the elements within each branch, are intricate, subtle, and in continuous change—affected by partisan politics, personalities, social forces, and public opinion. A few landmark stages in the evolution of the present system provide perspective.

In 1789 Alexander Hamilton, as the first Secretary of the Treasury, affirmed and successfully established a position of strong executive leadership in matters of public finance. His proposals on revenues, banking, and the assumption of prior debts of both national and state governments were based on his philosophy that federal fiscal policies should be designed to encourage economic growth. However, Hamilton's successors, and the Presidents under whom they served, did not follow his concept of executive responsibility for "plans of finance."

Partly through default, Congress took charge of all phases of fiscal policy. At the outset, each chamber was so small that coherent initiative was possible. (The first House had some 60 members—about the number of its present Appropriations Committee.) Spending estimates, considered in Committee of the Whole in 1789, were later referred to the Committee on Ways and Means. In 1865 expenditures were assigned to a new Appropriations Committee while revenues remained with the Ways and Means Committee. In 1885 most spending proposals were subdivided among the legislative committees so that appropriation bills came to be handled by numerous committees (14 in the House and 15 in the Senate), each dealing directly with the departments. The presidential role was minimal.

By the turn of the century there was a clear need for reform in financial management. At all levels of government, officials spent money on activities "as authorized by law" and in line with "appropriations" made by legislative bodies—usually after committee consideration. Other officials collected taxes and fees under various unrelated statutes. Such a system—or lack-of-system—worked within reason as long as governments had little to do. But as government activities grew, becoming more technical and closely interrelated, this lack-of-system bogged down.

Several factors played a part in the eventual breakthrough. In the first decade of the twentieth century, an "executive budget" came into successful use by some cities and states. President Taft's Commission on Efficiency and Economy prepared an illustrative federal budget which—while rejected by Congress—commanded broad public support. The more advanced methods developed by European governments came to American attention. World War I precipitated accounting chaos, with an aftermath of scandal. The need for new and better methods was established beyond dispute.

The Budget and Accounting Act of 1921 placed direct responsibility for preparation and execution of the federal budget upon the President, making a unified federal budget possible for the first time. The Act set up two new organizational units, the General Accounting Office (GAO) and the Bureau of the Budget. GAO is headed by the Comptroller General, appointed by the President *with* senate approval for a 15-year term, and is regarded as primarily a congressional rather than an executive resource. The Bureau, under a Director appointed by the President *without* senate confirmation and serving at his pleasure, has from its inception been the President's chief reliance in budgetary and related matters.

9. Alexander Hamilton's philosophy was that federal fiscal policies should

   (A) be expansionary
   (B) encourage economic growth
   (C) be determined by Congress
   (D) encourage a balanced budget
   (E) be determined by the President

10. Hamilton's successors

   I. Followed his economic philosophy of "plans of finance"
   II. Followed his social philosophy
   III. Did not follow his philosophy of strong executive leadership

   (A) I only
   (B) III only
   (C) I and II only
   (D) II and III only
   (E) I, II, and III

11. In the history of U.S. fiscal management, spending estimates were *first* considered by the

   (A) Committee of the Whole
   (B) Appropriations Committee
   (C) Ways and Means Committee
   (D) Commission on Efficiency and Economy
   (E) General Accounting Office

12. At the end of the nineteenth century, there was a need for

    (A) more restrained executive leadership
    (B) a new finance commission
    (C) more Congressional interest in finance
    (D) overall reform of financial management
    (E) creation of a new Appropriations committee

13. The "executive budget" was first used

    (A) by Alexander Hamilton
    (B) in the 19th century
    (C) in the first decade of the 20th century
    (D) by President Eisenhower
    (E) by President Truman

14. President Taft's federal budget was

    (A) based on procedures used by some European governments
    (B) enthusiastically accepted by Congress
    (C) a partial cause of accounting chaos during World War I
    (D) rejected by Congress
    (E) vilified by the public

15. In 1921, the responsibility for preparation and execution of the federal budget fell upon the

    (A) President
    (B) Congress
    (C) Bureau of the Budget
    (D) House of Representatives
    (E) Senate

16. All of the following are true about the Bureau of the Budget except

    (A) its Director is appointed by the President
    (B) it assists the President in budgetary matters
    (C) its Director need not be approved by the Senate
    (D) it was established in 1921
    (E) its Director serves for a 15-year term

Passage 3:

In describing the Indians of the various sections of the United States at different stages in their history, some of the factors which account for their similarity amid difference can be readily accounted for, others are difficult to discern.

The basic physical similarity of the Indians from Alaska to Patagonia is explained by the fact that they all came originally from Asia by way of the Bering Strait and the Aleutian Islands into Alaska and then southward. They came in different waves, the earliest around

25,000 years ago, the latest probably not long before America was discovered by Europeans. Because these people all came from Asia and were therefore drawn from the same pool of Asiatic people, they tended to look alike. But since the various waves of migration crossed into Alaska at widely separated times, there were differences among them in their physical characteristics.

There were also differences in cultural equipment. The earliest arrivals are known to science only through their simple tools of chipped stone and bone. Despite their limited technical equipment, some of the New Mexico Indians were very successful big game hunters. Twenty-five thousand years ago they were hunting the wooly mammoth, the giant bison, the ground sloth and the camel, all characteristic animals of the closing phases of the last ice age.

After their arrival from Asia in various waves across the Bering Strait, the early peoples in the Americas slowly spread southward into the vast empty spaces of the two continents. A group of people moving slowly down the Mackenzie River valley east of the Rockies into the general region of Southern Alberta, then eastward across the northern prairies reaching the wooded country around the upper Mississippi and the Western Great Lakes, then in a southeastward movement following the Mississippi valley until some final settlement was reached in the Gulf states, would encounter a wide variety of physical environments. At various stages of such wanderings they would have to evolve methods of coping with the cold, barren, tundra country of northern Canada; the prairies, cold, treeless but well stocked with large game; then later the completely different flora and fauna of the Minnesota-Wisconsin-Illinois area, thickly forested and well watered and providing an abundance of small game and wild vegetable foods; then the semi-tropical character of the lower Mississippi country as they neared the Gulf of Mexico. Since such a migration would be spread over many centuries, the modification of whatever basic culture they had on their arrival from Asia would be very slow. Yet the end result would be completely different from their original culture. It would also be different from the final culture of a closely allied group who became separated from them early in their wanderings and whose movements led them into different types of country. In its final form, the culture of this second group would have little in common with that of the first except perhaps a continuing resemblance in language and in physical type.

17. According to the passage, Indians who migrated to what is now the United States originated in

(A) Asia
(B) Africa
(C) South America
(D) Alaska
(E) Patagonia

18. Physical differences among Indians who migrated to Alaska can be accounted for by the fact that they came

(A) from different places
(B) from different tribes
(C) at different times
(D) from different races
(E) to different places

19. It is estimated that Indians first came to what is now the United States about

(A) 5,000 years ago
(B) 10,000 years ago
(C) 15,000 years ago
(D) 25,000 years ago
(E) 50,000 years ago

20. The author is most interested in discussing the Indians'

(A) cultural background
(B) eating habits
(C) technical abilities
(D) migration patterns
(E) physical characteristics

21. According to the passage, the southernmost area reached by the earliest Indians was the

(A) northern prairies
(B) upper Mississippi
(C) Great Lakes
(D) Mackenzie River valley
(E) Gulf States

22. Particularly noted for their hunting prowess were the Indians of

(A) Mississippi
(B) Southern Alberta
(C) the Mackenzie River valley
(D) New Mexico
(E) the American prairies

23. What characteristics of Indian culture remained fairly stable despite the Indian migrations?

I. Language
II. Physical type
III. Technical abilities

(A) I only
(B) III only
(C) I and II only
(D) II and III only
(E) I, II, and III

24. Which animals were hunted by the Indians when they first migrated to the Americas?

I. Bison
II. Wooly mammoth
III. Camel

(A) I only
(B) III only
(C) I and II only
(D) II and III only
(E) I, II, and III

25. The passage most likely was written by a(n)

(A) economist
(B) historian
(C) educator
(D) social scientist
(E) anthropologist

If there is still time remaining, you may review the questions in this section only.
You may not turn to any other section of the test.

Section II   Problem Solving

TIME: 40 minutes

DIRECTIONS: Solve each of the following problems; then indicate the correct answer on the answer sheet. [On the actual test you will be permitted to use any space available on the examination paper for scratch work.]

NOTE: A figure that appears with a problem is drawn as accurately as possible so as to provide information that may help in answering the question. Numbers in this test are real numbers.

26. If 64% of the students in a class got a grade of C and there are 200 students in the class, how many students in the class received a grade of C?

(A) 64
(B) 118
(C) 124
(D) 128
(E) 164

27. If $2x + y = 10$ and $x = 3$, what is $x - y$?

(A) −4
(B) −1
(C) 0
(D) 1
(E) 7

28. If a worker can pack $\frac{1}{6}$ of a carton of canned food in 15 minutes and there are 40 workers in a factory, how many cartons should be packed in the factory in $1\frac{2}{3}$ hours?

(A) 33
(B) $40\frac{2}{9}$
(C) $43\frac{1}{9}$
(D) $44\frac{4}{9}$
(E) $45\frac{2}{3}$

29. Potatoes cost 15¢ a pound. If the price of potatoes rises by 10%, how much will 10 pounds of potatoes cost?

(A) 17¢
(B) $1.50
(C) $1.60
(D) $1.65
(E) $1.75

30. A truck driver must complete a 180-mile trip in 4 hours. If he averages 50 miles an hour for the first three hours of his trip, how fast must he travel in the final hour?

(A) 30 mph
(B) 35 mph
(C) 40 mph
(D) 45 mph
(E) 50 mph

31. If a triangle has base B and the altitude of the triangle is twice the base, then the area of the triangle is

(A) $\frac{1}{2}AB$
(B) AB
(C) $\frac{1}{2}B^2$
(D) B^2
(E) $2B$

32. If the product of two numbers is 10 and the sum of the two numbers is 7, then the larger of the two numbers is

(A) -2

(B) 2

(C) 3

(D) $4\frac{1}{4}$

(E) 5

33. Oranges cost $\$x$ a bag for the first 100 bags a store buys from a wholesaler. All bags bought in addition to the first 100 get a discount of 10%. How much does it cost to buy 150 bags of oranges from the wholesaler?

(A) $100

(B) $140x

(C) $145x

(D) $150x

(E) $100x + \$50$

34. If the lengths of the two sides of a right triangle adjacent to the right angle are 8 and 15 respectively, then the length of the side opposite the right angle is.

(A) $\sqrt{258}$

(B) 15.8

(C) 16

(D) 17

(E) 17.9

35. It costs x¢ each to print the first 600 copies of a newspaper. It costs $\left(x - \frac{y}{10}\right)$¢ for every copy after the first 600. How much does it cost to print 1,500 copies of the newspaper?

(A) $1500x$¢

(B) $150y$¢

(C) $(1500x - 90y)$¢

(D) $\$(150x - 9y)$

(E) $\$15x$

36. If the side of a square increases by 40%, then the area of the square increases by

(A) 16%

(B) 40%

(C) 96%

(D) 116%

(E) 140%

37. If 28 cartons of soda cost $21.00, then 7 cartons of soda should cost

(A) $5.25

(B) $5.50

(C) $6.40

(D) $7.00

(E) $10.50

38. Plane P takes off at 2 A.M. and flies at an average speed of x mph. Plane Q takes off at 3:30 A.M. and flies the same route as P but travels at an average speed of y mph. Assuming that y is greater than x, how many hours after 3:30 A.M. will plane Q overtake plane P?

(A) $\frac{3}{2}x$ hrs.

(B) $\frac{3}{2}$ hrs.

(C) $\frac{3}{2y}$ hrs.

(D) $\frac{3}{2(y-x)}$ hrs.

(E) $\frac{3x}{2(y-x)}$ hrs.

39. A worker is paid $20 for each day he works, and he is paid proportionately for any fraction of a day he works. If during one week he works $\frac{1}{8}$, $\frac{2}{3}$, $\frac{3}{4}$, $\frac{1}{3}$, and 1 full day, what are his total earnings for the week?

(A) $40.75
(B) $52.50
(C) $54
(D) $57.50
(E) $58.25

Use the following table for questions 40-41.

DISTRIBUTION OF TEST SCORES IN A CLASS

Number of Students	Number of Correct Answers
10	36 to 40
16	32 to 35
i2	28 to 31
14	26 to 27
8	0 to 25

40. What percent of the class answered 32 or more questions correctly?

(A) 20
(B) 26
(C) $32\frac{1}{2}$
(D) $43\frac{1}{3}$
(E) 52

41. The number of students who answered 28 to 31 questions correctly is x times the number who answered 25 or fewer correctly, where x is

(A) $\frac{2}{3}$
(B) 1
(C) $\frac{3}{2}$
(D) $\frac{7}{4}$
(E) 2

42. If the product of 3 consecutive integers is 210, then the sum of the two smaller integers is

(A) 5
(B) 11
(C) 12
(D) 13
(E) 18

43. Cereal costs $\frac{1}{3}$ as much as bacon. Bacon costs $\frac{5}{4}$ as much as eggs. Eggs cost what fraction of the cost of cereal?

(A) $\frac{5}{12}$
(B) $\frac{5}{4}$
(C) $\frac{5}{3}$
(D) $\frac{12}{5}$
(E) $\frac{4}{5}$

44. A truck gets 15 miles per gallon of gas when it is empty. When the truck is full, it travels only 80% as far on a gallon of gas as when empty. How many gallons will the loaded truck use to travel 80 miles?

(A) $5\frac{1}{3}$
(B) 6
(C) $6\frac{1}{3}$
(D) $6\frac{2}{3}$
(E) $6\frac{3}{4}$

45. If x and y are negative numbers, which of the following statements are always true?

    I. $x - y$ is negative.   II. $-x$ is positive   III. $(-x)(-y)$ is positive.

(A) I only
(B) II only
(C) I and II only
(D) II and III only
(E) I and III only

46. A car travels at 70 miles an hour for the first hour and a half of a trip. After the first $1\frac{1}{2}$ hours the car travels at 50 miles an hour. How long will the car take to drive 200 miles?

(A) $1\frac{1}{2}$ hours
(B) 2 hours
(C) $2\frac{3}{5}$ hours
(D) $3\frac{1}{5}$ hours
(E) $3\frac{2}{5}$ hours

47. A manufacturer makes books at a cost of \$$x$ each for the first 1,000 copies. The second thousand copies cost \$$(x - 2y)$ each. How much will it cost to make 1,600 copies of a book?

(A) \$1600x
(B) \$160x + \$120y
(C) \$1600x + \$1200y
(D) \$1600x − \$1200y
(E) \$16,000x − \$1200y

48. If $\frac{1}{3} < x$, then

(A) x is greater than 1
(B) x is greater than 3
(C) $\frac{1}{x}$ is greater than 3
(D) $\frac{1}{x}$ is less than 3
(E) all of the above statements are true

49. $\frac{1}{3} + \frac{2}{7} = \frac{x}{42}$ where x is

(A) $\frac{13}{21}$
(B) 13
(C) 21
(D) 24.5
(E) 26

50. If $r + x + y + z = 12$ and x is less than 6, then at least k of the numbers $r, x, y,$ and z must be positive, where k is

(A) 0
(B) 1
(C) 2
(D) 3
(E) 4

51. If the radius of a sphere is increased by a factor of 2, then the volume of the sphere is increased by a factor of

(A) 1
(B) 2
(C) 4

(D) 6
(E) 8

52. If the two sides of a right triangle adjacent to the right angle have lengths $n - 1$ and $2\sqrt{n}$, then the length of the side of the triangle opposite the right angle is

(A) $n - 1$
(B) $4\sqrt{n}$
(C) $4n$

(D) $\sqrt{n^2 + 2n}$
(E) $n + 1$

53. A function is given by the rule $f(x) = x^2 + 2$. What is $f(a + 2)$?

(A) $a^2 + 2$
(B) $a^2 + 4$
(C) $a^2 + 6$

(D) $a^2 + 2a + 4$
(E) $a^2 + 4a + 6$

54. If $\frac{x}{y} = 2$, then $\frac{y^2}{x^2}$ is equal to

(A) $\frac{1}{4}$
(B) $\frac{1}{2}$
(C) 1

(D) 2
(E) 4

55. An employer pays two workers X and Y a total of \$550 a week. X is paid 120% of the amount that Y is paid. How much is Y paid each week?

(A) \$200
(B) \$235
(C) \$250

(D) \$260
(E) \$300

If there is still time remaining, you may review the questions in this section only.
You may not turn to any other section of the test.

Section III   Practical Judgment

TIME: 20 minutes

DIRECTIONS: Read the following passage. After you have completed it, you will be asked to answer two sets of questions. The first of these, data evaluation, involves determining the importance of specific factors included in the passage. The second, data application, consists of general questions relating to the passage. When answering questions, you may consult the passage.

For the past two years, Bennett Joseph, head of the regional firm R and S Packing Company, had been seriously considering the use of U.S. government grade labeling for its high-quality canned fruits and vegetables. Having enjoyed an excellent reputation with the public under the trademark "Delish" for more than 30 years, these canned goods were known throughout the area by distributors and consumers alike as among the best.

The grade-labeling problem had come to the fore as the result of a new food supermarket chain called *Gaynes.* The new chain, a national organization, was making a depth penetration in the region by spending a sizeable portion of its large advertising and promotion budget for pushing its own private brands of frozen and canned fruits and vegetables. Its advertising emphasized that the public could find both grade and descriptive labeling on each package and can. The descriptive labels listed the type of food, the can size, the number of servings per can, the net contents, and the name and address of the chain.

Joseph had always paid careful attention to the descriptive labeling on R and S products but had been most reluctant to commit the company to the use of grade labeling. Joseph's reluctance was supported by the company's advertising and promotion manager and the production boss, who believed with him that grade labeling could hardly bring out the fresh flavor and taste upon which the company prided itself and had been able to capture through its own special heating, processing, and canning techniques.

A factor that seriously concerned Joseph in the use of grade labels on canned fruits and vegetables was the possible use of a high grade on one of the grading characteristics to offset a low score on another. This method could hardly help R and S, whose pack was known by distributors and consumers alike to be much better even than the highest grades of its competitors.

While Joseph was pondering this problem, he mulled over what he had read about grade labeling. In the first place, grading and labeling of canned foods had been developed to protect and help the consumer. Through the Department of Agriculture, federal standards had been set up for standardization, grading, and inspection work. To encourage voluntary use of these standards, the Department of Agriculture hired inspectors who carried out the federal inspection program at production periods. For canned fruits and vegetables, the grades were A, B, and C, which were based on such criteria as uniformity, succulence, and color—not flavor or food value.

Joseph certainly agreed that grade labeling could provide additional information for the consumer. R and S could also use it in company advertisements to supplement its own descriptive labels. But didn't everyone know about the taste and quality of R and S products? He also wondered what happened when a company using grade labeling saw the qualities of fruits and vegetables change from year to year. At one period, that quality might be high for most growers; it might also be low during another. Too, some factors that were very important in their effect on consumer choice could not be subjected to a grading discipline. For example, the range of individual tastes was impossible to standardize. Certainly taste, Joseph felt, should be at least as important as the other, more tangible criteria used to grade canned goods.

Joseph's legal advisor pointed out that there was another aspect to the problem of grade labeling. He had been informed by colleagues employed at the Department of Commerce that while present use of standards was voluntary, such use might become mandatory in the not-too-distant future. His contacts explained that their information was based not on present government plans, but on possible Congressional legislation. The scenario went like this. Several consumer organizations were active in promoting "truth in labeling" legislation. Their objective was the provision of more information on packaging so that consumers could make better decisions on what products to buy. Simply put, it was argued that consumers could not distinguish between competing products on the basis of present labeling requirements. Present labels contained only the manufacturer's name and address, the fact that the contents conformed to Federal Drug and Agriculture food standards, and net weight. No mandatory criteria existed for grade standards. Consumers could judge quality only on the basis of trial-and-error, by trying the product or by reading the advertised claims of competing brands. Government officials believed that if several of the larger consumer organizations combined efforts to lobby in Congress for passage of consumer legislation, there was an even chance that a "truth in labeling" law could be passed within a year.

Joseph weighed the findings of his legal advisor. He realized that, while taste was the ultimate criterion for choosing one brand over another, the *initial* choice of a particular brand could be influenced by product grade. Moreover, since R and S products were of the highest quality, they would undoubtedly carry the highest possible federal grades. Joseph was most concerned about the timing of a decision to accept product grading, which was at the present time still voluntary. Would it be to R and S's advantage to adopt a voluntary labeling program, or would it be better to wait until grading became mandatory for all processors? What advantages and disadvantages would result from taking a wait-and-see attitude, rather than immediately commencing a voluntary grading program?

Before Joseph completed his study of the problem, one of his leading competitors, Taam Foods, commenced a voluntary label standardization program. Joseph was worried about the possibility that some of Taam Foods' products might be designated grade A quality. Taam Foods could quickly exploit this advantage at the expense of R and S. Thus, grading had now become a competitive issue. Joseph felt that he had to make a quick decision one way or the other.

Data Evaluation Questions

DIRECTIONS: The questions that follow relate to the preceding passage. Evaluate, in terms of the passage, each of the items given. Then select your answer from one of the following classifications, and blacken the corresponding space on the answer sheet.

(A) A MAJOR OBJECTIVE in making the decision: one of the goals sought by the decision maker

(B) A MAJOR FACTOR in making the decision: an aspect of the problem, specifically mentioned in the passage, that fundamentally affects and/or determines the decision

(C) A MINOR FACTOR in making the decision: a less important element bearing on or affecting a Major Factor, rather than a Major Objective directly

(D) A MAJOR ASSUMPTION in making the decision: a projection or supposition arrived at by the decision maker before considering the factors and alternatives

(E) AN UNIMPORTANT ISSUE in making the decision: an item lacking significant impact on, or relationship to, the decision

56. Establishment of a new supermarket chain

57. Mandatory standardization of food labeling practices

58. Effects on sales of grade labeling of R and S products

59. Federal food standards established by the Department of Agriculture

60. Maintaining the R and S brand image

61. Likelihood that grade labeling would become mandatory

62. Present label requirements established by law

63. Influence of consumer groups on government actions

64. Taam Foods' labels

65. The 30 years of experience behind R and S packing company

66. Superior taste of R and S products

67. Quality of R and S products

Data Application Questions

DIRECTIONS: Answer each of the following questions using information contained in the passage.

68. According to the passage, grade labeling was intended to

   I.   Increase the cost of canning
  II.   Increase competition
 III.   Protect and inform the consumer

(A) I only   (D) II and III only
(B) III only   (E) I, II, and III
(C) I and II only

69. R and S had not adopted grade labeling because

   I.   it had little reason to do so
  II.   its products would have received low grade ratings
 III.   it was too expensive

(A) I only
(B) III only
(C) I and II only
(D) II and III only
(E) I, II, and III

70. Which of the following R & S employees had doubts about the efficacy of adopting grade labeling?

    I.   Bennett Joseph
    II. The advertising manager
    III. The production manager

    (A) I only
    (B) III only
    (C) I and II only
    (D) II and III only
    (E) I, II, and III

71. Which government agencies supervised the labeling program?

    I.   Department of Commerce
    II. Department of Health
    III. Department of Agriculture

    (A) I only
    (B) III only
    (C) I and II only
    (D) II and III only
    (E) I, II, and III

72. Grading of fruits and vegetables was based on

    I.   taste
    II. color
    III. uniformity

    (A) I only
    (B) III only
    (C) I and II only
    (D) II and III only
    (E) I, II, and III

73. *Gaynes* labels included

    I.   food content
    II. net contents
    III. price per unit

    (A) I only
    (B) III only
    (C) I and II only
    (D) II and III only
    (E) I, II, and III

74. R and S management had doubts about grade labeling because

   I.   grading could not adequately describe the quality of the contents
  II.   a high grade on one characteristic might be used to offset a low grade on another
III.   consumers would be confused

  (A) I only
  (B) III only
  (C) I and II only
  (D) II and III only
  (E) I, II, and III

75. According to Mr. Bennett Joseph, one of the most important criteria used to grade canned goods should be

   I.   A,B,C values
  II.   Price
III.   Consumer tastes

  (A) I only
  (B) III only
  (C) I and II only
  (D) II and III only
  (E) I, II, and III

If there is still time remaining, you may review the questions in this section only.
You may not turn to any other section of the test.

Section IV   Data Sufficiency

TIME: 30 minutes

DIRECTIONS: Each of the following problems has a question and two statements which are labeled (1) and (2). Use the data given in (1) and (2) together with other available information (such as the number of hours in a day, the definition of *clockwise*, mathematical facts, etc.) to decide whether the statements are *sufficient* to answer the question. Then fill in space

(A) if you can get the answer from (1) alone but not from (2) alone;

(B) if you can get the answer from (2) alone but not from (1) alone;

(C) if you can get the answer from (1) and (2) together, although neither statement by itself suffices;

(D) if statement (1) alone suffices *and* statement (2) alone suffices;

(E) if you cannot get the answer from statements (1) and (2) together, but need even more data.

All numbers used in this section are real numbers. A figure given for a problem is intended to provide information consistent with that in the question, but not necessarily with the additional information contained in the statements.

76. In triangle *ABC*, find *x* if *y* = 40.

(1) *AB* = *BC*
(2)   *z* = 100

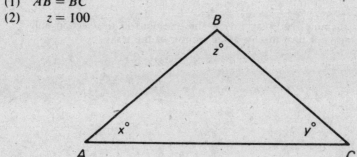

77. What is the area of the shaded part of the circle? *O* is the center of the circle.

(1) The radius of the circle is 4.
(2) *x* is 60.

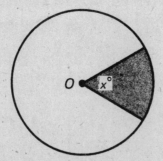

78. What was Mr. Kliman's income in 1970?

(1) His total income for 1968, 1969, and 1970 was $41,000.
(2) He made 20% more in 1969 than he did in 1968.

79. If l and l' are straight lines, find y.

    (1) $x = 100$
    (2) $z = 80$

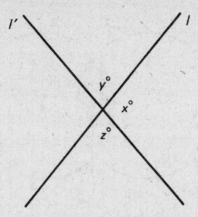

80. Fifty students have signed up for at least one of the courses German I and English I. How many of the 50 students are taking German I but not English I?

    (1) 16 students are taking German I and English I.
    (2) The number of students taking English I but not German I is the same as the number taking German I but not English I.

81. Is $ABCD$ a square?

    (1) $AD = AB$
    (2) $x = 90$

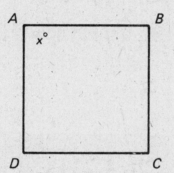

82. The XYZ Corporation has 7,000 employees. What is the average yearly wage of an employee of the XYZ Corporation?

    (1) 4,000 of the employees are executives.
    (2) The total amount the company pays in wages each year is $77,000,000.

83. Is $x > y$?

    (1) $(x + y)^2 > 0$
    (2) x is positive

84. What is the area of the shaded region if both circles have radius 4 and O and O' are the centers of the circles?

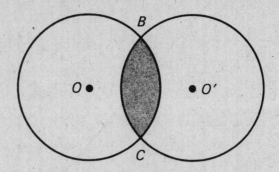

(1) The area enclosed by both circles is 29π.
(2) The line connecting O and O' is perpendicular to the line connecting B and C (B and C are the points where the two circles intersect).

85. How long will it take to travel from A to B? It takes 4 hours to travel from A to B and back to A.

(1) It takes 25% more time to travel from A to B than it does to travel from B to A.
(2) C is midway between A and B, and it takes 2 hours to travel from A to C and back to A.

86. l, l', and k are straight lines. Are l and l' parallel?

(1) $x = y$
(2) $y = z$

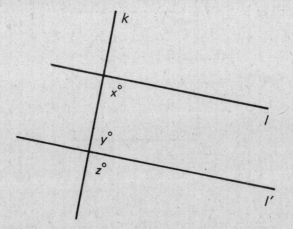

87. What is $x + y + z$?

(1) $x + y = 3$
(2) $x + z = 2$

88. How much cardboard will it take to make a rectangular box with a lid the length of whose base is 7 inches?

(1) The width of the box will be 5 inches.
(2) The height of the box will be 4 inches.

89. What is the profit on 15 boxes of detergent?

    (1)   The cost of a crate of boxes of detergent is $50.

    (2)   Each crate contains 100 boxes of detergent.

90. Which of the two figures, *ABCD* or *EFGH*, has the largest area?

    (1) The perimeter of *ABCD* is longer than the perimeter of *EFGH*.

    (2) *AC* is longer than *EG*.

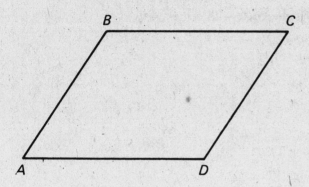
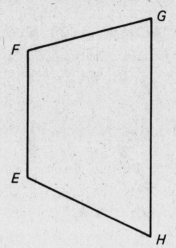

91. Is a number divisible by 9?

    (1)   The number is divisible by 3.

    (2)   The number is divisible by 27.

92. *PQRS* is a rectangle. The coordinates of the point *P* are (2,3). What is the area of *PQRS*?

    (1)   The coordinates of the point *S* are (2,5).

    (2)   The coordinates of the point *Q* are (6,3).

93. *ABCD* is a rectangle. Which region *ABEF* or *CDEF* has a larger area?

    (1)   *BE* is longer than *FD*.

    (2)   *BE* is longer than *CD*.

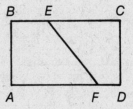

94. Is the integer *k* odd or even?

    (1) k^2 is odd.

    (2) $2k$ is even.

95. Does a car with 5 gallons of gas in its fuel tank have enough fuel to travel 100 miles?

    (1)   The car travels 25 miles on one gallon of gas.

    (2)   The car is driven at a speed of 50 miles per hour.

96. *ABCD* is a square.
    BCO is a semicircle.
    What is the area of *ABOCD*?

    (1) The length of *AC* is $4\sqrt{2}$.
    (2) The radius of the semicircle *BOC* is 2.

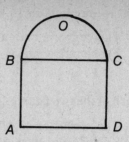

97. Do the points *P* and *Q* lie on the same circle with center (0,0)?

    (1) The coordinates of point *P* are (2,3).
    (2) The coordinates of point *Q* are (4,1).

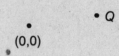

98. Did *ABC* Company make a profit in 1980?

    (1) *ABC* Company made a profit in 1979.
    (2) *ABC* Company made a profit in 1981.

99. Is 2^n divisible by 8?

    (1) *n* is an odd integer.
    (2) *n* is an integer greater than 5.

100. Did the price of a bushel of soybeans increase during every week of 1980?

    (1) The price of a bushel of soybeans was $2 on Jan 1, 1980.
    (2) The price of a bushel of soybeans was $4 on Jan 1, 1981.

101. What is the length of line
    segment *AB*? All lines that
    meet are perpendicular.
    AJ, JI, HI, BC, FE, GF and *DC* are each
    equal to *x*. *HG* and *DE* are each equal to *y*.

    (1) $y = 3$
    (2) $x = 2$

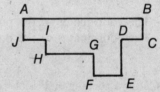

102. Is the angle *c* larger than 60°?

    (1) $a + b$ is greater than *c*.
    (2) *a* is greater than *b* which is greater than *c*.

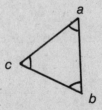

103. Which is larger, 2^a or 3^b?

    (1) *a* is greater than $2b$.
    (2) *a* is greater than or equal to $b + 3$.

104. Which number is the largest: *a*, *b*, or *c*?

   (1) *ab* is greater than *ac*.
   (2) *ba* is greater than *bc*.

105. Will the circle with center *O* fit inside the square *ABCD*?

   (1) The diameter of the circle is less than a side of the square.
   (2) The area of the circle is less than the area of the square.

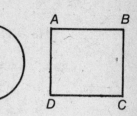

· If there is still time remaining, you may review the questions in this section only.
You may not turn to any other section of the test.

Section V   Writing Ability

TIME: 15 minutes

DIRECTIONS: Each of the sentences in this section is either correct or contains one error in grammar, usage, diction (choice of words), idiom or punctuation. If there is an error it will be found in one of the underlined parts of the sentence, labeled (A), (B), (C), or (D). If you identify an error mark the appropriate letter on your answer sheet. If there is no error in the sentence mark (E)—no error.

Note: Assume that all parts of the sentence that are not underlined are correct and cannot be changed.

106. Roberta is the one who seems convinced that we are trying to harm her, irregard-
                     A   B   C

     less of how much we have done for her benefit. No error
             D   E

107. Providing you have studied hard, you will be able to do this assignment quite easily
       A   B   C   D

     without any help from them. No error
                           E

108. Three people came into the study—his former wife, his best friend, and his
                A   B   C

     mother-in-law. No error
         D   E

109. The advise we had gotten had come just at the right time in our dealings in this most
        A   B   C   D

     unfortunate matter. No error
                 E

110. Margaret hung up all the clothes that had been laying around the room. No error
            A B   C   D   E

111. His conclusions are different from the ones that you and I am prepared to
                              A   B   C

     accept, even under the present circumstances. No error
          D   E

112. George, the foreman of the production line, told Mr. Crosby that he had inadvertently
     _____   _A_   _B_   _C_
     shipped out a defective batch. No error
             _D_   _E_

113. The assistant-in-chief immediately noticed the tapes' color; and called for his
         _____A_____ ___B___   _____C_____ ___D___
     superior. No error
            _E_

114. Let us now take account of these data that we have been given and use them as
                          _____A_____ _B_   _C_
     the bases for our further research. No error
       _D_   _E_

115. They had sent all their friends, except for Laura and I, a letter of greeting. No error
         _A_   _____B_____   _C_ _D_   _E_

116. Joan felt badly about losing the earrings which her husband had sent her for their
              ___A___   _____B_____ __C__   _D_
     anniversary. No error
                  _E_

117. The three advantages of his plan are: its simplicity, it can be applied immediately, and
                         _____A_____   ___B___   _____C_____
     its probable popularity among the local population. No error
                              __D__   _E_

118. After visiting the doctor, she decided to follow his instructions, and made plans to
                                        ____A____
     move without delay to Salt Springs where she could be sure of a healthy climate.
          ____B____   ___C___   ___D___
     No error
       _E_

119. There was scarcely no time given to think about the problem before the bell rang for
           _A_   _B_   __C__   ___D___
     the end of class. No error
                      _E_

120. You will have to intervene in this fight between Sandra and me. No error
         _A_   _B_   ___C___   _D_ _E_

121. If anyone in a position of genuine managerial responsibility approved the project,
                 _____A_____   ___B___
     they are largely to blame for its subsequent failure. No error
     _____C___   __D__   _E_

122. The President, together with the First Lady and three trusted advisors,
                    ____A____   _____B_____
     have arrived at Andrews Air Force Base for the flight to Zurich. No error
     _____C_____   ___D___   _E_

123. The city government, with <u>its large number</u> of agencies, commissions,
A

<u>and regulatory bodies,</u> <u>as well as</u> nearly a dozen deputy mayors, <u>are unable</u> to
   B   C   D

develop a single coherent plan for managing the current fiscal crisis. <u>No error</u>
                                                                         E

124. <u>That</u> Donovan is the man <u>whom</u> the President nominated to this post <u>is not enough;</u>
        A   B   C

the nominee's background must be carefully scrutinized by the Senate <u>as a whole</u>
                                                                       D

<u>before</u> final confirmation is given. <u>No error</u>
 E   E

125. <u>Realizing</u> the widespread public interest <u>in the discovery</u>, the manuscript <u>was placed</u>
        A   B   C

on display <u>in the foyer</u> of the university library. <u>No error</u>
            D   E

If there is still time remaining, you may review the questions in this section only.
You may not turn to any other section of the test.

Section VI Practical Judgment

TIME: 20 minutes

DIRECTIONS: Read the following passage. After you have completed it, you will be asked to answer two sets of questions. The first of these, data evaluation, involves determining the importance of specific factors included in the passage. The second, data application, consists of general questions relating to the passage. When answering questions, you may consult the passage.

Sam Hoe's small furniture factory was doing more business than ever before and had a solid backlog of orders that ensured continuous production. Its profits, however, had not kept pace with production. Rising machinery, lumber, and hardware costs, higher wages, and higher operating expenses all combined to eat into profits. Mr. Hoe was concerned about this situation and had thought about raising prices on many of his products. This was not practical at the present, however, because the prices of most items had been increased within the last six months. Among various alternatives, he had considered opening an outlet to retail his own products.

The Hoe Company had been established when Sam's father had started a small woodworking shop in his garage twenty years before. When Sam had come into the business about five years later, the shop had been moved to a warehouse on the outskirts of town. At that time, much of the space was used for storage of materials and finished goods. Through the next ten years more and more of the storage area had been taken over for equipment and work space; therefore an additional storage building had been constructed next to the original building. The payroll had grown to twenty craftsmen, who were supervised by a production manager. Mr. Hoe and one bookkeeper did the purchasing, accounting, and sales work.

The shop, located in a city of 25,000 people, had begun on a special-order custom basis, selling mainly to local residents. Through the years a standard line of tables and chairs had been developed, which now accounted for 78 percent of sales. Most of the standard line furniture was sold through four wholesalers to retail furniture stores in a five-state area. Two outlets in the city, a department store and a large furniture showroom, bought directly from the factory. Although most orders for custom-made items came from within the state, a few came from states from all areas of the country.

In examining his sales and profit records for the past two years, Mr. Hoe found that while sales had increased steadily, profits showed only a very slight increase over the preceding year. Further study showed that while the sale of custom-made merchandise netted a consistently good profit, standard items, sold on a slimmer margin, lost money in some cases. Rising material costs and more rigid specifications and demands from large retail purchasers had both contributed to the problem. Unfortunately, the number of orders for custom work had to be limited, for top craftsmen were in short supply and much of this work demanded highly skilled cabinetmakers.

Mr. Hoe believed that profits could be improved if the volume of standard furniture could be increased. Discussing the situation with his production manager, Mr. Hoe commented, "Lem, what would you think about opening a retail showroom here? The way I see it, our standard items are popular and almost sell themselves. There's plenty of room since we added the new building, and fixing up a nice-looking showroom shouldn't be too difficult or expensive. If we cut out the retailer's margin and split it between the customer and ourselves, we can cut prices—or hold them steady, anyway—and still make a decent profit." The retail showroom, Hoe explained, would not replace existing distribution channels, but rather complement them. The showroom could be located in the factory, thereby saving delivery and rental costs.

Another idea that Hoe raised was the possibility of increasing the number of retail stores that carried the Hoe Company's line. It was not suggested that furniture sales be extended geographically beyond the five states now served, but rather that a more intensive effort would be made to increase the number of retail outlets in these states. According to Hoe, this could be accomplished by adding more wholesalers, especially in the larger states.

Hoe's marketing manager, Norbert Ravis, agreed that the number of retail outlets should be increased by more intensive coverage of wholesalers or by adding additional wholesalers to the network. Norbert suggested that the company find a way to increase sales through moderate-sized retailers, rather than expand sales to department stores and large distributors. Norbert explained that although large retailers could order in bulk, the profit margin was lower. What was needed, according to Norbert, was a balance of sales between large and small retailers, with about three-fourths of total sales allocated to the smaller or moderate-sized retailer. To support his argument, Norbert supplied the following statistics: a standard set of a table and four chairs sold to a large department store earned a 25 percent profit to the factory. The same set sold to a small or moderate-sized retailer earned a 40 percent profit. Therefore, as far as Norbert was concerned, sales should be increased to smaller retailers only.

Sam Kander, Hoe's production manager, was worried about the production capabilities of the factory. With output reaching capacity, how could the marketing people plan for increased sales without taking into consideration the capacity of the plant? Even if an additional shift was added, the factory could only increase output by another 40 percent with existing machinery. Kander felt that the best way to increase sales would be to expand the custom-made merchandise. A special effort should be made to hire more cabinetmakers. Hoe could make a survey of the various vocational schools in the area to find young men who would work as apprentices in the factory. Demand was increasing for the sort of custom work that Hoe supplied. Moreover, custom work was the most profitable for the company.

Sam Hoe weighed all the alternatives. He came to the conclusion that increasing sales without improving profitability would be a waste of resources. He would have to determine which alternative would allow his company to grow, while at the same time contributing to profit improvement.

Data Evaluation Questions

DIRECTIONS: The questions that follow relate to the preceding passage. Evaluate, in terms of the passage, each of the items given. Then select your answer from one of the following classifications, and blacken the corresponding space on the answer sheet.

(A) A MAJOR OBJECTIVE in making the decision: one of the goals sought by the decision maker

(B) A MAJOR FACTOR in making the decision: an aspect of the problem, specifically mentioned in the passage, that fundamentally affects and/or determines the decision

(C) A MINOR FACTOR in making the decision: a less important element bearing on or affecting a Major Factor, rather than a Major Objective directly

(D) A MAJOR ASSUMPTION in making the decision: a projection or supposition arrived at by the decision maker before considering the factors and alternatives

(E) AN UNIMPORTANT ISSUE in making the decision: an item lacking significant impact on, or relationship to, the decision

126. Increased production costs incurred by Hoe's company

127. Increased demand for Hoe's furniture

128. Storage space needed by Hoe's company

129. Employment of 20 craftsmen in Hoe's factory

130. Opening of a retail showroom

131. Availability of skilled cabinetmakers

132. Improving profitability of Hoe's company

133. Number of states in which Hoe's furniture is sold

134. Ease of selling Hoe's standard furniture in an attached showroom

135. Addition of more wholesalers

136. Production capabilities of Hoe's factory

137. Direct sales to large retailers

138. Likelihood of recruiting apprentices through local schools

Data Application Questions

DIRECTIONS: Answer each of the following questions using information contained in the passage.

139. Among the problems faced by Sam Hoe's business was the fact that

    I. employee morale was low
    II. prices were fluctuating
    III. profits had increased only slightly

    (A) I only
    (B) III only
    (C) I and II only
    (D) II and III only
    (E) I, II, and III

140. Sam Hoe had decided against a price increase for his goods because

    I. competition was too intense
    II. his father was against it
    III. he had had a general price increase within the past six months

    (A) I only
    (B) III only
    (C) I and II only
    (D) II and III only
    (E) I, II, and III

141. Most of Sam Hoe's furniture sales were generated by his

    I. standard line items
    II. American colonial lines
    III. custom pieces

    (A) I only
    (B) III only
    (C) I and II only
    (D) II and III only
    (E) I, II, and III

142. Norbert Ravis favored increasing sales to smaller retailers rather than to larger ones mainly because

    (A) Hoe's profits on sales to smaller retailers were larger
    (B) this strategy would put less strain on Hoe's production capacity
    (C) this would reduce the number of steps between Hoe and the final consumer
    (D) bulk purchasing resulted in greater delivery costs for Hoe
    (E) this would allow Hoe's standards of quality to be maintained more easily

143. Mr. Hoe's furniture was sold mainly

    I. in areas throughout the United States
   II. to local residents
  III. within a five-state area

  (A) I only
  (B) III only
  (C) I and II only
  (D) II and III only
  (E) I, II, and III

144. Mr. Hoe wanted to open a retail showroom in order to

    I. increase his profitability
   II. sell excess stock
  III. cut down on advertising expenses

  (A) I only
  (B) III only
  (C) I and II only
  (D) II and III only
  (E) I, II, and III

145. Mr. Hoe's profits had eroded because

    I. large retailers demanded higher quality control
   II. raw materials had increased in price
  III. wholesale margins had increased

  (A) I only
  (B) III only
  (C) I and II only
  (D) II and III only
  (E) I, II, and III

If there is still time remaining, you may review the questions in this section only.
You may not turn to any other section of the test.

Section VII   Data Sufficiency

TIME: 30 minutes

DIRECTIONS: Each of the following problems has a question and two statements which are labeled (1) and (2). Use the data given in (1) and (2) together with other available information (such as the number of hours in a day, the definition of *clockwise,* mathematical facts, etc.) to decide whether the statements are *sufficient* to answer the question. Then fill in space

(A) if you can get the answer from (1) alone but not from (2) alone;

(B) if you can get the answer from (2) alone but not from (1) alone;

(C) if you can get the answer from (1) and (2) together, although neither statement by itself suffices;

(D) if statement (1) alone suffices *and* statement (2) alone suffices;

(E) if you cannot get the answer from statements (1) and (2) together, but need even more data.

All numbers used in this section are real numbers. A figure given for a problem is intended to provide information consistent with that in the question, but not necessarily with the additional information contained in the statements.

146. What percentage is Y's salary of X's salary?

    (1) X's salary is 80% of Z's salary.
    (2) Y's salary is 120% of Z's salary.

147. How long will it be before ABC stock is worth $63 per share?

    (1) ABC stock doubles in price every six months.
    (2) ABC company pays dividends of $3 a share.

148. What is the value of $x + 2y$?

    (1) $x + y - z = 10$
    (2) $y + z = 4$

149. What is the sum of the three numbers x, y, and z?

    (1) The average of x, y, and z is 12.
    (2) $x = 3, y = 20$

150. Which angle is smaller, x or y?

    (1) $AB = BC$
    (2) $x + y = 100°$

151. How much money did the Suppertime Theatre make from ticket sales? The theatre sells two kinds of tickets: reserved seat and general admission.

    (1) The theatre made $2,000 from sales of reserved seats.
    (2) The theatre sold 400 general admission tickets.

152. What is the value of $x + y$?

    (1) $x = 50\%$ of y
    (2) $2x + 2y = 6$

153. Does 3 evenly divide the integer x?

    (1) 6 evenly divides x.
    (2) 12 evenly divides x.

154. Are the lines l and m perpendicular?

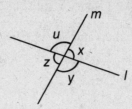

    (1) $z = x$
    (2) $u = y$

155. The expenses of the ABC corporation are each billed to one and only one of its three divisions: division A, division B, and division C. What percentage of the expenses of the ABC corporation were billed to division A?

    (1) The expenses of division A are twice as much as the expenses of division B.
    (2) The expenses of division B are the same as the expenses of division C.

156. The graph gives the distribution of expenses between Joe and Bill each month for their apartment. How much does Bill pay each month for the apartment?

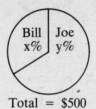

Total = $500

    (1) $X = 40$
    (2) $Y = 60$

157. Is $\dfrac{x}{12} > \dfrac{y}{40}$?

    (1) $10x > 3y$
    (2) $12x < 4y$

158. What is the value of $x - y$?

    (1) $x^2 - y^2 = 10$
    (2) $x + y = 2$

159. In a survey of 100 people, 70 people owned a television or a telephone or both. If 30 people owned both a television and a telephone, which group of surveyed people is larger: those who own a television or those who own a telephone?

    (1) 25 people own a television but do not own a telephone.
    (2) 45 people own a telephone.

160. Which is larger, x or x^2?

    (1) $x > 0$
    (2) $x < 0$

161. Which line segment is longer, AB or CD?

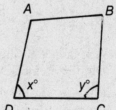

    (1) $x + y = 170$
    (2) CB is longer than AD

162. How many degrees Celsius is 100° Fahrenheit?

    (1) degrees Celsius = 5/9 (degrees Fahrenheit) -32
    (2) degrees Fahrenheit = 9/5 (degrees Celsius) $+$ 32

163. How much is Jane's salary?

    (1) Jane's salary is 70% of John's salary.
    (2) John's salary is 50% of Mary's salary.

164. What is the value of z? $z = x - (150\%$ of $y)$.

    (1) $x = \frac{3}{2}y$
    (2) $z = \sqrt{y}$

165. What is the length of AB?
    The length of $AC = 5$.

    (A) AC is perpendicular to CB.
    (2) The length of CB is 12.

166. Is $x > 1$?

    (1) $x + y = 2$
    (2) $y < 0$

167. Is x positive?

    (1) $x^2 + 3x - 4 = 0$
    (2) $x > -2$

168. Can x, y, z be the lengths of the sides of a triangle?

    (1) $x > y > z > 0$
    (2) $x + y > z$

169. Is n the square of a positive integer k?

    (1) $n = 4j^2$ with j an integer.
    (2) $n^2 = A^2 + B^2$ with A, B integers.

170. Train Y leaves New York at 1 a.m. and travels east at a constant speed of y m.p.h. Train Z leaves New York at 2 a.m. and travels east at a constant speed of z m.p.h. Which train will travel farther by 4 a.m.?

    (1) $y > z$
    (2) $y = 1.2z$

171. Is $xy < 0$?

    (1) $\frac{1}{x} < \frac{1}{y}$
    (2) $x > 0$

172. A square originally had sides with length s. The length of the side is increased by $x\%$. Did the area of the square increase by more than 10%?

    (1) x is greater than 5.
    (2) x is less than 10.

173. How much did the XYZ corporation make in 1970?

    (1) The XYZ corporation made twice as much in 1970 as it did in 1969.
    (2) The XYZ corporation made twice as much in 1971 as it did in 1970.

174. What is the value of $x + y$?

    (1) $x - y = 12$
    (2) $2x + 3y = 7$

175. How many books are on the bookshelf?

    (1)   The bookshelf is 12 feet long.
    (2)   The average weight of each book is 1.2 pounds.

If there is still time remaining, you may review the questions in this section only.
You may not turn to any other section of the test.

Answers

Section I — Reading Comprehension

1. (C)	8. (E)	15. (A)	22. (D)
2. (C)	9. (B)	16. (E)	23. (C)
3. (D)	10. (B)	17. (A)	24. (E)
4. (C)	11. (A)	18. (C)	25. (E)
5. (C)	12. (D)	19. (D)	
6. (B)	13. (C)	20. (D)	
7. (A)	14. (D)	21. (E)	

Section II — Problem Solving

(Numbers in parentheses indicate the section in the Mathematics Review where material concerning the question is discussed.)

26. (D) (I-4)	36. (C) (I-4, III-7)	46. (E) (II-3)
27. (B) (II-2)	37. (A) (II-6)	47. (D) (II-3)
28. (D) (II-3)	38. (E) (II-3)	48. (D) (II-7)
29. (D) (I-4)	39. (D) (I-2)	49. (E) (I-2)
30. (A) (I-7)	40. (D) (I-4)	50. (B) (I-6, II-7)
31. (D) (III-7)	41. (C) (II-3)	51. (E) (III-8)
32. (E) (II-2)	42. (B) (I-1)	52. (E) (III-4)
33. (C) (I-4)	43. (D) (I-2)	53. (E) (II-1)
34. (D) (III-4)	44. (D) (I-4)	54. (A) (II-2)
35. (C) (II-3)	45. (D) (I-6)	55. (C) (II-2)

Section III — Practical Judgment

56. (B)	61. (D)	66. (C)	71. (B)
57. (C)	62. (E)	67. (B)	72. (D)
58. (B)	63. (C)	68. (B)	73. (C)
59. (C)	64. (B)	69. (A)	74. (C)
60. (A)	65. (E)	70. (E)	75. (B)

Section IV   Data Sufficiency

76. **(D)**	84. **(A)**	92. **(C)**	100. **(E)**
77. **(C)**	85. **(A)**	93. **(A)**	101. **(C)**
78. **(E)**	86. **(C)**	94. **(A)**	102. **(B)**
79. **(D)**	87. **(E)**	95. **(A)**	103. **(A)**
80. **(C)**	88. **(C)**	96. **(D)**	104. **(E)**
81. **(E)**	89. **(E)**	97. **(C)**	105. **(A)**
82. **(B)**	90. **(E)**	98. **(E)**	
83. **(E)**	91. **(B)**	99. **(B)**	

Section V   Writing Ability

106. **(C)**	111. **(C)**	116. **(A)**	121. **(C)**
107. **(A)**	112. **(B)**	117. **(B)**	122. **(C)**
108. **(E)**	113. **(D)**	118. **(D)**	123. **(D)**
109. **(A)**	114. **(E)**	119. **(B)**	124. **(E)**
110. **(D)**	115. **(C)**	120. **(E)**	125. **(A)**

Section VI   Practical Judgment

126. **(B)**	131. **(B)**	136. **(B)**	141. **(A)**
127. **(B)**	132. **(A)**	137. **(E)**	142. **(A)**
128. **(C)**	133. **(E)**	138. **(D)**	143. **(D)**
129. **(E)**	134. **(D)**	139. **(B)**	144. **(A)**
130. **(A)**	135. **(A)**	140. **(B)**	145. **(C)**

Section VII   Data Sufficiency

146. **(C)**	154. **(E)**	162. **(D)**	170. **(D)**
147. **(E)**	155. **(C)**	163. **(E)**	171. **(C)**
148. **(C)**	156. **(D)**	164. **(A)**	172. **(A)**
149. **(A)**	157. **(A)**	165. **(C)**	173. **(E)**
150. **(C)**	158. **(C)**	166. **(C)**	174. **(C)**
151. **(E)**	159. **(D)**	167. **(C)**	175. **(E)**
152. **(B)**	160. **(B)**	168. **(E)**	
153. **(D)**	161. **(E)**	169. **(A)**	

Analysis

Section I   Reading Comprehension

1. **(C)** See paragraph 2, line 1.

2. **(C)** See paragraph 1, sentence 2: "His maturer theories of society . . ."

3. **(D)** See paragraph 1: ". . . he ended life as a major social theorist . . . sympathetic with violent revolution. . . ."

4. **(C)** See paragraph 3: ". . . Russia . . . is no longer a proletarian movement . . . but a camouflaged imperialistic effort.. . . ."

5. **(C)** See paragraph 3. Of course, it is accepted by those in (D) and (E), but also by those in (C).

6. **(B)** This can be deduced from the last paragraph.

7. **(A)** See paragraph 2.

8. **(E)** All these are mentioned in paragraph 1.

9. **(B)** See paragraph 2: ". . . fiscal policies should be designed to encourage economic growth."

10. **(B)** See paragraph 2: they did not.

11. **(A)** See paragraph 3: the Committee of the Whole.

12. **(D)** See paragraph 4, line 1.

13. **(C)** See paragraph 5: "In the first decade of the twentieth century, an 'executive budget' came into successful use. . . ."

14. **(D)** See paragraph 5: it was rejected.

15. **(A)** See paragraph 6, line 1: the responsibility was given by the Budget and Accounting Act of 1921.

16. **(E)** See paragraph 6: the Director of the Bureau of the Budget serves for an indefinite term.

17. **(A)** See paragraph 2.

18. **(C)** See paragraph 2: they came at different times.

19. **(D)** See paragraph 2.

20. **(D)** Paragraphs 2 and 4 especially mention the various points of migration which the Indians reached.

21. **(E)** See paragraph 4.

22. **(D)** See paragraph 3: ". . . the New Mexico Indians were very successful big game hunters."

23. **(C)** See the last line of paragraph 4.

24. **(E)** All these are given in paragraph 3.

25. **(E)** Certainly, alternatives (A) and (C) do not correspond to the contents of the passage, while (B) and (D) are too general. The main point in the passage is the migration of Indians, their cultures, and their acclimation to new surroundings. These subjects are in the domain of the anthropologist.

Section II   Problem Solving

26. **(D)** 64% of 200 is $(.64)(200)$, which equals 128. Therefore, 128 students received a grade of C.

27. **(B)** Since $x = 3$, $2x + y = 6 + y$; so $6 + y = 10$ and $y = 4$. Therefore, $x - y = 3 - 4 = -1$.

28. **(D)** Since 15 minutes is $\frac{1}{4}$ of an hour, each worker can pack $4 \times \frac{1}{6}$ or $\frac{2}{3}$ of a case an hour. The factory has 40 workers, so they should pack $40 \times \frac{2}{3}$ or $\frac{80}{3}$ cases each hour. Therefore, in $1\frac{2}{3}$ or $\frac{5}{3}$ hours the factory should pack $\left(\frac{5}{3} \times \frac{80}{3}\right)$, which equals $\frac{400}{9}$ or $44\frac{4}{9}$ cases.

29. **(D)** If potatoes cost 15¢ a pound, then 10 pounds will cost $1.50. If the price increases by 10%, then 10 pounds of potatoes will cost 110% of $1.50, which is $1.65.

30. **(A)** Since the truck driver averaged 50 miles per hour for the first three hours, he traveled 3×50 or 150 miles during the first three hours. Since he needs to travel $180 - 150$ miles in the final hour, he should drive at 30 mph.

31. **(D)** The area of a triangle is $\frac{1}{2}$ the base times the altitude. The altitude is $2B$, so the area is $(\frac{1}{2})(B)(2B)$ or B^2.

32. **(E)** If we denote the two numbers by x and y, then $xy = 10$ and $x + y = 7$. Then x is $7 - y$ and $(7 - y)y = 7y - y^2 = 10$ or $y^2 - 7y + 10 = 0$. But $y^2 - 7y + 10$ equals $(y - 5)(y - 2)$; so the two numbers are 5 and 2. The correct answer can be selected quickly by inspection of the choices.

33. **(C)** Since the first 100 bags cost $x each, the total cost of the first 100 bags is $100x. Since the remaining 50 bags are discounted 10%, each bag costs 90% of $x or $(.90)x$ and the 50 bags cost $45x. Thus, the total cost is $145x.

34. **(D)** According to the Pythagorean theorem, the length squared equals $8^2 + 15^2$, which is

289. So the length of the side opposite the right angle is 17.

35. **(C)** The first 600 copies cost a total of $600x$¢. There are $1,500 - 600$ or 900 copies after the first 600, each of which costs $\left(x - \frac{y}{10}\right)$¢; so the 900 copies cost $900\left(x - \frac{y}{y}\right)$¢, which equals $(900x - 90y)$¢. Therefore, the total cost is $(1500x - 90y)$¢.

36. **(C)** If s is the original side of the square, then s^2 is the area of the original square. The side of the increased square is 140% of s or $(1.4)s$. Therefore, the area of the increased square is $(1.4s)^2$ or $1.96s^2$, which is 196% of the original area. Thus, the area has increased by 96%.

37. **(A)** If P is the price of 7 cartons, then $\frac{7}{28} = \frac{P}{21}$, so $P = \frac{1}{4}$ of $21, which is $5.25.

38. **(E)** Plane P will travel $\frac{3}{2}$ of an hour before Q takes off, so it will be $\frac{3x}{2}$ miles away at 3:30 A.M. Let t denote the number of hours after 3:30 A.M. it takes Q to overtake P. By then P has flown $tx + \frac{3x}{2}$ miles and Q has flown ty miles. We want the value of t, where $ty = tx + \frac{3x}{2}$, or $t(y - x) = \frac{3x}{2}$. Therefore, $t = \frac{3x}{2(y - x)}$.

39. **(D)** Note that $\left(\frac{2}{3} + \frac{1}{3}\right)$ equals 1 full day, and that $\left(\frac{1}{8} + \frac{3}{4}\right)$ is shy $\frac{1}{8}$ of being 1 full day. So he works $2\frac{7}{8}$ days altogether.

$$\left(2\frac{7}{8}\right)(20) = \left(\frac{23}{8}\right)(20) = \frac{460}{8} = \$57.50.$$

40. **(D)** There were 26 $(16 + 10)$ students who answered 32 or more questions correctly. Since the total number of students is 60, and

$\frac{26}{60} = .43\frac{1}{3}$. $43\frac{1}{3}\%$ of the class answered 32 or more questions correctly.

41. **(C)** 12 students had scores of 28 to 31, and 8 scores of 25 or less; so $8x = 12$ and $x = \frac{12}{8} = \frac{3}{2}$.

42. **(B)** The product of 3 consecutive integers is of the form $(x - 1)(x)(x + 1)$ and a good approximation to this is x^3. Since $6^3 = 216$, a good guess for x is 6, 6 is correct since $5 \times 6 \times 7 = 210$. Therefore, the sum of the two smaller integers is $5 + 6$ or 11.

43. **(D)** Let C, B, and E denote the cost of cereal, bacon, and eggs respectively. Then $C = \frac{1B}{3}$ and $B = \frac{5E}{4}$, or $E = \frac{4B}{5}$. Therefore, $E = \frac{4B}{5}$ and $B = 3C$; so we conclude that $E = \left(\frac{4}{5}\right)3C = \frac{12C}{5}$.

44. **(D)** Since 80% of 15 is 12, the loaded truck travels 12 miles on a gallon of gas. Therefore, it will use $\frac{80}{12}$ or $6\frac{8}{12}$ or $6\frac{2}{3}$ gallons of gas to travel 80 miles.

45. **(D)**

STATEMENT I is true, since the band which denotes corporation income taxes is. wider in 1946 than in 1947.

STATEMENT II is false, since the top line on the receipts graph falls between 1945 and 1950.

STATEMENT III is true, since the top line on the expenditures graph is lower in 1948 than at any other time between 1945 and 1952.

Therefore, only STATEMENTS I and III can be inferred from the graph.

46. **(E)** In the first $1\frac{1}{2}$ hours, the car will travel $\frac{3}{2} \times 70$ or 105 miles. In order to travel a total of 200 miles the car has 95 miles left. At a speed of 50 miles per hour it will take $\frac{95}{50}$ or

$1\frac{9}{10}$ hours to travel 95 miles. Therefore, the total traveling time necessary to travel 200 miles is $1\frac{1}{2} + 1\frac{9}{10}$, which equals $3\frac{4}{10}$ or $3\frac{2}{5}$ hours.

47. **(D)** The first 1,000 copies will cost $\$1,000x$. There are 600 copies after the first thousand, each costing $\$(x - 2y)$, so all 600 cost $\$600x - \$1200y$. Therefore, the cost of 1,600 copies is $\$1600x - \$1200y$.

48. **(D)** If $\frac{1}{3} < x$, then since inverting positive numbers reverses inequalities, $\frac{1}{1/3} > \frac{1}{x}$. Since $\frac{1}{1/3} = 3$, 3 is greater than $\frac{1}{x}$ or $\frac{1}{x}$ is less than 3. (x is positive since it is greater than $\frac{1}{3}$.)

49. **(E)** $\frac{1}{3} = \frac{14}{42}$ and $\frac{2}{7} = \frac{12}{42}$, so $\frac{1}{3} + \frac{2}{7} = \frac{26}{42}$. Therefore, $x = 26$.

50. **(B)** Since 12 is positive, one of the numbers must be positive because the sum of negative numbers is negative. If r is 13, then $x = 0$, $y = -1$, and $z = 0$ satisfy $r + x + y + w = 12$ and $x < 6$.

51. **(E)** The volume of a sphere of radius r is $\frac{4}{3}\pi r^3$. If r is replaced by $2r$, the volume $= \frac{4}{3}\pi(2r)^3 = \frac{4}{3}\pi 8r^3 = 8\left(\frac{4}{3}\pi r^3\right)$, so the volume has increased by a factor of 8.

52. **(E)** According to the Pythagorean theorem, the length of the hypotenuse, the side opposite the right angle, is the square root of $(n - 1)^2 + (2\sqrt{n})^2$, which is $n^2 - 2n + 1 + 4n$ or $n^2 + 2n + 1$. This equals $(n + 1)^2$. Therefore, the answer is $\sqrt{(n + 1)^2}$, which is $n + 1$.

53. **(E)** According to the rule given $f(a + 2)$ is $(a + 2)^2 + 2$ which is $(a^2 + 4a + 4) + 2$ or $a^2 + 4a + 6$.

54. **(A)** Since $\frac{x}{y}$ is not zero, $\frac{y}{x} = 1/\frac{x}{y} = \frac{1}{2}$. But $\frac{y^2}{x^2} = \left(\frac{y}{x}\right)^2 = \left(\frac{1}{2}\right)^2 = \frac{1}{4}$.

55. **(C)** Let x be the amount X is paid and y be the amount Y is paid. Since $x = (1.2)y$, $x + y = (2.2)y$. But we know $x + y = \$550$; so $(2.2)y = \$550$. Dividing each side, we have $y = \$250$.

III   Practical Judgment

56. **(B)** The establishment of a new supermarket chain in the R and S market area, and its use of grade labeling, was a *Major Factor* considered by Joseph in his decision as to whether to adopt the practice.

57. **(C)** The fact that the government's program would standardize grading was a *Minor Factor* related to the consideration of whether or not to adopt the practice.

58. **(B)** The effect of grade labeling on sales was a *Major Factor* considered by R and S in determining the consequences of the adoption of the future of the firm.

59. **(C)** Federal food standards were a *Minor Factor* in making the decision.

60. **(A)** In deciding whether to adopt grade labeling, Mr. Joseph's major consideration was what effect it would have on consumer acceptance of his products. Since R and S already enjoyed a high reputation, Joseph did not want to take any action that would jeopardize it.

61. **(D)** *Major Assumption.* Joseph's legal advisor felt that grade labeling might become mandatory in the near future. It is clear from the passage that this was a matter of opinion only.

62. **(E)** Present label requirements, described in paragraph 7, were unimportant to Joseph's decision as to whether to adopt the government's voluntary program.

63. **(C)** Possible government legislation resulting from consumer pressure was a *Minor Factor* in Joseph's decision as to whether to adopt the voluntary labeling program.

64. **(B)** *Major Factor.* Taam Food's adoption of grading worried Joseph because of its possible competitive advantage.

65. **(E)** *Unimportant Issue.* R and S Packing's experience was not a real consideration in any decision alternative.

66. **(C)** *Minor Factor.* The superior flavor of R and S products was one aspect of the overall quality of the goods. Since the overall quality was a *Major Factor*, flavor was a *Minor Factor*.

67. **(B)** *Major Factor.* The quality of R and S products would largely determine their grade. The possibility of receiving a high grade was a major consideration in accepting the voluntary program.

68. **(B)** See the last paragraph. It is clear that grade labeling was intended to help the consumer identify brands by level of quality.

69. **(A)** R and S management felt that it enjoyed a good reputation as canners of high quality canned fruits and vegetables. Already having this favorable brand image, there was little reason to adopt grade labeling.

70. **(E)** All three. See the third paragraph.

71. **(B)** The Department of Agriculture. See paragraph 5.

72. **(D)** Taste was not a consideration in the Department of Agriculture's labeling procedure. See paragraph 5.

73. **(C)** The labels included type of food; can size; number of servings per can; net contents; and name and address of the chain. See paragraph 2, lines 6–8.

74. **(C)** See paragraph 3, lines 4–6 and paragraph 4, lines 1–3.

75. **(B)** See paragraph 6, lines 9–10.

Section IV   Data Sufficiency

76. **(D)** (1) alone is sufficient, since if two sides of a triangle are equal, the angles opposite the equal sides are equal. Since $AB = BC$ then $x = y$, so $x = 40$. (2) alone is sufficient since the sum of the angles of a triangle is $180°$. Therefore, if $z = 100$ and $y = 40$, x must

equal $180 - 100 - 40 = 40$. Therefore, each statement alone is sufficient.

77. **(C)** (1) tells us the area of the circle is $\pi 4^2 = 16\pi$. Since there are 360° in the whole circle, (2) tells us that the shaded area is $^{60}/_{360}$ or $\frac{1}{6}$ of the area of the circle. Thus, using both (1) and (2), we can answer the question, but since we need both the radius of the circle and the value of x, neither of them alone is sufficient. Therefore, the answer is (C).

78. **(E)** Using (1) we can find the income for 1970 if we know the income for 1968 and 1969, but (1) gives no more information about the income for 1968 and 1969. If we also use (2) we can get the income in 1969 if we know the income for 1968, but we still can't determine the income for 1968. Therefore, both together are not sufficient.

79. **(D)** Since a straight line forms an angle of 180° and l' is a straight line, we know $x + y = 180$. If we use (1) we get $y = 80$, so (1) alone is sufficient. When two straight lines intersect, the vertical angles are equal. So $y = z$; thus if we use (2) we have that $y = 80$. Therefore, (2) alone is sufficient. Thus, each statement alone is sufficient.

80. **(C)** In the figure, x denotes the number taking German I but not English I, and y the number taking English I but not German I. From (1) we know that $x + 16 + y = 50$; from (2), $x = y$. Neither statement alone can be solved for x, but both together are sufficient (and yield $x = 17$).

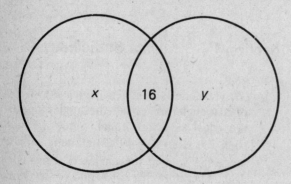

81. **(E)** (1) alone is not sufficient because it only says two sides are equal; in a square all four sides are equal. Even if we use (2) we don't know if $ABCD$ is a square since *all* angles have to be right angles in a square. Therefore, both statements together are insufficient.

82. **(B)** The average yearly wage per employee is the total amount of wages divided by the number of employees. So (2) alone is sufficient since it gives the total amount of wages and we are given the number of employees. (1) alone is not sufficient, since (1) by itself does not tell us the total wages. Therefore, the answer is (B).

83. **(E)** Since the square of any nonzero number is positive, (1) says $x + y \neq 0$ or $x \neq -y$. So (1) alone is not sufficient. If we also assume (2), we know only that x is positive and unequal to $-y$, not whether x is greater than or less than y. Thus (1) and (2) together are insufficient.

84. **(A)** Since the circles both have radius 4, the figure $OBO'C$ is a rhombus (each side is a radius) and the diagonals BC and OO' (of a rhombus) are perpendicular. So (2) does not give any new information, and is thus not sufficient alone. (1) alone is sufficient. The area of each circle is 16π since the radius of each circle is 4. If there were no shaded area, the area enclosed by both circles would be $16\pi + 16\pi = 32\pi$. Since the area enclosed by both circles is 29π, the shaded area is $32\pi - 29\pi$ or 3π. So (1) alone is sufficient but (2) alone is insufficient.

85. **(A)** Let x be the time it takes to travel from A to B and let y be the time it takes to travel from B to A. We know $x + y = 4$. (1) says x is 125% of y or $x = \frac{5}{4}y$. So using (1) we have $x + \frac{5}{4}x = 4$ which we can solve for x. Thus, (1) alone is sufficient. (2) alone is not sufficient since we need information about the relation of x to y to solve the problem and (2) says nothing about the relation between x and y. Therefore, (1) alone is sufficient but (2) alone is insufficient.

86. **(C)** (1) alone is insufficient. If x and y were right angles, (1) would imply that l and l' are

parallel, but if x and y are not right angles, (1) would imply that l and l' are not parallel. (2) alone is not sufficient since it gives information only about l' and says nothing about the relation of l and l'. (1) and (2) together give $x = z$ which means that l and l' are parallel. Therefore, (1) and (2) together are sufficient but neither alone is sufficient.

87. **(E)** If we use (1), we have $x + y + z = 3 + z$, but we have no information about z, so (1) alone is insufficient. If we use (2) alone, we have $x + y + z = y + 2$, but since we have no information about y, (2) alone is insufficient. If we use both (1) and (2), we obtain $x + y + z = y + 2 = 3 + z$. We can also add (1) and (2) to obtain $2x + y + z = 5$, but we can't find the value of $x + y + z$ without more information. So the answer is **(E)**.

88. **(C)** We need to know the surface area of the box. Since each side is a rectangle, we know the surface area will be $2LW + 2LH + 2HW$ where H is the height of the box, L is the length, and W is the width. We are given that $L = 7$, so to answer the question we need H and W. Since (1) gives only the value of W and (2) gives only the value of H, neither alone is sufficient. But both (1) and (2) together are sufficient.

89. **(E)** The profit is the selling price minus the cost, so to answer the question we need to know both the selling price and the cost of 15 boxes of detergent. Since (1) and (2) give information only about the cost but no information about the selling price, both statements together are insufficient.

90 **(E)** (1) alone is not sufficient. A four-sided figure can have both larger perimeter and smaller area than another four-sided figure, or it could have larger perimeter and larger area. (2) alone is also insufficient since the length of one diagonal does not determine the area of a four-sided figure. (1) and (2) together are also insufficient, as shown by the figure.

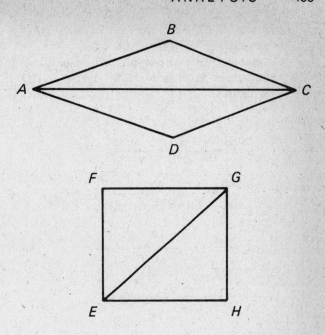

(1) and (2) are both satisfied and the area of $EFGH$ is larger than $ABCD$. But (1) and (2) could still be satisfied and the area of $ABCD$ be larger than the area of $EFGH$; so the answer is **(E)**.

91. **(B)** Statement (1) alone is not sufficient, since 12 is divisible by 3 but 12 is not divisible by 9. Statement (2) alone is sufficient, since if a number is divisible by 27 then, because $27 = 9 \times 3$, the number must be divisible by 9.

92. **(C)** Statement (1) is not sufficient. (1) will let you figure out the length of the side SP; however, you need to know the length of SR or PQ to find the area. Statement (2) alone is not sufficient. (2) will allow you to find the length of PQ, but you also need to know the length of SP or RQ.
Statements (1) and (2) together are sufficient.

93. **(A)** Both regions $ABEF$ and $CDEF$ are trapezoids, so their area is given by the formula a $(\frac{1}{2}[b_1 + b_2])$ where a is an altitude and b_1 and b_2 are the sides perpendicular to the altitude. Since $ABCD$ is a rectangle, $AB = CD$, which means the altitudes are the same length for each region. So it is sufficient to know whether $BE + AF$ is larger than $EC + FD$.

Statement (1) alone is sufficient, since, if BE is larger than FD, then $BC - BE$, which is EC, must be smaller than $AD - FD = AF$. ($AD =$

BC since *ABCD* is a rectangle.) So *BE* + *AF* is larger than *EC* + *FD*.
Statement (2) alone is not sufficient, since either region could be larger if *BE* is larger than *CD* (See figures).

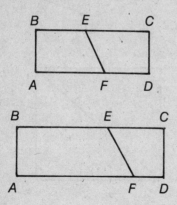

94. **(A)** The square of an even integer is always even. So if k^2 is odd, k can't be even. Therefore, k is odd and (1) alone is sufficient.
Statement (2) alone is not sufficient, since 2k is even for every integer k.

95. **(A)** Statement (1) alone is sufficient, since using (1) implies that the car can travel 125 miles using 5 gallons of fuel.
Statement (2) alone is not sufficient. The speed is not enough to determine how far the car can travel.

96. **(D)** The area of the region is the area of the square plus the area of the semicircle. So you must be able to determine the length of a side of the square and the length of the radius of the semicircle. Since the radius is ½ of *BC*, it is sufficient to determine either the radius or the length of a side of the square. Statement (1) alone is sufficient, since the diagonal of a square is $\sqrt{2}$ times the length of a side. Statement (2) alone is sufficient, since the length of a side of the square is twice the radius.

97. **(C)** Using statements (1) and (2), you can determine the distance from *P* to (0,0) and the distance from *Q* to (0,0). The distances are equal if and only if *P* and *Q* are on the same circle with center (0,0). Neither statement alone is sufficient, since you need to know both distances.

98. **(E)** Both statements together give no information about the year 1980.

99. **(B)** Since 2^n is n "copies" of 2 multiplied together, 2^n is divisible by 8 if and only if n is greater than or equal to 3. (This is because $8 = 2 \times 2 \times 2 = 2^3$). Therefore, (2) alone is sufficient.
Statement (1) alone is not sufficient, because there are odd numbers less than 3 and odd numbers greater than 3.

100. **(E)** The fact that the price is higher at the end of the year than it was at the beginning of the year does not imply that the price rose every week during the year. The price could have gone up and down many times during the year.

101. **(C)** Since *AB* = *JI* + *HG* + *FE* + *DC*, if we knew the lengths of *JI*, *HG*, *FE*, and *DC* we could find the length of *AB*. So we need to know both what x is and what y is. Therefore, statements (1) and (2) together are sufficient, but each one separately is not sufficient.

102. **(B)** Statement (1) alone is not sufficient. If $a = 70°$, $b = 25°$ and $c = 85°$, statement (1) would be true; however, if $a = 90°$, $b = 45°$, and $c = 45°$, statement (1) would also be true.
Statement (2) alone is sufficient. Since we know that the sum of the angles in a triangle is 180°, the smallest angle is always less than or equal to 60°. Notice that statement (2) gives enough information to answer the question, but the answer is *no*. Don't confuse answering a question with answering a question affirmatively.

103. **(A)** Statement (1) alone is sufficient. If a is greater than 2b, then 2^a is greater than $2^{2b} = (2^2)^b = 4^b$, and 4^b is greater than 3^b.
Statement (2) alone is not sufficient. If $b = 1$, then a could be 4 and 2^a would be greater than 3^b; however, if $b = 6$ and $a = 9$ then $2^a = 512$ and this is not greater than $3^a = 729$.

104. **(E)** If $a = 3, b = 2$, and $c = 1$, then statements (1) and (2) are both true, but if $a = 2, b = 3$, and $c = 1$, statements (1) and (2) are still true.

105. **(A)** Statement (1) alone is sufficient. Statement (2) is not sufficient. If the radius of the circle were $\sqrt{\pi}$ then the area of the circle would be $\pi r^2 = \pi^2$, but the diameter of the circle would be $2\sqrt{\pi}$, which is greater than π. So the circle could not fit inside a square with side of length π, although the area of the square would be π^2.

Section V Writing Ability

106.　**(C)** The word *irregardless* is nonstandard for *regardless*.

107.　**(A)** *Provided* is standard usage and not *Providing*.

108.　**(E)** No error.

109.　**(A)** The noun is *advice* and not *advise*.

110.　**(D)** The participle *lying* is required and not *laying*.

111.　**(C)** The plural subject *you and I* requires the plural verb *are*.

112.　**(B)** The pronoun *he* has no clear antecedent and therefore we do not know who *shipped out the defective batch;* George or Crosby.

113.　**(D)** The compound verb idea *noticed* and *called for* cannot be separated by a semicolon or any other punctuation mark.

114.　**(E)** No error.

115.　**(C)** *Me* is required as the object following the prepositional phrase *except for*.

116.　**(A)** She felt bad. The adjective is required following the linking verb *felt* and not the adverb *badly*.

117.　**(B)** Parallelism calls for a series of three noun phrases. (B) should read *the fact that it can be*.

118.　**(D)** People are *healthy* but the climate is *healthful*.

119.　**(B)** The word *scarcely* has a negative connotation and must be followed by *any* and not *no*.

120.　**(E)** No error.

121.　**(C)** *Anyone* is a singular pronoun. Therefore, the phrase *they are* should be changed to the singular *he is* in order to agree with the antecedent.

122.　**(C)** The subject of the verb is the singular *The President*. The verb should also be singular: *has arrived*. The long phrase about the First Lady and the advisers is merely parenthetical.

123.　**(D)** The subject of the verb is singular: *The city government*. Phrase (D), therefore, should be singular: *are unable*.

124.　**(E)** No error.

125.　**(A)** The opening phrase is a dangling modifier; it is unclear who or what realized the public interest. Phrase (A) should be changed to something like *Because of*.

Section VI Practical Judgment

126.　**(B)** The major decision to be made by Sam Hoe is whether to open a retail showroom for the sale of his custom line. He felt that this strategy might be a solution to his major problem of a declining profit position caused by higher costs. Therefore, the fact of higher production costs was a *Major Factor* in making his decision.

127.　**(B)** The increased demand for furniture which Sam Hoe had experienced was a *Major Factor* leading him to consider opening a retail showroom.

128.　**(C)** Storage space is an *Unimportant Issue* in making the decision; it bears no direct relation to the manufacture and sale of furniture in this problem.

129.　**(E)** Mr. Hoe's workshop employed 20 craftsmen but this fact wouldn't affect the opening of a showroom. It is an *Unimportant Issue*.

130.　**(A)** Sam's major decision is whether to open a retail showroom or not. This is the *Major Objective*. See the explanation to question 126 above.

131.　**(B)** The scarcity of cabinetmakers limited Mr. Hoe's output of custom-built furniture and therefore was a *Major Factor* in his contemplation of how to increase the profitability of his standard furniture line.

132. **(A)** Improving the profitability of the firm was one of Sam Hoe's primary objectives.

133. **(E)** The number of states in which the company sells its products was an *Unimportant Issue* in the consideration of the decision alternatives.

134. **(D)** Sam Hoe believed that his standard furniture items "are popular and almost sell themselves." However, this contention is not buttressed by facts in the passage.

135. **(A)** Adding more wholesalers was an objective of Norbert Ravis.

136. **(B)** The capacity of Hoe's plant to produce additional amounts of furniture was a *Major Factor* in the alternative course of action to increase sales.

137. **(E)** No special importance was attached to the fact that sales were made directly to a department store and a large retail furniture showroom (see paragraph 3).

138. **(D)** This is a *Major Assumption* because no definite facts were cited to demonstrate that skilled apprentices were actually available.

139. **(B)** See paragraphs 1 and 4. Profits were not increasing at the same rate as production. The other problems were not mentioned.

140. **(B)** See paragraph 1. Sam did consider a price increase, but did not take any action of the sort since he had raised prices of most items during the past six months.

141. **(A)** See paragraph 3. Custom furniture accounted for 78 percent of sales.

142. **(A)** See paragraph 7.

143. **(D)** See paragraph 3. Most of Mr. Hoe's standard line was sold within a five-state area, while most of his custom-made items were sold within the state. Only a few items in the latter category were sold throughout the country.

144. **(A)** By selling at a factory location, Mr. Hoe could reduce his distribution costs.

145. **(C)** No mention was made of wholesalers' margins. Answers I and II are given in paragraphs 1 and 4.

Section VII   Data Sufficiency

146. **(C)** Using statement (1), you can set up an equation involving X's salary and Z's salary. Using statement (2), you can set up an equation involving Y's salary and Z's salary. Thus, using both (1) and (2), you can relate X's salary to Y's salary. You need both statements to solve the problem.

147. **(E)** If you knew what a share of ABC stock was worth, then using statement (1) you could decide when the stock would be worth $63. However, statement (2) does not give the needed information. Therefore, (1) and (2) together are not sufficient.

148. **(C)** If you add statements (1) and (2), you obtain $x + 2y = 14$. Since you don't know the value of z, statement (1) or (2) alone is insufficient.

149. **(A)** Since the average of the three numbers is their sum divided by 3, statement (1) alone is sufficient. Statement (2) alone is not sufficient.

150. **(C)** Statement (1) alone implies that angle $x =$ the angle opposite side AB.
Statement (2) alone implies that the angle opposite side AB is 80°. So, using both, we can see that y is the smaller, but either statement alone is not sufficient.

151. **(E)** You need to know how much money was made from general admission ticket sales. Statement (2) only tells how many tickets were sold, not how much they cost.

152. **(B)** Statement (2) alone is sufficient, since $2x + 2y = 2(x + y)$. Generally you need to have two equations to solve for 2 unknowns. However, since $2x + 2y$ is a multiple of what you want, the extra equation, statement (1), is not needed.

153. **(D)** "3 evenly divides x" means $x = 3k$ for some integer k. Statement (1) alone is sufficient, since "6 evenly divides x" means $x = 6k$ for some integer k, so $x = 3(2k)$ and 3 evenly divides x. Statement (2) alone is sufficient since "12 evenly divides x" means $x = 12k$ for some integer k, so $x = 3(4k)$ and 3 divides x.

154. **(E)** When any two lines intersect, the vertical angles formed are equal. So for any pair of lines (perpendicular or non-perpendicular) statements (1) and (2) are true.

155. **(C)** The total of the percentage billed to A, the percentage billed to B, and the percentage billed to C is 100%. Using statement (1) and statement (2) together, you can set up an equation $A + \frac{1}{2}A + \frac{1}{2}A = 100$ and solve for A, where A is the percentage billed to A. If you use statement (1) alone or statement (2) alone, you can only get an equation that involves A and either B or C. So statement (1) alone is insufficient and statement (2) alone is insufficient.

156. **(D)** Statement (1) alone is sufficient, since it implies that Bill pays 40% of $500 each month. Statement (2) alone is sufficient, since $x + y = 100$.
Therefore statement (1) and statement (2) are equivalent.

157. **(A)** To compare two fractions, the fractions must have the same denominator. The least common denominator for both fractions is 120. Using this fact, $\frac{x}{12} = \frac{10x}{120}$ and $\frac{y}{40} = \frac{3y}{120}$. So the relation between the fractions is the same as the relation between $10x$ and $3y$. Therefore, statement (1) alone is sufficient. Statement (2) alone is not sufficient. Using $y = 13$ and $x = 4$, statement (2) is true and $\frac{x}{12}$ is greater than $\frac{y}{40}$. However, using $y = 10$ and $x = 2$, statement (2) is still true, but now $\frac{x}{12}$ is less than $\frac{y}{40}$.

158. **(C)** Since $x^2 - y^2 = (x + y)(x - y)$, statement (1) and statement (2) together are sufficient. Neither statement by itself is sufficient.

159. **(D)** The people can be divided into 3 distinct groups which do not overlap: A = people who own a television but do not own a telephone; B = people who own both a television and a telephone; C = people who own a telephone but do not own a television. You are given that the number of people in A plus the number of people in B plus the number of people in C equals 70. Furthermore, you know the number in B is 30. Since the groups you need to compare are those with a television (that is, those in A or B) and those with a telephone (that is, those in B or C), it is sufficient to know whether A or C has more members. By the above equations, if you know A, then you can determine C, and vice versa.
Statement (1) is sufficient, since it tells you how many people are in group A.
Statement (2) is sufficient, since it tells you how many people are in group B or in group C. Since there are 30 people in B, you can determine how many are in C. A Venn diagram is a useful way to visualize the information: A + B + C = 70.

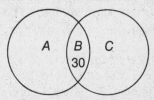

160. **(B)** Statement (2) alone is sufficient. If $x < 0$, then, since x^2 is always positive, x^2 is larger than x. Statement (1) alone is not sufficient. If x is > 1, then x^2 is larger, but if $0 < x < 1$, then x is larger. For example, if $x = 2$ then $x^2 = 4$, but if $x = \frac{1}{2}$ then $x^2 = \frac{1}{4}$.

161. **(E)** Statement (1) would imply that AB is shorter than CD if AD and CB were equal. However, even with statement (2) you can't deduce whether DC or AB is longer. If CB was "just a little bit" longer than AD, then CD would be longer, but if CB was "much" longer than AD, then AB would be longer than CD.

162. **(D)** Statement (1) alone is sufficient. Just use 100 for degrees Fahrenheit in the formula. Statement (2) alone is also sufficient, since the formula in statement (2) can be solved to give the formula of statement (1) which we know is sufficient.

163. **(E)** Statements (1) and (2) relate Jane's salary to other salaries, but none of those salaries is known. So statements (1) and (2) together are not sufficient.

164. **(A)** Statement (1) alone is sufficient because $\frac{3}{2}y$ is the same as 150% of y; thus statement (1) implies $z = 0$. Statement (2) alone is not sufficient, since you are given no value for y.

165. **(C)** Statement (1) means that the triangle ABC is a right triangle. So if two sides are known, the third side can be determined. Therefore, statements (1) and (2) together are sufficient. Statement (1) alone is not sufficient. You need to know the lengths of 2 sides, and you are only given one side.
Statement (2) alone is not sufficient. If you know the lengths of two sides but don't know an angle, you can't find the third side.

166. **(C)** Statements (1) and (2) together are sufficient.
Statement (1) alone is not sufficient, since it only relates x to y. Statement (2) alone is not sufficient since without (1) x and y are not related.

167. **(C)** Statement (1) alone is not sufficient. (1) implies x is equal to either -4 or 1.
Statement (2) alone is not sufficient, since there are positive numbers greater than -2 and negative numbers greater than -2.
Statements (1) and (2) together are sufficient, since the only possible value is 1.

168. **(E)** Statements (1) and (2) together are not sufficient. If $x = 10$, $y = 6$, and $z = 2$, then (1) and (2) are true, but since $6 + 2$ is not greater than 10, x, y, and z can't be the lengths of the sides of a triangle.

169. **(A)** Statement (1) alone is sufficient, since (1) implies that n is the square of $2j$.
Statement (2) alone is not sufficient. If $A = 3$, and $B = 4$, then $n^2 = 25$, so n is not the square of an integer.

170. **(D)** Statement (2) alone is sufficient. Since train Y travels for 3 hours and train Z travels for 2 hours, the distance train Y travels is $3y$, and the distance train Z travels is $2z$. Therefore, statement (1) alone is sufficient.

171. **(C)** Statement (1) alone is not sufficient. x could be negative or positive with y positive, and (1) would be true.
Statement (2) alone is not sufficient, since it gives no information about y.
Statements (1) and (2) together are sufficient. If $x > 0$ then (1) implies y is > 0, so $xy > 0$.

172. **(A)** Statement (1) alone is sufficient. If x is greater than 5, then the area must increase by more than 10%, since $(1.05s)^2 = 1.1025(s^2)$.
Statement (2) alone is not sufficient. If x is 1, then the area increases by less than 10%. However, if x is 9, then the area increases by more than 10%.

173. **(E)** Statements (1) and (2) together are not sufficient. You are only given comparisons between years.

174. **(C)** Statement (1) tells us only that $x = 6 + y$, so it is not sufficient. In the same way, statement (2) alone will give only one of the unknowns in terms of the other. However, if we use both (1) and (2), we obtain a system of two equations which can be solved for x and y.

175. **(E)** Statement (1) would be sufficient if there were information about the width of each book. Since statement (2) only gives information about the *weight* of each book, both statements together are not sufficient.

Evaluating Your Score

Tabulate your score for each section of Sample Test 3 according to the directions on pages 4–5 and record the results in the Self-scoring Table below. Then find your rating for each score on the Self-scoring Scale and record it in the appropriate blank.

Self-scoring Table

PART	SCORE	RATING
1		
2		
3		
4		
5		
6		
7		

Self-scoring Scale

RATING

PART	POOR	FAIR	GOOD	EXCELLENT
1	0–8	9–12	13–19	20–25
2	0–15	16–21	22–25	26–30
3	0–7	8–10	11–15	16–20
4	0–14	15–20	21–25	26–30
5	0–7	8–10	11–15	16–20
6	0–7	8–10	11–15	16–20
7	0–14	15–20	21–25	26–30

Study again the Review sections covering material in Sample Test 3 for which you had a rating of FAIR or POOR. Then go on to Sample Test 4.

To obtain an approximation of your actual GMAT score see page 5.

Answer Sheet—Sample Test 4

Sections I-II Reading Recall

1. Ⓐ Ⓑ Ⓒ Ⓓ Ⓔ
2. Ⓐ Ⓑ Ⓒ Ⓓ Ⓔ
3. Ⓐ Ⓑ Ⓒ Ⓓ Ⓔ
4. Ⓐ Ⓑ Ⓒ Ⓓ Ⓔ
5. Ⓐ Ⓑ Ⓒ Ⓓ Ⓔ
6. Ⓐ Ⓑ Ⓒ Ⓓ Ⓔ
7. Ⓐ Ⓑ Ⓒ Ⓓ Ⓔ
8. Ⓐ Ⓑ Ⓒ Ⓓ Ⓔ
9. Ⓐ Ⓑ Ⓒ Ⓓ Ⓔ
10. Ⓐ Ⓑ Ⓒ Ⓓ Ⓔ
11. Ⓐ Ⓑ Ⓒ Ⓓ Ⓔ
12. Ⓐ Ⓑ Ⓒ Ⓓ Ⓔ
13. Ⓐ Ⓑ Ⓒ Ⓓ Ⓔ
14. Ⓐ Ⓑ Ⓒ Ⓓ Ⓔ
15. Ⓐ Ⓑ Ⓒ Ⓓ Ⓔ
16. Ⓐ Ⓑ Ⓒ Ⓓ Ⓔ
17. Ⓐ Ⓑ Ⓒ Ⓓ Ⓔ
18. Ⓐ Ⓑ Ⓒ Ⓓ Ⓔ
19. Ⓐ Ⓑ Ⓒ Ⓓ Ⓔ
20. Ⓐ Ⓑ Ⓒ Ⓓ Ⓔ
21. Ⓐ Ⓑ Ⓒ Ⓓ Ⓔ
22. Ⓐ Ⓑ Ⓒ Ⓓ Ⓔ
23. Ⓐ Ⓑ Ⓒ Ⓓ Ⓔ
24. Ⓐ Ⓑ Ⓒ Ⓓ Ⓔ
25. Ⓐ Ⓑ Ⓒ Ⓓ Ⓔ
26. Ⓐ Ⓑ Ⓒ Ⓓ Ⓔ
27. Ⓐ Ⓑ Ⓒ Ⓓ Ⓔ
28. Ⓐ Ⓑ Ⓒ Ⓓ Ⓔ
29. Ⓐ Ⓑ Ⓒ Ⓓ Ⓔ
30. Ⓐ Ⓑ Ⓒ Ⓓ Ⓔ

Section III Problem Solving

31. Ⓐ Ⓑ Ⓒ Ⓓ Ⓔ
32. Ⓐ Ⓑ Ⓒ Ⓓ Ⓔ
33. Ⓐ Ⓑ Ⓒ Ⓓ Ⓔ
34. Ⓐ Ⓑ Ⓒ Ⓓ Ⓔ
35. Ⓐ Ⓑ Ⓒ Ⓓ Ⓔ
36. Ⓐ Ⓑ Ⓒ Ⓓ Ⓔ

37. Ⓐ Ⓑ Ⓒ Ⓓ Ⓔ
38. Ⓐ Ⓑ Ⓒ Ⓓ Ⓔ
39. Ⓐ Ⓑ Ⓒ Ⓓ Ⓔ
40. Ⓐ Ⓑ Ⓒ Ⓓ Ⓔ
41. Ⓐ Ⓑ Ⓒ Ⓓ Ⓔ
42. Ⓐ Ⓑ Ⓒ Ⓓ Ⓔ
43. Ⓐ Ⓑ Ⓒ Ⓓ Ⓔ
44. Ⓐ Ⓑ Ⓒ Ⓓ Ⓔ
45. Ⓐ Ⓑ Ⓒ Ⓓ Ⓔ
46. Ⓐ Ⓑ Ⓒ Ⓓ Ⓔ
47. Ⓐ Ⓑ Ⓒ Ⓓ Ⓔ
48. Ⓐ Ⓑ Ⓒ Ⓓ Ⓔ
49. Ⓐ Ⓑ Ⓒ Ⓓ Ⓔ
50. Ⓐ Ⓑ Ⓒ Ⓓ Ⓔ
51. Ⓐ Ⓑ Ⓒ Ⓓ Ⓔ
52. Ⓐ Ⓑ Ⓒ Ⓓ Ⓔ
53. Ⓐ Ⓑ Ⓒ Ⓓ Ⓔ
54. Ⓐ Ⓑ Ⓒ Ⓓ Ⓔ
55. Ⓐ Ⓑ Ⓒ Ⓓ Ⓔ
56. Ⓐ Ⓑ Ⓒ Ⓓ Ⓔ
57. Ⓐ Ⓑ Ⓒ Ⓓ Ⓔ
58. Ⓐ Ⓑ Ⓒ Ⓓ Ⓔ
59. Ⓐ Ⓑ Ⓒ Ⓓ Ⓔ
60. Ⓐ Ⓑ Ⓒ Ⓓ Ⓔ
61. Ⓐ Ⓑ Ⓒ Ⓓ Ⓔ
62. Ⓐ Ⓑ Ⓒ Ⓓ Ⓔ
63. Ⓐ Ⓑ Ⓒ Ⓓ Ⓔ
64. Ⓐ Ⓑ Ⓒ Ⓓ Ⓔ
65. Ⓐ Ⓑ Ⓒ Ⓓ Ⓔ
66. Ⓐ Ⓑ Ⓒ Ⓓ Ⓔ
67. Ⓐ Ⓑ Ⓒ Ⓓ Ⓔ
68. Ⓐ Ⓑ Ⓒ Ⓓ Ⓔ
69. Ⓐ Ⓑ Ⓒ Ⓓ Ⓔ
70. Ⓐ Ⓑ Ⓒ Ⓓ Ⓔ
71. Ⓐ Ⓑ Ⓒ Ⓓ Ⓔ
72. Ⓐ Ⓑ Ⓒ Ⓓ Ⓔ
73. Ⓐ Ⓑ Ⓒ Ⓓ Ⓔ
74. Ⓐ Ⓑ Ⓒ Ⓓ Ⓔ
75. Ⓐ Ⓑ Ⓒ Ⓓ Ⓔ
76. Ⓐ Ⓑ Ⓒ Ⓓ Ⓔ
77. Ⓐ Ⓑ Ⓒ Ⓓ Ⓔ
78. Ⓐ Ⓑ Ⓒ Ⓓ Ⓔ
79. Ⓐ Ⓑ Ⓒ Ⓓ Ⓔ
80. Ⓐ Ⓑ Ⓒ Ⓓ Ⓔ

81. Ⓐ Ⓑ Ⓒ Ⓓ Ⓔ
82. Ⓐ Ⓑ Ⓒ Ⓓ Ⓔ
83. Ⓐ Ⓑ Ⓒ Ⓓ Ⓔ
84. Ⓐ Ⓑ Ⓒ Ⓓ Ⓔ
85. Ⓐ Ⓑ Ⓒ Ⓓ Ⓔ

Section IV Practical Judgment

86. Ⓐ Ⓑ Ⓒ Ⓓ Ⓔ
87. Ⓐ Ⓑ Ⓒ Ⓓ Ⓔ
88. Ⓐ Ⓑ Ⓒ Ⓓ Ⓔ
89. Ⓐ Ⓑ Ⓒ Ⓓ Ⓔ
90. Ⓐ Ⓑ Ⓒ Ⓓ Ⓔ
91. Ⓐ Ⓑ Ⓒ Ⓓ Ⓔ
92. Ⓐ Ⓑ Ⓒ Ⓓ Ⓔ
93. Ⓐ Ⓑ Ⓒ Ⓓ Ⓔ
94. Ⓐ Ⓑ Ⓒ Ⓓ Ⓔ
95. Ⓐ Ⓑ Ⓒ Ⓓ Ⓔ
96. Ⓐ Ⓑ Ⓒ Ⓓ Ⓔ
97. Ⓐ Ⓑ Ⓒ Ⓓ Ⓔ
98. Ⓐ Ⓑ Ⓒ Ⓓ Ⓔ
99. Ⓐ Ⓑ Ⓒ Ⓓ Ⓔ
100. Ⓐ Ⓑ Ⓒ Ⓓ Ⓔ
101. Ⓐ Ⓑ Ⓒ Ⓓ Ⓔ
102. Ⓐ Ⓑ Ⓒ Ⓓ Ⓔ
103. Ⓐ Ⓑ Ⓒ Ⓓ Ⓔ
104. Ⓐ Ⓑ Ⓒ Ⓓ Ⓔ
105. Ⓐ Ⓑ Ⓒ Ⓓ Ⓔ

Section V Data Sufficiency

106. Ⓐ Ⓑ Ⓒ Ⓓ Ⓔ
107. Ⓐ Ⓑ Ⓒ Ⓓ Ⓔ
108. Ⓐ Ⓑ Ⓒ Ⓓ Ⓔ
109. Ⓐ Ⓑ Ⓒ Ⓓ Ⓔ
110. Ⓐ Ⓑ Ⓒ Ⓓ Ⓔ
111. Ⓐ Ⓑ Ⓒ Ⓓ Ⓔ
112. Ⓐ Ⓑ Ⓒ Ⓓ Ⓔ
113. Ⓐ Ⓑ Ⓒ Ⓓ Ⓔ
114. Ⓐ Ⓑ Ⓒ Ⓓ Ⓔ
115. Ⓐ Ⓑ Ⓒ Ⓓ Ⓔ
116. Ⓐ Ⓑ Ⓒ Ⓓ Ⓔ
117. Ⓐ Ⓑ Ⓒ Ⓓ Ⓔ
118. Ⓐ Ⓑ Ⓒ Ⓓ Ⓔ
119. Ⓐ Ⓑ Ⓒ Ⓓ Ⓔ
120. Ⓐ Ⓑ Ⓒ Ⓓ Ⓔ

Section VI Verbal Ability

121. Ⓐ Ⓑ Ⓒ Ⓓ Ⓔ
122. Ⓐ Ⓑ Ⓒ Ⓓ Ⓔ
123. Ⓐ Ⓑ Ⓒ Ⓓ Ⓔ
124. Ⓐ Ⓑ Ⓒ Ⓓ Ⓔ
125. Ⓐ Ⓑ Ⓒ Ⓓ Ⓔ
126. Ⓐ Ⓑ Ⓒ Ⓓ Ⓔ
127. Ⓐ Ⓑ Ⓒ Ⓓ Ⓔ
128. Ⓐ Ⓑ Ⓒ Ⓓ Ⓔ
129. Ⓐ Ⓑ Ⓒ Ⓓ Ⓔ
130. Ⓐ Ⓑ Ⓒ Ⓓ Ⓔ
131. Ⓐ Ⓑ Ⓒ Ⓓ Ⓔ
132. Ⓐ Ⓑ Ⓒ Ⓓ Ⓔ
133. Ⓐ Ⓑ Ⓒ Ⓓ Ⓔ
134. Ⓐ Ⓑ Ⓒ Ⓓ Ⓔ
135. Ⓐ Ⓑ Ⓒ Ⓓ Ⓔ
136. Ⓐ Ⓑ Ⓒ Ⓓ Ⓔ
137. Ⓐ Ⓑ Ⓒ Ⓓ Ⓔ
138. Ⓐ Ⓑ Ⓒ Ⓓ Ⓔ
139. Ⓐ Ⓑ Ⓒ Ⓓ Ⓔ
140. Ⓐ Ⓑ Ⓒ Ⓓ Ⓔ
141. Ⓐ Ⓑ Ⓒ Ⓓ Ⓔ
142. Ⓐ Ⓑ Ⓒ Ⓓ Ⓔ
143. Ⓐ Ⓑ Ⓒ Ⓓ Ⓔ
144. Ⓐ Ⓑ Ⓒ Ⓓ Ⓔ
145. Ⓐ Ⓑ Ⓒ Ⓓ Ⓔ
146. Ⓐ Ⓑ Ⓒ Ⓓ Ⓔ
147. Ⓐ Ⓑ Ⓒ Ⓓ Ⓔ
148. Ⓐ Ⓑ Ⓒ Ⓓ Ⓔ
149. Ⓐ Ⓑ Ⓒ Ⓓ Ⓔ
150. Ⓐ Ⓑ Ⓒ Ⓓ Ⓔ
151. Ⓐ Ⓑ Ⓒ Ⓓ Ⓔ
152. Ⓐ Ⓑ Ⓒ Ⓓ Ⓔ
153. Ⓐ Ⓑ Ⓒ Ⓓ Ⓔ
154. Ⓐ Ⓑ Ⓒ Ⓓ Ⓔ
155. Ⓐ Ⓑ Ⓒ Ⓓ Ⓔ
156. Ⓐ Ⓑ Ⓒ Ⓓ Ⓔ
157. Ⓐ Ⓑ Ⓒ Ⓓ Ⓔ
158. Ⓐ Ⓑ Ⓒ Ⓓ Ⓔ
159. Ⓐ Ⓑ Ⓒ Ⓓ Ⓔ
160. Ⓐ Ⓑ Ⓒ Ⓓ Ⓔ

Section VII Practical Judgment

161. Ⓐ Ⓑ Ⓒ Ⓓ Ⓔ
162. Ⓐ Ⓑ Ⓒ Ⓓ Ⓔ
163. Ⓐ Ⓑ Ⓒ Ⓓ Ⓔ
164. Ⓐ Ⓑ Ⓒ Ⓓ Ⓔ
165. Ⓐ Ⓑ Ⓒ Ⓓ Ⓔ
166. Ⓐ Ⓑ Ⓒ Ⓓ Ⓔ
167. Ⓐ Ⓑ Ⓒ Ⓓ Ⓔ
168. Ⓐ Ⓑ Ⓒ Ⓓ Ⓔ
169. Ⓐ Ⓑ Ⓒ Ⓓ Ⓔ
170. Ⓐ Ⓑ Ⓒ Ⓓ Ⓔ
171. Ⓐ Ⓑ Ⓒ Ⓓ Ⓔ
172. Ⓐ Ⓑ Ⓒ Ⓓ Ⓔ
173. Ⓐ Ⓑ Ⓒ Ⓓ Ⓔ
174. Ⓐ Ⓑ Ⓒ Ⓓ Ⓔ
175. Ⓐ Ⓑ Ⓒ Ⓓ Ⓔ
176. Ⓐ Ⓑ Ⓒ Ⓓ Ⓔ
177. Ⓐ Ⓑ Ⓒ Ⓓ Ⓔ
178. Ⓐ Ⓑ Ⓒ Ⓓ Ⓔ
179. Ⓐ Ⓑ Ⓒ Ⓓ Ⓔ
180. Ⓐ Ⓑ Ⓒ Ⓓ Ⓔ

Section VIII Data Sufficiency

181. Ⓐ Ⓑ Ⓒ Ⓓ Ⓔ
182. Ⓐ Ⓑ Ⓒ Ⓓ Ⓔ
183. Ⓐ Ⓑ Ⓒ Ⓓ Ⓔ
184. Ⓐ Ⓑ Ⓒ Ⓓ Ⓔ
185. Ⓐ Ⓑ Ⓒ Ⓓ Ⓔ
186. Ⓐ Ⓑ Ⓒ Ⓓ Ⓔ
187. Ⓐ Ⓑ Ⓒ Ⓓ Ⓔ
188. Ⓐ Ⓑ Ⓒ Ⓓ Ⓔ
189. Ⓐ Ⓑ Ⓒ Ⓓ Ⓔ
190. Ⓐ Ⓑ Ⓒ Ⓓ Ⓔ
191. Ⓐ Ⓑ Ⓒ Ⓓ Ⓔ
192. Ⓐ Ⓑ Ⓒ Ⓓ Ⓔ
193. Ⓐ Ⓑ Ⓒ Ⓓ Ⓔ
194. Ⓐ Ⓑ Ⓒ Ⓓ Ⓔ
195. Ⓐ Ⓑ Ⓒ Ⓓ Ⓔ

Sample Test 4

Section I   Reading Recall (Passages)

TIME: 15 minutes

DIRECTIONS: This part contains three reading passages. You are to read each one carefully. You will have fifteen minutes to study the three passages. In the next section, you will have twenty minutes to answer questions based on them. When answering the questions, you will *not* be allowed to refer back to the passages.

Passage 1:

The economic condition of the low-income regions of the world is one of the great problems of our time. Their progress is important to the high-income countries, not only for humanitarian and political reasons but also because rapid economic growth in the low-income countries could make a substantial contribution to the expansion and prosperity of the world economy as a whole.

The governments of most high-income countries have in recent years undertaken important aid programs, both bilaterally and multilaterally, and have thus demonstrated their interest in the development of low-income countries. They have also worked within the General Agreement on Tariffs and Trade (GATT) for greater freedom of trade and, recognizing the special problems of low-income countries, have made special trading arrangements to meet their needs. But a faster expansion of trade with high-income countries is necessary if the low-income countries are to enjoy a satisfactory rate of growth.

This statement is therefore concerned with the policies of high-income countries toward their trade with low-income countries. Our recommendations are based on the conviction that a better distribution of world resources and a more rational utilization of labor are in the general interest. A liberal policy on the part of high-income countries with respect to their trade with low-income countries will not only be helpful to the low-income countries but, when transitional adjustments have taken place, beneficial to the high-income countries as well.

It is necessary to recognize however, that in furthering the development of low-income countries, the high-income countries can play only a supporting role. If development is to be successful, the main effort must necessarily be made by the people of the low-income countries. The high-income countries are, moreover, likely to provide aid and facilitate trade more readily and extensively where the low-income countries are seen to be making sound and determined efforts to help themselves, and thus to be making effective use of their aid and trade opportunities.

It is, then, necessary that the low-income countries take full account of the lessons that have been learned from the experience of recent years, if they wish to achieve successful development and benefit from support from high-income countries. Among the most important of these lessons are the following:

465

Severe damage has been done by inflation. A sound financial framework evokes higher domestic savings and investment as well as more aid and investment from abroad. Budgetary and monetary discipline and a more efficient financial and fiscal system help greatly to mobilize funds for investment and thereby decisively influence the rate of growth. Foreign aid should also be efficiently applied to this end.

The energies of the people of low-income countries are more likely to be harnessed to the task of economic development where the policies of their governments aim to offer economic opportunity for all and to reduce excessive social inequalities.

Development plans have tended to concentrate on industrial investment. The growth of industry depends, however, on concomitant development in agriculture. A steady rise in productivity on the farms, where in almost all low-income countries a majority of the labor force works, is an essential condition of rapid over-all growth. Satisfactory development of agriculture is also necessary to provide an adequate market for an expanding industrial sector and to feed the growing urban population without burdening the balance of payments with heavy food imports. Diminishing surpluses in the high-income countries underline the need for a faster growth of agricultural productivity in low-income countries. Success in this should, moreover, lead to greater trade in agricultural products among the low-income countries themselves as well as to increased exports of some agricultural products to the high-income countries.

There can be no doubt about the urgency of the world food problem. Adequate nourishment and a balanced diet are not only necessary for working adults but are crucial for the mental and physical development of growing children. Yet, in a number of low-income countries where the diet is already insufficient the production of food has fallen behind the increase in population. A continuation of this trend must lead to endemic famine. The situation demands strenuous efforts in the low-income countries to improve the production, preservation, and distribution of food so that these countries are better able to feed themselves.

Passage 2:

The concept of "standard of living" is a wide and multifaceted one. In the absence of comprehensive measurement, it is commonly expressed empirically in terms of consumption or in terms of income.

One of the most comprehensive expressions of standard of living is total consumption over an extended period, where consumption is defined not only as family purchases but also as (1) consumption of goods and services produced by the family; (2) consumption of public services provided without payment; and (3) consumption of goods and services received as compensation for labor, over and above wages and salary. It may be assumed that total consumption is less subject to incidental fluctuations than income. Moreover, it reflects not only current income but also past income and savings, windfalls, and expectations regarding future income.

Current monetary income constitutes the main indicator for the standard of living; however, standard of living is not determined solely by current income, but also by past income, accumulated assets and expectations for future income. Moreover, the standard of living of a family is influenced by the value of the public services from which it benefits and the rate of taxes which it has to pay.

Between 1964 and 1970 the standard of living of the urban population rose. During this period, average real income increased by approximately 5% per annum. During the economic recession (1966–67), the income of all strata was adversely affected, particularly that of lower income groups. Since the end of the recession, a trend of decreasing inequality in income distribution has occurred, most noticeably among the lower income brackets. In 1970, the degree of income inequality was similar to that of the year 1964, despite the fact that during the latter period two external factors—an increase in welfare payments and the aging of the population—acted towards increasing the degree of inequality.

In the period under review, the standard of living of families originating from Asia and Africa improved relative to that of all families. This improvement found expression in higher income levels, better housing, a higher ownership rate of consumer durables and an increase in the proportion of families in higher income brackets. However, even after the improvement in their relative position during the past decade, their average income is still only 70% of the overall average for all families.

One of the important factors behind the income differential between families of African and Asian origins and the rest of the population is the level of education. In recent years the gap between these two groups has narrowed among the younger generation, but it is still substantial. Unless the education gap is significantly reduced between these two groups, other means employed in an attempt to produce more income equality will be thwarted. More resources must be immediately put to the task of improving educational opportunities for families of African and Asian origin, without of course, reducing the educational facilities and opportunities open to the rest of the population.

Passage 3:

Much has been written about the need for increasing our knowledge of marketing in other countries and how different marketing systems operate in delivering goods and services to consumers. American businessmen have long been interested in foreign markets for the purpose of stimulating trade. Analysis of the mechanisms of a given country's internal trade and the structural and environmental factors of its marketing system are necessary to the success of an American firm's marketing efforts abroad.

Knowledge of a country's marketing system is of equal importance to the potential investor. Information pertaining to channels of distribution, promotional facilities, and the marketing experience of management should have weight in the investment decision equal to factors such as financing, the possibility of expropriation, and plant location. Moreover, American businessmen are certainly not limited to investment in manufacturing industry abroad; there may be profitable opportunities for the introduction of American marketing institutions and techniques in other countries. The extent to which American dollars should be channeled into the introduction of American marketing innovations depends upon the answers to the following questions: (1) to what extent is it possible to "transplant" American marketing operations or institutions to foreign countries, and (2) would such transplantations, if successful, contribute to the economic development of the recipient country?

In light of the above, research is needed to determine the factors responsible for the acceptance and growth of marketing innovations so that an understanding of the adoption process can aid American businessmen contemplating the introduction of similar marketing techniques in other developing countries.

Take the case of an American marketing innovation: self-service. Whether self-service shops can be successful outside the United States depends upon sufficient population density, consumer income and the availability of suitable store locations and manpower. But even when these environmental forces are positive, cultural constraints may still serve as a barrier to the development of self-service. For example, a packaged foods industry cannot develop unless culturally developed habits of buying only "fresh" foods and produce can be overcome. Moreover, consumers must be sufficiently literate to select products from store shelves without the help of sales clerks.

The traditional pattern of shopping (in many countries) at different locations for each category of goods—e.g. dairy products, vegetables, meat, etc.—is a custom that has been learned and reinforced over many years. It does not break down easily. Daily shopping trips may be more of a social endeavor, providing the housewife contact with her friends at the local market or grocery, although hand-to-mouth buying may also result from low incomes and lack of refrigeration and storage facilities.

In Israel, the first supermarket was successful in changing the shopping patterns of many housewives who traditionally shopped at different stores for meat, dairy products, vegetables and fruit, and baked goods. Housewives preferred the self-service shop because it reduced total shopping time and offered quality food at lower prices. Working women switched to the self-service shop because it is open during their lunch hour, unlike the small shops that close at midday for several hours. Besides introducing a wider assortment of products at lower prices, standardized packaging, pricing, and quality was afforded the Israeli consumer. Although prepackaged meats and produce were not accepted by many consumers at first, there are indications that buying habits have changed. For example, packaged meat now accounts for about 25 percent of total sales of Israel's two major self-service food chains. In addition, the rate of increase of packaged meat sales at one chain (Consumer Union) is now greater than that of other commodities.

If there is still time remaining, review the passages until all 15 minutes have elapsed.
You may not turn to any other section of the test.

Section II   Reading Recall (Questions)

TIME: 20 minutes

QUESTIONS TO

Passage 1:

DIRECTIONS: Answer the following questions pertaining to information contained in the three passages from Section I. You may *not* turn back to these passages for assistance.

1. The economic conditions of low-income countries are important to high-income countries because of

    I.   economic reasons
    II. political reasons
    III. cultural reasons

    (A) I only
    (B) III only
    (C) I and II only
    (D) II and III only
    (E) I, II, and III

2. According to the passage, governments of most high-income countries have

    (A) not worked for freer trade with low-income countries
    (B) undertaken important aid programs for low-income countries
    (C) injected massive doses of capital into low-income countries
    (D) provided training programs for low-income country entrepreneurs
    (E) helped improve the educational systems of low-income countries

3. The major subject with which the passage is concerned is

    (A) trade policies of high-income countries towards low-income countries
    (B) foreign trade problems of low-income countries
    (C) fiscal and monetary problems of low-income countries
    (D) trade arrangements under the GATT organization
    (E) general economic problems of low-income countries

4. If low-income countries expect aid from high-income countries, they must do all of the following *except*

    (A) spend the aid wisely
    (B) put their own houses in order first
    (C) learn from the experience of developed countries
    (D) curb inflation
    (E) de-emphasize agricultural development in favor of industrial growth

5. Which of the following is mentioned for its influence upon the rate of economic growth?

    (A) an efficient financial and fiscal system
    (B) a trade surplus
    (C) a democratic government
    (D) little reliance upon foreign aid
    (E) a budgetary surplus

6. Industrial growth depends upon a parallel growth of the

(A) labor force
(B) agricultural system
(C) balance of payments
(D) urban population
(E) monetary system

7. The passage states that participation of high-income countries should be limited to

(A) ten percent of their GNP
(B) a supporting role
(C) regulations stipulated by GATT
(D) what low-income countries can absorb
(E) monetary aid only

8. In order to better enlist the support of the population in economic development efforts, low-income countries should

(A) not accept more foreign aid than they can use
(B) budget the capital wisely
(C) reduce excessive social inequalities
(D) concentrate on commercial development
(E) establish agricultural communes

9. Which of the following represents a major problem in the agricultural systems of low-income countries?

I. The increase in food production is less than population growth.
II. Food distribution is inefficient.
III. Food prices are too high.

(A) I only
(B) III only
(C) I and II only
(D) II and III only
(E) I, II, and III

10. If low-income countries could develop economically at a faster rate, the result would be

(A) less inflation
(B) lower deficits in their balance of trade
(C) liberal trade policies
(D) better distribution of world resources
(E) more equitable fiscal policies

QUESTIONS TO

Passage 2:

11. The author defines "standard of living" in terms of

    (A) total goods and services produced
    (B) consumption of goods and services
    (C) real income
    (D) per-capita income
    (E) discretionary income

12. Which income period(s) would be included in the author's definition of "standard of living"?

    I. Past income
    II. Current income
    III. Future income

    (A) I only   (C) I and II only   (E) Neither I, II, nor III
    (B) II only   (D) I, II, and III

13. Consumption is defined as

    (A) total family purchases
    (B) total family purchases plus goods and·services produced by the family
    (C) public services provided by the state
    (D) income minus expenditures on necessities
    (E) total family purchases plus other goods and services consumed

14. Between 1964 and 1970, average real income

    (A) remained stable
    (B) increased by about 5 percent annually
    (C) decreased slightly
    (D) decreased during the recession
    (E) decreased by 5 percent annually

15. According to the passage, between 1967 and 1970, income equality

    (A) declined among all strata
    (B) declined most significantly among lower income groups
    (C) widened between the rich and the poor strata
    (D) did not change appreciably
    (E) declined among older groups in the population

16. The author believes that inequality of income might be narrowed if

    (A) the tax structure were reformed
    (B) the educational gap between different population groups were reduced
    (C) more jobs could be found for people of Asian-African origin
    (D) real incomes increased
    (E) a system of price controls were implemented

17. The standard of living of Asian-African immigrants has improved as measured by all of the following factors *except*

    (A) higher income levels
    (B) better housing
    (C) increased ownership of consumer durables
    (D) a shift in population centers
    (E) an increased proportion of Asian-African families in higher income brackets

18. It may be inferred that the author of the passage is a(n)

    (A) engineer
    (B) food specialist
    (C) economist
    (D) bank president
    (E) efficiency expert

19. Even though the income level of families of Asian-African origin increased relatively, their average income is still

    (A) only about equal to that of other groups
    (B) about 70 percent of the overall national average
    (C) close to the national average, but slightly below
    (D) about 50 percent of the national average
    (E) about 25 percent of the national average

20. Between 1964 and 1970, the standard of living of the urban population

    (A) declined
    (B) increased
    (C) stagnated
    (D) remained about constant
    (E) doubled

QUESTIONS TO

Passage 3:

21. According to the author, knowledge of foreign marketing systems is essential because it

    (A) cements relations between countries
    (B) helps us to know about other people
    (C) can help to stimulate foreign trade
    (D) improves channels of distribution
    (E) teaches us something about our own marketing system

22. The passage implies that marketing can contribute to

    (A) improving goods and services
    (B) economic development
    (C) more efficient promotion and advertising
    (D) full employment
    (E) growth of economic institutions

23. Successful introduction of American marketing techniques abroad depends upon the

    (A) educational level in the host country
    (B) amount of investment capital available
    (C) use of efficient channels of distribution
    (D) extent to which the techniques can be "transplanted"
    (E) adaptability of American methods to foreign cultural conditions

24. A most important constraint on the introduction of self-service shops seems to be

    (A) cultural barriers
    (B) income
    (C) education
    (D) capital formation
    (E) population dispersion

25. In Israel, daily shopping trips to the food market occur because of

    (A) a lack of supermarkets
    (B) social reasons as much as economic ones
    (C) low per-capita incomes
    (D) poor transportation facilities
    (E) fluctuating food supplies

26. Working women in Israel prefer self-service shops owing to their

    (A) lower food prices
    (B) better quality food products
    (C) more convenient shopping hours
    (D) wider choice of commodities
    (E) pre-packaged meats and vegetables

27. Concerning the transfer of American marketing techniques abroad, the author concludes that

    (A) most countries can accept these techniques
    (B) they are not operable in most countries
    (C) more research is needed into this subject
    (D) the transfer depends upon capital availability
    (E) in general, only developed countries can use American marketing techniques

28. The author states that adoption of self-service is a function of

    I. household income
    II. cultural and structural constraints
    III. population destiny

    (A) I only   (C) I and II only   (E) I, II and III
    (B) III only   (D) II and III only

29. The article from which this passage was extracted probably appeared in a(n)

    (A) academic journal
    (B) accounting journal
    (C) consumer newsletter
    (D) popular magazine
    (E) newspaper editorial

30. Based on the Israeli experience, we can conclude that the adoption of self-service by developing countries

    (A) is hopeless
    (B) shows some promise
    (C) is likely to proceed with great rapidity
    (D) hinders development of local marketing expertise
    (E) depends upon a large population of working women

If there is still time remaining, you may review the questions in this section only.
You may not look at Part A or turn to any other section of the test.

Section III   Problem Solving

TIME: 75 minutes

DIRECTIONS: Solve each of the following problems; then indicate the correct answer on the answer sheet. [On the actual test you will be permitted to use any space available on the examination paper for scratch work.]

NOTE: A figure that appears with a problem is drawn as accurately as possible so as to provide information that may help in answering the question. Numbers in this test are real numbers.

31. If 32 students in a class are female and there are 18 male students in the class, what percentage of the class is female?

    (A) 32%   (D) 64%
    (B) 36%   (E) 72%
    (C) 56.25%

32. If $x + y = 2$ and $y = 5$ what is $x - y$?

    (A) -8 (D) 2
    (B) -5 (E) 8
    (C) -3

Use the following graph for questions 33–35.

SHARE OF COMPUTER MARKET
(Percentage of machines in domestic use)

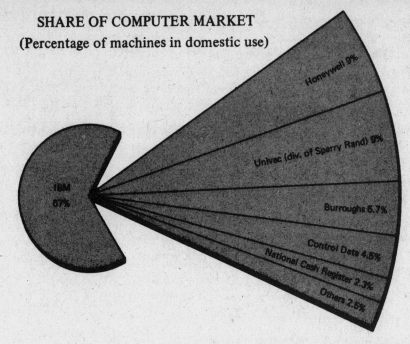

IBM 67%

Honeywell 9%

Univac (div. of Sperry Rand) 9%

Burroughs 5.7%

Control Data 4.5%

National Cash Register 2.3%

Others 2.5%

© 1973 by the New York Times Company. Reprinted by permission.

33. IBM's share of the computer market is roughly *x* times the total of all other companies; *x* equals

(A) $\frac{1}{10}$ (D) 2
(B) $\frac{1}{2}$ (E) 3
(C) $1\frac{1}{2}$

34. If Control Data and National Cash Register merged, the merged firm's new rank in share of the market would be

(A) 2   (D) 5
(B) 3   (E) 6
(C) 4

35. Consider the following statements

  I. Univac's share of the market is greater than those of Burroughs and Control Data combined.
  II. Honeywell and Univac together have less than a third of IBM's share of the market.
  III. IBM's share of the market is 30 times larger than that of National Cash Register.

Which of the above statements are true?

(A) II only
(B) III only
(C) I and II
(D) I and III
(E) I, II and III

36. If a job takes 12 men 4 hours to complete. how long should it take 15 men to complete the job?

 (A) 2 hrs. 40 min.
 (B) 3 hrs.
 (C) 3 hrs. 12 min.
 (D) 3 hrs. 24 min.
 (E) 3 hrs. 30 min.

37. Apples cost 10¢ each. If the price of apples rises by 12%, how much will a dozen apples cost?

 (A) 12¢
 (B) $1.20
 (C) $1.32
 (D) $1.34
 (E) $1.36

38. How long must a driver take to drive the final 70 miles of a trip if he wants to average 50 miles an hour for the entire trip and during the first part of the trip he drove 50 miles in $1\frac{1}{2}$ hours?

 (A) 54 min
 (B) 1 hr
 (C) 66 min
 (D) 70 min
 (E) 75 min

Use the following table for questions 39–41.

MAJOR WAGE NEGOTIATIONS IN 1973

Month	Employer	Unions	Workers Covered
January	Popular Price Dresses	Ladies Garment Workers	59,950
February	N.J. Apparel Contractors	Ladies Garment Workers	27,050
March	Con Edison	Utility Workers	16,800
April	Goodyear	Rubber Workers	23,000
May	General Electric Co.	Electrical Workers (I.U.E.)	90,000
	Int. Paper Kraft Division	United Paperworkers, Electrical Brotherhood	11,500
	Nat. Skirt and Sportswear Assn. N.Y. Coat and Suit Assn.	Ladies Garment Workers	51,500
June	Westinghouse Electric	Electrical Workers (I.U.E.)	36,300
	Calif. Processors	Teamsters	56,550
	Nat. Master Freight	Teamsters	450,000
	Railroads	United Transportation Union	135,000
July	U.S. Postal Service	Postal Workers	600,000
September	Major Automobile Makers	Auto Workers	670,250
October	Mack Truck	Auto Workers	13,900
December	Budd	Auto Workers	19,200

Source: U.S. Dept. of Labor.

39. For how many months in 1973 are there major wage negotiations which involve fewer than 150,000 workers?

(A) 4
(B) 5
(C) 6
(D) 7
(E) 8

40. How many workers will have wage negotiations handled by the Ladies Garment Workers Union in 1973?

(A) 51,500
(B) 87,000
(C) 102,000
(D) 130,000
(E) 138,500

41. Of those workers whose wages will be negotiated in 1973, which union represents the largest number?

(A) Ladies Garment Workers
(B) Meat Cutters
(C) Teamsters
(D) Postal Workers
(E) Auto Workers

42. If a rectangle has length L and the width is one half of the length, then the area of the rectangle is

(A) L
(B) L^2
(C) $\frac{1}{2}L^2$
(D) $\frac{1}{4}L^2$
(E) $2L$

43. Eggs cost 50¢ a dozen for the first 100 dozen a store buys from a wholesaler and 47¢ a dozen for all those bought in addition to the first 100 dozen. How much does it cost to buy 150 dozen eggs from the wholesaler?

(A) $70.50
(B) $72.00
(C) $73.50
(D) $123.50
(E) $150.00

44. If the product of two numbers is 5 and one of the numbers is $\frac{3}{2}$, then the sum of the two numbers is

(A) $4\frac{1}{3}$
(B) $4\frac{2}{3}$
(C) $4\frac{5}{6}$
(D) $5\frac{1}{6}$
(E) $6\frac{1}{2}$

45. Which of the following sets of numbers can be used as the lengths of the sides of a triangle?

I. [5,7,12]
II. [2,4,10]
III. [5,7,9]

(A) I only   (D) I and III only
(B) III only   (E) II and III only
(C) I and II only

46. What is the next number in the sequence 2,5,8 . . . ?

(A) 7   (D) 11
(B) 9   (E) 12
(C) 10

47. A dealer owns a group of station wagons and motorcycles. If the number of tires (excluding spare tires) on the vehicles is 30 more than twice the number of vehicles, then the number of station wagons the dealer owns is

(A) 10   (D) 30
(B) 15   (E) 45
(C) 20

Use this graph for questions 48–51.

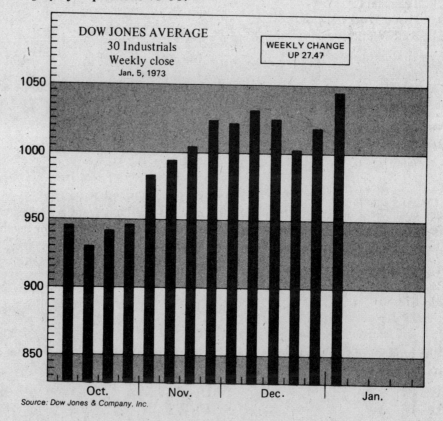

Source: Dow Jones & Company, Inc.

49. Between which two successive weeks (of those shown) did the average drop the most?

  (A) first and second weeks in Oct.
  (B) fourth week in Oct. and first week in Nov.
  (C) third and fourth weeks in Nov.
  (D) first and second weeks in Dec.
  (E) third and fourth weeks in Dec.

50. What was the lowest value of the average during the time shown?

  (A) 910
  (B) 922
  (C) 931

  (D) 939
  (E) 970

51. During how many weeks (of those shown) was the average close between 960 and 1000?

  (A) 2
  (B) 3
  (C) 4

  (D) 5
  (E) 6

52. If the two sides of a right triangle adjacent to the right angle are 5 and 12, then the third side of the triangle is

  (A) 7
  (B) 9
  (C) 11

  (D) 13
  (E) 15

53. Rich sold his skis for $160.00 and his ski boots for $96.00. He made a profit of 20% on his boots and took a 10% loss on his skis. He ended up with a

  (A) loss of $1.78
  (B) loss of $1.50
  (C) gain of $3.20
  (D) gain of $7.53
  (E) gain of $17.06

54. It costs 10¢ each to print the first 500 copies of a newspaper. It costs $(10 - x/50)$¢ each for every copy after the first 500. What is x if it cost $75.00 to print 1,000 copies of the newspaper?

  (A) 2.5
  (B) 100
  (C) 25

  (D) 250
  (E) 300

55. The amount of coal necessary to heat a home cost $53.00 in 1972 and will increase at the rate of 15% a year. The amount of oil necessary to heat the same home cost $45.00 in 1972 but will increase at the rate of 20% a year. In 1974 which of the following methods would heat the home for the cheapest price?

    (A) Use of only coal
    (B) Use of only oil
    (C) Use of coal or oil since they cost the same amount
    (D) Use of oil for 8 months and coal for 4 months
    (E) Use of coal for 8 months and oil for 4 months

56. If the side of a square increases by 30%, then its area increases by

    (A) 9%
    (B) 30%
    (C) 60%
    (D) 69%
    (E) 130%

57. Train Y leaves New York at 1 A.M. and travels east at an average speed of x mph. If train Z leaves New York at 2 A.M. and travels east, at what average rate of speed will train Z have to travel in order to catch train Y by 5:30 A.M.?

    (A) $\frac{5}{6}x$
    (D) $\frac{9}{7}x$

    (B) $\frac{9}{8}x$
    (E) $\frac{3}{2}x$

    (C) $\frac{6}{5}x$

Use this graph for question 58.

ANTIPOLLUTION FUNDING DURING THE 70s
(Cost in billions of dollars for 1971–1980)

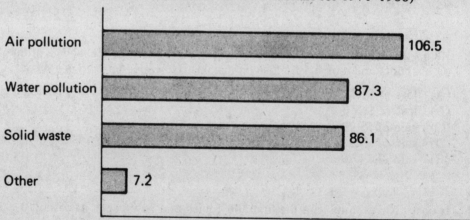

58. The ratio of air pollution funding to water pollution funding is about

    (A) 2 to 1
    (B) 3 to 2
    (C) 6 to 5
    (D) 5 to 6
    (E) 2 to 3

59. If 30 boxes of pencils cost a total of $5.10, then 4 boxes of pencils should cost

    (A) 52¢
    (B) 68¢
    (C) 78¢
    (D) 85¢
    (E) 93¢

60. A worker is paid r dollars for each hour he works up to 8 hours a day. For any time worked over 8 hours he is paid at the rate of $(1.5)r$ dollars an hour. The total amount of dollars the worker will earn if he works 11 hours in a day is

(A) $(4.5)r$

(B) $(5.5)r$

(C) $(9.25)r$

(D) $(11)r$

(E) $(12.5)r$

61. If the product of 3 consecutive integers is 120, then the sum of the integers is

(A) 9

(B) 12

(C) 14

(D) 15

(E) 17

Use the table below for questions 62 and 63.

Grants from the XYZ Foundation	1971	1972
Colleges	5.2	4.9
Medical research	3.1	3.5
Other	1.7	1.8
Total	10.0	10.2

62. Medical research grants between 1971 and 1972

(A) decreased by 4%

(B) stayed about the same

(C) increased by about 10%

(D) increased by about 13%

(E) increased by about 21%

63. What percent of the total grants of the *XYZ* Foundation for both years was received by colleges?

(A) 49.8

(B) 50

(C) 50.2

(D) 50.5

(E) 51

64. Mechanics are paid twice the hourly wage of salesmen. Custodial workers are paid one-third the hourly wage of mechanics. What fraction of the hourly wage of custodial workers are salesmen paid?

(A) $\frac{1}{3}$

(B) $\frac{1}{2}$

(C) $\frac{2}{3}$

(D) $\frac{4}{3}$

(E) $\frac{3}{2}$

65. If x and y are negative, then which of the following statements are always true?

  I. $x + y$ is positive

 II. xy is positive

III. $x - y$ is positive

(A) I only

(B) II only

(C) III only

(D) I and III only

(E) II and III only

66. An unloaded truck travels 10 miles on a gallon of gas. When the same truck is loaded it travels only 85% as far on a gallon of gas. How many gallons of gas will the loaded truck use to travel 50 miles?

(A) 5
(B) 5.67
(C) 5.88

(D) 6.02
(E) 6.3

67. If $8a = 6b$ and $3a = 0$ then

(A) a and b are equal
(B) $a = 6$
(C) $\dfrac{b}{a} = \dfrac{4}{3}$

(D) $a = 6$ and $b = 8$
(E) $\dfrac{a}{b} = \dfrac{3}{4}$

68. A horse can travel at the rate of 5 miles per hour for the first two hours of a trip. After the first two hours the horse's speed drops to 3 miles per hour. How many hours will it take the horse to travel 20 miles?

(A) 4
(B) 5
(C) $5\frac{1}{3}$

(D) $5\frac{1}{2}$
(E) $5\frac{2}{3}$

Use the following table for questions 69–72

THE BUDGET DOLLAR

1972
Fiscal year, estimated
Where it comes from

1973
Fiscal year, estimated
Where it comes from

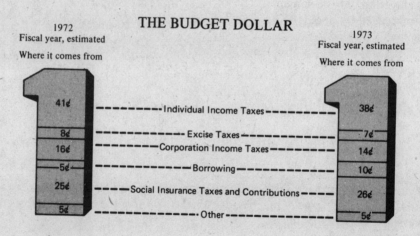

	1972	1973
Individual Income Taxes	41¢	38¢
Excise Taxes	8¢	7¢
Corporation Income Taxes	16¢	14¢
Borrowing	5¢	10¢
Social Insurance Taxes and Contributions	25¢	26¢
Other	5¢	5¢

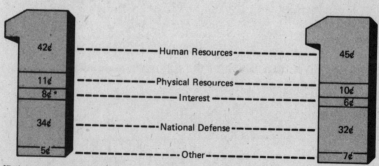

	1972	1973
Human Resources	42¢	45¢
Physical Resources	11¢	10¢
Interest	8¢*	6¢
National Defense	34¢	32¢
Other	5¢	7¢

*Excludes interest paid to trust funds

© 1973 by the New York Times Company. Reprinted by permission.

69. In each year the category which provided the most income was

   (A) borrowing
   (B) individual income taxes
   (C) human resources
   (D) social insurance taxes
   (E) national defense

70. The change in the percentage of the budget allocated to human resources between 1972 and 1973 is expected to be

   (A) −3%
   (B) −2%
   (C) 0%
   (D) +2%
   (E) +3%

71. In 1973 which one of the following categories was estimated to require the largest amount of the budget?

   (A) human resources
   (B) national defense
   (C) physical resources
   (D) interest and national defense
   (E) physical resources and national defense

72. Which of the following statements can be inferred from the graph?

   I. The amount of money collected from excise taxes declined from 1972 to 1973.
   II. The government will borrow twice as much money in 1973 as it did in 1972.
   III. Of the total amount of income in 1972 and 1973, 15% came from Corporation Income Taxes.

   (A) None
   (B) III only
   (C) I and II only
   (D) II and III only
   (E) I, II, and III

73. If the ratio of the radii of two circles is 3 to 2, then the ratio of the areas of the two circles is

   (A) 2 to 3   (D) 9 to 4
   (B) 3 to 4   (E) 3 to 2
   (C) 4 to 9

74. −5 times (−4) is

   (A) −20   (D) −54
   (B) 54   (E) −5
   (C) 20

75. If $\frac{1}{x} < \frac{1}{y}$ then

(A) $x > y$
(B) x and y are negative
(C) x and y are positive
(D) $x < y$
(E) none of the preceding statements follows

76. A manufacturer of boxes wants to make a profit of x dollars. When he sells 5,000 boxes it costs 5¢ a box to make the first 1,000 boxes and then it costs y¢ a box to make the remaining 4,000 boxes. What price in dollars should he charge for the 5,000 boxes?

(A) $5,000 + 1,000y$
(B) $5,000 + 1,000y + 100x$
(C) $50 + 10y + x$
(D) $5,000 + 4,000y + x$
(E) $50 + 40y + x$

Use the following graph for questions 77–80.

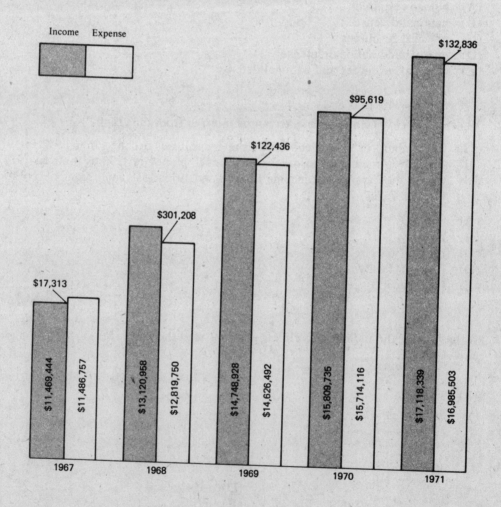

77. In what year was the profit (income minus expenses) the greatest?

(A) 1967
(B) 1968
(C) 1969

(D) 1970
(E) 1971

78. In how many of the years was the profit larger than in the preceding year?

(A) 0
(B) 1
(C) 2

(D) 3
(E) 4

79. Between which two successive years was the rise (in dollars) in income the greatest?

(A) 1967 and 1968
(B) 1968 and 1969
(C) 1969 and 1970
(D) 1970 and 1971
(E) insufficient information to determine

80. Which of the following statements can be inferred from the graph?

    I. The company made a profit in all the years shown on the graph.
   II. The company's profit increased in every year between 1969 and 1971.
  III. The company's expenses increased in each year shown on the graph.

(A) I only
(B) II only
(C) III only
(D) I and III only
(E) I, II, and III

81. If $x - 2$ is less than y then

(A) x and y are positive
(B) y is less than $x + 2$
(C) y is greater than x
(D) $y + 2$ is greater than x
(E) none of the preceding

82. Wheat costs $2.00 a bushel and corn costs $3.00 a bushel. If the price of wheat rises 10% a month and the price of corn is unchanged, how many months will it take before a bushel of corn costs less than a bushel of wheat?

(A) 2
(B) 3
(C) 4

(D) 5
(E) 6

83. If $\frac{1}{2} + \frac{1}{4} = \frac{x}{15}$, then x is

    (A) 10
    (B) 11.25
    (C) 12
    (D) 13.75
    (E) 14

84. If $x + y + z + w = 15$, then at least k of the numbers x, y, z, w must be positive where k is

    (A) 0
    (B) 1
    (C) 2
    (D) 3
    (E) 4

85. If the length of a rectangle is increased by 11%, then the area of the rectangle is increased by

    (A) 11%
    (B) 21%
    (C) 110%
    (D) 111%
    (E) 121%

If there is still time remaining. you may review the questions in this section only.
You may not turn to any other section of the test.

Section IV   Practical Judgment

TIME: 20 minutes

DIRECTIONS: Read the following passage. After you have completed it, you will be asked to answer two sets of questions. The first of these, data evaluation, involves determining the importance of specific factors included in the passage. The second, data application, consists of general questions relating to the passage. When answering questions, you may consult the passage.

The Parks Company, located in New York City, had engaged exclusively in the manufacture of baking powder in the seventy-five years since its founding. Sales were approximately $800,000 annually. The sales volume, measured in commodity units instead of dollars, had showed a decline of about 11 percent over the past decade. The company had a small office force and employed approximately 50 people in the production process, which was divided into (1) the mixing department, (2) the assembly department, and (3) the final inspection and packing department.

In 1935, distribution had been foreign as well as national. Forty years later, the sale of the product was confined to New England and the Middle Atlantic states. Mr. Andrew H. Pendler, the president, attributed this significant decrease in both market area and sales volume to high tariff rates, sterner competition, and trade dislocations caused by World War II.

Mr. Gordon Janis, the sales manager, after studying the market closely, arrived at a different set of reasons why sales had been dropping. In the first place, according to Janis, sales to commercial consumers had diminished to practically nothing. Many modern bakeries bought the necessary chemicals and manufactured their own baking powder. Secondly, the population had become urbanized. Formerly, when a larger portion of the citizenry was suburban, many housewives had done their own baking. People in cities were close to bakeries and other outlets where they could buy the finished product, and improved transportation had enabled fresh bakery products to be readily available at retail outlets. The third reason which Mr. Janis considered significant was the growing popularity of ready-mixes. The natural tendency of practically all human beings is to get as much as they can for a minimum of effort. Since ready-mixes did save housewives a good deal of labor, this type of product had been well received.

Mr. Janis believed that the company could not cope with the first two factors, and therefore his suggestion for increasing sales was to branch out and manufacture ready-mix baking products which would compare favorably with nationally-known brands. Management was particularly receptive to Janis's idea because production of ready-mixes would require only minor changes in personnel and the cost of additional machinery would be relatively small. Two additional machines were necessary, each costing approximately $10,000.

Mr. Pendler was determined to succeed in the marketing of the new products. He believed that a thorough market analysis was a prerequisite to making a final decision as to whether Janis's idea was commercially sound. Pendler wanted to know whether a small company like Parks could battle for a share of the ready-mix market against much bigger competitors. His concern centered on two key variables. First, he questioned the ability of his marketing people to develop a product which would be sufficiently differentiated from competitors' products. Parks would have to market a product which had some distinct advantage over competing products. This advantage could be in the form of an improvement over existing brands, for example, a mix that was easier to prepare. Second, a strong advertising campaign was necessary to enter the market with an unknown product. Potential consumers would have to be made aware of the new brand and its advantages. Pendler wanted to know how much such an advertising campaign would cost and whether the company had the financial resources to finance it.

Janis was given the task of preparing a marketing research report which would provide answers to Pendler's questions. Graduate students were hired to poll housewives as they entered supermarkets. Each student questioned a number of housewives about their purchases of ready-mixes, how frequently they used the products, what they liked and/or disliked about the mixes. Respondents were also asked to recall any advertising they remembered about ready-mixes. After about fifty interviews, Janis believed that the had collected enough information to reach certain conclusions.

Janis tabulated the research data and found the following trends. Most housewives said that they purchased ready-mixes and preferred to prepare their own cakes, rather than buy them from a bakery or supermarket. Housewives felt that ready-mixes were preferable to commercially-prepared cakes because of their freshness and economy. In particular, respondents liked the convenience of being able to bake a cake "in an emergency" if unexpected company came to visit. Other reasons mentioned for preferring ready-mixes were: "Tastes fresh," "modern thing to do," "my neighbors use it," and "I can choose some of the ingredients."

Few respondents using ready-mixes mentioned any dislikes. Some of the negative reactions mentioned were: "Lack of recipe variety," "my husband doesn't like them," and "all the mixes are the same."

Most of the housewives polled recalled seeing some advertising for ready-mixes during the last week. Half of the respondents recalled specific advertising themes of the major producers. Overall reaction to the advertising was favorable.

Examining the survey results, Janis concluded that Parks should market a ready-mix of its own. He reasoned that since consumer reaction was so favorable, there was room in the market for another brand. Janis recommended, however, that since the research did not reveal how Parks might differentiate its product from those already on the market, the best marketing strategy would be to charge a lower price than that of competing products. With a lower price, he asserted, Parks's ready-mix would sell well to the economy-minded housewife.

Advertising was a problem. It was clear that, given the relatively small marketing budget available to Janis, Parks could not emulate the sort of advertising campaign used by existing ready-mix manufacturers. Janis believed that if Parks would concentrate solely on the economy-minded market segment, advertising themes could be developed and a campaign launched within the company's budget constraints. Janis's report and conclusions were forwarded to Mr. Pendler. After a short deliberation, Pendler approved the ready-mix project.

Without further investigation, the manufacture of Parks's ready-mixes was started. After several months, ready-mix sales still amounted to less than 10 percent of gross sales, and 85 percent of ready-mix sales were in New York City. The entire position of the company was in jeopardy. Both Mr. Pendler and Mr. Janis were worried about the business, but neither seemed to know what to do.

Data Evaluation Questions

DIRECTIONS: The questions that follow relate to the preceding passage. Evaluate, in terms of the passage, each of the items given. Then select your answer from one of the following classifications, and blacken the corresponding space on the answer sheet.

(A) A MAJOR OBJECTIVE in making the decision: one of the goals sought by the decision maker

(B) A MAJOR FACTOR in making the decision: an aspect of the problem, specifically mentioned in the passage, that fundamentally affects and/or determines the decision

(C) A MINOR FACTOR in making the decision: a less important element bearing on or affecting a Major Factor, rather than a Major Objective directly

(D) A MAJOR ASSUMPTION in making the decision: a projection or supposition arrived at by the decision maker before considering the factors and alternatives

(E) AN UNIMPORTANT ISSUE in making the decision: an item lacking significant impact on, or relationship to, the decision

86. Declining sales volume

87. New York City location of Parks Company

88. Production of a successful ready-mix baking product

89. Urbanization of the population

90. Increased world trade

91. Start-up costs for development of ready-mix product

92. Differentiation of Parks's ready-mix from competing products

93. Specific advertising themes recalled by shoppers being interviewed

94. $10,000 cost for one additional machine

95. Size of the office staff employed at Parks

96. Parks's ability to compete with bigger companies

97. Number of housewives interviewed for marketing survey

98. Modern bakeries' practice of producing their own baking powder

99. Financial resources of Parks

100. Cost of Parks's advertising campaign

Data Application Questions

DIRECTIONS: Answer each of the following questions using information contained in the passage.

101. According to company management, the market area for Parks's baking powder had declined owing to

    I. high tariff rates
    II. increased competition
    III. World War II

    (A) I only
    (B) III only
    (C) I and II only
    (D) II and III only
    (E) I, II, and III

102. Over the last decade, Parks sales volume had declined by about

    (A) 5 percent
    (B) 10 percent
    (C) 11 percent
    (D) 15 percent
    (E) 25 percent

103. Baking powder sales had declined because

    I. bakeries made their own powder
    II. housewives had switched to ready-mixes
    III. manufacturing costs had increased

    (A) I only
    (B) III only
    (C) I and II only
    (D) II and III only
    (E) I, II, and III

104. Based on the evidence presented in the passage, the Parks Company management can be characterized as

    I.   good decision makers
   II. good market researchers
 III. poor businessmen

  (A) I only
  (B) III only
  (C) I and II only
  (D) II and III only
  (E) I, II, and III

105. According to the passage, the decision to make ready-mixes was based directly on which of the following considerations?

    I.   Management was worried about the business.
   II. Ready-mixes were growing in popularity.
 III. Production of ready-mixes was possible without incurring major additional capital and labor costs.

  (A) I only
  (B) III only
  (C) I and II only
  (D) II and III only
  (E) I, II, and III

If there is still time remaining, you may review the questions in this section only.
You may not turn to any other section of the test.

Section V   Data Sufficiency

TIME: 15 minutes

DIRECTIONS: Each of the following problems has a question and two statements which are labeled (1) and (2). Use the data given in (1) and (2) together with other available information (such as the number of hours in a day, the definition of *clockwise*, mathematical facts, etc.) to decide whether the statements are *sufficient* to answer the question. Then fill in space

- **(A)** if you can get the answer from (1) alone but not from (2) alone;
- **(B)** if you can get the answer from (2) alone but not from (1) alone;
- **(C)** if you can get the answer from (1) and (2) together, although neither statement by itself suffices;
- **(D)** if statement (1) alone suffices *and* statement (2) alone suffices;
- **(E)** if you cannot get the answer from statements (1) and (2) together, but need even more data.

All numbers used in this section are real numbers. A figure given for a problem is intended to provide information consistent with that in the question, but not necessarily with the additional information contained in the statements.

106. A rectangular field is 40 yards long. Find the area of the field.

  (1) A fence around the outside of the field is 140 yards long.
  (2) The distance from one corner of the field to the opposite corner is 50 yards.

107. Is x greater than 0?

  (1) $x^3 + 1 = 0$
  (2) $x^2 - \frac{1}{2} = 0$

108. There are 450 boxes to load on a truck. A and B working independently but at the same time take 30 minutes to load the truck. How long should it take B working by himself to load the truck?

  (1) A loads twice as many boxes as B.
  (2) A would take 45 minutes by himself.

109.

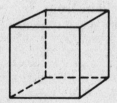

Is the figure above a cube?

  (1) The lengths of all edges are equal.
  (2) The angle between any two edges that meet is a right angle.

110. A car drives around a circular track once. A second car drives from point *A* to point *B* in a straight line. Which car travels farther?

   (1) The car driving around the circular track takes a longer time to complete its trip than the car traveling in a straight line.
   (2) The straight line from *A* to *B* is 1½ times as long as the diameter of the circular track.

111. Find *x* + *y*

   (1) *x* − *y* = 6
   (2) 2*x* + 3*y* = 7

112. Find the length of *AC* if *AB* has length 3 and *x* is 45.

   (1) *z* = 45
   (2) *y* = 90

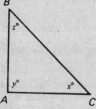

113. How much did it cost Mr. Jones to insure his car for the year 1971?

   (1) He spent $300.00 for car insurance in 1970.
   (2) The total amount he spent for car insurance in 1969, 1970, and 1971 was $905.00

114. It costs 50 cents in tolls, 2 dollars in gas, and at least 1 dollar for parking to drive (round trip) from Utopia to Green Acres each day. The train offers a weekly ticket. Which is the cheaper way to travel per week?

   (1) The weekly train ticket costs 15 dollars.
   (2) Parking costs a total of 6 dollars.

115. Is *ABDC* a rectangle?

   (1) *AD* and *BC* bisect each other at *E*.
   (2) Angle *ACD* is 90°.

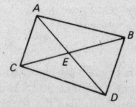

116. A worker is hired for five days. He is paid $5.00 more for each day of work than he was paid for the preceding day of work. What was the total amount he was paid for the five days of work?

   (1) He had made 50% of the total by the end of the third day.
   (2) He was paid twice as much for the last day as he was for the first day.

117. Is *y* larger than *x*?

   (1) *x* + *y* = 2
   (2) $\frac{x}{y} = 2$

118. Does a circle with diameter *d* have greater area than a square of side *s*?

   (1) $d < (\sqrt{2})s$
   (2) *d* < *s*

119. 5 apples cost 80 cents. How much will it cost to buy 10 apples and 3 oranges?

(1) Oranges cost 6 for 50 cents.
(2) 10 apples and 6 oranges cost $2.10.

120. A pair of skis originally sold for $160.00. After a discount of $x\%$, the skis were discounted $y\%$. Do the skis cost less than $130.00 after the discounts?

(1) $x = 20$ (2) $y = 15$

If there is still time remaining, you may review the questions in this section only. You may not turn to any other section of the test.

Section VI Verbal Ability

TIME: 20 minutes

Antonyms

DIRECTIONS: For each question below, select the lettered word or phrase that comes closest to being *opposite* in meaning to the word appearing in capital letters. Be sure to consider all meanings carefully.

121. SEDITIOUS: (A) mild (B) loyal (C) sedate (D) proper (E) quaint

122. REDOLENT: (A) clean (B) propitious (C) agreeable (D) odorless (E) unsure

123. PUERILE: (A) savory (B) aromatic (C) mature (D) sterile (E) weak

124. ABATE: (A) deter (B) proceed (C) deny (D) increase (E) animate

125. ACERBITY: (A) reluctance (B) weakness (C) lassitude (D) charm (E) sweetness

126. ACTUATE: (A) dismiss (B) dissuade (C) demote (D) deny (E) denigrate

127. IRRESOLUTE: (A) forceful (B) determined (C) unsound (D) sensitive (E) defensible

128. FRACTIOUS: (A) delicate (B) solid (C) agreeable (D) liberal (E) wholesome

129. DISAPPROVAL: (A) countenance (B) evasion (C) deposition (D) declaration (E) honor

130. ENMITY: (A) affection (B) security (C) awe (D) sanction (E) preponderance

131. GUILE: (A) opening (B) skill (C) honesty (D) reality (E) cupidity

132. CONDUCE: (A) confide (B) direct (C) confirm (D) counteract (E) disprove

133. DEBILITY: (A) credibility (B) strength (C) waste (D) lucidity (E) simplicity

134. EXTOL: (A) propose (B) upset (C) deprecate (D) erect (E) consult

Word-Pair Relationships

DIRECTIONS: For each question below, determine the relationship between the pair of capitalized words and then select the lettered pair of words which have a similar relationship to the first pair.

135. AVIARY : BIRDS :: (A) zoo : tigers (B) bank : money (C) post office : letters (D) arboretum : plants (E) beehive : honey

136. CONVICT : IMPRISONMENT :: (A) student : school (B) exile : banishment (C) delinquent : orphanage (D) prisoner : court (E) hostage : freedom

137. WATER : FLOOD :: (A) rain : river (B) wind : sleet (C) snow : blizzard (D) ice : floe (E) summer : winter

138. PENITENT : OBDURATE :: (A) pensive : thoughtless (B) vacuous : empty (C) cumulative : aggressive (D) happy : ecstatic (E) problematic : ponderous

139. FORTITUDE : RESOLUTION : : (A) timidity : cowardice   (B) heroics : stoicism   (C) medal : bravery   (D) poem : poet   (E) plan : execution

140. YARDSTICK : MEASUREMENT : : (A) scientist : observation   (B) microscope : observation   (C) dictator : control   (D) car : highway   (E) hypothesis : theory

141. EAR : AMPLIFIER : : (A) finger : instrument   (B) wind : velocity   (C) foot : distance   (D) automobile : accelerator   (E) eye : telescope

142. PHLEGMATIC : ENERGETIC : : (A) perfidious : faithful   (B) flagrant : swift   (C) motivated : static   (D) sickly : powerful   (E) egregious : atrocious

143. MURDER : GENOCIDE : : (A) accident : assault   (B) attack : war   (C) fire : holocaust   (D) wasteland : desert   (E) mortuary : sanctuary

144. NEBULOUS : CLARIFICATION : : (A) trite : aggrandizement   (B) erroneous : emendation   (C) broken : replacement   (D) mysterious : deception   (E) accused : proof

145. CLANDESTINE : SURREPTITIOUS : : (A) secret : subversive   (B) covert : concealed   (C) brazen : vivid   (D) mundane : corporeal   (E) unknown : imaginary

146. AMALGAMATE : UNITED : : (A) blend : assorted   (B) organize : arranged   (C) oscillate : displayed   (D) dissipate : anticipated   (E) analyze : scattered

147. EXORCISM : INCANTATION : : (A) confrontation : pandemonium   (B) petition : request   (C) liturgy : prayer   (D) eulogy : libation   (E) matrimony : march

Sentence Completions

DIRECTIONS: For each sentence below, select the lettered word or set of words which, when inserted in the sentence blanks, best completes the meaning of that sentence.

148. The ⎯⎯ source is so polluted that residents dare not ⎯⎯ it.

(A) water . . . drink   (B) air . . . imbibe   (C) river . . . navigate   (D) energy . . . tap   (E) atmospheric . . . test

149. The throbbing _____ of twenty _____ poured forth the music of Vivaldi, Mozart, and Bach.

    (A) soliloquy . . . voices (B) singing . . . musicians (C) sonority . . . instruments (D) boom . . . recorders (E) emotion . . . horns

150. Increased _____ would be seen as a step toward eventual resumption of diplomatic relations.

    (A) animosity (B) incentives (C) embargoes (D) trade (E) lobbying

151. That the _____ know their plight is clear from the way they dart in different directions in search of a(n) _____.

    (A) participants . . . solution (B) victims . . . exit (C) birds . . meal (D) animals . . . mate (E) rescuers . . . goal

152. Although superficially similar, the theories of the two anthropologists appear completely _____ when examined in detail.

    (A) unique (B) identical (C) absurd (D) opposed (E) compatible

153. The Reform Bills _____ the power of the common citizens of England by _____ the legal restrictions on manhood suffrage.

    (A) extended . . . reaffirming (B) underscored . . . redoubling (C) increased . . . reducing (D) augmented . . . raising (E) modified . . . simplifying

154. Despite the increasing importance of _____ to American businesses, study of foreign languages in U.S. schools has _____ in recent years.

    (A) government controls . . . grown
    (B) research spending . . . plummetted
    (C) world trade . . . dropped
    (D) science . . . decreased
    (E) international competition . . . risen

155. Tax reduction will increase the _____ and _____ of consumers.

    (A) savings . . . losses (B) mobility . . . gregariousness (C) spending . . . inflation (D) income . . . purchasing power (E) leisure time . . . consumption

156. Although he is most famous _____ as the greatest of the "Metaphysical" poets, John Donne was _____ in his own lifetime as a preacher.

    (A) among scholars . . . ridiculed
    (B) in America . . . respected
    (C) today . . . better known
    (D) in modern times . . . criticized
    (E) among critics . . . little known

157. It is the _____ attention given to this crucial issue which makes the report so _____.

(A) unflinching ... significant (B) scanty ... fascinating (C) constant ... meaningless (D) exaggerated ... important (E) enormous ... atypical

158. Auto sales have shown _____ in recent months, though not enough to _____ the trend towards layoffs and plant closings.

(A) losses ... support (B) improvement ... reverse (C) fluctuation ... lessen (D) increases ... strengthen (E) stability ... explain

159. He never stopped talking; he was _____.

(A) laconic (B) loquacious (C) pedantic (D) eccentric (E) restrained

160. For leaders in a democracy, dependent upon popular support, _____ considerations inevitably affect governmental decisions.

(A) economic (B) international (C) political (D) psychological (E) personal

If there is still time remaining, you may review the questions in this section only.
You may not turn to any other section of the test.

Section VII   Practical Judgment

TIME: 20 minutes

DIRECTIONS: Read the following passage. After you have completed it, you will be asked to answer two sets of questions. The first of these, data evaluation, involves determining the importance of specific factors included in the passage. The second, data application, consists of general questions relating to the passage. When answering questions, you may consult the passage.

The second day of Vespucci SpA's annual sales conference in Milan threatened to end in uproar. The business equipment manufacturer's 28 salesmen had received sales manager Guido Tulli's proposal to re-assign them to new territories with angry condemnation.

Explaining the reasons behind the drastic measures, Tulli had reminded the salesmen that the company was suffering from declining sales and had a serious cash flow problem. This was mainly due to slow payments by customers. Accounts receivable were increasing at an alarming rate, he had told them.

Under Tulli's plan, the company's top salesmen were to be switched from the areas with high sales to areas that currently yielded low sales. He had explained that this would mean that the more experienced salesmen could concentrate on building up sales in the less productive regions. The less experienced salesmen could easily handle the well-developed territories.

Some of the firm's leading salesmen immediately started to object. "I have spent years building up my territory," one of them protested. "I do not see why I should have to start all over again in a new region."

Tulli pointed out that he felt that the firm's best salesmen were being wasted in these well-developed sales regions. "You are simply going to well-established customers and taking orders," he argued.

An experienced salesman contested this view, observing that he had greatly increased sales in his territory the previous year by persuading existing customers to expand the amount of their orders in business stationery.

This supported his view, retorted Tulli, that the salesmen in the well-established territories were becoming stale, and were failing to uncover new customers. "This is only natural," he added. "When I was promoted to sales manager, I was amazed at how successful my successor was in getting new orders in my old territory. The company badly needs your experience to develop the weaker regions."

Another experienced salesman asked whether the new plan would mean that salesmen would get an extra bonus or higher commission rates for establishing new accounts. Tulli began to explain why he thought this was impractical, when he was interrupted by one of the younger salesmen who had been sitting at the back of the room quietly fuming. He told Tulli that he felt completely demotivated by the proposal to remove them from the undeveloped territories.

Tulli tried to reassure the young salesman that the company did not regard them as failures. The changes were being made simply because the company was having difficulties, and needed to boost sales quickly, he pointed out.

Tulli swallowed hard before announcing another new policy he knew was likely to upset the gathered salesmen. "The management board has also decided that in future sales commissions will be paid quarterly and only on those orders for which payments have been received from customers," he announced nervously. "As from today it will be your responsibility to raise the subject of slow payments with customers. Moreover, no new orders will be accepted from customers until all overdue payments are received."

This was too much for the salesmen to take and the meeting erupted into a noisy uproar. "Why shouldn't we be paid for orders we have succeeded in getting?" demanded one salesman furiously. "It is not our job to collect debts," protested another. "This contravenes our employment contract," shouted yet another.

The salesmen were all talking agitatedly at once when Tulli decided to close the proceedings for that day. He rushed to a nearby hotel where group managing director Leon Cavello was staying overnight. He was due to address the conference the following morning.

"Our proposals have met with even more hostility than we expected," Tulli told Cavello, relating how the meeting had broken up in disorder. "I'm afraid you will have a hard time of it tomorrow convincing them that the proposals are in everybody's interest. But I don't think we can dodge the issue now. We have to tackle it while we have them all together."

Cavello nodded gravely. His first inclination was to proceed with the proposals whether or not the salesmen approved. On the other hand, he reflected, salesmen are the key to a company's success. It might be unwise to impose a new system on them without their consent.

Cavello convinced Tulli that his plan, presented during the day at the sales meeting, could not be implemented because of the unequivocal opposition of the salesmen. A compromise plan had to be worked out. Tulli and Cavello worked long into the night putting together a plan which they believed would be acceptable to most of the salesmen and in harmony with the company's objectives.

Tulli suggested assigning quotas to salesmen in existing territories rather than shifting successful salesmen from high-sales territories. "By assigning quotas, we can measure individual performance and motivate salesmen towards a predetermined level of achievement. Annual quotas based on expected sales also help in planning production, inventory, and working capital needs. Shifting salesmen is easier under a quota system because quotas can be easily adjusted to reflect the area's potential. If a low-yielding territory has low sales potential, the quota would be relatively lower than in a high-yielding, high-potential territory."

Cavello agreed that a quota system might be the solution to their sales problem. However, quotas had some disadvantages. "Companies sometimes set lower quotas for less able salesmen, but this can be demoralizing. Better salesmen will feel that they are being discriminated against. They will not give their best effort under such a plan." Tulli insisted that a quota system would work. "We need to find a plan which will motivate our best as well as our younger, less experienced salesmen."

Cavello summarized the available options. The first option was a straight commission plan. No matter how much sales a salesman produced over his quota, he would earn the same commission rate. A second possibility was a combination of salary and commissions. "Salesmen drawing even nominal salaries tend to think as company men and they have less reason to resist sales plan changes that are justified in terms of goals." Cavello further pointed out that special incentives could be offered under such a plan, such as a new account bonus or higher commission rates for sales over 100% of quota. "By offering such incentives," Cavello added, "Salesmen in less productive regions would be motivated to spend more time in building new accounts."

Tulli agreed that both options suggested by Cavello might be accepted by the salesmen. "But," he asked, "are these options better for the company than the ones I proposed today?"

Data Evaluation Questions

DIRECTIONS: The questions that follow relate to the preceding passage. Evaluate, in terms of the passage, each of the items given. Then select your answer from one of the following classifications, and blacken the corresponding space on the answer sheet.

(A) A MAJOR OBJECTIVE in making the decision: one of the goals sought by the decision maker

(B) A MAJOR FACTOR in making the decision: an aspect of the problem, specifically mentioned in the passage, that fundamentally affects and/or determines the decision

(C) A MINOR FACTOR in making the decision: a less important element bearing on or affecting a Major Factor, rather than a Major Objective directly

(D) A MAJOR ASSUMPTION in making the decision: a projection or supposition arrived at by the decision maker before considering the factors and alternatives

(E) AN UNIMPORTANT ISSUE in making the decision: an item lacking significant impact on, or relationship to, the decision

161. Vespucci SpA's declining sales

162. Vespucci's accounts receivable problem

163. Vespucci's Italian location

164. Improved cash flow

165. Ease with which salesmen may be shifted under a quota system

166. Development of new customers

167. Late payments by customers

168. Ability of top salesmen to succeed in any territory

169. Assignment of quotas to salesmen

170. Flexibility in setting quotas at either high or low levels

171. Measurement of salesmen's individual performances

172. Likelihood that salesmen will accept Cavello's options

173. Disadvantages of sales quotas

174. Tulli's experience in dealing with salesmen

175. Number of salesmen working for Vespucci

Data Application Questions

DIRECTIONS: Answer each of the following questions using information contained in the passage.

176. According to the passage, Tulli proposed that Vespucci salesmen not be allowed to accept new orders from customers unless

    I. the sales manager approved
   II. the new orders were profitable
  III. customer payments were up to date

   (A) I only
   (B) III only
   (C) I and II only
   (D) II and III only
   (E) I, II, and III

177. Vespucci's cash flow problem was caused by

    I. poor salesmanship
   II. declining sales
  III. slow payments by customers

   (A) I only
   (B) III only
   (C) I and II only
   (D) II and III only
   (E) I, II, and III

178. According to Tulli, sales could be increased if salesmen would be

    I.   reassigned territories
    II.   responsible for collecting overdue accounts
   III.   spending more time in the field

    (A) I only
    (B) III only
    (C) I and II only
    (D) II and III only
    (E) I, II, and III

179. Tulli gave which of the following reasons in support of his reorganization plan?

    I.   Salesmen's morale was low.
    II.   Sales territories were too large.
   III.   Too few new customers were being obtained.

    (A) I only
    (B) III only
    (C) I and II only
    (D) II and III only
    (E) I, II, and III

180. It seems likely that reducing credit to customers would probably lead to

    I.   a reduction in accounts receivable
    II.   increased cash flow
   III.   more sales

    (A) I only
    (B) III only
    (C) I and II only
    (D) II and III only
    (E) I, II, and III

If there is still time remaining, you may review the questions in this section only.
You may not turn to any other section of the test.

Section VIII   Data Sufficiency

TIME: 15 minutes

DIRECTIONS: Each of the following problems has a question and two statements which are labeled (1) and (2). Use the data given in (1) and (2) together with other available information (such as the number of hours in a day, the definition of *clockwise*, mathematical facts, etc.) to decide whether the statements are *sufficient* to answer the question. Then fill in space

(A) if you can get the answer from (1) alone but not from (2) alone;

(B) if you can get the answer from (2) alone but not from (1) alone;

(C) if you can get the answer from (1) and (2) together, although neither statement by itself suffices;

(D) if statement (1) alone suffices *and* statement (2) alone suffices;

(E) if you cannot get the answer from statements (1) and (2) together, but need even more data.

All numbers used in this section are real numbers. A figure given for a problem is intended to provide information consistent with that in the question, but not necessarily with the additional information contained in the statements.

181. *k* is an integer. Is *k* divisible by 8?

(1) *k* is divisible by 4.
(2) *k* is divisible by 16.

182. How much is the average salary of the 30 assembly workers? The foreman is paid a salary of $12,000.

(1) The total salary paid to the assembly workers and the foreman is $312,000.
(2) The foreman's salary is 120% of the average salary of the assembly workers.

183. How far is it from town *A* to town *B*? Town *C* is 12 miles east of town *A*.

(1) Town *C* is south of town *B*.
(2) It is 9 miles from town *B* to town *C*.

184. How many vinyl squares with sides 5 inches long will be needed to cover the rectangular floor of a room?

(1) The floor is 10 feet long.
(2) The floor is 5 feet wide.

185. Mary must work 15 hours to make in wages the cost of a set of luggage. How many dollars does the set of luggage cost?

(1) Jim must work 12 hours to make in wages the cost of the set of luggage.
(2) Jim's hourly wage is 125% of Mary's hourly wage.

186. What is the value of x?

    (1) $\dfrac{x}{y} = 3$

    (2) $x - y = 9$

187. Is DE parallel to AB?

    (1)   The triangles DEC and ABC are similar.

    (2) $CE = EB$

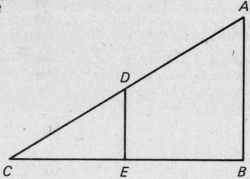

188. How many of the numbers x and y are positive? Both x and y are less than 20.

    (1) x is less than 5.

    (2) $x + y = 24$

189. What is the value of x? $PS = SR$.

    (1) $y = 30$

    (2) $PQ = QR$

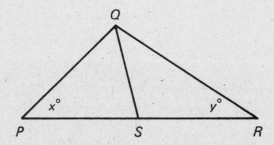

190. How much does the first volume of a 5 volume work weigh?

    (1)   The first 3 volumes weigh 4 pounds.

    (2)   The second, third and fourth volumes weigh a total of $3\frac{1}{2}$ pounds.

191. How much wood will it take to make a rectangular box with a top?

    (1)   The area of the bottom is 4 square feet.

    (2)   The area of a side is 6 square feet.

192. A sequence of numbers is given by the rule $a_n = a_{n-1} + 2$. Is a_{10} an even integer?

    (1) a_1 is even.
    (2) a_9 is 24.

193. Which side of triangle ABC is the longest? $y = 40°$.

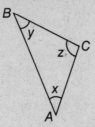

    (1) $z > y$
    (2) $x = 40°$

194. A worker was hired for 5 days. What was her average daily wage for the 5 days?

    (1) She was paid a total of $500 for the 5 days.
    (2) She earned $100 the first day and $100 the last day.

195. If $x = k$, is the expression $x^3 + ax^2 + bx$ equal to zero?

    (1) $a = 0$
    (2) $-b = k^2$

If there is still time remaining, you may review the questions in this section only.
You may not turn to any other section of the test.

Answers

Sections I and II   Reading Recall

1. **(C)**	9. **(C)**	17. **(D)**	25. **(B)**
2. **(B)**	10. **(D)**	18. **(C)**	26. **(C)**
3. **(A)**	11. **(B)**	19. **(B)**	27. **(C)**
4. **(E)**	12. **(D)**	20. **(B)**	28. **(E)**
5. **(A)**	13. **(E)**	21. **(C)**	29. **(A)**
6. **(B)**	14. **(B)**	22. **(B)**	30. **(B)**
7. **(B)**	15. **(B)**	23. **(D)**	
8. **(C)**	16. **(B)**	24. **(A)**	

Section III   Problem Solving

(Numbers in parentheses indicate the section in the Mathematics Review where material concerning the question is discussed.)

31. **(D)** (I–4)	50. **(C)** (IV–3)	69. **(B)** (IV–2)
32. **(A)** (II–2)	51. **(A)** (IV–3)	70. **(E)** (IV–2)
33. **(D)** (IV–2)	52. **(D)** (III–4)	71. **(A)** (IV–2)
34. **(C)** (IV–2)	53. **(A)** (I–4)	72. **(A)** (IV–2)
35. **(A)** (IV–2)	54. **(D)** (II–3)	73. **(D)** (III–7, II–5)
36. **(C)** (II–3)	55. **(B)** (I–4)	74. **(C)** (I–6)
37. **(D)** (I–4)	56. **(D)** (III–7)	75. **(E)** (II–7)
38. **(A)** (II–3)	57. **(D)** (II–3)	76. **(E)** (I–4, II–3)
39. **(E)** (IV–1)	58. **(C)** (IV–3, II–5)	77. **(B)** (IV–4)
40. **(E)** (IV–1)	59. **(B)** (II–5)	78. **(C)** (IV–4)
41. **(E)** (IV–1)	60. **(E)** (II–3)	79. **(A)** (IV–4)
42. **(C)** (III–7)	61. **(D)** (I–1)	80. **(C)** (IV–4)
43. **(C)** (II–3, II–2)	62. **(D)** (IV–1)	81. **(D)** (II–7)
44. **(C)** (II–2)	63. **(B)** (IV–2)	82. **(D)** (I–8)
45. **(B)** (III–4)	64. **(E)** (II–3)	83. **(B)** (I–2)
46. **(D)** (II–6)	65. **(B)** (II–7)	84. **(B)** (I–6)
47. **(B)** (II–2, II–3)	66. **(C)** (I–2)	85. **(A)** (III–7, I–4)
48. **(C)** (IV–3)	67. **(A)** (I–2, II–2)	
49. **(E)** (IV–4)	68. **(C)** (II–3)	

Section IV   Practical Judgment

86. **(B)**	91. **(B)**	96. **(D)**	101. **(E)**
87. **(E)**	92. **(A)**	97. **(E)**	102. **(C)**
88. **(A)**	93. **(E)**	98. **(C)**	103. **(C)**
89. **(B)**	94. **(C)**	99. **(B)**	104. **(B)**
90. **(E)**	95. **(E)**	100. **(B)**	105. **(D)**

Section V   Data Sufficiency

106.	(D)	110.	(B)	114.	(A)	118.	(B)
107.	(A)	111.	(C)	115.	(C)	119.	(D)
108.	(D)	112.	(D)	116.	(D)	120.	(A)
109.	(C)	113.	(E)	117.	(C)		

Section VI   Verbal Ability

121.	(B)	131.	(C)	141.	(E)	151.	(B)
122.	(D)	132.	(D)	142.	(A)	152.	(D)
123.	(C)	133.	(B)	143.	(C)	153.	(C)
124.	(D)	134.	(C)	144.	(B)	154.	(C)
125.	(E)	135.	(D)	145.	(B)	155.	(D)
126.	(B)	136.	(B)	146.	(B)	156.	(C)
127.	(B)	137.	(C)	147.	(C)	157.	(A)
128.	(C)	138.	(A)	148.	(A)	158.	(B)
129.	(A)	139.	(A)	149.	(C)	159.	(B)
130.	(A)	140.	(B)	150.	(D)	160.	(C)

Section VII   Practical Judgment

161.	(B)	166.	(A)	171.	(A)	176.	(D)
162.	(B)	167.	(C)	172.	(D)	177.	(D)
163.	(E)	168.	(D)	173.	(B)	178.	(C)
164.	(A)	169.	(A)	174.	(E)	179.	(B)
165.	(C)	170.	(E)	175.	(E)	180.	(A)

Section VIII   Data Sufficiency

181.	(B)	185.	(E)	189.	(C)	193.	(B)
182.	(D)	186.	(C)	190.	(E)	194.	(A)
183.	(C)	187.	(A)	191.	(E)	195.	(C)
184.	(C)	188.	(B)	192.	(D)		

Analysis

Sections I and II Reading Recall

1. **(C)** See the second sentence of paragraph 1.

2. **(B)** Paragraph 2: "governments of most high-income countries have in recent years undertaken important aid programs. . . ."

3. **(A)** See paragraphs 3 and 4 especially.

4. **(E)** Choices (A) through (D) are all mentioned. See paragraphs 4, 6, 7, and 8.

5. **(A)** Paragraph 6: "a more efficient financial and fiscal system help[s] greatly to mobilize funds for investment" and following.

6. **(B)** See paragraph 8, the section which states that industrial growth depends upon agricultural productivity.

7. **(B)** See paragraphs 2 and especially 4: "high-income countries can play only a supporting role."

8. **(C)** See paragraph 7: "The energies of the people . . . are more likely to be harnessed . . . where . . . governments aim . . . to reduce excessive social inequalities."

9. **(C)** Only the first two are mentioned. I is mentioned in paragraph 9, II is implied in paragraphs 8 and 9.

10. **(D)** See paragraph 3: If low income countries could speed their economic growth, then "a better distribution of world resources" would occur.

11. **(B)** In paragraph 2, this definition is given.

12. **(D)** See the last sentence of paragraph 2.

13. **(E)** See paragraph 2.

14. **(B)** This is given in paragraph 4.

15. **(B)** In paragraph 4, it is stated that "a trend of decreasing inequality . . . among the lower income brackets" had occurred since the end of the recession of 1966–67.

16. **(B)** See paragraph 6: "Unless the education gap is significantly reduced . . . more income equality will be thwarted."

17. **(D)** See paragraph 5: The standard of living improvement was expressed in "high income levels, better housing, a higher ownership rate of consumer durables and an increase in the proportion of families in higher income brackets."

18. **(C)** The entire passage deals with standards of living and income levels of population groups, an important subject of economics.

19. **(B)** See paragraph 5: "their average income is still only 70% of the overall average for all families."

20. **(B)** See the first sentence of paragraph 4: "Between 1964 and 1970 the standard of living of the urban population rose."

21. **(C)** See paragraph 1: "American businessmen have long been interested in foreign markets for the purpose of stimulating trade."

22. **(B)** See the statement that such "transplantations" could aid economic development as given in paragraph 2.

23. **(D)** Paragraphs 2 and 3 deal with this issue.

24. **(A)** See paragraph 4ff., concerning the resistance to packaged foods, new shopping behavior, etc.

25. **(B)** See paragraph 5: "Daily shopping trips may be more of a social endeavor."

26. **(C)** See paragraph 6: "working women switched . . . because it is open during their lunch hour."

27. **(C)** See paragraph 3: "research is needed to determine the factors responsible for the acceptance and growth of marketing innovations."

28. **(E)** All three. The first two are specifically stated in paragraph 4, the last is implied in the passage.

29. **(A)** is most appropriate.

30. **(B)** The Israeli experience shows that there is hope that similar countries might successfully adopt self-service.

Section III   Problem Solving

31. **(D)** There are 50 students in the class. Since $\frac{32}{50} = .64$, females make up 64% of the class.

32. **(A)** Since y is 5 and $x + y = 2$, $x + 5 = 2$. Add -5 to each side of the equation to obtain $x = -3$. Therefore, $x - y = -3 - (5) = -8$.

33. **(D)** IBM's share of the market is 67% and the total share of the other companies is 33%. Since $2(33)\% = 66\%$, the answer is roughly 2.

34. **(C)** If the two firms merge, their share would be $(4.5 + 2.3)\%$. The merged firm would have a 6.8% market share which would make it fourth behind IBM, Honeywell, and Univac.

35. **(A)** Statement I is false since Univac has 9% of the market which is less than 5.7% + 4.5% or 10.2%. Statement II is true since together Univac and Honeywell have a share amounting to 18% of the market which is less than one third of the 67% which

IBM controls. Statement III is false since $30(2.3)\% = 69\%$ which is larger than 67%.

36. **(C)** Since 15 is $\frac{5}{4}$ of 12, it takes 15 men only $\frac{4}{5}$ as long as 12 men to do the job. $\frac{4}{5}$ of 4 = $3\frac{1}{5}$ hours, or 3 hrs. 12 min.

37. **(D)** The new price of apples is $(1.12)10\cancel{c} = 11.2\cancel{c}$ each. Therefore, $12(11.2)\cancel{c} = 134.4\cancel{c} = \$1.34$.

38. **(A)** The total length of the trip will be 120 miles. Hence to average 50 mph for the trip, he must take 2.4 hrs. total traveling time. Since he has already traveled for 1.5 hrs., he must complete the trip in 2.4−1.5 or .9 hrs. or 54 min.

39. **(E)** Jan., Feb., March, April, Aug., Oct., Nov., and Dec.

40. **(E)** The wage negotiations will involve 87,000 in Jan. and Feb., and 51,500 in May. So the total is 138,500.

41. **(E)** The Auto Workers have one agreement involving 670,250. This agreement by itself makes their coverage the largest.

42. **(C)** Area = length times width = $(L)(\frac{1}{2}L) = \frac{1}{2}L^2$.

43. **(C)** The first 100 dozen cost $(100)(50\cancel{c}) = \$50.00$ Since the total purchase is 150 dozen, the last 50 dozen cost 47¢ each. So the total cost is $\$50.00 + 50(47\cancel{c}) = \$50.00 + \$23.50 = \$73.50$.

44. **(C)** Let x be the unknown number. Then $\left(\frac{3}{2}\right)x = 5$; so $x = (5)\left(\frac{2}{3}\right) = \frac{10}{3}$. The sum of the two numbers is $x + \frac{3}{2} = \frac{10}{3} + \frac{3}{2} = \frac{29}{6} = 4\frac{5}{6}$.

45. **(B)** The length of any side of a triangle must be less than the sum of the lengths of the other two sides. Since $5 + 7 = 12$ and 10 is greater than $2 + 4$, I and II cannot be the sides of a triangle. $5 + 7$ is greater than 9, $5 + 9$ is greater than 7, and $7 + 9$ is greater than 5. Therefore, there is a triangle whose sides have lengths of 5, 7, and 9.

46. **(D)** $2+3=5$ and $5+3=8$, so the next number is $8+3$ or 11.

47. **(B)** Each station wagon has 4 tires and each motorcycle has 2 tires. Let x be the number of station wagons and let y be the number of motorcycles. Then $4x + 2y$ is the total number of tires which must equal $2(x+y)+30$. Thus, $4x + 2y = 2x + 2y + 30$ yielding $4x = 2x+30$ with $2x=30$ or $x=15$.

48. **(C)** Use your pencil to compare the height of the columns.

49. **(E)** (B), (C), (D), are wrong since the average rose. The drop was roughly 35 pts. between the first and second weeks in October compared to about 25 pts. between the third and fourth weeks in December.

50. **(C)** The week with lowest value was the second week in October. (Each notch between 900 and 950 indicates 5 pts.)

51. **(A)** The average closed between 960 and 1,000 only at the end of the first and second weeks of November.

52. **(D)** The square of the hypotenuse, the side opposite the right angle, equals $(5)^2 + (12)^2$ or $25 + 144$ or 169. So the length of the side opposite the right angle is $\sqrt{169}$ or 13.

53. **(A)** Price = (cost)(rate). Let x be the original cost of the skis. Then $\$160 = x(.9)$, so $x = \$177.78$. Let y be the original cost of the boots then $\$96 = y(1.2)$, so $y = \$80$. So he made $\$96 - \$80 = \$16$ on the boots and lost $\$177.78 - \$160 = \$17.78$ on the skis. Therefore, he lost $\$1.78$.

54. **(D)** The cost in cents of printing 1000 copies equals $500(10) + (1000 - 500)\left(10 - \dfrac{x}{50}\right) = 5000 + 500\left(10 - \dfrac{x}{50}\right)$. Therefore, $7500 = 5000 + 5000 - 10x$, $10x = 2500$, and $x = 250$.

55. **(B)** The increase in cost between 1972 and 1973 is the product (cost in 1972) · (rate of increase). The cost in 1973 will be the cost in 1972 $(1 + $ rate of increase). Also, the cost in 1974 will equal (cost in 1973) $(1 + $ rate of increase) or (cost in 1972) $(1 + $ rate of increase)^2. So the cost of coal for 1974 $= \$(53)(1.15)^2 = \$(53)(1.32225) = \$70.09$, and the cost of oil for 1974 $= \$(45)(1.2)^2 = \$(45)(1.44) = \$64.80$. Since oil is cheaper than coal, (D) and (E) are incorrect because replacing oil by coal for any amount of time raises the cost.

56. **(D)** Let s be the side of the original square. Since the side of the increased square is $1.3s$, the area of the increased square is $1.69(s^2)$. Therefore, the area has increased by $1.69(s^2) - s^2$ or by $.69(s^2)$ or 69%.

57. **(D)** By 5:30 A.M. train Y will have traveled $(4\frac{1}{2})x$ miles. So train Z must travel $(4\frac{1}{2})x$ miles in $3\frac{1}{2}$ hours. The average rate of speed necessary is $\dfrac{4\frac{1}{2}x}{3\frac{1}{2}}$ which equals $\dfrac{\frac{9}{2}x}{\frac{7}{2}}$ or $\dfrac{9}{7}x$.

58. **(C)** $(6)(18) = 108$ and $(5)(18) = 90$. To make quick estimates, check the amount funded for water pollution if air pollution received 100. For example, if the ratio were 3 to 2, water pollution would get only 66,7 billion dollars.

59. **(B)** Let x be the cost in cents of 4 boxes of pencils. $\dfrac{4}{30} = \dfrac{x}{5.10}$, which means $x = \$\left(\dfrac{4}{30}\right)(5.10) = \$.68 = 68¢$.

60. **(E)** The amount the worker is paid for working T hours if T is larger than 8 is $8r + (T - 8)(1.5)r$. When $T = 11$, the worker will be paid $8r + 3(1.5)r = (12.5)r$.

61. **(D)** The product of three consecutive integers is of the form $x(x + 1)(x + 2)$. A good approximation to this is $(x + 1)^3$. Since $5^3 = 125$, a good guess is 4, 5, 6. This is correct because $(4)(5)(6) = 120$. The sum of these three numbers is 15.

62. **(D)** Medical research grants increased by .4 between 1971 and 1972. The fractional increase is $\dfrac{.4}{3.1}$. Since $\dfrac{.4}{3.2} = \dfrac{1}{8} = 12.5\%$, 13% is the best estimate.

63. **(B)** Total amount was 20.2 and the total amount the colleges received was 10.1. The colleges received $\dfrac{10.1}{20.2}$ or $\dfrac{1}{2}$ or 50%.

64. **(E)** Let M be the mechanic's hourly wage, C the custodial worker's hourly wage, and S the salesman's hourly wage. Then $M = 2S$, and $C = \frac{1}{3}M$ or $M = 3C$, hence $3C = 2S$, $S = \frac{3}{2}C$.

65. **(B)** Statement I is false since $(-1) + (-2) = -3$, and III is false since $(-1) - (-2) = 1$. But II is true since $(-x)(-y) = xy$, for all x and y.

66. **(C)** The loaded truck gets $(.85)10$ miles or 8.5 miles per gallon. The loaded truck will require $\frac{50}{8.5}$ or 5.88 gallons to travel 50 miles.

67. **(A)** Since $3a = 0$, a must equal 0, which implies that $b = 0$. Note that $\frac{b}{a}$ and $\frac{a}{b}$ are not defined.

68. **(C)** The horse will travel 10 miles in the first two hours. The horse will take $\frac{10}{3}$ or $3\frac{1}{3}$ hours to travel the final 10 miles. So the total time is $5\frac{1}{3}$ hours.

69. **(B)** Income is part of "Where it comes from."

70. **(E)** In 1972 human resources received 42% of each budget dollar and in 1973 it received 45% of each budget dollar. So this budget allocation was estimated to rise by 3%, thus the difference is +3%.

71. **(A)** Note that the question refers to 1973.

72. **(A)** Statement I is false since the graph indicates only that the percentage of the total collected was less. (If the total in 1973 was much larger, the amount collected from excise taxes could have increased.) II is false since, again, the graph gives only percentages not amounts. III is false for the same reason.

73. **(D)** Let r_1 be the radius of the first circle and r_2 the radius of the second circle. Then $\frac{r_1}{r_2} = \frac{3}{2}$, so $r_1 = \left(\frac{3}{2}\right)r_2$, and $\pi(r_1)^2 = \pi\frac{9}{4}(r_2)^2$. Since the area of a circle is π (radius)^2, then the ratio of the areas is 9 to 4.

74. **(C)** $(-5)(-4) = (5)(4)$.

75. **(E)** Let $x = -3$ and $y = 2$, then $\frac{1}{-3} < \frac{1}{2}$, so (A), (B), and (C) are false. Let $x = 3$ and $y = 2$; then $\frac{1}{3} < \frac{1}{2}$ so (D) is false. (E) is the only correct answer.

76. **(E)** The selling price of the boxes should equal x plus the cost. The cost in cents of making 5,000 boxes is $(1,000)5\text{¢} + (4,000)y$ which equals $50 + 40y$ in dollars. So the selling price should be $50 + 40y + x$.

77. **(B)** The profit is indicated by the arrow.

78. **(C)** 1968 and 1971.

79. **(A)** The rise in income was greater than $1,600,000 only between 1967 and 1968, and between 1968 and 1969. The gain was greater in the former.

80. **(C)** Statement I is false since there was a loss in 1967. II is false since the profits decreased from 1968 to 1969.

81. **(D)** If $x - 2 < y$, then $x < y + 2$.

82. **(D)** The price of wheat in dollars will be $2(1.10)^n$ a bushel after n months, and this will be greater than 3 when $(1.10)^n$ is greater than 1.5. $(1.1)^2 = 1.21$, $(1.1)^3 = 1.331$, $(1.1)^4 = 1.4641$, $(1.1)^5 = 1.61051$; therefore, after 5 months the price of wheat will be higher.

83. **(B)** If $\frac{1}{2} + \frac{1}{4} = \frac{x}{15}$, then since $\frac{1}{2} + \frac{1}{4} = \frac{3}{4}$, we have that $\frac{3}{4} = \frac{x}{15}$. So $x = \frac{45}{4} = 11\frac{1}{4} = 11.25$.

84. **(B)** If three of the numbers were negative, then as long as the fourth is greater than the absolute value of the sum of the other three, the sum of all four will be positive. For example, $(-50) + (-35) + (-55) + 155 = 15$.

85. **(A)** Area $= LW$. The increased length is $1.11L$ and W is unchanged; so the increased area is $(1.11L)W = (1.11)(LW) = (1.11)A$. Therefore, the increase in area is $1.11A - A = .11A$; and the area is increased by 11%.

Section IV   Practical Judgment

86. **(B)** Declining sales volume was a symptom of the company's problem; therefore, it is a *Major Factor* requiring a decision as to how the decline can be corrected.

87. **(E)** Company location had no direct bearing on the issues discussed in the passage.

88. **(A)** The production of profitable ready-mixes is the *Major Objective* of management. Whether or not the decision was a correct one can be discerned by the reader; nevertheless, this is the direction in which management decided to go.

89. **(B)** The urbanization of the population, leading to the consumption of commercially-baked food products, was a *Major Factor* in management's decision to manufacture a home-baking product.

90. **(E)** The increase in world trade had no direct bearing on the company's problem. As management saw it, an increase in *tariff rates* abroad had caused a decline in their overseas sales.

91. **(B)** The relatively low start-up cost was a *Major Factor* considered in the decision to produce ready-mixes. The passage states that management was "particularly receptive" to the idea of marketing a ready-mix partly because the cost of additional personnel and machinery was relatively small.

92. **(A)** Mr. Pendler raised the issue (in paragraph 6) of whether his company could develop a product that would be differentiated from competitors' products. Product differentiation was a *Major Objective*.

93. **(E)** Mr. Pendler was concerned with the cost of an advertising campaign, not primarily with its content. Although housewives were asked to recall advertising themes, the responses were not used by Mr. Pendler or Mr. Janis either in decision-making or in formulating recommendations. Therefore, the recall of advertising themes is an *Unimportant Issue*.

94. **(C)** The cost of a machine is a *Minor Factor*, whereas the *total* start-up cost is the *Major Factor*.

95. **(E)** An *Unimportant Issue*. The size of Parks's office staff was not a consideration in any decision alternative.

96. **(D)** The decision to produce ready-mixes shows that management concluded that Parks could compete with much bigger firms. This conclusion is a *Major Assumption* not supported by the facts in the passage. Mr. Pendler raised two conditions that had to be met for a "go" decision. First, Parks's product had to be differentiated from those of its competitors. The research did not reveal *how* Parks could differentiate its product. Second, the advertising campaign had to be of a magnitude that would promote market entry. Nothing was mentioned about the *magnitude* decided upon; only the target audience was determined (the economy-minded segment). To conclude, management's decision to market the product was apparently based more on intuition than on facts.

97. **(E)** Nothing in the passage suggests that any special significance should be attached to the *number* of persons interviewed in the marketing survey.

98. **(C)** A *Minor Factor*. According to Mr. Janis, one of the reasons for declining sales of Parks's baking powder was the fact that modern bakeries were producing their own powder. The *Major Factor* in the decision to produce ready-mixes was the declining sales of baking powder, not the reasons that caused it.

99. **(B)** A major consideration of Mr. Pendler was whether Parks had sufficient resources to undertake an advertising program large enough to enable the company to enter the market with its new product. The cost of the campaign, weighed against the available resources to finance it, was a *Major Factor* in the decision to produce the ready-mix.

100. **(B)** A *Major Factor* for the same reason as in question 14. Here the emphasis is on *cost*, rather than the other side of the equation—the financing of the campaign.

101. **(E)** See paragraph 2: high tariff rates, sterner competition, and trade distortions caused by World War II.

102. **(C)** It was 11 percent. See paragraph 1.

103. **(C)** Manufacturing costs were not a factor. See paragraph 3.

104. **(B)** To have let sales decline for so long without taking any action and then finally reacting in a superficial way—making decisions without adequate research and consideration—is poor managerial action.

105. **(D)** Management was certainly worried about the business, but this apprehension did not directly lead to *specific* action as factors I and II did.

Section V   Data Sufficiency

106. **(D)** Area = (length)(width) = 40(width). So to find the area we must know the width. The perimeter of a rectangle is twice (length + width). (1) tells us the perimeter equals 140 yds. Since the length is 40 yds, the width is 30 yds, so (1) is sufficient. If we connect 2 opposite corners of the field, then it is divided into 2 right triangles where the side opposite the right angle has length 50 and one of the other sides has length 40. Since $(40)^2 + (width)^2 = (50)^2$ the width is 30, and (2) is sufficient by itself.

107. **(A)** Statement (1) is $x^3 + 1 = 0$, which means $x^3 = -1$; the only solution to this equation is -1. So x is not greater than 0. Therefore, (1) alone is sufficient. Statement (2) says $x^2 - \frac{1}{2} = 0$ or $x^2 = \frac{1}{2}$. There are two possible solutions to this equation, one positive and the other negative. So (2) by itself is not sufficient.

108. **(D)** Statement (1) is sufficient since it implies that A loaded 300 boxes in 30 minutes and B loaded 150 boxes. So B should take 90 minutes to load the 450 boxes by himself. (2) is also sufficient since it implies A loads 10 boxes per minute; hence A loads 300 boxes in 30 minutes, and by the above argument we can deduce that B will take 90 minutes.

109. **(C)** A cube is a solid with 6 faces, all of which are congruent squares. Statement (1) is not sufficient since a solid with 2 of the faces as diamonds (rhombus) is not a cube but does satisfy (1). . Statement (2) is not sufficient since a solid with 2 or 4 of the faces congruent rectangles is not a cube But (1) and (2) together mean that each face is a congruent square.

110. **(B)** The first car will travel a distance equal to the circumference of the circle, which is π times the diameter. Since π is greater than $1\frac{1}{2}$, (2) is sufficient. (1) is not sufficient since one car might have traveled at a faster rate than the other.

111. **(C)** Statement (1) tells us only that $x = 6 + y$, so it is not sufficient. In the same way (2) alone will give only one of the unknowns in terms of the other. However, if we use both (1) and (2), we obtain a system of two equations which can be solved for x and y.

112. **(D)** Since we know that the sum of the angles in a triangle is 180° and that $x = 45$, (1) implies (2) and (2) implies (1). Either one is sufficient, since if $z = 45$, then $x = z$ and the sides opposite the equal angles are equal. Hence $AC = AB = 3$.

113. **(E)** Using (1) and (2) together it is possible to determine only the total paid in 1969 and 1971. No relation is given between the amounts paid in 1969 and 1971; thus there is not enough information to determine the cost in 1971.

114. **(A)** It costs $10 in gas, $2.50 in the tolls, and at least $5 in parking to drive each week. So driving costs at least $17.50 a week. (1) is sufficient. Without information on the price of the train ticket we can not compare the two methods, so (2) is not sufficient.

115. **(C)** Statement (1) is not sufficient since the diagonals of *any* parallelogram bisect each other. Statement (2) is not sufficient since the other angles of the figure do not have to be right angles. However, (1) and (2) together are sufficient. Statement (1) implies the figure is a parallelogram. In a parallelogram, opposite angles are equal and

the sum of all four angles must be 360°. Thus, if one of the angles in a parallelogram is 90°, all of the angles are right angles and the parallelogram is a rectangle.

116. **(D)** Let x be the amount he was paid on the first day; then he was paid $x + 5$, $x + 10$, $x + 15$, and $x + 20$ for the remaining days of work. The total amount he was paid is $5x + 50$. Thus if we can find x, we can find the total amount he was paid. Statement (1) is sufficient since after 3 days his total pay was $x + x + 5 + x + 10$ or $3x + 15$; this is equal to $\frac{1}{2}(5x + 50)$. So $3x + 15 = 2.5(x) + 25$ which implies $x = 20$. Statement (2) is sufficient since he was paid $x + 20$ on the last day and so $x + 20 = 2x$ which implies $x = 20$.

Remember that to answer the question it is not necessary to actually *solve* the equations given in statements 1 and 2. You only have to know that they will give you an equation which can be solved for x. Don't bother to actually solve the problem since you only have a limited amount of time to work all the questions in this section.

117. **(C)** Statement (1) alone is not sufficient since $x = 3$, $y = -1$, and $x = -1$, $y = 3$ satisfy $x + y = 2$. Statement (2) alone is not sufficient since $x = 2$, $y = 1$ and $x = -2$, $y = -1$ satisfy (2) However, since (2) says $x = 2y$, using (1) $x + y = 2y + y = 2$ we see that $y = \frac{2}{3}$ and $x = \frac{4}{3}$. So (1) and (2) together are sufficient.

118. **(B)** Area of the circle is $\pi r^2 = \pi\left(\frac{d}{2}\right)^2 = \frac{\pi}{4}d^2$ and the area of the square is s^2. Statement (2) is sufficient. $d < s$ implies $d^2 < s^2$ and $\frac{\pi}{4}$ is less than 1. So $\frac{\pi}{4}d^2 < d^2 < s^2$. (Note that since d and s are both positive $d < s$ does imply $d^2 < s^2$.) However, if $d < \sqrt{2}s$ then $d^2 < 2s^2$ so $\frac{\pi}{4}d^2 < \frac{\pi}{2}s^2$. But $\frac{\pi}{2}$ is larger than 1, so the area of the circle could be larger or smaller than s^2. Thus (1) alone is not sufficient.

119. **(D)** 10 apples will cost $1.60. Hence if we can discover the cost of three oranges we can solve the problem. Statement (1) is sufficient since (1) implies 3 oranges will cost 25¢. Statement (2) is also sufficient since we know 10 apples cost $1.60, thus (2) implies (1) which we know to be sufficient.

120. **(A)** Since 80% of $160 = $128, we know that after the first discount the skis cost less than $130. Any further discount will only lower the price. So (1) alone is sufficient. Statement (2) alone is not sufficient since if x were 10%, (2) would tell us the price was less than $130; but if x were 1%, (2) would imply that the price was greater than $130.

Section VI   Verbal Ability

121. **(B)** SEDITIOUS: factious, rebellious. *Antonym:* loyal

122. **(D)** REDOLENT: odorous, fragrant. *Antonym:* odorless

123. **(C)** PUERILE: youthful, juvenile. *Antonym:* mature

124. **(D)** ABATE: lessen, reduce. *Antonym:* increase

125. **(E)** ACERBITY: sharpness, acrimony. *Antonym:* sweetness

126. **(B)** ACTUATE: move, instigate. *Antonym:* dissuade

127. **(B)** IRRESOLUTE: undetermined, vacillating. *Antonym:* determined

128. **(C)** FRACTIOUS: petulant, testy. *Antonym:* agreeable

129. **(A)** DISAPPROVAL: condemnation, censure. *Antonym:* countenance

130. **(A)** ENMITY: animosity, hostility. *Antonym:* affection

131. **(C)** GUILE: deceit, duplicity. *Antonym:* honesty

132. **(D)** CONDUCE: lead, contribute. *Antonym:* counteract

133. **(B)** DEBILITY: languor, weakness. *Antonym:* strength

134. **(C)** EXTOL: praise, commend. *Antonym:* deprecate

135. **(D)** An aviary is a place where birds are kept, while an arboretum is a place for plants.

136. **(B)** A convict is sentenced to prison; an exile is sentenced to banishment.

137. **(C)** A flood is a large, violently moving mass of water. Blizzard and snow have the same relationship.

138. **(A)** The relationship is one of opposites. Penitent is an antonym for obdurate. The same relationship holds for pensive and thoughtless.

139. **(A)** The relationship is one of synonyms. Fortitude is a synonym for resolution, as timidity is a synonym for cowardice.

140. **(B)** A yardstick is a tool used in measurement; a microscope is a tool used for observation.

141. **(E)** An amplifier enlarges what is perceived by the ear, as a telescope enlarges what is perceived by the eye.

142. **(A)** The relationship is one of antonyms. Perfidious is an antonym for faithful.

143. **(C)** Genocide is an extreme and widespread form of murder, as a holocaust is an extreme and widespread form of fire.

144. **(B)** A clarification repairs or improves what is nebulous; an emendation improves what is erroneous.

145. **(B)** The relationship is one of synonyms. Covert means the same as concealed.

146. **(B)** The relationship is one of synonyms. To amalgamate something is to make it united, just as to organize something is to make it arranged.

147. **(C)** An incantation is recited during an exorcism, while a prayer is recited as part of a liturgy.

148. **(A)** Air is not imbibed (B); neither do the other alternatives fit the meaning of the sentence.

149. **(C)** Recorders do not "boom" (D); a soliloquy is a rendering by one person, while musicians do not sing (B).

150. **(D)** While incentives (B) might be a conceivable alternative, trade (D) is more specific.

151. **(B)** Victims has the most meaning in the context of plight.

152. **(D)** Opposed carries out the idea of contrast implied by the word "Although."

153. **(C)** Giving the vote to more people would be expected to increase the power of the "common citizens."

154. **(C)** Only this alternative develops the logical contrast implied by the word "Despite."

155. **(D)** Tax reductions increase (real) income and raise purchasing power.

156. **(C)** Alternative (C) is needed to fit the contrast established by the word "Despite."

157. **(A)** None of the other pairs work logically together.

158. **(B)** Improvement in auto sales could logically be expected to reverse the trend described.

159. **(B)** If he continued talking, he was loquacious (very talkative).

160. **(C)** Dependence on popular support would tend to make political considerations significant.

Section VII   Practical Judgment

161. **(B)** The company had two major problems. The first mentioned in the passage was declining sales. The only explanation found in the passage was that salesmen had not

developed enough new customers. Declining sales was a *Major Factor* in Tulli's decision to reassign salesmen, although one can argue whether his decision was correct. The second problem was the factor of increasing accounts receivable, because of slow customer payments. The problem, in turn, was a symptom of declining sales.

162. **(B)** As pointed out above, increasing accounts receivables was a major company problem and was a *Major Factor* in Tulli's decision to reassign salesmen and to change the company's compensation policy.

163. **(E)** The nationality of the company is an *Unimportant Issue*.

164. **(A)** The cash shortage is the problem uppermost in management's considerations. This condition was the primary issue which led to the change in compensation policy and the reassignment of salesmen.

165. **(C)** As one of the advantages attached by Tulli to a quota system, this is a *Minor Factor* in the decision process.

166. **(A)** *Major Objective*. The development of new customers by both experienced and less experienced salesmen was an outcome desired by Tulli.

167. **(C)** *Minor Factor*. The cash flow problem was caused by slow payments by customers. See paragraph 2 and the answers to questions 1 and 5.

168. **(D)** *Major Assumption*. Under Tulli's plan, top salesmen were to be re-assigned from high to low-sales areas. The underlying assumption of Tulli was that these salesmen would succeed in low-sales territories as well. However, low sales in a territory may be more owing to a lack of potential in the territory, rather than to a lack of experience or skill on the part of the salesmen.

169. **(A)** *Major Objective*. Tulli suggested assigning quotas to salesmen as a solution to the incentive problem. Cavello agreed in principle to Tulli's proposal and added some variations of his own as stated in paragraph 17 ff.

170. **(E)** *Unimportant Issue*. The quota rate does not influence the decision as to whether to adopt a quota system. The issue is whether a quota system will motivate salesmen to produce more sales.

171. **(A)** Through a quota system the individual performance of salesmen can be measured. This is one of the outcomes desired by Tulli.

172. **(D)** *Major Assumption*. That salesmen will accept Cavello's options is a *belief* held by Tulli. See the last paragraph.

173. **(B)** *Major Factor*. The disadvantages of sales quotas were considered by Cavello as factors that could determine the success or failure of a possible course of action (the quota option).

174. **(E)** *Unimportant Issue*. Nothing is stated in the passage which relates Tulli's experience in dealing with salesmen to the decision process.

175. **(E)** *Unimportant Issue*. The number of salesmen—although mentioned in the passage—is unrelated to the decision process.

176. **(D)** The only reason given was III. See pargraph 10.

177. **(D)** Whether or not poor salesmanship was a cause cannot be determined from the information contained in the passage.

178. **(C)** Spending more time in the field was not mentioned.

179. **(B)** Only III was mentioned in the passage. Salesmen's morale will certainly be affected if the reassignment plan is adopted by management.

180. **(A)** Reducing credit to customers will cause a decline in sales. It is likely that customers will switch to other companies whose credit policies are more liberal.

Section VIII   Data Sufficiency

181. **(B)**

An integer k is divisible by another integer m if $k = mr$, where r is an integer. So STATE-

MENT (1) implies $k = 4r$ for some integer r. STATEMENT (1) alone is insufficient because 12 is divisible by 4 ($4 \cdot 3 = 12$) but 12 is not divisible by 8.

STATEMENT (2) alone is sufficient. STATEMENT (2) implies that $k = 16r$ for some integer r, but since $16 = 8 \cdot 2$ that means $k = 8 \cdot 2r$ and $2r$ is an integer, so k is divisible by 8.

182. **(D)**

STATEMENT (1) is sufficient. Since the foreman's salary is $12,000, the total of the assembly workers' salaries is $300,000. Therefore, the average salary is $300,000 ÷ 30 = $10,000.

STATEMENT (2) is sufficient. If A is the average salary of the assembly workers, then 120% of A is $12,000. Therefore, $A = $12,000 ÷ $\frac{6}{5}$ = $10,000.

183. **(C)**

STATEMENT (2) alone is insufficient since you need to know what direction town B is from town C.

STATEMENT (1) alone is insufficient, since you need to know how far it is from town B to town C.

Using both STATEMENTS (1) and (2), A, B and C form a right triangle with legs of 9 miles and 12 miles. The distance from town A to town B is the hypotenuse of the triangle, so the distance from town A to town B is $\sqrt{9^2 + 12^2} = 15$ miles.

184. **(C)**

STATEMENTS (1) and (2) by themselves are insufficient since you need to know the area of the floor, and STATEMENT (1) only gives the length and STATEMENT (2) only gives the width. Using STATEMENTS (1) and (2) together, the area of the floor is $5 \times 10 = 50$ square feet. Since the area of each square is $5^2 = 25$ square inches, each square has area $\frac{25}{144}$ square feet. Therefore, the number of squares is $50 ÷ \frac{25}{144} = 288$.

185. **(E)**

STATEMENTS (1) and (2) only give relations between Mary's wages and Jim's wages

and tell you the cost of the set of luggage in terms of hours of wages. Since there is no information about the value of the hourly wages in dollars, STATEMENTS (1) and (2) together are not sufficient.

186. **(C)**

STATEMENT (1) alone implies $x = 3y$. Since there is no more information about y, STATEMENT (1) alone is insufficient.

STATEMENT (2) alone gives $x = 9 + y$ but there is no information about y, so STATEMENT (2) alone is not sufficient.

STATEMENTS (1) and (2) together are sufficient. If $x = 9 + y$ and $x = 3y$, then $3y = 9 + y$ which gives $y = \frac{9}{2}$, so $x = (3)(\frac{9}{2}) = \frac{27}{2}$.

187. **(A)**

Since in similar triangles corresponding angles are equal, angle CED = angle CBA. Therefore, DE is parallel to AB and STATEMENT (1) alone is sufficient.

STATEMENT (2) alone is insufficient since D could be *any* point on the line CA and there is at most one point on CA which will make DE parallel to AB.

188. **(B)**

If $x + y = 24$ then at least one of the numbers x or y is positive. If x is positive then $y = 24 - x$ and since x is less than 20, $24 - x = y$ is positive. The same argument shows that if y is positive so is x. Therefore, STATEMENT (2) alone is sufficient to show that both numbers are positive.

STATEMENT (1) alone is insufficient, since the fact that x is less than 5 does not tell whether x is positive and no information is given about y.

189. **(C)**

STATEMENT (2) alone implies $x = y$ since equal sides have equal angles in a triangle. Since there is no information about y, STATEMENT (2) alone is insufficient.

STATEMENT (1) alone is insufficient since there is no relation between x and y without STATEMENT (2).

STATEMENTS (1) and (2) together imply $x = y = 30$, so STATEMENTS (1) and (2) together are sufficient.

190. **(E)**

Denote by w_1 the weight of the first volume, by w_2 the weight of the second volume, by w_3 the weight of the third volume and by w_4 the weight of the fourth volume. STATEMENT (1) gives $w_1 + w_2 + w_3 = 4$ and STATEMENT (2) gives $w_2 + w_3 + w_4 = 3\frac{1}{2}$. Using STATEMENTS (1) and (2) you can obtain $w_1 - w_4 = \frac{1}{2}$ so $w_1 = w_4 + \frac{1}{2}$ but no other information is given about w_4. Therefore, STATEMENTS (1) and (2) together are insufficient.

191. **(E)** Since the box is rectangular, there are 4 sides which occur in 2 different pairs. Therefore, you can't determine the area of every side using statements (1) and (2).

192. **(D)** If any value of a_n is an even integer, then all succeeding values are even. (Any even integer $+ 2$ is an even integer.) Since a_{10} appears after a_1 and a_9, both statement (1) alone and statement (2) alone are sufficient.

193. **(B)** STATEMENT (2) alone is sufficient. Statement (2) allows you to find the values of x, y, and z, and the largest side is opposite the largest angle.
STATEMENT (1) alone is not sufficient. (1) implies that AB is longer than AC, but you have no information about BC.

194. **(A)** STATEMENT (1) alone is sufficient, since the average is the total divided by 5.
STATEMENT (2) alone is not sufficient. There is no information about her wages for the three days she worked between the first and last day.

195. **(C)** STATEMENT (1) alone is not sufficient. The expression becomes $x^3 + bx = x(x^2 + b)$, but there is no relationship between the expression and k.
STATEMENT (2) alone is not sufficient, since the roots of the expression will depend on the value of a.

STATEMENTS (1) and (2) together make the expression $x^3 + ax^2 + bx$ into $x^3 - k^2x = x(x^2 - k^2)$, which is equal to zero when $x = k$.

Evaluating Your Score

Tabulate your score for each section of Sample Test 4 according to the directions on pages 4–5 and record the results in the Self-scoring Table below. Then find your rating for each score on the Self-scoring Scale and record it in the appropriate blank.

Self-scoring Table

PART	SCORE	RATING
1-2		
3		
4		
5		
6		
7		
8		

Self-scoring Scale

RATING

PART	POOR	FAIR	GOOD	EXCELLENT
1-2	0-10	11-15	16-22	23-30
3	0-24	25-30	31-39	40-55
4	0-7	8-10	11-15	16-20
5	0-5	6-8	9-12	13-15
6	0-15	16-20	21-29	30-40
7	0-7	8-10	11-15	16-20
8	0-5	6-8	9-12	13-15

Study again the Review sections covering material in Sample Test 4 for which you had a rank of FAIR or POOR. Then go on to Sample Test 5.

To obtain an approximation of your actual GMAT score see page 5.

Answer Sheet—Sample Test 5

Section I
Reading
Comprehension

1. Ⓐ Ⓑ Ⓒ Ⓓ Ⓔ
2. Ⓐ Ⓑ Ⓒ Ⓓ Ⓔ
3. Ⓐ Ⓑ Ⓒ Ⓓ Ⓔ
4. Ⓐ Ⓑ Ⓒ Ⓓ Ⓔ
5. Ⓐ Ⓑ Ⓒ Ⓓ Ⓔ
6. Ⓐ Ⓑ Ⓒ Ⓓ Ⓔ
7. Ⓐ Ⓑ Ⓒ Ⓓ Ⓔ
8. Ⓐ Ⓑ Ⓒ Ⓓ Ⓔ
9. Ⓐ Ⓑ Ⓒ Ⓓ Ⓔ
10. Ⓐ Ⓑ Ⓒ Ⓓ Ⓔ
11. Ⓐ Ⓑ Ⓒ Ⓓ Ⓔ
12. Ⓐ Ⓑ Ⓒ Ⓓ Ⓔ
13. Ⓐ Ⓑ Ⓒ Ⓓ Ⓔ
14. Ⓐ Ⓑ Ⓒ Ⓓ Ⓔ
15. Ⓐ Ⓑ Ⓒ Ⓓ Ⓔ
16. Ⓐ Ⓑ Ⓒ Ⓓ Ⓔ
17. Ⓐ Ⓑ Ⓒ Ⓓ Ⓔ
18. Ⓐ Ⓑ Ⓒ Ⓓ Ⓔ
19. Ⓐ Ⓑ Ⓒ Ⓓ Ⓔ
20. Ⓐ Ⓑ Ⓒ Ⓓ Ⓔ
21. Ⓐ Ⓑ Ⓒ Ⓓ Ⓔ
22. Ⓐ Ⓑ Ⓒ Ⓓ Ⓔ
23. Ⓐ Ⓑ Ⓒ Ⓓ Ⓔ
24. Ⓐ Ⓑ Ⓒ Ⓓ Ⓔ
25. Ⓐ Ⓑ Ⓒ Ⓓ Ⓔ

Section II
Problem
Solving

26. Ⓐ Ⓑ Ⓒ Ⓓ Ⓔ
27. Ⓐ Ⓑ Ⓒ Ⓓ Ⓔ
28. Ⓐ Ⓑ Ⓒ Ⓓ Ⓔ
29. Ⓐ Ⓑ Ⓒ Ⓓ Ⓔ
30. Ⓐ Ⓑ Ⓒ Ⓓ Ⓔ
31. Ⓐ Ⓑ Ⓒ Ⓓ Ⓔ
32. Ⓐ Ⓑ Ⓒ Ⓓ Ⓔ
33. Ⓐ Ⓑ Ⓒ Ⓓ Ⓔ
34. Ⓐ Ⓑ Ⓒ Ⓓ Ⓔ
35. Ⓐ Ⓑ Ⓒ Ⓓ Ⓔ

36. Ⓐ Ⓑ Ⓒ Ⓓ Ⓔ
37. Ⓐ Ⓑ Ⓒ Ⓓ Ⓔ
38. Ⓐ Ⓑ Ⓒ Ⓓ Ⓔ
39. Ⓐ Ⓑ Ⓒ Ⓓ Ⓔ
40. Ⓐ Ⓑ Ⓒ Ⓓ Ⓔ
41. Ⓐ Ⓑ Ⓒ Ⓓ Ⓔ
42. Ⓐ Ⓑ Ⓒ Ⓓ Ⓔ
43. Ⓐ Ⓑ Ⓒ Ⓓ Ⓔ
44. Ⓐ Ⓑ Ⓒ Ⓓ Ⓔ
45. Ⓐ Ⓑ Ⓒ Ⓓ Ⓔ
46. Ⓐ Ⓑ Ⓒ Ⓓ Ⓔ
47. Ⓐ Ⓑ Ⓒ Ⓓ Ⓔ
48. Ⓐ Ⓑ Ⓒ Ⓓ Ⓔ
49. Ⓐ Ⓑ Ⓒ Ⓓ Ⓔ
50. Ⓐ Ⓑ Ⓒ Ⓓ Ⓔ
51. Ⓐ Ⓑ Ⓒ Ⓓ Ⓔ
52. Ⓐ Ⓑ Ⓒ Ⓓ Ⓔ
53. Ⓐ Ⓑ Ⓒ Ⓓ Ⓔ
54. Ⓐ Ⓑ Ⓒ Ⓓ Ⓔ
55. Ⓐ Ⓑ Ⓒ Ⓓ Ⓔ

Section III
Practical
Judgment

56. Ⓐ Ⓑ Ⓒ Ⓓ Ⓔ
57. Ⓐ Ⓑ Ⓒ Ⓓ Ⓔ
58. Ⓐ Ⓑ Ⓒ Ⓓ Ⓔ
59. Ⓐ Ⓑ Ⓒ Ⓓ Ⓔ
60. Ⓐ Ⓑ Ⓒ Ⓓ Ⓔ
61. Ⓐ Ⓑ Ⓒ Ⓓ Ⓔ
62. Ⓐ Ⓑ Ⓒ Ⓓ Ⓔ
63. Ⓐ Ⓑ Ⓒ Ⓓ Ⓔ
64. Ⓐ Ⓑ Ⓒ Ⓓ Ⓔ
65. Ⓐ Ⓑ Ⓒ Ⓓ Ⓔ
66. Ⓐ Ⓑ Ⓒ Ⓓ Ⓔ
67. Ⓐ Ⓑ Ⓒ Ⓓ Ⓔ
68. Ⓐ Ⓑ Ⓒ Ⓓ Ⓔ
69. Ⓐ Ⓑ Ⓒ Ⓓ Ⓔ
70. Ⓐ Ⓑ Ⓒ Ⓓ Ⓔ
71. Ⓐ Ⓑ Ⓒ Ⓓ Ⓔ
72. Ⓐ Ⓑ Ⓒ Ⓓ Ⓔ
73. Ⓐ Ⓑ Ⓒ Ⓓ Ⓔ
74. Ⓐ Ⓑ Ⓒ Ⓓ Ⓔ
75. Ⓐ Ⓑ Ⓒ Ⓓ Ⓔ

Section IV
Data
Sufficiency

76. Ⓐ Ⓑ Ⓒ Ⓓ Ⓔ
77. Ⓐ Ⓑ Ⓒ Ⓓ Ⓔ
78. Ⓐ Ⓑ Ⓒ Ⓓ Ⓔ
79. Ⓐ Ⓑ Ⓒ Ⓓ Ⓔ
80. Ⓐ Ⓑ Ⓒ Ⓓ Ⓔ
81. Ⓐ Ⓑ Ⓒ Ⓓ Ⓔ
82. Ⓐ Ⓑ Ⓒ Ⓓ Ⓔ
83. Ⓐ Ⓑ Ⓒ Ⓓ Ⓔ
84. Ⓐ Ⓑ Ⓒ Ⓓ Ⓔ
85. Ⓐ Ⓑ Ⓒ Ⓓ Ⓔ
86. Ⓐ Ⓑ Ⓒ Ⓓ Ⓔ
87. Ⓐ Ⓑ Ⓒ Ⓓ Ⓔ
88. Ⓐ Ⓑ Ⓒ Ⓓ Ⓔ
89. Ⓐ Ⓑ Ⓒ Ⓓ Ⓔ
90. Ⓐ Ⓑ Ⓒ Ⓓ Ⓔ
91. Ⓐ Ⓑ Ⓒ Ⓓ Ⓔ
92. Ⓐ Ⓑ Ⓒ Ⓓ Ⓔ
93. Ⓐ Ⓑ Ⓒ Ⓓ Ⓔ
94. Ⓐ Ⓑ Ⓒ Ⓓ Ⓔ
95. Ⓐ Ⓑ Ⓒ Ⓓ Ⓔ
96. Ⓐ Ⓑ Ⓒ Ⓓ Ⓔ
97. Ⓐ Ⓑ Ⓒ Ⓓ Ⓔ
98. Ⓐ Ⓑ Ⓒ Ⓓ Ⓔ
99. Ⓐ Ⓑ Ⓒ Ⓓ Ⓔ
100. Ⓐ Ⓑ Ⓒ Ⓓ Ⓔ
101. Ⓐ Ⓑ Ⓒ Ⓓ Ⓔ
102. Ⓐ Ⓑ Ⓒ Ⓓ Ⓔ
103. Ⓐ Ⓑ Ⓒ Ⓓ Ⓔ
104. Ⓐ Ⓑ Ⓒ Ⓓ Ⓔ
105. Ⓐ Ⓑ Ⓒ Ⓓ Ⓔ

Section V
Writing
Ability

106. Ⓐ Ⓑ Ⓒ Ⓓ Ⓔ
107. Ⓐ Ⓑ Ⓒ Ⓓ Ⓔ
108. Ⓐ Ⓑ Ⓒ Ⓓ Ⓔ
109. Ⓐ Ⓑ Ⓒ Ⓓ Ⓔ
110. Ⓐ Ⓑ Ⓒ Ⓓ Ⓔ

111. Ⓐ Ⓑ Ⓒ Ⓓ Ⓔ
112. Ⓐ Ⓑ Ⓒ Ⓓ Ⓔ
113. Ⓐ Ⓑ Ⓒ Ⓓ Ⓔ
114. Ⓐ Ⓑ Ⓒ Ⓓ Ⓔ
115. Ⓐ Ⓑ Ⓒ Ⓓ Ⓔ
116. Ⓐ Ⓑ Ⓒ Ⓓ Ⓔ
117. Ⓐ Ⓑ Ⓒ Ⓓ Ⓔ
118. Ⓐ Ⓑ Ⓒ Ⓓ Ⓔ
119. Ⓐ Ⓑ Ⓒ Ⓓ Ⓔ
120. Ⓐ Ⓑ Ⓒ Ⓓ Ⓔ
121. Ⓐ Ⓑ Ⓒ Ⓓ Ⓔ
122. Ⓐ Ⓑ Ⓒ Ⓓ Ⓔ
123. Ⓐ Ⓑ Ⓒ Ⓓ Ⓔ
124. Ⓐ Ⓑ Ⓒ Ⓓ Ⓔ
125. Ⓐ Ⓑ Ⓒ Ⓓ Ⓔ

Section VI
Practical
Judgment

126. Ⓐ Ⓑ Ⓒ Ⓓ Ⓔ
127. Ⓐ Ⓑ Ⓒ Ⓓ Ⓔ
128. Ⓐ Ⓑ Ⓒ Ⓓ Ⓔ
129. Ⓐ Ⓑ Ⓒ Ⓓ Ⓔ
130. Ⓐ Ⓑ Ⓒ Ⓓ Ⓔ
131. Ⓐ Ⓑ Ⓒ Ⓓ Ⓔ
132. Ⓐ Ⓑ Ⓒ Ⓓ Ⓔ
133. Ⓐ Ⓑ Ⓒ Ⓓ Ⓔ
134. Ⓐ Ⓑ Ⓒ Ⓓ Ⓔ
135. Ⓐ Ⓑ Ⓒ Ⓓ Ⓔ
136. Ⓐ Ⓑ Ⓒ Ⓓ Ⓔ
137. Ⓐ Ⓑ Ⓒ Ⓓ Ⓔ
138. Ⓐ Ⓑ Ⓒ Ⓓ Ⓔ
139. Ⓐ Ⓑ Ⓒ Ⓓ Ⓔ
140. Ⓐ Ⓑ Ⓒ Ⓓ Ⓔ
141. Ⓐ Ⓑ Ⓒ Ⓓ Ⓔ
142. Ⓐ Ⓑ Ⓒ Ⓓ Ⓔ
143. Ⓐ Ⓑ Ⓒ Ⓓ Ⓔ
144. Ⓐ Ⓑ Ⓒ Ⓓ Ⓔ
145. Ⓐ Ⓑ Ⓒ Ⓓ Ⓔ

Section VII
Writing
Ability

146. Ⓐ Ⓑ Ⓒ Ⓓ Ⓔ
147. Ⓐ Ⓑ Ⓒ Ⓓ Ⓔ
148. Ⓐ Ⓑ Ⓒ Ⓓ Ⓔ
149. Ⓐ Ⓑ Ⓒ Ⓓ Ⓔ
150. Ⓐ Ⓑ Ⓒ Ⓓ Ⓔ
151. Ⓐ Ⓑ Ⓒ Ⓓ Ⓔ
152. Ⓐ Ⓑ Ⓒ Ⓓ Ⓔ
153. Ⓐ Ⓑ Ⓒ Ⓓ Ⓔ
154. Ⓐ Ⓑ Ⓒ Ⓓ Ⓔ
155. Ⓐ Ⓑ Ⓒ Ⓓ Ⓔ
156. Ⓐ Ⓑ Ⓒ Ⓓ Ⓔ
157. Ⓐ Ⓑ Ⓒ Ⓓ Ⓔ
158. Ⓐ Ⓑ Ⓒ Ⓓ Ⓔ
159. Ⓐ Ⓑ Ⓒ Ⓓ Ⓔ
160. Ⓐ Ⓑ Ⓒ Ⓓ Ⓔ
161. Ⓐ Ⓑ Ⓒ Ⓓ Ⓔ
162. Ⓐ Ⓑ Ⓒ Ⓓ Ⓔ
163. Ⓐ Ⓑ Ⓒ Ⓓ Ⓔ
164. Ⓐ Ⓑ Ⓒ Ⓓ Ⓔ
165. Ⓐ Ⓑ Ⓒ Ⓓ Ⓔ
166. Ⓐ Ⓑ Ⓒ Ⓓ Ⓔ
167. Ⓐ Ⓑ Ⓒ Ⓓ Ⓔ
168. Ⓐ Ⓑ Ⓒ Ⓓ Ⓔ
169. Ⓐ Ⓑ Ⓒ Ⓓ Ⓔ
170. Ⓐ Ⓑ Ⓒ Ⓓ Ⓔ

Sample Test 5

Section I   Reading Comprehension

TIME: 30 minutes

DIRECTIONS: This part contains four reading passages. You are to read each one carefully. When answering the questions, you *will* be allowed to refer back to the passages. The questions are based on what is *stated* or *implied* in each passage. You have thirty minutes to complete this section.

Passage 1:

A newly-issued report reveals in facts and figures what should have been known in principle, that quite a lot of business companies are going to go under during the coming decade, as tariff walls are progressively dismantled. Labor and capital valued at $12 billion are to be made idle through the impact of duty-free imports. As a result, 35,000 workers will
(5)   be displaced. Some will move to other jobs and other departments within the same firm. Around 15,000 will have to leave the firm now employing them and work elsewhere.

The report is measuring exclusively the influence of free trade with Europe. The authors do not take into account the expected expansion of production over the coming years. On the other hand, they are not sure that even the export predictions they make
(10)   will be achieved. For this presupposes that a suitable business climate lets the pressure to increase productivity materialize.

There are two reasons why this scenario may not happen. The first one is that industry on the whole is not taking the initiatives necessary to adapt fully to the new price situation it will be facing as time goes by.

(15)   This is another way of saying that the manufacturers do not realize what lies ahead. The government is to blame for not making the position absolutely clear. It should be saying that in ten years time tariffs on all industrial goods imported from Europe will be eliminated. There will be no adjustment assistance for manufacturers who cannot adapt to this situation.

(20)   The second obstacle to adjustment is not stressed in the same way in the report; it is the attitude of the service sector. Not only are service industries unaware that the Common Market treaty concerns them too, they are artificially insulated from the physical pressures of international competition. The manufacturing sector has been forced to apply its nose to the
(25)   grindstone for some time now, by the increasingly stringent import-liberalization program.

The ancillary services on which the factories depend show a growing indifference to their work obligations. They seem unaware that overmanned ships, underutilized container equipment in the ports, and repeated work stoppages slow the country's attempts to narrow the trade gap. The remedy is to cut the fees charged by these services so as to reduce their
(30)   earnings—in exactly the same way that earnings in industrial undertakings are reduced by the tariff reduction program embodied in the treaty with the European Community.

There is no point in dismissing 15,000 industrial workers from their present jobs during the coming ten years if all the gain in productivity is wasted by costly harbor, transport,

(35)   financial, administrative and other services. The free trade treaty is their concern as well. Surplus staff should be removed, if need be, from all workplaces, not just from the factories. Efficiency is everybody's business.

1. The attitude of the report, as described in the passage, may best be expressed as

    (A) harshly condemnatory, because industry is not more responsive to the business climate
    (B) optimistic that government will induce industry to make needed changes
    (C) critical of labor unions
    (D) pessimistic that anything can be done to reduce the trade gap
    (E) objective in assessing the influence of free trade on employment

2. What is the meaning of *free trade* in line 7?

    (A) unlimited sale of goods in Europe
    (B) trade on a barter basis
    (C) the elimination of tariffs
    (D) sale of price-discounted goods to European countries
    (E) trade with only the so-called "free countries," i.e., Western Europe

3. It can be inferred that the term *adjustment assistance* in line 18 refers mainly to

    (A) unemployment compensation
    (B) some sort of financial assistance to manufacturers hurt by free trade
    (C) help in relocating plants to Europe
    (D) aid in reducing work stoppages
    (E) subsidy payments to increase exports

4. The author's central recommendation seems to be that

    (A) unemployment should be avoided at all costs
    (B) redundant labor should be removed in all sectors
    (C) government should control the service sector
    (D) tariffs should not be lowered
    (E) workers should be retrained

5. Which of the following titles best describes the content of the passage?

    (A) *The Prospects of Free Trade*
    (B) *Government Intervention in World Trade*
    (C) *Trade With the Common Market*
    (D) *What Lies Ahead?*
    (E) *Unemployment and Adjustment Assistance*

Passage 2:

The fundamental objectives of sociology are the same as those of science generally—discovery and explanation. To *discover* the essential data of social behavior and the connections among the data is the first objective of sociology. To *explain* the data and the connections is the second and larger objective. Science makes its advances in terms of
(5)   both of these objectives. Sometimes it is the discovery of a new element or set of elements that marks a major breakthrough in the history of a scientific discipline. Closely related to such discovery is the discovery of relationships of data that had never been noted

before. All of this is, as we know, of immense importance in science. But the drama of discovery, in this sense, can sometimes lead us to overlook the greater importance of ex-
(10) planation of what is revealed by the data. Sometimes decades, even centuries, pass before known connections and relationships are actually explained. Discovery and explanation are the two great interpenetrating, interacting realms of science.

The order of reality that interests the scientists is the *empirical* order, that is, the order of data and phenomena revealed to us through observation or experience. To be precise
(15) or explicit about what is, and is not, revealed by observation is not always easy, to be sure. And often it is necessary for our natural powers of observation to be supplemented by the most intricate of mechanical aids for a given object to become "empirical" in the sense just used. That the electron is not as immediately visible as is the mountain range does not mean, obviously, that it is any less empirical. That social behavior does not lend itself
(20) to as quick and accurate description as, say, chemical behavior of gases and compounds does not mean that social roles, statuses, and attitudes are any less empirical than mole-cules and tissues. What is empirical and observable today may have been nonexistent in scientific consciousness a decade ago. Moreover, the empirical is often data *inferred* from direct observation. All of this is clear enough, and we should make no pretense that
(25) there are not often shadow areas between the empirical and the nonempirical. Neverthe-less, the first point to make about any science, physical or social, is that its world of data is the empirical world. A very large amount of scientific energy goes merely into the work of expanding the frontiers, through discovery, of the known, observable, empirical world.

(30) From observation or discovery we move to *explanation*. The explanation sought by the scientist is, of course, not at all like the explanation sought by the theologian or meta-physician. The scientist is not interested—not, that is, in his role of scientist—in ulti-mate, transcendental, or divine causes of what he sets himself to explain. He is interested in explanations that are as empirical as the data themselves. If it is the high incidence of
(35) crime in a certain part of a large city that requires explanation, the scientist is obliged to offer his explanation in terms of factors which are empirically real as the phenomenon of crime itself. He does not explain the problem, for example, in terms of references to the will of God, demons, or original sin. A satisfactory explanation is not only one that is empirical, however, but one that can be stated in the terms of a *causal proposition*. De-
(40) scription is an indispensable point of beginning, but description is not explanation. It is well to stress this point, for there are all too many scientists, or would-be scientists, who are primarily concerned with data gathering, data counting, and data describing, and who seem to forget that such operations, however useful, are but the first step. Until we have accounted for the problem at hand, explained it causally by referring the data to some
(45) principle or generalization already established, or to some new principle or generalization, we have not explained anything.

6. According to the passage, scientists are not interested in theological explanations because

(A) scientists tend to be atheists
(B) theology cannot explain change
(C) theological explanations are not empirical
(D) theology cannot explain social behavior
(E) scientists are concerned primarily with data gathering

7. The major objective of the passage is to

   (A) show that explanation is more important than discovery
   (B) prove that sociology is a science
   (C) explain the major objectives of sociology
   (D) discuss scientific method
   (E) describe social behavior

8. Which of the following statements best agrees with the author's position?

   (A) Science is the formulation of unverified hypotheses.
   (B) Explanation is inferred from data.
   (C) Causation is a basis for explanation.
   (D) Generalization is a prerequisite for explanation.
   (E) Empiricism is the science of discovery.

9. Judging from the contents of the passage, the final step in a study of social behavior would be to

   (A) discover the problem
   (B) establish principles
   (C) offer an explanation of the data by determining causation
   (D) collect data
   (E) establish generalizations

10. According to the passage, which of the following activities contribute to the advance of science?

    I. Finding data relationships
    II. Expanding the limits of the empirical
    III. Establishing ultimate causes of phenomena

    (A) I only (B) II only (C) I and II only
    (D) I and III only (E) I, II, and III

11. The author's main point in the first paragraph may best be described by which of the following statements?

    (A) Science and sociology are interdisciplinary.
    (B) The first objective of sociology is discovery.
    (C) Discovery without explanation is meaningless.
    (D) Both discovery and explanation are fundamental to building a science.
    (E) It takes a long time before relationships of data are discovered.

Passage 3:

A polytheist always has favorites among the gods, determined by his own temperament, age, and condition, as well as his own interest, temporary or permanent. If it is true that everybody loves a lover, then Venus will be a popular deity with all. But from lovers she will elicit special devotion. In ancient Rome, when a young couple went out together to
(5) see a procession or other show, they would of course pay great respect to Venus, when her image appeared on the screen. Instead of saying, "Isn't love wonderful?" they would say, "Great art thou, O Venus." In a polytheistic society you could tell a good deal about a person's frame of mind by the gods he favored, so that to tell a girl you were trying to woo that you thought Venus overrated was hardly the way to win her heart. But in any
(10) case, a lovesick youth or, maiden would be spontaneously supplicating Venus.

The Greeks liked to present their deities in human form; it was natural to them to sym-
bolize the gods as human beings glorified, idealized. But this fact is also capable of misleading us. We might suppose that the ancients were really worshipping only themselves;
that they were, like Narcissus, beholding their own image in a pool, so that their worship
(15) was *anthropocentric* (man-centered) rather than *theocentric* (god-centered). We are in
danger of assuming that they were simply constructing the god in their own image. This is
not necessarily so. The gods must always be symbolized in one form or another. To give
them a human form is one way of doing this, technically called *anthropomorphism* (from
the Greek *anthropos*, a man, and *morphé*, form). People of certain temperaments and with-
(20) in certain types of culture seem to be more inclined to it than are others. It is, however,
more noticeable in others than in oneself, and those who affect to despise it are sometimes conspicuous for their addiction to it. A German once said an Englishman's idea of
God is an Englishman twelve feet tall. Such disparagement of anthropomorphism occurred in the ancient world, too. The Celts, for instance, despised Greek practice in this
(25) matter, preferring to use animals and other such symbols. The Egyptians favored more
abstract and stylized symbols, among which a well-known example is the solar disk, a
symbol of Rà, the sun-god.

Professor C. S. Lewis tells of an Oxford undergraduate he knew who, priggishly de-
spising the conventional images of God, thought he was overcoming anthropomorphism by
(30) thinking of the Deity as infinite vapor or smoke. Of course even the bearded-old-man
image can be a better symbol of Deity than ever could be the image, even if this were
psychologically possible, of an unlimited smog.

What is really characteristic of all polytheism, however, is not the worship of idols or
humanity or forests or stars; it is, rather, the worship of innumerable *powers* that confront
(35) and affect us. The powers are held to be valuable in themselves; that is why they are to
be worshipped. But the values conflict. The gods do not cooperate, so you have to play
them off against each other. Suppose you want rain. You know of two gods, the dry-god
who sends drought and the wet-god who sends rain. You do not suppose that you can
just pray to the wet-god to get busy, and simply ignore the dry-god. If you do so, the lat-
(40) ter may be offended, so that no matter how hard the wet-god tries to oblige you, the dry-
god will do his best to wither everything. Because both gods are powerful you must take
both into consideration, begging the wet-god to be generous and beseeching the dry-god
to stay his hand.

12. It can be inferred from the passage that polytheism means a belief in

(A) Greek gods
(B) more than one god
(C) a god-centered world
(D) powerful deities
(E) infinite numbers of gods

13. The author's statement in lines 7–8 that "you could tell a good deal about a person's frame of mind by the gods he favored" means that

(A) those who believed in gods were superstitious
(B) worship was either anthropocentric or theocentric
(C) gods were chosen to represent a given way of life
(D) the way a person thinks depends on the power of deities
(E) in certain cultures, the gods served as representations of what people thought of
themselves

14. It may be inferred from the passage that the author would most likely agree that ancient cultures

    I. symbolized their deities only in human form
    II. symbolized the gods in many forms
    III. were mainly self-worshippers
    (A) I only   (B) II only   (C) I and II only
    (D) I and III only   (E) I, II, and III

15. The main point the author makes about anthropomorphism in lines 19–22 is that

    (A) certain cultures are inclined to anthropomorphism
    (B) those who demean anthropomorphism may themselves practice it
    (C) the disparagement of anthropomorphism is common to both ancient and modern cultures
    (D) the Germans tend to be more theocentric than the English
    (E) anthropomorphism is a practice common to all cultures

16. It may be inferred from the last paragraph that polytheism entails

    (A) a commonality of interests among the deities
    (B) predictable consequences
    (C) incoherence and conflict among the "powers"
    (D) an orderly universe
    (E) worshipping one god at a time

Passage 4:

The following passage was written in 1970.

It appears that the easiest kind of occupation is that of the forecaster. If a dismal future is forecasted, and remedial actions are taken, and the future turns out better than predicted—the forecaster can claim that disaster was avoided because he was listened to. If, however, his pessimism was well founded, the forecaster can take credit for being an able
(5) predictor of future events. In this last case, if corrective action was taken—but failed—the forecaster can claim that the amount of action was insufficient, too late, or of the wrong kind.

One reason that the forecasting business has, in itself, become a growth industry is that every institution must plan ahead to stay ahead. Everyone today seems to be interested in
(10) gaining whatever insights are possible as to the trends of the near future. Unfortunately, many of the people that are telling us about the nature of expected changes are basing their predictions on an irrational interpretation of recent past events, and not on factual data. Most of these popular forecasts are inspirational but not very actionable.

(15) If we flash back to the early 1960s we can quickly retrace the course of events which are the basis for many popular predictions. John Gardner, in his then recently published book, *Self Renewal,* commented that many Americans were operating on the principal of "whatever is—is right." However, within a few years this mood drastically changed. Radical student movements, Vietnam peace marches, Civil Rights demonstrations, Women's
(20) Liberation, Consumerism, Ecology, and other events tended to make Gardner's doctrine no longer descriptive of Americans. Within a period of less than five years the rapidity of change in attitudes and values was overwhelming. We suddenly began to question everything and anything—from the institution of marriage to the government's right to engage in war.

(25)   The key question is not what happened but why it happened. To answer this question we must take account of the important factors which induced change, and attach to each its due weight. Also, we must attempt to specify how these factors interrelated and interacted with each other. Of course, this is very difficult because of the number of factors involved, and their far-reaching impact. If we analyze just one factor at a time, we may reach fuzzy or

(30)   erroneous conclusions. For example, let us illustrate the advantage of structuring the interconnections between interrelated factors. Suppose that you are in charge of a program to build low-income housing. You are working diligently to provide decent homes for poverty-stricken people. You are praised for your far-sighted genuine concern, having been quoted as saying that your housing projects will help eliminate poverty. You finally succeed,

(35)   but your success has the unintended result of increasing poverty. Why? Low-income housing merely draws more poor people into an area where very few jobs exist; this creates an even worse supply-and-demand situation for jobs; and the city's poverty problems are worsened.

(40)   In essence, we are saying that to arrive at any meaningful conclusion when studying a problem, we must first list all the factors which influence the final result or outcome, and the interrelation between these factors. The housing case demonstrates that a series of short-run answers to a problem may create worse problems in the long run.

17. With which of the following statements would the author be most likely to agree?

(A) Forecasting is a dismal business.
(B) Forecasters are generally pessimistic.
(C) There is a growing demand for forecasters.
(D) Forecasting is inspirational.
(E) Forecasters are always right.

18. Which of the following statements may be inferred from the first paragraph of the passage?

I.   Forecasting may help to avert calamities.
II. Forecasters are adept at hedging.
III. Forecasting should be improved.
(A) I only   (B) II only   (C) I and II only
(D) I and III only   (E) I, II, and III

19. Which of the following statements best describes the point the author is trying to make in his description of the housing case?

(A) Housing projects cannot eliminate poverty.
(B) Poor people resent low-income housing.
(C) The project was not a long-run solution to the poverty problem.
(D) The project director was guilty of "fuzzy" thinking.
(E) The project evidently suffered from cost overruns.

20. The author's main purpose in the passage is to

(A) introduce new hypotheses
(B) describe his experiences
(C) discuss the early 1960s
(D) explain the housing case
(E) improve the art of forecasting

21. According to the passage, Gardner's thesis

    (A) is not operative today
    (B) is operative today
    (C) was operative in the early 1960s
    (D) was never operative
    (E) is completely false

22. It can be inferred from the passage that the attitude of "whatever is—is right" was succeeded by an attitude of

    (A) "whatever is—is always wrong"
    (B) "whatever is—should be questioned"
    (C) "whatever is—should be opposed"
    (D) "whatever is—is meaningless"
    (E) "whatever is—should remain"

23. It is the author's opinion that to improve forecasting there must be better

    (A) interpretation of causal factors
    (B) description of events
    (C) insights into trends
    (D) interpretation of facts
    (E) statistical analysis of data

24. The author exhorts forecasters to

    (A) analyze one fact at a time
    (B) plan ahead to stay ahead
    (C) base predictions on past events
    (D) quickly retrace the course of events
    (E) analyze all interrelated causal factors

25. According to the passage, the author's attitude towards the environmental changes mentioned in lines 18–24 is one of

    (A) ambivalence
    (B) disapproval
    (C) approval
    (D) consternation
    (E) surprise

If there is still time remaining, you may review the questions in this section only.
You may not turn to any other section of the test.

Section II Problem Solving

TIME: 40 minutes

DIRECTIONS: Solve each of the following problems; then indicate the correct answer on the answer sheet. [On the actual test you will be permitted to use any space available on the examination paper for scratch work.]

NOTE: A figure that appears with a problem is drawn as accurately as possible so as to provide information that may help in answering the questions. Numbers in this test are real numbers.

26. What is the next number in the geometric progression 4, 12, 36?

(A) 44
(B) 60
(C) 72
(D) 108
(E) 144

27. An angle of x degrees has the property that its complement is equal to $\frac{1}{6}$ of its supplement where x is

(A) 30
(B) 45
(C) 60
(D) 63
(E) 72

28. If a company makes a profit of $250 on sales of $1,900, the profit was approximately what percentage of sales?

(A) 10%
(B) 12%
(C) 13%
(D) 15%
(E) 17%

29. Which of the following numbers is the least common multiple of the numbers 2, 3, 4, and 5?

(A) 12
(B) 24
(C) 30
(D) 40
(E) 60

30. In a certain town 40% of the people have brown hair, 25% have brown eyes, and 10% have both brown hair and brown eyes. What percentage of the people in the town have neither brown hair nor brown eyes?

(A) 35
(B) 40
(C) 45
(D) 50
(E) 55

31. If the altitude of a triangle increases by 5% and the base of the triangle increases by 7%, by what percent will the area of the triangle increase?

(A) 3.33%
(B) 5%
(C) 6%
(D) 12%
(E) 12.35%

32. A shipping firm charges 2¢ a pound for the first 20 pounds of package weight and 1.5¢ for each pound or fraction of a pound over 20 pounds of package weight. How much will it charge to ship a package which weighs 23½ pounds?

   (A) 6¢
   (B) 40¢
   (C) 45¢
   (D) 46¢
   (E) 52¢

33. If paper costs 1¢ a sheet, and a buyer gets a 2% discount on all the paper he buys after the first 1,000 sheets, how much will it cost to buy 5,000 sheets of paper?

   (A) $49.20
   (B) $50.00
   (C) $3,920.00
   (D) $4,920.00
   (E) $5,000.00

34. Tom's salary is 150% of John's salary. John's salary is 80% of Steve's salary. What is the ratio of Steve's salary to Tom's salary?

   (A) 1 to 2
   (B) 2 to 3
   (C) 5 to 6
   (D) 6 to 5
   (E) 5 to 4

35. A driver is taking a 5 hour trip. If he travels 135 miles in the first 3 hours, how far will he have to drive in the final 2 hours in order to average 50 miles an hour for the entire trip?

   (A) 50 miles
   (B) 55 miles
   (C) 110 miles
   (D) 115 miles
   (E) 165 miles

36. If it takes 50 workers 4 hours to dig a sewer, how long should it take 30 workers to dig the same sewer?

   (A) 2 hrs., 24 min.
   (B) 5 hrs., 12 min.
   (C) 6 hrs., 12 min.
   (D) 6 hrs., 20 min.
   (E) 6 hrs., 40 min.

37. Dictionaries weigh 6 pounds each and a set of encyclopedias weighs 75 pounds. 20 dictionaries are shipped in each box. 2 sets of encyclopedias are shipped in each box. A truck is loaded with 98 boxes of dictionaries and 50 boxes of encyclopedias. How much does the truck's load weigh?

   (A) 588 pounds
   (B) 7,500 pounds
   (C) 11,750 pounds
   (D) 19,260 pounds
   (E) 22,840 pounds

38. Mary is paid $600 a month on her regular job. During July in addition to her regular job, she makes $400 from a second job. Approximately what percentage of her annual income does Mary make in July?

   (A) 8
   (B) 8⅓
   (C) 12½
   (D) 13
   (E) 14

39. If the area of a triangle with base S is equal to the area of a square with side S, then the altitude of the triangle is

(A) ½S (D) $3S$
(B) S (E) $4S$
(C) $2S$

40. A train travels at an average speed of 20 mph through urban areas, 50 mph through suburban areas, and 75 mph through rural areas. If a trip consists of traveling half an hour through urban areas, 3½ hours through suburban areas, and 3 hours through rural areas, what is the train's average speed for the entire trip?

(A) 50 mph (D) 58⁴⁄₇ mph
(B) 53²⁄₇ mph (E) 59²⁄₇ mph
(C) 54³⁄₇ mph

41. $(x - y)(y + 3)$ is equal to

(A) $x^2 - 3y + 3$ (D) $xy - 3y + y^2 + 3x$
(B) $xy - 3y + y^2$ (E) $y^2 - 3y + 3x - xy$
(C) $xy - y^2 - 3y + 3x$

42. If $x < y$, $y < z$, and $z > w$, which of the following statements is always true?

(A) $x > w$ (D) $y > w$
(B) $x < z$ (E) $x < w$
(C) $y = w$

43. What is the ratio of ⅔ to ⅘?

(A) ¼ (D) ²⁰⁄₆
(B) ¹⁰⁄₁₂ (E) ²⁄₇
(C) ⁸⁄₁₅

44. Of the numbers 7, 9, 11, 13, 29, 33, how many are prime numbers?

(A) none (D) 5
(B) 3 (E) all
(C) 4

45. A company issues 100,000 shares of stock. In 1960 each of the shares was worth $9.50. In 1970 each share was worth $13.21. How much more were the 100,000 shares worth in 1970 than in 1960?

(A) $37,000 (D) $371,000
(B) $37,010 (E) $371,100
(C) $37,100

46. A worker's daily salary varies each day. In one week he worked five days. His daily salaries were $40.62, $41.35, $42.00, $42.50, and $39.53. What was his average daily salary for the week?

(A) $40.04 (D) $41.20
(B) $40.89 (E) $206.00
(C) $41.04

47. One dozen eggs and ten pounds of apples are currently the same price. If the price of a dozen eggs rises by 10% and the price of apples goes up by 2%, how much more will it cost to buy a dozen eggs and ten pounds of apples?

(A) 6%   (D) 20%
(B) 10%   (E) 30%
(C) 12%

48. Find x when $x + y = 4$, and $2y = 6$

(A) 1   (D) −3
(B) $\dfrac{3}{2}$ (E) −1
(C) −2

49. If 25 men an unload a truck in 1 hour and 30 minutes, how long should it take 15 men to unload the truck?

(A) 2 hours   (D) 2½ hours
(B) 2¼ hours   (E) 3 hours
(C) 2⅓ hours

50. A car gets 20 miles per gallon of gas when it travels at 50 miles per hour. The car gets 12% fewer miles to the gallon at 60 miles per hour. How far can the car travel at 60 miles per hour on 11 gallons of gas?

(A) 193.6 miles   (D) 204.3 miles
(B) 195.1 miles   (E) 220 miles
(C) 200 miles

51. Feathers cost $500 a ton for the first 12 tons and $(500 − x) a ton for any tons over 12. What is x, if it costs $10,000 for 30 tons of feathers?

(A) 270.00   (D) 277.78
(B) 277.00   (E) 280.00
(C) 277.70

52. The angles of a triangle are in the ratio 2:3:4. The largest angle in the triangle is

(A) 30°   (D) 75°
(B) 50°   (E) 80°
(C) 70°

53. Find the area of the trapezoid $ABCD$. $AB = CD = 5$, $BC = 10$, $AD = 16$, and BE is an altitude of the trapezoid.

(A) 50   (D) 80
(B) 52   (E) 160
(C) 64

54. If x is greater than 2, which of the following statements are true?

    I. x is negative.

   II. x is positive.

  III. $2x$ is greater than or equal to x.

  IV. x^2 is greater than or equal to x.

  (A) III only

  (B) IV only

  (C) I and III only

  (D) I, III, and IV only

  (E) II, III, and IV only

55. A worker is digging a ditch. He gets 2 assistants who work ⅔ as fast as he does. If all 3 work on a ditch they should finish it in what fraction of the time that the worker takes working alone?

  (A) 3/7   (D) 4/3

  (B) ½   (E) 7/3

  (C) ¾

If there is still time remaining, you may review the questions in this section only.
You may not turn to any other section of the test.

Section III   Practical Judgment

TIME: 20 minutes

DIRECTIONS: Read the following passage. After you have completed it, you will be asked to answer two sets of questions. The first of these, data evaluation, involves determining the importance of specific factors included in the passage. The second, data application, consists of general questions relating to the passage. When answering questions, you may consult the passage.

Luigi Cappa was beginning to wonder what had made him give up a smoothly running job in New York to tackle what had turned out to be a baffling problem in southern Italy.

He was a U.S. citizen, and if he had stayed with his company he might have had a seat on the board within two years.

Then an uncle in Turin, in northern Italy, had written to Cappa, imploring him to come and run his printing plant near Palermo in Sicily, which produced transfer designs and other specialized printing, some of it for export.

Cappa was 28 years old, unmarried and ambitious. The offer had appealed to him in several ways.

First, there was the chance to be his own boss immediately. Second, there was the challenge, as Cappa saw it, of bringing U.S. know-how to the Italian family firm. Third, there was the satisfaction of returning as a man of some authority to the country where his own father had been born.

He was a believer in scientific management. He also believed that people everywhere are basically alike and will respond in about the same way to the carrot of cash rewards and the stick of firm leadership.

After only a few months in Palermo, he knew differently. Cappa's uncle had set up the plant five years previously with the active encouragement of the Italian government. But the 300-strong labor force still had no loyalty to the company from the distant north. The workers dreamed of orange groves rather than production targets.

Indeed, on one occasion Cappa had found a worker blissfully cleaning equipment from one of the printing machines in an orange grove near the plant. When he had ordered him back into the plant the man had looked astonished and replied: "Why should I work inside when I can do my job here?"

Productivity was very low. When Cappa had visited a local barber, who knew that he worked in the printing plant but did not know he was the boss, the man had said: "Sir, can you get me a job with the printing company so that I no longer have to work?"

As Cappa walked round the plant he saw plenty of modern machines. He also saw a workforce that yearned to be out in the sun, and wondered how he could get his employees to change their attitudes.

First, he tried using his personal appeal as an American-Italian. That did not work. He would have been more successful, he ruefully admitted to himself, had he been born in Palermo.

He instituted production committees, which were supposed to generate their own ideas on improving productivity. He worked at them very hard but they too were a dismal failure.

When managers sat on the committees the workers seemed struck dumb, failing to produce constructive ideas. Then, when Cappa gave the committee more autonomy to run its own affairs, the members used the time allocated for meetings to leave the factory and take a siesta outside.

Cappa decided that a bonus system relating pay directly to output was the only solution. At first the union opposed this, saying it was the kind of piecework they had been fighting against. Then, to Cappa's surprise, they gave in. He thought he had won a victory.

If so, it was a hollow one. The workers began demanding the bonus as a right, whether or not they had worked extra hours or produced more. When Cappa refused to pay, the workers went on strike.

Cappa felt that he was dealing with forces beyond his control, with people whom he could not fully understand.

"They just don't seem to want to participate," he wrote to a friend in New York. "If you give them the chance to run their own affairs, they take advantage of it. If you offer them a carrot, they eat half your arm as well. And if you wave a stick, they strike."

Cappa's friend replied that he should investigate the possibility of instituting a system of co-determination management. Co-determination management gives workers a part in making decisions within the firm in areas that are traditionally the prerogative of management. What the system amounts to—in practical terms—is that it allows workers to have some managerial authority in deciding corporate policy, and in some cases, objectives. Once a decision is made in principle to institute such a system, the next step is to work out just how much authority management is willing to share with the workers and in what policy areas.

Cappa decided to give co-determination a try as a last resort. Rather than dictate specific areas in which to implement co-determination, Cappa felt that it would be best to consult with workers' committees and then make a joint decision. At first, the workers expressed some interest in the plan, but when they asked Cappa to explain how the system would add to their pay, he was taken aback. Cappa tried to explain to the workers that they would gain decision-making authority, not only on the plant floor but in policy-making. He further explained that they would have some power to influence, for example, whether profits should be re-invested in the company, or distributed to shareholders. In reply, the workers' representatives said that they had no interest in having responsibility for managerial decisions because they had enough problems of their own. With that response, Cappa realized that his co-determination scheme had no chance of being accepted by the workers.

Cappa seemed to have reached a dead end. He could advise his uncle to concentrate production in Turin and get rid of the Palermo plant. But then he would have to return to the U.S. without a job and with a feeling of defeat.

Alternatively, Cappa could find a way of motivating his workers. But *how*, he asked himself for the thousandth time.

Data Evaluation Questions

DIRECTIONS: The questions that follow relate to the preceding passage. Evaluate, in terms of the passage, each of the items given. Then select your answer from one of the following classifications, and blacken the corresponding space on the answer sheet.

(A)   A MAJOR OBJECTIVE in making the decision: one of the goals sought by the decision maker

(B)   A MAJOR FACTOR in making the decision: an aspect of the problem, specifically mentioned in the passage, that fundamentally affects and/or determines the decision

(C)   A MINOR FACTOR in making the decision: a less important element bearing on or affecting a Major Factor, rather than a Major Objective directly

(D)   A MAJOR ASSUMPTION in making the decision: a projection or supposition arrived at by the decision maker before considering the factors and alternatives

(E)   AN UNIMPORTANT ISSUE in making the decision: an item lacking significant impact on, or relationship to, the decision

56.   Location of company headquarters in northern Italy

57.   Basic similarity of the motivations of people everywhere

58.   Increasing the motivation of the Sicilian workers

59.   Low worker productivity

60.   Likelihood that higher pay would improve output

61.   Cappa's U.S. citizenship

62.   Degree of worker loyalty to the company

63.   Usefulness of cash rewards in motivating employees

64.   Desire of workers to run their own affairs

65.   Relating pay to output

66.   Quality of the machines used in the factory

67.   Proximity of orange groves to the plant

68. Cappa's desire to meet with workers' committees before settling on a plan

69. Cappa's high degree of personal ambition

70. Power of the union to influence worker attitudes and behavior

Data Application Questions

DIRECTIONS: Answer each of the following questions using information contained in the passage.

71. According to the passage, low productivity at the printing plant was the result of

    I. improper worker training
    II. low pay
  III. lack of worker commitment to the firm

    (A) I only
    (B) III only
    (C) I and II only
    (D) II and III only
    (E) I, II, and III

72. A major conclusion of the passage is that

    I. Sicilian workers probably cannot be motivated by methods appropriate in the United States
    II. expatriate managers are unsuitable in Italy
  III. scientific management is unworkable in Italy

    (A) I only
    (B) III only
    (C) I and II only
    (D) II and III only
    (E) I, II, and III

73. Cappa attempted which of the following means to motivate workers?

    I. Participative management
    II. Payment related to productivity
  III. His ethnic relation to the workers

    (A) I only
    (B) III only
    (C) I and II only
    (D) II and III only
    (E) I, II, and III

74. Cappa was induced to take the job at his uncle's plant because of

    I. monetary considerations
   II. his desire to return to his native land
  III. self-esteem

  (A) I only
  (B) III only
  (C) I and II only
  (D) II and III only
  (E) I, II, and III

75. Cappa's attempt to institute co-determination might have proven successful if he had

  (A) built a system of worker incentive payments into the plan
  (B) been willing to give a measure of true authority to the workers' committees
  (C) used greater tact in proposing the plan to the workers
  (D) previously decided the specific areas in which co-determination would be effective
  (E) given greater emphasis to the workers' influence over the use of profits when presenting the plan

If there is still time remaining, you may review the questions in this section only.
You may not turn to any other section of the test.

Section IV   Data Sufficiency

TIME: 30 minutes

DIRECTIONS: Each of the following problems has a question and two statements which are labeled (1) and (2). Use the data given in (1) and (2) together with other available information (such as the number of hours in a day, the definition of *clockwise,* mathematical facts, etc.) to decide whether the statements are *sufficient* to answer the question. Then fill in space

(A) if you can get the answer from (1) alone but not from (2) alone;

(B) if you can get the answer from (2) alone but not from (1) alone;

(C) if you can get the answer from (1) and (2) together, although neither statement by itself suffices;

(D) if statement (1) alone suffices *and* statement (2) alone suffices;

(E) if you cannot get the answer from statements (1) and (2) together, but need even more data.

All numbers used in this section are real numbers. A figure given for a problem is intended to provide information consistent with that in the question, but not necessarily with the additional information contained in the statements.

76. *ABC* is a triangle inscribed in circle *AOCB.* Is *AC* a diameter of the circle *AOCB?*

   (1)   Angle *x* is a right angle.
   (2)   The length of *AB* is ¾ the length of *BC*.

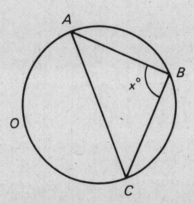

77. A cylindrical tank has a radius of 10 feet and its height is 20 feet. How many gallons of a liquid can be stored in the tank?

   (1)   A gallon of the liquid occupies about .13 cubic feet of space.
   (2)   The diameter of the tank is 20 feet.

78. How many books are on the bookshelf?

   (1)   The average weight of each book is 1.2 pounds.
   (2)   The books and the bookshelf together weigh 34 pounds.

79. Is the triangle *ABC* congruent to the triangle *DEF?* Angle *x* is equal to angle *y*.

   (1)   *AB* is equal to *DE.*
   (2)   *BC* is equal to *EF.*

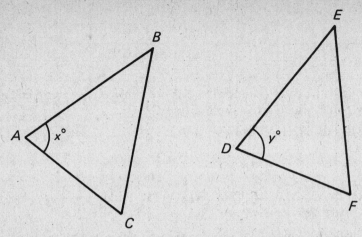

80. A plane flies over New York City. What is its speed in miles per hour?

(1) The plane is flying in a circle.
(2) The plane is flying at the speed of $\frac{1}{9}$ mile per second.

81. Mr. Carpenter wants to build a room in the shape of a rectangle. The area of the floor will be 32 square feet. What is the length of the floor?

(1) The length of the floor will be twice the width of the floor.
(2) The width of the floor will be 4 feet less than the length of the floor.

82. Do the rectangle $ABCD$ and the square $EFGH$ have the same area?

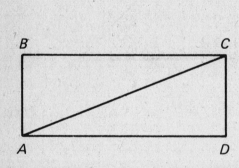
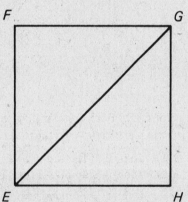

(1) $AC = EG$, $AB = \frac{1}{2} EH$
(2) The area of triangle ABC is not equal to the area of triangle EFG.

83. How much does Susan weigh?

(1) Susan and Joan together weigh 250 pounds.
(2) Joan weighs twice as much as Susan.

84. Two different holes, hole A and hole B, are put in the bottom of a full water tank. If the water drains out through the holes, how long before the tank is empty?

(1) If only hole A is put in the bottom, the tank will be empty in 24 minutes.
(2) If only hole B is put in the bottom, the tank will be empty in 42 minutes.

85. Find $x + y$

    (1) $x - y = 6$
    (2) $2x - 2y = 12$

86. C is a circle with center D and radius 2. E is a circle with center F and radius R. Are there any points which are on both E and C?

    (1) The distance from D to F is $1 + R$.
    (2) $R = 3$.

87. Mr. Parker made $20,000 in 1967. What is Mr. Parker's average yearly income for the three years 1967 to 1969?

    (1) He made 10% more in each year than he did in the previous year.
    (2) His total combined income for 1968 and 1969 was $46,200.

88. Is angle x a right angle?

    (1) $y = z$
    (2) $(AC)^2 + (CB)^2 = (AB)^2$

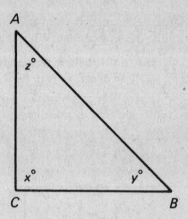

89. John and Paul are standing together on a sunny day. John's shadow is 10 feet long. Paul's shadow is 9 feet long. How tall is Paul?

    (1) John is 6 feet tall.
    (2) John is standing 2 feet away from Paul.

90. Is x greater than y?

    (1) x^2 is greater than y^2
    (2) $x + 3$ is greater than $y + 2$

91. A dozen eggs cost 90¢ in January 1980. Did a dozen eggs cost more than 90¢ in January 1981?

    (1) In January 1980, the average worker had to work 5 minutes to pay for a dozen eggs.
    (2) In January 1981, the average worker had to work 4 minutes to pay for a dozen eggs.

92. How many raffle tickets were sold if ticket sales brought in receipts of $10,000?

(1) Each ticket was sold for 25¢.
(2) 4000 books of tickets were sold.

93. What is the value of $\frac{x}{y}$? $x > 0$.

(1) $x = \frac{1}{4}y$
(2) $y = 400\%$ of x

94. What is the area of the circular sector AOB? A and B are points on the circle which has O as its center.

(1) Angle $AOB = 72°$.
(2) $OB = 4$

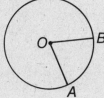

95. How many of the numbers x, y, and z are positive? x, y, and z are all less than 30.

(1) $x + y + z = 61$
(2) $x + y = 35$

96. How far is it from town A to town B? Town C is 15 miles west of town A.

(1) It is 10 miles from town B to town C.
(2) There is a river between town A and town B.

97. In 1980, the ratio of American cars sold to imported cars sold was 4 to 1. How many imported cars were sold in 1980?

(1) 6,000,000 American cars were sold in 1980.
(2) A total of 7,500,000 cars were sold in 1980.

98. What percentage of families in the state have annual incomes over $25,000 and own a sailboat?

(1) 28% of all the families in the state have an annual income over $25,000.
(2) 40% of families in the state with annual income over $25,000 own a sailboat.

99. What is the value of $x - y$?

(1) $x = 5$
(2) $x + 2y = 2x + y$

100. What is the radius of the circle with center O?

(1) The area of the circle is 25π.
(2) The area of the circle divided by the diameter of the circle is equal to π times $\frac{1}{2}$ of the radius of the circle.

101. A crate of oranges costs $1.00. What percent of the cost of an orange is the selling price of an orange?

(1) The oranges are sold for 6¢ each.
(2) There are 20 oranges in a crate.

102. What is the area of rectangle *ABCD*?

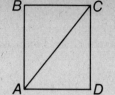

   (1) $AC = 5$
   (2) $AB = 4$

103. Is $xy < 0$?

   (1) $x > 2$
   (2) $y > -1$

104. Which is larger, a^b or b^a? $a > 0$ and $b > 0$.

   (1) $a = 1$
   (2) $b > 2$

105. Is x greater than y?

   (1) $xy = 5$
   (2) $x/y = 2$

If there is still time remaining, you may review the questions in this section only. You may not turn to any other section of the test.

Section V   Writing Ability

TIME: 20 minutes

DIRECTIONS: Each of the sentences in this section is either correct or contains one error in grammar, usage, diction (choice of words), idiom or punctuation. If there is an error it will be found in one of the underlined parts of the sentence, labeled (A), (B), (C), or (D). If you identify an error mark the appropriate letter on your answer sheet. If there is no error in the sentence mark E—no error.

Note: Assume that all parts of the sentence that are not underlined are correct and cannot be changed.

106. Historians <u>agree that,</u> <u>at the outbreak of</u> the war, neither Lincoln <u>nor</u> most members
              A   B   C
of the Republican Party <u>was primarily concerned</u> with the abolition of slavery.
                             D

<u>No error</u>
E

107. Blake is <u>among</u> the very few individuals <u>who</u> <u>critics regard</u> as genuinely significant
           A   B   C
<u>in both the</u> history of art and the history of literature. <u>No error</u>
    D   E

108. <u>Many scientists are alarmed</u> over the interest in such pseudo-scientific topics as ESP,
               A
flying saucers, and the occult, <u>fearing that</u> <u>it may herald</u> a new dark age of gullibility,
                               B   C
ignorance, and <u>thinking in superstitious ways.</u> <u>No error</u>
                   D   E

109. Having broken with Freud, Jung's later writings nevertheless bore signs of the
          A   B
    continued influence of Freudian doctrine and theories. No error
                C   D   E

110. Despite the revolutionary implications of Darwin's theories, which won
                                                 A
    practically universal acceptance among biologists and other scientists within a
                B   C
    relatively short time, as compared with other intellectual movements
    of similar importance. No error
            D   E

111. Scores of authors have tried to demonstrate that the plays we know as Shakespeare's
                              A   B
    were written by some other person, but no one, most critics agree, has produced much
                                                      C
    positive evidence for this belief. No error
                      D   E

112. The proposed statute requiring that all school textbooks be approved by the state
                          A   B
    board before adoption has been criticized by several civil liberties groups. No error
            C   D   E

113. That Giotto's paintings are significant in the history of the early Renaissance is
            A
    undeniable, but Giotto can not scarcely be considered the equal of such masters as
                              B   C   D
    Leonardo and Raphael. No error
                      E

114. Bismarck's distinctive quality was his methodical dedication to his pre-determined
                A   B
    goals, his refusal to be detracted by secondary pursuits or concerns. No error
                    C   D   E

115. Although the theory of continental drift was not widely accepted until
                                        A   B
    the mid-twentieth century, the basic concept has been described as early as 1620.
                                          C   D
    No error
     E

116. In the diagnosis of psychiatric ailments, it is essential that the practitioner approach
            A   B   C
    each subject without pre-judgments as relates to the nature or causes of the disorder.
                                          D
    No error
     E

117. Contrary to popular belief, during the Middle Ages, literary works <u>on secular topics</u>

                                                                 A

<u>were</u> probably <u>as numerous,</u> if not <u>more numerous than</u>, theological and devotional
   B   C   D

writings. <u>No error</u>
        E

118. Adaptive radiation is <u>the process whereby</u> a given species, <u>through gradual</u>
                           A   B

<u>adaptation</u> in several locations to a variety <u>of different habitats,</u> <u>eventually become</u>
   A   C   D

separate species with distinct characteristics and behaviors. <u>No error</u>
                                                        E

119. The U.S. Constitution <u>may be amended</u> by any of three methods: <u>by action of</u> the
                              A   B

Congress, by action of <u>the individual</u> state legislatures, and <u>by means of a</u>
                               C   D

Constitutional Convention. <u>No error</u>
                            E

120. Although legal suits are pending in several states <u>which</u> may <u>effect</u> the final tally, the
                                                 A   B

Census Bureau <u>has</u> officially deposited its population figures in order to meet the
                 C

deadline <u>prescribed by law.</u> <u>No error</u>
            D   E

121. The Senator's <u>extensive background</u> in foreign affairs <u>has made</u> her <u>uniquely</u>
                            A   B   C

<u>qualified to</u> a seat on this important sub-committee. <u>No error</u>
   D   E

122. Foreign auto makers <u>have not only made</u> major <u>inroads into</u> the American market;
                               A   B

manufacturers <u>of other</u> consumer goods have challenged the dominance of U.S.
               C

industry <u>as well.</u> <u>No error</u>
        D   E

123. <u>Of the numerous events</u> which helped bring about the U.S. Civil War, <u>perhaps</u> the
        A   B

most decisive <u>was</u> the election of Lincoln, <u>which</u> finally forced the disagreement to its
              C   D

crisis. <u>No error</u>
       E

124. Though the American political system <u>differs with</u> the British <u>in many respects,</u> the
                                  A   B

fundamental legal protections <u>it</u> affords the individual <u>are derived</u> almost entirely
                             C   D

from the British model. <u>No error</u>
                    E

125. After six months of study, the commission announced that some of the money
                    A   B

previously allocated for water supply projects be spent instead on pollution control
        C   D

measures. No error
         E

If there is still time remaining, you may review the questions in this section only.
You may not turn to any other section of the test.

Section VI   Practical Judgment

TIME: 20 minutes

DIRECTIONS: Read the following passage. After you have completed it, you will be asked to answer two sets of questions. The first of these, data evaluation, involves determining the importance of specific factors included in the passage. The second, data application, consists of general questions relating to the passage. When answering questions, you may consult the passage.

The Climax Corporation manufactured a line of major electrical appliances distributed through sixty wholesalers, many of which were company-owned. Retailers carried competitive lines, but wholesalers did not; portable appliances moved to market through nonexclusive distributors.

The company depended on wholesalers to provide service either directly or through supervision of retailers' service departments. When the warranty was involved, the manufacturer supplied the parts and the wholesaler the labor. Retailers who performed the service function were given a larger discount than those who returned the goods to the wholesaler to fulfill the guarantee.

In 1980, home office officials began questioning the adequacy of the service thus rendered either under the terms of the warranty or independently. Typical retailers carried several brands and, in general, did not have competent service personnel. The result was that the blame for the defect was passed back to the manufacturer. This, said the sales manager, was a major consideration. Others believed that reduction of service costs would follow from centralizing the entire operation in the hands of a relatively few factory service branches or in carefully trained service personnel employed by a relatively few widely distributed wholesalers. Costs would be thus reduced, and, at the same time, the quality of service rendered would be enhanced, it was claimed.

The product service manager argued that more money should be spent on training retail sales service personnel. Retailers like to render service, he claimed, since it helps to bring traffic into their stores and thus is profitable. A third possibility explored was the promotion of good service by concerns who service but do not sell appliances.

During the conference, the rise of the discount house was discussed. It was thought to be a phenomenon partly based on the realization that good independent service can be secured in most markets and for most appliances. There may be an exception in the case of TV sets, it was admitted, since it is common to find great resentment as to quality of service and delay in meeting calls.

The subsequent discussion raised questions as to the validity of the policy of requiring the retailer to give free service time under the terms of the guarantee. Often owners expected to receive this service free, even though they had bought the appliance elsewhere. Some company officials believed that the company should pay dealers for their time costs when they enabled the company to make good on its guarantee. One executive pointed out, during a heated discussion on this point, that at least one major automobile company now paid its dealers for making repairs under the warranty.

About this time the sales manager read about a consumer survey that found that the average owner gave little thought to service availability when buying an appliance, except perhaps in the case of TV sets. But, when trouble arose the owner expected the maker to "stand behind his product" and not fall back on any excuse as to costs or time involved, limitations which are found in the normal warranty.

Climax's operations manager was given the responsibility to set up a task force which would study each of the alternatives discussed during the conference. The alternatives were to be examined with regard to customer service and cost. The task force was asked to make its recommendations directly to the service manager.

Two of the alternative methods for increasing service were almost immediately discarded as impractical. It was found that retail sales personnel would not have adequate time to devote to servicing appliances. Investing capital in concerns which service but do not sell appliances might increase the level of service, but Climax would have little if any control over their operation. These concerns were independently owned and had no more allegiance to Climax than they did to any number of manufacturers whose appliances they serviced. Some concerns were highly reliable, but others had a record of spotty service. Weighed against other available alternatives, these options had few benefits to Climax.

It was the conclusion of the operations group that a choice had to be made among three options: (1) factory service branches, (2) wholesaler service departments and (3) a combination of both factory and wholesaler service.

The factory service alternative had a number of advantages to Climax. Because Climax would provide the service at its own locations with company personnel, it could closely supervise the quality of the work done. Factory supervision of service was more difficult whenever the work was done by independent dealers. Moreover, under the factory system, Climax could ensure that service personnel undergo the most rigorous initial and refresher training programs. Another advantage of centralized factory service was that parts inventories would be minimized by storage in only a few service locations. Finally, under this system, Climax would determine the price of service, thereby ensuring that consumers would not be overcharged.

The major disadvantage of centralized factory service was that Climax would have to invest in service locations, provide parts inventories, and train personnel. Because of the size of this investment, few locations could be established.

Compared to factory service, wholesaler-operated locations would be more difficult to supervise. As a result, the level of service was bound to vary from location to location. Even though the consumer survey indicated that service was not an important consideration in the pre-purchase decision as to whether to buy an appliance, poor service experienced by a customer might lower the chance that a Climax appliance would be bought again.

Wholesaler service would require less investment for Climax. Although Climax would have to take some of the responsibility for training wholesaler personnel, it would not have to invest in service locations nor in inventory parts. Initial investment and operating costs would not limit the number of service centers as it would in the case of factory service. Many of the wholesalers would be eager to offer the service as an added customer benefit. Climax's investment would be even smaller if service facilities were maintained by independent, non-factory-owned wholesalers.

A final alternative was a combination of both factory service centers and wholesaler-operated service departments. Under this option, wholesalers would be encouraged to offer service whenever possible, while Climax would maintain centralized service centers in areas where wholesaler service was inadequate or spotty.

Data Evaluation Questions

DIRECTIONS: The questions that follow relate to the preceding passage. Evaluate, in terms of the passage, each of the items given. Then select your answer from one of the following classifications, and blacken the corresponding space on the answer sheet.

(A) A MAJOR OBJECTIVE in making the decision: one of the goals sought by the decision maker

(B) A MAJOR FACTOR in making the decision: an aspect of the problem, specifically mentioned in the passage, that fundamentally affects and/or determines the decision

(C) A MINOR FACTOR in making the decision: a less important element bearing on or affecting a Major Factor, rather than a Major Objective directly

(D) A MAJOR ASSUMPTION in making the decision: a projection or supposition arrived at by the decision maker before considering the factors and alternatives

(E) AN UNIMPORTANT ISSUE in making the decision: an item lacking significant impact on, or relationship to, the decision

126. Training of retail service personnel

127. The rise of the discount house

128. Lack of competent service personnel at most typical retailers

129. Technical level of service demanded by consumers

130. Centralization of the service operation

131. Distribution of Climax products through 60 wholesalers

132. Increasing the level of service

133. Consumer belief that manufacturers are responsible for product defects

134. Investment required in service centers under each plan

135. Consumer pre-purchase decisions

136. Portable appliances sold by non-exclusive distributors

137. Cost of parts inventories

138. Increase in store traffic due to service calls

139. Pricing of service

Data Application Questions

DIRECTIONS: Answer each of the following questions using information contained in the passage.

140. Under Climax Corporation's warranty, which agency repaired defective appliances?

    I.   Wholesaler
    II. Retailer
    III. Manufacturer

    (A) I only
    (B) III only
    (C) I and II only
    (D) II and III only
    (E) I, II, and III

141. Which of the following reasons were given by executives of Climax Corporation for reconsidering their service system?

    I.   Retailers did not have competent service personnel
    II. Climax's service system was revised annually
    III. The customers were not utilizing the service

    (A) I only
    (B) III only
    (C) I and II only
    (D) II and III only
    (E) I, II, and III

142. Some executives believed that if service were centralized

    I.   quality of service would be improved
    II. service costs would decrease
    III. fewer call-backs would occur

    (A) I only
    (B) III only
    (C) I and II only
    (D) II and III only
    (E) I, II, and III

143. According to the passage, buyers of appliances at the time of purchase regarded service availability

    I.   as an important factor
    II. as a minor factor
    III. as an unimportant issue

    (A) I only
    (B) III only
    (C) I or II only
    (D) II or III only
    (E) I, II, or III

144. According to the passage, retailers liked to service appliances because it

    I. brought traffic to the store
   II. was profitable
  III. kept them busy

  (A) I only
  (B) III only
  (C) I and II only
  (D) II and III only
  (E) I, II, and III

145. Increased purchases of appliances through discount stores would mean that

    I. retailer service availability was not a strong motive in the buying decision
   II. discount stores must increase their service availability
  III. Climax Corporation's sales would decline

  (A) I only
  (B) III only
  (C) I and II only
  (D) I and III only
  (E) I, II, and III

**If there is still time remaining, you may review the questions in this section only.
You may not turn to any other section of the test.**

Section VII   Writing Ability

TIME: 20 minutes

DIRECTIONS: This test consists of a number of sentences, in each of which some part or the whole is underlined. Each sentence is followed by five alternative versions of the underlined portion. Select the alternative you consider both most correct and most effective according to the requirements of standard written English. Answer A is the same as the original version; if you think the original version is best, select answer A.

  In considering the answer choices, be attentive to matters of grammar, diction, and syntax, as well as clarity, precision, and fluency. Do not select an answer which alters the meaning of the original sentence.

146. Since neither of the agencies had submitted the necessary documentation, <u>each were required to re-apply for the grant the following year.</u>

  (A) each were required to re-apply for the grant the following year
  (B) each were required, the following year, to re-apply for the grant
  (C) each was required to re-apply for the grant the following year
  (D) both were required to re-apply, the following year, for the grant
  (E) it was required to re-apply for the grant the following year

147. Stationary missile launching sites are frequently criticized by military experts on the ground that, in comparison to mobile units, <u>they are the most</u> vulnerable to pre-emptive attack.

  (A) they are the most
  (B) such sites are the most
  (C) they are rather
  (D) stationary sites are most
  (E) they are more

148. The qualities needed in a president are scarcely tested in today's political campaigns, which call instead for showmanship, good looks, and being able to seem eloquent while saying nothing.

    (A) being able to seem eloquent
    (B) the ability to seem eloquent
    (C) having eloquence
    (D) a certain eloquence
    (E) that he seem eloquent

149. Anyone who would speak with authority on the poets of the Renaissance must have a broad acquaintance with the writers of classical antiquity.

    (A) Anyone who would speak
    (B) If one would speak
    (C) He which would speak
    (D) Anyone desirous for speaking
    (E) Those who have a wish to speak

150. Having chosen to demand an immediate vote on the issue, because of his belief that a sizable majority was within easy reach.

    (A) Having chosen to demand an immediate vote on the issue
    (B) An immediate vote on the issue having been demanded
    (C) He had chosen to demand an immediate vote on the issue
    (D) His demand had been for an immediate vote to be held on the issue
    (E) He had chosen that a vote on the issue should be held immediately

151. In its final report, the commission proposed, among other measures, that the legal drinking age be raised from eighteen to twenty-one.

    (A) that the legal drinking age be raised
    (B) a rise of the legal drinking age
    (C) that the legal drinking age should be raised
    (D) raising the age of drinking legally
    (E) to raise legally the drinking age

152. Since neither her nor the Dean were willing to veto the curriculum changes, they went into effect as of September 1.

    (A) her nor the Dean were willing
    (B) she nor the Dean was willing
    (C) her nor the Dean wished
    (D) she or the Dean was willing
    (E) she nor the Dean were willing

153. A broad range of opinions was represented between the various members of the steering committee.

    (A) A broad range of opinions was represented between
    (B) A broad range of opinions were represented between
    (C) A broad range of opinions had been held by
    (D) A broad range of opinions was represented among
    (E) Varying opinions were represented by

154. Undaunted by the political repercussions of his decision, the new gasoline rationing plan was announced by the Governor at the state office building last Friday.

(A) the new gasoline rationing plan was announced by the Governor
(B) the Governor's new gasoline rationing plan was announced
(C) the Governor made the announcement concerning the new gasoline rationing plan
(D) the new gasoline rationing plan of the Governor was announced
(E) the Governor announced the new gasoline rationing plan

155. Compelling historical reasons exist for the fragmented style and lack of coherence of modern art, however, they are none the less to be deplored by the honest critic.

(A) art, however, they are none the less to be deplored
(B) art; however, they are none the less deplorable
(C) art, however, they are nevertheless to be deplored
(D) art; still, they are equally to be deplored
(E) art; however, they are none the less to be deplored

156. Despite their avowed opposition to the strike, no one from among the dozens of non-union workers were willing to cross the picket line.

(A) from among the dozens of non-union workers were willing
(B) of the dozens of non-union workers were willing
(C) was willing from among the dozens of non-union workers
(D) from among the dozens of non-union workers was willing
(E) from the dozens of non-union workers were willing

157. According to one recent survey, gasoline economy, low price, and safety have replaced style and comfort as leading factors in the choice of a new car.

(A) and safety have replaced
(B) and safe driving have replaced
(C) and safety has replaced
(D) as well as safety has replaced
(E) along with safety have replaced

158. The poetry of George Herbert is regarded by many critics as equal in quality, though less influential, than the work of his more famous contemporary John Donne.

(A) equal in quality, though less influential, than the work
(B) equal in quality to, though less influential than, the work
(C) qualitatively equal, though less influential than, that
(D) equal in quality, though less influential, than the work
(E) of equal quality, though of less influence, than that

159. If it is the present administration whom we should blame for the economic crisis, the first step toward a solution is to reject the incumbent at the polls this November.

(A) whom we should blame
(B) whom is to blame
(C) who we should blame
(D) who should be blamed
(E) who one should blame

160. The assembly speaker has called for a shorter fall session of the legislature <u>in hopes that less amendments of a</u> purely symbolic nature will be proposed by the state's lawmakers.

   (A) in hopes that less amendments of a
   (B) hoping that fewer amendments that have a
   (C) in hopes that fewer amendments of a
   (D) in order that less amendments of a
   (E) in hope that fewer amendments of

161. <u>One of the costliest engineering projects ever undertaken, both public and private funds have been needed to support the space shuttle program.</u>

   (A) One of the costliest engineering projects ever undertaken, both public and private funds have been needed to support the space shuttle program.
   (B) One of the costliest engineering projects ever undertaken, support for the space shuttle program has come from both public and private funds.
   (C) The space shuttle program has been supported by both public and private funds, one of the costliest engineering projects ever undertaken.
   (D) From both public and private funds support has come for one of the costliest engineering projects ever undertaken; namely, the space shuttle program.
   (E) Both public and private funds have been needed to support the space shuttle program, one of the costliest engineering projects ever undertaken.

162. Parker's testimony made it clear that <u>he appointed Ryan before he had become aware</u> of Ryan's alleged underworld connections.

   (A) he appointed Ryan before he had become aware
   (B) he appointed Ryan before his awareness
   (C) he had appointed Ryan prior to his having become aware
   (D) his appointment of Ryan preceded awareness
   (E) he had appointed Ryan before becoming aware

163. <u>Despite its being smaller in size than are</u> conventional automobile engines, the new Alcock Engine can still deliver the horsepower needed for most short-distance city driving.

   (A) Despite its being smaller in size than are
   (B) In spite of its being smaller than
   (C) Although smaller than
   (D) Despite its size relative to
   (E) Though not comparable in size to

164. Seventy-four applications were received, <u>of whom the better were selected</u> for detailed review.

   (A) of whom the better were selected
   (B) from which were selected the better
   (C) the best of which were selected
   (D) from whom were selected the best
   (E) from which they selected the best

165. <u>If the British government had had no fear of</u> the increasing hostility of the Indian populace, Gandhi's non-violent tactics would have availed little.

    (A) If the British government had had no fear of
    (B) If the British government did not fear
    (C) Had the British government no fear
    (D) If the British government did not have fear of
    (E) Would the British government not have feared

166. The official imposition of "Lysenkoism" on Soviet biologists, with its chilling effects on scientists in countless related fields, <u>illustrate vividly the dangers of government interference with science.</u>

    (A) illustrate vividly the dangers of government interference with science
    (B) illustrate the dangers of government interference with science vividly
    (C) illustrates vividly the dangers of government interference with science
    (D) vividly illustrate the dangers of government interference with science
    (E) vividly illustrates how dangerous can be government interference with science

167. Health care costs have been forced upward less by increases in the salaries of nurses, technicians, and other personnel <u>than by increases in the amounts</u> spent on diagnostic machinery and electronic equipment.

    (A) than by increases in the amounts
    (B) than the amounts
    (C) but by increases in the amounts
    (D) and more by increases in the amounts
    (E) than by funds

168. The press secretary announced that <u>neither himself nor the President would be</u> available for questions until they had had more time to examine the report.

    (A) neither himself nor the President would be
    (B) neither he or the President was
    (C) neither he nor the President would be
    (D) he and the President will not be
    (E) he nor the President would be

169. In routine cases, the Civilian Review Board receives all complaints about police misconduct, weighs the evidence and the seriousness of the charges, and <u>then it decides whether a formal inquiry is needed.</u>

    (A) then it decides whether a formal inquiry is needed
    (B) then decides if a formal inquiry would be needed
    (C) then it decides whether to hold a formal inquiry
    (D) then decides whether a formal inquiry is needed
    (E) decides at that point if a formal inquiry is needed or not

170. Current scientific theory suggests that the dinosaurs were, in fact, one of the most spectacularly successful <u>groups of organisms ever developed</u> in the course of evolution.

    (A) groups of organisms ever developed
    (B) group of organisms that have been developed
    (C) groups of organisms to ever be developed
    (D) group of organisms to be developed
    (E) groups of organism developed

If there is still time remaining, you may review the questions in this section only.
You may not turn to any other section of the test.

Answers

Section I   Reading Comprehension

1. (E)	8. (C)	15. (B)	22. (B)
2. (C)	9. (C)	16. (C)	23. (A)
3. (B)	10. (C)	17. (C)	24. (E)
4. (B)	11. (D)	18. (B)	25. (A)
5. (A)	12. (B)	19. (C)	
6. (C)	13. (E)	20. (E)	
7. (C)	14. (B)	21. (C)	

Section II   Problem Solving

(Numbers in parentheses indicate the section in the Mathematics Review where material concerning the question is discussed.)

26. (D) (II–6)	36. (E) (II–3)	46. (D) (I–7)
27. (E) (III–1, II–2)	37. (D) (II–3)	47. (A) (I–4)
28. (C) (I–4)	38. (D) (I–4)	48. (A) (II–2)
29. (E) (I–1)	39. (C) (III–7)	49. (D) (II–3)
30. (C) (II–4)	40. (D) (I–7)	50. (A) (I–4, II–3)
31. (E) (III–7,I–4)	41. (C) (II–1)	51. (D) (II–3)
32. (D) (II–3)	42. (B) (II–7)	52. (E) (II–5, III–4)
33. (A) (I–4)	43. (C) (I–2, II–5)	53. (B) (III–7)
34. (C) (II–3,II–5)	44. (C) (I–1)	54. (E) (II–7)
35. (D) (II–3)	45. (D) (II–3)	55. (A) (II–3)

Section III   Practical Judgment

56. (B)	61. (E)	66. (E)	71. (B)
57. (D)	62. (B)	67. (E)	72. (A)
58. (A)	63. (D)	68. (C)	73. (E)
59. (B)	64. (D)	69. (C)	74. (B)
60. (D)	65. (A)	70. (B)	75. (A)

Section IV   Data Sufficiency

76. (A)	84. (C)	92. (A)	100. (A)
77. (A)	85. (E)	93. (D)	101. (C)
78. (E)	86. (A)	94. (C)	102. (C)
79. (E)	87. (D)	95. (A)	103. (E)
80. (B)	88. (B)	96. (E)	104. (C)
81. (D)	89. (A)	97. (D)	105. (E)
82. (D)	90. (E)	98. (C)	
83. (C)	91. (E)	99. (B)	

Section V   Writing Ability

106. **(D)**	111. **(E)**	116. **(D)**	121. **(D)**
107. **(B)**	112. **(E)**	117. **(C)**	122. **(A)**
108. **(D)**	113. **(B)**	118. **(D)**	123. **(E)**
109. **(A)**	114. **(C)**	119. **(E)**	124. **(A)**
110. **(A)**	115. **(C)**	120. **(B)**	125. **(D)**

Section VI   Practical Judgment

126. **(C)**	131. **(E)**	136. **(E)**	141. **(A)**
127. **(C)**	132. **(A)**	137. **(C)**	142. **(C)**
128. **(B)**	133. **(B)**	138. **(D)**	143. **(B)**
129. **(D)**	134. **(B)**	139. **(C)**	144. **(C)**
130. **(A)**	135. **(E)**	140. **(C)**	145. **(A)**

Section VII   Writing Ability

146. **(C)**	153. **(D)**	160. **(C)**	167. **(A)**
147. **(E)**	154. **(E)**	161. **(E)**	168. **(C)**
148. **(B)**	155. **(E)**	162. **(E)**	169. **(D)**
149. **(A)**	156. **(D)**	163. **(C)**	170. **(A)**
150. **(C)**	157. **(A)**	164. **(C)**	
151. **(A)**	158. **(B)**	165. **(A)**	
152. **(B)**	159. **(A)**	166. **(C)**	

Analysis

1. **(E)** The report (on which the passage is based) is certainly not optimistic (B), but rather pessimistic in its assessment, although not specifically about the trade gap (D). Nor can the report be characterized as harshly condemnatory (A) or critical of labor unions (C). After all, as pointed out in the passage, it is labor that will suffer. The answer is (E). This is specifically supported by the first and second paragraphs.

2. **(C)** Free trade is the reduction or elimination of tariffs and duties on exports. See lines 3 and 16–18.

3. **(B)** Manufacturers that cannot increase productivity in order to lower prices will not be able to compete with duty-free imports, and will not receive adjustment assistance, i.e., subsidies or some other financial payments to buttress them in the face of foreign competition.

4. **(B)** The author's recommendation is that redundant labor should be removed. See lines 36–37.

5. **(A)** Even though the subject of trade with the Common Market (C) is discussed, the major thrust of the passage is on the consequences of free trade—in this case, with the Common Market.

6. **(C)** This is stated in paragraph 3 of the passage.

7. **(C)** The major objective is to explain the objectives of sociology, which are the same as those of science. See line 1.

8. **(C)** A discussion of this point is given in paragraph 3. The other answers are either factually incorrect or incomplete.

9. **(C)** The final step or objective of science—according to the passage—is explanation (line 3), best stated as a causal proposition. See lines 38–39.

10. **(C)** I and II are mentioned in the first and second paragraphs. III is mentioned in lines 32–33 as one of the activities in which the scientist is *not* interested.

11. **(D)** Answers (B) and (E) are mentioned in the passage, but are secondary in importance to (D). Answer (C) is not correct, and answer (A) is not mentioned in the passage.

12. **(B)** This is mentioned in the first and the final paragraphs. In any case, the prefix *poly* means many and the suffix *theist* means one who believes in a god or gods.

13. **(E)** Answers (A), (B) and (D) cannot be inferred from the passage. Answer (C) is roughly consonant with what the author has to say, but (E) is a stronger example of the question statement.

14. **(B)** I is incorrect since they worshipped gods in both human and other forms. See lines 24ff.

15. **(B)** Although the author states that certain cultures are more inclined to anthropocentric worship (A), he mentions it while making the point that there are those who attribute it to others, even though practicing it themselves.

16. **(C)** The paragraph indicates that if the universe is partly controlled by the "wet-god" (it rains), then the "dry-god" lacks control. This is an example of incoherence. If you pray for rain, you must also pray to prevent the "dry-god" from exercising his powers, an example of potential conflict. Hence there is hardly a commonality of interests or order in a polytheistic system.

17. **(C)** This statement is made in line 8. While it would seem that (E) is implied in the first paragraph, this thought is negated in line 13.

18. **(B)** The first paragraph illustrates the author's belief that if a forecaster predicts a dismal future, no matter what the outcome, he can claim credit for action taken (if it worked), or disassociate himself from a wrong decision.

19. **(C)** While the project director might be guilty of "fuzzy" thinking (D), the main point the author is trying to make is that the housing project was a short-term solution to what was essentially a long-run problem. This point is also stated in lines 42–43.

20. **(E)** Clearly, the author's primary purpose is to point out some of the problems in forecasting and how they might be eliminated.

21. **(C)** Gardner's thesis is discussed in lines 16–18. His thesis was that in the early 1960s (when his book was written), Americans were operating on the basis of a no-questioning value system. According to the passage, this value system changed after several years, but we cannot infer that it is not operative today (A), for it may have changed again since the passage was written. For the same reason, we cannot infer that the thesis applies today.

22. **(B)** Answer (B) can be inferred from the examples given in lines 19–21 and also the statement contained in lines 22–24. Answer (A) is unacceptable because of the word "always"— this does not appear in the passage.

23. **(A)** This opinion is explicitly stated in lines 26 and 27.

24. **(E)** This exhortation is stated in lines 40–42.

25. **(A)** The author makes no comment about these environmental changes, except that they represent a change in attitudes and values of the population. The author makes no value judgment of his own, so we can say that his attitude is one of ambivalence.

Section II   Problem Solving

26. **(D)** Since $\frac{12}{4} = 3 = \frac{36}{12}$ the ratio of one term to the previous term is 3. So if x is the next term, $\frac{x}{36} = 3$ and $x = 3(36) = 108$.

27. **(E)** The complement of x is an angle of $90 - x$ degrees, and the supplement of x is an angle of $180 - x$ degrees. Thus, we have $90 - x = \frac{1}{6}$ $(180 - x) = 30 - \frac{1}{6}x$, so $60 = \frac{5}{6}x$ or $x = 72$.

28. **(C)** The profit was $250 on sales of $1,900, so the ratio of profit to sales is $\frac{250}{1,900} = \frac{25}{190}$ which is approximately .132 or about 13%.

29. **(E)** Since 4 is a multiple of 2, the least common multiple of 3, 4, and 5 will be the least common multiple of 2, 3, 4, and 5. 3, 4, and 5 have no common factors so the least common multiple is $3 \cdot 4 \cdot 5 = 60$.

30. **(C)** Since 10% have both brown eyes and brown hair, and 25% have brown eyes, 15% of the people have brown eyes but do not have brown hair. Thus, 40% + 15% or 55% of the people have brown eyes or brown hair or both. Therefore, 100% — 55% or 45% of the people have neither brown eyes nor brown hair.

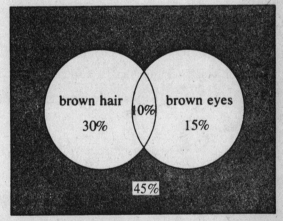

31. **(E)** Area = ½ (altitude) (base). The increased altitude is (1.05) altitude and the increased base is (1.07) base. Therefore, the increased area is ½(1.05)(1.07)(altitude)(base). So the increased area is (1.1235) area. Thus, the area has increased by 12.35%.

32. **(D)** The first 20 pounds cost $20 \cdot 2¢ = 40¢$. The package weighs 3½ pounds more than 20 pounds, so there are 3 pounds and one fraction of a pound over 20 pounds. The weight over 20 pounds will cost. $4 \cdot (1.5)¢ = 6¢$. Therefore, the total cost will be 46¢.

33. **(A)** Since $5,000 - 1,000 = 4,000$, there are 4,000 sheets which will be discounted. The 4,000 sheets cost $4,000¢$ or $40.00 before the discount, so they will cost $(.98)($40.00)$ or $39.20 after the 2% discount. The first 1,000 sheets cost 1¢ each so they cost $1,000¢$ or $10.00. Therefore, the total cost of the 5,000 sheets will be $49.20.

34. **(C)** Let T be Tom's salary, J be John's salary, and S be Steve's salary, then the given information is $T = (1.5)J$ and $J = (.8)S$. Changing to fractions we get $T = \frac{3}{2}J$ and $J = \frac{4}{5}S$ so $S = \frac{5}{4}J$. Therefore, $\frac{S}{T} = \frac{5}{4}J / \frac{3}{2}J = \frac{5}{4} / \frac{3}{2} = \frac{5}{4} \cdot \frac{2}{3} = \frac{5}{6}$. The ratio is 5 to 6.

35. **(D)** If the average speed is 50 mph, then in 5 hours the driver will travel $5 \cdot 50$ miles or 250 miles. He traveled 135 miles in the first 3 hours, so he needs to travel $250 - 135 = 115$ miles in the final 2 hours.

36. **(E)** 30 workers are $\frac{3}{5}$ of 50 workers, so it should take the 30 workers $\frac{5}{3}$ as long as the 50 workers. Therefore, the 30 workers should take $\frac{5}{3} \cdot 4 = \frac{20}{3} = 6\frac{2}{3}$ hours = 6 hours and 40 minutes.

37. **(D)** Each box of dictionaries weighs $6 \times 20 = 120$ pounds. Each box of encyclopedias weighs $2 \times 75 = 150$ pounds. So the load weighs $98 \times 120 + 50 \times 150 = 19,260$ pounds.

38. **(D)** Mary makes $600 a month on her regular job. Therefore, she receives $600 \cdot 12 = $7,200 a year from her regular job. Her only other income is $400. So her total yearly income is $7,600. She makes $600 + $400 = $1,000 during July, so she makes $1,000/7,600 = \frac{5}{38}$ which is about .13 of her annual income during July. Therefore, Mary makes about 13% of her annual income in July.

39. **(C)** The area of the triangle is ½(altitude)(base) = ½ (altitude)S. The area of the square is S^2. Therefore, ½S(altitude) = S^2, so the altitude must be $2S$.

40. **(D)** The train will average 50 mph for 3½ hours, 75 mph for 3 hours and 20 mph for half an hour. So the distance of the trip is $(3½)(50) + (3)(75) + (½)(20) = 175 + 225 + 10 = 410$ miles. The trip takes 7 hours. Therefore, the average speed is $410/7 = 58\frac{4}{7}$ mph.

41. **(C)** $(x - y)(y + 3) = x(y + 3) - y(y + 3)$
$$= xy + 3x - y^2 - 3y$$
$$= xy - y^2 - 3y + 3x$$

42. **(B)** If $x < y$ and $y < z$, then $x < z$. All the other statements may be true but are not always true.

43. **(C)** The ratio is $\frac{2}{3} / \frac{5}{4}$ which is equal to $\frac{2}{3} \cdot \frac{4}{5} = \frac{8}{15}$

44. **(C)** 3 divides 9 evenly and 3 divides 33 evenly, so 9 and 33 are not primes. 7, 11, 13, and 29 have no divisors except 1 and themselves, so they are all primes. Thus, the set of numbers contain 4 prime numbers.

45. **(D)** Each share is worth $13.21 - $9.50 or $3.71 more in 1970 than it was in 1960. So 100,000 shares are worth $($3.71)(100,000)$ or $371,000.00 more in 1970 than they were in 1960.

46. **(D)** Add up all the daily wages for the week: $40.62 + 41.35 + 42.00 + 42.50 + 39.53 = $206.00. Divide $206.00 by 5 to get the average daily wage, $41.20.

47. **(A)** If the price of a pound of apples rises 2%, then the price of ten pounds of apples rises 2%. This is because the percentage change is the same for any amount sold. Since a dozen eggs and ten pounds of apples currently cost the same, each costs one half of the total price. Therefore, one half of the total is increased by 10% and the other half is increased by 2%, so the total price is increased by ½(10%) + ½(2%) = 6%.

48. **(A)** $2y = 6$, so $y = 3$. Therefore, $x + 3 = 4$; so $x = 1$.

49. **(D)** Each man does $\frac{1}{25}$ of the job in $1\frac{1}{2}$ hours.

Thus, 15 men will do $\frac{15}{25}$ or $\frac{3}{5}$ of the job in $1\frac{1}{2}$ hours. So 15 men will complete the job in $\frac{5}{3} \cdot \frac{3}{2} = \frac{5}{2} = 2\frac{1}{2}$ hours. Another method gives $\frac{15}{25} = \frac{3/2}{x}$ where x is the time 15 men will take to complete the job. Therefore, $15x = \frac{3}{2} \cdot 25 = \frac{75}{2}$ so $x = \frac{5}{2} = 2\frac{1}{2}$.

50. **(A)** The car gets $100\% - 12\%$ or 88% of 20 miles to the gallon at 60 miles per hour. Thus, the car gets $(.88)(20)$ or 17.6 miles to the gallon at 60 mph. Therefore, it can travel $(11)(17.6)$ or 193.6 miles.

51. **(D)** The first 12 tons cost $(12)(\$500)$ or $\$6,000$. When you purchase 30 tons, you are buying 18 tons in addition to the first 12 tons costing additionally $\$(500 - x)(18)$. Since $\$10,000 - \$6,000 = \$4,000$, we get $\$9,000 - 18x = \$4,000$, and $18x = \$5,000$. So $x = 277.78$.

52. **(E)** The sum of the angles of a triangle is $180°$. Let x be the number of degrees in the largest angle; then the other angles are $\frac{1}{2}x$ and $\frac{3}{4}x$ degrees. Therefore, $\frac{1}{2}x + \frac{3}{4}x + x = \frac{9}{4}x = 180°$, so $x = 80°$.

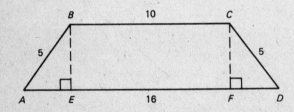

53. **(B)** If we draw $CF \perp AD$, then $\triangle ABE \cong \triangle DCF$ and $AE = FD = 3$. Then $BE = 4$. Thus the area of the trapezoid, which equals the product of the altitude and the average of the bases, equals $(4)(\frac{1}{2})(10 + 16) = 52$.

54. **(E)** Since x is greater than 2 and 2 is greater than 0, x is greater than 0. Therefore, STATEMENT I is false but STATEMENT II is true.

If we add x to each side of the inequality $x > 0$ we obtain $x + x > x + 0$, so $2x > x$. Therefore, STATEMENT III is true.

Since x is greater than 2 which is greater than 1, we know $x > 1$. Multiply the inequality by x (x is positive so the inequality is preserved); the result is $x^2 > x$, so STATEMENT IV is true. Therefore, STATEMENTS II, III, and IV are true.

55. **(A)** Since each assistant does $\frac{2}{3}$ as much as the worker, all 3 will accomplish $1 + 2(\frac{2}{3})$ or $\frac{7}{3}$ as much as the worker by himself. So they will finish the job in $1 \div \frac{7}{3}$ or $\frac{3}{7}$ as much time as it would take the worker by himself.

Section III   Practical Judgment

56. **(B)** The workers had no loyalty to the company from the "distant north." This was a *Major Factor* as far as their will to work was concerned.

57. **(D)** This was an assumption initially made by Cappa upon which he developed his managerial style. It was erroneous, of course.

58. **(A)** Motivating the workers is Cappa's *Major Objective*.

59. **(B)** Low productivity, caused mainly by lack of motivation, is a *Major Factor*.

60. **(D)** Cappa's desire to institute a bonus system (that failed) was not supported by any evidence that it could succeed.

61. **(E)** The fact that Cappa was a U.S. citizen had no apparent impact on the major problem of motivating workers or on his deciding whether to return to the U.S.

62. **(B)** Worker loyalty—or lack of it—was a *Major Factor* in determining what sort of plan would motivate workers to increase productivity.

63. **(D)** Cappa *believed* that people everywhere are alike and will respond to cash incentives. This was an unsupported assumption on his part.

64. **(D)** Cappa *believed* that productivity would increase if workers received more authority. This assumption was not based on any facts given in the passage.

65. **(A)** Relating pay to output was a *Major Objective* desired by Cappa. Its purpose was to increase productivity, another major objective.

66. **(E)** The quality of the machinery was not a factor in any alternative course of action.

67. **(E)** Nothing in the passage mentions the location of the orange groves as an element in the decision process.

68. **(C)** Cappa tried to establish co-determination in order to increase worker motivation—an objective. Meeting with the committees was a less important consideration than implementing co-determination itself.

69. **(C)** Cappa's ambitions were a *Minor Factor* in Cappa's decision to leave for Italy. Note the three reasons for his accepting his uncle's proposition, as given in the passage: (1) the chance to be his own boss, (2) his wish to bring U.S. know-how to the firm, and (3) his desire to return to his father's homeland with some personal authority. Ambition is probably connected with these three factors, but it is of lesser importance.

70. **(B)** Cappa's plans had been stymied on more than one occasion by the recalcitrance of the union. Therefore, the power of the union was a *Major Factor* which Cappa had to take into consideration in making his final decision.

71. **(B)** Since worker productivity was linked to a bonus system, poor worker output could be attributed (from facts in the passage) to lack of worker commitment.

72. **(A)** Answers II and III are general statements that are not necessarily supported by the case. It is clear, however, that answer I is a conclusion supported by facts in the passage.

73. **(E)** Cappa tried all three. See paragraphs 11, 12, and 14.

74. **(B)** Cappa wanted to manage a company on his own in order to prove his ability. See paragraphs 3–5.

75. **(A)** The workers rejected the co-determination plan after learning that it would not benefit them financially.

Section IV   Data Sufficiency

76. **(A)**
STATEMENT (1) alone is sufficient. If angle x is a right angle, then AOC is a semi-circle. Therefore, AC is a diameter.
STATEMENT (2) alone is insufficient. There are many (an infinite number) triangles we can inscribe in the circle such that $AB = \frac{3}{4}BC$. Not all of these will have AC as a diameter.
Therefore, STATEMENT (1) alone is sufficient, but STATEMENT (2) alone is not sufficient.

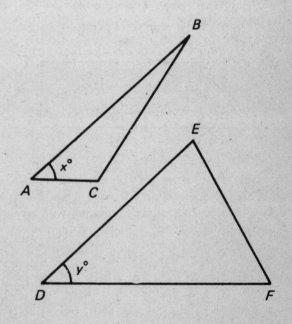

77. **(A)**

To find how many gallons the tank will hold, we need to calculate the volume of the tank and then divide this by the volume of one gallon of the liquid. Therefore, STATEMENT (1) alone is sufficient.

STATEMENT (2) alone is not sufficient (note that it gives no further information about the tank). We need to know how much space a gallon of the liquid occupies.

Therefore, STATEMENT (1) alone is sufficient, but STATEMENT (2) alone is not.

78. **(E)**

STATEMENT (1) alone is not sufficient. We still need the total weight of the books; then we can divide by the average weight to obtain the number of books.

STATEMENT (2) tells us how much the books and the bookshelf together weigh, but we don't know how much the books weigh.

So STATEMENTS (1) and (2) together are not sufficient.

79. **(E)**

STATEMENT (1) alone is not sufficient, since many noncongruent triangles can have a side and an angle which are equal.

By the same reasoning, STATEMENT (2) alone is not sufficient.

STATEMENTS (1) and (2) together are not sufficient. For two triangles to be congruent, they must have two pairs of corresponding sides and the *included* angles equal. For example, the following two triangles satisfy STATEMENTS (1) and (2) and angle $x =$ angle y but they are not congruent.

Therefore, STATEMENTS (1) and (2) together are not sufficient.

80. **(B)**

STATEMENT (2) alone is sufficient, since we can multiply $\frac{1}{9}$ by (60×60) to obtain the speed in mph.

STATEMENT (1) alone is not sufficient, because the plane's flying in a circle gives us no information about the exact speed of the plane.

So STATEMENT (2) alone is sufficient, but STATEMENT (1) alone is not.

81. **(D)**

STATEMENT (1) alone is sufficient. If $L =$ the length of the floor, then STATEMENT (1) says the width is $\frac{1}{2}L$. The area of the floor is length times width or $(L)(\frac{1}{2}L)$ or $\frac{1}{2}L^2$. Since the area is equal to 32 square feet, we have $\frac{1}{2}L^2 = 32$ so $L^2 = 64$ and $L = 8$ feet.

STATEMENT (2) alone is sufficient. Let $W =$ the width of the floor. Then STATEMENT (2) says $W = L - 4$. So the area is $L(L - 4)$ or $L^2 - 4L$ which equals 32. Therefore, L satisfies $L^2 - 4L - 32 = 0$, and since $L^2 - 4L - 32 = (L - 8)(L + 4)$, $L^2 - 4L - 32 = 0$ if and only if $L = 8$ or $L = -4$. Since $L = -4$ has no meaning for the problem, $L = 8$.

So STATEMENT (1) alone is sufficient, and STATEMENT (2) alone is sufficient.

82. **(D)** We have to determine whether $(AB)(BC)$ which is the area of the rectangle $ABCD$ is equal to $(EH)^2$ which is the area of the square $EFGH$.

STATEMENT (1) alone is sufficient. Since ABC is a right triangle, $BC = \sqrt{(AC)^2 - (AB)^2}$, and using STATEMENT (1) we have $BC = \sqrt{(EG)^2 - \frac{1}{4}(EH)^2}$. Using the fact that $EFGH$ is a square, we know $(EG)^2 = 2(EH)^2$, so we can express BC in terms of EH. Using STATEMENT (1) we can express AB as $\frac{1}{2}EH$, so $(AB)(BC)$ can be expressed as a multiple of $(EH)^2$. Notice that to answer the question you don't have to actually set up the equation. If you work it out you will find that the area of $ABCD$ is $\frac{\sqrt{7}}{4}(EH)^2$, so the areas are not equal. *Don't* waste time carrying out the extra work on the test.

STATEMENT (2) alone is sufficient since the diagonal of a rectangle divides the rectangle into two congruent triangles. Therefore, the area of $ABCD$ is equal to the area of $EFGH$ if and only if the area of ABC is equal to the area of EFG.

83. **(C)**

STATEMENT (2) says $J = 2S$, where $J =$ Joan's weight and $S =$ Susan's weight. But since we don't know Joan's weight, STATEMENT (2) alone is not sufficient.

STATEMENT (1) says $J + S = 250$; so if we use STATEMENT (2) we have $2S + S = 250$

or $S = \dfrac{250}{3} = 83\frac{1}{3}$. But STATEMENT (1) alone is not sufficient. If we use only STATEMENT (1), we don't know how much Joan weighs. Therefore, STATEMENTS (1) and (2) together are sufficient, but neither statement alone is sufficient.

84. **(C)**
In each minute, hole A drains $\frac{1}{24}$ of the tank according to STATEMENT (1). Since we have no information about B, STATEMENT (1) alone is not sufficient.
In each minute, hole B drains $\frac{1}{42}$ of the tank according to STATEMENT (2), but STATEMENT (2) gives no information about hole A. So STATEMENT (2) alone is not sufficient.
If we use STATEMENTS (1) and (2), then both holes together will drain $\dfrac{1}{24} + \dfrac{1}{42}$ or $\dfrac{7+4}{6 \times 28}$ or $\frac{11}{168}$ of the tank each minute. Therefore, it will take $\frac{168}{11}$ or $15\frac{3}{11}$ minutes for the tank to be empty. So STATEMENTS (1) and (2) together are sufficient, but neither statement alone is sufficient.

85. **(E)** STATEMENTS (1) and (2) are equivalent, since $x - y = 6$ if and only if $2x - 2y = 2(x - y) = 2 \cdot 6 = 12$. Each statement tells us only what $x - y$ is, and we have no other information. Therefore, each statement alone is insufficient. But since the two statements are the same, even together they are not sufficient.

86. **(A)**
STATEMENT (2) alone is not sufficient, since we must know how close the circles are and we know only the radius of each circle.
STATEMENT (1) alone is sufficient. The centers of the two circles are closer than the sum of the radii. (So we can form a triangle with DF as one side and the two other sides with length 2 and R respectively; but this means that the third vertex of the triangle will be on both circle E and circle C.)
So STATEMENT (1) alone is sufficient, but STATEMENT (2) alone is not sufficient.

87. **(D)** It is sufficient to be able to find his total income for the years 1967 through 1969 since we divide the total income by 3 to obtain the average income.

STATEMENT (1) alone is sufficient. Since we know his income for 1967, we can find his income in 1968 and 1969 by using STATEMENT (1). Therefore, we can find the total income. STATEMENT (2) alone is sufficient. Add the combined income from 1968 and 1969 to the income from 1967 (which is given), and we have the total income.
Therefore, STATEMENTS (1) and (2) are each sufficient.

88. **(B)**
STATEMENT (1) alone is not sufficient. $y = z$ does not imply $x = 90°$. For example, in an equilateral triangle, $x = y = z$ and $x = 60°$.
STATEMENT (2) alone is sufficient. Pythagoras' theorem says x is a right angle if and only if $(AC)^2 + (BC)^2 = (AB)^2$.

89. **(A)**
STATEMENT (1) alone is sufficient. If $P =$ Paul's height, then we can write a proportion $\dfrac{P}{6} = \dfrac{9}{10}$ since their shadows are proportional to their heights. $\left[\text{Thus, } P = \dfrac{54}{10} = 5.4 \text{ feet.}\right]$
STATEMENT (2) alone is not sufficient. The distance they are apart does not give us any information about their heights.
Therefore, STATEMENT (1) alone is sufficient, but STATEMENT (2) alone is not sufficient.

90. **(E)**
STATEMENT (1) alone is not sufficient. Note that $4 = (-2)^2 > 1 = (-1)^2$ but $-2 < -1$.
STATEMENT (2) alone is not sufficient. If $x + 3$ is greater than $y + 2$, then x can be less than y or greater than y. For example, $\frac{1}{2}$ is greater than 0, and $\frac{1}{2} + 3$ is greater than $0 + 2$. However, $\frac{1}{2}$ is less than 1, while $\frac{1}{2} + 3$ is greater than $1 + 2$.
STATEMENTS (1) and (2) together are not sufficient. For example, $-\frac{1}{2}$ is less than $\frac{1}{4}$, $-\frac{1}{2} + 3$ is greater than $2 + \frac{1}{4}$, and $(-\frac{1}{2})^2 = \frac{1}{4}$ is greater than $\frac{1}{16} = (\frac{1}{4})^2$. Also, $\frac{1}{4}$ is less than 2, $(\frac{1}{4})^2$ is less than 2^2, and $2 + 3$ is greater than $\frac{1}{4} + 2$. So STATEMENTS (1) and (2) together are not sufficient.

91. **(E)** STATEMENTS (1) and (2) together are insufficient. You need to know whether the wages of the average worker changed. 4 minutes of work in January 1981 could be worth more or less than 90¢.

92. **(A)** STATEMENT (1) alone is sufficient. STATEMENT (2) alone is not sufficient, since you do not know how many tickets are in a book.

93. **(D)** STATEMENT (1) alone is sufficient. Since $x > 0$, (1) implies $y > 0$. Hence, we can divide the equation $x = \frac{1}{4}y$ by y to get the value of x/y.

    STATEMENT (2) alone is sufficient since $y = 4x$ is equivalent to statement (1).

94. **(C)** STATEMENT (1) alone is not sufficient. Using (1) you can deduce that the area of the sector is 72/360 of the area of the circle, but you can't find the area of the circle.

    STATEMENT (2) alone is not sufficient. OB is a radius of the circle, so (2) gives you the area of the circle but you can't deduce what fraction of the circle the sector is. However, statement (1) gives that information, so statements (1) and (2) together are sufficient.

95. **(A)** STATEMENT (1) alone is sufficient. Since all the numbers are less than 30, all three must be positive for their sum to be larger than 60.

    STATEMENT (2) alone is insufficient. (2) implies that x and y are positive, but gives no information about z.

96. **(E)** STATEMENTS (1) and (2) together are not sufficient. You need to know what direction it is from town B to town C, besides the distance between the towns.

97. **(D)** STATEMENT (1) is sufficient. The fact that the ratio is 4 to 1 means that the number of imported cars sold was ¼ the number of American cars sold.

    STATEMENT (2) alone is sufficient, since the ratio of 4 to 1 means that 20% of all cars sold were imported cars.

98. **(C)** STATEMENTS (1) and (2) are sufficient. 40% of the 28% are families who both have income over $25,000 and own a sailboat. Note that STATEMENT (2) alone is not sufficient. The percentage of families who own a sailboat and have an income over $25,000 is a percentage of families in the state. In statement (2), the percentage given is a percentage of families with income over $25,000.

99. **(B)** STATEMENT (2) alone is sufficient. Solving the equation in (2) gives $x = y$, which implies that $x - y = 0$. STATEMENT (1) alone is obviously not sufficient, since no information about y is supplied.

100. **(A)** Since the area of a circle is equal to πr^2 and the radius is positive, STATEMENT (1) alone is sufficient.

    STATEMENT (2) is true for all circles, so it gives no information about the radius of this particular circle.

101. **(C)** STATEMENT (2) is needed to find the cost of each orange and STATEMENT (1) is needed to know the selling price of an orange.

102. **(C)** Since the figure is a rectangle, ABC is a right triangle. Therefore, using STATEMENT (1) and (2) you can find BC, which will enable you to compute the area.

    STATEMENT (2) alone is not sufficient, since BC could be any value without contradicting statement (2).

    STATEMENT (1) alone is not sufficient. If $AB = 4$ and $BC = 3$, then $AC = 5$, and the area is 12. However, if $AB = 1$ and $BC = \sqrt{24}$, then $AC = 5$, but the area is $\sqrt{24}$, which is not 12.

103. **(E)** STATEMENTS (1) and (2) together are not sufficient. If $x = 3$ and $y = -\frac{1}{2}$, then $xy = -\frac{3}{2}$. But if $x = 3$ and $y = 1$, then $xy = 3$.

104. **(C)** STATEMENT (1) reduces a^b to $1^b = 1$, and $b^a = b$.

    STATEMENT (2) then allows us to decide, since $b > 2$ implies $b > 1$.

    STATEMENT (2) alone is not sufficient. If $a = 1$ and $b = 3$, then $a^b = 1$ is less than $b^a = 3$. However, if $a = 3$ and $b = 4$, then $a^b = 81$, which is greater than $b^a = 64$.

105. **(E)** STATEMENT (2) implies $x = 2y$. This is not sufficient since if x is negative, then x will be less than y, but if x is positive, then x will be greater than y. If we also use STATEMENT (1), we

obtain $(2y)y = 2y^2 = 5$, which has two solutions, one positive, the other negative. Thus, both statements together are not sufficient.

Section V   Writing Ability

106. **(D)** With a *neither . . . nor* construction, the verb should agree with the *nearer* subject. Since *members* is plural, the verb should be *were concerned*.

107. **(B)** The pronoun *who* is the object of the verb *regard;* therefore, it should be in the objective case, *whom*.

108. **(D)** To maintain parallel construction, phrase (D) should simply read *superstition*.

109. **(A)** The opening phrase is a dangling modifier, since *Jung's later writings* had not *broken with Freud*. Phrase (A) should read something like *Although Jung had broken with Freud . . .*

110. **(A)** This is a fragment. It can be made into a complete sentence by replacing the word *which* with *they*.

111. **(E)** No error.

112. **(E)** No error.

113. **(B)** *Not scarcely* is a double negative; one word or the other should be deleted.

114. **(C)** The word *detracted* has been mistakenly used in place of *distracted*.

115. **(C)** To make clear the order in which the events occurred, the verb in phrase (C) should be the past perfect *had been*.

116. **(D)** Phrase (D) is awkward and non-idiomatic. A preferable substitute would be *as to* or *about*.

117. **(C)** To complete the idea, phrase (C) should read *as numerous as*.

118. **(D)** The subject of the verb is the singular *a given species*. Therefore, the verb should be the singular *becomes*.

119. **(E)** No error.

120. **(B)** The verb *affect* is needed here, since the desired meaning is *influence*.

121. **(D)** The usual idiom is *qualified for*.

122. **(A)** The words in phrase (A) are placed awkwardly and confusingly, and should be moved. The opening part of the sentence should read *Not only have foreign auto makers made major inroads . . .*

123. **(E)** No error.

124. **(A)** The usual idiom is *differs from*.

125. **(D)** The sentence should read *the commission announced that some of the money . . . would be spent . . .*

Section VI   Practical Judgment

126. **(C)** The major decision to be made by the executives of Climax Corporation was whether to maintain their present service operation, or, if not, what alternative would be best. The training of retail service personnel was a *Minor Factor* in making that decision; it was suggested by the product service manager that more money be spent on such training.

127. **(C)** The rise of the discount house was a *Minor Factor,* to be considered only because consumers who buy appliances at such stores do so under the realization that discount houses do not have service facilities. The question, of course, was why consumers bought appliances at discount stores when they knew the dealers would not provide service.

128. **(B)** The fact that typical (i.e., average) retailers did not have competent service personnel was a *Major Factor* in making a decision about Climax's service system. The other important factor, of course, was whether consumers really expected service facilities in each retail store.

129. **(D)** The technical level of service demanded by consumers is a *Major Assumption* that had to be examined before a decision about service could be made. In simple terms, how much service do consumers really want? Where do they want this service—from retailers, wholesalers, the manufacturer? In several places in the passage, some concern about this problem is expressed. See the discussion about discount stores and TV sets.

130. **(A)** Centralizing the service operation was a *Major Objective* of some home company officials. See paragraph 3.

131. **(E)** The number of wholesalers was unimportant; the fact that they were company-owned (and -controlled) was an important issue.

132. **(A)** *Major Objective*. Increasing the level of service was an objective desired by Climax's management. This was mentioned explicitly in paragraph 9.

133. **(B)** *Major Factor*. A major consideration in the option of improving service was that consumers blame the manufacturer for product defects. See paragraph 3.

134. **(B)** *Major Factor*. The magnitude of the investment required by each service alternative was a major factor in the decision as to which one to select.

135. **(E)** *Unimportant Issue*. Consumer pre-purchase decisions are important in the selection of a particular appliance. However, according to the survey, "the average owner gave little thought to service availability when buying an appliance, except perhaps in the case of TV sets" (paragraph 7). Therefore, the service component gained importance only after the purchase, i.e., when service was actually needed.

136. **(E)** *Unimportant Issue*. It is a fact that portable appliances are sold by nonexclusive distributors (paragraph 1). However, this fact was not a consideration relative to any decision alternative.

137. **(C)** The cost of parts inventories is a *Minor Factor*, as it is only one element in the *total* cost of service facilities. The total cost or invest-ment includes—in addition to parts—personnel training and facilities (for factory service).

138. **(D)** Climax's product service manager *claimed* (paragraph 4) that good service increases store traffic. His claim, however, was not substantiated in the passage.

139. **(C)** *Minor Factor*. The price of service is mentioned once in the passage (paragraph 11) and is understood in the context of factory control over service. The point is that, under the alternative of factory service, Climax would have control over the pricing of service, thus preventing overcharging of consumers. Control is a major consideration in the choice of an alternative service function, and pricing is but one element of control.

140. **(C)** In paragraph two, it is stated that repairs are made either by retailers or wholesalers. In the case of wholesalers, the manufacturer supplies the parts, the wholesaler the labor.

141. **(A)** The adequacy of service rendered by retailers was given as the major reason for the review of Climax's service operation. It was felt that present service was inadequate owing to the lack of competent service personnel among retailers.

142. **(C)** See paragraph 3. The sales manager and others believed that if the service operation were centralized, its quality would increase while its costs would decrease.

143. **(B)** According to the results of the consumer survey quoted in paragraph 7, consumers did not pay much attention to the availability of service at the *time of purchase*.

144. **(C)** See paragraph 4. Retailers liked to service appliances because of the profit and store traffic generated.

145. **(A)** Discount stores were able to cut prices because they did not bear the cost of service departments. Therefore, if consumer purchases increased through these outlets, it meant that they did not regard service availability when making a decision to purchase. Moreover, it was mentioned in the passage that a consumer survey found that the "average owner gave little thought to service availability when buying an appliance."

Section VII   Writing Ability

146. **(C)** The pronoun *each* is singular, and requires the singular verb *was required*.

147. **(E)** When only two things are being compared (in this case, stationary sites and mobile sites), the word *more* rather than *most* should be used.

148. **(B)** To maintain parallel structure, a phrase beginning with a noun (*ability*) is needed.

149. **(A)** The original wording is the clearest and simplest.

150. **(C)** As originally written, the sentence is a fragment, since it lacks an independent subject and verb. Choice (C) supplies them (*He had chosen*).

151. **(A)** No error in the original sentence.

152. **(B)** The pronoun *she* is needed, since it is the subject of the verb *was willing*; the verb must be singular, because of the *neither . . . nor* construction.

153. **(D)** Use *among* when three or more people or things are involved.

154. **(E)** The underlined phrase must begin with *the Governor*; otherwise, the phrase which precedes it has no clear reference. Choice (C) is verbose and rather vague.

155. **(E)** A semi-colon must be used to separate two independent clauses; otherwise, the sentence is a run-on sentence.

156. **(D)** The pronoun *no one* is singular, and requires the singular verb *was*. Choice (C) is awkward in comparison to choice (D).

157. **(A)** The sentence is correct as originally written. Note that the compound subject ("X, Y, and Z") requires a plural verb—in this case, *have replaced*.

158. **(B)** The comparative phrases *equal . . . to* and *less . . . than* must be complete in order for the sentence to make sense.

159. **(A)** Correct as originally written. The pronoun *whom* is correct, since it is the object of the verb *should blame*.

160. **(C)** Use *fewer* for countable items (such as amendments); use *less* for non-countable substances (for example, sand, water, or time).

161. **(E)** The phrase beginning *one of the costliest* must be adjacent to the phrase *the space shuttle program,* in order to make the reference clear.

162. **(E)** The past perfect tense *had appointed* is needed to clarify the order in which the events occurred.

163. **(C)** The other choices are verbose, vague, or both.

164. **(C)** Use the pronoun *whom* only for people, never for things.

165. **(A)** In most *if* clauses, the past subjunctive form of the verb—with *had*—must be used.

166. **(C)** The singular verb *illustrates* is needed, since the subject is the singular *imposition*.

167. **(A)** Correct as originally written. Parallelism calls for repetition of the pronoun *by* (*less by . . . than by . . .*).

168. **(C)** The pronoun should be *he*, since it is the subject of the verb *would be*.

169. **(D)** The pronoun *it* is unnecessary, since the subject of the verb—*the Civilian Review Board*—has already appeared.

170. **(A)** Correct as originally written.

Evaluating Your Score

Tabulate your score for each section of Sample Test 5 according to the directions on pages 4–5 and record the results in the Self-scoring Table below. Then find your rating for each score on the Self-scoring Scale and record it in the appropriate blank.

Self-scoring Table

PART	SCORE	RATING
1		
2		
3		
4		
5		
6		
7		

Self-scoring Scale

RATING

PART	POOR	FAIR	GOOD	EXCELLENT
1	0–8	9–12	13–19	20–25
2	0–15	16–21	22–25	26–30
3	0–7	8–10	11–15	16–20
4	0–14	15–20	21–25	26–30
5	0–7	8–10	11–15	16–20
6	0–7	8–10	11–15	16–20
7	0–8	9–12	13–19	20–25

Study again the Review sections covering material in Sample Test 5 for which you had a rating of FAIR or POOR.

To obtain an approximation of your actual GMAT score see page 5.

SIX

EXPERIMENTAL QUESTION TYPES

Each form of the GMAT includes one or more sections made up of experimental or trial questions. These sections are not counted towards your GMAT score. They are used by the test-makers for various purposes: to help in the statistical process known as "equating," by which the various forms of the exam are placed on the same scoring scale; to pre-test new questions before they are used in scored portions of the exam; and to pre-test new question types which may or may not be incorporated in future versions of the GMAT.

Experimental sections are never labeled as such, so it's impossible to be completely sure that a given test section is experimental. Therefore, you should do your best on every section of the test. On the other hand, do remember that new question types are frequently included in forms of the GMAT on a purely experimental basis. If you encounter a completely unfamiliar question type on your GMAT, don't become alarmed; the chances are great that it is experimental and will not affect your score.

In this chapter, we'll present samples of a few experimental question types which have appeared with some frequency on recent GMATs. Any of these question types may or may not appear on the GMAT you take; if they do appear, they may or may not be counted towards your score. It will be worthwhile, then, to become familiar with these question types before taking the GMAT, but be sure to concentrate your studies primarily on the other more common question types reviewed earlier in this book.

Analysis of Explanations

This question type is designed to measure your ability to recognize logical relationships, draw conclusions from statements, and make inferences. Each set of questions consists of a short passage describing a situation, a statement of the result of this situation, and several statements relating to the situation which you must analyze using the procedure outlined below.

DIRECTIONS: For each set of questions, a fact situation and a result are presented. Several numbered statements follow the result. Each statement is to be evaluated in relation to the fact situation and result.

Consider each statement separately from the other statements. For each one, examine the following sequence of decisions, in the order A, B, C, D, E. Each decision results in selecting or eliminating a choice. *The first choice that cannot be eliminated* is the correct answer.

A   Is the statement *inconsistent* with, or contradictory to, something in the fact situation, the result, or both together? If so, choose A.
     If not,

B   Does the statement present a *possible adequate explanation* of the result? If so, choose B.
    If not,

C   Does the statement have to be true if the fact situation and the result are as stated? If so, the statement is *deducible* from something in the fact situation, the result, or both together; choose C.
    If not,

D   Does the statement either support or weaken a possible explanation of the result? If so, the statement is *relevant* to an explanation. Choose D.
    If not,

E   The statement is *irrelevant* to an explanation of the result. Choose E.

Use common sense to decide whether explanations are adequate and whether statements are inconsistent or deducible. No formal system of logic is presupposed. Do not consider extremely unlikely or remote possibilities.

Sample Analysis of Explanation Question Sets

Use the directions given above to answer the following sample Analysis of Explanations Question Sets. Check the answer explanations at the end of the chapter to see how you did. Study any questions you missed until you understand the reasoning involved.

Question Set 1

Situation: When the will of industrialist Michael MacPherson was read upon his death in December, 1972, it was found that he had left the sum of $500,000, or half of his estate, whichever was less, to Nutmeg State University to endow a MacPherson Chair of Anglo-Scottish Literature. The will specified that a noted Scottish writer should be chosen each year to hold the chair and lecture at the university on his own works. At a meeting the following month, a special faculty committee voted to invite William Worthington, a Scottish novelist, to occupy the MacPherson chair for 1973–74. Worthington immediately replied, by telegram, that he was deeply honored but was unsure whether his other commitments would allow him to remain away from Scotland for a full year. Worthington asked for one month in which to decide whether to accept the post.

Result: In April, 1973, the university officially withdrew its invitation to Worthington.

1. At the end of two months, Worthington had failed to make any further response to the university's offer.   1. Ⓐ Ⓑ Ⓒ Ⓓ Ⓔ

2. The university's message withdrawing the invitation was in the mail at the same time as Worthington's message of acceptance.   2. Ⓐ Ⓑ Ⓒ Ⓓ Ⓔ

3. The occupant of the MacPherson Chair was to be newly selected each year.   3. Ⓐ Ⓑ Ⓒ Ⓓ Ⓔ

4. Worthington was unqualified for the MacPherson Chair because he lacked knowledge of American literature and culture.   4. Ⓐ Ⓑ Ⓒ Ⓓ Ⓔ

5. The school withdrew its invitation when the trustees of the university bowed to widespread public demands that Worthington be dropped.   5. Ⓐ Ⓑ Ⓒ Ⓓ Ⓔ

6. Nutmeg State University is located in an extremely conservative community with strict religious and moral standards.   6. Ⓐ Ⓑ Ⓒ Ⓓ Ⓔ

7. MacPherson himself had attended Nutmeg State University but had been expelled after one year for cheating on an exam.   7. Ⓐ Ⓑ Ⓒ Ⓓ Ⓔ

8. Ⓐ Ⓑ Ⓒ Ⓓ Ⓔ   **8.** Worthington was the author of several novels which were controversial because of their explicit sexual content.

9. Ⓐ Ⓑ Ⓒ Ⓓ Ⓔ   **9.** Worthington was eager to accept the post since he knew it would leave him ample time for writing.

10. Ⓐ Ⓑ Ⓒ Ⓓ Ⓔ   **10.** After extensive claims by creditors had been settled, it was found that MacPherson's entire estate amounted to $316.44.

Question Set 2

Situation: In January, 1977, the Sevigne Brewing Company of France decided that the time was right to introduce Sevigne Beer on the U.S. market. Observing the success in America of beers imported from Germany, Holland, Austria, and even Japan, the directors of Sevigne reasoned that a properly promoted French product might, within two years, win up to 10% of the growing U.S. import market. Among the advantages of their product, the directors felt, were the novelty of French beer, which should arouse consumer curiosity; the light, dry taste of Sevigne, which was well adapted to American palates; and the image of France as a producer of high-quality gourmet foods and beverages. The retail price of Sevigne was tentatively set at a level comparable to that of the leading import, and the firm began testing the product in four U.S. cities preparatory to a full-scale move into the market planned for October, 1977.

Result: In November, 1978, Sevigne Beer was dropped from the U.S. market, at a loss to the firm of over $16 million.

11. Ⓐ Ⓑ Ⓒ Ⓓ Ⓔ   **11.** The American public was unwilling to accept French beer as more than a curiosity.

12. Ⓐ Ⓑ Ⓒ Ⓓ Ⓔ   **12.** At the time Sevigne Beer was introduced in America, no French beer had a significant portion of the U.S. market.

13. Ⓐ Ⓑ Ⓒ Ⓓ Ⓔ   **13.** The directors of Sevigne hoped to establish a price for their product competitive with that of other imported beers.

14. Ⓐ Ⓑ Ⓒ Ⓓ Ⓔ   **14.** In January, 1978, two major brewers of imported beers began costly new advertising campaigns across the U.S.

15. Ⓐ Ⓑ Ⓒ Ⓓ Ⓔ   **15.** Sales of domestic beers in the U.S. rose by 4% in 1978.

16. Ⓐ Ⓑ Ⓒ Ⓓ Ⓔ   **16.** Changes in the value of U.S. currency drove up the retail price of Sevigne Beer by 75% during the first half of 1978.

17. Ⓐ Ⓑ Ⓒ Ⓓ Ⓔ   **17.** The Sevigne test-marketing strongly indicated that the beer was unlikely to succeed on the U.S. market.

18. Ⓐ Ⓑ Ⓒ Ⓓ Ⓔ   **18.** The success of Japanese beer in the U.S. was due almost entirely to the relatively large Japanese-American population in certain cities.

19. Ⓐ Ⓑ Ⓒ Ⓓ Ⓔ   **19.** The Sevigne company felt that their beer's identification with France would help establish its popularity in the U.S.

20. Ⓐ Ⓑ Ⓒ Ⓓ Ⓔ   **20.** The formula by which Sevigne Beer was brewed had been significantly changed in June, 1975.

Question Set 3

Situation: Planning for the Himalayan expedition led by Sir Aubrey Cathcart, which would attempt to scale the notorious western slope of K9, fourth tallest mountain in the world, began a year in advance. A staff of mountaineering experts spent hundreds of hours analyzing the extremes of terrain, temperature, and atmospheric conditions with which the climbers would have to contend, and selected or designed dozens of top quality mountaineering items especially for the expedition. Before the climbers left for Tibet, every item on the thirty-eight page checklist of needed gear was shipped ahead in hermetically sealed crates, with the exception of a few specially-designed products still being custom manufactured at the time. These would be sent on by air freight in time to meet the climbers at Bashitar, their last checkpoint before beginning the ascent.

Result: In the final check of equipment at Bashitar, it was discovered that six pairs of custom-made Swiss binoculars were missing, delaying the start of the expedition by nearly two months.

21. Sir Aubrey personally supervised the expedition's planning stages.　21. (A) (B) (C) (D) (E)

22. The Swiss firm commissioned to make the binoculars had gone bankrupt three months before, but had failed to notify its clients.　22. (A) (B) (C) (D) (E)

23. All the equipment for the climb had been shipped to Tibet in the same freighter.　23. (A) (B) (C) (D) (E)

24. Before the final equipment check, the binoculars, worth over $900 each, had been stored on the first floor of an unlocked, unguarded warehouse.　24. (A) (B) (C) (D) (E)

25. The plane carrying the binoculars to Bashitar crashed over Soviet Georgia because of engine trouble.　25. (A) (B) (C) (D) (E)

26. The staff member responsible for ordering the binoculars had failed to do so.　26. (A) (B) (C) (D) (E)

27. The equipment for the climb was chosen partly for its ability to withstand extreme cold.　27. (A) (B) (C) (D) (E)

28. The special Swiss binoculars were crucial to the success of the climb.　28. (A) (B) (C) (D) (E)

29. The airport at Bashitar is only large enough to serve small, two-engine propeller craft.　29. (A) (B) (C) (D) (E)

30. Those in charge of selecting the gear for the climb had little real knowledge of the demands of mountain climbing.　30. (A) (B) (C) (D) (E)

Question Set 4

Situation: In June, 1961, Dr. Hugo Danube, a researcher into extra-sensory perception (ESP), began a series of ESP tests involving volunteer pairs of twins. In each experimental trial, one twin selected a card from a set of five and signalled "Ready" by pressing a button which lit a light in an adjoining room, where the other twin waited. Upon seeing the light flash, the second twin would guess which card the first had selected. The choices made by each twin were recorded by trained researchers, who had no way of knowing which cards were being chosen in the other room. "Hits" and "misses" were determined by comparing the two lists later. Dr. Danube was exultant when Robert and Edna Fleming, the third set of twins he tested, recorded an 88% "hit" rate, far higher than would be predicted by the laws of probability.

Result: Over the next twelve years, no other set of twins tested by Dr. Danube recorded a "hit" rate significantly above the chance level.

31. During the testing, the twins received no immediate confirmation of their rate of success or failure.　31. (A) (B) (C) (D) (E)

32. Upon testing, it was found that the Flemings had hearing nearly 60% more acute than that of the average person.　32. (A) (B) (C) (D) (E)

33. The five cards used by Dr. Danube carried pictures of a star, a wave, a circle, a square, and a triangle.　33. (A) (B) (C) (D) (E)

34. ESP has no scientific validity; the Flemings had used an ingenious code to reveal their card choices to one another.　34. (A) (B) (C) (D) (E)

35. Ⓐ Ⓑ Ⓒ Ⓓ Ⓔ   **35.** During the twelve years of testing, over thirty different graduate students served on Dr. Danube's staff.

36. Ⓐ Ⓑ Ⓒ Ⓓ Ⓔ   **36.** Dr. Danube's experimental method was a closely-guarded secret.

37. Ⓐ Ⓑ Ⓒ Ⓓ Ⓔ   **37.** The researcher charged with recording the guesses of the second Fleming twin unconsciously revealed the choices of the first twin by slight, involuntary movements.

38. Ⓐ Ⓑ Ⓒ Ⓓ Ⓔ   **38.** Dr. Danube regarded the Flemings' "hit" rate as evidence for the existence of ESP.

39. Ⓐ Ⓑ Ⓒ Ⓓ Ⓔ   **39.** In Dr. Danube's experiment, no control was exerted over the length of time between flashes of the "Ready" light.

40. Ⓐ Ⓑ Ⓒ Ⓓ Ⓔ   **40.** The Flemings were children of the Remarkable Andi, a professional magician known for his clever "mind-reading" stunts.

Question Set 5

Situation: In 1959, the government of Tambul, a small east Asian nation, became concerned about the country's shortage of physicians, and began a drive to encourage Tambuli citizens to study medicine. Six years later, the prime minister appointed a commission to report on the results of this drive. The commission's report was optimistic. It pointed out that, as of 1965, over 8,000 Tambulis were attending medical schools abroad, mainly in the United States; within three years, the report declared, a steady stream of doctors would be returning to practice in Tambul. In addition, the new national medical college in Hamistan, the capital city of Tambul, has just opened its doors; in five years, the first class of physicians, numbering 350, was expected to be graduated. The commission concluded that within six to eight years Tambul should have a surplus of physicians.

Result: In 1975, eight of the ten provinces of Tambul reported severe shortages of physicians.

41. Ⓐ Ⓑ Ⓒ Ⓓ Ⓔ   **41.** The average annual income of a physician in Tambul is about $4,000.

42. Ⓐ Ⓑ Ⓒ Ⓓ Ⓔ   **42.** The national medical college was not founded until six years after the government drive for more doctors had begun.

43. Ⓐ Ⓑ Ⓒ Ⓓ Ⓔ   **43.** In 1965, 150 Tambuli doctors practiced medicine in the United States.

44. Ⓐ Ⓑ Ⓒ Ⓓ Ⓔ   **44.** The national medical college and eight out of nine Tambuli hospitals were destroyed in warfare between 1969 and 1974.

45. Ⓐ Ⓑ Ⓒ Ⓓ Ⓔ   **45.** Almost none of the Tambuli doctors trained abroad returned to their native land to practice medicine.

46. Ⓐ Ⓑ Ⓒ Ⓓ Ⓔ   **46.** Between 1959 and 1965, Tambuli government policy emphasized bringing foreign-born doctors to settle and practice in Tambul.

47. Ⓐ Ⓑ Ⓒ Ⓓ Ⓔ   **47.** The eight provinces which lacked doctors were among the most rural, most sparsely populated, and poorest regions in Asia.

48. Ⓐ Ⓑ Ⓒ Ⓓ Ⓔ   **48.** From 1969 to 1974, Tambul was at war.

49. Ⓐ Ⓑ Ⓒ Ⓓ Ⓔ   **49.** The spread of disease in Tambul was facilitated by the lack in many villages of sanitation and adequate nutrition.

50. Ⓐ Ⓑ Ⓒ Ⓓ Ⓔ   **50.** Language differences made it nearly impossible for natives of Tambul to win acceptance from American medical colleges.

Question Set 6

Situation: In the field of historical romance, Pierrot Books, publishers of such multi-million selling books as *Love's Tender Torment* and *Passion's Savage Caress*, had long been dominant. Worldwide sales of Pierrot books in 1978 numbered over 32 million. However, in

June, 1979, a new firm known as Airedale House announced plans to publish a competing line of romances. Airedale House intended to produce six new titles each month, the same number published by Pierrot, and had signed a long-term contract with a major book marketing firm providing for international distribution in the same regions where Pierrot had been successful. They planned a forty-six city U.S. tour by several of their most important authors to gain exposure for the new imprint beginning in November of 1979. Pierrot officials publicly expressed confidence that their firm would maintain and strengthen its control of the market.

Result: In 1982, over 40 million Airedale House books were sold.

51. Airedale House lured away two of Pierrot's authors with lucrative multi-book contracts.　　51. Ⓐ Ⓑ Ⓒ Ⓓ Ⓔ

52. In May, 1981, motion picture rights to *Cruel Kiss of Surrender*, a Pierrot romance, were sold for over $2 million.　　52. Ⓐ Ⓑ Ⓒ Ⓓ Ⓔ

53. The romances published by Airedale House won a large following relatively quickly.　　53. Ⓐ Ⓑ Ⓒ Ⓓ Ⓔ

54. Airedale House used "mass production" techniques in the writing and editing of books which enabled them to rush more new titles onto the market than could Pierrot Books.　　54. Ⓐ Ⓑ Ⓒ Ⓓ Ⓔ

55 A massive publicity campaign by Airedale House succeeded in capturing a dominant share of the romance market.　　55. Ⓐ Ⓑ Ⓒ Ⓓ Ⓔ

56. Pierrot's most prolific and best-loved author, Frances E. Braithewaite, died suddenly in February, 1980.　　56. Ⓐ Ⓑ Ⓒ Ⓓ Ⓔ

57. The marketing firm which had contracted to handle Airedale House books also distributed lines of reference books, non-fiction best sellers, and serious fiction.　　57. Ⓐ Ⓑ Ⓒ Ⓓ Ⓔ

58. Sales of Pierrot Books in 1982 numbered about 50 million.　　58. Ⓐ Ⓑ Ⓒ Ⓓ Ⓔ

59. Airedale House invaded several major marketing territories previously untapped by Pierrot.　　59. Ⓐ Ⓑ Ⓒ Ⓓ Ⓔ

60. Pierrot Books suffered a financial collapse in 1981, leaving control of the romance field to Airedale House.　　60. Ⓐ Ⓑ Ⓒ Ⓓ Ⓔ

Question Set 7

Situation: In March, 1974, foul-smelling sludge was discovered rapidly spreading over the southern third of Lake Wataguse in upstate New York. Investigators found that hundreds of drums of toxic chemical wastes in a long-forgotten dumping ground adjacent to the lake had begun to leak their contents. A battle began over who was responsible for cleaning up the dangerous mess. It was found that the wastes had been deposited during the 1940s and 50s by Peristar Plastics, an Ithaca, New York firm since absorbed by International Synthetics, Inc., a London-based conglomerate which disclaimed all responsibility. State environmental authorities declared that they had no resources to handle the multi-million dollar clean-up job, and the federal government cited a series of complex regulations which, they said, took the matter out of their hands. In June, 1976, a New York state court finally ruled that the state Environmental Safety Commission should perform the clean-up, after which, however, International Synthetics must reimburse the state for all costs.

Result: In December, 1978, the dump had still not been cleaned up.

61. Peristar Plastics had produced the wastes in the manufacture of petroleum-based synthetic materials.　　61. Ⓐ Ⓑ Ⓒ Ⓓ Ⓔ

62. The wastes had been gradually polluting Lake Wataguse for over twenty years.　　62. Ⓐ Ⓑ Ⓒ Ⓓ Ⓔ

63. Ⓐ Ⓑ Ⓒ Ⓓ Ⓔ   **63.** International Synthetics appealed the state court's ruling all the way to the U.S. Supreme Court, delaying a final ruling for nearly three years.

64. Ⓐ Ⓑ Ⓒ Ⓓ Ⓔ   **64.** The leakage from the dump constituted a health hazard to those in the community.

65. Ⓐ Ⓑ Ⓒ Ⓓ Ⓔ   **65.** State courts do not rule in cases involving businesses whose headquarters are located outside of the United States.

66. Ⓐ Ⓑ Ⓒ Ⓓ Ⓔ   **66.** The New York State Supreme Court overturned the June, 1976 ruling.

67. Ⓐ Ⓑ Ⓒ Ⓓ Ⓔ   **67.** The Ithaca, New York plant of Peristar Plastics was over 175 miles away from Lake Wataguse.

68. Ⓐ Ⓑ Ⓒ Ⓓ Ⓔ   **68.** In 1977, International Synthetics was absorbed by Interworld Technologies, Ltd., which disclaimed responsibility for the pollution of Lake Wataguse.

69. Ⓐ Ⓑ Ⓒ Ⓓ Ⓔ   **69.** Prior to the discovery of the toxic leakage, Lake Wataguse had been a popular year-round resort area.

70. Ⓐ Ⓑ Ⓒ Ⓓ Ⓔ   **70.** The total funds available to the Environmental Safety Commission varied between $95,000 and $170,000 annually during 1976–78.

Question Set 8

Situation: Despite protests from many members of the university community, as well as disagreement among its own membership, the Political Science Association (PSA) of Brownso University voted to include a showing of a film prepared by the American Fascist Party in a series of films by various political organizations. The decision drew promises of picketing and protests from several campus groups, along with anonymous threats to physically disrupt the screening. On October 3, two days before the movie was scheduled, the rented film arrived at the PSA office in Bainbridge Hall. Ellen Frampton, president of the PSA and a strong advocate of the film's showing, asked Marc Thompsen, the PSA secretary, to accept the delivery and store the film safely. "Where should I put it?" Marc asked. Ellen replied, "In the closet," and left the office, asking Marc to be sure to lock the office door when he left.

Result: On October 5, one hour before the movie was scheduled to be shown, Ellen looked in the closet where films were usually kept and was dismayed to find no sign of the film.

71. Ⓐ Ⓑ Ⓒ Ⓓ Ⓔ   **71.** The PSA planned to show the film despite threats of possible violence at the screening.

72. Ⓐ Ⓑ Ⓒ Ⓓ Ⓔ   **72.** A university-based socialist club had publicly announced that it would take "any steps necessary" to prevent the showing of the fascist film.

73. Ⓐ Ⓑ Ⓒ Ⓓ Ⓔ   **73.** The university president telephoned Ellen on October 4 to personally request that the PSA reconsider its decision to show the film.

74. Ⓐ Ⓑ Ⓒ Ⓓ Ⓔ   **74.** Marc Thompsen, who had voted against the showing of the film, had hidden it in his home to prevent its being screened.

75. Ⓐ Ⓑ Ⓒ Ⓓ Ⓔ   **75.** The Fascist Party provided the movie free as a way of publicizing their beliefs and activities.

76. Ⓐ Ⓑ Ⓒ Ⓓ Ⓔ   **76.** Ellen Frampton was not actually present at the time the film was delivered.

77. Ⓐ Ⓑ Ⓒ Ⓓ Ⓔ   **77.** A handful of angry students broke into the PSA office on October 4 and stole the film.

78. Ⓐ Ⓑ Ⓒ Ⓓ Ⓔ   **78.** Some members of the PSA were opposed to the presentation of a film advocating fascism.

79. Ⓐ Ⓑ Ⓒ Ⓓ Ⓔ   **79.** When the planned showing of the fascist film was announced, six left-wing political groups demanded equal time to respond.

80. Ⓐ Ⓑ Ⓒ Ⓓ Ⓔ   **80.** There were three closets in the PSA office.

Question Set 9

Situation: The incidence of lateness at Crest Haven High School had risen to such a point that the principal made it the central focus of a faculty conference in early November. Pointing out that the epidemic of lateness was affecting the concentration and attitude of teachers and students alike, the principal appointed a three-member faculty committee to offer concrete suggestions on how to remedy the situation. At the next faculty conference, held four weeks later, the committee made several recommendations: a school-wide punctuality drive, featuring awards for classes maintaining top punctuality records; the posting of guards at entrances to the school to take down the names of all late arrivals for the principal's records; and strict punishments for lateness, including suspension from school after five offenses were recorded.

Result: By February 1, the incidence of lateness at Crest Haven had increased still further.

81. Nearly all students at Crest Haven lived within walking distance of school.

81. Ⓐ Ⓑ Ⓒ Ⓓ Ⓔ

82. Angered by the principal's authoritarian manner, a popular group of student leaders organized a successful "Anti-Punctuality Drive" among their classmates.

82. Ⓐ Ⓑ Ⓒ Ⓓ Ⓔ

83. Over 90% of Crest Haven graduates go on to college or university study.

83. Ⓐ Ⓑ Ⓒ Ⓓ Ⓔ

84. The faculty committee had prepared its recommendations prior to the Christmas-New Year holiday break in classes.

84. Ⓐ Ⓑ Ⓒ Ⓓ Ⓔ

85. The administration of Crest Haven failed to recognize the seriousness of the tardiness problem.

85. Ⓐ Ⓑ Ⓒ Ⓓ Ⓔ

86. The faculty committee's recommendations were approved by an overwhelming majority at the December faculty conference.

86. Ⓐ Ⓑ Ⓒ Ⓓ Ⓔ

87. The faculty committee's program called for the use of both rewards and punishments in the battle to reduce lateness.

87. Ⓐ Ⓑ Ⓒ Ⓓ Ⓔ

88. The worst winter weather in fifty-seven years caused student travel delays on twenty-four school days in December and January.

88. Ⓐ Ⓑ Ⓒ Ⓓ Ⓔ

89. The faculty committee was unable to agree on appropriate methods of combatting student tardiness.

89. Ⓐ Ⓑ Ⓒ Ⓓ Ⓔ

90. Due to budget cuts, the transit system serving the Crest Haven school district was forced to reduce bus service starting January 1.

90. Ⓐ Ⓑ Ⓒ Ⓓ Ⓔ

Question Set 10

Situation: On March 15, 1977, the Institute for Cancer Research (ICR) released the results of a study of nine Texas counties with a heavy concentration of petroleum refineries. The study showed an unusually high incidence of cancers of the lung, nasal cavity, and skin among residents of these counties. Concurrently, the ICR began a campaign calling for more stringent regulation of the petroleum industry. In particular, it favored creation of a State Petroleum Industry Safety Board with the power to shut down any refinery not meeting strict health and safety standards. Aided by favorable publicity in the national press, the ICR succeeded in getting Proposition 11, which mandated the creation of such a State Board, on the 1977 Texas ballot. Two months before election day, the Stringfellow Opinion Poll showed voters favoring Proposition 11 by a margin of nearly two to one.

Result: Texas voters defeated Proposition 11 by over 100,000 votes.

91. At the last minute, the Texas Supeme Court bowed to petroleum industry pressure and removed Proposition 11 from the ballot on a technicality.

91. Ⓐ Ⓑ Ⓒ Ⓓ Ⓔ

92. Ⓐ Ⓑ Ⓒ Ⓓ Ⓔ   **92.** The proposed State Petroleum Industry Safety Board would have been responsible for enforcing health requirements for oil refineries.

93. Ⓐ Ⓑ Ⓒ Ⓓ Ⓔ   **93.** The many Texans employed by the petroleum industry who voted against Proposition 11 formed a disproportionately high percentage of those casting ballots on election day.

94. Ⓐ Ⓑ Ⓒ Ⓓ Ⓔ   **94.** Lucius Stringfellow, President of the Stringfellow Polling Institute, was also Chairman of the Board of the ICR.

95. Ⓐ Ⓑ Ⓒ Ⓓ Ⓔ   **95.** The nine counties studied by the ICR also contain dumping grounds for toxic industrial wastes.

96. Ⓐ Ⓑ Ⓒ Ⓓ Ⓔ   **96.** Three close relatives of the principle author of the ICR report, including her husband, were themselves employed by the petroleum industry.

97. Ⓐ Ⓑ Ⓒ Ⓓ Ⓔ   **97.** After the 1977 election, the ICR immediately launched a drive to re-introduce Proposition 11 on the 1978 ballot.

98. Ⓐ Ⓑ Ⓒ Ⓓ Ⓔ   **98.** The ICR campaign received attention outside the state of Texas as well as locally.

99. Ⓐ Ⓑ Ⓒ Ⓓ Ⓔ   **99.** The ICR study came under increasing attack in the local press for alleged statistical inaccuracies and methodological errors.

100. Ⓐ Ⓑ Ⓒ Ⓓ Ⓔ   **100.** A massive television and newspaper ad campaign sponsored by the major oil companies succeeded in swaying thousands of Texas voters.

ANSWERS AND ANALYSIS

1. **D** This statement supports one possible explanation of the result: that the university was forced to withdraw its invitation by Worthington's failure to give a yes or no answer. The withdrawal would be necessary under the circumstances in order to leave enough time to select another author to occupy the chair.

2. **E** This does not help to strengthen or weaken any likely explanation of the result.

3. **C** This is deducible from the statement in the situation that "a noted Scottish writer should be chosen each year."

4. **A** The notion that knowledge of American literature and culture were pre-requisites to holding the position contradicts the statement in the situation that the occupant of the MacPherson Chair was to lecture "on his own works."

5. **B** This statement explains why the result occurred; therefore, it is a (B).

6. **D** This statement is a (D) because it suggests and strengthens a possible explanation of the result: that outside pressures of some kind forced the university to act as it did. An extremely conservative community would be likely to object to the presence of university lecturers who in some way offended the moral sense of the local residents.

7. **E** This is irrelevant to an explanation of the result, which took place many years later and had really nothing to do with MacPherson's academic career. (If you thought the university might have *refused* the gift of half a million dollars when it discovered that MacPherson had been expelled years earlier, you were violating the rule against considering extremely unlikely possibilities. After all, would *you* refuse the gift?)

8. **D** Place this statement alongside statement 6, and you can see why statement 8 is a (D). The two statements *together* provide almost enough to adequately explain the result, which makes each one *alone* deserve a (D) rating. (Remember not to *combine* the two items; this could lead to an erroneous answer of B.)

9. **A** This is contradictory, since the passage describes how Worthington hesitated to accept the position.

10. **B** This is enough to explain the result, since half of MacPherson's $316.44 estate wouldn't even be enough for Worthington's airfare.

11. **B** If Sevigne Beer was unpopular in America, it's easy to see why it would be dropped from the U.S. market.

12. **C** This is deducible from the reference in the situation to the "novelty" of French beer in America.

13. **C** This statement is deducible from the first half of the last sentence of the situation.

14. **D** One possible explanation of the result is that Sevigne Beer was swamped by costly advertising campaigns by competitors, with which the Sevigne Company was unable or unwilling to compete. This statement strengthens this explanation.

15. **E** Sales of domestic beers are irrelevant to the fate of Sevigne, especially since we have no way of knowing whether a 4% increase is unusually high, unusually low, or just average.

16. **D** Higher prices will often hurt the sales of a product so this statement certainly supports one possible explanation for the failure of Sevigne Beer.

17. **A** This is contradicted by the fact that *after* testing the product, the company went ahead with its move into the market (deducible from the result). The firm would not have done so if statement 17 were true.

18. **E** Beers from many nations had been successful in the U.S.; the factors influential in making another nation's beers successful don't really help to explain the failure of Sevigne.

19. **C** This is deducible from the situation; reread the third sentence.

20. **E** This event occurred well before the start of the narrative, and does not have any direct bearing on the situation or the result.

21. **E** This statement is irrelevant, since it doesn't help to establish who or what was responsible for the absence of the binoculars.

22. **B** This could well explain why the absence of the binoculars was not discovered until the equipment check at Bashitar.

23. **A** This statement contradicts the information in the passage that a few items were to be shipped by air separately from the other gear.

24. **D** This suggests that the absence of the binoculars was due to theft.

25. **B** This provides an adequate explanation for the results.

26. **A** This contradicts the passage, since we're told that *every* item needed for the expedition was either shipped to Tibet or was being manufactured for later shipment. Otherwise, this could be a (B) item.

27. **C** This is deducible from the second sentence of the situation.

28. **C** This is deducible from the result. If the missing binoculars had not been crucial, there would have been no need to delay the start of the expedition for two months.

29. **E** This statement is unlikely to have a bearing on the whereabouts of the missing binoculars.

30. **A** This is contradicted by the fact that the equipment was chosen by "mountaineering experts," according to the situation.

31. **C** This is deducible from the next-to-last sentence of the situation, which states that "hits" and "misses" were not determined until after the testing had been completed.

32. **D** This suggests and supports one possible explanation for the result: that there is no such thing as ESP, and the Flemings in fact made use of normal sensory clues in transmitting information about the cards selected. The situation does *not* specify that the rooms were soundproofed to prevent this.

33. **E** This hardly helps to explain the experimental results Dr. Danube obtained.

34. **B** This statement explains why the Flemings—and *only* the Flemings—were able to show "ESP" in Dr. Danube's tests.

35. **E** Since we're told that those who assisted Dr. Danube were "trained researchers," it seems to make no real difference who in particular served on the staff.

36. **D** This statement *weakens* the ingenious-trickery hypothesis, since it would be far more difficult for pranksters to carry out such a hoax if they were not able to plan their trickery in advance.

37. **A** This is impossible, given the statement in the situation that the researchers "had no way of knowing which cards were being chosen."

38. **C** This is obviously true, based on the whole purpose of the experiments and Dr. Danube's "exultant" reaction to the Flemings' performance.

39. **D** This supports the ingenious-trickery hypothesis, by suggesting one possible method the Flemings could have used to transmit their choices to one another: a code based on varying intervals between flashes of the "Ready" light.

40. **D** This strengthens the ingenious-trickery hypothesis, by suggesting a source from which the Fleming twins might have learned their techniques.

41. **D** This supports one possible explanation of the result that Tambuli nationals who earned medical degrees were unwilling to practice in their own country and instead chose to work in other countries where the economic rewards were greater.

42. **C** This is deducible from the fact that, according to the report prepared in 1965, six years after the start of the government drive, the new medical college "had just opened its doors."

43. **E** The number of Tambuli doctors practicing medicine in the United States in 1965 is irrelevant to an explanation of the shortage of doctors in Tambul ten years later.

44. **B** The virtual destruction of the Tambuli medical system by warfare is sufficient to explain the shortage of doctors. The doctors to be graduated from the medical college never completed their studies; others were doubtless killed when their hospitals were destroyed; and still others probably fled.

45. **B** This is sufficient to explain the result, especially since a comparison of the numbers of Tambuli doctors being trained in America (over 8,000) with the numbers to be produced by the Tambuli medical college (only 350 per year) indicates that the former was to be the major source of Tambuli physicians.

46. **A** This contradicts the situation, which describes the attempts of the Tambuli government to fill medical posts from within its own citizenry.

47. **D** This supports the same explanation suggested by statement 41, with the added refinement of suggesting that, possibly, all the doctors in Tambul were concentrated in the two most well-to-do provinces; that is, the problem may have been one of *distribution* rather than numbers.

48. **D** This strengthens the likelihood of the explanation made explicit in statement 44.

49. **E** This statement might help explain the prevalence of infectious diseases in Tambul, but it has no bearing on the shortage of doctors *per se*.

50. **A** This is contradicted by the fact that many Tambulis *did* attend medical colleges in the U.S., according to the situation.

51. **D** This certainly might help explain the result. It is not in itself adequate to explain the result, however, since we don't know how important these authors were to Pierrot Books or whether they proved to be highly successful with Airedale House.

52. **E** Sale of motion picture rights to a book (as opposed to release of a finished film) has no direct bearing on sales of that book, much less on sales by a completely different publisher.

53. **C** This is obviously true, according to the result.

54. **A** This sounds like a (B) or at least a (D), doesn't it? Unfortunately, it contradicts the statement in the situation that Airedale House planned to publish the same number of new books each month as Pierrot Books.

55. **B** This statement explains the result all by itself.

56. **D** This strengthens one possible explanation of the result: that a sudden decline in the popularity of Pierrot Books helped Airedale House win over a large number of former Pierrot readers.

57. **E** It's hard to see why this statement should affect an explanation of the result, since book sales are not normally affected by factors like this one.

58. **D** This weakens the most obvious explanation of the result: namely, that Airedale House won out in a bitter competitive struggle with Pierrot Books. If true, this statement suggests that, in fact, the market for historical romances grew enormously from 1978–82—meaning that some other explanation must be sought.

59. **A** This contradicts the situation, which states that the distribution of Airedale House books was to be roughly equal to Pierrot's.

60. **B** This explains the result neatly and completely. Note that this statement and statement 58 are completely contradictory. Don't be thrown by this: each statement is to be evaluated on its own, and such contradictions between statements may, in fact, occur.

61. **E** Exactly *how* the wastes were produced 'way back in the 40s and 50s does not help explain why they were not cleaned up in 1978.

62. **A** This contradicts the situation. We're told that the sludge, when discovered, was "rapidly spreading" over the lake. The leak had evidently started only recently; otherwise, "rapidly spreading" wastes would surely have covered the lake or, at least, have been noticed earlier.

63. **B** A delay of nearly three years would mean that no final decision was reached until 1979—an adequate explanation, then, for the lack of action as of December, 1978.

64. **C** This is deducible from the fact that the sludge is described in the situation as "toxic" and a "dangerous mess."

65. **A** This is inconsistent with the situation, since a court ruling had in fact been handed down (see the last sentence).

66. **D** This strengthens the explanation provided in more complete form by statement 63.

67. **E** This is irrelevant. No matter how far away the Peristar plant may have been, the problem regarding the toxic wastes is unaffected.

68. **D** Like statement 66, this one strengthens the likelihood that complicated legal maneuvering prevented any action to clean up Lake Wataguse.

69. **E** This does not help to explain the result one way or the other.

70. **B** This explains the result, since the clean-up job was a "multi-million dollar" task, and the business interests involved were instructed to repay the state agency only *after* the clean-up.

71. **C** This is deducible from the entire course of the narrative. The threats are mentioned in the second sentence of the situation.

72. **D** This strengthens one possible explanation by establishing the socialist club as the number one suspect in the Case of the Missing Movie.

73. **E** This is irrelevant to the disappearance of the film, unless we assume that the president of the university was capable of sneaking over to the PSA office and stealing it—probably too far-fetched. Note also that Ellen's surprise at finding the film missing precludes her having agreed to the president's request.

74. **B** This clearly explains the result all by itself.

75. **A** This contradicts the reference in the situation to "the rented film."

76. **A** This contradicts the statement in the situation that Ellen Frampton "left the office" after asking Marc Thompsen to accept the delivery.

77. **B** This statement provides an adequate explanation of the result.

78. **C** This is deducible from the situation. Note the reference to disagreements among the membership of the PSA in the first sentence.

79. **E** This does not help explain why the film was missing.

80. **D** Ellen told Marc to put the film "in the closet," and then left. *But,* if there are three closets in the PSA office . . . you guessed it. Marc might have simply put the film in the wrong closet. Twenty seconds *after* the result, Ellen may well have checked the other two closets and found the film.

81. **D** This weakens a possible explanation of the result: that the increase in lateness could have been caused by a breakdown in the transit system or the school bus service.

82. **B** This explains the result quite adequately.

83. **E** This neither strengthens nor weakens a possible explanation of the result.

84. **C** This is deducible from the fact that the faculty committee presented its proposals four weeks after a meeting which took place in early November.

85. **A** This is obviously inconsistent with the action of the principal in appointing the committee.

86. **D** This weakens a possible explanation that may not have occurred to you: that the faculty committee's recommendations were never approved by the faculty as a whole or were not put into effect for some other reason.

87. **C** This is deducible from the description of the program: "awards" for punctual classes would constitute rewards; "suspension from school" would constitute punishment (unless you consider getting away from this particular principal a kind of backhanded reward).

88. **B** This provides an adequate explanation for the poor punctuality records for December and January.

89. **A** This is contradicted by the fact that the committee did present a complete program at the December meeting.

90. **D** This supports the possible explanation alluded to in the discussion of statement 81.

91. **A** This statement is contradicted by the result: Proposition 11 must have been on the ballot if it was defeated by the voters.

92. **C** This is deducible from the fourth sentence of the situation.

93. **B** This explains the result adequately. It's possible for an opinion poll to differ markedly from the actual election results if those voting on election day constitute an unrepresentative sample of the population as a whole.

94. **D** This statement suggests a possible conflict of interest which may have caused the Stringfellow Poll to be seriously biased in favor of Proposition 11. The explanation which is strengthened by this statement would be: most Texans opposed the Proposition; the Stringfellow Poll results were simply wrong.

95. **D** This statement suggests a possible weakness in the evidence being used by the ICR to support tighter controls on the petroleum industry: it may be the toxic wastes, and not the refineries, which caused the cancer rates to rise. Exposure of such flaws in the ICR study could well lead to the defeat of Proposition 11 at the polls, and this possible explanation is strengthened by this statement.

96. **E** This statement, which superficially resembles statement 94, is irrelevant to the result, since it is obvious that the author of the ICR report was not biased in favor of the petroleum industry. Therefore, this statement cannot be a factor in our search for an explanation of the result.

97. **E** Events occurring after the result are usually irrelevant to an explanation of the result.

98. **C** This is deducible from the reference to "favorable publicity in the national press."

99. **D** This supports the possible explanation of the result mentioned in the discussion of statement 95.

100. **B** This explains the result.

Logical Reasoning

This question type requires the application of logic to familiar situations and ideas. Thus, emphasis is placed on common sense, not legal precision or a formal training in logic.

DIRECTIONS: In this section you must judge the logic and reasoning employed in short sentences or paragraphs. You should choose the *best* answer to each question, that is, the one which most logically follows from the application of common sense. The best answer selection should not involve any logical inconsistency or any data not related to the logical issue presented. After making your choice, blacken your answer in the space provided.

1. Since rice serves the function in oriental cuisines that is served by bread in western cuisines, rice and bread must be very similar in taste.

    The writer's argument would be considerably weakened if attention were focused on the fact that

    (A) bread is made from wheat, not rice
    (B) bread and rice have differing nutritional value
    (C) oriental cuisines are based on foods and tastes not found in western cuisines
    (D) bread and rice are substantially different in shape
    (E) bread and rice come from related grains processed in the same manner

1. Ⓐ Ⓑ ©️ Ⓓ Ⓔ

2. Ⓐ Ⓑ Ⓒ Ⓓ Ⓔ   **2.** Since Phil always gets good marks in chemistry, he must be a good all-around student.

Which of the following statements most closely parallels the reasoning used in the above statement?

(A) Since all automobiles I have owned have four wheels, four must be the most economical number of wheels for an auto.

(B) Since all racing horses are fast, horses which never race must be slower.

(C) Since John always talks loudly, he must be hard of hearing.

(D) Since all mechanisms for social control that I know of are repressive, all forms of government are probably counterproductive.

(E) Since Tom is a good bowler, he probably excels at all sports.

Questions 3–4 are based on missing portions of the passage below. In completing each question, choose the answer which best fits the context of the passage.

Serum cholesterol levels in human blood have been linked to various physiological changes. These changes have ramifications both somatic and psychological, both desirable and dysfunctional. For example, it has been conclusively demonstrated that as the cholesterol level rises in the male bloodstream, hormonal output of pituitary and most other glandular organs increases proportionately. However, testosterone production increases geometrically with an arithmetic increase in serum level, thereby producing a sexual vitality inconsonant with other physiological impulses resulting from glandular product. Thus, increasing levels of serum cholesterol, especially in young males, can result in _3_. Continuously high serum levels can also result in higher incidence of all forms of heart disease, especially in males aged 40 through 54. Chances of contracting any type of heart disease increase by a factor of four if serum levels are 50% above normal for a period of three or more consecutive years. If this high serum level is present in combination with other casual factors of heart disease, such as obesity, smoking, and lack of exercise, the chances of a heart attack during the given years can increase by as much as a factor of ten. Since high serum cholesterol levels usually result from these other causal elements of heart disease, it follows that _4_.

3. Ⓐ Ⓑ Ⓒ Ⓓ Ⓔ   **3.** (A) disturbing discontinuities in physiological and psychological development
(B) lengthening of the prepubescent period
(C) a dangerous pattern of antisocial behavior
(D) severe psychological damage
(E) abnormal development of personality

4. Ⓐ Ⓑ Ⓒ Ⓓ Ⓔ   **4.** (A) the actual increase in chances of heart attack cannot be calculated precisely
(B) the actual increase in chances of heart attack is much greater than either given factor
(C) the actual increase in chances of heart attack is much lower than either given factor
(D) high levels of serum cholesterol are as much a warning symptom as they are a cause of heart disease
(E) individuals exhibiting all such characteristics are especially susceptible

5. Ⓐ Ⓑ Ⓒ Ⓓ Ⓔ   **5.** Since all people that I know are of the Protestant faith, Protestantism is probably the universal religion.

Which of the following statements most closely parallels the kind of reasoning used in the above statement?

(A) Since all Russian novels that I have read involve passion, Russians are probably very passionate people.

(B) Since all light bulbs I have seen operate electrically, all light probably results from electrical power.

(C) Since all carrots that I have seen are orange in color, carrots probably taste like oranges.

(D) Since all people that I know smile when they are happy, smiling is probably the universal way of expressing happiness.

(E) Since all clocks I have seen have hands, there is probably no better way to tell time.

6. If the cinema has replaced the theatre, technological advances have replaced spontaneous exhibitions as a source of entertainment.

6. Ⓐ Ⓑ Ⓒ Ⓓ Ⓔ

Which of the following statements most closely parallels the kind of reasoning used in the above statement?

(A) If lighters have replaced matches, butane has replaced sulfur as a source of light.

(B) If plastic has replaced glass, technology has replaced art.

(C) If Vitamin C pills have replaced oranges, synthetics have replaced natural foods as sources of essential nutrients.

(D) If pens have replaced pencils, science has replaced tradition.

(E) If soy has replaced wheat, the need for economy has surpassed the desire for flavor.

7. Since white is the amalgam of all colors, this paper is also blue.

7. Ⓐ Ⓑ Ⓒ Ⓓ Ⓔ

Which of the following statements most closely parallels the reasoning used in the above statement?

(A) Since I am holding up 4 fingers, I am also holding up 3 fingers.

(B) Since Portugal is on the Iberian Peninsula, it must be part of Spain.

(C) Since Alaska is part of the U.S., it must also be part of the North American continent.

(D) Since penguins are also birds, they must have wings.

(E) Since light is made up of rays, heat is a form of radiation.

8. New York City has a population of 8 million and spends $10 billion a year; the State of New Jersey has a population of 8 million, and spends $4 billion a year. New Jersey must be more efficient.

8. Ⓐ Ⓑ Ⓒ Ⓓ Ⓔ

The writer's argument would be considerably weakened if attention were focused on the fact that

(A) New Jersey is much larger geographically.

(B) New York is dissected by rivers.

(C) the cost of living is high in both states.

(D) New York City provides services that New Jersey does not.

(E) tax revenue in New York City is twice that of N.J.

9. Last year, inflation ran at 17% and the stock market dropped by 28%, but gold increased by almost 300%. Obviously, gold is the best investment there is.

9. Ⓐ Ⓑ Ⓒ Ⓓ Ⓔ

The writer's argument would be considerably weakened if attention were focused on the fact that

(A) silver appreciated by 150% last year.
(B) the U.S. dollar is not so strong in the world currency market as it once was.
(C) certain antiques nearly tripled in value last year.
(D) prior to last year and for a period of 40 years, gold appreciated in value by only 10%.
(E) the stock market has appreciated by nearly 40% since the first of the new year.

10. Ⓐ Ⓑ Ⓒ Ⓓ Ⓔ 10. I've smoked cigars from Jamaica, the Canary Islands, and Nicaragua. I say there are no cigars better than the Havanas I used to smoke 10 years ago. Unfortunately, Havanas are no longer imported here.

The writer's argument would be considerably weakened if attention were focused on the fact that

(A) Jamaican weather is identical to Havana weather.
(B) most of the former great Havana cigar growers are now located elsewhere.
(C) the soil in the Canary Islands is identical to Havana soil.
(D) the types of tobacco grown in Havana are identical to those grown in Nicaragua.
(E) ten years ago, Havana tobaccos were considerably inferior as compared with their present-day quality.

11. Ⓐ Ⓑ Ⓒ Ⓓ Ⓔ 11. Since amphibians predated all forms of life on land, intelligent life on this planet evolved from early sea creatures.

The writer's argument would be considerably strengthened if attention were focused on the fact that

(A) certain sea mammals exhibit great intelligence.
(B) landlocked reptiles eliminated all forms of amphibian life during the Paleozoic era.
(C) Darwin's theory of natural selection has never been conclusively proven.
(D) fossil remains indicate that the brains of amphibian creatures were very small.
(E) a human lung is qualitatively different from the gills of an amphibian.

12. Ⓐ Ⓑ Ⓒ Ⓓ Ⓔ 12. Since Napoleon was the best military strategist who ever lived, Patton's success in battle can be attributed to his emulation of Napoleon.

The writer's argument would be considerably weakened if attention were focused on the fact that

(A) Napoleon was beaten decisively at Waterloo.
(B) Patton's command was transferred to Omar Bradley.
(C) success in battle results from many factors in addition to strategies.
(D) Patton had modern missiles at his disposal.
(E) Napoleon fought against Britain and Russia; both of these countries were allies of Patton.

Questions 13–17 are based on missing portions of the passages below. In completing each question, choose the area which best fits the context of the respective passage.

"Conglomerate" is a term recently coined to describe a uniquely modern, uniquely American corporate phenomenon. The nomenclature refers to corporations whose primary tactic of expansion is diversification. That is, conglomerates are companies that grow by buying or somehow gaining control of other companies in unrelated fields of commerce. Conglomerates are uniquely modern because only an efficient large-scale system of capital funding could support such an acquisitive appetite on a regular basis. They are uniquely American, for only in this country is growth *per se* a legitimate corporate goal. The anti-trust law has limited certain kinds of "normal" growth in that corporations are often prohibited from controlling other corporations in the same or a related field of endeavor. Hence 13. This clearly reveals the American ambivalence to the corporate form since the industrial revolution—on the one hand, a blind faith in the ethos of growth, and on the other, an equally blind fear of "big business." This, in turn, explains the cyclical nature of America's trust-busting fervor.

The economic justification for conglomerates is at once simple and simplistic. It is argued that significant efficiency is to be found through the conglomerate form in terms of 14. Indeed, in his 1968 work *The American Challenge,* J. J. Servan-Schrieber argued that the threat of a global economy dominated by the U.S. is at bottom the result of American sophistication in, and monopoly of, modern, efficient management techniques. If all efficient managers are American, then all 15; if all efficient bureaucratic systems are American, then all of international business will adopt those systems. But an analysis of the first American conglomerate, the huge executive departments of government, can quickly dispel Mr. Servan-Schrieber's fear.

13. (A) the corporate lust for growth can be satiated only by expansion *across* industry lines   13. Ⓐ Ⓑ Ⓒ Ⓓ Ⓔ
   (B) the problem is stated
   (C) American corporations are forced to try to circumvent the law
   (D) corporate entities strive for true monopoly
   (E) a schism has developed between different types of corporate managers

14. (A) bureaucratic systems and high-level management services   14. Ⓐ Ⓑ Ⓒ Ⓓ Ⓔ
   (B) one corporation owning others in the same field
   (C) the supply of raw materials
   (D) personnel selection
   (E) intra-industry consolidation

15. (A) others are doomed to failure at the outset   15. Ⓐ Ⓑ Ⓒ Ⓓ Ⓔ
   (B) Americans will manage all efficient foreign companies
   (C) international business will be effectively monopolized
   (D) foreign companies will seek to learn from America's management intelligentsia
   (E) domestic American business will achieve great success

The dialectic was originally described by Hegel as a system which causes social movement. The process began with a thesis, the status quo, the extant system of distribution of social and economic power. The thesis is invariably attacked by the antithesis, the insurgent, the new solution to societal problems. Out of the conflict of these two emerges the synthesis, or that social structure or set of beliefs which combines elements of both the original thesis and the consequent antithesis. It is the synthesis that, in time, becomes the new thesis, and thus the dialectic process is 16. The notion of the dialectic in and of itself is merely an intellectually appealing way of describing that which is intuitively obvious. And since things obvious are rarely controversial, the dialectic 17. But Marx's interpretation of the dialectic cast it in the role of the metronome of history, guiding the inexorable rhythm of the human parade toward the best of all possible worlds—Communism.

16. Ⓐ Ⓑ Ⓒ Ⓓ Ⓔ   **16.** (A) perpetual
                        (B) redundant
                        (C) self-regenerative
                        (D) a circular process
                        (E) occasionally socially regressive

17. Ⓐ Ⓑ Ⓒ Ⓓ Ⓔ   **17.** (A) in its original form was merely descriptive
                        (B) passed permanently into the realm of obscurity
                        (C) was debated only in academic circles
                        (D) died the death of rhetoric
                        (E) became an analytic tool of conventional social theory

ANSWERS AND ANALYSIS

1. **C** It demonstrates that the two cuisines are essentially different, and thus function might be the only similarity between the two. Electricity does for some vehicles what gas does for others, but there is no similarity other than function between electricity and gas. (E) actually strengthens the author's argument. (A) is incorrect because the fact that the two come from different sources does not necessarily affect taste, e.g., sugar and saccharine. (B) does not relate to taste at all, yet taste is the obvious focus of the conclusion. (D) is equally irrelevant.

2. **E** The reasoning in this statement exactly parallels the reasoning in the given sentence, i.e., that what is true of someone in one context is true for that someone in all similar contexts. The logic of (A) is that what is true of some things predicates a different truth about all such things. The logic of (B) is that if a segment of a class of things exhibits a certain characteristic all members of the class not included in that segment do not exhibit that characteristic. (C) is obviously unrelated logically to the given sentence. (D) represents the same reasoning as (A).

3. **A** This relates to the focus of the first part of the passage. Since one gland's hormonal production outpaces the production of the others as the serum level rises, discontinuities in development are the likely result. (B) runs contrary to the author's logic, (C) is much too strong a statement relative to the author's previous tone, as is (D); (E) is unjustifiable because the author never mentions the effect of serum level on personality.

4. **D** Because high serum in combination with other factors results in a high risk of heart disease, and because high serum typically results from these other factors, cholesterol is both a warning and a cause of the disease. (A) is not at all justified by the text, and (B) and (C) contradict the sentence immediately preceding. (E) is just a rephrasing of the previous sentence.

5. **D** The reasoning in the given statement is a classic specific-to-general conclusion. (A) assumes that Russian novels accurately reflect Russian personality, mixing the metaphors in the specific-to-general process. If the first clause of (A) read "Since all Russians I have met are passionate," this might be the best answer. (B) also mixes metaphors in assuming that light bulbs are the sole source of light. (C) is ridiculous. (E) bears no relationship to the given statement whatsoever since it makes a value (qualitative) judgment, i.e., "no *better* way," rather than a purely quantitative conclusion, i.e., "no *other* way."

6. **C** The basic logic involved in the given statement is that X replaces Y, the basic nature of X has displaced the basic nature of Y in terms of a specific function. (C) parallels the given statement. (A) is defective in several ways, one of which being that not all lighters are butane, and thus the "function" described in the second clause of (A) is imprecise. (B)'s second clause contains no mention of function whatsoever; (D) and (E) are flawed in the same manner.

7. **A** The logic of the given statement is that the whole contains all and any of its constituent parts even though this may not be observable by merely usual scrutiny, i.e., salt contains both sodium and chloride. None of the answer selections parallels such reasoning except (A).

8. **D** This offers an explanation as to why New York City's budget might be larger and yet equally efficient. Therefore, the given statement is weakened. (A) is incorrect because there is no reason to assume a relationship between geographical size and higher spending. (B) has no reasonable relationship to budgetary spending. (C) is explicitly true for both states, and therefore could neither strengthen nor weaken the argument. (E) is flawed but seductive. Although higher tax revenues imply a revenue/expenditure efficiency in New York, the facts presented show New Jersey's tax revenue—one-half of New York City's—producing expenditures of less: For example, if revenue in New York equals $20B, then New Jersey revenue equals $10B. Efficiency ratio in New York City is thus 2/1, but in New Jersey, 2.5/1. Besides, unless it can be demonstrated that New York City gets more for its $10B than New Jersey gets for its $4B, the author's statement is not weakened.

9. **D** This shows that return on gold investments fluctuate widely, and thus, in some years, there were probably better investments than gold. (A) simply demonstrates that, at least last year, gold was a better investment relative to silver, thus *strengthening* the author's argument. (B) has no relevance to the statement, especially since the change in relative value is not specifically denominated in dollars (as opposed to francs or rubles). (C) has two flaws: first, only "certain antiques" tripled in value; secondly, they increased in value by only 200%. (E) has no relevance whatsoever.

10. **E** This demonstrates that present-day Havanas are superior to those the author used to smoke. (A), (B), (C) and (D) do not weaken the author's argument since they all relate solely to *one* component of cigar quality, no one of which can be evaluated against any other.

11. **A** This is the only selection which *strengthens* the author's statement; all others *weaken* his logic.

12. **C** If true, this weakens the writer's tautological consideration of "strategies" and "success." (A) and (B) merely state that both Patton and Napoleon were "defeated" in one way or another (on the battlefield or by the bureaucrats). Both choices are therefore neutral in terms of the writer's statement, particularly because he uses "best" instead of "perfect." (D) and (E) again state facts which do not relate to the logic of the writer's point.

13. **A** This follows logically since if *intra*-industry expansion is illegal, the only alternative is inter-industry expansion. (B), while not explicitly contrary to prior statements in the passage, in no way explains the sentence that it precedes. (C) is not

inferred in the passage, (D) contradicts the immediately foregoing sentence, and (E) has no basis anywhere in the passage.

14. **A** It is logical that all companies require roughly similar bureaucratic systems and high-level management services, since the higher the management the less need for day-to-day familiarity with the business of the various companies. (B) is stated earlier in the passage as being illegal. (C) assumes that companies operating in different industries, but under the "conglomorate" umbrella, have similar new materials requirements. This is not likely given the way "conglomerate" is earlier defined. (D) is completely irrelevant, since presumably different companies in unrelated fields need, for the most part, different personnel. (E) has no basis, since each company under the conglomerate superstructure retains a separate identity as well as a separate business.

15. **B** This follows logically, and is consistent with the author's tone. (A) states the converse of the first clause of the question sentence, and thus cannot logically flow from it. The fact that all efficient managers are American does not imply that all non-American managers are "doomed to failure at the outset." (C) is wrong because efficiency does not inevitably lead to monopoly. (D) is flawed because although true, it fits neither the content nor the tone of the rest of the passage; (E) suffers similarly.

16. **C** An accurate summation of the foregoing description. (A) is wrong because logically, no social system can be absolutely perpetual. (B) is wrong because earlier in the passage, the dialectic is called the source of social movement, and, as such could not be redundant. (D) and (E) are similarly contradictory.

17. **E** This both sums up the foregoing two sentences and provides excellent groundwork for the "But" of the next sentence. (A), while appealing, is too pejorative relative to the earlier parts of the passage. (*Note.* An incorrect answer to question 16 could easily cause another mistake here. This is often true in sections of this type.) (B) is contradicted by the rest of the passage, as is (D). (C) contradicts the previous sentence, since it indicates that the dialectic *was*, at some *level* (not frequency) controversial.

Case Evaluation

The objective of this question type is to test your ability to evaluate the validity of a conclusion that is based on facts given in a presented case, when new factors are introduced. The section consists of a reading passage (the case) which describes a situation and includes a principle or set of rules that apply to that situation. This is followed by a conclusion that may be drawn from the case. You are then given a set of statements that may change the nature of the case. Your job is to evaluate the effect that each statement has on the validity of the conclusion. You have to choose:

(A) if the statement clearly proves the conclusion.
(B) if the statement strengthens or reinforces the conclusion but does not clearly prove it.
(C) if the statement clearly disproves the conclusion.
(D) if the statement weakens the conclusion but does not clearly disprove it.
(E) if the statement has no relevance to the conclusion.

We have included several sample cases for practice. Before you begin you should bear in mind the following:

a. Each case includes a principle of law or a set of rules upon which the conclusion is based. These principles or rules may be limited to one section of the text or may be scattered throughout the text. *Make sure you identify and understand ALL the principles involved.*

b. The principles may be sound legal principles or they may be artificially constructed for the purpose of the particular case. In either case *you must accept them as valid and base your reasoning on them.*

c. The *Conclusion* for each case may follow logically from what you have read in the text or may seem inappropriate according to your understanding of the case. This is because the statements which follow may change the nature of the case entirely. *Make sure you read the Conclusion carefully and understand its implications.*

d. The *Statements* that come after the conclusion will either add facts to the case, change factual details quoted in the case, or in effect remove facts from the case. You should read each Statement and readapt the case accordingly. Each Statement must be taken individually. *Do not base your decision regarding one Statement on information presented in any other statement.*

e. When *Evaluating* the effect of each statement on the conclusion you will choose one of the five *Criteria,* listed above. *Make sure you understand what each one of the Criteria implies.* Pay particular attention to (B) and (D) which tend to be tricky.

f. When reading the *Case* pay particular attention to the way the facts are presented. *Distinguish between specific description of events and loose implications* which are designed to fool you into drawing false conclusions. Although the cases are written in very readable language you should pay attention to what seem like trivial details; *assume that every detail is important.*

g. Finally, as the cases are drawn from real life situations that you may have experienced, you may tend to take sides or sympathize with certain characters. *Try to avoid letting your personal feelings influence your judgment.*

You can now begin to test yourself. Do each case separately and check the answers and analysis that appear after the third sample case.

DIRECTIONS: The following section contains three sample cases. Each case includes a principle of law or a set of rules relating to that particular case. Each case is followed by a conclusion concerning the nature of the case and a set of five statements which may affect the nature of the case. You must evaluate what effect each statement has on the validity of the conclusion and choose:

(A)   if the statement clearly proves the conclusion.
(B)   if the statement strengthens or reinforces the conclusion but does not clearly prove it.
(C)   if the statement clearly disproves the conclusion.
(D)   if the statement weakens the conclusion but does not clearly disprove it.
(E)   if the statement has no relevance to the conclusion.

Case 1

Dagwood Bumble has been out of work five months and in final desperation begs Archie Plunkett to give him a job in his grocery store. Plunkett tells him that he can have a job as a packer in the back room on condition that he agrees to work for three-quarter pay and do anything he is told without question.

Thinking of his wife and five hungry children, Bumble agrees and begins packing sugar into five-pound bags, but according to his boss's instructions he short-weights each bag by a quarter pound. That day Plunkett's store gets raided by an inspector from the Department of Weights and Measures, and Bumble gets caught red-handed and is arrested.

Under the law a person is considered guilty of an illegal act which he commits under the direction of his superior unless it is committed under direct personal duress or compulsion, or under the immediate threat of death or serious bodily harm.

Conclusion: Dagwood Bumble is guilty of an illegal act.

Statements

1. Ⓐ Ⓑ Ⓒ Ⓓ Ⓔ   1. Bumble had not started packing the sugar when he was arrested.

2. Ⓐ Ⓑ Ⓒ Ⓓ Ⓔ   2. Bumble, who was afraid of losing his job, was prepared to carry out Plunkett's instructions.

3. Ⓐ Ⓑ Ⓒ Ⓓ Ⓔ   3. Plunkett was in the back room while Bumble was packing the short-weight sugar, to make sure that he was doing what he was told.

4. Ⓐ Ⓑ Ⓒ Ⓓ Ⓔ   4. Plunkett had been short-weighting his sugar for years.

5. Ⓐ Ⓑ Ⓒ Ⓓ Ⓔ   5. Plunkett was bigger and stronger than Bumble, and Bumble knew that he had a violent temper.

Case 2

Dr. Egon Lanolin, a brilliant industrial chemist, was employed by Tru-bute Soap Company in their research laboratories where he had been unsuccessfully working on a new formula synthetic soap for over a year. Roger Trube, owner-director of the company, impatient for results, confronted Dr. Lanolin and accused him of inefficiency and sheer laziness in his project. As a result Lanolin quit on the spot and found immediate employment with Fancilon Cosmetics, one of Tru-bute's major competitors.

Within a month Fancilon was on the market with a new synthetic soap called Synthilon. Tru-Bute sued Fancilon and Lanolin for the ownership and production rights for the new soap on the basis of an existing law.

A company or an individual shall have ownership rights to a product, invention or process that was initiated and developed wholly or partially by an employee during his period of employment by the said company or individual, provided that the product, invention or process is related to the employee's duties.

Conclusion: Tru-Bute should be awarded ownership of the synthetic soap formula.

Statements

6. Ⓐ Ⓑ Ⓒ Ⓓ Ⓔ   6. Fancilon had been working on a synthetic soap formula prior to Egon Lanolin's joining them.

7. Ⓐ Ⓑ Ⓒ Ⓓ Ⓔ   7. Dr. Lanolin did not quit Tru-bute, but was fired for not advancing on the formula.

8. Ⓐ Ⓑ Ⓒ Ⓓ Ⓔ   8. The process of setting up the production line and manufacturing the synthetic soap took three months.

9. Synthilon soap is based on Dr. Lanolin's formula which he completed only after the termination of his employment with Tru-Bute.

9. Ⓐ Ⓑ Ⓒ Ⓓ Ⓔ

10. Fancilon did not have its own research laboratories and operated chiefly by buying ready-made and proven formulas for its products.

10. Ⓐ Ⓑ Ⓒ Ⓓ Ⓔ

Case 3

George Funk buys his son, Bernie, a .22 caliber rifle for his thirteenth birthday. Funk gives Bernie careful instructions in gun care and maintenance and particularly in gun safety. Bernie is a bright and responsible youngster so his father assumes that he will not use the rifle in the house or environs, as they live in a crowded residential area.

One day when Funk is at work, Bernie takes the rifle into the back yard and starts shooting at birds. A stray bullet hits and injures Jock Bull, the Funks' neighbor, who was pruning his fruit trees in his own back yard. Jock sues Bernie's father for personal injury.

The law pertaining to this case states that a parent who has entrusted his child with a dangerous instrument is responsible for damages which the child causes with the instrument if the parent has not exercised sufficient care in letting the child use the instrument.

Conclusion: George Funk is responsible for Jock Bull's injury.

Statements

11. George Funk had locked the bullets in his safe and Bernie used bullets he had gotten from a friend.

11. Ⓐ Ⓑ Ⓒ Ⓓ Ⓔ

12. George Funk has no sons.

12. Ⓐ Ⓑ Ⓒ Ⓓ Ⓔ

13. It was Bernie's friend Manny who fired Bernie's rifle and injured Jock Bull that morning.

13. Ⓐ Ⓑ Ⓒ Ⓓ Ⓔ

14. The Funks did not live in a crowded residential area.

14. Ⓐ Ⓑ Ⓒ Ⓓ Ⓔ

15. George Funk knew that the key to the rifle cabinet where he kept Bernie's .22 rifle was identical to the key of Bernie's bicycle lock.

15. Ⓐ Ⓑ Ⓒ Ⓓ Ⓔ

ANSWERS AND ANALYSIS

1. **C** This statement *clearly disproves the conclusion* as Bumble had not yet carried out the illegal act of short-weighting the sugar.

2. **B** Although this does not clearly prove the conclusion, it certainly *strengthens* it as it shows Bumble's agreement to carry out an illegal act, while his fear of losing his job does not constitute *direct personal duress or compulsion.*

3. **C** Plunkett's presence in the room to supervise Bumble, who is desperate to keep his job, can be considered as *direct personal duress* and thus *clearly disproves* the conclusion that he is guilty.

4. **E** This fact has no bearing on the conclusion that Bumble is guilty.

5. **D** Although there is no evidence that Plunkett threatened Bumble physically, Bum-

592 • EXPERIMENTAL QUESTION TYPES

ble's knowledge of Plunkett's violent temper may have been seen as a *threat of bodily harm* by Bumble and thus it *weakens the conclusion*.

6. **D** This statement *weakens the conclusion* as it allows for the possibility of Fancilon's independent development of the formula, but it does not *clearly disprove* it because the text does not say on whose formula the new soap is based.

7. **E** Whether Lanolin quit or was fired is totally *irrelevant to the conclusion*.

8. **C** This statement *clearly disproves* the conclusion as it dates the completion of the Synthilon formula two months before Lanolin joined Fancilon.

9. **A** The fact that the formula was Lanolin's *clearly proves* the conclusion as the text tells us that he had been working on it while employed by Tru-Bute. The time of completion of the formula does not affect the principle of ownership.

10. **B** This statement *strengthens the conclusion* by precluding Fancilon's independent development of the new soap, but as it does not establish that the formula for its soap is clearly Dr. Lanolin's, it does not prove the conclusion.

11. **D** This fact *weakens the conclusion* in that it shows that George Funk had exercised some care in his son's use of the rifle. But the key is *sufficient care,* and hiding the bullets was not sufficient in this case.

12. **C** Since George Funk has no sons, Bernie cannot be his son and so he is not responsible for any of Bernie's actions. This *clearly disproves* the conclusion.

13. **C** According to the cited law, George Funk is only responsible for damages caused by his child. This statement therefore *clearly disproves the conclusion*.

14. **E** Where the Funks lived *is not relevant to the conclusion,* which deals with George Funk's responsibility.

15. **A** This *clearly proves the conclusion* as it shows that George Funk had not exercised sufficient care in controlling his son's use of the rifle by knowingly allowing his automatic access to it.

SEVEN

A LIST OF SCHOOLS REQUIRING THE GMAT

The following list represents graduate schools of business which require GMAT scores as part of their admissions procedure. All the schools included are members of the American Assembly of Collegiate Schools of Business.

Adelphi University
School of Business Administration
Garden City, NY 11530

Advanced Management Institute
at Lake Forest College
Lake Forest, IL 60045

American Graduate School of International Management
Thunderbird Campus
Glendale, AZ 85306

The American University
School of Business Administration
Washington, DC 20016

Arizona State University
College of Business Administration
Tempe, AZ 85281

Atlanta University
School of Business Administration
Atlanta, GA 30314

Auburn University
School of Business
Auburn, AL 36830

Augusta College
Department of Business Administration
Augusta, GA 30904

Babson College
Babson Park, MA 02157

Baldwin-Wallace College
Division of Business Administration
Berea, OH 44017

Ball State University
College of Business
Muncie, IN 47306

Baylor University
Hankamer School of Business
Waco, TX 76706

Bentley College
Waltham, MA 02154

Bloomsburg State College
School of Business
Bloomsburg, PA 17815

Boise State University
School of Business
1910 College Boulevard
Boise, ID 83725

Boston College
School of Management
Chestnut Hill, MA 02167

Boston University
School of Management
685 Commonwealth Avenue
Boston, MA 02215

Bowling Green State University
College of Business Administration
Bowling Green, OH 43403

Bradley University
College of Business Administration
Peoria, IL 61625

Brigham Young University
Graduate School of Business
Provo, Utah 84602

Bryant College
Smithfield, RI 02917

Butler University
College of Business Administration
Indianapolis, IN 46208

California State College, Bakersfield
School of Business and
    Public Administration
9001 Stockdale Highway
Bakersfield, CA 93309

California State College, Dominguez Hills
School of Management
Dominguez Hills, CA 90747

California State College, San Bernardino
School of Administration
5500 State College Parkway
San Bernardino, CA 92407

California State College, Stanislaus
Division of Business Administration
Turlock, CA 95380

**California Polytechnic State University,
    San Luis Obispo**
School of Business and Social Sciences
San Luis Obispo, CA 93407

**California State Polytechnic University,
    Pomona**
School of Business Administration
Pomona, CA 91768

California State University, Chico
School of Business
Chico, CA 95929

California State University, Fresno
School of Business and Administrative
    Sciences
Fresno, CA 93740

California State University, Fullerton
School of Business Administration and
    Economics
Fullerton, CA 92634

California State University, Hayward
School of Business and Economics
Hayward, CA 94542

California State University, Long Beach
School of Business Administration
Long Beach, CA 90840

California State University, Los Angeles
School of Business and Economics
Los Angeles, CA 90032

California State University, Northridge
School of Business Administration
    and Economics
Northridge, CA 91330

California State University, Sacramento
School of Business and
    Public Administration
6000 Jay Street
Sacramento, CA 95819

Canisius College
School of Business Administration
Buffalo, NY 14208

Capital University
Graduate School of Administration
Columbus, OH 43209

Carnegie-Mellon University
Graduate School of Industrial
    Administration
Pittsburgh, PA 15213

Case Western Reserve University
School of Management
Cleveland, OH 44106

Central Michigan University
School of Business Administration
Mt. Pleasant, MI 48859

Central Missouri State University
School of Business and Economics
Warrensburg, MO 64093

Central State University
School of Business
Edmond, OK 73034

Chaminade University of Honolulu
Department of Business Administration
3140 Waialae Avenue
Honolulu, HI 96816

City University of New York
The Bernard M. Baruch College
School of Business and Public
 Administration
17 Lexington Avenue
New York, NY 10010

Clarion State College
School of Business Administration
Clarion, PA 16214

Clark University
Department of Management
Worcester, MA 01610

Clemson University
College of Industrial Management and
 Textile Science
Clemson, SC 29631

Cleveland State University
The James J. Nance College of Business
 Administration
Cleveland, OH 44115

College of St. Thomas
Department of Business Administration
St. Paul, MN 55105

College of William and Mary
School of Business Administration
Williamsburg, VA 23185

Colorado State University
College of Business
Fort Collins, CO 80523

Columbia University
Graduate School of Business
New York, NY 10027

Cornell University
Graduate School of Business and Public
 Administration
Ithaca, NY 14853

Creighton University
College of Business Administration
Omaha, NE 68178

Dartmouth College
The Amos Tuck School of Business
 Administration
Hanover, NH 03755

DePaul University
College of Commerce
Chicago, IL 60604

Dowling College
Business Administration Programs
Oakdale, NY 11769

Drake University
College of Business Administration
25th and University
Des Moines, IA 50311

Drexel University
College of Business and Administration
Philadelphia, PA 19104

Drury College
Breech School of Business Administration
Springfield, MO 65802

Duke University
Graduate School of Business Administration
Durham, NC 27706

Duquesne University
Graduate School of Business and
 Administration
Pittsburgh, PA 15219

East Carolina University
School of Business
Greenville, NC 27834

East Tennessee State University
College of Business
Johnson City, TN 37601

East Texas State University
College of Business Administration
Commerce, TX 75428

Eastern Illinois University
School of Business
Charleston, IL 61920

Eastern Kentucky University
College of Business
Richmond, KY 40475

Eastern Michigan University
College of Business
Ypsilanti, MI 48197

Eastern New Mexico University
College of Business
University Station No. 19
Portales, NM 88130

Eastern Washington University
School of Business and Administration
Cheney, WA 99004

Emory University
Graduate School of Business
  Administration
Atlanta, GA 30322

Emporia State University
Division of Business and Business Education
Emporia, KS 66801

Florida Atlantic University
College of Business and Public Administration
Boca Raton, FL 33432

Florida International University
School of Business and Organizational
  Sciences
Tamiami Campus
Miami, FL 33199

Florida State University
College of Business
Tallahassee, FL 32306

Florida Technological University
College of Business Administration
P.O. Box 25000
Orlando, FL 32816

Fordham University
College of Business Administration
Bronx, NY 10458

Furman University
Department of Economics and
  Business Administration
Greenville, SC 29613

Gannon College
Division of Business Administration
Erie, PA 16501

George Mason University
School of Business Administration
4400 University Drive
Fairfax, VA 22030

George Washington University
School of Government and Business
  Administration
Washington, DC 20052

Georgetown University
School of Business Administration
Washington, D.C. 20057

Georgia College
Department of Business Administration and
  Economics
Campus Box 554
Milledgeville, GA 31061

Georgia Institute of Technology
College of Industrial Management
225 North Avenue, NW
Atlanta, GA 30332

Georgia Southern College
School of Business
Statesboro, GA 30458

Georgia State University
College of Business Administration
University Plaza
Atlanta, GA 30303

Gonzaga University
School of Business Administration
Spokane, WA 99258

Governors State University
College of Business and
    Public Service
Park Forest South, IL 60466

Grand Valley State Colleges
F. E. Seidman Graduate College of
    Business and Administration
Allendale, MI 49401

Harvard University
Graduate School of Business
    Administration
Soldiers Field
Boston, MA 02163

Hofstra University
School of Business
1000 Fulton Avenue
Hempstead, NY 11550

Howard University
School of Business and Public
    Administration
Washington, DC 20059

Humboldt State University
School of Business and Economics
Arcata, CA 95521

Idaho State University
College of Business
Pocatello, ID 83209

Illinois Institute of Technology
Stuart School of Management and Finance
Chicago, IL 60616

Illinois State University
College of Business
Normal, IL 61761

Indiana State University
School of Business
Terre Haute, IN 47809

Indiana University
The Graduate School of Business
Bloomington, IN 47401

Iona College
School of Business Administration
New Rochelle, NY 10801

Jackson State University
School of Business and Economics
Jackson, MS 39217

John Carroll University
School of Business
Cleveland, OH 44118

Kansas State University
College of Business Administration
Manhattan, KS 66506

Kent State University
Graduate School of Business
    Administration
Kent, OH 44242

LaSalle College
School of Business Administration
Philadelphia, PA 19141

Lehigh University
College of Business and Economics
Bethlehem, PA 18015

Lindenwood Colleges
Department of Business Administration
St. Charles, MO 63301

Long Island University
Brooklyn Center
School of Business Administration
Brooklyn, NY 11201

Long Island University
C. W. Post Center
School of Business Administration
Greenvale, NY 11548

Louisiana State University
College of Business Administration
Baton Rouge, LA 70803

Louisiana Tech University
College of Administration and Business
Box 5796, Tech Station
Ruston, LA 71272

Loyola College
Department of Business Administration
4501 North Charles Street
Baltimore, MD 21210

Loyola Marymount University
College of Business Administration
Los Angeles, CA 90045

Loyola University
School of Business Administration
Lewis Towers
820 North Michigan Avenue
Chicago, IL 60611

Loyola University
College of Business Administration
New Orleans, LA 70118

Manhattan College
School of Business
Riverdale, NY 10471

Mankato State University
College of Business
Mankato, MN 56001

Marist College
Department of Business and Economics
North Road
Poughkeepsie, NY 12601

Marquette University
The Robert A. Johnston College of
Business Administration
Milwaukee, WI 53233

Marshall University
College of Business and Applied Science
Huntington, WV 25701

Massachusetts Institute of Technology
Alfred P. Sloan School of Management
Cambridge, MA 02139

McNeese State University
School of Business
Lake Charles, LA 70609

Memphis State University
College of Business Administration
Memphis, TN 38152

Miami University
School of Business Administration
Oxford, OH 45056

Michigan State University
The Graduate School of Business
Administration
East Lansing, MI 48824

Michigan Technological University
School of Business and Engineering
Administration
Houghton, MI 49931

Middle Tennessee State University
School of Business
Murfreesboro, TN 37132

Mississippi College
School of Business and Public Administration
Clinton, MS 39058

Mississippi State University
College of Business and Industry
Mississippi State, MS 39762

Monmouth College
Department of Business Administration
West Long Branch, NJ 07764

Moorhead State University
Business, Industry, and Applied Programs
Moorhead, MN 56560

Morehead State University
School of Business and Economics
Morehead, KY 40351

Morgan State University
School of Business and Management
Baltimore, MD 21239

Mount Saint Mary's College
Department of Business
Emmitsburg, MD 21727

Murray State University
College of Business and Public Affairs
Murray, KY 42071

New Hampshire College
Manchester, NH 03104

New Mexico State University
College of Business Administration and
    Economics
Las Cruces, NM 88003

New York Institute of Technology
Division of Business and Management
1855 Broadway
New York, NY 10023

New York University
College of Business and Public
    Administration
Washington Square
New York, NY 10003

New York University
Graduate School of Business Administration
100 Trinity Place
New York, NY 10006

Nicholls State University
College of Business Administration
Thibodaux, LA 70301

North Texas State University
College of Business Administration
Denton, TX 76203

Northeast Louisiana University
College of Business Administration
Monroe, LA 71209

Northeast Missouri State University
Business Division
Kirksville, MO 63501

Northeastern University
College of Business Administration
Boston, MA 02115

Northern Arizona University
College of Business Administration
C.U. Box 15066
Flagstaff, AZ 86011

Northern Illinois University
College of Business
DeKalb, IL 60115

Northern Michigan University
School of Business and Management
Marquette, MI 49855

Northrop University
College of Business and Management
1155 West Arbor Vitae Street
Inglewood, CA 90306

Northwest Missouri State University
Department of Business and Economics
Maryville, MO 64468

Northwestern State University of Louisiana
College of Business
Natchitoches, LA 71457

Northwestern University
Graduate School of Management
Leverone Hall
2001 Sheridan Road
Evanston, IL 60201

Oakland University
School of Economics and Management
Rochester, MI 48063

Ohio State University
College of Administrative Science
Columbus, OH 43210

Ohio University
College of Business Administration
Athens, OH 45701

Oklahoma City University
School of Management and Business Sciences
Oklahoma City, OK 73106

Oklahoma State University
College of Business Administration
Stillwater, OK 74074

Old Dominion University
School of Business Administration
Norfolk, VA 23508

Oregon State University
School of Business
Corvallis, OR 97331

Pace University
Lubin School of Business Administration
New York, NY 10028

Pacific Lutheran University
School of Business Administration
Tacoma, WA 98447

Pan American University
School of Business Administration
Edinburg, TX 78539

The Pennsylvania State University
College of Business Administration
106 Business Administration Building
University Park, PA 16802

Pennsylvania State University,
  Capitol Campus
Master of Administration Program
Middletown, PA 17057

Pepperdine University
School of Business and Management
Los Angeles, CA 90044

Philadelphia College of Textiles and Science
School of Business Administration
Philadelphia, PA 19144

Polytechnic Institute of New York
Department of Management
Brooklyn, NY 11201

Portland State University
School of Business Administration
P.O. Box 751
Portland, OR 97207

Prairie View A & M University
College of Business
Prairie View, TX 77445

Providence College
Department of Business Administration
Providence, RI 02918

Purdue University
School of Management
Krannert Graduate School of Management
West Lafayette, IN 47907

Rensselaer Polytechnic Institute
School of Management
Troy, NY 12181

Rider College
School of Business Administration
Lawrenceville, NJ 08648

Rochester Institute of Technology
College of Business
Rochester, NY 14623

Rollins College
Roy E. Crummer School of Finance
  and Business Administration
Winter Park, FL 32789

Roosevelt University
Walter E. Heller College of Business
  Administration
430 South Michigan Avenue
Chicago, IL 60605

Rutgers The State University
Graduate School of Business
  Administration
Newark, NJ 07102

Rutgers University, Camden
Department of Business and Economics
Camden, NJ 08102

Saginaw Valley State College
School of Business and Management
2250 Pierce Road
University Center, MI 48710

Saint Bonaventure University
School of Business Administration
St. Bonaventure, NY 14778

Saint Cloud State University
College of Business
Saint Cloud, MN 56301

St. John's University
College of Business Administration
Utopia and Grand Central Parkways
Jamaica, NY 11439

St. Joseph's College
Department of Business Administration
Philadelphia, PA 19131

Saint Louis University
School of Business and Administration
St. Louis, MO 63108

St. Mary's University
School of Business and Administration
One Camino Santa Maria
San Antonio, TX 78284

Samford University
School of Business
Birmingham, AL 35209

San Diego State University
School of Business Administration
San Diego, CA 92110

San Francisco State University
School of Business
1600 Holloway Avenue
San Francisco, CA 94132

San Jose State University
School of Business
San Jose, CA 95192

Savannah State College
Division of Business Administration
Savannah, GA 31404

Seattle University
Albers School of Business
Seattle, WA 98122

Seton Hall University
W. Paul Stillman School of Business
South Orange, NJ 07079

Shippensburg State College
School of Business
Shippensburg, PA 17257

Southeastern Massachusetts University
College of Business and Industry
North Dartmouth, MA 02747

Southeastern Oklahoma State University
School of Business and Industry
Durant, OK 74701

Southern Illinois University at Carbondale
College of Business and Administration
Carbondale, IL 62901

Southern Illinois University at Edwardsville
School of Business
Edwardsville, IL 62026

Southern Methodist University
School of Business Administration
Dallas, TX 75275

Stanford University
Graduate School of Business
Stanford, CA 94305

State University of New York at Albany
School of Business
Albany, NY 12222

State University of New York at Binghamton
School of Management
Binghamton, NY 13901

State University of New York at Buffalo
School of Management
Crosby Hall, Library Circle
Buffalo, NY 14214

Stephen F. Austin State University
School of Business
Nacogdoches, TX 75962

Suffolk University
College of Business Administration
47 Mt. Vernon Street
Boston, MA 02108

Syracuse University
School of Management
116 College Place
Syracuse, NY 13210

Temple University
School of Business Administration
Philadelphia, PA 19122

Tennessee Technological University
College of Business Administration
Cookeville, TN 38501

Texas Christian University
M. J. Neeley School of Business
Fort Worth, TX 76129

Texas Eastern University
School of Business Administration
Tyler, TX 75701

Thomas College
West River Road
Waterville, ME 04901

Trinity University
Faculty of Business and Management
    Studies
San Antonio, TX 78284

Troy State University
School of Business
Troy, AL 36081

Tulane University
Graduate School of Business
    Administration
New Orleans, LA 70118

United States International University
School of Business and Management
San Diego, CA 92131

University of Akron
College of Business Administration
Akron, OH 44325

University of Alabama
College of Commerce and Business
    Administration
Graduate School of Business
University, AL 35486

University of Alabama in Birmingham
School of Business
Birmingham, AL 35294

University of Alaska
School of Management
Fairbanks, AK 99701

University of Alaska, Anchorage
School of Business and Public Administration
3221 Providence Drive
Anchorage, AK 99504

University of Arizona
College of Business and Public
    Administration
Tucson, AZ 85721

University of Arkansas
College of Business Administration
Fayetteville, AR 72701

University of Arkansas at Little Rock
College of Business Administration
Little Rock, AR 72204

University of Baltimore
School of Business
Baltimore, MD 21201

University of Bridgeport
College of Business Administration
Bridgeport, CT 06602

University of California
School of Business Administration
    Graduate School of Business
    Administration
Berkeley, CA 94720

University of California, Irvine
Graduate School of Administration
Irvine, CA 92717

University of California, Los Angeles
Graduate School of Management
Los Angeles, CA 90024

University of Chicago
Graduate School of Business
5836 South Greenwood Avenue
Chicago, IL 60637

University of Cincinnati
College of Business Administration
Cincinnati, OH 45221

University of Colorado
Graduate School of Business
    Administration
Boulder, CO 80309

University of Connecticut
School of Business Administration
Storrs, CT 06268

University of Dallas
Graduate School of Management
University of Dallas Station
Irving, TX 75061

University of Dayton
School of Business Administration
Dayton, OH 45469

University of Delaware
College of Business and Economics
Newark, DE 19711

University of Denver
Graduate School of Business and Public
   Management
University Park
Denver, CO 80208

University of Detroit
College of Business and Administration
Graduate School
McNichols Road at Livernois
Detroit, MI 48221

University of Evansville
School of Business Administration
Evansville, IN 47702

University of Georgia
College of Business Administration
Athens, GA 30602

University of Hawaii
College of Business Administration
2404 Maile Way
Honolulu, HI 96822

University of Houston
College of Business Administration
4800 Calhoun Street
Houston, TX 77004

University of Idaho
College of Business and Economics
Moscow, ID 83843

University of Illinois at Chicago Circle
College of Business Administration
Box 4348
Chicago, IL 60680

**University of Illinois at Urbana-
   Champaign**
College of Commerce and Business
   Administration
Urbana, IL 61801

University of Iowa
College of Business Administration
Iowa City, IA 52242

University of Kansas
School of Business
Lawrence KS 66045

University of Kentucky
College of Business and Economics
Lexington, KY 40506

University of Louisville
School of Business
Louisville, KY 40208

University of Lowell
College of Management Science
Lowell, MA 01854

University of Maine at Orono
College of Business Administration
Orono, ME 04473

University of Maryland
College of Business and Management
College Park, MD 20742

University of Massachusetts
School of Business Administration
Amherst, MA 01002

University of Miami
School of Business Administration
Coral Gables, FL 33124

The University of Michigan
Graduate School of Business
   Administration
Ann Arbor, MI 48109

University of Michigan, Dearborn
School of Management
4901 Evergreen Road
Dearborn, MI 48128

University of Minnesota
Graduate School of Business
   Administration
Minneapolis, MN 55455

University of Minnesota, Duluth
School of Business and Economics
Duluth, MN 55812

University of Mississippi
School of Business Administration
University, MS 38677

University of Missouri, Columbia
College of Business and Public
    Administration
Columbia, MO 65201

University of Missouri, Kansas City
School of Administration
5100 Rockhill Road
Kansas City, MO 64110

University of Missouri, St. Louis
School of Business Administration
8001 Natural Bridge Road
St. Louis, MO 63121

University of Montana
School of Business Administration
Missoula, MT 59801

University of Nebraska, Lincoln
College of Business Administration
Lincoln, NE 68588

University of Nebraska, Omaha
College of Business Administration
Omaha, NE 68101

University of Nevada, Las Vegas
College of Business and Economics
Las Vegas, NV 89154

University of Nevada, Reno
College of Business Administration
Reno, NV 89557

University of New Hampshire
Whittemore School of Business and
    Economics
Durham, NH 03824

The University of New Mexico
The Robert O. Anderson Graduate
    School of Business and Administrative
    Sciences
Albuquerque, NM 87131

University of New Orleans
College of Business Administration
New Orleans, LA 70122

University of North Carolina, Chapel Hill
Graduate School of Business
    Administration
Chapel Hill, NC 27514

**The University of North Carolina,
    Charlotte**
College of Business Administration
UNCC Station
Charlotte, NC 28223

**University of North Carolina,
    Greensboro**
School of Business and Economics
Greensboro, NC 27412

University of North Dakota
College of Business and Public
    Administration
Grand Forks, ND 58201

University of Northern Iowa
College of Business and Behavioral
    Sciences
Cedar Falls, IA 50613

University of Notre Dame
College of Business Administration
Notre Dame, IN 46556

University of Oklahoma
College of Business Administration
Norman, OK 73019

University of Oregon
Graduate School of Management
    and Business
Eugene, OR 97403

University of Pennsylvania
The Wharton School
3620 Locust Walk
Philadelphia, PA 19174

University of Pittsburgh
Graduate School of Business
Pittsburgh, PA 15260

University of Portland
School of Business Administration
Portland, OR 97203

University of Puget Sound
School of Business and Public
  Administration
Tacoma, WA 98416

University of Rhode Island
College of Business Administration
302 Ballentine Hall
Kingston, RI 02881

University of Richmond
School of Business Administration
University of Richmond, VA 23173

University of Rochester
Graduate School of Management
Rochester, NY 14627

University of San Diego
School of Business Administration
San Diego, CA 92110

University of San Francisco
College of Business Administration
San Francisco, CA 94117

University of Santa Clara
Graduate School of Business and
  Administration
Santa Clara, CA 95053

University of South Carolina
Graduate School of Business
Columbia, SC 29208

University of South Dakota
School of Business
Vermillion, SD 57069

University of South Florida
College of Business Administration
4202 Fowler Avenue
Tampa, FL 33620

University of Southern California
Graduate School of Business
  Administration
University Park
Los Angeles, CA 90007

University of Southern Mississippi
College of Business Administration
Hattiesburg, MS 39401

University of Tennessee, Chattanooga
School of Business Administration
Chattanooga, TN 37401

University of Tennessee, Knoxville
College of Business Administration
Knoxville, TN 37916

University of Tennessee, Nashville
Division of Business Administration
Nashville, TN 37203

University of Texas, Arlington
College of Business Administration
Arlington, TX 76019

University of Texas, Dallas
School of Management and Administration
P.O. Box 688
Richardson, TX 75080

University of Texas, San Antonio
College of Business
San Antonio, TX 78285

University of Toledo
College of Business Administration
Toledo, OH 43606

University of Tulsa
College of Business Administration
Tulsa, OK 74104

University of Utah
College of Business
Salt Lake City, UT 84112

University of Vermont
Business Administration Department
Burlington, VT 05410

University of Virginia
The Colgate Darden Graduate School
  of Business Administration
P.O. Box 6550
Charlottesville, VA 22906

University of Virginia
McIntire School of Commerce
Monroe Hall
Charlottesville, VA 22903

University of Washington
School and Graduate School of Business
  Administration
Seattle, WA 98195

University of Wisconsin, Eau Claire
School of Business
Eau Claire, WI 54701

University of Wisconsin, LaCrosse
School of Business Administration
La Crosse, WI 54601

University of Wisconsin, Madison
Graduate School of Business
Madison, WI 53706

University of Wisconsin, Milwaukee
School of Business Administration
Milwaukee, WI 53201

University of Wisconsin, Oshkosh
College of Business Administration
Oshkosh, WI 54901

University of Wisconsin, Whitewater
College of Business and Economics
Whitewater, WI 53190

University of Wyoming
College of Commerce and Industry
Laramie, WY 82070

Utah State University
College of Business
Logan, UT 84322

Valdosta State College
School of Business Administration
Valdosta, GA 31601

Vanderbilt University
Graduate School of Management
Nashville, TN 37203

Virginia Commonwealth University
School of Business
Richmond, VA 23284

**Virginia Polytechnic Institute and
  State University**
College of Business
Blacksburg, VA 24061

Wake Forest University
Babcock Graduate School of Management
Winston-Salem, NC 27109

Washington State University
College of Economics and Business
Pullman, WA 99163

Washington University
The Graduate School of Business
  Administration
St. Louis, MO 63130

Wayne State University
School of Business Administration
Detroit, MI 48202

West Georgia College
School of Business
Carrollton, GA 30117

West Texas State University
School of Business
Canyon, TX 79016

West Virginia College of Graduate Studies
Division of Business and Management
2300 MacCorkle Avenue, S.E.,
Charleston, WV 25304

West Virginia University
College of Business and Economics
Morgantown, WV 26506

Western Carolina University
School of Business
Cullowhee, NC 28723

Western Connecticut State College
School of Business and Public Administration
Danbury, CT 06810

Western Illinois University
College of Business
Macomb, IL 61455

Western Kentucky University
Bowling Green College of Business and
  Public Affairs
Bowling Green, KY 42101

Western Michigan University
College of Business
Kalamazoo, MI 49001

Wichita State University
College of Business Administration
Wichita, KS 67208

Widener College
Center of Management and Applied
    Economics
Chester, PA 19013

Willamette University
Atkinson Graduate School of Administration
Salem, OR 97301

Woodbury University
Los Angeles, CA 90017

Wright State University
College of Business and Administration
Dayton, OH 45435

Xavier University
College of Business Administration
Cincinnati, OH 45207

Youngstown State University
School of Business Administration
Youngstown, OH 44555

BARRON'S GUIDE TO

GRADUATE
BUSINESS
SCHOOLS

EASTERN EDITION

SECOND EDITION

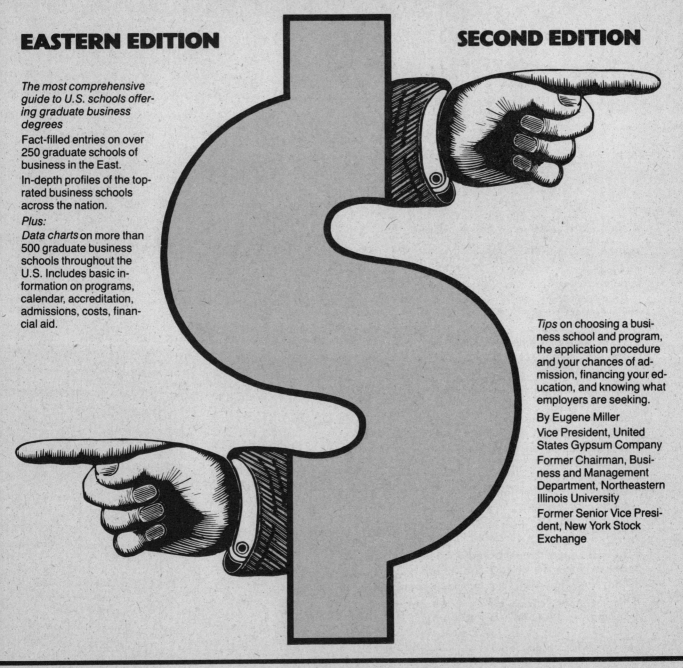

The most comprehensive guide to U.S. schools offering graduate business degrees

Fact-filled entries on over 250 graduate schools of business in the East.

In-depth profiles of the top-rated business schools across the nation.

Plus:

Data charts on more than 500 graduate business schools throughout the U.S. Includes basic information on programs, calendar, accreditation, admissions, costs, financial aid.

Tips on choosing a business school and program, the application procedure and your chances of admission, financing your education, and knowing what employers are seeking.

By Eugene Miller

Vice President, United States Gypsum Company

Former Chairman, Business and Management Department, Northeastern Illinois University

Former Senior Vice President, New York Stock Exchange

Barron's Educational Series, Inc. $5.95

Barron's New Guide to the Law School Admission Test
LSAT

A comprehensive 6-week study program.

Extensive test tips, strategies,
and practice in:
Common Question Types
   Practical Judgment
   Cases and Principles
   Logical Reasoning
   Quantitative Comparison
   Data Interpretation
   Writing Ability

**Experimental and Infrequent
Question Types**
   Validity of Conclusions
   Evaluations of Facts
   Reading Comprehension
   Reading Recall
   Artificial Language
   Analysis of Explanations
   Logical Diagrams

with a special mathematics review section.

**Four Full-Length Model Examinations
Patterned After the Latest Forms of the LSAT.
All questions have fully explained answers.**

With at-a-glance chart on all
ABA-approved American law schools.

by Jerry Bobrow
in collaboration with
   William A. Covino,
   David A. Kay,
   Brian N. Siegel,
   Daniel C. Spencer,
   Merritt L. Weisinger

Barron's Educational Series, Inc. $6.95

BARRON'S
GMAT
UPDATE

To be sure of getting the latest information on the Graduate Management Admission Test, register now for the Barron's free Test Update Service. If there are any changes in the types of questions asked, the subject areas covered, or the format of the test, Barron's UPDATE NEWS will describe these changes and offer practice items. This timely and informative newsletter is available free of charge to those who register for our Test Update Service. Just mail your request to:

TEST UPDATE SERVICE/GMAT
Barron's Educational Series, Inc.
113 Crossways Park Drive
Woodbury, New York 11797.